CHARACTER AND CONFLICT

An Introduction to Drama

CHARACTER
AND
CONFLICT

An Introduction to Drama

ALVIN B. KERNAN

YALE UNIVERSITY

HARCOURT, BRACE & WORLD, INC.
NEW YORK & BURLINGAME

Library of Congress Catalog Card Number: 63-10700

Printed in the United States of America

CONTENTS

MEANING
323

KING HENRY THE FOURTH, Part I,
William Shakespeare,

NOTES BY G. B. HARRISON
335

PART II
Plays for Further Reading

PART III
Glossary

INTRODUCTION

The plays in this volume are drawn from all the great periods of the theater. There is a Greek tragedy from the fifth century B.C., a late medieval morality play, two works from the Renaissance, a comedy from the baroque theater in France, several instances of modern realism, and a number of plays from our own century in which the dramatists have broken out of traditional forms in order to express the modern consciousness of the world. This collection therefore offers a panorama of the development of the theater in the West and a history of the way in which the dramatists of various ages have adapted and exploited the resources of the play to show, as Hamlet puts it, "the very age and body of the time his form and pressure."

But why the particular plays chosen for this volume? Why not Sophocles' *Oedipus Rex* rather than his *Antigone* as an example of Greek tragedy? Or Tolstoy's *The Power of Darkness* rather than Brecht's *Mother Courage* as an example of modern naturalism? The answer is that the plays included here were chosen not only because they are great drama, or because they represent a particular theatrical period, but because each provides a particularly clear and well-defined instance of the use of one fundamental element of drama. For example, a playwright creates characters; *Hedda Gabler,* according to one critic, is: "a character study pure and simple. . . . The poet does not even pass judgment on his heroine; he simply paints her full-length portrait with scientific impassivity. But what a portrait! How searching in insight, how brilliant in coloring, how rich in detail!" *Hedda Gabler,* of course, is not all character; the play has a plot and it shows us a great deal of the world in which Hedda lives, but it is the character of Hedda Gabler that stands out and that is most carefully developed. The play is, therefore, an ideal place to begin the study of the ways in which a dramatist creates his characters and the uses he makes of them.

In *Mother Courage* the world, or the environment, in which the characters of the play live is most important; in *Antigone* the plot stands out
particularly clearly; and *I Henry IV* is almost a catalogue of the ways
in which the dramatist can create and elaborate the "meaning" of his
stage action.

To supplement these examples each of the first three long plays is
followed by a short play in which the same dramatic element is presented in a different manner or on a different level. *Hedda Gabler* is
followed by *Everyman*. Here the dramatist abandons realism and reveals
the mind of his chief character by presenting his thoughts as characters.
Mother Courage, which presents the world in "realistic" terms, is
followed by Archibald MacLeish's *The Fall of the City,* in which the
forces at work in the world are represented by an "unrealistic" robot-
warrior. In *Antigone* the pattern of events that takes place in the City of
Thebes *and* in the minds of the principals, Antigone and Creon, constitutes the plot. But since it is always difficult to understand that plot
takes place within the mind as well as outside of it in the physical
world, *Antigone* is followed by Strindberg's *The Stronger,* a play in
which there is a very definite psychological plot but almost no external
action.

The "Plays for Further Reading" provide additional examples of the
dramatic techniques dealt with in the first section. These four plays,
however, have been selected and arranged to focus on another aspect
of drama, the relationship between comedy and tragedy. Chekhov's
The Cherry Orchard and Saroyan's *The Time of Your Life* are both
dramatic presentations of our modern, unheroic world—one set in a
country house of the decaying Russian aristocracy and the other in a
San Francisco honky-tonk. Despite strong efforts to control their own
destinies, no character in either play is very talented or very effective
in his dealings with reality. But one play moves to a tragic conclusion,
the other to a comic one. *Hamlet* and *The Misanthrope* are related in
somewhat the same way. In both plays the leading character believes
that his "time is out of joint" and that it is up to him "to set it right."
But Hamlet's Denmark and the fashionable Paris salons in which
Alceste moves are very different places; in one the action moves toward
tragedy, while in the other the movement is toward something like
comedy.

The total selection of plays offered in this volume, then, can be approached in a number of ways, and the critical discussions, the introductions, the questions, and the glossary provide materials that will be of use to anyone who wishes to deal with the historical development of the drama, the nature of comedy and tragedy, or dramatic modes such as expressionism, realism, naturalism, and poetic drama. But the focus of the book is critical. By means of the selections, the critical discussions that precede seven of the plays, and the questions that follow all of the plays, this book aims to provide what might be called "a grammar of the play." Just as a grammar of language deals with such fundamentals as the parts of speech, definitions of words, and syntax, so this grammar of the play deals with such fundamentals as character, setting, plot, and meaning, with the constituent parts of each of these, and with the ways in which the components of the play can be connected and related to produce the whole. In other words, the purpose of the editorial material is to present as clearly and as simply as possible the elements, not the refinements, of drama.

This approach has required the elimination, or at least the devaluation, of some of the established terms of dramatic criticism, which, however important they may once have seemed, are no longer such useful critical tools. That is, instead of illuminating the play by pointing to what is important in it, the terms tend to obscure meaning by directing attention to what is unimportant or peripheral. For example, that traditional triad of terms—exposition, rising action, and climax—used for so many years to describe the way in which a playwright puts his play together, tends to limit rather than to enhance our understanding of plays. In using this terminology we may think that we know something about a play when we know that it begins with an introduction of the characters and a description of their situation in the first act, multiplies their problems and raises the audience's expectation in the second act, and then in the third act resolves all questions raised. But a description of this kind merely brings us to the threshold of useful critical inquiry. If we are really to understand a play, we need to know the answers to such questions as: What is being exposed in the exposition? Why do the characters have these particular personal and social problems? What causes the action to rise? In what ways and for what reasons does the action move toward the particular conclusion it reaches? What does this particular resolution mean? A too frequent use of the exposition-rising action-resolution pattern, and the use of similar terms, creates an illusion that this is the only proper way of putting a play together. In fact it is only one way—primarily the way of the nineteenth-century "well-made play" and early realistic drama; the majority of the great plays conform only loosely, if at all, to this pattern.

Because these traditional terms are so familiar, wherever possible they have been referred to in the text and fitted into the explanation of the nature of drama offered there. They are also gathered together and defined, along with other information about the theater and plays, in a glossary at the back of the book. Any reader who wants to know how a term like "rising action'" or "obligatory scene" can be adjusted to the theory of drama proposed in the critical discussions in this book can find the answer in the glossary.

If the approach to drama offered here were shining new and the invention of one critic's mind, it would be highly suspect. But the critical material in this book presents in a condensed and simplified form the methods of analysis now used in the majority of college classrooms where an effort is made to describe the dynamics of a play and get down to its basic elements. Any reader familiar with the literary criticism of the last thirty or forty years will also recognize that the theory of drama offered here is an attempt to gather together and to apply to the study of drama at an introductory level the work of many modern critics—T. S. Eliot, William Empson, Kenneth Burke, R. P. Blackmur, Francis Fergusson, Alan Downer, W. K. Wimsatt, and Northrop Frye, to name a few—who have tried to get closer to the nature of literature and to construct a more effective vocabulary for criticism.

The major categories of dramatic art discussed in this book, far from being new, ultimately derive from the first piece of dramatic criticism: Aristotle's *Poetics,* written in the fourth century B.C. Aristotle says that "all tragedy must necessarily contain six parts," and these are "fable, manners, diction, sentiments, decoration, and music." By the fable (*mythos*) is meant roughly what we call "plot." Manners (*ethos*) refers in part to what is now known as "character." Diction (*lexis*) is the language used in the play. (I have, in agreement with modern criticism, chosen not to consider language as a separate element of drama but as a component of character and setting.) Sentiment (*dianoia*) apparently refers to the "theme" of a play, the ideas in it, and this I have enlarged to the topic "Meaning." By decoration (*opsis*) Aristotle means the scenery—he considered it unimportant—which I have expanded, following the practice of working dramatists since Aristotle's time, to cover all that part of creation represented by scenery, the "world" around man, his environment. Music (*melos*) refers to the dances and chanting of the chorus in Greek tragedy, which is no longer an important part of drama other than opera, though plays still have a "rhythm of action," and the language of poetic drama is still metrical.

Having said what this book tries to do, it now remains to say briefly what it does not try to do. First of all, it avoids as much as possible any analysis of a play before it is read. Each section of critical commentary discusses dramatic principles pertinent to the play that follows and draws examples from a number of other plays. But the play is not interpreted. The questions that follow each play ask the student to consider the play in the light of the general discussion and to examine the way it exploits various dramatic possibilities. Similarly, the introduction to each play provides general information, not an interpretation.

Second, no attempt has been made to present here a complete catalogue of the dramatic techniques developed over the last 2,500 years. Examples are offered of the basic ways in which a dramatist works, and it is then left to the reader to discover the variation and extension of technique introduced in the plays printed here.

PART

I

CRITICISM
AND
PLAYS

CHARACTER IN DRAMA

When we see a play our attention first focuses on character. We are interested in the people on the stage, and we want to know more about them: What moves them to act as they do? What happens to them? Why does it happen? Are they responsible? These are legitimate interests, because a play is valuable only insofar as it tells us something about human nature and about the way the world goes for men. The characters are a dramatist's primary images of human nature; they are his statements in speech and gestures about the elusive creature man. The character Hamlet, for example, can be thought of as a *dramatic proposition*, similar to one philosopher's definition of man as "a featherless biped," or to the economist's definition of human beings as "consumers and producers of goods and services." Hamlet, featherless biped, consumers and producers—all are attempts to sum up, to find an adequate image for, the essential quality of man. Obviously, however, the character Hamlet is more complex than these other definitions. A summary statement about him must take into account, for example, his sorrow over the death of his father and the lust of his mother, his disturbed preoccupation with change and death, his mysterious assumption of a suit of black clothes, his staging of a play, and, finally, his killing of a king. Besides being too simple to encompass the complex actions and feelings of Hamlet, the philosopher's and economist's definitions are also too abstract, too general, for the specific terms of the play. Hamlet is the Prince of Denmark, the lover—perhaps —of Ophelia, the son of Gertrude, the man who as a child was carried on the shoulders of Yorick, whose skull has been turned up by a gravedigger in making room for Ophelia's body.

The degree of complexity and the amount of detail are not the only ways in which these definitions differ. The philosopher's and the economist's definitions *fix* man, place him in a static condition. No matter what happens, he will always be two-footed and without feathers, always a user or producer of articles and work. But in drama man is dynamic, a restless seeker of some particular end. The forces at work within him—his *motives*—drive him forward to do or to attempt to do some particular thing in the outer world: to achieve freedom, control nature, or create order and stability from chaos and change. If we are to understand a character in a play we must think of him not as a static collection of qualities—a still portrait—but as a doer of something. Our aim as readers should not be the fine analysis of a fixed, unchanging character; it should be an attempt to discover the fundamental motive that finds expression in everything the character does. Because dramatists conceive of their characters as doers or as attempters, every detail of costume and figure, every movement and gesture, every statement—on even the most trivial subjects—is a partial expression of the basic motive of the character. As the play progresses, this motive, lightly sounded in the opening movements of the play, takes more obvious form in a major goal such as to bring peace to Rome, to marry Juliet, or to become the master of the world. The immediate obvious goal the character seeks is not itself, however, to be thought of as his basic motive. It is only one of the ways he seeks the realization of his motive, one expression of some more fundamental desire that in its less heroic forms is common to all men. For example, Hamlet's obvious aim is to kill Claudius and fulfill the Ghost's command, but this is only one expression of his deeper motive, which is to seek out and destroy the infection that is poisoning every area of life in Denmark: politics, marriage, religion, and friendship. This general motive, which is expressed in his aim to kill Claudius, is equally present, though muted, in most of Hamlet's words and actions. He is, for example, trying to pierce the surface of fair-seeming and locate corruption when he asks Ophelia if she is honest, when he breaks through his mother's illusions and shows her the real meaning of her marriage to Claudius, when he stabs through the hangings and kills Polonius, or when he "penetratingly" remarks that man who seems "the beauty of the world" is no more than a "quintessence of dust." As we perceive Hamlet's motive, he ceases to be merely a fictitious prince struggling in a dark castle to kill an ogre king and becomes a representation of the characteristic human desire to locate and eradicate those elements in life that subvert our hopes and ideals. Hamlet does not have every common characteristic of man, such as the ability to produce and consume goods and services, but he does embody an enduring, fundamental—and troublesome—human motive.

Since a character's actions and speech express his motive, it follows that we must look carefully at *all* he says and does. The simplest scheme to follow in our discussion of the components of character will be to begin by looking at the visible elements of dramatic character—physical features, clothing, movements, and gestures. From there we can move inward to consider other expressions of character, such as thought and language. This movement from the external to the internal should strike us as natural, for it approximates the manner in which we come to know not only characters in plays but also people in actual life. In life, however, some details are irrelevant; it may be, for example, no indication of a person's character that he has a humpback, or thin hair, or is enormously fat. But in a play these physical details express character. In Shakespeare's *Richard III* the crookbacked Richard's motive is to twist and destroy; this motive is expressed as much in his deformed back as it is in the disorders he contrives in his family, his society, and his kingdom. Similarly, Hedda Gabler's thin hair and her desire to pull out another woman's luxurious hair mark her as a woman who not only lacks vitality but also actively seeks the lifeless, a woman whose motive is to kill. Falstaff's great belly shows us that he wants to make the world all flesh, that he seeks a purely physical existence. To think of physical traits in this manner may at first require some readjustments, for nowadays we assume—or so we say—that a physical handicap is an accident. But in plays, though there are a few exceptions, physical features are usually expressions of motives. Even such obvious physical attributes as youth and old age, beauty and ugliness, should be taken in this way. Juliet's extreme youth—she is only thirteen—and her startling beauty are properly understood as physical realizations of her inner innocence and harmony of being.

While playwrights have always made use of the theory that the outer man expresses the inner one, they have often dramatized circumstances in which appearance and reality do not square, where, as Duncan says in *Macbeth,* "There's no art to find the mind's construction in the face." Oedipus' clubfoot shows us that for all his grandeur —King of Thebes and the greatest of living men—he is flawed, but no physical traits reveal that Iago in *Othello* is not the honest and trustworthy officer he seems, or that Claudius, the usurping king in *Hamlet,* is not the wise and efficient ruler he appears to be. Wherever physical appearance, actions, or words conceal rather than express directly the "mind's construction" we have what is known as *irony.*

The word has many shades of meaning, which we shall have cause to examine, but basically *irony* is used to describe circumstances in which what seems to be and what actually is are in some way opposed: for example, where a devil seems to be a god, where death masquerades as life, or where slavery presents itself as freedom.

The fact of irony complicates but does not invalidate our general point that physical appearance helps us understand the basic nature of a character. In the simplest kind of irony there is a direct and obvious contradiction between appearance and reality, between body and mind. The contradiction sets up a contrast, and a contrast is almost as useful as a similarity in defining something. White may be defined by black as well as by other instances of white. The "well compact dimensions," the straight, powerful, handsome bodies, of such hypocrites as Edmund, in *King Lear,* and Iago both conceal and reveal their twisted, ugly minds. The straightness of body defines by contrast the crookedness of mind. Irony complicates character in many ways by creating ambivalent or complex motives, but for the present it is only necessary to remember that the physical attributes of a dramatic character are never mere accidents. They are symbols or indexes, direct or ironic, of his basic nature.

Clothing—costume—also makes visible a character's motives. The realization of motive may be direct and obvious, as it is in Tennessee Williams' *A Streetcar Named Desire* where the bright, primary colors worn by the men in the play express their brutal directness, their emotional simplicity, and their reduction of life to elemental appetites. Clothing may also express more subtle motives; in the same play Blanche DuBois' longing to disguise the crude, painful facts of life is represented by the cosmetics (makeup may be considered part of costume), fake furs, and costume jewelry with which she attempts to veil her loss of youth, money, and social prominence. Even less obvious uses of clothing may express character. Correct but unremarkable clothing may suggest, for example, that a character is proper, that his basic drive is to do the accepted thing.

Since clothing often manifests the man, a change of clothing may signify a radical change in him. In *King Lear,* Lear first appears clad in rich robes and wearing a golden crown, secure and certain of his worth as a man and as a ruler. Two acts later, on the stormy heath, when he comes to doubt his own value, his changed condition is reflected in his attempt to strip himself naked so that his outward appearance will conform to his new-found knowledge that man is no more than "a poor, bare, forked animal." Clothing, like physical appearance, may also be employed in an ironic manner to reveal the distinction between what a man is and what he pretends to be. Blanche DuBois' cheap furs and Macbeth's kingly garments, which "hang loose about him, like a giant's robe upon a dwarfish thief," provide grim comments on the inadequacy of these characters to live up to their pretensions. The key to understanding the function of costume in the theater is to remember that dress is seldom decorative or realistic detail, but is an expression of the wearer's motives.

Just as a character's motives are visible in his person and in his clothing, so his gestures and movements are *an acting out* of his motives. Care must be exercised to catch the meaning of deceptively simple and ordinary movements such as pacing a room, breaking free from an embrace, turning away from a conversation, frequently withdrawing from the stage, or retiring to an isolated corner. Taken together, all these seemingly innocent actions may suggest that a character's primary motive is to remain unencumbered by human relationships, to be free and unattached. While every stage action in a well-written play, no matter how trivial, will help express motives, dramatists usually provide more obviously significant actions to manifest the primary drives of their characters. In Shakespeare's *Antony and Cleopatra*, for example, everything passes away in time. Love, friendship, power, beauty, wealth, youth—all disintegrate. Caught up in this ceaseless change, the major characters' motive is to create some kind of permanence, to hold together something that they value. They express this motive by their frequent attempts to hold something or to embrace someone: firm handshakes to seal bargains, tight embraces to bind love to love, buckling of the body into armor to preserve reputation and to hold the empire together. Romeo and Juliet insist (though they consistently fail) that they can be united in soul and mind, without concern for such earthly matters as body, family, civil disorders, or other practical concerns of life. Their suicides by poison and dagger are their final attempts to be rid of the body and earthly cares and to be joined at last with one another in spirit in a "triumphant grave." Of course, a subtle irony plays through this definitive act, because in rejecting, finally, their earthly part, the body, Romeo and Juliet may have thrown everything away and become no more than corpses. Spirit and body, the play seems to say, are inextricably intertwined.

But in attempting to understand dramatic characters, we must focus first on what they try to do, not on what they succeed in doing. In the plays of Anton Chekhov, for example, the characters often have a simple aim: to go to Moscow, to buy a farm. They are, however, futile people who fail to achieve what they want. Chekhov illustrates their basic ineffectiveness by showing their consistent failure to achieve smaller aims as well: They stumble when they try to walk, bump into furniture and knock things over when they try to move gracefully, fall down when they attempt to dance, and go to sleep when they intend to stay awake. To understand them we must first see what they try to do and then discover the way in which these motives combine with what they actually do to make up their total characters.

The greatest dramatists use action in such a skillful fashion that stage movements often provide a summary of the entire play and an insight into the basic motives of all the major characters. In the duel between Hamlet and Laertes, which comes at the close of *Hamlet,* what appears to be a polite fencing match is in fact deadly serious, for Laertes' rapier is poisoned. The combatants occupy the foreground of the stage, while Claudius stands waiting behind them with the cup of poison. To one side stand the Queen and courtiers, apparently without knowledge of what is actually taking place. When the duel begins, Hamlet proves a far better fencer than he was thought to be. After Hamlet has hit Laertes several times, a scuffle occurs, the rapiers are dropped, and by chance Hamlet picks up the one with the poisoned tip. These actions are endlessly suggestive, but they obviously summarize in visual terms the principal activities of the major characters throughout the play. First of all, the weapons are fencing foils, and the rapid thrust and parry of these light, flexible swords duplicates the quick interplay of the minds of Claudius and Hamlet as each has sought during the play to counter the attacks of the other and in turn to open his antagonist up for the fatal thrust. (Obviously a duel using battle-axes or lances would not fit the situation here.) Claudius' position behind Laertes restates his method of procedure throughout the play: he has never attacked Hamlet directly but has always gotten at him through an agent—the Queen, Polonius, Ophelia, or Rosencrantz and Guildenstern. His major source of dupes has been Polonius and his family, and now he is using the last of them. Whenever Claudius has dealt with Hamlet, he has masked his true intentions behind a pretense of honest concern and fair dealing; his method is reflected in the pretense that the duel is no more than honest exercise, a courtly game involving a small wager. But behind Claudius' pretenses of honesty, he has always been a poisoner—he has metaphorically poisoned the kingdom and literally poisoned its king—and so the poisoned rapier and cup. The Queen and courtiers innocently looking on estab-

lish visually their simple-minded acceptance of all that has gone on in
Elsinore and demonstrate that the majority of men look but do not
see. The chance exchange of rapiers and the deaths of Laertes, Gertrude, and Claudius condense into a few, swift actions the role that
fate has played in the drama; the inevitable deaths of the stupid and
innocent, who stumble between "the pass and fell-incensed points of
mighty opposites"; and the frequent recoil of the invention on the in-
ventor. Finally, Hamlet's death shows once again the cost of ridding
the court of Claudius. Not many dramatists employ actions as effectively as Shakespeare does in *Hamlet,* but in most plays action will
tell us a great deal about character.

Important as the "visual language" may be, playwrights seldom provide us with much physical description of their characters, nor do
they often elaborate on costume and action. A few swift, strong strokes
of the descriptive brush in a stage direction or in a speech make the
necessary point; it is up to the reader or the producer to enlarge upon
these hints. The reason for the brevity of description is that dramatists
do not write to be read in a classroom or study. They write with
the theater in mind—actors, costumes, movement, scenery, placement,
gesture, sound. The text of the completed play is thus a kind of musical
score that does not finally exist as a play until it is produced on a
stage. This does not mean that it is futile to read plays; it only means
that we must read in a special way, that we must stage the play in
our heads as we read, providing form and voice for the actor, costumes, makeup, scenery, and movement. We must read as if we were
directors placing the characters on stage for the maximum effect, directing them in their gestures and movements, providing the correct
intonation for a given line, telling them what to do during awkward
intervals when they remain on stage without lines to speak. Only by
reading in this way can we hope to arrive at something approximating
an ideal "performance." Some readers—Charles Lamb is the most
famous of them—have preferred never to go to the theater, insisting
that a live performance can never match the magnificent acting and
superb effects of the theater of the imagination.

But a word of caution is necessary here. Reading the text of a play
in this fashion is not an invitation to rewrite the play. We are not
free to costume the characters in any fashion that appeals to us, nor
are we free to have them do anything that strikes our fancy. Costumes, action, and all other details of the production must be controlled by the play as we have it in the text. When the author does

not provide specific directions, our theatrical additions must be material images of the fundamental ideas of the text. For example, while Shakespeare provides no directions about the physical appearance of Macbeth, it would clearly be inappropriate to make him short, thin, and supple. His brutal doggedness in battle, his determination to control the kingdom by any means once he has committed himself to this course, and the ponderous quality of his speech and mind dictate that he be powerful and heavy-set in body, slow and steady in movement, deep and peremptory in voice.

Some historians of the theater have argued that drama began with miming, that is, the wordless acting out of ritual patterns. Many modern men of the theater have used this theory to argue that the play is essentially, as well as originally, a visual art that makes its statements about human nature and life primarily by means of costume, scenery, and action. No great play fails to make use of these and other forms of visual expression, but our greatest drama has always had a verbal dimension as well, and it is difficult to understand how characters could convey their intricate motives by their bodies, clothing, and actions alone. The visual and verbal elements of a play are not in opposition. Rather, they are complementary; motives expressed in visual terms will be echoed and refined by language. Dramatic language works in the same way that stage movement works. The lines spoken by a character are not flat statements of fact or description; they are living language taut with effort. Bertolt Brecht, the German playwright, once described the nature of dramatic language—*language that is action*—by pointing out that the sentence, "Pluck out the eye that offends thee," is essentially still and undramatic; but the sentence, "If thine eye offend thee, pluck it out," is fully dramatic because it contains and compels an action. Brecht called this kind of language *Gestisch*, or "gestural." In other words, in dramatic speech the speaker accomplishes or tries to accomplish with words what he also tries to accomplish with his hands and feet. Words, after all, can wound or destroy as well as a knife, or nourish as well as food. Making and breaking, forming and separating, soaring and falling, covering and uncovering, and other such actions take place constantly in dramatic language, even when no visual objects are handled or no physical action takes place. A character's physical actions provide us with rough estimates of his motive, but his language confirms these estimates and provides more delicate shadings of motive.

Motive as expressed in language is most obvious in what we may call *thought*. This term refers to the ideas of a character, his expressed opinions on any subject, his general pronouncements, his statements of values. Most people express a good many random ideas in their conversation, and it is difficult to trace a simple pattern in their thought; but a playwright, working under very severe demands of economy, gives many of his characters only one central idea, one unchanging motive. This idea or motive will be expressed in a variety of ways and will appear in what the character says about such diverse subjects as the weather, foreign affairs, the lastest novel, or the condition of the garden. The motive is obvious enough in the comic character, for example, who reduces every topic of conversation to food or turns always to the subject of money. It is nearly as apparent in a character like Parson Manders in Ibsen's *Ghosts,* who in the course of the first act discusses a great many topics: Which of the latest books should be read? Are the artists living in Paris moral? Should a child be sent away from his family to school? Ought an orphanage be insured against fire? No matter what the subject, Manders' speech implies that the conventional and socially accepted ways of thinking should serve as a guide to conduct. This simple pattern of thought reveals Manders as a spokesman, almost a *personification,* of propriety, a man whose rather undistinguished motive is to do what is generally thought to be correct.

The thought patterns of more interesting characters than Manders are usually more difficult to establish, and it is more difficult, too, for the audience to determine by his language what a character like Cassius in *Julius Caesar,* for example, is trying to do. Cassius talks about whether or not the heavens have any effect on human destiny, he describes Caesar, he persuades Brutus to join a conspiracy, he argues about a battle plan, and he discusses the necessity of wringing taxes from captive provinces. But when we look closely at what he has to say on each of these points we discover that his motive, while it is always half-hidden and partially obscured, is in every case to manifest his belief that he is the master of his own destiny, that no other man or force is superior to him or controls him. In the attempt to understand a character, one of the first steps should always be to gather together all of his statements to see if a single idea runs through them: What thought or motive does he consistently voice? Since playwrights do not attempt to hide the nature of their characters, they will usually state their central idea succinctly and openly at some point in the play. Cassius' central motive is revealed perfectly in his famous lines,

> The fault, dear Brutus, is not in our stars,
> But in ourselves, that we are underlings.

Because they lack variety and depth, characters like Parson Manders who have only one simple value to which they return predictably are known as *type* or *flat characters.* This kind of character is found in all drama but is the staple of *comedy,* for in the comic vision of life character is not very diverse or complicated. Comic characters usually fall into well-known types—the young lover, the clever servant, the old merchant, the pedantic doctor; and these types mechanically and laughably seek their one goal—money, a particular young woman, food, or mischief. What happens to these characters in comedy is equally predictable: the young lovers overcome the obstacles of birth and fortune; the old merchant is cuckolded and robbed; and the world goes merrily on its way, not because the direction of events has been shaped very much by character, but simply because this is the way of the comic world.

In *tragedy,* however, the major characters are usually more complex, for tragedy dramatizes the inner life of man with all its conflicts, its ambiguities, its crosscurrents of value. Characters with conflicting motives, who sustain internal struggles, are often described as *rounded* or *three-dimensional,* meaning that they show some of the complexity that is believed to exist in actual men. But in the drama the most complex character seldom embodies more than two or three conflicting values, though this conflict will be expressed in a variety of ways. Hamlet is the perfect example: "To be or not to be," to act or to remain passive, to revenge his father or to let the opportunity go by, to love or not to love Ophelia, to accept the corruption of the world or to strike out at it.

In tragedy this conflict of thought may be realized in several ways. One way—the way used by Shakespeare in *Hamlet*—is for the character himself to be aware of the conflicts within him and to express his duality of motive directly. An equally common technique uses irony to create a character who is not self-aware, who is not conscious of the conflict within himself. He thinks that he is single-minded and that since he knows his own mind perfectly he can move to assert his principal value in a direct and uncomplicated fashion. By the end of the play, at the point called the *reversal,* it becomes clear that the character is not what he thought he was, that his nature is dual, and that he has been moving in a direction contrary to what he supposed. Let us take, for example, the case of Brutus in Shakespeare's *Julius Caesar.* Brutus thinks of himself as a cool rationalist who approaches all problems, whether they be as trivial as where he placed a book he was reading or as important as the decision to kill the prospective dictator Julius Caesar, in a purely objective manner. Yet the play makes clear that Brutus is moved, in part at least, by common human passions such as pride, envy, fear, and hatred. Brutus remains throughout the play totally unaware of the division in his character, and he is unified, we might say, only in being consistently divided. Like most men, he acts at once rationally and passionately.

In most tragic drama, man "ever but slenderly knows himself," as Goneril says of her father in *King Lear,* and the motives of characters of this order are not easily understood. The dramatist uses language as precisely as he can to present these farther ranges of character where the irrational and the rational meet and where motives originate. Long before psychologists demonstrated the existence of the unconscious mind and its role in human speech, dramatists had created characters who said far more than they consciously knew they were saying—whose actions and words expressed aims and conflicts of which they were unaware. In examining dramatic language at this level we must remember that a character's words are not to be thought of as mere signs that such and such a quality is present, as a flashing red light at a railroad crossing signals that a train is passing. Instead, dramatic language is used to act out on the verbal level—as if the flashing red light expressed the nature of the train—a basic motive, or motives (if the character is complicated). R. P. Blackmur has used the term "language as gesture" to describe this type of speech. Furthermore, language used in this way not only expresses motive and verbalizes the characteristic gesture, but it also defines the quality of the gesture, whether it is direct or involved, quick or slow, optimistic or despairing. A few examples will make this point clear.

A characteristic speech pattern may manifest motive. A character who habitually begins sentences bravely enough but trails off without finishing his thought because he realizes that no one is listening has verbalized both his desire to accomplish some aim and his despair of achieving it in the face of the world's indifference. The repetition of stock phrases at crucial moments is a realization in words of an unoriginal and inflexible mind, a mind that does the same thing again and again. Long pauses or a slow, involved speech express a hesitant and tangled mind; quick, flowing lines express a mind moving rapidly and with assurance toward a goal.

Carefully controlled *rhythms* of speech provide some of the most subtle and acute effects of this order. Macbeth's lines,

> Tomorrow, and tomorrow, and tomorrow
> Creeps in this petty pace from day to day,
> To the last syllable of recorded time, . . .

make audible in the long, slow, dragging, regular movements—coupled with the repetition of words—his sense that the one movement left in life for him is to creep through tedious sameness to a meaningless death.

A character may also express his motives in his *imagery*—the general term for *comparisons, metaphors, and similes.*[1] When Romeo sees Juliet in the Capulet garden he compares her to brilliant things: to the sun, to a bright angel, to a rich treasure, and to the stars in the heavens. All this, of course, is perfectly standard love imagery, but it nonetheless reveals that Romeo, like other lovers, is seeking, and realizes his aspiration for a magical instant in language, to reach and be one with the highest, the transcendent. Juliet is for him, for at least this one moment, not a flesh-and-blood woman but the symbol of an unearthly ideal toward which he strains upward in his language just as he strains upward with his body from the ground to the balcony on which Juliet stands. Metaphor may reveal and attempt to move in the reverse direction as well. Iago in *Othello* regularly compares men and women to animals—a black ram, a dog, a white ewe, a Barbary horse, a fly; and he reduces all human actions, such as love or friendship, to physical functions—disgorging, disrelishing, feeding, heating, and tasting. His images express his constant wish to diminish life to no more than animal activity. In this last example it becomes obvious that two *strains of imagery*, or *image patterns*, those of animals and of physical functions, combine to suggest the same motive. Ordi-

[1] In actual usage the terms *image* and *imagery* have a much wider range of meaning. Basically an image is "the representation through language of sense experience" (Laurence Perrine, *Sound and Sense in Poetry*, p. 40). The representation through language of a meadow or a brilliant scene at court is therefore an image, and it follows that since all literature is made up of a series of images of this kind, writing itself can be defined as image making. In the theater, of course, images are presented not through language alone but through clothing, voices, bodies, settings, and sounds. Here we seem to have not an image, a representation, but the sense experience itself in all its fullness. The theater gives us images, not phenomena, because its pictures are constructed not to imitate reality, but to provide by the selection and structuring of details some insight into the nature of the thing represented by or associated with the image. An image is not finally a recreation of sense experience but a designed rearrangement of it, which provides in turn not only sense experience, but also knowledge about the object imaged. It is thus always a metaphor: it stands for something.

narily a character uses a variety of images, and in order to understand what motives he is expressing in them we must look for the common aim implicit in each image. But images sometimes jar against one another. The imagery of a complex character will also be complex, for they will express his mixed motives. When Hamlet describes man as "this quintessence of dust," his reverence for man and his wish to glorify him appear in "quintessence," while his disdain, disgust, and repulsion for the flesh is carried by the word "dust." Dramatists use imagery in a great many ways to express character, but the general rule holds that the images a character uses are expressions in language of either his basic motive or his unresolved conflict of motives.

Patterns, rhythms, and images are but three components of *style;* a character's style—the *way* he puts things—is in each of its details an enunciation of his motives. Consider, for example, the following speech from Congreve's *The Way of the World*. Mirabell is explaining to a friend the ways he tried to gain the confidence of an old lady so that she would permit him to marry her ward.

I did as much as a man could, with any reasonable conscience; I proceeded to the very last act of flattery with her, and was guilty of a song in her commendation. Nay, I got a friend to put her into a lampoon, and compliment her with the imputation of an affair with a young fellow, which I carried so far that I told her the malicious town took notice that she was grown fat of a sudden; and when she lay in of a dropsy, persuaded her she was reported to be in labor.

Leaving aside its sprightly and irreverent humor, the most impressive quality of the speech is its breath-taking speed, its swift, certain, un-hesitating forward movement. Yet despite its steady advance the lines are nicely balanced, phrase is played off against phrase and sentence against sentence, so that the over-all effect is one of both force and order. The *diction,* i.e., the choice of words, is adequate and precise without being ornate, and there are no figures of speech. The lines dramatize a perfectly functioning, naturally keen, powerful, realistic, and ordered mind.

At the other end of the scale is a speech such as this:

Come, come, you are malicious now, and would breed debates. Petulant's my friend, and a very honest fellow, and a very pretty fellow, and has a smattering—faith and troth, a pretty deal of an odd sort of a small wit: nay, I'll do him justice. I'm his friend, and I won't wrong him neither. And if he had any judgement in the world, he would not be altogether contemptible.

These lines of Witwoud's, also from *The Way of the World,* progress, if at all, slowly and haltingly with painful breaks and hesitations. They are filled with deadwood, with needless repetition that only darkens the sense of what Witwould is trying to say. The diction is vague and imprecise. The several mild exclamations, such as "Come, come" and "faith and troth," emphasize the painful slowness, the eddying drift, the lack of sense with which his mind is working.

These few examples are not intended as a catalogue of the stylistic resources of the dramatist; they only suggest the kind of linguistic devices the dramatist may use to bring his characters to life. Grammar, figures of speech, and even so humble a device as punning tell a great deal about character, and the dramatist who wishes to do so can use all of the stylistic techniques developed in rhetoric and poetry over the last 2,000 years. Dramatic speech in all its details does serve as gesture, and an understanding of a character must be based on a close examination of at least the main features of his style. In poetic drama, where the language seems stretched to its maximum expressiveness, style will, of course, be more complex and precise in what it says about a character; but good prose speech, while not as packed and taut as poetry, makes use of the same stylistic devices that poetry does. The difference between good poetry and good prose is one of degree, not of kind.

Up to this point we have considered only those ways in which a character expresses *himself,* but playwrights often throw oblique light on their *dramatis personae* by relating them to objects, places, and people outside themselves. An association with some *prop* (stage property) often suggests some deep-lying interest. Falstaff's fondness for a cup of sack reveals his concern for bodily pleasure. (Does it also suggest that he prefers the pleasures of inebriation to the difficulties of looking steadily at reality?) The unshaded, harsh electric light that hangs in the center of Stanley Kowalski's house in *A Streetcar Named Desire* is the physical image of his unblinking way of looking at people and things. Both the light and the man expose pretense and cruelly reveal the objective truth. Light and man are finally joined when Stanley thrusts the bare bulb into the face of a woman who has been pretending that she is younger than she is to reveal every wrinkle, every sign of age in her painted face. Props used in this way are called *symbols,* and they should always be approached with a good deal of care. In the case of the bare light, for example, it should be noticed that it is an "artificial" light, a man-made way of "looking at things." Stanley would be quite a different kind of person if he were identified with the sunlight, and if he used its light to reveal Blanche's age.

A great deal may be revealed by a character's preference for a particular place; the nature of the place may establish his primary concerns. Willy Loman in Arthur Miller's *Death of a Salesman* gives form to his fierce desire to grow something in the world—sons, friends, dignity, reputation—by his frequent references to gardens and by his return to a barren, backyard garden to plant seeds in the middle of the night after his world has collapsed around him. Alceste in Molière's *The Misanthrope* gives symbolic statement to his desire for isolation and total self-dependence by his reiterated decision to leave the polite drawing rooms of Paris for the wilds of the desert.

What one character says about another often provides crucial information, though it is wise to remember that such descriptions may be biased or incomplete. Claudius' statements about Hamlet's motives are revealing, but they scarcely tell the whole story. One character's comments on another character usually results in a *double perspective;* the first tells us something about the second, but he also tells us a good deal about the way he himself thinks. When Gertrude, for example, attributes her son's melancholy to the death of his father and to her "o'er hasty marriage," she provides a partial and rather obvious insight into the character of Hamlet, but she reveals her own feelings of guilt as well.

Minor characters frequently serve both as commentators and *reflectors* of forces at work within the major figures. The calm, stoic Horatio who stands so often silent behind Hamlet makes visible the unruffled acceptance of a confused and evil world that Hamlet, in one part of his complicated being, himself longs to achieve. In Ibsen's *Ghosts,* Parson Manders is apparently a figure of the utmost respectability, who argues that men should always accept traditional moral standards because they are right and because they lead ultimately to happiness. The grotesque figure of the carpenter Engstrand, whose oily platitudes about duty and right are simply obvious attempts to mask his greed and selfish interests, reflects Manders' character. Manders is not the conscious hypocrite that Engstrand is, but in all that he says and does there is a concern for being well thought of by other people; it is this hidden, self-seeking part of his nature that is constantly reflected by the parody figure of Engstrand. The identification is ultimately objectified when after Engstrand has done Manders a favor they shake hands and Manders says with great feeling that from this time they "will travel together."

Formal relationships such as the partnership of Engstrand and Manders usually provide significant clues to the characters involved. In family relationships blood kinship frequently represents metaphorically a more essential kinship of nature. King Lear has three daughters, two of them evil, grasping materialists, the other the soul of kindness and love. While each daughter remains a character in her own right, at the same time she personifies some of Lear's attitudes and values. The daughters act out for us—somewhat in the manner of an allegorical play—the struggle that is going on in Lear's mind between the forces of good and evil, and their words and actions reveal the full meaning of certain choices that Lear makes. All relationships—between master and servant, king and subject, husband and wife, father and child, sister and brother, friend and friend—should be examined closely. They are used by the dramatist to reveal the nature of the characters involved. In a play, even more than in life, a man is known by the company he keeps.

Since playwrights make their points by *contrast* as well as by *similarity,* a play will often contain characters whose radically different natures help to define one another. Iago's hatred for man and his attempts to destroy everyone around him are more distinct and more meaningful because he appears in the same play with Desdemona, whose nature it is to love and to be concerned for the welfare of everyone. The stark, brutal realism of Stanley Kowalski in *A Streetcar Named Desire* is set off by the vague, fumbling romanticism of Blanche DuBois; the practical vision of Oedipus stands in direct contrast to the spiritual vision of the prophet Teiresias. The latter contrast is reinforced by the ironic fact that Teiresias is literally blind while Oedipus' physical vision is excellent.

Here then are a few of the techniques playwrights have used to construct dramatic characters. It will be useful at this point to sum up the general principles that have emerged from our discussion. First of all, let us consider the status of a character in a play. Dramatic characters, such as Oedipus, Falstaff, or Hamlet, often seem more "real," more vital, more essentially alive than do most of the people one meets. That a fictional character should seem more alive than a human being is a paradoxical result of the great dramatist's ability to concentrate and sustain in his characters those qualities that we consider the essence of life: perfect expression of self in language and action, fullness of thought, intensity of feelings, and relentless movement toward the realization of basic goals.

The "genuineness" of the more interesting dramatic characters is further established by the fact that they have about them an ultimate air of mystery. Here we arrive at one of the fundamental peculiarities of the dramatic form. In a novel or lyric poem the author is free to tell us the true nature of a person, the springs of character can be laid open directly. But in the more traditional realistic or semi-realistic drama there can be no such thing as absolute certainty about character. We see, as in life, only the outside of the person, hear what he says, watch what he does, listen to what others say about him, and we proceed from these phenomena to make informed guesses about what kind of person he finally is. We attempt to define the unknown and invisible principle of being from the known and visible, and we can do so with considerable certainty in the case of such simple characters as Macduff in *Macbeth*, Cassio in *Othello*, or Polonius in *Hamlet*. But the great figures of the stage—Oedipus, Lear, Hamlet—defy our efforts to pluck out the heart of their mystery. Even when they speak directly to us of the currents of feeling that stir the bottoms of their souls, their words manage to suggest areas of being and motives that cannot be directly stated, for which the character himself cannot find adequate language.

But dramatic characters for all their "realness" are not finally living people, complete human beings materialized on the stage by the magic of the playwright's words and the voice and body of the actor. Characters in drama are artistic constructions in which form, voice, and movement give life to the playwright's vision of human nature. Dramatic characters possess *no qualities or attributes other than those the author provides them with,* and we are not free to guess about the existence of other unstated qualities as we might be in trying to understand a real human being. For example, if a character in a play shows constant feelings of inferiority we should not conjecture that in childhood he had dominating parents and a superior brother. He is an invented character, and as such he had no childhood except that which the playwright may have given him. There is no point in trying to imagine what a character does before the play opens or after it closes, unless the author provides pertinent information.

This distinction between what we may call the *symbolic* and *realistic* theories of dramatic character might seem to be critical hair-splitting without practical value for understanding a play, but it is in fact a crucial matter. If we approach the characters as real people, we risk taking the details of the play for granted and thus missing their meaning. Drama becomes for us a mere imitation of life, which intrigues us because, like the photograph, it duplicates reality. Using the realistic approach we might conclude that King Lear has three daughters simply because he is a man who happens to have three daughters, and that Oedipus has a clubfoot simply because of an unfortunate childhood accident. This "realtistic" approach in which things *are* just because they are leads to an uncritical acceptance of the play. Conversely, by taking the characters as real people we may see too much at the same time that we understand too little. If we assume that characters are real people, or at any rate just like real people, it seems reasonable to explain them in the same way that we explain real people. Encountering a man like Macbeth in real life we might conclude, if we were simple moralists, that here was a man who should have gone to church more regularly and read the Bible more carefully; or if we were psychologists we might argue that here was a man who had been repressed by his father and therefore spent his life attempting to destroy authority and father-figures such as the King. Nothing of this, of course, is in Shakespeare's play; Macbeth kills the King because he, like other men, is ambitious to rise in the world and control others rather than be controlled by them. He himself wants to be a king, and this motive is a *given,* a basic part of his nature, for which no explanation or cause is offered in the play. The drive to absolute power is, the play suggests, a standard part of man's will, one of the inexplicable facts of being. In providing moral or psychological interpretations that have no foundation in the play we are substituting our own understanding of life for the very specific information that the play provides.

If, on the other hand, we approach characters not as real people, but as symbolic forms, like the images painters create, designed to present in a schematic fashion the basic and essential qualities of general human nature as the playwright perceives it, then our eye for detail and meaning is sharpened, and we are alert to the subtle portrayal of character presented. Our work as readers is to see *all* there is in the play, but no more.

The second major point to be made is that dramatic character is *coherent.* Characters are made up of many different details: physical features, clothing, movements, opinions, statements, and ways of speaking. These details are not a random collection of unrelated fragments. Instead, each detail reinforces the others, gives expression in a different mode or on a different level to the same "characteristic." As a result, a dramatic character is unified: what his clothes tell us about him in one way, his movements and his words will tell us in another

HEDDA GABLER

BY

HENRIK IBSEN

It is difficult for us to imagine the state of the theater in the 1870's when Henrik Ibsen (1828–1906) began to write the realistic drama for which he is most famous. The standard theatrical fare in most European theaters during the nineteenth century, except for revivals of the classics, consisted of what we today would call melodramas: plays that show little concern for the realities of human nature and deal with sensational materials such as young officers falsely accused of betraying their country and entangled with fascinating female spies, or honest and beautiful women who by some mistake are thought to be adulteresses and banished from their homes and children. Usually both officer and wife are saved in the end by some trusting, warmhearted admirer who has believed in them all along. A mechanical formula even existed for plotting such plays to maintain maximum suspense and to extract the last tear.

Ibsen borrowed some of the techniques of this theater, but he revolutionized its subject matter. Beginning with *The Pillars of Society* (1875) and continuing with such plays as *A Doll's House* (1878), *Ghosts* (1881), *An Enemy of the People* (1882), *The Wild Duck* (1883), *Hedda Gabler* (1890), and *The Master Builder* (1891), he brought to the stage frank, penetrating discussions of such real human problems as the struggles of just men with corrupt societies, the confinement of women to their homes, the effects of lies and pretenses on human relations, the desperate need of weak men for illusion, and the human failings that prevent men from achieving absolute freedom.

Not only did Ibsen revolutionize the subject of the drama, but he also reformed methods of dramatic construction and the mode of presentation. Gone from his plays were the faraway castles and snow-covered, moonlit mountains of romantic melodrama. In their place were realistic sets of nineteenth-century, middle-class homes, of business offices, and of town halls. To take the place of fantastic heroes and heroines with their outsize gestures and language, Ibsen created characters who act, talk, and think like human beings. For the type of construction designed to exploit the audiences' love of the sensational, the unusual, and the sentimental, Ibsen substituted careful workmanship and detailed plotting in which each event of the play was the inevitable result of what had gone before. The illusion of reality was carefully maintained: entrances and exits were convincingly motivated, and at no point were characters allowed to do anything that they might not reasonably do in real life.

We take this kind of play to be the theatrical norm, but it is, nonetheless, a very new kind of play. No one had written quite like this before the nineteenth century, and the fashion seems already to be passing. Dramatists in our own time are seeking new, more openly theatrical forms that do not bind the playwright to recreating life as it commonly appears to the eye, but that allow him to present the world as man experiences it in his mind.

It would be a mistake to think, however, that Ibsen, like some of his followers, did no more in his plays than dramatize actual social problems in a manner as much like ordinary life as possible. He was not a photographer; his realistic method merely guarantees fidelity to the truth of life. Beneath the commonplace realities of his sets and the ordinary manners of his characters lie age-old energies and desires; within an everyday problem, such as a woman who is bored with her lot, enduring human questions and ancient antagonisms come once again to life. But so smooth and unexceptional is the surface of a play like *Hedda Gabler* that it may be difficult at first to see that its petty, realistic movements and flat, unadorned speeches express these primal powers. To see the meaning of such simple matters as Hedda's thin hair, the pistols she inherits from her father, or the placement of her writing desk, requires even more care and sensitivity than is necessary to interpret the brief words and acts by which people reveal themselves in actual life. But while such details often have no meaning, or we lack enough knowledge to see their meaning, in reality, in *Hedda Gabler* each action and word reveals the mind in which it originated.

ACT I

᠍᠍꒜ Scene: *A spacious, handsome, and tastefully furnished drawing room, decorated in dark colors. In the back, a wide doorway with curtains drawn back, leading into a smaller room decorated in the same style as the drawing room. In the right-hand wall of the front room, a folding door leading out to the hall. In the opposite wall, on the left, a glass door, also with curtains drawn back. Through the panes can be seen part of a verandah outside, and trees covered with autumn foliage. An oval table, with a cover on it, and surrounded by chairs, stands well forward. In front, by the wall on the right, a wide stove of dark porcelain, a high-backed armchair, a cushioned footrest, and two footstools. A settee, with a small round table in front of it, fills the upper right-hand corner. In front, on the left, a little way from the wall, a sofa. Farther back than the glass door, a piano. On either side of the doorway at the back a whatnot with terra-cotta and majolica ornaments. Against the back wall of the inner room a sofa, with a table, and one or two chairs. Over the sofa hangs the portrait of a handsome elderly man in a General's uniform. Over the table a hanging lamp, with an opal glass shade. A number of bouquets are arranged about the drawing room, in vases and glasses. Others lie upon the tables. The floors in both rooms are covered with thick carpets. Morning light. The sun shines in through the glass door.*

MISS JULIANA TESMAN, *with her bonnet on and carrying a parasol, comes in from the hall, followed by* BERTA, *who carries a bouquet wrapped in paper.* MISS TESMAN *is a comely and pleasant-looking lady of about sixty-five. She is nicely but simply dressed in a gray walking costume.* BERTA *is a middle-aged woman of plain and rather countrified appearance.*

MISS TESMAN (*stops close to the door, listens, and says softly*). Upon my word, I don't believe they are stirring yet!

BERTA (*also softly*). I told you so, Miss. Remember how late the steamboat got in last night. And then, when they got home!—good

Lord, what a lot the young mistress had to unpack before she could get to bed.

MISS TESMAN. Well, well—let them have their sleep out. But let us see that they get a good breath of the fresh morning air when they do appear. (*She goes to the glass door and throws it open.*)

BERTA (*beside the table, at a loss what to do with the bouquet in her hand*). I declare there isn't a bit of room left. I think I'll put it down here, Miss. (*She places it on the piano.*)

MISS TESMAN. So you've got a new mistress now, my dear Berta. Heaven knows it was a wrench to me to part with you.

BERTA (*on the point of weeping*). And do you think it wasn't hard for me too, Miss? After all the blessed years I've been with you and Miss Rina.

MISS TESMAN. We must make the best of it, Berta. There was nothing else to be done. George can't do without you, you see—he absolutely can't. He has had you to look after him ever since he was a little boy.

BERTA. Ah, but, Miss Julia, I can't help thinking of Miss Rina lying helpless at home there, poor thing. And with only that new girl, too! She'll never learn to take proper care of an invalid.

MISS TESMAN. Oh, I shall manage to train her. And of course, you know, I shall take most of it upon myself. You needn't be uneasy about my poor sister, my dear Berta.

BERTA. Well, but there's another thing, Miss. I'm so mortally afraid I shan't be able to suit the young mistress.

MISS TESMAN. Oh, well—just at first there may be one or two things——

BERTA. Most like she'll be terrible grand in her ways.

MISS TESMAN. Well, you can't wonder at that—General Gabler's daughter! Think of the sort of life she was accustomed to in her father's time. Don't you remember how we used to see her riding down the road along with the General? In that long black habit—and with feathers in her hat?

BERTA. Yes, indeed—I remember well enough—! But good Lord, I should never have dreamt in those days that she and Master George would make a match of it.

MISS TESMAN. Nor I. But, by-the-bye, Berta—while I think of it: in future you mustn't say Master George. You must say Dr. Tesman.

BERTA. Yes, the young mistress spoke of that too—last night—the moment they set foot in the house. Is it true, then, Miss?

MISS TESMAN. Yes, indeed it is. Only think, Berta—some foreign university has made him a doctor—while he has been abroad, you understand. I hadn't heard a word about it, until he told me himself upon the pier.

BERTA. Well, well, he's clever enough for anything, he is. But I didn't think he'd have gone in for doctoring people too.

MISS TESMAN. No, no, it's not that sort of doctor he is. (*Nods significantly.*) But let me tell you, we may have to call him something still grander before long.

BERTA. You don't say so! What can that be, Miss?

MISS TESMAN (*smiling*). H'm—wouldn't you like to know! (*With emotion.*) Ah, dear, dear—if my poor brother could only look up from his grave now, and see what his little boy has grown into! (*Looks around.*) But bless me, Berta—why have you done this? Taken the chintz covers off all the furniture?

BERTA. The mistress told me to. She can't abide covers on the chairs, she says.

MISS TESMAN. Are they going to make this their everyday sitting room then?

BERTA. Yes, that's what I understood—from the mistress. Master George—the doctor—he said nothing.

> [GEORGE TESMAN *comes from the right into the inner room, humming to himself, and carrying an unstrapped empty portmanteau. He is a middle-sized, young-looking man of thirty-three, rather stout, with a round, open, cheerful face, fair hair and beard. He wears spectacles, and is somewhat carelessly dressed in comfortable indoor clothes.*]

MISS TESMAN. Good morning, good morning, George.

TESMAN (*in the doorway between the rooms*). Aunt Julia! Dear Aunt Julia! (*Goes up to her and shakes hands warmly.*) Come all this way—so early! Eh?

MISS TESMAN. Why of course I had to come and see how you were getting on.

TESMAN. In spite of your having had no proper night's rest?

MISS TESMAN. Oh, that makes no difference to me.

TESMAN. Well, I suppose you got home all right from the pier? Eh?

MISS TESMAN. Yes, quite safely, thank goodness. Judge Brack was good enough to see me right to my door.

TESMAN. We were so sorry we couldn't give you a seat in the carriage. But you saw what a pile of boxes Hedda had to bring with her.

MISS TESMAN. Yes, she had certainly plenty of boxes.

BERTA (*to* TESMAN). Shall I go in and see if there's anything I can do for the mistress?

TESMAN. No, thank you, Berta—you needn't. She said she would ring if she wanted anything.

BERTA (*going towards the right*). Very well.

TESMAN. But look here—take this portmanteau with you.

BERTA (*taking it*). I'll put it in the attic. (*She goes out by the hall door.*)

TESMAN. Fancy, Aunty—I had the whole of that portmanteau chock full of copies of documents. You wouldn't believe how much I have picked up from all the archives I have been examining—curious old details that no one has had any idea of——

MISS TESMAN. Yes, you don't seem to have wasted your time on your wedding trip, George.

TESMAN. No, that I haven't. But do take off your bonnet, Auntie. Look here! Let me untie the strings—eh?

MISS TESMAN (*while he does so*). Well, well—this is just as if you were still at home with us.

TESMAN (*with the bonnet in his hand, looks at it from all sides*). Why, what a gorgeous bonnet you've been investing in!

MISS TESMAN. I bought it on Hedda's account.

TESMAN. On Hedda's account? Eh?

MISS TESMAN. Yes, so that Hedda needn't be ashamed of me if we happened to go out together.

TESMAN (*patting her cheek*). You always think of everything, Aunt Julia. (*Lays the bonnet on a chair beside the table.*) And now, look here—suppose we sit comfortably on the sofa and have a little chat, till Hedda comes.

> [*They seat themselves. She places her parasol in the corner of the sofa.*]

MISS TESMAN (*takes both his hands and looks at him*). What a delight it is to have you again, as large as life, before my very eyes, George! My George—my poor brother's own boy!

TESMAN. And it's a delight for me, too, to see you again, Aunt Julia! You, who have been father and mother in one to me.

MISS TESMAN. Oh, yes, I know you will always keep a place in your heart for your old aunts.

TESMAN. And what about Aunt Rina? No improvement—eh!

MISS TESMAN. Oh, no—we can scarcely look for any improvement in her case, poor thing. There she lies, helpless, as she has lain for all these years. But heaven grant I may not lose her yet awhile! For if I did, I don't know what I should make of my life, George—especially now that I haven't you to look after any more.

TESMAN (*patting her back*). There, there, there——!

MISS TESMAN (*suddenly changing her tone*). And to think that here you are a married man, George!—And that you should be the one to carry off Hedda Gabler, the beautiful Hedda Gabler! Only think of it—she, that was so beset with admirers!

TESMAN (*hums a little and smiles complacently*). Yes, I fancy I have several good friends about town who would like to stand in my shoes—eh?

MISS TESMAN. And then this fine long wedding tour you have had! More than five—nearly six months——

TESMAN. Well, for me it has been a sort of tour of research as well. I have had to do so much grubbing among old records—and to read no end of books too, Auntie.

MISS TESMAN. Oh, yes, I suppose so. (*More confidentially, and lowering her voice a little.*) But listen now, George—have you nothing—nothing special to tell me?

TESMAN. As to our journey?

MISS TESMAN. Yes.

TESMAN. No, I don't know of anything except what I have told you in my letters. I had a doctor's degree conferred on me—but that I told you yesterday.

MISS TESMAN. Yes, yes, you did. But what I mean is—haven't you any —any—expectations——?

TESMAN. Expectations?

MISS TESMAN. Why, you know, George—I'm your old auntie!

TESMAN. Why, of course I have expectations.

MISS TESMAN. Ah!

TESMAN. I have every expectation of being a professor one of these days.

MISS TESMAN. Oh, yes, a professor——

TESMAN. Indeed, I may say I am certain of it. But my dear Auntie—you know all about that already!

MISS TESMAN (*laughing to herself*). Yes, of course I do. You are quite right there. (*Changing the subject.*) But we were talking about your journey. It must have cost a great deal of money, George?

TESMAN. Well, you see—my handsome traveling scholarship went a good way.

MISS TESMAN. But I can't understand how you can have made it go far enough for two.

TESMAN. No, that's not so easy to understand—eh?

MISS TESMAN. And especially traveling with a lady—they tell me that makes it ever so much more expensive.

TESMAN. Yes, of course—it makes it a little more expensive. But Hedda had to have this trip, Auntie! She really had to. Nothing else would have done.

MISS TESMAN. No, no, I suppose not. A wedding tour seems to be quite indispensable nowadays. But tell me now—have you gone thoroughly over the house yet?

TESMAN. Yes, you may be sure I have. I have been afoot ever since daylight.

MISS TESMAN. And what do you think of it all?

TESMAN. I'm delighted! Quite delighted! Only I can't think what we are to do with the two empty rooms between this inner parlor and Hedda's bedroom.

MISS TESMAN (*laughing*). Oh, my dear George, I dare say you may find some use for them—in the course of time.

TESMAN. Why of course you are quite right, Aunt Julia! You mean as my library increases—eh?

MISS TESMAN. Yes, quite so, my dear boy. It was your library I was thinking of.

TESMAN. I am specially pleased on Hedda's account. Often and often, before we were engaged, she said that she would never care to live anywhere but in Secretary Falk's villa.

MISS TESMAN. Yes, it was lucky that this very house should come into the market, just after you had started.

TESMAN. Yes, Aunt Julia, the luck was on our side, wasn't it—eh?

MISS TESMAN. But the expense, my dear George! You will find it very expensive, all this.

TESMAN (*looks at her, a little cast down*). Yes, I suppose I shall, Aunt!

MISS TESMAN. Oh, frightfully!

TESMAN. How much do you think? In round numbers?—Eh?

MISS TESMAN. Oh, I can't even guess until all the accounts come in.

TESMAN. Well, fortunately, Judge Brack has secured the most favorable terms for me—so he said in a letter to Hedda.

MISS TESMAN. Yes, don't be uneasy, my dear boy. Besides, I have given security for the furniture and all the carpets.

TESMAN. Security? You? My dear Aunt Julia—what sort of security could you give?

MISS TESMAN. I have given a mortgage on our annuity.

TESMAN (*jumps up*). What! On your—and Aunt Rina's annuity!

MISS TESMAN. Yes, I knew of no other plan, you see.

TESMAN (*placing himself before her*). Have you gone out of your senses, Auntie! Your annuity—it's all that you and Aunt Rina have to live upon.

MISS TESMAN. Well, well, don't get so excited about it. It's only a matter of form you know—Judge Brack assured me of that. It was he that was kind enough to arrange the whole affair for me. A mere matter of form, he said.

TESMAN. Yes, that may be all very well. But nevertheless——

MISS TESMAN. You will have your own salary to depend upon now. And, good heavens, even if we did have to pay up a little——! To eke things out a bit at the start——! Why, it would be nothing but a pleasure to us.

TESMAN. Oh, Auntie—will you never be tired of making sacrifices for me!

MISS TESMAN (*rises and lays her hands on his shoulders*). Have I had any other happiness in this world except to smooth your way for you, my dear boy? You, who have had neither father nor mother to depend on. And now we have reached the goal, George! Things have looked black enough for us, sometimes; but, thank heaven, now you have nothing to fear.

TESMAN. Yes, it is really marvelous how everything has turned out for the best.

MISS TESMAN. And the people who opposed you—who wanted to bar the way for you—now you have them at your feet. They have fallen, George. Your most dangerous rival—his fall was the worst. And now he has to lie on the bed he has made for himself—poor misguided creature.

TESMAN. Have you heard anything of Eilert? Since I went away, I mean.

MISS TESMAN. Only that he is said to have published a new book.

TESMAN. What! Eilert Lövborg! Recently—eh?

MISS TESMAN. Yes, so they say. Heaven knows whether it can be worth anything! Ah, when your new book appears—that will be another story, George! What is it to be about?

TESMAN. It will deal with the domestic industries of Brabant during the Middle Ages.

MISS TESMAN. Fancy—to be able to write on such a subject as that.

TESMAN. However, it may be some time before the book is ready. I have all these collections to arrange first, you see.

MISS TESMAN. Yes, collecting and arranging—no one can beat you at that. There you are my poor brother's own son.

TESMAN. I am looking forward eagerly to setting to work at it; especially now that I have my own delightful home to work in.

MISS TESMAN. And, most of all, now that you have got the wife of your heart, my dear George.

TESMAN (*embracing her*). Oh, yes, yes, Aunt Julia. Hedda—she is the best part of all! (*Looks towards the doorway.*) I believe I hear her coming—eh?

> [HEDDA *enters from the left through the inner room.*
> *She is a woman of nine-and-twenty. Her face and*
> *figure show refinement and distinction. Her com-*
> *plexion is pale and opaque. Her steel-gray eyes ex-*
> *press a cold, unruffled repose. Her hair is of an agree-*
> *able medium brown, but not particularly abundant.*
> *She is dressed in a tasteful, somewhat loose-fitting*
> *morning gown.*]

MISS TESMAN (*going to meet* HEDDA). Good morning, my dear Hedda! Good morning, and a hearty welcome.

HEDDA (*holds out her hand*). Good morning, dear Miss Tesman! So early a call! That is kind of you.

MISS TESMAN (*with some embarrassment*). Well—has the bride slept well in her new home?

HEDDA. Oh yes, thanks. Passably.

TESMAN (*laughing*). Passably! Come, that's good, Hedda! You were sleeping like a stone when I got up.

HEDDA. Fortunately. Of course one has always to accustom one's self to new surroundings, Miss Tesman—little by little. (*Looking towards the left.*) Oh—there the servant has gone and opened the verandah door, and let in a whole flood of sunshine.

MISS TESMAN (*going towards the door*). Well, then, we will shut it.

HEDDA. No, no, not that! Tesman, please draw the curtains. That will give a softer light.

TESMAN (*at the door*). All right—all right. There now, Hedda, now you have both shade and fresh air.

HEDDA. Yes, fresh air we certainly must have, with all these stacks of flowers—— But—won't you sit down, Miss Tesman?

MISS TESMAN. No, thank you. Now that I have seen that everything is all right here—thank heaven! I must be getting home again. My sister is lying longing for me, poor thing.

TESMAN. Give her my very best love, Auntie; and say I shall look in and see her later in the day.

MISS TESMAN. Yes, yes, I'll be sure to tell her. But by-the-bye, George —(*feeling in her dress pocket*)—I have almost forgotten—I have something for you here.

TESMAN. What is it, Auntie? Eh?

MISS TESMAN (*produces a flat parcel wrapped in newspaper and hands it to him*). Look here, my dear boy.

TESMAN (*opening the parcel*). Well, I declare! Have you really saved them for me, Aunt Julia! Hedda! isn't this touching—eh?

HEDDA (*beside the whatnot on the right*). Well, what is it?

TESMAN. My old morning shoes! My slippers.

HEDDA. Indeed. I remember you often spoke of them while we were abroad.

TESMAN. Yes, I missed them terribly. (*Goes up to her.*) Now you shall see them, Hedda!

HEDDA (*going towards the stove*). Thanks, I really don't care about it.

TESMAN (*following her*). Only think—ill as she was, Aunt Rina embroidered these for me. Oh, you can't think how many associations cling to them.

HEDDA (*at the table*). Scarcely for me.

MISS TESMAN. Of course not for Hedda, George.

TESMAN. Well, but now that she belongs to the family, I thought——

HEDDA (*interrupting*). We shall never get on with this servant, Tesman.

MISS TESMAN. Not get on with Berta?

TESMAN. Why, dear, what puts that in your head? Eh?

HEDDA (*pointing*). Look there! She has left her old bonnet lying about on a chair.

TESMAN (*in consternation, drops the slippers on the floor*). Why, Hedda——

HEDDA. Just fancy, if any one should come in and see it.

TESMAN. But Hedda—that's Aunt Julia's bonnet.

HEDDA. Is it!

MISS TESMAN (*taking up the bonnet*). Yes, indeed it's mine. And what's more, it's not old, Madame Hedda.

HEDDA. I really did not look closely at it, Miss Tesman.

MISS TESMAN (*trying on the bonnet*). Let me tell you it's the first time I have worn it—the very first time.

TESMAN. And a very nice bonnet it is too—quite a beauty!

MISS TESMAN. Oh, it's no such great thing, George. (*Looks around her.*) My parasol——? Ah, here. (*Takes it.*) For this is mine too—(*mutters*)—not Berta's.

TESMAN. A new bonnet and a new parasol! Only think, Hedda!

HEDDA. Very handsome indeed.

TESMAN. Yes, isn't it? But Auntie, take a good look at Hedda before you go! See how handsome she is!

MISS TESMAN. Oh, my dear boy, there's nothing new in that. Hedda was always lovely. (*She nods and goes towards the right.*)

TESMAN (*following*). Yes, but have you noticed what splendid condition she is in? How she has filled out on the journey?

HEDDA (*crossing the room*). Oh, do be quiet——!

MISS TESMAN (*who has stopped and turned*). Filled out?

TESMAN. Of course you don't notice it so much now that she has that dress on. But I, who can see——

HEDDA (*at the glass door, impatiently*). Oh, you can't see anything.

TESMAN. It must be the mountain air in the Tyrol——

HEDDA (*curtly, interrupting*). I am exactly as I was when I started.

TESMAN. So you insist; but I'm quite certain you are not. Don't you agree with me, Auntie?

MISS TESMAN (*who has been gazing at her with folded hands*). Hedda is lovely—lovely—lovely. (*Goes up to her, takes her head between both hands, draws it downwards, and kisses her hair*). God bless and preserve Hedda Tesman—for George's sake.

HEDDA (*gently freeing herself*). Oh! Let me go.

MISS TESMAN (*in quiet emotion*). I shall not let a day pass without coming to see you.

TESMAN. No you won't, will you, Auntie? Eh?

MISS TESMAN. Good-by—good-by!

> [*She goes out by the hall door.* TESMAN *accompanies her. The door remains half open.* TESMAN *can be heard repeating his message to Aunt Rina and his thanks for the slippers.*
>
> [*In the meantime,* HEDDA *walks about the room raising her arms and clenching her hands as if in desperation. Then she flings back the curtains from the glass door, and stands there looking out.*

[*Presently* TESMAN *returns and closes the door behind him.*]

TESMAN (*picks up the slippers from the floor*). What are you looking
at, Hedda?

HEDDA (*once more calm and mistress of herself*). I am only looking at
the leaves. They are so yellow—so withered.

TESMAN (*wraps up the slippers and lays them on the table*). Well you
see, we are well into September now.

HEDDA (*again restless*). Yes, to think of it! Already in—in September.

TESMAN. Don't you think Aunt Julia's manner was strange, dear? Almost solemn? Can you imagine what was the matter with her? Eh?

HEDDA. I scarcely know her, you see. Is she often like that?

TESMAN. No, not as she was today.

HEDDA (*leaving the glass door*). Do you think she was annoyed about
the bonnet?

TESMAN. Oh, scarcely at all. Perhaps a little, just at the moment——

HEDDA. But what an idea, to pitch her bonnet about in the drawing
room! No one does that sort of thing.

TESMAN. Well you may be sure Aunt Julia won't do it again.

HEDDA. In any case, I shall manage to make my peace with her.

TESMAN. Yes, my dear, good Hedda, if you only would.

HEDDA. When you call this afternoon, you might invite her to spend
the evening here.

TESMAN. Yes, that I will. And there's one thing more you could do that
would delight her heart.

HEDDA. What is it?

TESMAN. If you could only prevail on yourself to say *du*[1] to her. For
my sake, Hedda? Eh?

HEDDA. No, no, Tesman—you really musn't ask that of me. I have told
you so already. I shall try to call her "Aunt"; and you must be
satisfied with that.

TESMAN. Well, well. Only I think now that you belong to the family,
you——

HEDDA. H'm—I can't in the least see why——

[*She goes up towards the middle doorway.*]

TESMAN (*after a pause*). Is there anything the matter with you, Hedda?
Eh?

HEDDA. I'm only looking at my old piano. It doesn't go at all well with
all the other things.

TESMAN. The first time I draw my salary, we'll see about exchanging
it.

HEDDA. No, no—no exchanging. I don't want to part with it. Suppose
we put it there in the inner room, and then get another here in its
place. When it's convenient, I mean.

[1] *Du*—thou, the familiar form of the pronoun *you.*

TESMAN (*a little taken aback*). Yes—of course we could do that.

HEDDA (*takes up the bouquet from the piano*). These flowers were not here last night when we arrived.

TESMAN. Aunt Julia must have brought them for you.

HEDDA (*examining the bouquet*). A visiting card. (*Takes it out and reads.*) "Shall return later in the day." Can you guess whose card it is?

TESMAN. No. Whose? Eh?

HEDDA. The name is "Mrs. Elvsted."

TESMAN. Is it really? Sheriff Elvsted's wife? Miss Rysing that was.

HEDDA. Exactly. The girl with the irritating hair, that she was always showing off. An old flame of yours, I've been told.

TESMAN (*laughing*). Oh, that didn't last long; and it was before I knew you, Hedda. But fancy her being in town!

HEDDA. It's odd that she should call upon us. I have scarcely seen her since we left school.

TESMAN. I haven't seen her either for—heaven knows how long. I wonder how she can endure to live in such an out-of-the-way hole— eh?

HEDDA (*after a moment's thought says suddenly*). Tell me, Tesman— isn't it somewhere near there that he—that—Eilert Lövborg is living?

TESMAN. Yes, he is somewhere in that part of the country.

[BERTA *enters by the hall door.*]

BERTA. That lady, ma'am, that brought some flowers a little while ago, is here again. (*Pointing.*) The flowers you have in your hand, ma'am.

HEDDA. Ah, is she? Well, please show her in.

[BERTA *opens the door for* MRS. ELVSTED, *and goes out herself.* MRS. ELVSTED *is a woman of fragile figure, with pretty, soft features. Her eyes are light blue, large, round, and somewhat prominent, with a startled, inquiring expression. Her hair is remarkably light, almost flaxen, and unusually abundant and wavy. She is a couple of years younger than* HEDDA. *She wears a dark visiting dress, tasteful, but not quite in the latest fashion.*]

HEDDA (*receives her warmly*). How do you do, my dear Mrs. Elvsted? It's delightful to see you again.

MRS. ELVSTED (*nervously, struggling for self-control*). Yes, it's a very long time since we met.

TESMAN (*gives her his hand*). And we too—eh?

HEDDA. Thanks for your lovely flowers——

MRS. ELVSTED. Oh, not at all—— I would have come straight here yesterday afternoon; but I heard that you were away——

TESMAN. Have you just come to town? Eh?

MRS. ELVSTED. I arrived yesterday, about midday. Oh, I was quite in despair when I heard that you were not at home.

HEDDA. In despair! How so?

TESMAN. Why, my dear Mrs. Rysing—I mean Mrs. Elvsted——

HEDDA. I hope that you are not in any trouble?

MRS. ELVSTED. Yes, I am. And I don't know another living creature here that I can turn to.

HEDDA (*laying the bouquet on the table*). Come—let us sit here on the sofa——

MRS. ELVSTED. Oh no, I am too restless to sit down.

HEDDA. Oh no, you're not. Come here. (*She draws* MRS. ELVSTED *down upon the sofa and sits at her side.*)

TESMAN. Well? What is it, Mrs. Elvsted?

HEDDA. Has anything particular happened to you at home?

MRS. ELVSTED. Yes—and no. Oh—I am so anxious you should not misunderstand me——

HEDDA. Then your best plan is to tell us the whole story, Mrs. Elvsted.

TESMAN. I suppose that's what you have come for—eh?

MRS. ELVSTED. Yes, yes—of course it is. Well then, I must tell you—if you don't already know—that Eilert Lövborg is in town, too.

HEDDA. Lövborg——!

TESMAN. What! Has Eilert Lövborg come back? Fancy that, Hedda!

HEDDA. Well, well—I hear it.

MRS. ELVSTED. He has been here a week already. Just fancy—a whole week! In this terrible town, alone! With so many temptations on all sides.

HEDDA. But my dear Mrs. Elvsted—how does he concern you so much?

MRS. ELVSTED (*looks at her with a startled air, and says rapidly*). He was the children's tutor.

HEDDA. Your children's?

MRS. ELVSTED. My husband's. I have none.

HEDDA. Your step-children's, then?

MRS. ELVSTED. Yes.

TESMAN (*somewhat hesitatingly*). Then was he—I don't know how to express it—was he—regular enough in his habits to be fit for the post? Eh?

MRS. ELVSTED. For the last two years his conduct has been irreproach-able.

TESMAN. Has it indeed? Fancy that, Hedda!

HEDDA. I hear it.

MRS. ELVSTED. Perfectly irreproachable, I assure you! In every respect. But all the same—now that I know he is here—in this great town —and with a large sum of money in his hands—I can't help being in mortal fear for him.

TESMAN. Why did he not remain where he was? With you and your husband? Eh?

MRS. ELVSTED. After his book was published he was too restless and un-settled to remain with us.

TESMAN. Yes, by-the-bye, Aunt Julia told me he had published a new book.

MRS. ELVSTED. Yes, a big book, dealing with the march of civilization —in broad outline, as it were. It came out about a fortnight ago. And since it has sold so well, and been so much read—and made such a sensation——

TESMAN. Has it indeed? It must be something he has had lying by since his better days.

MRS. ELVSTED. Long ago, you mean?

TESMAN. Yes.

MRS. ELVSTED. No, he has written it all since he has been with us— within the last year.

TESMAN. Isn't that good news. Hedda? Think of that.

MRS. ELVSTED. Ah, yes, if only it would last!

HEDDA. Have you seen him here in town?

MRS. ELVSTED. No, not yet. I have had the greatest difficulty in finding out his address. But this morning I discovered it at last.

HEDDA (*looks searchingly at her*). Do you know, it seems to me a little odd of your husband—h'm——

MRS. ELVSTED (*starting nervously*). Of my husband! What?

HEDDA. That he should send you to town on such an errand—that he does not come himself and look after his friend.

MRS. ELVSTED. Oh no, no—my husband has no time. And besides, I—I had some shopping to do.

HEDDA (*with a slight smile*). Ah, that is a different matter.

MRS. ELVSTED (*rising quickly and uneasily*). And now I beg and implore you, Mr. Tesman—receive Eilert Lövborg kindly if he comes to you! And that he is sure to do. You see you were such great friends in the old days. And then you are interested in the same studies—the same branch of science—so far as I can understand.

TESMAN. We used to be, at any rate.

MRS. ELVSTED. That is why I beg so earnestly that you—you too— will keep a sharp eye upon him. Oh, you will promise me that, Mr. Tesman—won't you?

TESMAN. With the greatest of pleasure, Mrs. Rysing——

HEDDA. Elvsted.

TESMAN. I assure you I shall do all I possibly can for Eilert. You may rely upon me.

MRS. ELVSTED. Oh, how very, very kind of you! (*Presses his hands.*) Thanks, thanks, thanks! (*Frightened.*) You see, my husband is very fond of him!

HEDDA (*rising*). You ought to write to him, Tesman. Perhaps he may not care to come to you of his own accord.

TESMAN. Well, perhaps it would be the right thing to do, Hedda? Eh?

HEDDA. And the sooner the better. Why not at once?

MRS. ELVSTED (*imploringly*). Oh, if you only would!

TESMAN. I'll write this moment. Have you his address. Mrs.—Mrs. Elvsted.

MRS. ELVSTED. Yes. (*Takes a slip of paper from her pocket, and hands it to him.*) Here it is.

TESMAN. Good, good. Then I'll go in—— (*Looks about him.*) By-the-bye—my slippers? Oh, here. (*Takes the packet, and is about to go.*)

HEDDA. Be sure you write him a cordial, friendly letter. And a good long one too.

TESMAN. Yes, I will.

MRS. ELVSTED. But please, please don't say a word to show that I have suggested it.

TESMAN. No, how could you think I would? Eh? (*He goes out to the right, through the inner room.*)

HEDDA (*goes up to* MRS. ELVSTED, *smiles, and says in a low voice*). There. We have killed two birds with one stone.

MRS. ELVSTED. What do you mean?

HEDDA. Could you not see that I wanted him to go?

MRS. ELVSTED. Yes, to write the letter——

HEDDA. And that I might speak to you alone.

MRS. ELVSTED (*confused*). About the same thing?

HEDDA. Precisely.

MRS. ELVSTED (*apprehensively*). But there is nothing more, Mrs. Tesman! Absolutely nothing!

HEDDA. Oh, yes, but there is. There is a great deal more—I can see that. Sit here—and we'll have a cosy, confidential chat. (*She forces* MRS. ELVSTED *to sit in the easy chair beside the stove, and seats herself on one of the footstools.*)

MRS. ELVSTED (*anxiously, looking at her watch*). But, my dear Mrs. Tesman—I was really on the point of going.

HEDDA. Oh, you can't be in such a hurry. Well? Now tell me something about your life at home.

MRS. ELVSTED. Oh, that is just what I care least to speak about.

HEDDA. But to me, dear——? Why, weren't we schoolfellows?

MRS. ELVSTED. Yes, but you were in the class above me. Oh, how dreadfully afraid of you I was then!

HEDDA. Afraid of me?

MRS. ELVSTED. *Yes*, dreadfully. For when we met on the stairs you used always to pull my hair.

HEDDA. Did I, really?

MRS. ELVSTED. Yes, and once you said you would burn it off my head.

HEDDA. Oh, that was all nonsense, of course.

MRS. ELVSTED. Yes, but I was so silly in those days. And since then, too—we have drifted so far—far apart from each other. Our circles have been so entirely different.

HEDDA. Well then, we must try to drift together again. Now listen! At school we said *du* to each other; and we called each other by our Christian names——

MRS. ELVSTED. No, I am sure you must be mistaken.

HEDDA. No, not at all! I can remember quite distinctly. So now we are going to renew our old friendship. (*Draws the footstool closer to* MRS. ELVSTED.) There now! (*Kisses her cheek.*) You must say *du* to me and call me Hedda.

MRS. ELVSTED (*presses and pats her hands*). Oh, how good and kind you are! I am not used to such kindness.

HEDDA. There, there, there! And I shall say *du* to you, as in the old days, and call you my dear Thora.

MRS. ELVSTED. My name is Thea.

HEDDA. Why, of course! I meant Thea. (*Looks at her compassionately.*) So you are not accustomed to goodness and kindness, Thea? Not in your own home?

MRS. ELVSTED. Oh, if I only had a home! But I haven't any; I have never had a home.

HEDDA (*looks at her for a moment*). I almost suspected as much.

MRS. ELVSTED (*gazing helplessly before her*). Yes—yes—yes.

HEDDA. I don't quite remember—was it not as housekeeper that you first went to Mr. Elvsted's?

MRS. ELVSTED. I really went as governess. But his wife—his late wife —was an invalid—and rarely left her room. So I had to look after the housekeeping as well.

HEDDA. And then—at last—you became mistress of the house.

MRS. ELVSTED (*sadly*). Yes, I did.

HEDDA. Let me see—about how long ago was that?

MRS. ELVSTED. My marriage?

HEDDA. Yes.

MRS. ELVSTED. Five years ago.

HEDDA. To be sure; it must be that.

MRS. ELVSTED. Oh, those five years——! Or at all events the last two or three of them! Oh, if you[2] could only imagine——

HEDDA (*giving her a little slap on the hand*). De? Fie, Thea!

MRS. ELVSTED. Yes, yes, I will try—— Well if—you could only imagine and understand——

HEDDA (*lightly*). Eilert Lövborg has been in your neighborhood about three years, hasn't he?

MRS. ELVSTED (*looks at her doubtfully*). Eilert Lövborg? Yes—he has.

HEDDA. Had you known him before, in town here?

MRS. ELVSTED. Scarcely at all. I mean—I knew him by name of course.

HEDDA. But you saw a good deal of him in the country?

[2] Mrs. Elvsted here uses the formal pronoun *De*, whereupon Hedda rebukes her. In her next speech Mrs. Elvsted says *du*.

MRS. ELVSTED. Yes, he came to us every day. You see, he gave the children lessons; for in the long run I couldn't manage it all myself.

HEDDA. No, that's clear. And your husband——? I suppose he is often away from home?

MRS. ELVSTED. Yes. Being Sheriff, you know, he has to travel about a good deal in his district.

HEDDA (*leaning against the arm of the chair*). Thea—my poor, sweet Thea—now you must tell me everything—exactly as it stands.

MRS. ELVSTED. Well then, you must question me.

HEDDA. What sort of a man is your husband, Thea? I mean—you know —in everyday life. Is he kind to you?

MRS. ELVSTED (*evasively*). I am sure he means well in everything.

HEDDA. I should think he must be altogether too old for you. There is at least twenty years' difference between you, is there not?

MRS. ELVSTED (*irritably*). Yes, that is true, too. Everything about him is repellent to me! We have not a thought in common. We have no single point of sympathy—he and I.

HEDDA. But is he not fond of you all the same? In his own way?

MRS. ELVSTED. Oh, I really don't know. I think he regards me simply as a useful property. And then it doesn't cost much to keep me. I am not expensive.

HEDDA. That is stupid of you.

MRS. ELVSTED (*shakes her head*). It cannot be otherwise—not with him. I don't think he really cares for any one but himself—and perhaps a little for the children.

HEDDA. And for Eilert Lövborg, Thea.

MRS. ELVSTED (*looking at her*). For Eilert Lövborg? What puts that into your head?

HEDDA. Well, my dear—I should say,when he sends you after him all the way to town—— (*Smiling almost imperceptibly.*) And besides, you said so yourself, to Tesman.

MRS. ELVSTED (*with a little nervous twitch*). Did I? Yes, I suppose I did. (*Vehemently, but not loudly.*) No—I may just as well make a clean breast of it at once! For it must all come out in any case.

HEDDA. Why, my dear Thea——?

MRS. ELVSTED. Well, to make a long story short: My husband did not know that I was coming.

HEDDA. What! Your husband didn't know it!

MRS. ELVSTED. No, of course not. For that matter, he was away from home himself—he was traveling. Oh, I could bear it no longer, Hedda! I couldn't indeed—so utterly alone as I should have been in future.

HEDDA. Well? And then?

MRS. ELVSTED. So I put together some of my things—what I needed most—as quietly as possible. And then I left the house.

HEDDA. Without a word?

MRS. ELVSTED. Yes—and took the train straight to town.

HEDDA. Why, my dear, good Thea—to think of you daring to do it!

MRS. ELVSTED (*rises and moves about the room*). What else could I possibly do?

HEDDA. But what do you think your husband will say when you go home again?

MRS. ELVSTED (*at the table, looks at her*). Back to him.

HEDDA. Of course.

MRS. ELVSTED. I shall never go back to him again.

HEDDA (*rising and going towards her*). Then you have left your home —for good and all?

MRS. ELVSTED. Yes. There was nothing else to be done.

HEDDA. But then—to take flight so openly.

MRS. ELVSTED. Oh, it's impossible to keep things of that sort secret.

HEDDA. But what do you think people will say of you, Thea?

MRS. ELVSTED. They may say what they like for aught *I* care. (*Seats herself wearily and sadly on the sofa.*) I have done nothing but what I had to do.

HEDDA (*after a short silence*). And what are your plans now? What do you think of doing?

MRS. ELVSTED. I don't know yet. I only know this, that I must live here, where Eilert Lövborg is—if I am to live at all.

HEDDA (*takes a chair from the table, seats herself beside her, and strokes her hands*). My dear Thea—how did this—this friendship— between you and Eilert Lövborg come about?

MRS. ELVSTED. Oh, it grew up gradually. I gained a sort of influence over him.

HEDDA. Indeed?

MRS. ELVSTED. He gave up his old habits. Not because I asked him to, for I never dared do that. But of course he saw how repulsive they were to me; and so he dropped them.

HEDDA (*concealing an involuntary smile of scorn*). Then you have re-claimed him—as the saying goes—my little Thea.

MRS. ELVSTED. So he says himself, at any rate. And he, on his side, has made a real human being of me—taught me to think, and to under-stand so many things.

HEDDA. Did he give you lessons too, then?

MRS. ELVSTED. No, not exactly lessons. But he talked to me—talked about such an infinity of things. And then came the lovely, happy time when I began to share in his work—when he allowed me to help him!

HEDDA. Oh, he did, did he?

MRS. ELVSTED. Yes! He never wrote anything without my assistance.

HEDDA. You were two good comrades, in fact?

MRS. ELVSTED (*eagerly*). Comrades! Yes, fancy, Hedda—that is the very word he used! Oh, I ought to feel perfectly happy; and yet I cannot; for I don't know how long it will last.

HEDDA. Are you no surer of him than that?

MRS. ELVSTED (*gloomily*). A woman's shadow stands between Eilert Lövborg and me.

HEDDA (*looks at her anxiously*). Who can that be?

MRS. ELVSTED. I don't know. Some one he knew in his—in his past. Some one he has never been able wholly to forget.

HEDDA. What has he told you—about this?

MRS. ELVSTED. He has only once—quite vaguely—alluded to it.

HEDDA. Well! And what did he say?

MRS. ELVSTED. He said that when they parted, she threatened to shoot him with a pistol.

HEDDA (*with cold composure*). Oh, nonsense! No one does that sort of thing here.

MRS. ELVSTED. No. And that is why I think it must have been that red-haired singing woman whom he once——

HEDDA. Yes, very likely.

MRS. ELVSTED. For I remember they used to say of her that she carried loaded firearms.

HEDDA. Oh—then of course it must have been she.

MRS. ELVSTED (*wringing her hands*). And now just fancy, Hedda—I hear that this singing woman—that she is in town again! Oh, I don't know what to do——

HEDDA (*glancing towards the inner room*). Hush! Here comes Tesman. (*Rises and whispers.*) Thea—all this must remain between you and me.

MRS. ELVSTED (*springing up*). Oh, yes, yes! for heaven's sake——!

[GEORGE TESMAN, *with a letter in his hand, comes from the right through the inner room.*]

TESMAN. There now—the epistle is finished.

HEDDA. That's right. And now Mrs. Elvsted is just going. Wait a moment—I'll go with you to the garden gate.

TESMAN. Do you think Berta could post the letter, Hedda dear?

HEDDA (*takes it*). I will tell her to.

[BERTA *enters from the hall.*]

BERTA. Judge Brack wishes to know if Mrs. Tesman will receive him.

HEDDA. Yes, ask Judge Brack to come in. And look here—put this letter in the post.

BERTA (*taking the letter*). Yes, ma'am.

[*She opens the door for* JUDGE BRACK *and goes out herself.* BRACK *is a man of forty-five; thickset, but well built and elastic in his movements. His face is roundish with an aristocratic profile. His hair is short, still almost black, and carefully dressed. His eyes are lively and sparkling. His eyebrows thick. His moustaches are also thick, with short-cut ends. He wears a well-cut walking suit, a little too youthful for his age. He uses an eyeglass, which he now and then lets drop.*]

JUDGE BRACK (*with his hat in his hand, bowing*). May one venture to call so early in the day?

HEDDA. Of course one may.

TESMAN (*presses his hand*). You are welcome at any time. (*Introducing him.*) Judge Brack—Miss Rysing——

HEDDA. Oh——!

BRACK (*bowing*). Ah—delighted——

HEDDA (*looks at him and laughs*). It's nice to have a look at you by daylight, Judge!

BRACK. Do you find me—altered?

HEDDA. A little younger, I think.

BRACK. Thank you so much.

TESMAN. But what do you think of Hedda—eh? Doesn't she look flourishing? She has actually——

HEDDA. Oh, do leave me alone. You haven't thanked Judge Brack for all the trouble he has taken——

BRACK. Oh, nonsense—it was a pleasure to me——

HEDDA. Yes, you are a friend indeed. But here stands Thea all impatience to be off—so *au revoir*, Judge. I shall be back again presently. (*Mutual salutations.* MRS. ELVSTED *and* HEDDA *go out by the hall door.*)

BRACK. Well, is your wife tolerably satisfied——

TESMAN. Yes, we can't thank you sufficiently. Of course she talks of a little rearrangement here and there; and one or two things are still wanting. We shall have to buy some additional trifles.

BRACK. Indeed!

TESMAN. But we won't trouble you about these things. Hedda says she herself will look after what is wanting.—— Shan't we sit down? Eh?

BRACK. Thanks, for a moment. (*Seats himself beside the table.*) There is something I wanted to speak to you about, my dear Tesman.

TESMAN. Indeed? Ah, I understand! (*Seating himself.*) I suppose it's the serious part of the frolic that is coming now. Eh?

BRACK. Oh, the money question is not so very pressing; though, for that matter, I wish we had gone a little more economically to work.

TESMAN. But that would never have done, you know! Think of Hedda, my dear fellow! You, who know her so well—— I couldn't possibly ask her to put up with a shabby style of living!

BRACK. No, no—that is just the difficulty.

TESMAN. And then—fortunately—it can't be long before I receive my appointment.

BRACK. Well, you see—such things are often apt to hang fire for a time.

TESMAN. Have you heard anything definite? Eh?

BRACK. Nothing exactly definite——— (*Interrupting himself.*) But, by-the-bye—I have one piece of news for you.

TESMAN. Well?

BRACK. Your old friend, Eilert Lövborg, has returned to town.

TESMAN. I know that already.

BRACK. Indeed! How did you learn it?

TESMAN. From that lady who went out with Hedda.

BRACK. Really? What was her name? I didn't quite catch it.

TESMAN. Mrs. Elvsted.

BRACK. Aha—Sheriff Elvsted's wife? Of course—he has been living up in their regions.

TESMAN. And fancy—I'm delighted to hear that he is quite a reformed character!

BRACK. So they say.

TESMAN. And then he has published a new book—eh?

BRACK. Yes, indeed he has.

TESMAN. And I hear it has made some sensation!

BRACK. Quite an unusual sensation.

TESMAN. Fancy—isn't that good news! A man of such extraordinary talents——— I felt so grieved to think that he had gone irretrievably to ruin.

BRACK. That was what everybody thought.

TESMAN. But I cannot imagine what he will take to now! How in the world will he be able to make his living? Eh?

    [*During the last words,* HEDDA *has entered by the hall door.*]

HEDDA (*to* BRACK, *laughing with a touch of scorn*). Tesman is forever worrying about how people are to make their living.

TESMAN. Well, you see, dear—we were talking about poor Eilert Lövborg.

HEDDA (*glancing at him rapidly*). Oh, indeed? (*Seats herself in the arm-chair beside the stove and asks indifferently.*) What is the matter with him?

TESMAN. Well—no doubt he has run through all his property long ago; and he can scarcely write a new book every year—eh? So I really can't see what is to become of him.

BRACK. Perhaps I can give you some information on that point.

TESMAN. Indeed!

BRACK. You must remember that his relations have a good deal of influence.

TESMAN. Oh, his relations, unfortunately, have entirely washed their hands of him.

BRACK. At one time they called him the hope of the family.

TESMAN. At one time, yes! But he has put an end to all that.

HEDDA. Who knows? (*With a slight smile.*) I hear they have reclaimed him up at Sheriff Elvsted's———

BRACK. And then this book that he has published——

TESMAN. Well, well, I hope to goodness they may find something for him to do. I have just written to him. I asked him to come and see us this evening, Hedda dear.

BRACK. But, my dear fellow, you are booked for my bachelors' party this evening. You promised on the pier last night.

HEDDA. Had you forgotten, Tesman?

TESMAN. Yes, I had utterly forgotten.

BRACK. But it doesn't matter, for you may be sure he won't come.

TESMAN. What makes you think that? Eh?

BRACK (*with a little hesitation, rising and resting his hands on the back of his chair*). My dear Tesman—and you too, Mrs. Tesman—I think I ought not to keep you in the dark about something that—that——

TESMAN. That concerns Eilert——?

BRACK. Both you and him.

TESMAN. Well, my dear Judge, out with it.

BRACK. You must be prepared to find your appointment deferred longer than you desired or expected.

TESMAN (*jumping up uneasily*). Is there some hitch about it? Eh?

BRACK. The nomination may perhaps be made conditional on the result of a competition——

TESMAN. Competition! Think of that, Hedda!

HEDDA (*leans farther back in the chair*). Aha—aha!

TESMAN. But who can my competitor be? Surely not——?

BRACK. Yes, precisely—Eilert Lövborg.

TESMAN (*clasping his hands*). No, no—it's quite inconceivable! Quite impossible! Eh?

BRACK. H'm—that is what it may come to, all the same.

TESMAN. Well but, Judge Brack—it would show the most incredible lack of consideration for me. (*Gesticulates with his arms.*) For—just think—I'm a married man. We have been married on the strength of these prospects, Hedda and I; and run deep into debt; and borrowed money from Aunt Julia too. Good heavens, they had as good as promised me the appointment. Eh?

BRACK. Well, well, well—no doubt you will get it in the end; only after a contest.

HEDDA (*immovable in her armchair*). Fancy, Tesman, there will be a sort of sporting interest in that.

TESMAN. Why, my dearest Hedda, how can you be so indifferent about it.

HEDDA (*as before*). I am not at all indifferent. I am most eager to see who wins.

BRACK. In any case, Mrs. Tesman, it is best that you should know how matters stand. I mean—before you set about the little purchases I hear you are threatening.

HEDDA. This can make no difference.

BRACK. Indeed! Then I have no more to say. Good-by! (*To* TESMAN.) I shall look in on my way back from my afternoon walk, and take you home with me.

TESMAN. Oh yes, yes—your news has quite upset me.

HEDDA (*reclining, holds out her hand*). Good-by, Judge; and be sure you call in the afternoon.

BRACK. Many thanks. Good-by, good-by!

TESMAN (*accompanying him to the door*). Good-by, my dear Judge! You must really excuse me—— (JUDGE BRACK *goes out by the hall door.*)

TESMAN (*crosses the room*). Oh, Hedda—one should never rush into adventures. Eh?

HEDDA (*looks at him, smiling*). Do you do that?

TESMAN. Yes, dear—there is no denying—it was adventurous to go and marry and set up house upon mere expectations.

HEDDA. Perhaps you are right there.

TESMAN. Well—at all events, we have our delightful home, Hedda! Fancy, the home we both dreamed of—the home we were in love with, I may almost say. Eh?

HEDDA (*rising slowly and wearily*). It was part of our compact that we were to go into society—to keep open house.

TESMAN. Yes, if you only knew how I had been looking forward to it! Fancy—to see you as hostess—in a select circle? Eh? Well, well, well—for the present we shall have to get on without society, Hedda —only to invite Aunt Julia now and then. Oh, I intended you to lead such an utterly different life, dear——!

HEDDA. Of course I cannot have my man in livery just yet.

TESMAN. Oh no, unfortunately. It would be out of the question for us to keep a footman, you know.

HEDDA. And the saddle horse I was to have had——

TESMAN (*aghast*). The saddle horse!

HEDDA. ——I suppose I must not think of that now.

TESMAN. Good heavens, no!—that's as clear as daylight.

HEDDA (*goes up the room*). Well, I shall have one thing at least to kill time with in the meanwhile.

TESMAN (*beaming*). Oh, thank heaven for that! What is it, Hedda? Eh?

HEDDA (*in the middle doorway, looks at him with covert scorn*). My pistols, George.

TESMAN (*in alarm*). Your pistols!

HEDDA (*with cold eyes*). General Gabler's pistols. (*She goes out through the inner room, to the left.*)

TESMAN (*rushes up to the middle doorway and calls after her*). No, for heaven's sake, Hedda darling—don't touch those dangerous things! For my sake, Hedda! Eh?

ACT II

≈⌐ Scene: *The room at the* TESMANS' *as in the first Act, except that the piano has been removed, and an elegant little writing table with bookshelves put in its place. A smaller table stands near the sofa at the left. Most of the bouquets have been taken away.* MRS. ELVSTED'S *bouquet is upon the large table in front. It is afternoon.*

HEDDA, *dressed to receive callers, is alone in the room. She stands by the open glass door, loading a revolver. The fellow to it lies in an open pistol case on the writing table.*

HEDDA (*looks down the garden, and calls*). So you are here again, Judge!

BRACK (*is heard calling from a distance*). As you see, Mrs. Tesman!

HEDDA (*raises the pistol and points*). Now I'll shoot you, Judge Brack!

BRACK (*calling unseen*). No, no, no! Don't stand aiming at me!

HEDDA. This is what comes of sneaking in by the back way.[1] (*She fires.*)

BRACK (*nearer*). Are you out of your senses——!

HEDDA. Dear me—did I happen to hit you?

BRACK (*still outside*). I wish you would let these pranks alone!

HEDDA. Come in then, Judge.

> [JUDGE BRACK, *dressed as though for a men's party, enters by the glass door. He carries a light overcoat over his arm.*]

BRACK. What the deuce—haven't you tired of that sport, yet? What are you shooting at?

HEDDA. Oh, I am only firing in the air.

BRACK (*gently takes the pistol out of her hand*). Allow me, madam! (*Looks at it.*) Ah—I know this pistol well! (*Looks around.*) Where is the case? Ah, here it is. (*Lays the pistol in it, and shuts it.*) Now we won't play at that game any more today.

---

[1] "Bagveje" means both "back ways" and "underhand courses."

HEDDA. Then what in heaven's name would you have me do with myself?

BRACK. Have you had no visitors?

HEDDA (*closing the glass door*). Not one. I suppose all our set are still
out of town.

BRACK. And is Tesman not at home either?

HEDDA (*at the writing table, putting the pistol case in a drawer which
she shuts*). No. He rushed off to his aunt's directly after lunch; he
didn't expect you so early.

BRACK. H'm—how stupid of me not to have thought of that!

HEDDA (*turning her head to look at him*). Why stupid?

BRACK. Because if I had thought of it I should have come a little—
earlier.

HEDDA (*crossing the room*). Then you would have found no one to
receive you; for I have been in my room changing my dress ever
since lunch.

BRACK. And is there no sort of little chink that we could hold a parley
through?

HEDDA. You have forgotten to arrange one.

BRACK. That was another piece of stupidity.

HEDDA. Well, we must just settle down here—and wait. Tesman is not
likely to be back for some time yet.

BRACK. Never mind; I shall not be impatient.

       [HEDDA *seats herself in the corner of the sofa.* BRACK
       *lays his overcoat over the back of the nearest chair,
       and sits down, but keeps his hat in his hand. A short
       silence. They look at each other.*]

HEDDA. Well?

BRACK (*in the same tone*). Well?

HEDDA. I spoke first.

BRACK (*bending a little forward*). Come, let us have a cosy little chat,
Mrs. Hedda.

HEDDA (*leaning further back in the sofa*). Does it not seem like a
whole eternity since our last talk? Of course I don't count those few
words yesterday evening and this morning.

BRACK. You mean since our last confidential talk? Our last tête-à-tête?

HEDDA. Well, yes—since you put it so.

BRACK. Not a day has passed but I have wished that you were home
again.

HEDDA. And I have done nothing but wish the same thing.

BRACK. You? Really, Mrs. Hedda? And I thought you had been enjoying your tour so much!

HEDDA. Oh, yes, you may be sure of that!

BRACK. But Tesman's letters spoke of nothing but happiness.

HEDDA. Oh, Tesman! You see, he thinks nothing so delightful as grubbing in libraries and making copies of old parchments, or whatever you call them.

BRACK (*with a spice of malice*). Well, that is his vocation in life—or part of it at any rate.

HEDDA. Yes, of course; and no doubt when it's your vocation—— But *I!* Oh, my dear Mr. Brack, how mortally bored I have been.

BRACK (*sympathetically*). Do you really say so? In downright earnest?

HEDDA. Yes, you can surely understand it——! To go for six whole months without meeting a soul that knew anything of our circle, or could talk about the things we are interested in.

BRACK. Yes, yes—I too should feel that a deprivation.

HEDDA. And then, what I found most intolerable of all——

BRACK. Well?

HEDDA. ——was being everlastingly in the company of—one and the same person——

BRACK (*with a nod of assent*). Morning, noon, and night, yes—at all possible times and seasons.

HEDDA. I said "everlastingly."

BRACK. Just so. But I should have thought, with our excellent Tesman, one could——

HEDDA. Tesman is—a specialist, my dear Judge.

BRACK. Undeniably.

HEDDA. And specialists are not at all amusing to travel with. Not in the long run at any rate.

BRACK. Not even—the specialist one happens to love?

HEDDA. Faugh—don't use that sickening word!

BRACK (*taken aback*). What do you say, Mrs. Hedda?

HEDDA (*half laughing, half irritated*). You should just try it! To hear of nothing but the history of civilization, morning, noon, and night——

BRACK. Everlastingly.

HEDDA. Yes, yes, yes! And then all this about the domestic industry of the middle ages——! That's the most disgusting part of it!

BRACK (*looks searchingly at her*). But tell me—in that case, how am I to understand your——? H'm——

HEDDA. My accepting George Tesman, you mean?

BRACK. Well, let us put it so.

HEDDA. Good heavens, do you see anything so wonderful in that?

BRACK. Yes and no—Mrs. Hedda.

HEDDA. I had positively danced myself tired, my dear Judge. My day was done—— (*With a slight shudder.*) Oh no—I won't say that; nor think it either!

BRACK. You have assuredly no reason to.

HEDDA. Oh, reasons—— (*Watching him closely.*) George Tesman—after all, you must admit that he is correctness itself.

BRACK. His correctness and respectability are beyond all question.

HEDDA. And I don't see anything absolutely ridiculous about him. Do you?

BRACK. Ridiculous? N—no—I shouldn't exactly say so——

HEDDA. Well—and his powers of research, at all events, are untiring. I see no reason why he should not one day come to the front, after all.

BRACK (*looks at her hesitatingly*). I thought that you, like every one else, expected him to attain the highest distinction.

HEDDA (*with an expression of fatigue*). Yes, so I did.—And then, since he was bent, at all hazards, on being allowed to provide for me—I really don't know why I should not have accepted his offer?

BRACK. No—if you look at it in that light——

HEDDA. It was more than my other adorers were prepared to do for me, my dear Judge.

BRACK (*laughing*). Well, I can't answer for all the rest; but as for myself, you know quite well that I have always entertained a—a certain respect for the marriage tie—for marriage as an institution, Mrs. Hedda.

HEDDA (*jestingly*). Oh, I assure you I have never cherished any hopes with respect to you.

BRACK. All I require is a pleasant and intimate interior, where I can make myself useful in every way, and am free to come and go as—as a trusted friend——

HEDDA. Of the master of the house, do you mean?

BRACK (*bowing*). Frankly—of the mistress first of all; but of course of the master, too, in the second place. Such a triangular friendship—if I may call it so—is really a great convenience for all parties, let me tell you.

HEDDA. Yes, I have many a time longed for some one to make a third on our travels. Oh—those railway-carriage tête-à-têtes——!

BRACK. Fortunately your wedding journey is over now.

HEDDA (*shaking her head*). Not by a long—long way. I have only arrived at a station on the line.

BRACK. Well, then the passengers jump out and move about a little, Mrs. Hedda.

HEDDA. I never jump out.

BRACK. Really?

HEDDA. No—because there is always some one standing by to——

BRACK (*laughing*). To look at your ankles, do you mean?

HEDDA. Precisely.

BRACK. Well but, dear me——

HEDDA (*with a gesture of repulsion*). I won't have it. I would rather keep my seat where I happen to be—and continue the tête-à-tête.

BRACK. But suppose a third person were to jump in and join the couple.

HEDDA. Ah—that is quite another matter!

BRACK. A trusted, sympathetic friend——

HEDDA. ——with a fund of conversation on all sorts of lively topics——

BRACK. ——and not the least bit of a specialist!

HEDDA (*with an audible sigh*). Yes, that would be a relief indeed.

BRACK (*hears the front door open, and glances in that direction*). The triangle is completed.

HEDDA (*half aloud*). And on goes the train.

> [GEORGE TESMAN, *in a gray walking suit, with a soft felt hat, enters from the hall. He has a number of unbound books under his arm and in his pockets.*]

TESMAN (*goes up to the table beside the corner settee*). Ouf—what a load for a warm day—all these books. (*Lays them on the table.*) I'm positively perspiring, Hedda. Hallo—are you there already, my dear Judge? Eh? Berta didn't tell me.

BRACK (*rising*). I came in through the garden.

HEDDA. What books have you got there?

TESMAN (*stands looking them through*). Some new books on my special subjects—quite indispensable to me.

HEDDA. Your special subjects?

BRACK. Yes, books on his special subjects, Mrs. Tesman. (BRACK *and* HEDDA *exchange a confidential smile.*)

HEDDA. Do you need still more books on your special subjects?

TESMAN. Yes, my dear Hedda, one can never have too many of them. Of course one must keep up with all that is written and published.

HEDDA. Yes, I suppose one must.

TESMAN (*searching among his books*). And look here—I have got hold of Eilert Lövborg's new book too. (*Offering it to her.*) Perhaps you would like to glance through it, Hedda? Eh?

HEDDA. No, thank you. Or rather—afterwards perhaps.

TESMAN. I looked into it a little on the way home.

BRACK. Well, what do you think of it—as a specialist?

TESMAN. I think it shows quite remarkable soundness of judgment. He never wrote like that before. (*Putting the books together.*) Now I shall take all these into my study. I'm longing to cut the leaves——! And then I must change my clothes. (*To* BRACK.) I suppose we needn't start just yet? Eh?

BRACK. Oh, dear no—there is not the slightest hurry.

TESMAN. Well then, I will take my time. (*Is going with his books, but stops in the doorway and turns.*) By-the-bye, Hedda—Aunt Julia is not coming this evening.

HEDDA. Not coming? Is it that affair of the bonnet that keeps her away?

TESMAN. Oh, not at all. How could you think such a thing of Aunt Julia? Just fancy——! The fact is, Aunt Rina is very ill.

HEDDA. She always is.

TESMAN. Yes, but today she is much worse than usual, poor dear.

HEDDA. Oh, then it's only natural that her sister should remain with her. I must bear my disappointment.

TESMAN. And you can't imagine, dear, how delighted Aunt Julia seemed to be—because you had come home looking so flourishing!

HEDDA (*half aloud, rising*). Oh, those everlasting aunts!

TESMAN. What?

HEDDA (*going to the glass door*). Nothing.

TESMAN. Oh, all right. (*He goes through the inner room, out to the right.*)

BRACK. What bonnet were you talking about?

HEDDA. Oh, it was a little episode with Miss Tesman this morning. She had laid down her bonnet on the chair there—(*Looks at him and smiles.*)—and I pretended to think it was the servant's.

BRACK (*shaking his head*). Now my dear Mrs. Hedda, how could you do such a thing? To that excellent old lady, too!

HEDDA (*nervously crossing the room*). Well, you see—these impulses come over me all of a sudden; and I cannot resist them. (*Throws herself down in the easy chair by the stove.*) Oh, I don't know how to explain it.

BRACK (*behind the easy chair*). You are not really happy—that is at the bottom of it.

HEDDA (*looking straight before her*). I know of no reason why I should be—happy. Perhaps you can give me one?

BRACK. Well—amongst other things, because you have got exactly the home you had set your heart on.

HEDDA (*looks up at him and laughs*). Do you too believe in that legend?

BRACK. Is there nothing in it, then?

HEDDA. Oh, yes, there is something in it.

BRACK. Well?

HEDDA. There is this in it, that I made use of Tesman to see me home from evening parties last summer——

BRACK. I, unfortunately, had to go quite a different way.

HEDDA. That's true. I know you were going a different way last summer.

BRACK (*laughing*). Oh fie, Mrs. Hedda! Well, then—you and Tesman——?

HEDDA. Well, we happened to pass here one evening; Tesman, poor fellow, was writhing in the agony of having to find conversation; so I took pity on the learned man——

BRACK (*smiles doubtfully*). You took pity? H'm——

HEDDA. Yes, I really did. And so—to help him out of his torment—I happened to say, in pure thoughtlessness, that I should like to live in this villa.

BRACK. No more than that?

HEDDA. Not that evening.

BRACK. But afterwards?

HEDDA. Yes, my thoughtlessness had consequences, my dear Judge.

BRACK. Unfortunately that too often happens, Mrs. Hedda.

HEDDA. Thanks! So you see it was this enthusiasm for Secretary Falk's villa that first constituted a bond of sympathy between George Tesman and me. From that came our engagement and our marriage, and our wedding journey, and all the rest of it. Well, well, my dear Judge—as you make your bed so you must lie, I could almost say.

BRACK. This is exquisite! And you really cared not a rap about it all the time.

HEDDA. No, heaven knows I didn't.

BRACK. But now? Now that we have made it so homelike for you?

HEDDA. Uh—the rooms all seem to smell of lavender and dried rose leaves.—But perhaps it's Aunt Julia that has brought that scent with her.

BRACK (*laughing*). No, I think it must be a legacy from the late Mrs. Secretary Falk.

HEDDA. Yes, there is an odor of mortality about it. It reminds me of a bouquet—the day after the ball. (*Clasps her hands behind her head, leans back in her chair and looks at him.*) Oh, my dear Judge—you cannot imagine how horribly I shall bore myself here.

BRACK. Why should not you, too, find some sort of vocation in life, Mrs. Hedda?

HEDDA. A vocation—that should attract me?

BRACK. If possible, of course.

HEDDA. Heaven knows what sort of a vocation that could be. I often wonder whether—— (*Breaking off.*) But that would never do either.

BRACK. Who can tell? Let me hear what it is.

HEDDA. Whether I might not get Tesman to go into politics, I mean.

BRACK (*laughing*). Tesman? No, really now, political life is not the thing for him—not at all in his line.

HEDDA. No, I daresay not. But if I could get him into it all the same?

BRACK. Why—what satisfaction could you find in that? If he is not fitted for that sort of thing, why should you want to drive him into it?

HEDDA. Because I am bored, I tell you! (*After a pause.*) So you think it quite out of the question that Tesman should ever get into the ministry?

BRACK. H'm—you see, my dear Mrs. Hedda—to get into the ministry, he would have to be a tolerably rich man.

HEDDA (*rising impatiently*). Yes, there we have it! It is this genteel poverty I have managed to drop into——! (*Crosses the room.*) That is what makes life so pitiable! So utterly ludicrous! For that's what it is.

BRACK. Now *I* should say the fault lay elsewhere.

HEDDA. Where, then?

BRACK. You have never gone through any really stimulating experience.

HEDDA. Anything serious, you mean?

BRACK. Yes, you may call it so. But now you may perhaps have one in store.

HEDDA (*tossing her head*). Oh, you're thinking of the annoyances about this wretched professorship! But that must be Tesman's own affair. I assure you I shall not waste a thought upon it.

BRACK. No, no, I daresay not. But suppose now that what people call— in elegant language—a solemn responsibility were to come upon you? (*Smiling.*) A new responsibility, Mrs. Hedda?

HEDDA (*angrily*). Be quiet! Nothing of that sort will ever happen!

BRACK (*warily*). We will speak of this again a year hence—at the very outside.

HEDDA (*curtly*). I have no turn for anything of the sort, Judge Brack. No responsibilities for me!

BRACK. Are you so unlike the generality of women as to have no turn for duties which——?

HEDDA (*beside the glass door*). Oh, be quiet, I tell you! I often think there is only one thing in the world I have any turn for.

BRACK (*drawing near to her*). And what is that, if I may ask?

HEDDA (*stands looking out*). Boring myself to death. Now you know it. (*Turns, looks towards the inner room, and laughs.*) Yes, as I thought! Here comes the Professor.

BRACK (*softly, in a tone of warning*). Come, come, come, Mrs. Hedda!

> [GEORGE TESMAN, *dressed for the party, with his gloves and hat in his hand, enters from the right through the inner room.*]

TESMAN. Hedda, has no message come from Eilert Lövborg? Eh?

HEDDA. No.

TESMAN. Then you'll see he'll be here presently.

BRACK. Do you really think he will come?

TESMAN. Yes, I am almost sure of it. For what you were telling us this morning must have been a mere floating rumor.

BRACK. You think so?

TESMAN. At any rate, Aunt Julia said she did not believe for a moment that he would ever stand in my way again. Fancy that!

BRACK. Well then, that's all right.

TESMAN (*placing his hat and gloves on a chair on the right*). Yes, but you must really let me wait for him as long as possible.

BRACK. We have plenty of time yet. None of my guests will arrive before seven or half-past.

TESMAN. Then meanwhile we can keep Hedda company, and see what happens. Eh?

HEDDA (*placing* BRACK'S *hat and overcoat upon the corner settee*). And at the worst Mr. Lövborg can remain here with me.

BRACK (*offering to take his things*). Oh, allow me, Mrs. Tesman! What do you mean by "At the worst"?

HEDDA. If he won't go with you and Tesman.

TESMAN (*looks dubiously at her*). But, Hedda dear—do you think it would quite do for him to remain with you? Eh? Remember, Aunt Julia can't come.

HEDDA. No, but Mrs. Elvsted is coming. We three can have a cup of tea together.

TESMAN. Oh, yes, that will be all right.

BRACK (*smiling*). And that would perhaps be the safest plan for him.

HEDDA. Why so?

BRACK. Well, you know, Mrs. Tesman, how you used to gird at my little bachelor parties. You declared they were adapted only for men of the strictest principles.

HEDDA. But no doubt Mr. Lövborg's principles are strict enough now. A converted sinner—— (BERTA *appears at the hall door*.)

BERTA. There's a gentleman asking if you are at home, ma'am——

HEDDA. Well, show him in.

TESMAN (*softly*). I'm sure it is he! Fancy that!

[EILERT LÖVBORG *enters from the hall. He is slim and lean; of the same age as* TESMAN, *but looks older and somewhat worn-out. His hair and beard are of a blackish brown, his face long and pale, but with patches of color on the cheekbones. He is dressed in a well-cut black visiting suit, quite new. He has dark gloves and a silk hat. He stops near the door, and makes a rapid bow, seeming somewhat embarrassed.*]

TESMAN (*goes up to him and shakes him warmly by the hand*). Well, my dear Eilert—so at last we meet again!

LÖVBORG (*speaks in a subdued voice*). Thanks for your letter, Tesman. (*Approaching* HEDDA.) Will you too shake hands with me, Mrs. Tesman?

HEDDA (*taking his hand*). I am glad to see you, Mr. Lövborg. (*With a motion of her hand.*) I don't know whether you two gentle-men——?

LÖVBORG (*bowing slightly*). Judge Brack, I think.

BRACK (*doing likewise*). Oh, yes, in the old days——

TESMAN (*to* LÖVBORG, *with his hands on his shoulders*). And now you must make yourself entirely at home, Eilert! Mustn't he, Hedda? For I hear you are going to settle in town again? Eh?

LÖVBORG. Yes, I am.

TESMAN. Quite right, quite right. Let me tell you, I have got hold of your new book; but I haven't had time to read it yet.

LÖVBORG. You may spare yourself the trouble.

TESMAN. Why so?

LÖVBORG. Because there is very little in it.

TESMAN. Just fancy—how can you say so?

BRACK. But it has been very much praised, I hear.

LÖVBORG. That was what I wanted; so I put nothing into the book but what every one would agree with.

BRACK. Very wise of you.

TESMAN. Well but, my dear Eilert——!

LÖVBORG. For now I mean to win myself a position again—to make a fresh start.

TESMAN (*a little embarrassed*). Ah, that is what you wish to do? Eh?

LÖVBORG (*smiling, lays down his hat, and draws a packet, wrapped in paper, from his coat pocket*). But when this one appears, George Tesman, you will have to read it. For this is the real book—the book I have put my true self into.

TESMAN. Indeed? And what is it?

LÖVBORG. It is the continuation.

TESMAN. The continuation? Of what?

LÖVBORG. Of the book.

TESMAN. Of the new book?

LÖVBORG. Of course.

TESMAN. Why, my dear Eilert—does it not come down to our own days?

LÖVBORG. Yes, it does; and this one deals with the future.

TESMAN. With the future! But, good heavens, we know nothing of the future!

LÖVBORG. No; but there is a thing or two to be said about it all the same. (*Opens the packet.*) Look here——

TESMAN. Why, that's not your handwriting.

LÖVBORG. I dictated it. (*Turning over the pages.*) It falls into two sections. The first deals with the civilizing forces of the future. And here is the second—(*running through the pages towards the end*)—forecasting the probable line of development.

TESMAN. How odd now! I should never have thought of writing anything of that sort.

HEDDA (*at the glass door, drumming on the pane*). H'm—I daresay not.

LÖVBORG (*replacing the manuscript in its paper and laying the packet on the table*). I brought it, thinking I might read you a little of it this evening.

TESMAN. That was very good of you, Eilert. But this evening——? (*Looking at* BRACK.) I don't quite see how we can manage it——

LÖVBORG. Well then, some other time. There is no hurry.

BRACK. I must tell you, Mr. Lövborg—there is a little gathering at my house this evening—mainly in honor of Tesman, you know——

LÖVBORG (*looking for his hat*). Oh—then I won't detain you——

BRACK. No, but listen—will you not do me the favor of joining us?

LÖVBORG (*curtly and decidedly*). No, I can't—thank you very much.

BRACK. Oh, nonsense—do! We shall be quite a select little circle. And I assure you we shall have a "lively time," as Mrs. Hed—as Mrs. Tesman says.

LÖVBORG. I have no doubt of it. But nevertheless——

BRACK. And then you might bring your manuscript with you, and read it to Tesman at my house. I could give you a room to yourselves.

TESMAN. Yes, think of that, Eilert,—why shouldn't you? Eh?

HEDDA (*interposing*). But, Tesman, if Mr. Lövborg would really rather not! I am sure Mr. Lövborg is much more inclined to remain here and have supper with me.

LÖVBORG (*looking at her*). With you, Mrs. Tesman?

HEDDA. And with Mrs. Elvsted.

LÖVBORG. Ah—— (*Lightly.*) I saw her for a moment this morning.

HEDDA. Did you? Well, she is coming this evening. So you see you are almost bound to remain, Mr. Lövborg, or she will have no one to see her home.

LÖVBORG. That's true. Many thanks, Mrs. Tesman—in that case I will remain.

HEDDA. Then I have one or two orders to give the servant——

[*She goes to the hall door and rings.* BERTA *enters.* HEDDA *talks to her in a whisper, and points toward the inner room.* BERTA *nods and goes out again.*]

TESMAN (*at the same time, to* LÖVBORG). Tell me, Eilert—is it this new subject—the future—that you are going to lecture about?

LÖVBORG. Yes.

TESMAN. They told me at the bookseller's, that you are going to deliver a course of lectures this autumn.

LÖVBORG. That is my intention. I hope you won't take it ill, Tesman.

TESMAN. Oh no, not in the least! But——?

LÖVBORG. I can quite understand that it must be disagreeable to you.

TESMAN (*cast down*). Oh, I can't expect you, out of consideration for me, to——

LÖVBORG. But I shall wait till you have received your appointment.

TESMAN. Will you wait? Yes, but—yes, but—are you not going to compete with me? Eh?

LÖVBORG. No; it is only the moral victory I care for.

TESMAN. Why, bless me—then Aunt Julia was right after all! Oh yes— I knew it! Hedda! Just fancy—Eilert Lövborg is not going to stand in our way!

HEDDA (*curtly*). Our way? Pray leave me out of the question.
> [*She goes up towards the inner room, where* BERTA
> *is placing a tray with decanters and glasses on the
> table.* HEDDA *nods approval, and comes forward again.*
> BERTA *goes out.*]

TESMAN (*at the same time*). And you, Judge Brack—what do you say to this? Eh?

BRACK. Well, I say that a moral victory—h'm—may be all very fine——

TESMAN. Yes, certainly. But all the same——

HEDDA (*looking at* TESMAN *with a cold smile*). You stand there looking as if you were thunderstruck——

TESMAN. Yes—so I am—I almost think——

BRACK. Don't you see, Mrs. Tesman, a thunderstorm has just passed over?

HEDDA (*pointing towards the inner room*). Will you not take a glass of cold punch, gentlemen?

BRACK (*looking at his watch*). A stirrup cup? Yes, it wouldn't come amiss.

TESMAN. A capital idea, Hedda! Just the thing? Now that the weight has been taken off my mind——

HEDDA. Will you not join them, Mr. Lövborg?

LÖVBORG (*with a gesture of refusal*). No, thank you. Nothing for me.

BRACK. Why, bless me—cold punch is surely not poison.

LÖVBORG. Perhaps not for every one.

HEDDA. I will keep Mr. Lövborg company in the meantime.

TESMAN. Yes, yes, Hedda dear, do.
> [*He and* BRACK *go into the inner room, seat them-
> selves, drink punch, smoke cigarettes, and carry on
> a lively conversation during what follows.* EILERT
> LÖVBORG *remains beside the stove.* HEDDA *goes to the
> writing table.*]

HEDDA (*raising her voice a little*). Do you care to look at some photographs, Mr. Lövborg? You know Tesman and I made a tour in the Tyrol on our way home?
> [*She takes up an album, and places it on the table be-
> side the sofa, in the further corner of which she seats
> herself.* EILERT LÖVBORG *approaches, stops, and looks
> at her. Then he takes a chair and seats himself at her
> left, with his back towards the inner room.*]

HEDDA (*opening the album*). Do you see this range of mountains, Mr. Lövborg? It's the Ortler group. Tesman has written the name underneath. Here it is: "The Ortler group near Meran."

LÖVBORG (*who has never taken his eyes off her, says softly and slowly*). Hedda—Gabler!

HEDDA (*glancing hastily at him*). Ah! Hush!

LÖVBORG (*repeats softly*). Hedda Gabler!

HEDDA (*looking at the album*). That was my name in the old days—when we two knew each other.

LÖVBORG. And I must teach myself never to say Hedda Gabler again—never, as long as I live.

HEDDA (*still turning over the pages*). Yes, you must. And I think you ought to practice in time. The sooner the better, I should say.

LÖVBORG (*in a tone of indignation*). Hedda Gabler married? And married to—George Tesman!

HEDDA. Yes—so the world goes.

LÖVBORG. Oh, Hedda, Hedda—how could you[2] throw yourself away!

HEDDA (*looks sharply at him*). What? I can't allow this!

LÖVBORG. What do you mean? (TESMAN *comes into the room and goes toward the sofa.*)

HEDDA (*hears him coming and says in an indifferent one*). And this is a view from the Val d'Ampezzo, Mr. Lövborg. Just look at these peaks! (*Looks affectionately up at* TESMAN.) What's the name of these curious peaks, dear?

TESMAN. Let me see? Oh, those are the Dolomites.

HEDDA. Yes, that's it! Those are the Dolomites, Mr. Lövborg.

TESMAN. Hedda dear, I only wanted to ask whether I shouldn't bring you a little punch after all? For yourself at any rate—eh?

HEDDA. Yes, do, please; and perhaps a few biscuits.

TESMAN. No cigarettes?

HEDDA. No.

TESMAN. Very well.

[*He goes into the inner room and out to the right.*
BRACK *sits in the inner room, and keeps an eye from
time to time on* HEDDA *and* LÖVBORG.]

LÖVBORG (*softly, as before*). Answer me, Hedda—how could you go and do this?

HEDDA (*apparently absorbed in the album*). If you continue to say *du* to me I won't talk to you.

LÖVBORG. May I say *du* when we are alone?

HEDDA. No. You may think it; but you mustn't say it.

LÖVBORG. Ah, I understand. It is an offense against George Tesman, whom you[3]—love.

HEDDA (*glances at him and smiles*). Love? What an idea!

LÖVBORG. You don't love him then!

HEDDA. But I won't hear of any sort of unfaithfulness! Remember that.

LÖVBORG. Hedda—answer me one thing——

[2] He uses the familiar *du*.

[3] From this point onward Lövborg uses the formal *De*.

HEDDA. Hush! (TESMAN *enters with a small tray from the inner room.*)

TESMAN. Here you are! Isn't this tempting? (*He puts the tray on the table.*)

HEDDA. Why do you bring it yourself?

TESMAN (*filling the glasses*). Because I think it's such fun to wait upon you, Hedda.

HEDDA. But you have poured out two glasses. Mr. Lövborg said he wouldn't have any——

TESMAN. No, but Mrs. Elvsted will soon be here, won't she?

HEDDA. Yes, by-the-bye—Mrs. Elvsted——

TESMAN. Had you forgotten her? Eh?

HEDDA. We were so absorbed in these photographs. (*Shows him a picture.*) Do you remember this little village?

TESMAN. Oh, it's that one just below the Brenner Pass. It was there we passed the night——

HEDDA. ——and met that lively party of tourists.

TESMAN. Yes, that was the place. Fancy—if we could only have had you with us, Eilert! Eh? (*He returns to the inner room and sits beside* BRACK.)

LÖVBORG. Answer me this one thing, Hedda——

HEDDA. Well?

LÖVBORG. Was there no love in your friendship for me either? Not a spark—not a tinge of love in it?

HEDDA. I wonder if there was? To me it seems as though we were two good comrades—two thoroughly intimate friends. (*Smilingly.*) You especially were frankness itself.

LÖVBORG. It was you that made me so.

HEDDA. As I look back upon it all, I think there was really something beautiful, something fascinating—something daring—in—in that secret intimacy—that comradeship which no living creature so much as dreamed of.

LÖVBORG. Yes, yes, Hedda! Was there not? When I used to come to your father's in the afternoon—and the General sat over at the window reading his papers—with his back towards us——

HEDDA. And we two on the corner sofa——

LÖVBORG. Always with the same illustrated paper before us——

HEDDA. For want of an album, yes.

LÖVBORG. Yes, Hedda, and when I made my confessions to you—told you about myself, things that at that time no one else knew! There I would sit and tell you of my escapades—my days and nights of devilment. Oh, Hedda—what was the power in you that forced me to confess these things?

HEDDA. Do you think it was any power in me?

LÖVBORG. How else can I explain it? And all those—those roundabout questions you used to put to me——

HEDDA. Which you understood so particularly well——

LÖVBORG. How could you sit and question me like that? Question me quite frankly——

HEDDA. In roundabout terms, please observe.

LÖVBORG. Yes, but frankly nevertheless. Cross-question me about—all that sort of thing?

HEDDA. And how could you answer, Mr. Lövborg?

LÖVBORG. Yes, that is just what I can't understand—in looking back upon it. But tell me now, Hedda—was there not love at the bottom of our friendship? On your side, did you not feel as though you might purge my stains away if I made you my confessor? Was it not so?

HEDDA. No, not quite.

LÖVBORG. What was your motive, then?

HEDDA. Do you think it quite incomprehensible that a young girl—when it can be done—without any one knowing——

LÖVBORG. Well?

HEDDA. ——should be glad to have a peep, now and then, into a world which——

LÖVBORG. Which——?

HEDDA. ——which she is forbidden to know anything about?

LÖVBORG. So that was it?

HEDDA. Partly. Partly—I almost think.

LÖVBORG. Comradeship in the thirst for life. But why should not that, at any rate, have continued?

HEDDA. The fault was yours.

LÖVBORG. It was you that broke with me.

HEDDA. Yes, when our friendship threatened to develop into something more serious. Shame upon you, Eilert Lövborg! How could you think of wronging your—your frank comrade?

LÖVBORG (*clenching his hands*). Oh, why did you not carry out your threat? Why did you not shoot me down?

HEDDA. Because I have such a dread of scandal.

LÖVBORG. Yes, Hedda, you are a coward at heart.

HEDDA. A terrible coward. (*Changing her tone.*) But it was a lucky thing for you. And now you have found ample consolation at the Elvsteds'.

LÖVBORG. I know what Thea has confided to you.

HEDDA. And perhaps you have confided to her something about us?

LÖVBORG. Not a word. She is too stupid to understand anything of that sort.

HEDDA. Stupid?

LÖVBORG. She is stupid about matters of that sort.

HEDDA. And I am cowardly. (*Bends over towards him, without looking him in the face, and says more softly.*) But now I will confide something to you.

LÖVBORG (*eagerly*). Well?

HEDDA. The fact that I dared not shoot you down——

LÖVBORG. Yes!

HEDDA. ——that was not my most arrant cowardice—that evening.

LÖVBORG (*looks at her a moment, understands, and whispers passionately*). Oh, Hedda! Hedda Gabler! Now I begin to see a hidden reason beneath our comradeship! You[4] and I——! After all, then, it was your craving for life——

HEDDA (*softly, with a sharp glance*). Take care! Believe nothing of the sort!

> [*Twilight has begun to fall. The hall door is opened
> from without by* BERTA.]

HEDDA (*closes the album with a bang and calls smilingly*). Ah, at last! My darling Thea, come along!

> [MRS. ELVSTED *enters from the hall. She is in evening
> dress. The door is closed behind her.*]

HEDDA (*on the sofa, stretches out her arms towards her*). My sweet Thea—you can't think how I have been longing for you!

> [MRS. ELVSTED, *in passing, exchanges slight saluta-
> tions with the gentlemen in the inner room, then goes
> up to the table and gives* HEDDA *her hands.* EILERT
> LÖVBORG *has risen. He and* MRS. ELVSTED *greet each
> other with a silent nod.*]

MRS. ELVSTED. Ought I to go in and talk to your husband for a moment?

HEDDA. Oh, not at all. Leave those two alone. They will soon be going.

MRS. ELVSTED. Are they going out?

HEDDA. Yes, to a supper party.

MRS. ELVSTED (*quickly, to* LÖVBORG). Not you?

LÖVBORG. No.

HEDDA. Mr. Lövborg remains with us.

MRS. ELVSTED (*takes a chair and is about to seat herself at his side*) Oh, how nice it is here!

HEDDA. No, thank you, my little Thea! Not there! You'll be good enough to come over here to me. I will sit between you.

MRS. ELVSTED. Yes, just as you please.

> [*She goes round the table and seats herself on the
> sofa on* HEDDA'S *right.* LÖVBORG *reseats himself on his
> chair.*]

LÖVBORG (*after a short pause, to* HEDDA). Is not she lovely to look at?

HEDDA (*lightly stroking her hair*). Only to look at?

LÖVBORG. Yes. For we two—she and I—we are two real comrades. We have absolute faith in each other; so we can sit and talk with perfect frankness——

___

[4] In this speech he once more says *du*. Hedda addresses him throughout as *De*.

HEDDA. Not round about, Mr. Lövborg?

LÖVBORG. Well——

MRS. ELVSTED (*softly clinging close to* HEDDA). Oh, how happy I am, Hedda; for, only think, he says I have inspired him too.

HEDDA (*looks at her with a smile*). Ah! Does he say that, dear?

LÖVBORG. And then she is so brave, Mrs. Tesman!

MRS. ELVSTED. Good heavens—am I brave?

LÖVBORG. Exceedingly—where your comrade is concerned.

HEDDA. Ah, yes—courage! If one only had that!

LÖVBORG. What then? What do you mean?

HEDDA. Then life would perhaps be liveable, after all. (*With a sudden change of tone.*) But now, my dearest Thea, you really must have a glass of cold punch.

MRS. ELVSTED. No, thanks—I never take anything of that kind.

HEDDA. Well then, you, Mr. Lövborg.

LÖVBORG. Nor I, thank you.

MRS. ELVSTED. No, he doesn't either.

HEDDA (*looks fixedly at him*). But if I say you shall?

LÖVBORG. It would be no use.

HEDDA (*laughing*). Then I, poor creature, have no sort of power over you?

LÖVBORG. Not in that respect.

HEDDA. But seriously, I think you ought to—for your own sake.

MRS. ELVSTED. Why, Hedda——!

LÖVBORG. How so?

HEDDA. Or rather on account of other people.

LÖVBORG. Indeed?

HEDDA. Otherwise people might be apt to suspect that—in your heart of hearts—you did not feel quite secure—quite confident of yourself.

MRS. ELVSTED (*softly*). Oh please, Hedda——

LÖVBORG. People may suspect what they like—for the present.

MRS. ELVSTED (*joyfully*). Yes, let them!

HEDDA. I saw it plainly in Judge Brack's face a moment ago.

LÖVBORG. What did you see?

HEDDA. His contemptuous smile, when you dared not go with them into the inner room.

LÖVBORG. Dared not? Of course I preferred to stop here and talk to you.

MRS. ELVSTED. What could be more natural, Hedda?

HEDDA. But the Judge could not guess that. And I saw, too, the way he smiled and glanced at Tesman when you dared not accept his invitation to this wretched little supper party of his.

LÖVBORG. Dared not! Do you say I dared not?

HEDDA. *I* don't say so. But that was how Judge Brack understood it.

LÖVBORG. Well, let him.

HEDDA. Then you are not going with them?

LÖVBORG. I will stay here with you and Thea.

MRS. ELVSTED. Yes, Hedda—how can you doubt that?

HEDDA (*smiles and nods approvingly to* LÖVBORG). Firm as a rock! Faithful to your principles, now and forever! Ah, that is how a man should be! (*Turns to* MRS. ELVSTED *and caresses her.*) Well now, what did I tell you, when you came to us this morning in such a state of distraction——

LÖVBORG (*surprised*). Distraction!

MRS. ELVSTED (*terrified*). Hedda—oh Hedda——!

HEDDA. You can see for yourself; you haven't the slightest reason to be in such mortal terror—— (*Interrupting herself.*) There! Now we can all three enjoy ourselves!

LÖVBORG (*who has given a start*). Ah—what is all this, Mrs. Tesman?

MRS. ELVSTED. Oh my God, Hedda! What are you saying? What are you doing?

HEDDA. Don't get excited! That horrid Judge Brack is sitting watching you.

LÖVBORG. So she was in mortal terror! On my account!

MRS. ELVSTED (*softly and piteously*). Oh, Hedda—now you have ruined everything!

LÖVBORG (*looks fixedly at her for a moment. His face is distorted*). So that was my comrade's frank confidence in me?

MRS. ELVSTED (*imploringly*). Oh, my dearest friend—only let me tell you——

LÖVBORG (*takes one of the glasses of punch, raises it to his lips, and says in a low, husky voice*). Your health, Thea!

[*He empties the glass, puts it down, and takes the second.*]

MRS. ELVSTED (*softly*). Oh, Hedda, Hedda—how could you do this?

HEDDA. *I* do it? I? Are you crazy?

LÖVBORG. Here's to your health too, Mrs. Tesman. Thanks for the truth. Hurrah for the truth!

[*He empties the glass and is about to refill it.*]

HEDDA (*lays her hand on his arm*). Come, come—no more for the present. Remember you are going out to supper.

MRS. ELVSTED. No, no, no!

HEDDA. Hush! They are sitting watching you.

LÖVBORG (*putting down the glass*). Now, Thea—tell me the truth——

MRS. ELVSTED. Yes.

LÖVBORG. Did your husband know that you had come after me?

MRS. ELVSTED (*wringing her hands*). Oh, Hedda—do you hear what he is asking?

LÖVBORG. Was it arranged between you and him that you were to come to town and look after me? Perhaps it was the Sheriff himself that urged you to come? Aha, my dear—no doubt he wanted my help in his office! Or was it at the card table that he missed me?

MRS. ELVSTED (*softly, in agony*). Oh, Lövborg, Lövborg——!

LÖVBORG (*seizes a glass and is on the point of filling it*). Here's a glass for the old Sheriff too!

HEDDA (*preventing him*). No more just now. Remember you have to read your manuscript to Tesman.

LÖVBORG (*calmly, putting down the glass*). It was stupid of me all this, Thea—to take it in this way, I mean. Don't be angry with me, my dear, dear comrade. You shall see—both you and the others— that if I was fallen once—now I have risen again! Thanks to you, Thea.

MRS. ELVSTED (*radiant with joy*). Oh, heaven be praised——!

[BRACK *has in the meantime looked at his watch. He and* TESMAN *rise and come into the drawing room.*]

BRACK (*takes his hat and overcoat*). Well, Mrs. Tesman, our time has come.

HEDDA. I suppose it has.

LÖVBORG (*rising*). Mine too, Judge Brack.

MRS. ELVSTED (*softly and imploringly*). Oh, Lövborg, don't do it!

HEDDA (*pinching her arm*). They can hear you!

MRS. ELVSTED (*with a suppressed shriek*). Ow!

LÖVBORG (*to* BRACK). You were good enough to invite me.

BRACK. Well, are you coming after all?

LÖVBORG. Yes, many thanks.

BRACK. I'm delighted——

LÖVBORG (*to* TESMAN, *putting the parcel of MS. in his pocket*). I should like to show you one or two things before I send it to the printer's.

TESMAN. Fancy—that will be delightful. But, Hedda dear, how is Mrs. Elvsted to get home? Eh?

HEDDA. Oh, that can be managed somehow.

LÖVBORG (*looking towards the ladies.*) Mrs. Elvsted? Of course, I'll come again and fetch her. (*Approaching.*) At ten or thereabouts, Mrs. Tesman? Will that do?

HEDDA. Certainly. That will do capitally.

TESMAN. Well, then, that's all right. But you must not expect me so early, Hedda.

HEDDA. Oh, you may stop as long—as long as ever you please.

MRS. ELVSTED (*trying to conceal her anxiety*). Well then, Mr. Lövborg—I shall remain here until you come.

LÖVBORG (*with his hat in his hand*). Pray do, Mrs. Elvsted.

BRACK. And now off goes the excursion train, gentlemen! I hope we shall have a lively time, as a certain fair lady puts it.

HEDDA. Ah, if only the fair lady could be present unseen——!

BRACK. Why unseen?

HEDDA. In order to hear a little of your liveliness at first hand, Judge Brack.

BRACK (*laughing*). I should not advise the fair lady to try it.

TESMAN (*also laughing*). Come, you're a nice one, Hedda! Fancy that!

BRACK. Well, good-by, good-by, ladies.

LÖVBORG (*bowing*). About ten o'clock, then.

> [BRACK, LÖVBORG, *and* TESMAN *go out by the hall door. At the same time* BERTA *enters from the inner room with a lighted lamp, which she places on the dining room table; she goes out by the way she came.*]

MRS. ELVSTED (*who has risen and is wandering restlessly about the room*). Hedda—Hedda—what will come of all this?

HEDDA. At ten o'clock—he will be here. I can see him already—with vine leaves in his hair—flushed and fearless——

MRS. ELVSTED. Oh, I hope he may.

HEDDA. And then, you see—then he will have regained control over himself. Then he will be a free man for all his days.

MRS. ELVSTED. Oh God!—if he would only come as you see him now!

HEDDA. He will come as I see him—so, and not otherwise! (*Rises and approaches* THEA). You may doubt him as long as you please; I believe in him. And now we will try——

MRS. ELVSTED. You have some hidden motive in this, Hedda!

HEDDA. Yes, I have. I want for once in my life to have power to mold a human destiny.

MRS. ELVSTED. Have you not the power?

HEDDA. I have not—and have never had it.

MRS. ELVSTED. Not your husband's?

HEDDA. Do you think that is worth the trouble? Oh, if you could only understand how poor I am. And fate has made you so rich! (*Clasps her passionately in her arms.*) I think I must burn your hair off, after all.

MRS. ELVSTED. Let me go! Let me go! I am afraid of you, Hedda!

BERTA (*in the middle doorway*). Tea is laid in the dining room, ma'am.

HEDDA. Very well. We are coming.

MRS. ELVSTED. No, no, no! I would rather go home alone! At once!

HEDDA. Nonsense! First you shall have a cup of tea, you little stupid. And then—at ten o'clock—Eilert Lövborg will be here—with vine leaves in his hair. (*She drags* MRS. ELVSTED *almost by force towards the middle doorway.*)

ACT III

᭐᭟ Scene: *The room at the* TESMANS'. *The curtains are drawn over the middle doorway, and also over the glass door. The lamp, half turned down, and with a shade over it, is burning on the table. In the stove, the door of which stands open, there has been a fire, which is now nearly burnt out.*

MRS. ELVSTED, *wrapped in a large shawl, and with her feet upon a footrest, sits close to the stove, sunk back in the armchair.* HEDDA, *fully dressed, lies sleeping upon the sofa, with a sofa blanket over her.*

MRS. ELVSTED (*after a pause, suddenly sits up in her chair, and listens eagerly. Then she sinks back again wearily, moaning to herself*). Not yet!—Oh God—oh God—not yet!
  [BERTA *slips in by the hall door. She has a letter in*
        her hand.]
MRS. ELVSTED (*turns and whispers eagerly*). Well—has any one come?
BERTA (*softly*). Yes, a girl has brought this letter.
MRS. ELVSTED (*quickly, holding out her hand*). A letter! Give it to me!
BERTA. No, it's for Dr. Tesman, ma'am.
MRS. ELVSTED. Oh, indeed.
BERTA. It was Miss Tesman's servant that brought it. I'll lay it here on the table.
MRS. ELVSTED. Yes, do.
BERTA (*laying down the letter*). I think I had better put out the lamp. It's smoking.
MRS. ELVSTED. Yes, put it out. It must soon be daylight now.
BERTA (*putting out the lamp*). It is daylight already, ma'am.
MRS. ELVSTED. Yes, broad day! And no one come back yet——!
BERTA. Lord bless you, ma'am! I guessed how it would be.
MRS. ELVSTED. You guessed?
BERTA. Yes, when I saw that a certain person had come back to town —and that he went off with them. For we've heard enough about that gentleman before now.

MRS. ELVSTED. Don't speak so loud. You will waken Mrs. Tesman.

BERTA (*looks towards the sofa and sighs*). No, no—let her sleep, poor thing. Shan't I put some wood on the fire?

MRS. ELVSTED. Thanks, not for me.

BERTA. Oh, very well. (*She goes softly out by the hall door.*)

HEDDA (*is awakened by the shutting of the door, and looks up*). What's that——?

MRS. ELVSTED. It was only the servant——

HEDDA (*looking about her*). Oh, we're here——! Yes, now I remember. (*Sits erect upon the sofa, stretches herself, and rubs her eyes.*) What o'clock is it, Thea?

MRS. ELVSTED (*looks at her watch*). It's past seven.

HEDDA. When did Tesman come home?

MRS. ELVSTED. He has not come.

HEDDA. Not come home yet?

MRS. ELVSTED (*rising*). No one has come.

HEDDA. Think of our watching and waiting here till four in the morning——

MRS. ELVSTED (*wringing her hands*). And how I watched and waited for him!

HEDDA (*yawns, and says with her hand before her mouth*). Well, well—we might have spared ourselves the trouble.

MRS. ELVSTED. Did you get a little sleep?

HEDDA. Oh yes; I believe I have slept pretty well. Have you not?

MRS. ELVSTED. Not for a moment. I couldn't, Hedda—not to save my life.

HEDDA (*rises and goes towards her*). There, there, there! There's nothing to be so alarmed about. I understand quite well what has happened.

MRS. ELVSTED. Well, what do you think? Won't you tell me?

HEDDA. Why, of course it has been a very late affair at Judge Brack's——

MRS. ELVSTED. Yes, yes, that is clear enough. But all the same——

HEDDA. And then, you see, Tesman hasn't cared to come home and ring us up in the middle of the night. (*Laughing.*) Perhaps he wasn't inclined to show himself either—immediately after a jollification.

MRS. ELVSTED. But in that case—where can he have gone?

HEDDA. Of course he has gone to his aunts' and slept there. They have his old room ready for him.

MRS. ELVSTED. No, he can't be with them; for a letter has just come for him from Miss Tesman. There it lies.

HEDDA. Indeed? (*Looks at the address.*) Why yes, it's addressed in Aunt Julia's own hand. Well then, he has remained at Judge Brack's. And as for Eilert Lövborg—he is sitting, with vine leaves in his hair, reading his manuscript.

MRS. ELVSTED. Oh Hedda, you are just saying things you don't believe a bit.

HEDDA. You really are a little blockhead, Thea.

MRS. ELVSTED. Oh yes, I suppose I am.

HEDDA. And how mortally tired you look.

MRS. ELVSTED. Yes, I am mortally tired.

HEDDA. Well then, you must do as I tell you. You must go into my room and lie down for a little while.

MRS. ELVSTED. Oh no, no—I shouldn't be able to sleep.

HEDDA. I am sure you would.

MRS. ELVSTED. Well, but your husband is certain to come soon now; and then I want to know at once——

HEDDA. I shall take care to let you know when he comes.

MRS. ELVSTED. Do you promise me, Hedda?

HEDDA. Yes, rely upon me. Just you go in and have a sleep in the meantime.

MRS. ELVSTED. Thanks; then I'll try to. (*She goes off through the inner room.*)

[*Hedda goes up to the glass door and draws back the curtains. The broad daylight streams into the room. Then she takes a little hand glass from the writing table, looks at herself in it, and arranges her hair. Next she goes to the hall door and presses the bell button.*]

[BERTA *presently appears at the hall door.*]

BERTA. Did you want anything, ma'am?

HEDDA. Yes; you must put some more wood in the stove. I am shivering.

BERTA. Bless me—I'll make up the fire at once. (*She rakes the embers together and lays a piece of wood upon them; then stops and listens.*) That was a ring at the front door, ma'am.

HEDDA. Then go to the door. I will look after the fire.

BERTA. It'll soon burn up. (*She goes out by the hall door.*)

[HEDDA *kneels on the footrest and lays some more pieces of wood in the stove.*]

[*After a short pause,* GEORGE TESMAN *enters from the hall. He looks tired and rather serious. He steals on tiptoe towards the middle doorway and is about to slip through the curtains.*]

HEDDA (*at the stove, without looking up*). Good morning.

TESMAN (*turns*). Hedda! (*Approaching her.*) Good heavens—are you up so early? Eh?

HEDDA. Yes, I am up very early this morning.

TESMAN. And I never doubted you were still sound asleep! Fancy that, Hedda!

HEDDA. Don't speak so loud. Mrs. Elvsted is resting in my room.

TESMAN. Has Mrs. Elvsted been here all night?

HEDDA. Yes, since no one came to fetch her.

TESMAN. Ah, to be sure.

HEDDA (*closes the door of the stove and rises*). Well, did you enjoy yourself at Judge Brack's?

TESMAN. Have you been anxious about me? Eh?

HEDDA. No, I should never think of being anxious. But I asked if you had enjoyed yourself.

TESMAN. Oh yes—for once in a way. Especially the beginning of the evening; for then Eilert read me part of his book. We arrived more than an hour too early—fancy that! And Brack had all sorts of arrangements to make—so Eilert read to me.

HEDDA (*seating herself by the table on the right*). Well? Tell me, then——

TESMAN (*sitting on a footstool near the stove*). Oh Hedda, you can't conceive what a book that is going to be! I believe it is one of the most remarkable things that have ever been written. Fancy that!

HEDDA. Yes, yes; I don't care about that——

TESMAN. I must make a confession to you, Hedda. When he had finished reading—a horrid feeling came over me.

HEDDA. A horrid feeling?

TESMAN. I felt jealous of Eilert for having had it in him to write such a book. Only think, Hedda!

HEDDA. Yes, yes, I am thinking!

TESMAN. And then how pitiful to think that he—with all his gifts—should be irreclaimable after all.

HEDDA. I suppose you mean that he has more courage than the rest?

TESMAN. No, not at all—I mean that he is incapable of taking his pleasures in moderation.

HEDDA. And what came of it all—in the end?

TESMAN. Well, to tell the truth, I think it might best be described as an orgy, Hedda.

HEDDA. Had he vine leaves in his hair?

TESMAN. Vine leaves? No, I saw nothing of the sort. But he made a long, rambling speech in honor of the woman who had inspired him in his work—that was the phrase he used.

HEDDA. Did he name her?

TESMAN. No, he didn't; but I can't help thinking he meant Mrs. Elvsted. You may be sure he did.

HEDDA. Well—where did you part from him?

TESMAN. On the way to town. We broke up—the last of us at any rate

—all together; and Brack came with us to get a breath of fresh air. And then, you see, we agreed to take Eilert home; for he had had far more than was good for him.

HEDDA. I daresay.

TESMAN. But now comes the strange part of it, Hedda; or, I should rather say, the melancholy part of it. I declare I am almost ashamed —on Eilert's account—to tell you——

HEDDA. Oh, go on——

TESMAN. Well, as we were getting near town, you see, I happened to drop a little behind the others. Only for a minute or two—fancy that!

HEDDA. Yes, yes, yes, but——?

TESMAN. And then, as I hurried after them—what do you think I found by the wayside? Eh?

HEDDA. Oh, how should I know!

TESMAN. You mustn't speak of it to a soul, Hedda! Do you hear! Promise me, for Eilert's sake. (*Draws a parcel, wrapped in paper, from his coat pocket*). Fancy, dear—I found this.

HEDDA. Is not that the parcel he had with him yesterday?

TESMAN. Yes, it is the whole of his precious, irreplaceable manuscript! And he had gone and lost it, and knew nothing about it. Only fancy, Hedda! So deplorably——

HEDDA. But why did you not give him back the parcel at once?

TESMAN. I didn't dare to—in the state he was then in——

HEDDA. Did you not tell any of the others that you had found it?

TESMAN. Oh, far from it! You can surely understand that, for Eilert's sake, I wouldn't do that.

HEDDA. So no one knows that Eilert Lövborg's manuscript is in your possession?

TESMAN. No. And no one must know it.

HEDDA. Then what did you say to him afterwards?

TESMAN. I didn't talk to him again at all; for when we got in among the streets, he and two or three of the others gave us the slip and disappeared. Fancy that!

HEDDA. Indeed! They must have taken him home then.

TESMAN. Yes, so it would appear. And Brack, too, left us.

HEDDA. And what have you been doing with yourself since?

TESMAN. Well, I and some of the others went home with one of the party, a jolly fellow, and took our morning coffee with him; or perhaps I should rather call it our night coffee—eh? But now, when I have rested a little, and given Eilert, poor fellow, time to have his sleep out, I must take this back to him.

HEDDA (*holds out her hand for the packet*). No—don't give it to him! Not in such a hurry, I mean. Let me read it first.

TESMAN. No, my dearest Hedda, I mustn't, I really mustn't.

HEDDA. You must not?

TESMAN. No—for you can imagine what a state of despair he will be in when he awakens and misses the manuscript. He has no copy of it, you must know! He told me so.

HEDDA (*looking searchingly at him*). Can such a thing not be reproduced? Written over again?

TESMAN. No, I don't think that would be possible. For the inspiration, you see——

HEDDA. Yes, yes—I suppose it depends on that. (*Lightly.*) But, by-the-bye—here is a letter for you.

TESMAN. Fancy——!

HEDDA (*handing it to him.*) It came early this morning.

TESMAN. It's from Aunt Julia! What can it be? (*He lays the packet on the other footstool, opens the letter, runs his eye through it, and jumps up.*) Oh, Hedda—she says that poor Aunt Rina is dying!

HEDDA. Well, we were prepared for that.

TESMAN. And that if I want to see her again, I must make haste. I'll run in to them at once.

HEDDA (*suppressing a smile*). Will you run?

TESMAN. Oh, dearest Hedda—if you could only make up your mind to come with me! Just think!

HEDDA (*rises and says wearily, repelling the idea*). No, no, don't ask me. I will not look upon sickness and death. I loathe all sorts of ugliness.

TESMAN. Well, well, then——! (*Bustling around.*) My hat—my overcoat——? Oh, in the hall—I do hope I mayn't come too late, Hedda! Eh?

HEDDA. Oh, if you run——

[BERTA *appears at the hall door.*]

BERTA. Judge Brack is at the door, and wishes to know if he may come in.

TESMAN. At this time! No, I can't possibly see him.

HEDDA. But I can. (*To* BERTA.) Ask Judge Brack to come in. (BERTA *goes out.*)

HEDDA (*quickly whispering*). The parcel, Tesman! (*She snatches it up from the stool.*)

TESMAN. Yes, give it to me!

HEDDA. No, no, I will keep it till you come back.

[*She goes to the writing table and places it in the bookcase.* TESMAN *stands in a flurry of haste, and cannot get his gloves on.*]

[JUDGE BRACK *enters from the hall.*]

HEDDA (*nodding to him*). You are an early bird, I must say.

BRACK. Yes, don't you think so? (*To* TESMAN.) Are you on the move, too?

TESMAN. Yes, I must rush off to my aunts'. Fancy—the invalid one is lying at death's door, poor creature.

BRACK. Dear me, is she indeed? Then on no account let me detain you. At such a critical moment——

TESMAN. Yes, I must really rush——Good-by! Good-by! (*He hastens out by the hall door.*)

HEDDA (*approaching*). You seem to have made a particularly lively night of it at your rooms, Judge Brack.

BRACK. I assure you I have not had my clothes off, Mrs. Hedda.

HEDDA. Not you, either?

BRACK. No, as you may see. But what has Tesman been telling you of the night's adventures?

HEDDA. Oh, some tiresome story. Only that they went and had coffee somewhere or other.

BRACK. I have heard about that coffee-party already. Eilert Lövborg was not with them, I fancy?

HEDDA. No, they had taken him home before that.

BRACK. Tesman, too?

HEDDA. No, but some of the others, he said.

BRACK (*smiling*). George Tesman is really an ingenuous creature, Mrs. Hedda.

HEDDA. Yes, heaven knows he is. Then is there something behind all this?

BRACK. Yes, perhaps there may be.

HEDDA. Well then, sit down, my dear Judge, and tell your story in comfort.

[*She seats herself to the left of the table.* BRACK *sits near her, at the long side of the table.*]

HEDDA. Now then?

BRACK. I had special reasons for keeping track of my guests—or rather of some of my guests—last night.

HEDDA. Of Eilert Lövborg among the rest, perhaps?

BRACK. Frankly, yes.

HEDDA. Now you make me really curious——

BRACK. Do you know where he and one or two of the others finished the night, Mrs. Hedda?

HEDDA. If it is not quite unmentionable, tell me.

BRACK. Oh no, it's not at all unmentionable. Well, they put in an appearance at a particularly animated soirée.

HEDDA. Of the lively kind?

BRACK. Of the very liveliest——

HEDDA. Tell me more of this, Judge Brack——

BRACK. Lövborg, as well as the others, had been invited in advance. I knew all about it. But he had declined the invitation; for now, as you know, he has become a new man.

HEDDA. Up at the Elvsteds', yes. But he went after all, then?

BRACK. Well, you see, Mrs. Hedda—unhappily the spirit moved him at my rooms last evening——

HEDDA. Yes, I hear he found inspiration.

BRACK. Pretty violent inspiration. Well, I fancy that altered his purpose; for we men folk are unfortunately not always so firm in our principles as we ought to be.

HEDDA. Oh, I am sure you are an exception, Judge Brack. But as to Lövborg——?

BRACK. To make a long story short—he landed at last in Mademoiselle Diana's rooms.

HEDDA. Mademoiselle Diana's?

BRACK. It was Mademoiselle Diana that was giving the soirée, to a select circle of her admirers and her lady friends.

HEDDA. Is she a red-haired woman?

BRACK. Precisely.

HEDDA. A sort of a—singer?

BRACK. Oh yes—in her leisure moments. And moreover a mighty huntress—of men—Mrs. Hedda. You have no doubt heard of her. Eilert Lövborg was one of her most enthusiastic protectors—in the days of his glory.

HEDDA. And how did all this end?

BRACK. Far from amicably, it appears. After a most tender meeting, they seem to have come to blows——

HEDDA. Lövborg and she?

BRACK. Yes. He accused her or her friends of having robbed him. He declared that his pocketbook had disappeared—and other things as well. In short, he seems to have made a furious disturbance.

HEDDA. And what came of it all?

BRACK. It came to a general scrimmage, in which the ladies as well as the gentlemen took part. Fortunately the police at last appeared on the scene.

HEDDA. The police too?

BRACK. Yes. I fancy it will prove a costly frolic for Eilert Lövborg, crazy being that he is.

HEDDA. How so?

BRACK. He seems to have made a violent resistance—to have hit one of the constables on the head and torn the coat off his back. So they had to march him off to the police station with the rest.

HEDDA. How have you learnt all this?

BRACK. From the police themselves.

HEDDA (gazing straight before her). So that is what happened. Then he had no vine leaves in his hair.

BRACK. Vine leaves, Mrs. Hedda?

HEDDA (*changing her tone*). But tell me now, Judge—what is your real reason for tracking out Eilert Lövborg's movements so carefully?

BRACK. In the first place, it could not be entirely indifferent to me if it should appear in the police court that he came straight from my house.

HEDDA. Will the matter come into court, then?

BRACK. Of course. However, I should scarcely have troubled so much about that. But I thought that, as a friend of the family, it was my duty to supply you and Tesman with a full account of his nocturnal exploits.

HEDDA. Why so, Judge Brack?

BRACK. Why, because I have a shrewd suspicion that he intends to use you as a sort of blind.

HEDDA. Oh, how can you think such a thing!

BRACK. Good heavens, Mrs. Hedda—we have eyes in our head. Mark my words! This Mrs. Elvsted will be in no hurry to leave town again.

HEDDA. Well, even if there should be anything between them, I suppose there are plenty of other places where they could meet.

BRACK. Not a single home. Henceforth, as before, every respectable house will be closed against Eilert Lövborg.

HEDDA. And so ought mine to be, you mean?

BRACK. Yes. I confess it would be more than painful to me if this personage were to be made free of your house. How superfluous, how intrusive, he would be, if he were to force his way into——

HEDDA. ——into the triangle?

BRACK. Precisely. It would simply mean that I should find myself homeless.

HEDDA (*looks at him with a smile*). So you want to be the one cock in the basket—that is your aim.

BRACK (*nods slowly and lowers his voice*). Yes, that is my aim. And for that I will fight—with every weapon I can command.

HEDDA (*her smile vanishing*). I see you are a dangerous person—when it comes to the point.

BRACK. Do you think so?

HEDDA. I am beginning to think so. And I am exceedingly glad to think —that you have no sort of hold over me.

BRACK (*laughing equivocally*). Well, well, Mrs. Hedda—perhaps you are right there. If I had, who knows what I might be capable of?

HEDDA. Come, come now, Judge Brack. That sounds almost like a threat.

BRACK (*rising*). Oh, not at all! The triangle, you know, ought, if possible, to be spontaneously constructed.

HEDDA. There I agree with you.

BRACK. Well, now I have said all I had to say; and I had better be getting back to town. Good-by, Mrs. Hedda. (*He goes towards the glass door.*)

HEDDA (*rising*). Are you going through the garden?

BRACK. Yes, it's a short cut for me.

HEDDA. And then it is the back way, too.

BRACK. Quite so. I have no objection to back ways. They may be piquant enough at times.

HEDDA. When there is ball practice going on, you mean?

BRACK (*in the doorway, laughing to her*). Oh, people don't shoot their tame poultry, I fancy.

HEDDA (*also laughing*). Oh no, when there is only one cock in the basket——

[*They exchange laughing nods of farewell. He goes. She closes the door behind him.*

[HEDDA, *who has become quite serious, stands for a moment looking out. Presently she goes and peeps through the curtain over the middle doorway. Then she goes to the writing table, takes* LÖVBORG'S *packet out of the bookcase, and is on the point of looking through its contents.* BERTA *is heard speaking loudly in the hall.* HEDDA *turns and listens. Then she hastily locks up the packet in the drawer, and lays the key on the inkstand.*

[EILERT LÖVBORG, *with his great coat on and his hat in his hand, tears open the hall door. He looks somewhat confused and irritated.*]

LÖVBORG (*looking towards the hall*). And I tell you I must and will come in! There!

[*He closes the door, turns and sees* HEDDA, *at once regains his self-control, and bows.*]

HEDDA (*at the writing table*). Well, Mr. Lövborg, this is rather a late hour to call for Thea.

LÖVBORG. You mean rather an early hour to call on you. Pray pardon me.

HEDDA. How do you know that she is still here?

LÖVBORG. They told me at her lodgings that she had been out all night.

HEDDA (*going to the oval table*). Did you notice anything about the people of the house when they said that?

LÖVBORG (*looks inquiringly at her*). Notice anything about them?

HEDDA. I mean, did they seem to think it odd?

LÖVBORG (*suddenly understanding*). Oh yes, of course! I am dragging her down with me! However, I didn't notice anything.—I suppose Tesman is not up yet?

HEDDA. No—I think not——

LÖVBORG. When did he come home?

HEDDA. Very late.

LÖVBORG. Did he tell you anything?

HEDDA. Yes, I gathered that you had had an exceedingly jolly evening at Judge Brack's.

LÖVBORG. Nothing more?

HEDDA. I don't think so. However, I was so dreadfully sleepy——

[MRS. ELVSTED *enters through the curtains of the middle doorway.*]

MRS. ELVSTED (*going towards him*). Ah, Lövborg! At last——!

LÖVBORG. Yes, at last. And too late!

MRS. ELVSTED (*looks anxiously at him*). What is too late?

LÖVBORG. Everything is too late now. It is all over with me.

MRS. ELVSTED. Oh no, no—don't say that!

LÖVBORG. You will say the same when you hear——

MRS. ELVSTED. I won't hear anything!

HEDDA. Perhaps you would prefer to talk to her alone! If so, I will leave you.

LÖVBORG. No, stay—you too. I beg you to stay.

MRS. ELVSTED. Yes, but I won't hear anything, I tell you.

LÖVBORG. It is not last night's adventures that I want to talk about.

MRS. ELVSTED. What is it then——?

LÖVBORG. I want to say that now our ways must part.

MRS. ELVSTED. Part!

HEDDA (*involuntarily*). I knew it!

LÖVBORG. You can be of no more service to me, Thea.

MRS. ELVSTED. How can you stand there and say that! No more service to you! Am I not to help you now, as before? Are we not to go on working together?

LÖVBORG. Henceforward I shall do no work.

MRS. ELVSTED (*despairingly*). Then what am I to do with my life?

LÖVBORG. You must try to live your life as if you had never known me.

MRS. ELVSTED. But you know I cannot do that!

LÖVBORG. Try if you cannot, Thea. You must go home again——

MRS. ELVSTED (*in vehement protest*). Never in this world! Where you are, there will I be also! I will not let myself be driven away like this! I will remain here! I will be with you when the book appears.

HEDDA (*half aloud, in suspense*). Ah yes—the book!

LÖVBORG (*looks at her*). My book and Thea's; for that is what it is.

MRS. ELVSTED. Yes, I feel that it is. And that is why I have a right to be with you when it appears! I will see with my own eyes how respect and honor pour in upon you afresh. And the happiness—the happiness—oh, I must share it with you!

LÖVBORG. Thea—our book will never appear.

HEDDA. Ah!

MRS. ELVSTED. Never appear!

LÖVBORG. Can never appear.

MRS. ELVSTED (*in agonized foreboding*). Lövborg—what have you done with the manuscript?

HEDDA (*looks anxiously at him*). Yes, the manuscript——?

MRS. ELVSTED. Where is it?

LÖVBORG. Oh Thea—don't ask me about it!

MRS. ELVSTED. Yes, yes, I will know. I demand to be told at once.

LÖVBORG. The manuscript—Well then—I have torn the manuscript into a thousand pieces.

MRS. ELVSTED (*shrieks*). Oh no, no——!

HEDDA (*involuntarily*). But that's not——

LÖVBORG (*looks at her*). Not true, you think?

HEDDA (*collecting herself*). Oh well, of course—since you say so. But it sounded so improbable——

LÖVBORG. It is true, all the same.

MRS. ELVSTED (*wringing her hands*). Oh God—oh God, Hedda—torn his own work to pieces!

LÖVBORG. I have torn my own life to pieces. So why should I not tear my lifework too——?

MRS. ELVSTED. And you did this last night?

LÖVBORG. Yes, I tell you! Tore it into a thousand pieces and scattered them on the fiord—far out. There there is cool sea water at any rate—let them drift upon it—drift with the current and the wind. And then presently they will sink—deeper and deeper—as I shall, Thea.

MRS. ELVSTED. Do you know, Lövborg, that what you have done with the book—I shall think of it to my dying day as though you had killed a little child.

LÖVBORG. Yes, you are right. It is a sort of child murder.

MRS. ELVSTED. How could you, then——! Did not the child belong to me too?

HEDDA (*almost inaudibly*). Ah, the child——

MRS. ELVSTED (*breathing heavily*). It is all over then. Well, well, now I will go, Hedda.

HEDDA. But you are not going away from town?

MRS. ELVSTED. Oh, I don't know what I shall do. I see nothing but darkness before me. (*She goes out by the hall door.*)

HEDDA (*stands waiting for a moment*). So you are not going to see her home, Mr. Lövborg?

LÖVBORG. I? Through the streets? Would you have people see her walking with me?

HEDDA. Of course I don't know what else may have happened last night. But is it so utterly irretrievable?

LÖVBORG. It will not end with last night—I know that perfectly well.

And the thing is that now I have no taste for that sort of life either. I won't begin it anew. She has broken my courage and my power of braving life out.

HEDDA (*looking straight before her*). So that pretty little fool has had her fingers in a man's destiny. (*Looks at him.*) But all the same, how could you treat her so heartlessly?

LÖVBORG. Oh, don't say that it was heartless!

HEDDA. To go and destroy what has filled her whole soul for months and years! You do not call that heartless!

LÖVBORG. To you I can tell the truth, Hedda.

HEDDA. The truth?

LÖVBORG. First promise me—give me your word—that what I now confide to you Thea shall never know.

HEDDA. I give you my word.

LÖVBORG. Good. Then let me tell you that what I said just now was untrue.

HEDDA. About the manuscript?

LÖVBORG. Yes. I have not torn it to pieces—nor thrown it into the fiord.

HEDDA. No, n— But—where is it then!

LÖVBORG. I have destroyed it none the less—utterly destroyed it, Hedda!

HEDDA. I don't understand.

LÖVBORG. Thea said that what I had done seemed to her like a child murder.

HEDDA. Yes, so she said.

LÖVBORG. But to kill his child—that is not the worst thing a father can do to it.

HEDDA. Not the worst?

LÖVBORG. No. I wanted to spare Thea from hearing the worst.

HEDDA. Then what is the worst?

LÖVBORG. Suppose now, Hedda, that a man—in the small hours of the morning—came home to his child's mother after a night of riot and debauchery, and said: "Listen—I have been here and there—in this place and in that. And I have taken our child with me—to this place and to that. And I have lost the child—utterly lost it. The devil knows into what hands it may have fallen—who may have had their clutches on it."

HEDDA. Well—but when all is said and done, you know—that was only a book——

LÖVBORG. Thea's pure soul was in that book.

HEDDA. Yes, so I understand.

LÖVBORG. And you can understand, too, that for her and me together no future is possible.

HEDDA. What path do you mean to take then?

LÖVBORG. None. I will only try to make an end of it all—the sooner the
better.

HEDDA (*a step nearer to him*). Eilert Lövborg—listen to me. Will you
not try to—to do it beautifully?

LÖVBORG. Beautifully? (*Smiling.*) With vine leaves in my hair, as you
used to dream in the old days——?

HEDDA. No, no. I have lost my faith in the vine leaves. But beautifully,
nevertheless! For once in a way!—Good-by! You must go now—
and do not come here any more.

LÖVBORG. Good-by, Mrs. Tesman. And give George Tesman my love.
(*He is on the point of going.*)

HEDDA. No, wait! I must give you a memento to take with you.
  [*She goes to the writing table and opens the drawer
  and the pistol case; then returns to* LÖVBORG *with one
  of the pistols.*]

LÖVBORG Good-by, Hedda Gabler. (*He goes out by the hall door.*)

HEDDA (*nodding slowly*). Do you recognize it? It was aimed at you
once.

LÖVBORG. You should have used it then.

HEDDA. Take it—and do you use it now.

LÖVBORG (*puts the pistol in his breast pocket*). Thanks!

HEDDA. And beautifully, Eilert Lövborg. Promise me that!

LÖVBORG. Good-by, Hedda Gabler. (*He goes out by the hall door.*)
  [HEDDA *listens for a moment at the door. Then she
  goes up to the writing table, takes out the packet of
  manuscript, peeps under the cover, draws a few of the
  sheets half out, and looks at them. Next she goes over
  and seats herself in the armchair beside the stove,
  with the packet in her lap. Presently she opens the
  stove door, and then the packet.*]

HEDDA (*throws one of the quires into the fire and whispers to herself*).
Now I am burning your child, Thea!—Burning it, curlylocks!
(*Throwing one or two more quires into the stove.*) Your child and
Eilert Lövborg's. (*Throws the rest in.*) I am burning—I am burning
your child.

ACT IV

Scene: *The same rooms at the* TESMANS'. *It is evening. The drawing room is in darkness. The back room is lighted by the hanging lamp over the table. The curtains over the glass door are drawn close.*

HEDDA, *dressed in black, walks to and fro in the dark room. Then she goes into the back room and disappears, for a moment to the left. She is heard to strike a few chords on the piano. Presently she comes in sight again, and returns to the drawing room.*

BERTA *enters from the right, through the inner room, with a lighted lamp, which she places on the table in front of the corner settee in the drawing room. Her eyes are red with weeping, and she has black ribbons in her cap. She goes quietly and circumspectly out to the right.*

HEDDA, *goes up to the glass door, lifts the curtain a little aside, and looks out into the darkness.*

Shortly afterwards, MISS TESMAN, *in mourning, with a bonnet and veil on, comes in from the hall.* HEDDA *goes towards her and holds out her hand.*

MISS TESMAN. Yes, Hedda, here I am, in mourning and forlorn; for now my poor sister has at last found peace.

HEDDA. I have heard the news already, as you see. Tesman sent me a card.

MISS TESMAN. Yes, he promised me he would. But nevertheless I thought that to Hedda—here in the house of life—I ought myself to bring the tidings of death.

HEDDA. That was very kind of you.

MISS TESMAN. Ah, Rina ought not to have left us just now. This is not the time for Hedda's house to be a house of mourning.

HEDDA (*changing the subject*). She died quite peacefully, did she not, Miss Tesman?

MISS TESMAN. Oh, her end was so calm, so beautiful. And then she had the unspeakable happiness of seeing George once more—and bidding him good-by. Has he come home yet?

HEDDA. No. He wrote that he might be detained. But won't you sit down?

MISS TESMAN. No thank you, my dear, dear Hedda. I should like to, but I have so much to do. I must prepare my dear one for her rest as well as I can. She shall go to her grave looking her best.

HEDDA. Can I not help you in any way?

MISS TESMAN. Oh, you must not think of it! Hedda Tesman must have no hand in such mournful work. Nor let her thoughts dwell on it either—not at this time.

HEDDA. One is not always mistress of one's thoughts——

MISS TESMAN (*continuing*). Ah yes, it is the way of the world. At home we shall be sewing a shroud; and here there will soon be sewing too, I suppose—but of another sort, thank God!

[GEORGE TESMAN *enters by the hall door.*]

HEDDA. Ah, you have come at last!

TESMAN. You here, Aunt Julia? With Hedda? Fancy that!

MISS TESMAN. I was just going, my dear boy. Well, have you done all you promised?

TESMAN. No; I'm really afraid I have forgotten half of it. I must come to you again tomorrow. Today my brain is all in a whirl. I can't keep my thoughts together.

MISS TESMAN. Why, my dear George, you mustn't take it in this way.

TESMAN. Mustn't——? How do you mean?

MISS TESMAN. Even in your sorrow you must rejoice, as I do—rejoice that she is at rest.

TESMAN. Oh yes, yes—you are thinking of Aunt Rina.

HEDDA. You will feel lonely now, Miss Tesman.

MISS TESMAN. Just at first, yes. But that will not last very long, I hope. I daresay I shall soon find an occupant for poor Rina's little room.

TESMAN. Indeed? Who do you think will take it? Eh?

MISS TESMAN. Oh, there's always some poor invalid or other in want of nursing, unfortunately.

HEDDA. Would you really take such a burden upon you again?

MISS TESMAN. A burden! Heaven forgive you, child—it has been no burden to me.

HEDDA. But suppose you had a total stranger on your hands——

MISS TESMAN. Oh, one soon makes friends with sick folk; and it's such an absolute necessity for me to have some one to live for. Well, heaven be praised, there may soon be something in this house, too, to keep an old aunt busy.

HEDDA. Oh, don't trouble about anything here.

TESMAN. Yes, just fancy what a nice time we three might have together, if——?

HEDDA. If——?

TESMAN (*uneasily*). Oh, nothing. It will all come right. Let us hope so—eh?

MISS TESMAN. Well, well, I daresay you two want to talk to each other. (*Smiling.*) And perhaps Hedda may have something to tell you too, George. Good-by! I must go home to Rina. (*Turning at the door.*) How strange it is to think that now Rina is with me and with my poor brother as well!

TESMAN. Yes, fancy that, Aunt Julia! Eh?

[MISS TESMAN *goes out by the hall door.*]

HEDDA (*follows* TESMAN *coldly and searchingly with her eyes*). I almost believe your Aunt Rina's death affects you more than it does your Aunt Julia.

TESMAN. Oh, it's not that alone. It's Eilert I am so terribly uneasy about.

HEDDA (*quickly*). Is there anything new about him?

TESMAN. I looked in at his rooms this afternoon, intending to tell him the manuscript was in safe keeping.

HEDDA. Well, did you not find him?

TESMAN. No. He wasn't at home. But afterwards I met Mrs. Elvsted, and she told me that he had been here early this morning.

HEDDA. Yes, directly after you had gone.

TESMAN. And he said that he had torn his manuscript to pieces—eh?

HEDDA. Yes, so he declared.

TESMAN. Why, good heavens, he must have been completely out of his mind! And I suppose you thought it best not to give it back to him, Hedda?

HEDDA. No, he did not get it.

TESMAN. But of course you told him that we had it?

HEDDA No. (*Quickly.*) Did you tell Mrs. Elvsted?

TESMAN. No, I thought I had better not. But you ought to have told him. Fancy, if, in desperation, he should go and do himself some injury! Let me have the manuscript, Hedda! I will take it to him at once. Where is it?

HEDDA (*cold and immovable, leaning on the armchair*). I have not got it.

TESMAN. Have not got it? What in the world do you mean?

HEDDA. I have burnt it—every line of it.

TESMAN (*with a violent movement of terror*). Burnt! Burnt Eilert's manuscript!

HEDDA. Don't scream so. The servant might hear you.

TESMAN. Burnt! Why, good God——! No, no, no! It's impossible!

HEDDA. It is so, nevertheless.

TESMAN. Do you know what you have done, Hedda? It's unlawful appropriation of lost property. Fancy that! Just ask Judge Brack, and he'll tell you what it is.

HEDDA. I advise you not to speak of it—either to Judge Brack, or to any one else.

TESMAN. But how could you do anything so unheard-of? What put it into your head? What possessed you? Answer me that—eh?

HEDDA (*suppressing an almost imperceptible smile*). I did it for your sake, George.

TESMAN. For my sake!

HEDDA. This morning, when you told me about what he had read to you——

TESMAN. Yes, yes—what then?

HEDDA. You acknowledged that you envied him his work.

TESMAN. Oh, of course I didn't mean that literally.

HEDDA. No matter—I could not bear the idea that any one should throw you into the shade.

TESMAN (*in an outburst of mingled doubt and joy*). Hedda! Oh, is this true? But—but—I never knew you to show your love like that before. Fancy that!

HEDDA. Well, I may as well tell you that—just at this time—— (*Impatiently, breaking off.*) No, no; you can ask Aunt Julia. She will tell you, fast enough.

TESMAN. Oh, I almost think I understand you, Hedda! (*Clasps his hands together.*) Great heavens! do you really mean it! Eh?

HEDDA. Don't shout so. The servant might hear.

TESMAN (*laughing in irrepressible glee*). The servant! Why, how absurd you are, Hedda. It's only my old Berta! Why, I'll tell Berta myself.

HEDDA (*clenching her hands together in desperation*). Oh, it is killing me—it is killing me, all this!

TESMAN. What is, Hedda? Eh?

HEDDA (*coldly, controlling herself*). All this—absurdity—George.

TESMAN. Absurdity! Do you see anything absurd in my being overjoyed at the news! But after all perhaps I had better not say anything to Berta.

HEDDA. Oh—why not that too?

TESMAN. No, no, not yet! But I must certainly tell Aunt Julia. And then that you have begun to call me George too! Fancy that! Oh, Aunt Julia will be so happy—so happy.

HEDDA. When she hears that I have burnt Eilert Lövborg's manuscript —for your sake?

TESMAN. No, by-the-bye—that affair of the manuscript—of course nobody must know about that. But that you love me so much, Hedda— Aunt Julia must really share my joy in that! I wonder, now, whether this sort of thing is usual in young wives? Eh?

HEDDA. I think you had better ask Aunt Julia that question too.

TESMAN. I will indeed, some time or other. (*Looks uneasy and downcast again.*) And yet the manuscript—the manuscript! Good God! It is terrible to think what will become of poor Eilert now.

[MRS. ELVSTED, *dressed as in the first Act, with hat
and cloak, enters by the hall door.*]

MRS. ELVSTED (*greets them hurriedly, and says in evident agitation*).
Oh, dear Hedda, forgive my coming again.

HEDDA. What is the matter with you, Thea?

TESMAN. Something about Eilert Lövborg again—eh?

MRS. ELVSTED. Yes! I am dreadfully afraid some misfortune has happened to him.

HEDDA (*seizes her arm*). Ah, do you think so?

TESMAN. Why, good Lord—what makes you think that, Mrs. Elvsted?

MRS. ELVSTED. I heard them talking of him at my boarding house—
just as I came in. Oh, the most incredible rumors are afloat about
him today.

TESMAN. Yes, fancy, so I heard too! And I can bear witness that he
went straight home to bed last night. Fancy that!

HEDDA. Well, what did they say at the boarding house?

MRS. ELVSTED. Oh, I couldn't make out anything clearly. Either they
knew nothing definite, or else—— They stopped talking when they
saw me; and I did not dare to ask.

TESMAN (*moving about uneasily*). We must hope—we must hope that
you misunderstood them, Mrs. Elvsted.

MRS. ELVSTED. No, no; I am sure it was of him they were talking. And
I heard something about the hospital or——

TESMAN. The hospital?

HEDDA. No—surely that cannot be!

MRS. ELVSTED. Oh, I was in such mortal terror! I went to his lodgings
and asked for him there.

HEDDA. You could make up your mind to that, Thea!

MRS. ELVSTED. What else could I do? I really could bear the suspense
no longer.

TESMAN. But you didn't find him either—eh?

MRS. ELVSTED. No. And the people knew nothing about him. He hadn't
been home since yesterday afternoon, they said.

TESMAN. Yesterday! Fancy, how could they say that?

MRS. ELVSTED. Oh, I am sure something terrible must have happened to
him.

TESMAN. Hedda dear—how would it be if I were to go and make in-
quiries——?

HEDDA. No, no—don't you mix yourself up in this affair.

[JUDGE BRACK, *with his hat in his hand, enters by the
hall door, which* BERTA *opens, and closes behind him.
He looks grave and bows in silence.*]

TESMAN. Oh, is that you, my dear Judge? Eh?

BRACK. Yes. It was imperative I should see you this evening.

TESMAN. I can see you have heard the news about Aunt Rina.

BRACK. Yes, that among other things.

TESMAN. Isn't it sad—eh?

BRACK. Well, my dear Tesman, that depends on how you look at it.

TESMAN (*looks doubtfully at him*). Has anything else happened?

BRACK. Yes.

HEDDA (*in suspense*). Anything sad, Judge Brack?

BRACK. That, too, depends on how you look at it, Mrs. Tesman.

MRS. ELVSTED (*unable to restrain her anxiety*). Oh! it is something about Eilert Lövborg!

BRACK (*with a glance at her*). What makes you think that, Madam? Perhaps you have already heard something——?

MRS. ELVSTED (*in confusion*). No, nothing at all, but——

TESMAN. Oh, for heaven's sake, tell us!

BRACK (*shrugging his shoulders*). Well, I regret to say Eilert Lövborg has been taken to the hospital. He is lying at the point of death.

MRS. ELVSTED (*shrieks*). Oh God! Oh God——

TESMAN. To the hospital! And at the point of death.

HEDDA (*involuntarily*). So soon then——

MRS. ELVSTED (*wailing*). And we parted in anger, Hedda!

HEDDA (*whispers*). Thea—Thea—be careful!

MRS. ELVSTED (*not heeding her*). I must go to him! I must see him alive!

BRACK. It is useless, Madam. No one will be admitted.

MRS. ELVSTED. Oh, at least tell me what has happened to him? What is it?

TESMAN. You don't mean to say that he has himself—— Eh?

HEDDA. Yes, I am sure he has.

TESMAN. Hedda, how can you——?

BRACK (*keeping his eyes fixed upon her*). Unfortunately you have guessed quite correctly, Mrs. Tesman.

MRS. ELVSTED. Oh, how horrible!

TESMAN. Himself, then! Fancy that!

HEDDA. Shot himself!

BRACK. Rightly guessed again, Mrs. Tesman.

MRS. ELVSTED (*with an effort at self-control*). When did it happen, Mr. Brack?

BRACK. This afternoon—between three and four.

TESMAN. But, good Lord, where did he do it? Eh?

BRACK (*with some hesitation*). Where? Well—I suppose at his lodgings.

MRS. ELVSTED. No, that cannot be; for I was there between six and seven.

BRACK. Well, then, somewhere else. I don't know exactly. I only know that he was found——. He had shot himself—in the breast.

MRS. ELVSTED. Oh, how terrible! That he should die like that!

HEDDA (*to* BRACK). Was it in the breast?

BRACK. Yes—as I told you.

HEDDA. Not in the temple?

BRACK. In the breast, Mrs. Tesman.

HEDDA. Well, well—the breast is a good place, too.

BRACK. How do you mean, Mrs. Tesman?

HEDDA (*evasively*). Oh, nothing—nothing.

TESMAN. And the wound is dangerous, you say—eh?

BRACK. Absolutely mortal. The end has probably come by this time.

MRS. ELVSTED. Yes, yes, I feel it. The end! The end! Oh, Hedda——!

TESMAN. But tell me, how have you learnt all this?

BRACK (*curtly*). Through one of the police. A man I had some business with.

HEDDA (*in a clear voice*). At last a deed worth doing!

TESMAN (*terrified*). Good heavens, Hedda! what are you saying?

HEDDA. I say there is beauty in this.

BRACK. H'm, Mrs. Tesman——

TESMAN. Beauty! Fancy that!

MRS. ELVSTED. Oh, Hedda, how can you talk of beauty in such an act!

HEDDA. Eilert Lövborg has himself made up his account with life. He has had the courage to do—the one right thing.

MRS. ELVSTED. No, you must never think that was how it happened! It must have been in delirium that he did it.

TESMAN. In despair!

HEDDA. That he did not. I am certain of that.

MRS. ELVSTED. Yes, yes! In delirium! Just as when he tore up our manuscript.

BRACK (*starting*). The manuscript? Has he torn that up?

MRS. ELVSTED. Yes, last night.

TESMAN (*whispers softly*). Oh, Hedda, we shall never get over this.

BRACK. H'm, very extraordinary.

TESMAN (*moving about the room*). To think of Eilert going out of the world in this way! And not leaving behind him the book that would have immortalized his name——

MRS. ELVSTED. Oh, if only it could be put together again!

TESMAN. Yes, if it only could! I don't know what I would not give——

MRS. ELVSTED. Perhaps it can, Mr. Tesman.

TESMAN. What do you mean?

MRS. ELVSTED (*searches in the pocket of her dress*). Look here. I have kept all the loose notes he used to dictate from.

HEDDA (*a step forward*). Ah——!

TESMAN. You have kept them, Mrs. Elvsted! Eh?

MRS. ELVSTED. Yes, I have them here. I put them in my pocket when I left home. Here they still are——

TESMAN. Oh, do let me see them!

MRS. ELVSTED (*hands him a bundle of papers*). But they are in such disorder—all mixed up.

TESMAN. Fancy, if we could make something out of them, after all! Perhaps if we two put our heads together——

MRS. ELVSTED. Oh, yes, at least let us try——

TESMAN. We will manage it! We must! I will dedicate my life to this task.

HEDDA. You, George? Your life?

TESMAN. Yes, or rather all the time I can spare. My own collections must wait in the meantime. Hedda—you understand, eh? I owe this to Eilert's memory.

HEDDA. Perhaps.

TESMAN. And so, my dear Mrs. Elvsted, we will give our whole minds to it. There is no use in brooding over what can't be undone—eh? We must try to control our grief as much as possible, and——

MRS. ELVSTED. Yes, yes, Mr. Tesman, I will do the best I can.

TESMAN. Well then, come here. I can't rest until we have looked through the notes. Where shall we sit? Here? No, in there, in the back room. Excuse me, my dear Judge. Come with me, Mrs. Elvsted.

MRS. ELVSTED. Oh, if only it were possible!

> [TESMAN *and* MRS. ELVSTED *go into the back room.*
> *She takes off her hat and cloak. They both sit at the*
> *table under the hanging lamp, and are soon deep in*
> *an eager examination of the papers.* HEDDA *crosses to*
> *the stove and sits in the armchair. Presently* BRACK
> *goes up to her.*]

HEDDA (*in a low voice*). Oh, what a sense of freedom it gives one, this act of Eilert Lövborg's.

BRACK. Freedom, Mrs. Hedda? Well, of course, it is a release for him——

HEDDA. I mean for me. It gives me a sense of freedom to know that a deed of deliberate courage is still possible in this world—a deed of spontaneous beauty.

BRACK (*smiling*). H'm—my dear Mrs. Hedda——

HEDDA. Oh, I know what you are going to say. For you are a kind of a specialist too, like—you know!

BRACK (*looking hard at her*). Eilert Lövborg was more to you than perhaps you are willing to admit to yourself. Am I wrong?

HEDDA. I don't answer such questions. I only know Eilert Lövborg has had the courage to live his life after his own fashion. And then— the last great act, with its beauty! Ah! that he should have the will and the strength to turn away from the banquet of life—so early.

BRACK. I am sorry, Mrs. Hedda—but I fear I must dispel an amiable illusion.

HEDDA. Illusion?

BRACK. Which could not have lasted long in any case.

HEDDA. What do you mean?

BRACK. Eilert Lövborg did not shoot himself voluntarily.

HEDDA. Not voluntarily?

BRACK. No. The thing did not happen exactly as I told it.

HEDDA (*in suspense*). Have you concealed something? What is it?

BRACK. For poor Mrs. Elvsted's sake I idealized the facts a little.

HEDDA. What are the facts?

BRACK. First, that he is already dead.

HEDDA. At the hospital?

BRACK. Yes—without regaining consciousness.

HEDDA. What more have you concealed?

BRACK. This—the event did not happen at his lodgings.

HEDDA. Oh, that can make no difference.

BRACK. Perhaps it may. For I must tell you—Eilert Lövborg was found shot in—in Mademoiselle Diana's boudoir.

HEDDA (*makes a motion as if to rise, but sinks back again*). That is impossible, Judge Brack! He cannot have been there again today.

BRACK. He was there this afternoon. He went there, he said, to demand the return of something which they had taken from him. Talked wildly about a lost child——

HEDDA. Ah—so that was why——

BRACK. I thought probably he meant his manuscript; but now I hear he destroyed that himself. So I suppose it must have been his pocket-book.

HEDDA. Yes, no doubt. And there—there he was found?

BRACK. Yes, there. With a pistol in his breast-pocket, discharged. The ball had lodged in a vital part.

HEDDA. In the breast—yes.

BRACK. No—in the bowels.

HEDDA (*looks up at him with an expression of loathing*). That too! Oh what curse is it that makes everything I touch turn ludicrous and mean?

BRACK. There is one point more, Mrs. Hedda—another disagreeable feature in the affair.

HEDDA. And what is that?

BRACK. The pistol he carried——

HEDDA (*breathless*). Well? What of it?

BRACK. He must have stolen it.

HEDDA (*leaps up*). Stolen it! That is not true! He did not steal it!

BRACK. No other explanation is possible. He must have stolen it—— Hush!

> [TESMAN *and* MRS. ELVSTED *have risen from the table
> in the back room, and come into the drawing room.*]

TESMAN (*with the papers in both his hands*). Hedda dear, it is almost impossible to see under that lamp. Think of that!

HEDDA. Yes, I am thinking.

TESMAN. Would you mind our sitting at your writing table—eh?

HEDDA. If you like. (*Quickly.*) No, wait! Let me clear it first!

TESMAN. Oh, you needn't trouble, Hedda. There is plenty of room.

HEDDA. No, no; let me clear it, I say! I will take these things in and put them on the piano. There! (*She has drawn out an object, covered with sheet music, from under the bookcase, places several other pieces of music upon it, and carries the whole into the inner room, to the left.* TESMAN *lays the scraps of paper on the writing table, and moves the lamp there from the corner table.* HEDDA *returns.*)

HEDDA (*behind* MRS. ELVSTED'S *chair, gently ruffling her hair*). Well, my sweet Thea, how goes it with Eilert Lövborg's monument?

MRS. ELVSTED (*looks dispiritedly up at her*). Oh, it will be terribly hard to put in order.

TESMAN. We must manage it. I am determined. And arranging other people's papers is just the work for me.

[HEDDA *goes over to the stove, and seats herself on one of the footstools.* BRACK *stands over her, leaning on the armchair.*]

HEDDA (*whispers*). What did you say about the pistol?

BRACK (*softly*). That he must have stolen it.

HEDDA. Why stolen it?

BRACK. Because every other explanation ought to be impossible, Mrs. Hedda.

HEDDA. Indeed?

BRACK (*glances at her*). Of course Eilert Lövborg was here this morning. Was he not?

HEDDA. Yes.

BRACK. Were you alone with him?

HEDDA. Part of the time.

BRACK. Did you not leave the room whilst he was here?

HEDDA. No.

BRACK. Try to recollect. Were you not out of the room a moment?

HEDDA. Yes, perhaps just a moment—out in the hall.

BRACK. And where was your pistol case during that time?

HEDDA. I had it locked up in——

BRACK. Well, Mrs. Hedda?

HEDDA. The case stood there on the writing table.

BRACK. Have you looked since, to see whether both the pistols are there?

HEDDA. No.

BRACK. Well, you need not. I saw the pistol found in Lövborg's pocket, and I knew it at once as the one I had seen yesterday—and before, too.

HEDDA. Have you it with you?

BRACK. No; the police have it.

HEDDA. What will the police do with it?

BRACK. Search till they find the owner.

HEDDA. Do you think they will succeed?

BRACK (*bends over her and whispers*). No, Hedda Gabler—not so long as I say nothing.

HEDDA (*looks frightened at him*). And if you do not say nothing—what then?

BRACK (*shrugs his shoulders*). There is always the possibility that the pistol was stolen.

HEDDA (*firmly*). Death rather than that.

BRACK (*smiling*). People say such things—but they don't do them.

HEDDA (*without replying*). And supposing the pistol was stolen, and the owner is discovered? What then?

BRACK. Well, Hedda—then comes the scandal.

HEDDA. The scandal!

BRACK. Yes, the scandal—of which you are mortally afraid. You will, of course, be brought before the court—both you and Mademoiselle Diana. She will have to explain how the thing happened—whether it was an accidental shot or murder. Did the pistol go off as he was trying to take it out of his pocket, to threaten her with? Or did she tear the pistol out of his hand, shoot him, and push it back into his pocket? That would be quite like her; for she is an able-bodied young person, this same Mademoiselle Diana.

HEDDA. But *I* have nothing to do with all this repulsive business.

BRACK. No. But you will have to answer the question: Why did you give Eilert Lövborg the pistol? And what conclusions will people draw from the fact that you did give it to him?

HEDDA (*lets her head sink*). That is true. I did not think of that.

BRACK. Well, fortunately, there is no danger, so long as I say nothing.

HEDDA (*looks up at him*). So I am in your power, Judge Brack. You have me at your beck and call, from this time forward.

BRACK (*whispers softly*). Dearest Hedda—believe me—I shall not abuse my advantage.

HEDDA. I am in your power none the less. Subject to your will and your demands. A slave, a slave then! (*Rises impetuously.*) No, I cannot endure the thought of that! Never!

BRACK (*looks half-mockingly at her*). People generally get used to the inevitable.

HEDDA (*returns his look*). Yes, perhaps. (*She crosses to the writing table. Suppressing an involuntary smile, she imitates* TESMAN's *intonations.*) Well? Are you getting on, George? Eh?

TESMAN. Heaven knows, dear. In any case it will be the work of months.

HEDDA (*as before*). Fancy that! (*Passes her hands softly through* MRS. ELVSTED's *hair.*) Doesn't it seem strange to you, Thea? Here are you sitting with Tesman—just as you used to sit with Eilert Lövborg?

MRS. ELVSTED. Ah, if I could only inspire your husband in the same way.

HEDDA. Oh, that will come too—in time.

TESMAN. Yes, do you know, Hedda—I really think I begin to feel something of the sort. But won't you go and sit with Brack again?

HEDDA. Is there nothing I can do to help you two?

TESMAN. No, nothing in the world. (*Turning his head.*) I trust to you to keep Hedda company, my dear Brack.

BRACK (*with a glance at* HEDDA). With the very greatest of pleasure.

HEDDA. Thanks. But I am tired this evening. I will go in and lie down a little on the sofa.

TESMAN. Yes, do dear—eh?

> [HEDDA *goes into the back room and draws the curtains. A short pause. Suddenly she is heard playing a wild dance on the piano.*]

MRS. ELVSTED (*starts from her chair*). Oh—what is that?

TESMAN (*runs to the doorway*). Why, my dearest Hedda—don't play dance music tonight! Just think of Aunt Rina! And of Eilert too!

HEDDA (*puts her head out between the curtains*). And of Aunt Julia. And of all the rest of them. After this, I will be quiet. (*Closes the curtains again.*)

TESMAN (*at the writing table*). It's not good for her to see us at this distressing work. I'll tell you what, Mrs. Elvsted, you shall take the empty room at Aunt Julia's, and then I will come over in the evenings, and we can sit and work there—eh?

HEDDA (*in the inner room*). I hear what you are saying, Tesman. But how am *I* to get through the evenings out here?

TESMAN (*turning over the papers*). Oh, I daresay Judge Brack will be so kind as to look in now and then, even though I am out.

BRACK (*in the armchair, calls out gaily*). Every blessed evening, with all the pleasure in life, Mrs. Tesman! We shall get on capitally together, we two!

HEDDA (*speaking loud and clear*). Yes, don't you flatter yourself we will, Judge Brack? Now that you are the one cock in the basket——

> [*A shot is heard within.* TESMAN, MRS. ELVSTED, *and* BRACK *leap to their feet.*]

TESMAN. Oh, now she is playing with those pistols again.

> [*He throws back the curtains and runs in, followed by* MRS. ELVSTED. HEDDA *lies stretched on the sofa, lifeless. Confusion and cries.* BERTA *enters in alarm from the right.*]

TESMAN (*shrieks to* BRACK). Shot herself! Shot herself in the temple! Fancy that!

BRACK (*half-fainting in the armchair*). Good God!—people don't do such things.

QUESTIONS

ACT I

1. Miss Tesman's character is not very complex. She is the spokesman for one human value only. What is this value, and how is it estab-

lished? Does Miss Tesman's character help us understand Hedda Gabler when she enters?

2. "Collecting and arranging," Miss Tesman says, is Tesman's strong point. Is this a good description of his total character? What other details, such as peculiarities of speech, manner of dress, typical concerns, tie in with Tesman's character as a scholar?

3. Hedda has an interesting, though not unusual, way of speaking. The surface of what she says is always polite, but there is often another meaning lurking below the surface. Select several examples of this manner, discuss them, and then show how her speech reveals her character.

4. Look at the variety of subjects Hedda expresses herself on in Act I (e.g., old slippers, sunshine, Miss Tesman's bonnet, a new piano, pregnancy, etc.); see if you can find a common denominator, some basic attitude that appears in each statement and opinion.

5. Forget for a moment the language in Act I and imagine it as a mime, that is, as action without words. Do Hedda's actions taken by themselves suggest the same type of character as her way of speaking and her opinions do?

6. Thea Elvsted's situation in life—her marriage to Elvsted, etc.—parallels Hedda Gabler's in some ways and contrasts it in others. What does this tell us about Hedda?

ACT II

7. You will notice that Hedda goes certain places on the stage and does certain things only when she is in a particular state of mind. Trace her movements to the glass doors, to the stove, to the small private room at the rear, and her return to her pistols; try to describe the way she feels when she goes to each.

8. Why did Hedda marry Tesman? Is this characteristic of her?

9. What kind of "triangle" do both Judge Brack and Hedda want to arrange? Why is this particular type of human relationship the kind that both are apt to favor?

10. Tesman and Lövborg are both historians, but they are interested in quite different kinds of history. What do their professional interests tell us about them? Is Lövborg contrasted with Tesman in any other ways?

11. When Hedda speaks to Lövborg of their past relationship, she remarks that he wanted to spoil their friendship, to allow it "to develop into something more serious." Do you find signs of this distaste for reality, for seriousness, in Hedda's other actions?

12. It becomes progressively clearer that Hedda is a complex character, that there is a conflict within her between two basic values. Describe these two conflicting values and show how they are manifested in her speech, her movements, and her relations with the other characters.

13. What is the meaning of Hedda's determination to wrest control of

Lövborg from Mrs. Elvsted? Why does she wish to send him back to drinking?

ACT III

14. Consider the details of the scene—the dying fire, the cold dawn—with which Act III opens. How does the scene reflect the situation of the characters?

15. In the notes he wrote while working on *Hedda Gabler,* Ibsen describes Thea Elvsted as "the conventional, sentimental, hysterical Philistine." Is this a fair description of the actual character created in the play?

16. By Act III it becomes fairly obvious that Lövborg's manuscript is a crucial object in the play. We might say, in fact, that the manuscript has in a curious way come to represent "meaningful life." Discuss the significance of the subject matter of the manuscript, and then describe the relationship of each of the major characters to the manuscript. What does their relationship to the manuscript tell us about their basic values, their fundamental characters?

17. Tesman says of Lövborg that he is "utterly incapable of . . . moderation." What actions of Lövborg's, past and present, bear this statement out? Is his lack of moderation shown as less or more attractive than Tesman's excessive caution?

18. What is the significance of the fact that Hedda gives Lövborg a pistol at the end of Act III? (In his notes for the play Ibsen planned to have Lövborg ask for a flower at parting.)

ACT IV

19. Judge Brack has a prominent part in the play, but his character lacks the complexity of Hedda's or Lövborg's. After collecting all the information provided about Brack—his clothes, what he knows about events in the town, his position, etc.—see if you can decide what value or quality is central to his character.

20. Hedda's desperate fear of scandal emerges in Act IV. Has there been evidence of this fear earlier in the play?

21. What is the significance of the terrible manner in which Lövborg dies? Why does the manner of his death upset Hedda?

22. In his notes Ibsen clearly planned to arrange the last scene to end with Tesman and Mrs. Elvsted puzzling over Lövborg's notes and able to make nothing of them because they both lack imagination. The play, however, ends quite differently. How does the present ending change the meaning?

23. Hedda's final act is suicide, which at first seems surprising, but on reflection seems peculiarly appropriate: the action that finally expresses fully and unambiguously Hedda's nature. Go back through the play and see if you can relate any of Hedda's earlier actions and statements to her final self-defining act.

Character in Expressionistic Drama

"People don't do such things" Judge Brack exclaims after Hedda Gabler commits suicide. But people, of course, *do* do such things, and there is nothing in *Hedda Gabler* that could not occur in the real world. Ibsen's play is a masterpiece of the dramatic mode known as *realism*. *Realism* and *realistic* are tricky terms, which are apt to shift meaning from age to age, or even from user to user, but for working purposes we may define *dramatic realism* as the maintenance of an appearance of life as it is ordinarily experienced. In the realistic theater characters seem to talk as people we know talk, to do the things we normally expect people will do, and to move about in the familiar world of other people, solid furniture, and familiar settings. Realism is, of course, an illusion, because every dramatist, whether or not he preserves the appearance of reality, inevitably selects and shapes his material in order to construct not a photograph of the real world, but a revealing image of it. Art and life are not, finally, the same thing.

In our earlier discussion of the ways in which a dramatist constructs a character, we considered only realistic techniques. In life as well as in a play, character may also be expressed indirectly by clothing, movement, thought, and style—though seldom as obviously, as precisely, as relentlessly, in short as "dramatically," as in the theater. In life perhaps only the genius and the insane man achieve that concentration of being and that economy of gesture which we find in dramatic characters. But every artist tries to express his ideas as fully as possible within his chosen form, and many playwrights have wanted to present the deeper layers of consciousness more directly than realistic dramatic techniques will allow. To do this they have developed over the ages a number of devices for shifting the dramatic focus inward in order to portray motives as they take shape within the mind itself. Probably the simplest and most realistic device of this kind is the use of a *confidant,* a type of character whose sole function is to listen to the hero's frank explanation of his inmost thoughts. In the *soliloquy* there no longer is a confidant present, and the hero, alone on stage, speaks as if he were thinking aloud, as Hamlet does, for example, in his famous "To be or not to be" speech. Another simple form of spoken private thought is the *aside,* a few words delivered by a character when several actors are present on the stage but by convention heard only by the audience.

Masks have also been used as a way of presenting man's deepest thoughts and feelings. They were used in the Greek and Roman theaters where, in addition to serving several practical functions, they probably portrayed the nature of the tragic or comic character wearing them, much as the demonic mask of the witch doctor expresses the nature of the forces with which he is working. In our own century the American playwright Eugene O'Neill reintroduced masks in a number of plays in an attempt to dramatize "those profound hidden conflicts of the mind which the probings of psychology continue to disclose to us." In *The Great God Brown,* for example, the face of the chief character, Dion Anthony, is described as "dark, spiritual, poetic, passionately supersensitive, helplessly unprotected in its childlike, religious faith in life." But in order to protect himself from the world, he wears a mask with the "expression of a mocking, reckless, defiant, gayly scoffing and sensual young Pan." The face and the mask portray the two sides of Dion's character, his true personality and the one he creates in order to live in a world that has little use for such sensitive, trusting beings. The use of the mask not only permitted O'Neill to present basic complexities of character, but it also allowed him to dramatize the fact that most men make use of a public character, a mask that they show to the world.

Another device—which has been extremely popular in recent years —for staging the relatively inaccessible parts of the mind is the *flashback.* Its function is to make visible the memories stored in man's mind, which are so crucial a part of his character. The flashback has been used frequently in the movies, a form well suited to handle it: the camera comes in closer and closer on a face as the face begins to dissolve into the scene the character is thinking of. The modern theater too has made good use of the flashback, despite the fact that it is technically somewhat more difficult to work on the stage than in the film. In Arthur Miller's *Death of a Salesman,* Willy Loman's intense preoccupation with his past and his continuing search among his memories for the point at which life began to go wrong is presented in a series of scenes in which the lights dim as his mind begins to wander from the present and come up again on a re-enactment of some event twenty years past. One by-product of the use of the flashback should be noted: since the scenes from the past are as vivid and actual as the scenes of the present, we must conclude that past and present are equally real in the mind. Most dramatic techniques entail such secondary implications, and the skillful dramatist is aware of and utilizes every possible meaning inherent in his techniques.

While such dramatic devices for revealing character as asides, flashbacks, and masks are unrealistic—the general term for them is *expressionistic*—playwrights have frequently used them in plays that otherwise maintain the pretense of showing life as we ordinarily experience it. Some of these devices are by now so commonplace that they have become theatrical *conventions,* and audiences accept them as realistic. When Hamlet steps out on stage and delivers a long soliloquy in blank verse in a play that is otherwise quite realistic, no one considers this any less lifelike than his speeches directed to other characters. In the West realistic and expressionistic devices have usually been mixed, but some playwrights have been unwilling to accept this compromise. Instead they have wanted to open up the human mind directly and concentrate on what goes on inside the head. There are a number of terms for this kind of dramatic writing—*allegory, surrealism, morality play, expressionism,* etc.—but all refer to a type of play in which the pretense of realism has been largely or altogether abandoned in order to stage directly what goes on in the mind, without concern for whether these events in any way resemble the familiar world we perceive with our senses.

In an allegorical play the conflicting forces and desires at work within each man become the separate characters of the drama. The attributes of each, such as clothing, movement, and speech, reveal the nature of that particular component of the human psyche; each has a motive that presses "him" toward some goal. The arguments and struggles between these "characters" act out man's mental conflicts. *Everyman,* the best known English allegorical play, dramatizes the thoughts of man at the moment death seizes him. He at first refuses to believe what Death—a character in the play—tells him, but as the dreadful truth is borne home, he begins to cast about for someone to help him, to accompany him on the long journey he must now undertake. Each of the values he has based his life upon—friendship, material wealth, beauty, etc.—is *personified,* made into a character, and Everyman tests each in turn, only to be disappointed when each refuses to go into the grave with him. Finally he discovers that only "Good Deeds" will accompany him, and Good Deeds is terribly weak because Everyman, like most men, has never taken very good care of "him." Some of the characters of the allegory, such as Fellowship and Goods may be thought of as having existence outside of Everyman's mind, but his examination of their worth within his own mind, not their separate existence, is dramatized. Probably allegorical plays of this kind can only be written at times when there is some accepted theory about the constituent parts of the mind and the way it works. No allegorical play dramatizing Freudian psychology has yet been written, but it is possible to imagine a modern *Everyman* in which "Ego," by pointing out practical reasons for a particular course of action, tries to mediate between a raging, selfish "Id" and a stern, puritanical "Superego," while "Pleasure Principle" is locked in a grim combat with "Death Wish."

In the modern *expressionistic* play, authors have not been certain enough of their theory of the mind to construct a complete *dramatis personae* out of mental characteristics. Instead, expressionistic dramatists have offered bizarre, unrealistic images of existence, not as it appears to the senses and not as we ordinarily agree that it is, but as— so they maintain—we actually experience it within ourselves. For example, in one scene of Georg Kaiser's *From Morn to Midnight* life is presented as a seven-day bicycle race in which a few active riders drive themselves to exhaustion to win fame and cash prizes, while the mass of people look on hoping that there will be a serious accident. This extended image is complicated in all of its details, but essentially it dramatizes in the round-and-round of the race the repetitive sameness of life and the sense of futility involved in going faster and faster to get to the same place, which is no place. Seven-day bicycle races have actually occurred of course, but all life is not in any literal sense a bicycle race. What Kaiser has found is a dramatic equivalent for a feeling about life, living as it is sensed, not seen.

Samuel Beckett, an Irish writer living in France, has created an even more unreal stage than did such early expressionists as Kaiser. In *Waiting for Godot* two characters spend the entire play waiting on a stage empty of all objects but a stunted tree for the arrival of someone who never comes. In fact, they are not sure of the name of the person they expect, they don't know whether he plans to come, and they are not even certain that he exists. A great deal of argument has raged over this play, but whatever else *Godot* may mean, clearly it gives concrete form to that inner sense of life in which the material world becomes unreal and living becomes only an anxious, uncertain wait for someone or something to save us from the bleakness of a meaningless existence.

Ionesco's *The Chairs,* a recent expressionistic play, dramatizes man's frustrated desire to communicate to others anything that he learns about himself or about his life. An old man and his wife, living alone on an island, prepare a large party and hire an orator to tell the guests what the old man has learned about life. The couple believe that a number of guests arrive, and they speak to them and provide chairs for each. But no guests actually appear, and the stage continues to fill with empty chairs. Later the orator really does arrive, but he proves to be a deaf mute. The old man and his wife commit suicide shortly after this, and the orator then tries to communicate his message by writing on a blackboard, but all he produces is a meaningless scribble.

Waiting for Godot and *The Chairs* are extreme examples of expressionism; they seem very strange to modern audiences brought up to expect that plays will be in large part "realistic." But we should not think of an expressionistic play like *The Chairs* as fundamentally different from a realistic play like *Hedda Gabler* or a semi-realistic play like *Hamlet.* Each type of play presents characters who are images of man, and in each these characters are moved by one or two basic motives, which are expressed by their bodies, their clothes, their movements, and their words. In fact, while plays like *Waiting for Godot* and *The Chairs* may seem at first glance much more difficult than a play like *Hedda Gabler,* they are really much simpler and easier to understand. It takes a good deal of very careful reading to see that Hedda's motive is to seek freedom from all control, but it requires very little effort to see that the motive of the characters in *Waiting for Godot* is to wait for salvation, and the motive of the old man in *The Chairs* is to communicate what he knows to others. In expressionistic drama everything is exaggerated and obvious once we adjust to the unfamiliar idiom, but in realistic drama gesture and language are muted so that we are in danger of missing the meaning. No matter how much the characters of an expressionistic play may seem like a fantastic dream or how much the characters of a realistic play may seem like real people, in both cases they are the playwright's images, definitions, of man.

EVERYMAN

The Moral Play of Everyman, to give the work its full title, is preserved in only two printed editions from the early sixteenth century. It was written, however, at some time during the fifteenth century, probably by a monk or clerk. Versions of Everyman exist in Dutch and German, and scholars have argued a good deal about the priority and relative literary merits of the different versions, particularly the Dutch and English. Nowadays scholars are less concerned with comparisons and dates than they are with the fact that Everyman is the play of medieval Christendom. It reveals that society's understanding of life, its assumptions about the world, and its major problems in a manner comparable to the way in which Oedipus Rex, say, reveals the Greek mind and Hamlet expresses the mind of Renaissance England. Before beginning to read Everyman, it will be helpful to look briefly at some of the more obvious facts that the play assumes about the medieval Christian view of man and his world.

Everyman dramatizes the major crisis in the life of man, the moment of his death—when the world that had seemed so substantial slips away to the reality of God's judgment, to life or damnation eternal. True life, then, begins with death, and the crucial event of living is dying. Everyman has not committed any grave sins during his life, but neither has he done very much good; therefore, if justice were strictly rendered by God, Everyman would not fare very well. But God is merciful and has provided for such ordinary people who are neither saints nor devils. Besides a minimum of good works, repentance and humility before God are all that are necessary for salvation. Man is aided in achieving this condition of mind by the Church and its sacraments.

The most revealing insight into the medieval world view comes, however, not from the direct statements of doctrine in Everyman, but from the form of the play. While *Oedipus Rex* is set in the square of a Greek city, Thebes, and *Hamlet* is set in the castle of the King of Denmark, Elsinore; in *Everyman* the setting becomes *the mind of a man*. Reality, the play says, is not the physical world or the political and social scene in which man lives out his mortal life; it is, instead, his interior consciousness of himself as a soul created by God, owing certain duties to Him, and returning to Him for a final accounting. All else in the world is unreal and fleeting and therefore need not be represented on the stage. Strictly speaking, none of the personifications that make up the cast of characters in *Everyman* has any life of his own; their words and actions merely reflect the realization of Everyman as, dying, he turns his mind to each of these things that has meant so much to him, and finds that each lacks essential realness, or the ability to pass over from this false world to the real one beyond. This is not to say, however, that medieval man did not love the world of the here and now. Quite the reverse. Everyman endures his greatest agony in being torn away from the familiar and intensely valued world known to his senses.

Everyman is a fine companion piece for *Hedda Gabler* because between them they mark the full range of ways to present character in drama. In both plays the dramatists offer studies of the human mind and its operations. The anonymous author of *Everyman* presents this mind directly as the only reality. Ibsen, because he believed like most modern men that the workings of the mind are mysterious and that the material world in which the mind exists is very real indeed, presents that mind struggling to express itself in the present, out of the muddle of daily life. Because Ibsen renders so perfectly the solid world of bodies and furniture, we become aware not only of Hedda Gabler's complex mind, but, perhaps even more powerfully, of her desperate attempts to find some satisfactory way of expressing her mind using the forms of the solid world. Mind or consciousness escapes the material world in *Everyman,* but in *Hedda Gabler* the spirit of man is entangled, inextricably, with its immediate surroundings.

CHARACTERS

MESSENGER   GOOD DEEDS
GOD: *Adonai*   KNOWLEDGE
DEATH   CONFESSION
EVERYMAN   BEAUTY
FELLOWSHIP   STRENGTH
COUSIN   DISCRETION
KINDRED   FIVE WITS
GOODS   ANGEL
          DOCTOR

EVERYMAN

Here beginneth a treatise how the High Father of Heaven sendeth Death to summon every creature to come and give account of their lives in this world, and is in manner of a moral play.

MESSENGER. I pray you all give your audience,
    And hear this matter with reverence,
    By figure° a moral play—
    The *Summoning of Everyman* called it is,
    That of our lives and ending shows   5
    How transitory we be all day.°
    This matter is wondrous precious,
    But the intent of it is more gracious,
    And sweet to bear away.
    The story saith: Man, in the beginning,   10
    Look well, and take good heed to the ending,
    Be you never so gay!
    Ye think sin in the beginning full sweet,
    Which in the end causeth the soul to weep,
    When the body lieth in clay.   15
    Here shall you see how Fellowship and Jollity,
    Both Strength, Pleasure, and Beauty,
    Will fade from thee as flower in May.
    For ye shall hear how our Heaven King
    Calleth Everyman to a general reckoning.   20

3. In the form of.   6. Always.

Give audience, and hear what he doth say.   [*Exit.*]

[GOD *speaketh.*]

GOD. I perceive, here in my majesty,
How that all creatures be to me unkind,°
Living without dread in worldly prosperity.
Of ghostly° sight the people be so blind,   25
Drowned in sin, they know me not for their God.
In worldly riches is all their mind,
They fear not my rightwiseness, the sharp rod;
My love that I showed when I for them died
They forget clean, and shedding of my blood red;   30
I hanged between two, it cannot be denied;
To get them life I suffered to be dead;
I healed their feet, with thorns hurt was my head.
I could do no more than I did, truly;
And now I see the people do clean forsake me.   35
They use the seven deadly sins damnable,
As pride, covetise, wrath, and lechery,
Now in the world be made commendable;
And thus they leave of angels the heavenly company.
Every man liveth so after his own pleasure,   40
And yet of their life they be nothing sure.
I see the more that I them forbear
The worse they be from year to year;
All that liveth appaireth° fast.
Therefore I will, in all the haste,   45
Have a reckoning of every man's person;
For, and I leave the people thus alone
In their life and wicked tempests,
Verily they will become much worse than beasts;
For now one would by envy another up eat;   50
Charity they all do clean forget.
I hoped well that every man
In my glory should make his mansion,
And thereto I had them all elect;
But now I see, like traitors deject,   55
They thank me not for the pleasure that I to them meant,
Nor yet for their being that I them have lent.
I proffered the people great multitude of mercy,
And few there be that asketh it heartily;
They be so cumbered with worldly riches,   60
That needs on them I must do justice,

23. Unnatural.   25. Spiritual.   44. Degenerates.

On every man living without fear.
Where art thou, Death, thou mighty messenger?
                    [*Enter* DEATH.]
DEATH. Almighty God, I am here at your will,
    Your commandment to fulfil.   65
GOD. Go thou to Everyman,
    And show him, in my name,
    A pilgrimage he must on him take,
    Which he in no wise° may escape;
    And that he bring with him a sure reckoning   70
    Without delay or any tarrying. [*Exit* GOD.]
DEATH. Lord, I will in the world go run over all,
    And cruelly out search both great and small.
    Every man will I beset that liveth beastly
    Out of God's laws, and dreadeth not folly.   75
    He that loveth riches I will strike with my dart,
    His sight to blind, and from heaven to depart,°
    Except that alms° be his good friend,
    In hell for to dwell, world without end.   [*Enter* EVERYMAN.]
    Lo, yonder I see Everyman walking;   80
    Full little he thinketh on my coming.
    His mind is on fleshly lusts and his treasure,
    And great pain it shall cause him to endure
    Before the Lord, Heaven King.
    Everyman, stand still! Whither art thou going   85
    Thus gaily? Hast thou thy Maker forgot?
EVERYMAN. Why askest thou?
    Wouldst thou wete?°
DEATH. Yea, sir, I will show you:
    In great haste I am sent to thee
    From God out of his Majesty.   90
EVERYMAN. What, sent to me?
DEATH. Yea, certainly.
    Though thou have forgot him here,
    He thinketh on thee in the heavenly sphere,   95
    As, ere we depart, thou shalt know.
EVERYMAN. What desireth God of me?
DEATH. That shall I show thee:
    A reckoning he will needs have
    Without any longer respite.   100
EVERYMAN. To give a reckoning, longer leisure I crave.
    This blind matter troubleth my wit.°

---

69. Manner, way. **77.** Separate. **78.** Almsgiving, charity. **88.** Know.
102. "This dark problem confuses me."

DEATH. On thee thou must take a long journey;
    Therefore thy book of count° with thee thou bring;
    For turn again° thou can not by no way.   105
    And look thou be sure of thy reckoning,
    For before God thou shalt answer and show
    Thy many bad deeds, and good but a few,
    How thou hast spent thy life, and in what wise,
    Before the Chief Lord of paradise.   110
    Have ado that we were in that way,°
    For, wete thou well, thou shalt make none attorney.°
EVERYMAN. Full unready I am such reckoning to give.
    I know thee not. What messenger art thou?
DEATH. I am Death, that no man dreadeth.°   115
    For every man I 'rest,° and no man spareth;
    For it is God's commandment
    That all to me should be obedient.
EVERYMAN. O Death! thou comest when I had thee least in mind!
    In thy power it lieth me to save.   120
    Yet of my goods will I give thee, if thou will be kind;
    Yea, a thousand pound shalt thou have,
    If thou defer this matter till another day.
DEATH. Everyman, it may not be, by no way!
    I set not by° gold, silver, nor riches,   125
    Nor by pope, emperor, king, duke, nor princes.
    For, and I would receive gifts great,
    All the world I might get;
    But my custom is clean contrary.
    I give thee no respite. Come hence, and not tarry.   130
EVERYMAN. Alas! shall I have no longer respite?
    I may say Death giveth no warning.
    To think on thee, it maketh my heart sick,
    For all unready is my book of reckoning.
    But twelve year and I might have abiding,°   135
    My counting-book I would make so clear,
    That my reckoning I should not need to fear.
    Wherefore, Death, I pray thee, for God's mercy,
    Spare me till I be provided of remedy.°
DEATH. Thee availeth not to cry, weep, and pray;   140
    But haste thee lightly that thou were gone that journey,
    And prove thy friends if thou can.
    For wete thou well the tide abideth no man;

104. Accounts. 105. Return. 111. "Get ready to go." 112. Shall have
no lawyer. 115. "That fears no man." 116. Arrest. 125. Care not for.
135. "If I could remain for only twelve years." 139. With help.

And in the world each living creature
For Adam's sin must die of nature.   145
EVERYMAN. Death, if I should this pilgrimage take,
And my reckoning surely make,
Show me, for saint charity,
Should I not come again shortly?
DEATH. No, Everyman; and thou be once there,   150
Thou mayst never more come here,
Trust me verily.
EVERYMAN. O gracious God, in the high seat celestial,
Have mercy on me in this most need!
Shall I have no company from this vale terrestrial   155
Of mine acquaintance that way me to lead?
DEATH. Yea, if any be so hardy,
That would go with thee and bear thee company.
Hie thee that thou were gone° to God's magnificence,
Thy reckoning to give before his presence.   160
What! weenest° thou thy life is given thee,
And thy worldly goods also?
EVERYMAN. I had weened so, verily.
DEATH. Nay, nay; it was but lent thee;
For, as soon as thou art gone,   165
Another a while shall have it, and then go therefrom
Even as thou hast done.
Everyman, thou art mad! Thou hast thy wits five,
And here on earth will not amend thy life;
For suddenly I do come.   170
EVERYMAN. O wretched caitiff! whither shall I flee,
That I might 'scape endless sorrow?
Now, gentle Death, spare me till tomorrow,
That I may amend me
With good advisement.°   175
DEATH. Nay, thereto I will not consent,
Nor no man will I respite,
But to the heart suddenly I shall smite
Without any advisement.
And now out of thy sight I will me hie;   180
See thou make thee ready shortly,
For thou mayst say this is the day
That no man living may 'scape away.   [*Exit* DEATH.]
EVERYMAN. Alas! I may well weep with sighs deep.
Now have I no manner of company
To help me in my journey and me to keep;   185

159. "Hurry and go."   161. Judgest.   175. Warning.

And also my writing° is full unready.
How shall I do now for to excuse me?
I would to God I had never been get!°
To my soul a full great profit it had be,   190
For now I fear pains huge and great.
The time passeth; Lord, help, that all wrought.
For though I mourn it availeth naught.
The day passeth, and is almost a-go;
I wot° not well what for to do.   195
To whom were I best my complaint° to make?
What if I to Fellowship thereof spake,
And showed him of this sudden chance?
For in him is all mine affiance,°
We have in the world so many a day   200
Been good friends in sport and play.
I see him yonder, certainly;
I trust that he will bear me company;
Therefore to him will I speak to ease my sorrow.
Well met, good Fellowship, and good morrow!   205
            [FELLOWSHIP *speaketh*.]
FELLOWSHIP. Everyman, good morrow, by this day!
   Sir, why lookest thou so piteously?
   If any thing be amiss, I pray thee me say,
   That I may help to remedy.
EVERYMAN. Yea, good Fellowship, yea,   210
   I am in great jeopardy.
FELLOWSHIP. My true friend, show to me your mind.
   I will not forsake thee to my life's end
   In the way of good company.
EVERYMAN. That was well spoken, and lovingly.   215
FELLOWSHIP. Sir, I must needs know your heaviness;
   I have pity to see you in any distress;
   If any have you wronged, ye shall revenged be,
   Though I on the ground be slain for thee,
   Though that I know before that I should die.   220
EVERYMAN. Verily, Fellowship, gramercy.
FELLOWSHIP. Tush! by thy thanks I set not a straw!
   Show me your grief, and say no more.
EVERYMAN. If I my heart should to you break,°
   And then you to° turn your mind from me,   225
   And would not me comfort when you hear me speak,
   Then should I ten times sorrier be.

---

187. Accounts. **189.** Begotten. **195.** Know. **196.** Lament. **199.** Trust
224. Reveal. **225.** Were to.

FELLOWSHIP. Sir, I say as I will do, indeed.
EVERYMAN. Then be you a good friend at need;
    I have found you true here before.   230
FELLOWSHIP. And so ye shall evermore;
    For, in faith, and° thou go to hell,
    I will not forsake thee by the way!
EVERYMAN. Ye speak like a good friend. I believe you well;
    I shall deserve° it, and I may.°   235
FELLOWSHIP. I speak of no deserving, by this day!
    For he that will say and nothing do
    Is not worthy with good company to go;
    Therefore show me the grief of your mind,
    As to your friend most loving and kind.   240
EVERYMAN. I shall show you how it is:
    Commanded I am to go a journey,
    A long way, hard and dangerous,
    And give a strait count° without delay
    Before the high judge, Adonai.   245
    Wherefore, I pray you, bear me company,
    As ye have promised, in this journey.
FELLOWSHIP. That is matter indeed! Promise is duty;
    But, and I should take such a voyage on me,
    I know it well, it should be to my pain.   250
    Also it maketh me afeared, certain.
    But let us take counsel here as well as we can,
    For your words would fright a strong man.
EVERYMAN. Why, ye said if I had need,
    Ye would me never forsake, quick nor dead,   255
    Though it were to hell, truly.
FELLOWSHIP. So I said, certainly,
    But such pleasures be set aside, the sooth to say.°
    And also, if we took such a journey,
    When should we come again?   260
EVERYMAN. Nay, never again till the day of doom.
FELLOWSHIP. In faith, then will not I come there!
    Who hath you these tidings brought?
EVERYMAN. Indeed, Death was with me here.
FELLOWSHIP. Now, by God that all hath bought,°   265
    If Death were the messenger,
    For no man that is living today
    I will not go that loath journey—
    Not for the father that begat me!

232. If. 235. Repay. If possible. 244. Strict accounting. 258. "Such
pleasantries are, truly, only a way of speaking." 265. Redeemed.

EVERYMAN. Ye promised otherwise, pardie.°   270
FELLOWSHIP. I wot well I said so, truly;
    And yet if thou wilt eat, and drink, and make good cheer,
    Or haunt to women the lusty company,°
    I would not forsake you while the day is clear,
    Trust me verily!   275
EVERYMAN. Yea, thereto ye would be ready.
    To go to mirth, solace, and play,
    Your mind will sooner apply
    Than to bear me company in my long journey.
FELLOWSHIP. Now, in good faith, I will not that way.   280
    But and thou wilt murder, or any man kill,
    In that I will help thee with a good will!
EVERYMAN. O, that is a simple advice indeed!
    Gentle fellow, help me in my necessity;
    We have loved long, and now I need,   285
    And now, gentle Fellowship, remember me!
FELLOWSHIP. Whether ye have loved me or no,
    By Saint John, I will not with thee go.
EVERYMAN. Yet, I pray thee, take° the labor, and do so much for
    me
    To bring me forward,° for saint charity,   290
    And comfort me till I come without the town.
FELLOWSHIP. Nay, and thou would give me a new gown,
    I will not a foot with thee go;
    But, and thou had tarried, I would not have left thee so.
    And as now God speed thee in thy journey,   295
    For from thee I will depart as fast as I may.
EVERYMAN. Whither away, Fellowship? Will you forsake me?
FELLOWSHIP. Yea, by my fay, to God I betake° thee.
EVERYMAN. Farewell, good Fellowship! For thee my heart is sore;
    Adieu for ever! I shall see thee no more.   300
FELLOWSHIP. In faith, Everyman, farewell now at the end!
    For° you I will remember that parting is mourning.
                                  [Exit FELLOWSHIP.]
EVERYMAN. Alack! shall we thus depart indeed
    (Ah, Lady, help!) without any more comfort?
    Lo, Fellowship forsaketh me in my most need.   305
    For help in this world whither shall I resort?
    Fellowship here before with me would merry make,
    And now little sorrow for me doth he take.
    It is said, "In prosperity men friends may find,

270. *Par dieu,* by God.   **273.** Enjoy the companionship of joyful women.
289. Undertake.   **290.** Accompany me.   **298.** Commit.   **302.** Because of.

Which in adversity be full unkind." 310
Now whither for succor shall I flee,
Sith° that Fellowship hath forsaken me?
To my kinsmen I will,° truly,
Praying them to help me in my necessity;
I believe that they will do so, 315
For "kind will creep where it may not go." °
I will go say,° for yonder I see them go.
Where be ye now, my friends and kinsmen?

                [*Enter* KINDRED *and* COUSIN.]

KINDRED. Here be we now, at your commandment.
    Cousin,° I pray you show us your intent 320
    In any wise, and do not spare.
COUSIN. Yea, Everyman, and to us declare
    If ye be disposed to go any whither,
    For, wete you well, we will live and die together.
KINDRED. In wealth and woe we will with you hold, 325
    For over his kin a man may be bold.
EVERYMAN. Gramercy, my friends and kinsmen kind.
    Now shall I show you the grief of my mind.
    I was commanded by a messenger
    That is a high king's chief officer; 330
    He bade me go a pilgrimage, to my pain,
    And I know well I shall never come again;
    Also I must give a reckoning straight,°
    For I have a great enemy that hath me in wait,°
    Which intendeth me for to hinder.° 335
KINDRED. What account is that which ye must render?
    That would I know.
EVERYMAN. Of all my works I must show
    How I have lived, and my days spent;
    Also of ill deeds that I have used° 340
    In my time, sith life was me lent;
    And of all virtues that I have refused.
    Therefore I pray you go thither with me,
    To help to make mine account, for saint charity.
COUSIN. What, to go thither? Is that the matter? 345
    Nay, Everyman, I had liefer fast bread and water
    All this five year and more.
EVERYMAN. Alas, that ever I was bore!

---

312. Since. 313. Will go. 316. "Natural relationship will creep where it may not walk," i.e. "blood is thicker than water." 317. Test. 320. A term used at this time for any relative, except brother or sister. 333. Both "severe" and "immediately." 334. In waiting, i.e. "controls me." 335. Harm. 340. Practiced. 341. Since.

     For now shall I never be merry
     If that you forsake me.   350
KINDRED. Ah, sir, what! Ye be a merry man!
     Take good heart to you, and make no moan.
     But one thing I warn you, by Saint Anne,
     As for me, ye shall go alone.
EVERYMAN. My Cousin, will you not with me go?   355
COUSIN. No, by our Lady! I have the cramp in my toe.
     Trust not to me, for, so God me speed,°
     I will deceive you in your most need.
KINDRED. It availeth not us to tice.°
     Ye shall have my maid with all my heart;   360
     She loveth to go to feasts, there to be nice,°
     And to dance, and abroad to start;°
     I will give her leave to help you in that journey,
     If that you and she may agree.
EVERYMAN. Now show me the very effect of your mind.   365
     Will you go with me, or abide behind?
KINDRED. Abide behind? Yea, that will I, and I may!
     Therefore, farewell till another day.   *[Exit* KINDRED.]
EVERYMAN. How should I be merry or glad?
     For fair promises men to me make,   370
     But when I have most need, they me forsake.
     I am deceived; that maketh me sad.
COUSIN. Cousin Everyman, farewell now,
     For verily I will not go with you;
     Also of mine own life an unready reckoning   375
     I have to account; therefore I make tarrying.°
     Now, God keep thee, for now I go.   *[Exit* COUSIN.]
EVERYMAN. Ah, Jesus! is all come hereto?
     Lo, fair words maketh fools fain;°
     They promise and nothing will do, certain.   380
     My kinsmen promised me faithfully
     For to abide with me steadfastly,
     And now fast away do they flee.
     Even so Fellowship promised me.
     What friend were best me of to provide?   385
     I lose my time here longer to abide.
     Yet in my mind a thing there is:
     All my life I have loved riches;
     If that my good now help me might,
     He would make my heart full light.   390

---

357. Prosper. **359.** Entice. **361.** Wanton. **362.** Travel about. **376.** I
tarry. **379.** Joyful.

I will speak to him in this distress.

Where art thou, my Goods and riches?

GOODS [*To one side*.] Who calleth me? Everyman? What, hast
thou haste?

I lie here in corners, trussed and piled so high,

And in chests I am locked so fast, 395

Also sacked in bags—thou mayest see with thine eye—

I cannot stir; in packs low I lie.

What would ye have? Lightly° me say.

EVERYMAN. Come hither, Goods, in all the haste thou may.

For of counsel I must desire thee. 400

[*Enter* GOODS.]

GOODS. Sir, and ye in the world have sorrow or adversity,

That can I help you to remedy shortly.

EVERYMAN. It is another disease that grieveth me;

In this world it is not, I tell thee so.

I am sent for another way to go, 405

To give a strict count general

Before the highest Jupiter of all;

And all my life I have had joy and pleasure in thee,

Therefore I pray thee go with me,

For, peradventure, thou mayest before God Almighty 410

My reckoning help to clean and purify;

For it is said ever among,

That "money maketh all right that is wrong."

GOODS. Nay, Everyman; I sing another song,

I follow no man in such voyages;

For, and I went with thee, 415

Thou shouldst fare much the worse for me;

For because on me thou did set thy mind,

Thy reckoning I have made blotted and blind,°

That thine account thou cannot make truly; 420

And that hast thou for the love of me.

EVERYMAN. That would grieve me full sore,

When I should come to that fearful answer.

Up, let us go thither together.

GOODS. Nay, not so! I am too brittle, I may not endure; 425

I will follow no man one foot, be ye sure.

EVERYMAN. Alas! I have thee loved, and had great pleasure

All my life-days on goods and treasure.

GOODS. That is to thy damnation, without lesing!°

For my love is contrary to the love everlasting. 430

But if thou had me loved moderately during,°

398. Quickly. 419. Obscure. 429. Lying. 431. While living.

As to the poor to give part of me,
Then shouldst thou not in this dolor be,
Nor in this great sorrow and care.
EVERYMAN. Lo, now was I deceived ere I was ware,°   435
    And all I may wyte my spending of time.°
GOODS. What, weenest thou that I am thine?
EVERYMAN. I had weened so.
GOODS. Nay, Everyman, I say no;
    As for a while I was lent thee,   440
    A season thou hast had me in prosperity.
    My condition is man's soul to kill;
    If I save one, a thousand I do spill;°
    Weenest thou that I will follow thee
    From this world? Nay, verily.   445
EVERYMAN. I had weened otherwise.
GOODS. Therefore to thy soul Goods is a thief;
    For when thou art dead, this is my guise,°
    Another to deceive in the same wise
    As I have done thee, and all to his soul's reprief.° 450
EVERYMAN. O false Goods, curséd may thou be!
    Thou traitor to God, that hast deceived me
    And caught me in thy snare.
GOODS. Marry! thou brought thyself in care,
    Whereof I am right glad.   455
    I must needs laugh, I cannot be sad.
EVERYMAN. Ah, Goods, thou hast had long my heartly love;
    I gave thee that which should be the Lord's above.
    But wilt thou not go with me indeed?
    I pray thee truth to say.   460
GOODS. No, so God me speed!
    Therefore farewell, and have good day.   [*Exit* GOODS.]
EVERYMAN. O, to whom shall I make my moan
    For to go with me in that heavy journey?
    First Fellowship said he would with me gone;   465
    His words were very pleasant and gay,
    But afterward he left me alone.
    Then spake I to my kinsmen, all in despair,
    And also they gave me words fair,
    They lacked no fair speaking,   470
    But all forsook me in the ending.
    Then went I to my Goods, that I loved best,
    In hope to have comfort, but there had I least;

435. Aware.   436. "And I may blame all on the way I spent my time."
443. Kill, destroy.   448. Practice.   450. Reproof.

For my Goods sharply did me tell
That he bringeth many into hell.   475
Then of myself I was ashamed,
And so I am worthy to be blamed;
Thus may I well myself hate.
Of whom shall I now counsel take?
I think that I shall never speed°   480
Till that I go to my Good Deeds.
But alas! she is so weak
That she can neither go° nor speak.
Yet will I venture° on her now.
My Good Deeds, where be you?   485
>   [GOOD DEEDS *speaks from below*.]
GOOD DEEDS. Here I lie, cold in the ground.
Thy sins hath me sore bound,
That I cannot stir.
EVERYMAN. O Good Deeds, I stand in fear!
I must you pray of counsel,   490
For help now should come right well.°
GOOD DEEDS. Everyman, I have understanding
That ye be summoned account to make
Before Messias, of Jerusalem King;
And you do by me,° that journey with you will I take.   495
EVERYMAN. Therefore I come to you my moan to make;
I pray you that ye will go with me.
GOOD DEEDS. I would full fain, but I cannot stand, verily.
EVERYMAN. Why, is there anything on you fall?
GOOD DEEDS. Yea, sir, I may thank you of all;°   500
If ye had perfectly cheered° me,
Your book of count full ready had be.
Look, the books of your works and deeds eke.°
Behold how they lie under the feet,
To your soul's heaviness.   505
EVERYMAN. Our Lord Jesus help me!
For one letter here I can not see.
GOOD DEEDS. There is a blind reckoning in time of distress!°
EVERYMAN. Good Deeds, I pray you, help me in this need,
Or else I am for ever damned indeed.   510
Therefore help me to make my reckoning
Before the Redeemer of all thing,
That King is, and was, and ever shall.

---

480. Prosper. **483.** Walk. **484.** Chance. **491.** Be welcome. **495.** "If you follow my advice." **500.** For everything. **501.** Properly cared for. **503.** Also. **508.** I.e., the sinner discovers that his account of good works is hard to read when he is in trouble.

GOOD DEEDS. Everyman, I am sorry of your fall,
  And fain would I help you, and I were able.   515
EVERYMAN. Good Deeds, your counsel I pray you give me.
GOOD DEEDS. That shall I do verily;
    Though that on my feet I may not go,°
    I have a sister that shall with you also,
    Called Knowledge,° which shall with you abide,   520
    To help you to make that dreadful reckoning.
                    [*Enter* KNOWLEDGE.]
KNOWLEDGE. Everyman, I will go with thee, and be thy guide,
    In thy most need to go by thy side.
EVERYMAN. In good condition I am now in every thing,
    And am wholly content with this good thing;   525
    Thanked be God my Creator.
GOOD DEEDS. And when he hath brought thee there,°
    Where thou shalt heal thee of thy smart,°
    Then go you with your reckoning and your Good Deeds to-
        gether
    For to make you joyful at heart   530
    Before the blesséd Trinity.
EVERYMAN. My Good Deeds, gramercy!
    I am well content, certainly,
    With your words sweet.
KNOWLEDGE. Now go we together lovingly   535
    To Confession, that cleansing river.
EVERYMAN. For joy I weep; I would we were there!
    But, I pray you, give me cognition°
    Where dwelleth that holy man, Confession.
KNOWLEDGE. In the house of salvation,   540
    We shall find him in that place,
    That shall us comfort, by God's grace.
            [KNOWLEDGE *leads* EVERYMAN *to* CONFESSION.]
    Lo, this is Confession. Kneel down and ask mercy,
    For he is in good conceit° with God almighty.
EVERYMAN. O glorious fountain, that all uncleanness doth clarify, 545
    Wash from me the spots of vice unclean,
    That on me no sin may be seen.
    I come, with Knowledge, for my redemption,
    Redempt with hearty and full contrition;°
    For I am commanded a pilgrimage to take,   550
    And great accounts before God to make.
    Now, I pray you, Shrift,° mother of salvation,

518. Walk. 520. Knowledge here is knowledge of sin. 527. To that
place. 528. Pain. 538. Understanding. 544. Esteem. 549. "Saved by
sincere and complete sorrow (for my sins)." 552. Confession.

Help my Good Deeds for my piteous exclamation.

CONFESSION. I know your sorrow well, Everyman.

    Because with Knowledge ye come to me,   555

    I will you comfort as well as I can,

    And a precious jewel I will give thee,

    Called penance, voider of adversity.

    Therewith shall your body chastised be

    With abstinence and perseverance in God's service.   560

    Here shall you receive that scourge of me

                    [*Gives* EVERYMAN *a scourge.*]

    Which is penance strong that ye must endure

    To remember thy Savior was scourged for thee

    With sharp scourges and suffered it patiently.

    So must thou ere thou 'scape° that painful pilgrimage.   565

    Knowledge, keep him in this voyage,°

    And by that time Good Deeds will be with thee.

    But in any wise° be sure of mercy,

    For your time draweth fast,° and ye will saved be;

    Ask God mercy, and He will grant truly;   570

    When with the scourge of penance man doth him bind,

    The oil of forgiveness then shall he find. [*Exit* CONFESSION.]

EVERYMAN. Thanked be God for his gracious work!

    For now I will my penance begin;

    This hath rejoiced and lighted my heart,   575

    Though the knots be painful and hard within.

KNOWLEDGE. Everyman, look your penance that ye fulfil,

    What pain that ever it to you be,

    And Knowledge shall give you counsel at will°

    How your account ye shall make clearly.   580

EVERYMAN. O eternal God! O heavenly figure!

    O way of rightwiseness! O goodly vision!

    Which descended down in a virgin pure

    Because he would Everyman redeem,

    Which Adam forfeited by his disobedience.   585

    O blessèd Godhead! elect and high divine,

    Forgive me my grievous offence;

    Here I cry thee mercy in this presence.

    O ghostly° treasure! O ransomer and redeemer!

    Of all the world hope and conductor,   590

    Mirror of joy, and founder of mercy,

    Which illumineth heaven and earth thereby,

    Hear my clamorous complaint, though it late be.

---

565. Finish. **566.** "Moving in this direction." **568.** Case. **569.** To an end. **579.** Whenever you desire it. **589.** Spiritual.

Receive my prayers; unworthy in this heavy life.
Though I be a sinner most abominable,   595
Yet let my name be written in Moses' table.°
O Mary! pray to the Maker of all thing,
Me for to help at my ending,
And save me from the power of my enemy,
For Death assaileth me strongly.   600
And, Lady, that I may by means of thy prayer
Of your Son's glory to be partner,
By the means of his passion I it crave.
I beseech you, help my soul to save.
Knowledge, give me the scourge of penance.   605
My flesh therewith shall give a quittance.°
I will now begin, if God give me grace.
KNOWLEDGE. Everyman, God give you time and space.
Thus I bequeath you in the hands of our Savior,
Now may you make your reckoning sure.   610
EVERYMAN. In the name of the Holy Trinity,
My body sore punished shall be.   [*Scourges himself.*]
Take this, body, for the sin of the flesh.
Also thou delightest to go gay and fresh,°
And in the way of damnation thou did me bring;   615
Therefore suffer now strokes of punishing.
Now of penance I will wade the water clear,
To save me from purgatory, that sharp fire.
                    [GOOD DEEDS *rises from below.*]
GOOD DEEDS. I thank God, now I can walk and go,
And am delivered of my sickness and woe.   620
Therefore with Everyman I will go, and not spare;
His good works I will help him to declare.
KNOWLEDGE. Now, Everyman, be merry and glad!
Your Good Deeds cometh now, ye may not be sad.
Now is your Good Deeds whole and sound,   625
Going upright upon the ground.
EVERYMAN. My heart is light, and shall be evermore.
Now will I smite faster than I did before.
GOOD DEEDS. Everyman, pilgrim, my special friend,
Blesséd be thou without end.   630
For thee is prepared the eternal glory.
Ye have me made whole and sound,
Therefore I will bide by thee in every stound.°
EVERYMAN. Welcome, my Good Deeds; now I hear thy voice,

596. Tablets, i.e., among the saved.   **606.** Full payment (for sins).   **614.**
Handsomely dressed.   **633.** Trial.

I weep for very sweetness of love. 635
KNOWLEDGE. Be no more sad, but ever rejoice;
    God seeth thy living° in his throne above.
    Put on this garment to thy behoof,°

              [*Handing* EVERYMAN *a cloak.*]
    Which is wet with your tears,
    Or else before God you may it miss,° 640
    When you to your journey's end come shall.
EVERYMAN. Gentle Knowledge, what do ye it call?
KNOWLEDGE. It is the garment of sorrow;
    From pain it will you borrow;°
    Contrition it is 645
    That getteth forgiveness;
    It pleaseth God passing well.
GOOD DEEDS. Everyman, will you wear it for your heal?
           [EVERYMAN *puts on the cloak.*]
EVERYMAN. Now blesséd be Jesu, Mary's Son,
    For now have I on true contrition. 650
    And let us go now without tarrying;
    Good Deeds, have we clear our reckoning?
GOOD DEEDS. Yea, indeed I have it here.
EVERYMAN. Then I trust we need not fear.
    Now, friends, let us not part in twain.° 655
KNOWLEDGE. Nay, Everyman, that will we not, certain.
GOOD DEEDS. Yet must thou lead with thee
    Three persons of great might.
EVERYMAN. Who should they be?
GOOD DEEDS. Discretion and Strength they hight,° 660
    And thy Beauty may not abide behind.
KNOWLEDGE. Also ye must call to mind
    Your Five Wits° as for your counselors.
GOOD DEEDS. You must have them ready at all hours.
EVERYMAN. How shall I get them hither? 665
KNOWLEDGE. You must call them all together,
    And they will hear you incontinent.°
EVERYMAN. My friends, come hither and be present,
    Discretion, Strength, my Five Wits, and Beauty.
    [*Enter* DISCRETION, STRENGTH, FIVE WITS, *and* BEAUTY.]
BEAUTY. Here at your will we be all ready. 670
    What will ye that we should do?
GOOD DEEDS. That ye would with Everyman go,
    And help him in his pilgrimage.

---

637. Way of living. **638.** Advantage. **640.** Lack (when you need it). **644.** Release. **655.** Separate. **660.** Are called. **663.** Senses. **667.** At once.

Advise° you, will ye with him or not in that voyage?   675
STRENGTH. We will bring him all thither,
    To his help and comfort, ye may believe me.
DISCRETION. So will we go with him all together.
EVERYMAN. Almighty God, lovéd may thou be!
    I give thee laud° that I have hither brought
    Strength, Discretion, Beauty, and Five Wits. Lack I naught.   680
    And my Good Deeds, with Knowledge clear,
    All be in company at my will here.
    I desire no more to my business.
STRENGTH. And I, Strength, will by you stand in distress,
    Though thou would in battle fight on the ground.   685
FIVE WITS. And though it were through the world round,
    We will not depart for sweet nor sour.°
BEAUTY. No more will I, unto death's hour,
    Whatsoever thereof befall.
DISCRETION. Everyman, advise you° first of all,   690
    Go with a good advisement and deliberation.
    We all give you virtuous monition°
    That all shall be well.
EVERYMAN. My friends, hearken what I will tell:
    I pray God reward you in his heavenly sphere.   695
    Now hearken, all that be here,
    For I will make my testament
    Here before you all present:
    In alms half my goods I will give with my hands twain
    In the way of charity, with good intent,   700
    And the other half still shall remain,
    I it bequeath to be returned there° it ought to be.
    This I do in despite of the fiend of hell,
    To go quite out of his peril°
    Ever after and this day.   705
KNOWLEDGE. Everyman, hearken what I say;
    Go to Priesthood, I you advise,
    And receive of him in any wise
    The holy sacrament and ointment together;°
    Then shortly see ye turn again hither;   710
    We will all abide you here.
FIVE WITS. Yea, Everyman, hie you that ye ready were.
    There is no emperor, king, duke, nor baron,
    That of God hath commission

674. Say. 679. Praise. 687. I.e., no matter what. 690. Be assured.
692. Forewarning. 702. When. Everyman is probably disposing of his body.
704. "To escape his perilous power." 709. Communion and Extreme Unction.

As hath the least priest in the world being;   715
For of the blesséd sacraments pure and benign
He beareth the keys, and thereof hath the cure°
For man's redemption—it is ever sure—
Which God for our soul's medicine
Gave us out of his heart with great pain,   720
Here in this transitory life, for thee and me.
The blesséd sacraments seven there be:
Baptism, confirmation, with priesthood good,
And the sacrament of God's precious flesh and blood,
Marriage, the holy extreme unction, and penance.   725
These seven be good to have in remembrance,
Gracious sacraments of high divinity.
EVERYMAN. Fain would I receive that holy body
And meekly to my ghostly father I will go.
FIVE WITS. Everyman, that is the best that ye can do.   730
God will you to salvation bring,
For priesthood exceedeth all other thing;
To us Holy Scripture they do teach,
And converteth man from sin, heaven to reach;
God hath to them more power given,   735
Than to any angel that is in heaven.
With five words° he may consecrate
God's body in flesh and blood to make,
And handleth his Maker between his hands.
The priest bindeth and unbindeth all bands,°   740
Both in earth and in heaven.
Thou, ministers all the sacraments seven,
Though we kissed thy feet, thou wert worthy;
Thou art the surgeon that cureth sin deadly:
No remedy we find under God   745
But all only priesthood.
Everyman, God gave priests that dignity,
And setteth them in his stead° among us to be;
Thus be they above angels, in degree.   [Exit EVERYMAN.]
KNOWLEDGE. If priests be good, it is so, surely.   750
But when Jesus hanged on the cross with great smart,°
There he gave out of his blesséd heart
The same sacrament in great torment.
He sold them not to us, that Lord omnipotent.
Therefore Saint Peter the Apostle doth say   755
That Jesus' curse hath all they
Which God their Savior do buy or sell,

---

717. Charge.   **737.** I.e., *Hoc est enim corpus meum.*   **740.** Bonds, contracts.
748. Place, i.e., as his officers.   **751.** Pain.

Or they for any money do take or tell.°
Sinful priests giveth the sinners example bad;
Their children sitteth by other men's fires, I have heard;   760
And some haunteth women's company
With unclean life, as lusts of lechery.
These be with sin made blind.
FIVE WITS. I trust to God no such may we find.
Therefore let us priesthood honor,   765
And follow their doctrine for our souls' succour.
We be their sheep, and they shepherds be
By whom we all be kept in surety.
Peace! for yonder I see Everyman come,
Which hath made true satisfaction.   770
GOOD DEEDS. Methinketh it is he indeed.
                    [*Re-enter* EVERYMAN.]
EVERYMAN. Now Jesu be your alder speed.°
I have received the sacrament for my redemption,
And then mine extreme unction.
Blesséd be all they that counseled me to take it!   775
And now, friends, let us go without longer respite.
I thank God that ye have tarried so long.
Now set each of you on this rood your hand,
And shortly follow me.
I go before, there I would be. God be our guide.   780
STRENGTH. Everyman, we will not from you go,
Till ye have done this voyage long.
DISCRETION. I, Discretion, will bide by you also.
KNOWLEDGE. And though this pilgrimage be never so strong,
I will never part you fro.   785
Everyman, I will be as sure by thee
As ever I did by Judas Maccabee.
                    [*They go to a grave.*]
EVERYMAN. Alas! I am so faint I may not stand,
My limbs under me do fold.
Friends, let us not turn again to this land,   790
Not for all the world's gold;
For into this cave must I creep
And turn to earth, and there to sleep.
BEAUTY. What, into this grave? Alas!
EVERYMAN. Yea, there shall you consume, more and less.°   795
BEAUTY. And what, should I smother here?
EVERYMAN. Yea, by my faith, and never more appear.
In this world live no more we shall,
But in heaven before the highest Lord of all.

758. Count.   **772.** "The help of all of you."   **778.** Cross.   **795.** Entirely.

BEAUTY. I cross out all this;° adieu, by Saint John!   800
    I take my cap in my lap° and am gone.
EVERYMAN. What, Beauty, whither will ye?
BEAUTY. Peace! I am deaf. I look not behind me,
    Not and thou would give me all the gold in thy chest.
                                            [*Exit* BEAUTY.]
EVERYMAN. Alas, whereto may I trust?   805
    Beauty goeth fast away from me;
    She promised with me to live and die.
STRENGTH. Everyman, I will thee also forsake and deny.
    Thy game liketh me not at all.
EVERYMAN. Why, then ye will forsake me all?   810
    Sweet Strength, tarry a little space.
STRENGTH. Nay, sir, by the rood of grace,
    I will hie me from thee fast,
    Though thou weep till thy heart to-brast.°
EVERYMAN. Ye would ever bide by me, ye said.   815
STRENGTH. Yea, I have you far enough conveyed.
    Ye be old enough, I understand,
    Your pilgrimage to take on hand.
    I repent me that I hither came.
EVERYMAN. Strength, you to displease I am to blame;   820
    Yet promise is debt, this ye well wot.
STRENGTH. In faith, I care not!
    Thou art but a fool to complain.
    You spend your speech and waste your brain.
    Go, thrust thee into the ground.   [*Exit* STRENGTH.]   825
EVERYMAN. I had weened surer I should you have found.
    He that trusteth in his Strength
    She him deceiveth at the length.
    Both Strength and Beauty forsaketh me,
    Yet they promised me fair and lovingly.   830
DISCRETION. Everyman, I will after Strength be gone;
    As for me I will leave you alone.
EVERYMAN. Why, Discretion,° will ye forsake me?
DISCRETION. Yea, in faith, I will go from thee;
    For when Strength goeth before   835
    I follow after evermore.
EVERYMAN. Yet, I pray thee, for the love of the Trinity,
    Look in my grave once piteously.°
DISCRETION. Nay, so nigh will I not come.
    Farewell, every one!   [*Exit* DISCRETION.]   840
EVERYMAN. O all thing faileth, save God alone,

---

800. I.e., his former promises. **801.** "Doff my cap low." **814.** Break in
pieces. **833.** Discretion here means judgment, or what we would now
call reason. **838.** With pity.

Beauty, Strength, and Discretion;
For when Death bloweth his blast,
They all run from me full fast.
FIVE WITS. Everyman, my leave now of thee I take; 845
I will follow the other, for here I thee forsake.
EVERYTHING. Alas! then may I wail and weep,
For I took you for my best friend.
FIVE WITS. I will no longer thee keep;
Now farewell, and there an end. [*Exit* FIVE WITS.] 850
EVERYMAN. O Jesu, help! All hath forsaken me!
GOOD DEEDS. Nay, Everyman; I will bide with thee,
I will not forsake thee indeed;
Thou shalt find me a good friend at need.
EVERYMAN. Gramercy, Good Deeds! Now may I true friends see. 855
They have forsaken me, every one;
I loved them better than my Good Deeds alone.
Knowledge, will ye forsake me also?
KNOWLEDGE. Yea, Everyman, when ye to death shall go;
But not yet, for no manner of danger. 860
EVERYMAN. Gramercy, Knowledge, with all my heart.
KNOWLEDGE. Nay, yet I will not from hence depart
Till I see where ye shall be come.
EVERYMAN. Methink, alas, that I must be gone
To make my reckoning and my debts pay, 865
For I see my time is nigh spent away.
Take example, all ye that this do hear or see,
How they that I loved best do forsake me,
Except my Good Deeds that bideth truly.
GOOD DEEDS. All earthly things is but vanity. 870
Beauty, Strength, and Discretion do man forsake,
Foolish friends and kinsmen, that fair spake,
All fleeth save Good Deeds, and that am I.
EVERYMAN. Have mercy on me, God most mighty;
And stand by me, thou Mother and Maid, holy Mary! 875
GOOD DEEDS. Fear not, I will speak for thee.
EVERYMAN. Here I cry God mercy!
GOOD DEEDS. Short our end, and 'minish our pain.°
Let us go and never come again.
EVERYMAN. Into thy hands, Lord, my soul I commend. 880
Receive it, Lord, that it be not lost.
As thou me boughtest, so me defend,
And save me from the fiend's boast,
That I may appear with that blessèd host
That shall be saved at the day of doom. 885
In manus tuas—of might's most

878. "Shorten our deaths and diminish our pains."

For ever—*commendo spiritum meum.*°

        [EVERYMAN *and* GOOD DEEDS *go into the grave.*]

KNOWLEDGE. Now hath he suffered that we all shall endure;
    The Good Deeds shall make all sure.
    Now hath he made ending.   890
    Methinketh that I hear angels sing
    And make great joy and melody
    Where Everyman's soul received shall be.

ANGEL. Come, excellent elect spouse to Jesu!
    Here above thou shalt go   895
    Because of thy singular virtue.
    Now the soul is taken the body fro,
    Thy reckoning is crystal clear.
    Now shalt thou into the heavenly sphere,
    Unto the which all ye shall come   900
    That liveth well before the day of doom.

            [*Exit* KNOWLEDGE. *Enter* DOCTOR.]

DOCTOR.° This moral men may have in mind;
    Ye hearers, take it of worth,° old and young,
    And forsake Pride, for he deceiveth you in the end,
    And remember Beauty, Five Wits, Strength, and Discretion,   905
    They all at the last do Everyman forsake,
    Save his Good Deeds there doth he take.
    But beware, and they be small
    Before God he hath no help at all.
    None excuse may be there for Everyman.   910
    Alas, how shall he do then?
    For, after death, amends may no man make,
    For then mercy and pity doth him forsake.
    If his reckoning be not clear when he doth come,
    God will say, *"Ite, maledicti, in ignem aeternum."*   915
    And he that hath his account whole and sound,
    High in heaven he shall be crowned.
    Unto which place God bring us all thither,
    That we may live body and soul together.
    Thereto help the Trinity!   920
    Amen, say ye, for saint charity.

      THUS ENDETH THIS MORAL PLAY OF EVERYMAN.

886–87. "Into thy hands, most mighty, I give my spirit forever." 902.
Teacher. 903. Value it. 915. "Hence, cursed one, into eternal fire."

QUESTIONS

1. For what reasons does God send Death to Everyman?
2. A character's manner of speaking tells us nearly as much about him

as the words he uses. Can you distinguish between God's manner and Death's? between Death's and Everyman's? What is the significance of the shift in Everyman's manner of speech after he realizes who Death is?

3. The characters of *Everyman* are personifications of such abstract ideas as death, man, and friendship; at the same time they are remarkably real and individual. How does the playwright make his characters seem so intensely alive and understandable?

4. Draw up a brief statement of the religious doctrine that the play teaches and then discuss the ways in which this doctrine is embodied in the characters and the action.

5. You will notice that there are no directions for costumes, no references to a setting, and no designation of physical characteristics for any of the characters. The original scribe or printer may simply have failed to include it, but the absence of such material seems curiously right for *Everyman*. Do you agree, or would you costume all the characters and design scenery for the bare stage?

6. How would you describe Everyman's "motive"? Show how this motive appears in everything he does.

7. Is Everyman a simple or a complex character? Do you find evidence of conflict within him? Does he change during the course of the action?

8. Are the characters Everyman visits in his attempt to find someone to accompany him into the grave sufficiently individualized so that it is possible to distinguish among them? Are these characters complex or simple?

9. Do you see any dramatic value in the particular sequence of the visits: Fellowship, Kindred, and Goods? Could the playwright have rearranged the sequence without affecting the meaning of the play?

10. What is the significance of placing Good Deeds "in the ground"?

11. Consider yourself for the moment a modern playwright who wants to make the same statements about human nature and human life that the anonymous *Everyman* playwright makes. You would be forced to work in the realistic rather than the allegorical mode; you would be unable to present personifications of his worldly possessions and his bodily and mental resources to dramatize Everyman's thoughts upon learning that death is at hand. Make an outline of a play that would permit you to make the same points as *Everyman* without destroying the illusion of reality. Would some points, some statements about human nature, be impossible to make in the realistic mode?

12. Are the different attitudes taken toward the priesthood by Knowledge and Five Wits consistent with the nature of each?

13. Why has the playwright placed the encounters with Beauty, Five Wits and Discretion after the meetings with such figures as Goods and Kindred? What is the significance of the fact that Beauty, Five Wits, and the others first agree to go into the grave with Everyman and then refuse?

THE WORLD
OF THE PLAY

Every literary form uses certain essential means of expression, which a writer may exploit or enlarge upon in whatever manner he chooses, but which he must continue to use so long as he wishes to work within the particular form he has chosen. The essentials of drama are only two: the actor and the stage. Anyone writing a play necessarily makes use of at least one actor, and he must also take into account the space around the actor, even if it be only a small plot of grass or two boards on trestles. No doubt you can think immediately of many borderline cases: perhaps puppet shows, in which the actors are only animated figures, or travel films—movies are, after all, only a special kind of drama—which are nearly all "stage"; but the rule holds that drama uses actors of some kind and a stage of some kind. Abandon either and you are no longer writing drama. We already have seen what the playwright does with his actors—he uses them as characters, images of man in his many aspects. In this section we shall be concerned with what the playwright does with the space around his characters, how he uses it and enlarges it until it comes to represent the world in which his characters live.

In reading or seeing a play our attention usually centers on character and we sometimes pay too little attention to the *setting*—the scenery and furnishings placed on stage. It is enough, we feel, that the scenery and properties provide the characters with the objects necessary for the action and a suitable background against which they can play out their parts. Ibsen in *Hedda Gabler,* for example, deals most immediately with life in Norway in the late nineteenth century, and appropriately enough sets his play in a middle-class drawing room of that period, complete with furniture contemporary to it—stove, carpets, and pictures. The set, looked at in this way, serves only to locate the play in time and perhaps to contribute something to the *mood:* a tragic set is usually heavy and somber, a comic set light, airy, and gaily colored.

But the care with which a dramatist like Ibsen sets his scene suggests that he makes use of it to supply more than the historical context, or even the mood. The scene of *Hedda Gabler* is carefully described before the action begins. Ibsen prescribes the general style and coloring of the furniture, drapes, and carpets; he is explicit about the pieces to be used in the set and where they are to be placed on the stage; and he provides a detailed plan of the room, locating doors and windows, marking the existence of another small room to the back of the main one, designating a veranda beyond the glass doors. Nor does he forget his room arrangement during the course of the play. Not only are there carefully noted changes in the furniture, such as the removal of the old piano to the back room and the addition of a small writing desk, but the characters are always specifically placed in the set: for example, "She forces Mrs. Elvsted to sit in the easy chair beside the stove, and seats herself on one of the footstools," or "She goes out through the inner room, to the left." (Directions are always given in relation to the stage; right is the right of an actor on stage facing the audience.)

A floor plan of the set for *Hedda Gabler* marked with the movements of the characters—in the theater this locating of characters on the stage is known as *blocking*—makes it obvious that certain places or objects are associated with certain moods or conditions of the characters' minds; It is clear enough that Hedda brings out the pistols whenever she is frustrated and in a "killing" mood. It is less obvious, perhaps, that she goes to the stove to warm herself—she is an unusually "cold" woman—only when she wants to hear the "warming" experiences of some other person; or that she goes to the glass doors and looks out only when she longs to escape the confinement of her life. Similarly, she moves into the small back room, which is peculiarly her own, and which is dominated, significantly, by a portrait of her father, General Gabler, only when she is retreating into herself, withdrawing from circumstances that do not suit her and that she can no longer control. In this way parts of the stage and the objects on it become associated with certain emotions and attitudes; a movement to one of these places or the handling of a certain prop gives a clue to what is occurring in the character's mind. Hedda's physical location often suggests her psychic or emotional location.

The use of a physical set to make visible a state of mind is a common dramatic technique, and we must always look carefully for the relation between place and character. Ibsen is unusual in the exactitude with which he plans his settings and the care with which he moves his characters about, but all good dramatists have used their stage in this way to some degree. In Shakespeare's *Julius Caesar,* for example, after the conspirators have murdered Caesar, Brutus goes to the Forum to explain to the citizens the necessity for the murder. His motives are lofty and his address appeals to such lofty abstractions as patriotism, duty, and reason. His idealism is apparent enough from what he says, but Shakespeare underlines it by presenting it in visual as well as verbal terms: while the mob remains below, Brutus ascends the rostrum and speaks from above. (In the Elizabethan theater for which the play was written he probably went to the upper stage, a balcony above and at the rear of the main platform stage.) After Brutus has finished, Mark Antony delivers a speech in which he fires the mob against the conspirators by appealing to their lower instincts—their greed, materialism, love of the sensational, and primitive delight in destruction. Antony begins on the rostrum above the crowd; as his appeals to baser emotions become cruder and more pronounced he descends from the rostrum and mingles with them on the stage. Language, action, and scene have combined to express the difference between Brutus and Antony.

In the Forum scene from *Julius Caesar* we would hesitate to assign any definite value to the places on stage unless the dramatist arranged matters in such a way as to suggest that a particular attitude was associated with a particular place. It is the high idealism of Brutus' speech which first suggests that the elevated stand he has taken above the crowd presents in visual terms his mental attitude and his relationship to the common people. The stove in *Hedda Gabler* seems to represent visually the warm energy of life that Hedda seeks since she goes to it when she wishes to extract from some other character the "warming" details of his life in the active, violent world beyond the walls of her house. Brutus' position on the rostrum or Hedda's near the stove become perfect symbols for idealism or for warmth when fitted into a larger pattern, but they would never yield these meanings by themselves.

While the meaning of certain places or objects to a character must often be sought out, dramatists frequently use scenes and objects that have immediately powerful symbolic values. To choose a few examples from Shakespeare: storm scenes, wild places such as the barren heaths in *Macbeth* and *Lear,* battle scenes composed of "alarums and excursions," and savage woods suggest destruction, waste, and disorder;

these qualities are often transferred to the characters placed in these scenes. An unnatural and disordered place can imply that the characters are in unnatural and disordered states of mind. On the other hand, calm pastoral scenes, solemn social occasions (such as feasts, marriages, and coronations), fertile gardens, and ordered domestic scenes can reflect characters in a state of harmony, productive order, and social concord. Certain objects—i.e., props—also have innate values: pistols, for example, or a cross, a marriage ring, a crown, even a loaf of bread.

But scenes and props do not always reflect character directly—a good man in a "good" setting; often they provide an illuminating contrast to the character by setting up an ironic perspective—a bad man in a "good" setting. The fresh, romantic love of Romeo and Juliet and their exclusive concern for one another is mirrored perfectly by the walled, isolated garden of the Capulets where they declare their love; but outside the walls of that enchanted, moonlit place are the sunbaked square, the countinghouses, and the graveyard of the city of Verona, where a deadly feud boils up. The realities of life—feuds, money, politics, death—stated by these other scenes set off by contrast Romeo and Juliet's personal, private, and idealistic love. But whatever the manner in which a scene is related to a character, it usually provides some perspective on him, and the first question to be asked about any scene is how it helps to define the characters placed in it. Does it state their values in physical terms? Does it suggest contrasting values?

While every effective dramatist uses his scene, at least in part, to tell us something about the characters he places in it, the scene has other functions to perform as well; the most important of these is to record in symbolic form the world that exists outside the individual. The scenes set in the pantry, the graveyard, the church, and the town square of Verona do not exist merely to provide an illuminating contrast to the ideal, impractical lovers, Romeo and Juliet. These city scenes represent the solid, objective world in which men have to eat, where they kill rather than love one another, and where in the end they die. We can say, then, that as a general rule the playwright uses his stage to represent the world in which his characters live. If the characters in a play are representations of human nature, of personality, the scene reflects the nature of the world, the environment of man. Besides being fundamental elements of the drama, personality and environment are the basic terms used in most philosophies and in most theories of history. At different times and in different places men have believed that one or the other of these forces dominates human destiny. Christianity, for example, emphasizes "character" and assumes that man is free to achieve his own salvation, with the grace of God, no matter what the condition of the world around him. The theory of evolution, on the other hand, assumes environment to be the crucial factor of life: the nature of a living thing is the result of its successful adaptation to the changing world in which it lives. In the Marxist view of history man's personality is not determined so much by climatic conditions as by economic facts. Behaviorist psychology makes man little more than the product of external stimuli to which he must respond in a mechanical fashion. Dramatists always reflect some prevalent world view in their plays; the environmental determinists, for example, have had their exponents in the theater in the dramatic movement called *naturalism*. Naturalistic plays, as you might expect, show little interest in the complexities and depths of character; instead they emphasize the external world and the social conditions that are believed to shape human personality. Gerhart Hauptmann's *The Weavers* (1892) is a naturalistic play on the revolt of the Silesian workers in 1844 when the steam-powered loom eliminated the jobs of the old hand-weavers. The play lacks a hero (heroism is impossible when all actions are determined by environment); the characters introduced are extremely simple, almost rudimentary, versions of human beings—types rather than individuals. But the play details with elaborate care the economic facts of life, such as the rising cost of food, the operations of the new spinning mills, and the high tariffs, which force the manufacturers to turn to cheaper means of production. So important are the objective realities of life in this play that the dramatist specifies even the kind of bread eaten and the type of beer drunk, not because they contribute much to meaning, but simply because they help to suggest that environment, not man, is *the* fact of life.

If the world is everything in a naturalistic play and character merely one of its effects, the reverse is true of expressionistic drama. Here the world is shown not as it objectively is, but as man experiences it in his mind. In *Waiting for Godot*, for example, the real world of cities, factories, fields, and multitudes is dissolved into the subjective reality of a bare, nearly empty space, and two men waiting. But naturalism and expressionism are extreme dramatic tendencies; the greater part of our drama has struck a balance somewhere between these two extremes by presenting both characters and the world. The mighty figures of Elizabethan drama reflect Renaissance optimism about the ability of man to shape himself and his world to a desired form; but these same "outstretched heroes," as Hamlet calls them, are always placed squarely in a society and in a natural world that influence their actions and their ultimate ends. Modern dramatists have been vitally concerned with the possibility that the world controls man, but they have been equally aware that individual man still has special needs, unique values, and a will that drives him to struggle to achieve what he conceives of as his proper ends. Whatever the relative emphasis placed on world or character in a play, the world is usually one of the basic ingredients.

Some brief explanation of how dramatists conceive of their theatrical worlds is necessary at this point. Just as stage characters are not total human beings but only dramatic representations of those motives that the dramatist considers the essential part of man, so the stage worlds he creates are not reproductions of everything in the real world, but symbolic renderings of what he thinks of as the essential qualities of our environment—human, social, or natural. Just as the dramatist thinks of man as a doer, as a power moving toward some fulfillment, so he thinks of the world not as a static object but as a force exerting pressure in some direction. What we must look for in the world of a play is that force, or forces, expressed by the furniture, scenery, sounds, and words out of which a dramatist constructs his stage world.

A further consideration of *Hedda Gabler* will illustrate one way in which a dramatist constructs his image of the world. The set is furnished in the formal, middle-class fashion of the late nineteenth century. The pieces are heavy, dark, ornate; the hangings and rugs rich and somber. Furthermore, if all the furniture Isben stipulates in his stage directions were used in a production, most stages would be difficult to move about on. The actors would be forced to thread their way between pieces of furniture to get from place to place. This room—typical of the houses of the Victorian well-to-do: formal, rich, crowded, and dark (which Hedda further darkens by insisting that the curtains be closed against the sunlight)—embodies nineteenth-century middle-class society with its emphasis on propriety, restraint of emotion, and material wealth, with its constriction of free, natural movement, and with its insistence that pretenses be maintained. The set makes visible, as a painting might, the stodgy, deadening, constrictive society, the polite world into which Hedda has married, which exerts a powerful influence on her and checks her free will.

All dramatists objectify their concept of the world in the immediate sets of their plays, and we must be careful to note stage descriptions and all other references to the arrangement of the stage. The information about the world of *Hedda Gabler* provided in the dialogue is almost as important as the explicit directions to the stage manager. Tesman's inability to afford the house that Hedda demands and that Judge Brack furnishes reminds us that this is a world in which appearances are more important than truth. The fact that the limited, unimaginative Tesman can pay for his house and furnishings only if he wins the professorship from the undisciplined but creative Lövborg, suggests that the kind of society represented by the set can survive only if vitality and imagination are suppressed.

Ibsen's single scene—an interior, realistically presented—is the usual way of setting the stage in the modern theater, which simply means that most modern plays present man in a limited, social context. But this is only one of many possible scenes, one of a nearly infinite number of worlds that can be created on the stage. If the play is set in a wild forest, on a battlefield, or in a crowded tenement, its world is one of primitive passions, rawness, and struggle. Set in a law court or place of government, it presents a man-made, orderly, traditional world. A stony wasteland suggests a hostile, ominous world; rich, fertile fields, a generous, burgeoning world. A consistently dark scene suggests a mysterious world filled with unknowns, while a brightly lighted scene suggests a reasonable, understandable world. Confining a play to a single scene creates a narrow, constricted world, while the presentation of a number of different scenes creates a varied, open world. An inside scene presents a man-made or social world, while an outdoor scene shows us a natural one. A bare stage implies a world in which all seemingly solid objects—buildings, mountains, trees—are no more than passing dreams; and if no attempt is made to disguise the working parts of the theater with wings and scenery, the implication is that "all the world's a stage." It seems likely that even the physical details and structure of the theaters of a given period constitute an image of the world; the glossary contains discussions of the world views suggested by the theaters of various ages.

Fortunately, playwrights are not limited to the use of the technical resources of the theater—lumber, canvas, paint, furniture, lights—in the construction of their dramatic worlds. "Characters" too can be employed as expressions of the play's world. Characters used in this way are really not *personalities* so much as they are parts of the scene, personified expressions of the elemental forces of the world. The witches in *Macbeth* are not individuals interesting in their own right, but aspects of a world shot through with dark, disorderly powers. The mob in *Julius Caesar,* and in other Shakespearean plays, is not properly understood as a collection of people so much as a representation in human form of a senseless, directionless power, which is a crucial part of the world in which true characters like Brutus and Caesar have to live. Judge Brack in *Hedda Gabler* is little more than a personification of the social forces that constitute the immediate world in which the characters live. He is linked to the other expression of that world, the set, for it was he who selected the furnishings and arranged for the house—though Miss Tesman had to pay. Furthermore, Brack's title of "Judge," his conventional way of looking at everything, his formal dress on all occasions, and his intimate knowledge at all times of "what people think," show that he, as much as the drawing-room set, represents bourgeois values.

Once we have identified a character with the world, it follows that all the components of his character—physical appearance, clothing, movements, thought, and style—will express the nature of that world. Characters of this type "act out" the world for us; they are not free agents but simply manifestations of the scene. When Judge Brack, for example, argues with Hedda that she must conceal the fact that Lövborg was killed with her pistol, it becomes clear that this formal, carefully mannered society for which he speaks is more concerned with avoiding scandal than with being truthful. And when Hedda discovers that he is willing to suppress the facts in order to gain power over her, we learn not only that the law he represents is corrupt but also that in his world men may conceal the truth not out of kindness but because the threat of scandal can be held over the heads of those they wish to dominate. The Judge's unmarried, childless state, his stag parties, his exceptional politeness and urbanity, his prosperity, and his concern for being properly dressed for all occasions—all these facts provide insights into the society for which he is the spokesman.

So far we have concentrated on the visible means used by the playwright—and enlarged upon by the scene designer—to create a world for the characters to move in. Considering the limited physical resources of the theater, particularly the Greek and Elizabethan theaters, which lacked artificial lights and had very little scenery, dramatists have by technical means achieved some remarkable effects and managed to present on the stage larger, more complex and mysterious worlds than would seem possible. The witches in *Macbeth,* for example, stirring their cauldron on a bare Elizabethan stage must have evoked then as now a vision of a universe filled with dark, primitive forces. The sentries in the opening scene of *Hamlet,* peering out from the upper balcony of the Elizabethan stage and straining their eyes for a ghost to appear out of that area where the physical vision ceases to operate, evoke a world of vast, mysterious spaces about which man, who knows only the limited area of the castle behind the battlements, and that imperfectly, can only guess. While Yank dies below deck, in Eugene O'Neill's *Bound East for Cardiff*, the regular sounding of the ship's whistle as she moves through the fog creates an ominous world where man knows his direction only by instruments and where collision is an ever-present danger.

Remarkable as these achievements are, a playwright still would be severely limited if he were forced to rely entirely on sound effects lights, scenery, and personifications to create his world. Since playing time is limited, and scene shifting takes a great deal of time, how can a very complex and enormously various world be set forth in the theater? The answer is, of course, through language. Every playwright brings his world into being largely, though not entirely, with words. In *Hedda Gabler* Ibsen confines his scene to a single set: the interior of the heavily furnished Tesman house. But the characters of the play speak of a much larger world just beyond our sight. This larger world is composed of such things as wild parties in Judge Brack's rooms and drunken brawls in Mademoiselle Diana's establishment. It extends from frozen and isolated villages in the north, where a widower marries to provide himself with a housekeeper and a nursemaid, to the Dolomites and the Brenner Pass, visited on the Tesmans' wedding trip. In this world beyond the walls of Hedda's drawing room an old lady is dying, and just beyond the closed doors the sun is shining in a garden where late fall flowers grow. The range of this world is even greater than these details suggest, for it reaches back to busy medieval households where cloth and other necessities of life were made (the subject of Tesman's book), and it goes onward into the future (the subject of Lövborg's book). No single detail of this larger world is very important by itself, but taken together these details make up a world of pain and passion, growth and decay, vitality and movement. Within Hedda's house, however, we hear only the echoes of this large world of doing and suffering. Life stops at her doorway and its sounds are muted. In the immediate scene of the play the drapes are closed against the sun, only "polite" subjects are discussed, the fire burns to provide artificial warmth, flowers with their sweet odors are not permitted, and Hedda's pregnancy, an unwelcome intrusion, is considered too indelicate or too painful for discussion.

As vast as the world Ibsen calls into being with his language is, it seems quite small compared with the world created by Shakespeare or the Greek dramatists. These playwrights present us with images of society and of the natural world, as does Ibsen, but they pass from houses and gardens to the realms of the cosmic and the supernatural. Disorders in the arrangement of the heavens, such as eclipses and meteors, the appearance of ghosts and witches, unusual changes in the pattern of nature—drought, plague, or flood, the voices of oracles, and the references to the gods, serve to tell us that the characters in Greek and Elizabethan drama play out their lives in a much larger world than can usually be found in modern drama.

The reasons for the narrowing of the "world" in modern drama are complicated, but one point about the change should be made. Until approximately the end of the Renaissance—in England, the latter part of the seventeenth century—most, though not all, serious drama was written in poetic form. Shakespeare, for example, usually writes in blank verse, although he mingles a good deal of prose with his poetry. The most important drama of the modern period—to stretch the term "modern" to include everything since about 1700—has been in prose. One result of this change has been the narrowing of the world that playwrights create in their plays, for in prose drama every element of the world just outside the range of vision has to be either inserted realistically as a topic in the dialogue or suggested somehow in the setting. Thus in *Hedda Gabler* someone has to sit down with a collection of photographs and describe the pictures of the Brenner Pass and the Dolomites, and someone has to come in and say that Aunt Rina is dying in order to admit the power of nature and the fact of death into the world the playwright is constructing. Ibsen is marvelously economical in his management of such details; every event in the play does double or triple duty. The introduction of some experience from the outside world is used to reveal still more about the characters and at the same time to advance the plot. But even in the hands of so great a dramatist, prose severely limits the variety and detail that a playwright can use to build the world of his play.

The use of poetry, and specifically the use of metaphor, which is a prominent feature of that way of using language which we call poetry, permits the dramatist to construct a vast and full world with the utmost economy. The famous line spoken by Macbeth as he feels the emptiness of his life coming over him at the end of his play, "I 'gin to be aweary of the sun," is a metaphorical way of saying, "I am tired of life." When Ibsen wishes to remind us of the sun shining bright and hot outside Hedda's dark room, he must arrange for her to see the sunlight pouring into the room, to register disapproval, and to have the drapes closed. In each case the playwright wants to suggest that the sun is the source of life and growth in the natural world from which his hero has cut himself off. Both techniques for bringing the sun in are effective, but Shakespeare's poetry gets the job done in a fraction of the time required by Ibsen. Because of this poetic economy, verse drama always makes the world of the play seem denser and more extensive, and therefore more actual, than does realistic prose drama. We can see the full value of poetry as a tool for constructing a dramatic world if we take such lines of poetry as the following and try to imagine what kind of dialogue or scenes the realistic prose dramatist would have to construct in order to build the same elements into his dramatic world. Here is Romeo speaking when he catches his first glimpse of Juliet on her balcony:

> But soft! What light through yonder window breaks?
> It is the east, and Juliet is the sun!

Othello as he looks at the sleeping Desdemona before he kills her reflects:

> But once put out thy light,
> Thou cunning'st pattern of excelling nature,
> I know not where is that Promethean heat
> That can thy light relume. When I have plucked the rose,
> I cannot give it vital growth again,
> It needs must wither.

Hamlet expresses his disgust with the world soon after Claudius has become king:

> How weary, stale, flat, and unprofitable
> Seem to me all the uses of this world!
> Fie on't, ah, fie! 'Tis an unweeded garden,
> That grows to seed; things rank and gross in nature
> Possess it merely.

Such passages demonstrate not only that poetry is more economical than prose, but that it permits associations to be made which would be impossible, or nearly so, in realistic prose drama.

So far we have concentrated on the ways a dramatist constructs single scenes to image his world, but now we must consider other ways of handling scenes. Some plays offer a multiple world constructed from many different scenes. In *Julius Caesar*, for example, there is a scene at Caesar's house in which Calpurnia warns him of her dream that he will be assassinated; there is a night scene in the city where lions roam the streets and strange fires appear in the heavens; there is

Brutus' garden where the cloaked conspirators meet to plan the assassination of Caesar; there is the senate chamber and its bloody murder; there is a short scene where the mob tears the poet Cinna to pieces because he bears the same name as one of the conspirators; and there is a battlefield where a series of accidents causes the defeat of Brutus and Cassius. On the surface these scenes are all quite different, yet a close examination reveals the presence in each of a supernatural, mysterious, primitive force flooding through the world and affecting the lives of men. Taken together these scenes, along with the others in the play, create a single world in which the irrational and inexplicable are manifested on many levels of being: in unnatural events in the cosmos, in the strange dreams and wild actions of men, and in the unforeseeable chances that shape history. Shakespeare has condensed the world of *Julius Caesar* to an essential force, and this force is shown to be not local and limited but pervasive and universal. In a play made up of many scenes, we should first try to determine whether or not these scenes present different aspects of the same world —show the same force at work in different places, on different social levels, and on such different planes of existence as nature, society, history, and man.

Often, however, the play presents not one world, but two or more, and to complicate matters even further, these worlds may be mutually exclusive, each denying the validity of the other as a true image of reality. When two worlds that deny or qualify one another are juxtaposed, we have another form of *dramatic irony*. In *Hedda Gabler* Ibsen achieves his ironic effect by using language to superimpose the large, active world outside the Tesman house on the small, still bourgeois world within. This common way of managing *scenic irony* is often supplemented or reinforced by the use of other methods. Two mutually exclusive worlds may be presented in physical terms on the same stage, as in Tennessee Williams' *Summer and Smoke*, in which one half of the stage is a bare doctor's office complete with microscope, skull, and anatomical chart, while the other side of the stage is a rectory with green plush sofa, a romantic landscape in a gilt frame, and a love seat. Between these two sets is the town square, which centers on a stone angel whose joined hands form a drinking basin for a fountain. Behind all this is the vast, intense blue sky of the cyclorama, a neutral background, as it were, for the scientific, materialistic world of the doctor, and the religious, moralistic world of the minister. Worlds that question one another in this way may be presented in sequence rather than simultaneously. Shakespeare is the master of this technique, and the alternation of city scenes with country scenes, indoor scenes with outdoor scenes, court scenes with tavern scenes, is one of his trademarks. A good example occurs in his *Henry V* where on the eve of the battle of Agincourt the English common soldiers facing death the next day gather in darkness around a small fire to talk of the plain realities of their world, the pain of dying, the wives and children left to starve, the sin of killing other men. The next scene shows the French nobles preparing for battle. Theirs is a splendid, chivalric world of glittering armor, brave banners, colorful clothing, and they talk of honor, courage, glory—and ransom.

Scenic irony always raises the question of appearance and reality. If two or more opposing worlds are created in a play, which is the false image and which is the true? The answer will depend on what the playwright wants to say about the nature of things, and the only sure way of finding the answer is to look carefully at what happens in the play. In *Hedda Gabler* we need not look very long. The placidity of that small, polite world within Hedda's house is constantly being shattered by events such as Lövborg's messy death in the larger, more vital world outside; and the bourgeois vision of the world is finally revealed as a total sham by the crack of Hedda's pistol and Judge Brack's fatuous attempt to maintain the pretense, "People don't do such things." Similarly, in *Henry V* the battlefield of Agincourt covered with the bodies of the French knights, slain by the arrows of soldiers who took war more seriously, blows away the wisps of French dreams of chivalry. One world drives out another, demonstrating its validity by continuing to exist when the other has vanished. In *Summer and Smoke,* however, though the characters have undergone changes by the end of the play, the vast, neutral sky remains, and before it the two worlds of religion and science continue to stand. The play shows that both are valid and invalid ways of describing ultimate reality.

Where more than one world is presented as a possible image of man's environment, the progression of scenes, the unfolding of reality is often important. This unfolding usually shows the characters' growth in understanding or illustrates the results that past actions have on their lives. The scene in *Hedda Gabler* is restricted to one narrow space, which tells us that no matter what has happened Hedda continues to move within that stifling, restrictive society she and her age have considered the proper setting for man. What a different play it would be if at some point in the third or fourth act Hedda were to rush out of the house into the streets of the town! In other plays, in which characters do change and are forced to confront new experiences and do come to new understandings of the world, this developing knowledge is expressed in the changes of scene. For example, the opening scene of *King Lear* is a rich, well-ordered palace. Lear's mistake of giving up his rule and banishing his truthful daughter, Cordelia, has fearful consequences. The changes of scene within the play dramatize these consequences. Never again does Lear regain his palace or his earlier certainty; he is forced out onto a bare heath in the middle of the night while the elements rage at him, and he can only conclude that man, far from being a king, is no more than a "poor, bare, forked animal." He runs wild like a hunted beast through the fields trying to elude his pursuers, he is cast into prison, and he ends his life on a desolate battlefield with all his daughters dead before him. His initial act forced him to move from a limited scene, which suggested that life was prosperous, orderly, and centered on man, to the bleak reality of a battlefield and the confrontation of a vast world extending through all time and space in which man seems *almost* insignificant.

MOTHER COURAGE
AND HER
CHILDREN

BY

BERTOLT BRECHT

Bertolt Brecht (1898–1956) remarks in his *Short Organum for the Theater* (1948) on the suspicious, inquiring way in which Galileo looked at a swinging chandelier, as if he had not expected it to swing and could not at first understand why it should move. From this detached, surprised point of view Galileo was able to see the phenomenon of the chandelier afresh and ultimately discover the rules of its operation. Brecht wanted a theater that would show our world in the same fresh, surprising way and thereby lead to a new understanding of life: "Here is the outlook, disconcerting but fruitful, which the theater must provoke with its representations of human social life. It must amaze its public, and it achieves this by a technique of making the familiar seem strange."

Brecht was born with an inquiring eye to which the familiar always looked strange, and this faculty was intensified by the events of an age in which, without the playwright's shaping hand, the familiar face of the world began to assume grotesque, unexpected forms. Brecht was a medical student in Munich during World War I and became an orderly in a military hospital. The mutilations he saw there, as he helped to patch up the wounded as quickly as possible in order to send them back to be killed, shocked him profoundly and made a pacifist of him for the remainder of his life. He began writing poems and plays after the war and found his way to Berlin, where he saw the poverty and hunger, the moral decadence, the futile political squabbling, and the gross commercialism of the postwar world at its worst. He showed this corrupt and crumbling society in a number of plays and musical dramas—in which he collaborated with the composer Kurt Weill—in the 1920's and early 1930's. The most famous of these works is the well-known *Threepenny Opera*. But then Hitler came to power, and Brecht, by now the most famous dramatist in Germany, had to flee. The Nazis considered his work decadent, unpatriotic, and defeatist. For years Brecht lived in exile, mostly in Denmark, where *Mother Courage* was written in 1939. In 1941 he escaped through Finland to the United States and for several years made a precarious living writing for the movies. In 1948 he returned to Europe and went to East Berlin. The Communist government provided him with a magnificent theater and a fine acting company to produce his plays. He had never, even in the days of fame in Germany, been free to produce his plays the way he wanted; indeed for nearly fifteen years he had had the greatest difficulty in getting a play of his staged in any fashion. For the remaining eight years of his life he concentrated on work in the theater, revising and bringing out a collected edition of his works, and trying to stay out of trouble with the politicians.

It was this strange, distorted world in which he lived that Brecht wanted to show in his plays; consequently he rejected the realistic theater of Ibsen and his followers, where every effort is made to show the familiar and the expected. Instead Brecht invented what he called "the epic theater." Here the illusion of reality and the setting of the middle-class drawing room are abandoned in favor of such bizarre settings as a fantastic city in Florida in which the only crime is to lack money. Scenery in the epic theater is openly theatrical: newsreels are projected on the backdrop, the price of bread is flashed on a sign, lights representing the moon are left undisguised. The epic style of acting emphasizes *acting;* that is, the actors do not pretend to *be* the person they play, but make it clear that they are *pretending.* The effect of all this is to create plays that are openly *images* of the world, not reproductions of it, in order to make the spectator think, to say, as Brecht describes it: "I should never have thought so.—That is not the way to do it.—This is most surprising, hardly credible.—This will have to stop. This human being's suffering moves me, because there would have been a way out for him. This is great art: nothing here seems inevitable—I am laughing about those who weep on the stage, weeping about those who laugh."

One other important distinction between Ibsen's realistic theater and Brecht's epic theater is the different emphasis placed on character. However much society may operate to control the actions of Hedda Gabler, it remains clear that she is free to choose her own fate. The focus of the play is on her character, what goes on inside of her head and what she does. But Brecht was a Marxist—whether he was ever a member of the Communist party remains doubtful—and for him character could be defined as "the totality of all social conditions." Man is at any given moment not an immutable entity but the product of his time and world. Brecht once put it this way, "Character should not be regarded like a stain of grease on a pair of trousers, which, however much you try to rub and wipe it away, will always come up again. In actual fact the question is always how a given person is going to act in a specified set of circumstances and conditions." This means that in his plays he was not so interested in probing deeply into character in order to get down to the permanent constituents of human nature as he was in showing the social and natural forces operating on man and moving him in certain directions. It means, in short, that his plays feature the "world."

While Brecht's critical pronouncements on drama provide interesting insights into his plays, they should never be taken as absolute descriptions of what you will find in them. Character is not very complicated in *Mother Courage,* but it is an important ingredient of the play; and, similarly, though Brecht thought that he was illustrating the Marxist theory of history—the eternal class struggle for the control of the means of production in which the individual counts for very little—it is possible to read his plays as dramatizations of man's attempt to establish his particular values in a hostile world, always the subject of tragedy.

CHARACTERS

RECRUITING OFFICER	COOK
SERGEANT	COMMANDER
MOTHER COURAGE	CHAPLAIN
EILIF	ORDNANCE OFFICER
SWISS CHEESE	YVETTE POTTIER
KATTRIN	ONE EYE

COLONEL
SCRIVENER
OLDER SOLDIER
YOUNGER SOLDIER
FIRST SOLDIER
OLD PEASANT
SECOND SOLDIER
PEASANT WOMAN

SOLDIER, *singing*
OLD WOMAN
VOICES, *two*
YOUNG MAN
VOICE, *girl singing*
LIEUTENANT
YOUNG PEASANT

(ONE SUPER)
(TWO EXTRAS)

THE TIME: *1624–1636.*
THE PLACE: *Sweden, Poland, Germany.*

Scene I

Spring, 1624. In Dalarna, the Swedish Commander Oxenstierna is recruiting for the campaign in Poland. The canteen woman Anna Fierling, commonly known as Mother Courage, loses a son.

Highway outside a town. A SERGEANT *and a* RECRUITING OFFICER *stand shivering.*

RECRUITING OFFICER. How the hell can you line up a company in a place like this? You know what I keep thinking about, Sergeant? Suicide. I'm supposed to knock four platoons together by the twelfth —four platoons the Chief's asking for! And they're so friendly around here, I'm scared to go to sleep at night. Suppose I do get my hands on some character and squint at him so I don't notice he's pigeon-chested and has varicose veins. I get him drunk and relaxed, he signs on the dotted line. I pay for the drinks, he steps outside for a minute. I have a hunch I should follow him to the door, and am I right? Away he's gone like a louse from a scratch. You can't take a man's word any more, Sergeant. There's no loyalty left in the world, no trust, no faith, no sense of honour. I'm losing my confidence in mankind, Sergeant.

SERGEANT. What they could do with around here is a good war. What else can you expect with peace running wild all over the place? You know what the trouble with peace is? No organization. And when do you get organization? In a war. Peace is one big waste of equipment. Anything goes, no one gives a damn. See the way they eat? Cheese on pumpernickel, bacon on the cheese? Disgusting! How many horses have they got in this town? How many young men?

Nobody knows! They haven't bothered to count 'em! That's peace for you! I've been in places where they haven't had a war for seventy years and you know what? The people haven't even been given names! They don't know who they are! It takes a war to fix that. In a war, everyone registers, everyone's name's on a list. Their shoes are stacked, their corn's in the bag, you count it all up—cattle, men, *et cetera*—and you take it away! That's the story: no organization, no war!

RECRUITING OFFICER. It's God's truth, you know.

SERGEANT. Of course, a war's like any good deal: hard to get going. But when it does get moving, it's a winner, and they're all scared of peace, like a dice player who daren't stop—'cause when peace comes they have to pay up. Of course, *until* it gets going, they're just as scared of war, it's such a novelty!

RECRUITING OFFICER. Hey, look, here's a canteen wagon. Two women and a couple of young lads. Stop the old lady, Sergeant. And if there's nothing doing this time, you won't catch me freezing my arse in the April wind a minute longer.

[*A harmonica is heard. A canteen wagon rolls on, drawn by two young fellows.* MOTHER COURAGE *is sitting on it with her dumb daughter,* KATTRIN.]

MOTHER COURAGE. A good day to you, Sergeant!

SERGEANT (*barring the way*). Good day to *you*! Who d'you think you are?

MOTHER COURAGE. Tradespeople.

[*She sings.*]

Here's Mother Courage and her wagon!
    Hey, Captain, let them come and buy!
Beer by the keg! Wine by the flagon!
    Let your men drink before they die!
Sabres and swords are hard to swallow:
    First you must give them beer to drink.
Then they can face what is to follow—
    But let 'em swim before they sink!

        Christians, awake! The winter's gone!
        The snows depart, the dead sleep on.
        And though you may not long survive,
        Get out of bed and look alive!

Your men will march till they are dead, sir.
    But cannot fight unless they eat.
The blood they spill for you is red, sir,
    What fires that blood is my red meat.
For meat and soup and jam and jelly
    In this old cart of mine are found:

So fill the hole up in your belly
    Before you fill one underground.
           Christians, awake! The winter's gone!
           The snows depart, the dead sleep on.
           And though you may not long survive,
           Get out of bed and look alive!
                [She prepares to go.]

SERGEANT. Halt! Where are you from, riffraff?

EILIF. Second Finnish Regiment!

SERGEANT. Where are your papers?

MOTHER COURAGE. Papers?

SWISS CHEESE. But this is Mother Courage!

SERGEANT. Never heard of her. Where'd she get a name like that?

MOTHER COURAGE. They call me Mother Courage 'cause I was afraid I'd be ruined. So I drove through the bombardment of Riga like a madwoman, with fifty loaves of bread in my cart. They were going moldy, I couldn't please myself.

SERGEANT. No funny business! Where are your papers?

    [MOTHER COURAGE *rummages among papers in a tin*
    box and clambers down from her wagon.]

MOTHER COURAGE. Here, Sergeant! Here's a Bible—I got it in Altötting to wrap my cucumbers in. Here's a map of Moravia—God knows if I'll ever get there—the birds can have it. And here's a document saying my horse hasn't got foot and mouth disease—pity he died on us, he cost fifteen gilders, thank God I didn't pay it. Is that enough paper?

SERGEANT. Are you making a pass at me? Well, you've got another guess coming. You need a license and you know it.

MOTHER COURAGE. Show a little respect for a lady and don't go telling these half-grown children of mine I'm making a pass at you. What would I want with you? My license in the Second Protestant Regiment is an honest face. If *you* wouldn't know how to read it, that's not my fault, I want no rubber stamp on it anyhow.

RECRUITING OFFICER. Sergeant, we have a case of insubordination on our hands. Do you know what we need in the army? Discipline!

MOTHER COURAGE. I was going to say sausages.

SERGEANT. Name?

MOTHER COURAGE. Anna Fierling.

SERGEANT. So you're all Fierlings.

MOTHER COURAGE. I was talking about me.

SERGEANT. And I was talking about your children.

MOTHER COURAGE. Must they all have the same name?
        [Pointing to the elder son.]
This fellow, for instance, I call him Eilif Noyocki—he got the name from his father who told me he was called Koyocki. Or was it

Moyocki? Anyhow, the lad remembers him to this day. Only the man he remembers is someone else, a Frenchman with a pointed beard. But he certainly has his father's brains—that man could whip the breeches off a farmer's backside before he could turn around. So we all have our own names.

SERGEANT. You're all called something different?

MOTHER COURAGE. Are you trying to make out you don't understand?

SERGEANT. (*Pointing at the younger son*). He's a Chinese, I suppose.

MOTHER COURAGE. Wrong again. A Swiss.

SERGEANT. After the Frenchman?

MOTHER COURAGE. Frenchman? What Frenchman? Don't confuse the issue, Sergeant, or we'll be here all day. He's a Swiss, but he happens to be called Feyos, a name that has nothing to do with his father, who was called something else—a military engineer, if you please, and a drunkard.

[SWISS CHEESE *nods, beaming; even* KATTRIN *smiles.*]

SERGEANT. Then how is it his name's Feyos?

MOTHER COURAGE. Oh, Sergeant, you have no imagination. *Of course* he's called Feyos: When he came, I was with a Hungarian. He didn't mind. He had a floating kidney, though he never touched a drop. He was a very *honest* man. The boy takes after him.

SERGEANT. But that wasn't his father!

MOTHER COURAGE. I said: he took after him. I call him Swiss Cheese. Why? Because he's good at pulling wagons.

[*Pointing to her daughter.*]

And that is Kattrin Haupt, she's half German.

SERGEANT. A nice family, I must say!

MOTHER COURAGE. And we've seen the whole wide world together—this wagonload and me.

SERGEANT. We'll need all that in writing.

[*He writes.*]

You're from Bamberg in Bavaria. What are you doing here?

MOTHER COURAGE. I can't wait till the war is good enough to come to Bamberg.

RECRUITING OFFICER. And you two oxen pull the cart. Jacob Ox and Esau Ox! D'you ever get out of harness?

EILIF. Mother! May I smack him in the kisser?

MOTHER COURAGE. You stay where you are. And now, gentlemen, what about a brace of pistols? Or a belt? Sergeant? Yours is worn clean through.

SERGEANT. It's something else *I'm* looking for. These lads of yours are straight as birch trees, strong limbs, massive chests . . . What are such fine specimens doing out of the army?

MOTHER COURAGE (*quickly*). A soldier's life is not for sons of mine.

RECRUITING OFFICER. Why not? It means money. It means fame. Peddling shoes is woman's work.

[*To* EILIF.]

Step this way and let's see if that's muscle or chicken fat.

MOTHER COURAGE. It's chicken fat. Give him a good hard look, and he'll fall right over.

RECRUITING OFFICER. Yes, and kill a calf in the falling!

[*He tries to hustle* EILIF *away.*]

MOTHER COURAGE. Let him alone! He's not for you!

RECRUITING OFFICER. He called my face a kisser. That is an insult. The two of us will now go and settle the affair on the field of honor.

EILIF. Don't worry, Mother, I can handle him.

MOTHER COURAGE. Stay here. You're never happy till you're in a fight. He has a knife in his boot and he knows how to use it.

RECRUITING OFFICER. I'll draw it out of him like a milk tooth. Come on, young fellow-me-lad!

MOTHER COURAGE. Officer, I'll report you to the Colonel, and he'll throw you in jail. His lieutenant is courting my daughter.

SERGEANT (*to* OFFICER). Go easy.

[*To* MOTHER COURAGE.]

What have you got against the service, wasn't his own father a soldier? Didn't you say he died a soldier's death?

MOTHER COURAGE. This one's just a baby. You'll lead him like a lamb to the slaughter. I know you. You'll get five gilders for him.

RECRUITING OFFICER (*to* EILIF). First thing you know, you'll have a lovely cap and high boots, how about it?

EILIF. Not from you.

MOTHER COURAGE. "Let's you and me go fishing," said the angler to the worm.

[*To* SWISS CHEESE.]

Run and tell everybody they're trying to steal your brother!

[*She draws a knife.*]

Yes, just you try, and I'll cut you down like dogs! We sell cloth, we sell ham, we are peaceful people!

SERGEANT. You're peaceful all right: your knife proves that. Why, you should be ashamed of yourself. Give me that knife, you hag! You admit you live off the war, what else *could* you live off? Now tell me, how can we have a war without soldiers?

MOTHER COURAGE. Do they have to be mine?

SERGEANT. So that's the trouble. The war should swallow the peach-stone and spit out the peach, hm? Your brood should get fat off the war, but the poor war must ask nothing in return, it can look after itself, can it? Call yourself Mother Courage and then get scared of the war, your breadwinner? Your sons aren't scared, I know that much.

EILIF. Takes more than a war to scare me.

SERGEANT. Correct! Take me. The soldier's life hasn't done *me* any harm, has it? I enlisted at seventeen.

MOTHER COURAGE. You haven't reached seventy.

SERGEANT. I will, though.

MOTHER COURAGE. Above ground?

SERGEANT. Are you trying to rile me, telling me I'll die?

MOTHER COURAGE. Suppose it's the truth? Suppose I see it's your fate? Suppose I *know* you're just a corpse on furlough?

SWISS CHEESE. She can look into the future. Everyone says so.

RECRUITING OFFICER. Then by all means look into the sergeant's future. It might amuse him.

SERGEANT. I don't believe in that stuff.

MOTHER COURAGE. Helmet!

[SERGEANT *gives her his helmet.*]

SERGEANT. It means less than a shit in the grass. Anything for a laugh.

[MOTHER COURAGE *takes a sheet of parchment and tears it in two.*]

MOTHER COURAGE. Eilif, Swiss Cheese, Kattrin! So shall we all be torn in two if we let ourselves get too deep into this war!

[*To the* SERGEANT.]

I'll give you the bargain rate, and do it free. Watch! Death is black, so I draw a black cross.

SWISS CHEESE. And the other she leaves blank, see?

MOTHER COURAGE. I fold them, put them in the helmet, and mix 'em up, the way all of us are mixed from our mother's womb on. Now draw!

[*The* SERGEANT *hesitates.*]

RECRUITING OFFICER (*to* EILIF). I don't take just anybody. I'm choosy. And you've got guts, I like that.

SERGEANT. It's silly. Means as much as blowing your nose.

SWISS CHEESE. The black cross! Oh, his number's up!

RECRUITING OFFICER. Don't let them get under your skin. There aren't enough bullets to go round.

SERGEANT (*hoarsely*). You cheated me!

MOTHER COURAGE. You cheated yourself the day you enlisted. And now we must drive on. There isn't a war every day in the week, we must get to work.

SERGEANT. Hell, you're not getting away with this! We're taking that bastard of yours with *us!*

EILIF. I'd like that, Mother.

MOTHER COURAGE. Quiet—you Finnish devil, you!

EILIF. And Swiss Cheese wants to be a soldier, too.

MOTHER COURAGE. That's news to me. I see I'll have to draw lots for all three of you.

[*She goes to the back to draw the crosses on bits of paper.*]

RECRUITING OFFICER (*to* EILIF). People've been saying the Swedish soldier is religious. That kind of loose talk has hurt us a lot. One verse of a hymn every Sunday—and then only if you have a voice . . .

[MOTHER COURAGE *returns with the slips and puts them in the* SERGEANT'S *helmet.*]

MOTHER COURAGE. So they'd desert their old mother, would they, the rascals? They take to war like a cat to cream. But I'll consult these slips, and they'll see the world's no promised land, with a "Join up, son, you're officer material!" Sergeant, I'm afraid for them, very afraid they won't get through this war. They have terrible qualities, all three.

[*She holds the helmet out to* EILIF.]

There. Draw your lot.

[EILIF *fishes in the helmet, unfolds a slip. She snatches it from him.*]

There you have it: a cross. Unhappy mother that I am, rich only in a mother's sorrows! He dies. In the springtime of his life, he must go. If he's a soldier, he must bite the dust, that's clear. He's too brave, like his father. And if he doesn't use his head, he'll go the way of all flesh, the slip proves it.

[*Hectoring him.*]

Will you use your head?

EILIF. Why not?

MOTHER COURAGE. It's using your head to stay with your mother. And when they make fun of you and call you a chicken, just laugh.

RECRUITING OFFICER. If you're going to wet your pants, I'll try your brother.

MOTHER COURAGE. I told you to laugh. Laugh! Now it's your turn, Swiss Cheese. You should be a better bet, you're honest.

[*He fishes in the helmet.*]

Oh, dear, why are you giving that slip such a funny look? You've drawn a blank for sure. It can't be there's a cross on it. It can't be I'm going to lose *you.*

[*She takes the slip.*]

A cross? Him too! Could it be 'cause he's so simple-minded? Oh, Swiss Cheese, you'll be a goner too, if you aren't honest, honest, honest the whole time, the way I always brought you up to be, the way you always bring me all the change when you buy me a loaf. It's the only way you can save yourself. Look, Sergeant, if it isn't a black cross!

SERGEANT. It's a cross! I don't understand how *I* got one. I always stay well in the rear.

[*To the* OFFICER.]
But it can't be a trick: it gets *her* children too.

SWISS CHEESE. It gets me too. But I don't accept it!

MOTHER COURAGE (*to* KATTRIN). And now all I have left for certain is you, you're a cross in yourself, you have a good heart.

[*She holds the helmet up high toward the wagon
but takes the slip out herself.*]

Oh, I could give up in despair! There must be some mistake, I didn't mix them right. Don't be too kind, Kattrin, just don't, there's a cross in your path too. Always be very quiet, it can't be hard since you're dumb. Well, so now you know, all of you: be careful, you'll need to be. Now let's climb on the wagon and move on.

[*She returns the helmet to the* SERGEANT *and climbs
on the wagon.*]

RECRUITING OFFICER (*to the* SERGEANT). Do something!

SERGEANT. I don't feel very well.

RECRUITING OFFICER. Maybe you caught a chill when you handed over your helmet in all this wind. Get her involved in a business transaction!

[*Aloud.*]

That belt, Sergeant, you could at least take a look at it. These good people live by trade, don't they? Hey, all of you, the Sergeant wants to buy the belt!

MOTHER COURAGE. Half a gilder. A belt like that is worth two gilders.

[*She clambers down again from the wagon.*]

SERGEANT. It isn't new. But there's too much wind here. I'll go and look at it behind the wagon. (*He does so.*)

MOTHER COURAGE. I don't find it windy.

SERGEANT. Maybe it's worth half a gilder at that. There's silver on it.

MOTHER COURAGE (*following him behind the wagon*). A solid six ounces worth!

RECRUITING OFFICER (*to* EILIF). And we can have a drink, just us men. I'll advance you some money to cover it. Let's go.

[EILIF *stands undecided.*]

MOTHER COURAGE. Half a gilder, then.

SERGEANT. I don't understand it. I always stay in the rear. There's no safer spot for a sergeant to be. You can send the others on ahead in quest of fame. My appetite is ruined. I can tell you right now: I won't be able to get anything down.

MOTHER COURAGE. You shouldn't take on so, just because you can't eat. Just stay in the rear. Here, take a slug of brandy, man.

[*She gives him brandy.*]

RECRUITING OFFICER (*who has taken* EILIF *by the arm and is making
off toward the back*). Ten gilders in advance and you're a soldier of the king and a stout fellow and the women will be mad about

you. And you can give me a smack in the kisser for insulting you. (*Both leave.*)

[*Dumb* KATTRIN *jumps down from the wagon and lets out harsh cries.*]

MOTHER COURAGE. Coming, Kattrin, coming! The sergeant's just paying up.

[*She bites the half gilder.*]

I'm suspicious of all money, I've been badly burned, Sergeant. But this money's good. And now we'll be going. Where's Eilif?

SWISS CHEESE. Gone with the recruiting officer.

MOTHER COURAGE (*stands quite still, then*). Oh, you simpleton!

[*To* KATTRIN.]

You *can't s*peak, I know. You are innocent.

SERGEANT. That's life, Mother Courage. Take a slug yourself, Mother. Being a soldier isn't the worst that could happen. You want to live off war and keep you and yours out of it, do you?

MOTHER COURAGE. You must help your brother now, Kattrin.

[BROTHER *and* SISTER *get into harness together and pull the wagon.* MOTHER COURAGE *walks at their side.*

The wagon gets under way.]

SERGEANT (*looking after them*).

When a war gives you all you earn
One day it may claim something in return!

Scene 2

*in the years 1625 and 1626 Mother Courage journeys through
Poland in the baggage train of the Swedish army. She meets her
son again before Wallhof castle. Of the successful sale of a
capon and great days for the brave son.*

> *Tent of the Swedish Commander. Kitchen next to
> it. Thunder of cannon. The* COOK *is quarreling with*
> MOTHER COURAGE *who is trying to sell him a capon.*

COOK. Sixty hellers for that paltry piece of poultry?

MOTHER COURAGE. Paltry poultry? Why, he's the fattest fowl you ever
saw! I see no reason why I shouldn't get sixty hellers for him—this
Commander can eat till the cows come home—and woe betide you
when there's nothing in your pantry . . .

COOK. They're ten hellers a dozen on every street corner.

MOTHER COURAGE. A capon like this on every street corner! With a
siege going on and people all skin and bones? Maybe you can get
a field rat! I said maybe. Because we're all out of *them* too. Didn't
you see the soldiers running five deep after one hungry little field
rat? All right then, in a siege, my price for a giant capon is fifty
hellers.

COOK. But we're not "in a siege," we're doing the besieging, it's the
other side that's "in a siege," when will you get this into your head?

MOTHER COURAGE. A fat lot of difference that makes, *we* haven't got
a thing to eat either. They took everything in the town with them
before all this started, and now they've nothing to do but eat and
drink, I hear. It's us I'm worried about. Look at the farmers round
here, they haven't a thing.

COOK. Certainly they have. They hide it.

MOTHER COURAGE (*triumphant*). They have not! They're ruined, that's what. They're so hungry I've seen 'em digging up roots to eat. I could boil your leather belt and make their mouths water with it. That's how things are round here. And I'm expected to let a capon go for forty hellers!

COOK. Thirty. Not forty. I said thirty hellers.

MOTHER COURAGE. I say this is no ordinary capon. It was a talented animal, so I hear. It would only feed to music—one march in particular was its favorite. It was so intelligent it could count. Forty hellers is too much for all this? I know *your* problem: if you don't find something to eat and quick, the Chief will—cut—your—fat—head—off!

COOK. All right, just watch.

[*He takes a piece of beef and lays his knife on it.*]

Here's a piece of beef, I'm going to roast it. I give you one more chance.

MOTHER COURAGE. Roast it, go ahead, it's only one year old.

COOK. One *day* old! Yesterday it was a cow. I saw it running around.

MOTHER COURAGE. In that case it must have started stinking before it died.

COOK. I don't care if I have to cook it five hours: I *must* know if it'll still be hard.

[*He cuts into it.*]

MOTHER COURAGE. Put plenty of pepper in, so the Commander won't smell the smell.

[*The* SWEDISH COMMANDER: *a* CHAPLAIN *and* EILIF *enter the tent.*]

COMMANDER (*clapping* EILIF *on the shoulder*). In the Commander's tent with you, my son! Sit at my right hand, you happy warrior! You've played a hero's part, you've served the Lord in his own Holy War, *that's* the thing! And you'll get a gold bracelet out of it when we take the town if *I* have any say in the matter! We come to save their souls and what do they do, the filthy, irreligious sons of bitches? Drive their cattle away from us, while they stuff their priests with beef at both ends! But you showed 'em. So here's a can of red wine for you, we'll drink together!

[*They do so.*]

The chaplain gets the dregs, he's pious. Now what would you like for dinner, my hearty?

EILIF. How about a slice of meat?

COMMANDER. Cook, meat!

COOK. Nothing to eat, so he brings company to eat it!

[MOTHER COURAGE *makes him stop talking, she wants to listen.*]

EILIF. Tires you out, skinning peasants. Gives you an appetite.

MOTHER COURAGE. Dear God, it's my Eilif!

COOK. Who?

MOTHER COURAGE. My eldest. It's two years since I saw him, he was stolen from me right off the street. He must be in high favor if the Commander's invited him to dinner. And what do you have to eat? Nothing. You hear what the Commander's guest wants? Meat! Better take my advice, buy the capon. The price is one gilder.

COMMANDER (*who has sat down with* EILIF *and the* CHAPLAIN, *roaring*). Cook! Dinner, you pig, or I'll have your head!

COOK. This is blackmail. Give me the damn thing!

MOTHER COURAGE. Paltry poultry like this?

COOK. You were right. Give it here. It's highway robbery, fifty hellers.

MOTHER COURAGE. I said one gilder. Nothing's too high for my eldest, the Commander's guest of honor.

COOK (*giving her the money*). Well, you might at least pluck it till I have a fire going.

MOTHER COURAGE (*sitting down to pluck the capon*). I can't wait to see his face when he sees me. This is my brave and clever son. I also have a stupid one but he's honest. The daughter is nothing. At least, she doesn't talk: we must be thankful for small mercies.

COMMANDER. Have another glass, my son, it's my favorite Falernian. There's only one cask left—two at the most—but it's worth it to meet a soldier that still believes in God! The shepherd of our flock here just looks on, he only preaches, he hasn't a clue how anything gets done. So now, Eilif, my son, give us the details: tell us how you fixed the peasants and grabbed the twenty bullocks. And let's hope they'll soon be here.

EILIF. In one day's time. Two at most.

MOTHER COURAGE. Now that's considerate of Eilif—to bring the oxen tomorrow—otherwise my capon wouldn't have been so welcome today.

EILIF. Well, it was like this. I found out that the peasants had hidden their oxen and—on the sly and chiefly at night—had driven them into a certain wood. The people from the town were to pick them up there. I let them get their oxen in peace—they ought to know better than me where they are, I said to myself. Meanwhile I made my men crazy for meat. Their rations were short and I made sure they got shorter. Their mouths'd water at the sound of any word beginning with M, like mother.

COMMANDER. Smart fella.

EILIF. Not bad. The rest was a walkover. Only the peasants had clubs and outnumbered us three to one and made a murderous attack on us. Four of them drove me into a clump of trees, knocked my good sword from my hand, and yelled, "Surrender!" What now, I said to myself, they'll make mincemeat of me.

COMMANDER. What did you do?

EILIF. I laughed.

COMMANDER. You what?

EILIF. I laughed. And so we got to talking. I came right down to business and said: "Twenty gilders an ox is too much, I bid fifteen." Like I wanted to buy. That foxed 'em. So while they were scratching their heads, I reached for my good sword and cut 'em to pieces. Necessity knows no law, huh?

COMMANDER. What do *you* say, shepherd of the flock?

CHAPLAIN. Strictly speaking, that saying is not in the Bible. Our Lord made five hundred loaves out of five so that no such necessity would arise. When he told men to love their neighbors, their bellies were full. Nowadays things are different.

COMMANDER (*laughing*). Quite different. A swallow of wine for those wise words, you pharisee!

[*To* EILIF.]

You cut 'em to pieces in a good cause, our chaps were hungry and you gave 'em to eat. Doesn't it say in the Bible "Whatsoever thou doest to the least of these my children, thou doest unto me?" And what *did* you do to 'em? You got 'em the best steak dinner they ever tasted. Moldy bread is not what they're used to. They always ate white bread, and drank wine in their helmets, before going out to fight for God.

EILIF. I reached for my good sword and cut 'em to pieces.

COMMANDER. You have the makings of a Julius Caesar, why, you should be presented to the King!

EILIF. I've seen him—from a distance of course. He seemed to shed a light all around. I must try to be like him!

COMMANDER. I think you're succeeding, my boy! Oh, Eilif, you don't know how I value a brave soldier like you! I treat such a chap as my very own son.

[*He takes him to the map.*]

Take a look at our position, Eilif, it isn't all it might be, is it?

MOTHER COURAGE (*who has been listening and is now plucking angrily at her capon*). He must be a very bad commander.

COOK. Just a greedy one. Why bad?

MOTHER COURAGE. Because he needs *brave* soldiers, that's why. If his plan of campaign was any good, why would he need *brave* soldiers, wouldn't plain, ordinary soldiers do? Whenever there are great virtues, it's a sure sign something's wrong.

COOK. You mean, it's a sure sign something's right.

MOTHER COURAGE. I mean what I say. Listen. When a general or a king is stupid and leads his soldiers into a trap, they need this virtue of courage. When he's tightfisted and hasn't enough soldiers, the few he does have need the heroism of Hercules—another virtue. And if he's a sloven and doesn't give a damn about anything, they have to be wise as serpents or they're finished. Loyalty's another virtue and you need plenty of it if the king's always asking too much of you. All virtues which a well-regulated country with a good king or a good general wouldn't need. In a good country virtues wouldn't be necessary. Everybody could be quite ordinary, middling, and, for all I care, cowards.

COMMANDER. I bet your father was a soldier.

EILIF. I've heard he was a great soldier. My mother warned me. I know a song about that.

COMMANDER. Sing it to us.

[*Roaring.*]

Bring that meat!

EILIF. It's called "The Song of the Fishwife and the Soldier."

[*He sings and at the same time does a war dance
with his sabre.*]

To a soldier lad comes an old fishwife
  And this old fishwife, says she:
A gun will shoot, a knife will knife,
  You will drown if you fall in the sea.
Keep away from the ice if you want my advice,
  Says the old fishwife, says she.
The soldier laughs and loads his gun
Then grabs his knife and starts to run:
  It's the life of a hero for me!
From the north to the south I shall march through the land
With a knife at my side and a gun in my hand!
  Says the soldier lad, says he.

When the lad defies the fishwife's cries
  The old fishwife, says she:
The young are young, the old are wise,
  You will drown if you fall in the sea.
Don't ignore what I say or you'll rue it one day!
  Says the old fishwife, says she.
But gun in hand and knife at side
The soldier steps into the tide:
  It's the life of a hero for me!
When the new moon is shining on shingle roofs white
We are all coming back, go and pray for that night!
  Says the soldier lad, says he.

[MOTHER COURAGE *continues the song from her
kitchen, beating on a pan with a spoon.*]

And the fishwife old does what she's told:
　　Down upon her knees drops she.
When the smoke is gone, the air is cold,
　　Your heroic deeds won't warm me!
See the smoke, how it goes! May God scatter his foes!
　　Down upon her knees drops she.

EILIF. What's that?

MOTHER COURAGE (*singing on*).

But gun in hand and knife at side
The lad is swept out by the tide:
　　He floats with the ice to the sea.
And the new moon is shining on shingle roofs white
But the lad and his laughter are lost in the night:
　　He floats with the ice to the sea.

COMMANDER. What a kitchen I've got! There's no end to the liberties they take!

EILIF (*has entered the kitchen and embraced his mother*). To see you again! Where are the others?

MOTHER COURAGE (*in his arms*). Happy as ducks in a pond. Swiss Cheese is paymaster with the Second Regiment, so at least he isn't in the fighting. I couldn't keep him out altogether.

EILIF. Are your feet holding up?

MOTHER COURAGE. I've a bit of trouble getting my shoes on in the morning.

COMMANDER (*who has come over*). So, you're his mother! I hope you have more sons for me like this chap.

EILIF. If I'm not the lucky one: you sit there in the kitchen and hear your son being feasted!

MOTHER COURAGE. Yes. I heard all right.

[*Gives him a box on the ear.*]

EILIF (*his hand to his cheek*). Because I took the oxen?

MOTHER COURAGE. No. Because you didn't surrender when the four peasants let fly at you and tried to make mincemeat of you! Didn't I teach you to take care of yourself? You Finnish devil, you!

[*The* COMMANDER *and the* CHAPLAIN *stand laughing
in the doorway.*]

Scene 3

Three years pass and Mother Courage, with parts of a Finnish regiment, is taken prisoner. Her daughter is saved, her wagon likewise, but her honest son dies.

A camp. The regimental flag is flying from a pole. Afternoon. All sorts of wares hanging on the wagon. MOTHER COURAGE's *clothes line is tied to the wagon at one end, to a cannon at the other. She and* KATTRIN *are folding the washing on the cannon. At the same time she is bargaining with an* ORDNANCE OFFICER *over a bag of bullets.* SWISS CHEESE, *in paymaster's uniform now, looks on.* YVETTE POTTER, *a very good-looking young person, is sewing at a colored hat, a glass of brandy before her. She is in stocking feet. Her red boots are near by.*

OFFICER. I'm letting you have the bullets for two gilders. Dirt cheap. 'Cause I need the money. The Colonel's been drinking with the officers for three days and we've run out of liquor.

MOTHER COURAGE. They're army property. If they find 'em on me, I'll be courtmartialed. You sell your bullets, you bastards, and send your men out to fight with nothing to shoot with.

OFFICER. Oh, come on, if you scratch my back, I'll scratch yours.

MOTHER COURAGE. I won't take army stuff. Not at *that* price.

OFFICER. You can resell 'em for five gilders, maybe eight, to the Ordnance Officer of the Fourth Regiment. All you have to do is give him a receipt for twelve. He hasn't a bullet left.

MOTHER COURAGE. Why don't you do it yourself?

OFFICER. I don't trust him. We're friends.

MOTHER COURAGE (*takes the bag*). Give it here.

[*To* KATTRIN.]

Take it round the back and pay him a gilder and a half.

[*As the* OFFICER *protests.*]

I said a gilder and a half!

[KATTRIN *drags the bag away. The* OFFICER *follows.*

MOTHER COURAGE *speaks to* SWISS CHEESE.]

Here's your underwear back, take care of it; it's October now, autumn may come at any time; I purposely don't say it must come, I've learnt from experience there's nothing that must come, not even the seasons. But your books *must* balance now you're the regimental paymaster. *Do* they balance?

SWISS CHEESE. Yes, Mother.

MOTHER COURAGE. Don't forget they made you paymaster because you're honest and so simple you'd never think of running off with the cash. Don't lose that underwear.

SWISS CHEESE. No, Mother. I'll put it under the mattress.

[*He starts to go.*]

OFFICER. I'll go with you, paymaster.

MOTHER COURAGE. Don't teach him any hanky-panky.

[*Without a good-bye the* OFFICER *leaves with* SWISS CHEESE.]

YVETTE (*waving to him*). You might at least say good-bye!

MOTHER COURAGE (*to* YVETTE). I don't like that. *He's* no sort of company for my Swiss Cheese. But the war's not making a bad start. Before all the different countries get into it, four or five years'll have gone by like nothing. If I look ahead and make no mistakes, business will be good. Don't you know you shouldn't drink in the morning with your illness?

YVETTE. Who says I'm ill? That's libel!

MOTHER COURAGE. They all say so.

YVETTE. They're all liars. I'm desperate, Mother Courage. They all avoid me like a stinking fish. Because of those lies. So what am I fixing my hat for?

[*She throws it down.*]

That's why I drink in the morning. I never used to, it gives you crow's feet. But now it's all one, every man in the regiment knows me. I should have stayed home when my first was unfaithful. But pride isn't for the likes of us, you eat dirt or down you go.

MOTHER COURAGE. Now don't you start again with your friend Peter and how it all happened—in front of my innocent daughter.

YVETTE. She's the one that should hear it. So she'll get hardened against love.

MOTHER COURAGE. That's something no one ever gets hardened against.

YVETTE. I'll tell you about it, and get it off my chest. I grew up in

Flanders' fields, that's where it starts, or I'd never even have caught
sight of him and I wouldn't be here in Poland today. He was an army
cook, blond, a Dutchman, but thin. Kattrin, beware of thin men! I
didn't. I didn't even know he'd had another girl before me and she
called him Peter Piper because he never took his pipe out of his
mouth the whole time, it meant so little to him.

[*She sings "The Fraternization Song."*]

Scarce seventeen was I when
   The foe came to our land
And laid aside his sabre
   And took me by the hand.
      And we performed by day
      The sacred rite of May
      And we performed by night
      Another sacred rite.
      The regiment, well exercised,
      Presented arms, then stood at ease,
      Then took us off behind the trees
      Where we fraternized.

Each of us had her foe and
   A cook fell to my lot.
I hated him by daylight
   But in the dark did not.
      So we perform by day
      The sacred rite of May
      And we perform by night
      That other sacred rite.
      The regiment, well exercised,
      Presents its arms, then stands at ease,
      Then takes us off behind the trees
      Where we fraternize.

Ecstasy filled my heart, O
   My love seemed heaven-born!
But why were people saying
   It was not love but scorn?
      The springtime's soft amour
      Through summer may endure
      But swiftly comes the fall
      And winter ends it all.
      December came. All of the men
      Filed past the trees where once we hid
      Then quickly marched away and did
      Not come back again.

I made the mistake of running after him, I never found him. It's ten years ago now.

[*With swaying gait she goes behind the wagon.*]

MOTHER COURAGE. You're leaving your hat.

YVETTE. For the birds.

MOTHER COURAGE. Let this be a lesson to you, Kattrin, never start anything with a soldier. Love does seem heaven-born, so watch out! Even with those who're not in the army life's no honey pot. He tells you he'd like to kiss the ground under your feet—did you wash 'em yesterday, while we're on the subject? And then if you don't look out, your number's up, you're his slave for life. Be glad you're dumb, Kattrin: you'll never contradict yourself, you'll never want to bite your tongue off because you spoke out of turn. Dumbness is a gift from God. Here comes the Commander's Cook, what's bothering *him*?

[*Enter the* COOK *and the* CHAPLAIN.]

CHAPLAIN. I bring a message from your son Eilif. The Cook came with me. You've made, ahem, an impression on him.

COOK. I thought I'd get a little whiff of the balmy breeze.

MOTHER COURAGE. You're always welcome to that if you behave yourself and, even if you don't, I think I can handle you. But what does Eilif want? I've no money to spare.

CHAPLAIN. Actually, I have something to tell his brother, the paymaster.

MOTHER COURAGE. He isn't here. And he isn't anywhere else either. He's not his brother's paymaster, and I won't have him led into temptation. Let Eilif try it on with someone else!

[*She takes money from the purse at her belt.*]

Give him this. It's a sin. He's speculating in mother love, he ought to be ashamed of himself.

COOK. Not for long. He has to go with his regiment now—to his death maybe. Send some more money, or you'll be sorry. You women are hard—and sorry afterwards. A glass of brandy wouldn't cost very much, but you refuse to provide it, and six feet under goes your man and you can't dig him up again.

CHAPLAIN. All very touching, my dear Cook, but to fall in this war is not a misfortune, it's a blessing. This is a war of religion. Not just any old war but a special one, a religious one, and therefore pleasing unto God.

COOK. Correct. In one sense it's a war because there's fleecing, bribing, plundering, not to mention a little raping, but it's different from all other wars because it's a war of religion. That's clear. All the same, it makes you thirsty.

CHAPLAIN (to MOTHER COURAGE, *pointing at the* COOK). I tried to hold him off but he said you'd bewitched him. He dreams about you.

COOK (*lighting a clay pipe*). Brandy from the fair hand of a lady, that's

for me. And don't embarrass me any more: the stories the chaplain
was telling on the way over still have me blushing.

MOTHER COURAGE. A man of his cloth! I must get you both something
to drink or you'll be making improper advances out of sheer boredom.

CHAPLAIN. That is indeed a temptation, said the Court Chaplain, and
gave way to it.

> [*Turning toward* KATTRIN *as he walks.*]

And who is this captivating young person?

MOTHER COURAGE. She's not a captivating young person, she's a respectable young person.

> [*The* CHAPLAIN *and the* COOK *go with* MOTHER COUR-
> AGE *behind the cart, and one hears them talk politics.*]

MOTHER COURAGE. The trouble here in Poland is that the Poles *would*
keep meddling. It's true our King moved in on them with man,
beast, and wagon, but instead of keeping the peace the Poles were
always meddling in their own affairs. They attacked the Swedish
King when he was in the act of peacefully withdrawing. So they
were guilty of a breach of the peace and their blood is on their own
heads.

CHAPLAIN. Anyway, our King was thinking of nothing but freedom.
The Kaiser enslaved them all, Poles and Germans alike, so our King
had to liberate them.

COOK. Just what *I* think. Your health! Your brandy is first rate, I'm
never mistaken in a face.

> [KATTRIN *looks after them, leaves the washing, and
> goes to the hat, picks it up, sits down, and takes up
> the red boots.*]

And the war is a war of religion.

> [*Singing while* KATTRIN *puts the boots on.*]

"A mighty fortress is our God . . ."

> [*He sings a verse or so of Luther's hymn.*]

And talking of King Gustavus, this freedom he tried to bring to
Germany cost him a pretty penny. Back in Sweden he had to levy
a salt tax, the poorer folks didn't like it a bit. Then, too, he had
to lock up the Germans and even cut their heads off, they clung
so to slavery and their Kaiser. Of course, if no one had *wanted* to
be free, the King wouldn't have had any fun. First it was just
Poland he tried to protect from bad men, specially the Kaiser, then
his appetite grew with eating, and he ended up protecting Germany
too. Now Germany put up a pretty decent fight. So the good King
had nothing but worries in return for his outlay and his goodness,
and of course he had to get his money back with taxes, which
made bad blood, but he didn't shrink even from that. For he had
one thing in his favor anyway, God's Holy Word, which was all to

the good, because otherwise they could have said he did it for himself or for profit. That's how he kept his conscience clear. He always put conscience first.

MOTHER COURAGE. It's plain you're no Swede, or you'd speak differently of the Hero King.

CHAPLAIN. What's more, you eat his bread.

COOK. I don't eat his bread. I bake his bread.

MOTHER COURAGE. He can never be conquered, and I'll tell you why: his men believe in him.

[*Earnestly.*]

To hear the big chaps talk, they wage the war from fear of God and for all things bright and beautiful, but just look into it, and you'll see they're not so silly: they want a good profit out of it, or else the little chaps like you and me wouldn't back 'em up.

COOK. That's right.

CHAPLAIN. And as a Dutchman you'd do well to see which flag's flying here before you express an opinion!

MOTHER COURAGE. All good Protestants for ever!

COOK. A health!

[KATTRIN *has begun to strut around with* YVETTE'S *hat on, copying* YVETTE'S *sexy walk. Suddenly cannon and shots. Drums.* MOTHER COURAGE, *the* COOK, *and the* CHAPLAIN *rush round to the front of the cart, the two last with glasses in their hands. The* ORDNANCE OFFICER *and a* SOLDIER *come running to the cannon and try to push it along.*]

MOTHER COURAGE. What's the matter? Let me get my washing off that gun, you slobs!

[*She tries to do so.*]

OFFICER. The Catholics! Surprise attack! We don't know if we can get away!

[*To the* SOLDIER.]

Get that gun!

[*Runs off.*]

COOK. For heaven's sake! I must go to the Commander. Mother Courage, I'll be back in a day or two—for a short conversation.

[*Rushes off.*]

MOTHER COURAGE. Hey, you've left your pipe!

COOK (*off*). Keep it for me, I'll need it!

MOTHER COURAGE. This *would* happen when we were just making money.

CHAPLAIN. Well, I must be going too. Yes, if the enemy's so close, it can be dangerous. "Blessed are the peacemakers," a good slogan in wartime! If only I had a cloak.

MOTHER COURAGE. I'm lending no cloaks. Not even to save a life I'm not. I've had experience in that line.

CHAPLAIN. But I'm in special danger. Because of my religion!

MOTHER COURAGE (*brings him a cloak*). It's against my better judgment. Now run!

CHAPLAIN. I thank you, you're very generous, but maybe I'd better stay and sit here. If I run, I might attract the enemy's attention. I might arouse suspicion.

MOTHER COURAGE (*to the* SOLDIER). Let it alone, you dolt, who's going to pay you for this? It'll cost you your life, let me hold it for you.

SOLDIER (*running away*). You're my witness: I tried!

MOTHER COURAGE. I'll swear to it!

[*Seeing* KATTRIN *with the hat.*]

What on earth are you up to—with a whore's hat! Take it off this minute! Are you crazy? With the enemy coming?

[*She tears the hat off her head.*]

Do you want them to find you and make a whore of you? And she has the boots on too, straight from Babylon. I'll soon fix that.

[*She tries to get them off.*]

Oh God, Chaplain, help me with these boots, I'll be back straightaway.

[*She runs to the wagon.*]

YVETTE (*entering and powdering her face*). What's that you say: the Catholics are coming? Where's my hat? Who's been trampling on it? I can't run around in that, what will they think of me? And I've no mirror either.

[*To the* CHAPLAIN.]

How do I look—too much powder?

CHAPLAIN. Just, er, right.

YVETTE. And where are my red boots?

[*She can't find them because* KATTRIN *is hiding her feet under her skirt.*]

I left them here! Now I've got to go barefoot to my tent, it's a scandal!   [*Exit.*]

[SWISS CHEESE *comes running in carrying a cashbox.*]

[MOTHER COURAGE *enters with her hands full of ashes.*]

[*To* KATTRIN.]

Ashes!

[*To* SWISS CHEESE.]

What have you got there?

SWISS CHEESE. The regimental cashbox.

MOTHER COURAGE. Throw it away! Your paymastering days are over!

SWISS CHEESE. It's a trust!

[*He goes to the back.*]

MOTHER COURAGE (*to the* CHAPLAIN). Off with your pastor's coat, Chaplain, or they'll recognize you, cloak or no cloak.

[*She is rubbing ashes into* KATTRIN'S *face.*]

Keep still. A little dirt, and you're safe. A calamity! The sentries were drunk. Well, one must hide one's light under a bushel, as they say. When a soldier sees a clean face, there's one more whore in the world. Specially a Catholic soldier. For weeks on end, no grub. Then, when they get some by way of plunder, they jump on top of the womenfolk. That should do. Let me look at you. Not bad. Looks like you've been rolling in muck. Don't tremble. Nothing can happen to you now.

[*To* SWISS CHEESE.]

Where've you left the cashbox?

SWISS CHEESE. I thought I'd just put it in the wagon.

MOTHER COURAGE (*horrified*). What!? In my wagon? God punish you for a prize idiot! If I just look away for a moment! They'll hang all three of us!

SWISS CHEESE. Then I'll put it somewhere else. Or escape with it.

MOTHER COURAGE. You'll stay where you are. It's too late.

CHAPLAIN (*still changing his clothes*). For Heaven's sake: the flag!

MOTHER COURAGE (*taking down the flag*). God in Heaven! I don't notice it any more. I've had it twenty-five years.

[*The thunder of cannon grows.*]

[*Three days later. Morning. The cannon is gone.*
MOTHER COURAGE, KATTRIN, *the* CHAPLAIN *and* SWISS
CHEESE *sit anxiously eating.*]

SWISS CHEESE. This is the third day I've been sitting here doing nothing, and the Sergeant, who's always been patient with me, may be slowly beginning to ask, "Where on earth is Swiss Cheese with that cashbox?"

MOTHER COURAGE. Be glad they're not on the scent.

CHAPLAIN. What about me? I can't hold service here or I'll be in hot water. It is written, "Out of the abundance of the heart, the tongue speaketh." But woe is me if *my* tongue speaketh!

MOTHER COURAGE. That's how it is. Here you sit—one with his religion, the other with his cashbox, I don't know which is more dangerous.

CHAPLAIN. We're in God's hands now!

MOTHER COURAGE. I hope we're not as desperate as *that*, but it *is* hard to sleep at night. 'Course it'd be easier if *you* weren't here, Swiss Cheese, all the same I've not done badly. I told them I was against the Antichrist, who's a Swede with horns on his head. I told them I noticed his left horn's a bit threadbare. When they cross-questioned me, I always asked where I could buy holy candles a bit cheaper.

I know these things because Swiss Cheese's father was a Catholic and made jokes about it. They didn't quite believe me but they needed a canteen, so they turned a blind eye. Maybe it's all for the best. We're prisoners. But so are lice in fur.

CHAPLAIN. The milk is good. As far as quantity goes, we may have to reduce our Swedish appetites somewhat. We are defeated.

MOTHER COURAGE. Who's defeated? The defeats and victories of the chaps at the top aren't always defeats and victories for the chaps at the bottom. Not at all. There've been cases where a defeat is a victory for the chaps at the bottom, it's only their honor that's lost, nothing serious. In Livonia once, our Chief took such a knock from the enemy, in the confusion I got a fine gray mare out of the baggage train, it pulled my wagon seven months—till we won and inventory was taken. But in general both defeat and victory are a costly business for us that haven't got much. The best thing is for politics to kind of get stuck in the mud.

[*To* SWISS CHEESE.]

Eat!

SWISS CHEESE. I don't like it. How will the Sergeant pay his men?

MOTHER COURAGE. Soldiers in flight don't get paid.

SWISS CHEESE. Well, they could claim to be. No pay, no flight. They can refuse to budge.

MOTHER COURAGE. Swiss Cheese, your sense of duty worries me. I've brought you up to be honest because you're not very bright. But don't go too far! And now I'm going with the Chaplain to buy a Catholic flag and some meat. There's no one can hunt out meat like him, sure as a sleepwalker. He can tell a good piece of meat from the way his mouth waters. A good thing they let me stay in the business. In business you ask what price, not what religion. And Protestant trousers keep you just as warm.

CHAPLAIN. As the mendicant monk said when there was talk of the Lutherans standing everything on its head in town and country: Beggars will *always* be needed.

[MOTHER COURAGE *disappears into the wagon.*]

She's worried about the cashbox. Up to now they've ignored us— as if we were part of the wagon—but can it last?

SWISS CHEESE. I can get rid of it.

CHAPLAIN. That's almost *more* dangerous. Suppose you're seen. They have spies. Yesterday morning one jumped out of the very hole I was relieving myself in. I was so off guard I almost broke out in prayer—*that* would have given me away all right! I believe their favorite way of finding a Protestant is smelling his, um, excrement. The spy was a little brute with a bandage over one eye.

MOTHER COURAGE (*clambering out of the wagon with a basket*). I've found you out, you shameless hussy!

[*She holds up* YVETTE'S *red boots in triumph.*]

Yvette's red boots! She just swiped them—because you went and told her she was a captivating person.

[*She lays them in the basket.*]

Stealing Yvette's boots! But *she* disgraces herself for money, *you* do it for nothing—for pleasure! I told you, you must wait for the peace. No soldiers! Save your proud, peacock ways for peacetime!

CHAPLAIN. I don't find her proud.

MOTHER COURAGE. Prouder than she can afford to be. I like her when people say "I never noticed the poor thing." I like her when she's a stone in Dalarna where there's nothing but stones.

[*To* SWISS CHEESE.]

Leave the cashbox where it is, do you hear? And pay attention to your sister, she needs it. Between the two of you, you'll be the death of me yet. I'd rather take care of a bag of fleas.

[*She leaves with the* CHAPLAIN.]

[KATTRIN *clears the dishes away.*]

SWISS CHEESE. Not many days more when you can sit in the sun in your shirt sleeves.

[KATTRIN *points to a tree.*]

Yes, the leaves are yellow already.

[*With gestures,* KATTRIN *asks if he wants a drink.*]

I'm not drinking, I'm thinking.

[*Pause.*]

She says she can't sleep. So I *should* take the cashbox away. I've found a place for it. I'll keep it in the mole hole by the river till the time comes. I might get it tonight before sunrise and take it to the regiment. How far can they have fled in three days? The Sergeant's eyes'll pop out of his head. "You've disappointed me most pleasantly, Swiss Cheese," he'll say, "*I* trust you with the cashbox and *you* bring it back!" Yes, Kattrin, I *will* have a glass now!

[*When* KATTRIN *reappears behind the wagon two men
confront her. One of them is a sergeant. The other
doffs his hat and flourishes it in a showy greeting. He
has a bandage over one eye.*]

THE MAN WITH THE BANDAGE. Good morning, young lady. Have you seen a man from the Second Protestant Regiment?

[*Terrified,* KATTRIN *runs away, spilling her brandy.
The two men look at each other and then withdraw
after seeing* SWISS CHEESE.]

SWISS CHEESE (*starting up from his reflection*). You're spilling it! What's the matter with you, can't you see where you're going? I don't understand you. Anyway, I must be off, I've decided it's the thing to do.

[*He stands up. She does all she can to make him
aware of the danger he is in. He only pushes her
away.*]

I'd like to know what you mean. I know you mean well, poor thing,
you just can't get it out. And don't trouble yourself about the
brandy, I'll live to drink so much of it, what's one glass?

[*He takes the cashbox out of the wagon and puts it
under his coat.*]

I'll be back straightaway. But don't hold me up or I'll have to scold
you. Yes, I know you mean well. If you could only speak!

[*When she tries to hold him back he kisses her and
pulls himself free. Exit. She is desperate and runs up
and down, emitting little sounds.* MOTHER COURAGE
and the CHAPLAIN *return.* KATTRIN *rushes at her
mother.*]

MOTHER COURAGE. What *is* it, what *is* it, Kattrin? Control yourself!
Has someone done something to you? Where is Swiss Cheese?

[*To the* CHAPLAIN.]

Don't stand around, get that Catholic flag up!

[*She takes a Catholic flag out of her basket and the*
CHAPLAIN *runs it up the pole.*]

CHAPLAIN (*bitterly*). All good Catholics forever!

MOTHER COURAGE. Now, Kattrin, calm down and tell all about it, your
mother understands. What, that little bastard of mine's taken the
cashbox away? I'll box his ears for him, the rascal! Now take your
time and don't try to talk, use your hands. I don't like it when you
howl like a dog, what'll the Chaplain think of you? See how shocked
he looks. A man with one eye was here?

CHAPLAIN. That fellow with one eye is an informer! Have they caught
Swiss Cheese?

[KATTRIN *shakes her head, shrugs her shoulders.*]

This is the end.

[*Voices off. The two men bring in* SWISS CHEESE.]

SWISS CHEESE. Let me go. I've nothing on me. You're breaking my
shoulder! I am innocent.

SERGEANT. This is where he comes from. These are his friends.

MOTHER COURAGE. Us? Since when?

SWISS CHEESE. I don't even know 'em. I was just getting my lunch
here. Ten hellers it cost me. Maybe you saw me sitting on that
bench. It was too salty.

SERGEANT. Who *are* you people, anyway?

MOTHER COURAGE. Law abiding citizens! It's true what he says. He
bought his lunch here. And it was too salty.

SERGEANT. Are you pretending you don't know him?

MOTHER COURAGE. I can't know all of them, can I? *I don't ask,* "What's your name and are you a heathen?" If they pay up, they're not heathens to me. Are you a heathen?

SWISS CHEESE. Oh, no!

CHAPLAIN. He sat there like a law-abiding chap and never once opened his mouth. Except to eat. Which is necessary.

SERGEANT. Who do you think *you* are?

MOTHER COURAGE. Oh, he's my barman. And you're thirsty, I'll bring you a glass of brandy. You must be footsore and weary!

SERGEANT. No brandy on duty.

[*To* SWISS CHEESE.]

You were carrying something. You must have hidden it by the river. We saw the bulge in your shirt.

MOTHER COURAGE. Sure it was him?

SWISS CHEESE. I think you mean another fellow. There *was* a fellow with something under his shirt, I saw him. I'm the wrong man.

MOTHER COURAGE. I think so too. It's a misunderstanding. Could happen to anyone. Oh, I know what people are like, I'm Mother Courage, you've heard of me, everyone knows about me, and I can tell you this: he looks honest.

SERGEANT. We're after the regimental cashbox. And we know what the man looks like who's been keeping it. We've been looking for him two days. It's you.

SWISS CHEESE. No, it's not!

SERGEANT. And if you don't shell out, you're dead, see? Where is it?

MOTHER COURAGE (*urgently*). 'Course he'd give it to you to save his life. He'd up and say, I do have it, here it is, you're stronger than me. He's not *that* stupid. Speak, little stupid, the Sergeant's giving you a chance!

SWISS CHEESE. What if I haven't got it?

SERGEANT. Come with us. We'll get it out of you.

[*They take him off.*]

MOTHER COURAGE (*shouting after them*). He'd tell you! He's not *that* stupid! And don't you break his shoulder blade! (*She runs after them.*)

[*The same evening. The* CHAPLAIN *and* KATTRIN *are rinsing glasses and polishing knives.*]

CHAPLAIN. Cases of people getting caught like this are by no means unknown in the history of religion. I am reminded of the Passion of Our Lord and Saviour. There's an old song about it.

[*He sings.*]

"The Song of the Hours"

In the first hour of the day
Simple Jesus Christ was

Presented as a murderer
To the heathen Pilate.

Pilate found no fault in him
No cause to condemn him
So he sent the Lord away.
Let King Herod see him!

Hour the third: the Son of God
Was with scourges beaten
And they set a crown of thorns
On the head of Jesus.

And they dressed him as a king
Joked and jested at him
And the cross to die upon
He himself must carry.

Six: they stripped Lord Jesus bare.
To the cross they nailed him.
When the blood came gushing, he
Prayed and loud lamented.

From their neighbour crosses, thieves
Mocked him like the others.
And the bright sun crept away
Not to see such doings.

Nine: Lord Jesus cried aloud
That he was forsaken!
In a sponge upon a pole
Vinegar was fed him.

Then the Lord gave up the ghost
And the earth did tremble.
Temple curtain split in twain.
Rocks fell in the ocean.

Evening: they broke the bones
Of the malefactors.
Then they took a spear and pierced
The side of gentle Jesus.

And the blood and water ran
And they laughed at Jesus.
Of this simple son of man
Such and more they tell us.

MOTHER COURAGE (*entering, excited*). It's life and death. But the
Sergeant will still listen to us. The only thing is, he mustn't know

it's our Swiss Cheese, or they'll say we helped him. It's only a matter of money, but where can *we* get money? Wasn't Yvette here? I met her on the way over. She's picked up a Colonel! Maybe he'll buy her a canteen business!

CHAPLAIN. You'd sell the wagon, everything?

MOTHER COURAGE. Where else would I get the money for the Sergeant?

CHAPLAIN. What are you to live off?

MOTHER COURAGE. That's just it.

[*Enter* YVETTE POTTIER *with a hoary old* COLONEL.]

YVETTE (*embracing* MOTHER COURAGE). *Dear* Mistress Courage, we meet again!

[*Whispering.*]

He didn't say no.

[*Aloud.*]

This is my friend, my, um, business adviser. I happened to hear you might like to sell your wagon. Due to special circumstances, I'd like to think about it.

MOTHER COURAGE. I want to pawn it, not sell it. And nothing hasty. In war time you don't find another wagon like that so easy.

YVETTE (*disappointed*). Only pawn it? I thought you wanted to sell, I don't know if I'm interested.

[*To the* COLONEL.]

What do *you* think, my dear?

COLONEL. I quite agree with you, ducky.

MOTHER COURAGE. It's only for pawn.

YVETTE. I thought you *had* to have the money.

MOTHER COURAGE (*firmly*). I do have to have it. But I'd rather wear my feet off looking for an offer than just sell. We live off the wagon. It's an opportunity for you, Yvette. Who knows when you'll have another such? Who knows when you'll find another . . . business adviser?

COLONEL. Take it, take it!

YVETTE. My friend thinks I should go ahead, but I'm not sure, if it's only for pawn. You think we should buy it outright, don't you?

COLONEL. I do, ducky, I do!

MOTHER COURAGE. Then you must hunt up something that's for sale. Maybe you'll find it—if you have the time, and your friend goes with you, let's say in about a week, or two weeks, you may find the right thing.

YVETTE. Yes, we can certainly look around for something. I love going around looking, I love going around with you, Poldy . . .

COLONEL. Really? Do you?

YVETTE. Oh, it's lovely! I could take two weeks of it!

COLONEL. Really, could you?

YVETTE. If you get the money, when are you thinking of paying it back?

MOTHER COURAGE. In two weeks. Maybe one.

YVETTE. I can't make up my mind. Poldy, advise me, *chéri!*

[*She takes the* COLONEL *to one side.*]

She'll *have* to sell, don't worry. That lieutenant—the blond one—you know the one I mean—he'll lend me the money. He's *mad* about me, he says I remind him of someone. What do you advise?

COLONEL. Oh, I have to warn you against *him*. He's no good. He'll exploit the situation. I told you, ducky, I told you *I'd* buy you something, didn't I tell you that?

YVETTE. I simply can't let you!

COLONEL. Oh, please, please!

YVETTE. Well, if you think the lieutenant might exploit the situation I *will* let you!

COLONEL. I do think so.

YVETTE. So you advise me to?

COLONEL. I do, ducky, I do!

YVETTE (*returning to* MOTHER COURAGE). My friend says all right. Write me out a receipt saying the wagon's mine when the two weeks are up—with everything in it. I'll just run through it all now, the two hundred gilders can wait.

[*To the* COLONEL.]

You go on ahead to the camp, I'll follow, I must go over all this so nothing'll be missing later from *my* wagon!

COLONEL. Wait, I'll help you up!

[*He does so.*]

Come soon, ducky-wucky!

[*Exit.*]

MOTHER COURAGE. Yvette, Yvette!

YVETTE. There aren't many boots left!

MOTHER COURAGE. Yvette, this is no time to go through the wagon, yours or not yours. You promised you'd talk to the Sergeant about Swiss Cheese. There isn't a minute to lose. He's up before the court martial one hour from now.

YVETTE. I just want to check through these shirts.

MOTHER COURAGE (*dragging her down the steps by the skirt*). You hyena, Swiss Cheese's life's at stake! And don't say who the money comes from. Pretend he's your sweetheart, for heaven's sake, or we'll all get it for helping him.

YVETTE. I've arranged to meet One Eye in the bushes. He must be there by now.

CHAPLAIN. And don't hand over all two hundred, a hundred and fifty's sure to be enough.

MOTHER COURAGE. Is it your money? I'll thank you to keep your nose out of this, I'm not doing *you* out of your porridge. Now run, and no haggling, remember his life's at stake.

[*She pushes* YVETTE *off.*]

CHAPLAIN. I didn't want to talk you into anything, but what are we going to live on? You have an unmarriageable daughter round your neck.

MOTHER COURAGE. I'm counting on that cashbox, smart alec. They'll pay his expenses out of it.

CHAPLAIN. You think she can work it?

MOTHER COURAGE. It's to her interest: I pay the two hundred and she gets the wagon. She knows what she's doing, she won't have her colonel on the string forever. Kattrin, go and clean the knives, use pumice stone. And don't *you* stand around like Jesus in Gethsemane. Get a move on, wash those glasses. There'll be over fifty cavalry-men here tonight, and you'll be saying you're not used to running around, "oh my poor feet, in church I never had to run around like this!" I think they'll let us have him. Thanks be to God they're corruptible. They're not wolves, they're human and after money. God is merciful, and men are bribable, that's how His will is done on earth as it is in Heaven. Corruption is our only hope. As long as there's corruption, there'll be merciful judges and even the innocent may get off.

YVETTE (*comes panting in*). They'll do it for two hundred if you make it snappy, these things change from one minute to the next. I'd better take One Eye to my colonel at once. He confessed he had the cashbox, they put the thumb screws on him. But he threw it in the river when he noticed them coming up behind him. So it's gone. Shall I run and get the money from my colonel?

MOTHER COURAGE. The cashbox gone? How'll I ever get my two hundred back?

YVETTE. So you thought you could get it from the cashbox? I *would* have been sunk. Not a hope, Mother Courage. If you want your Swiss Cheese, you'll have to pay. Or should I let the whole thing drop, so you can keep your wagon?

MOTHER COURAGE. I wasn't reckoning on this. But you needn't hound me, you'll get the wagon, it's yours already, and it's been mine seventeen years. I need a minute to think it over, it's all so sudden. What can I do? I *can't* pay two hundred. I *should* have haggled with them. I must hold on to something, or any passer-by can kick me in the ditch. Go and say I'll pay a hundred and twenty or the deal's off. Even then I lose the wagon.

YVETTE. I won't do it. And anyway, One Eye's in a hurry. He keeps looking over his shoulder all the time, he's so worked up. Hadn't I better give them the whole two hundred?

MOTHER COURAGE (*desperate*). I can't pay it! I've been working thirty
    years. She's twenty-five and still no husband. I have her to think
    of. So leave me alone, I know what I'm doing. A hundred and
    twenty or no deal.
YVETTE. You know best.   [*Runs off.*]
        [MOTHER COURAGE *turns away and slowly walks a*
        few paces to the rear. Then she turns round, looks
        neither at the CHAPLAIN *nor her daughter, and sits*
            down to help KATTRIN *polish the knives.*]
MOTHER COURAGE. Don't break the glasses, they're not ours. Watch
    what you're doing, you're cutting yourself. Swiss Cheese will be
    back, I'll give two hundred, if it's necessary. You'll get your brother
    back. With eighty gilders we could pack a hamper with goods and
    begin again. It wouldn't be the end of the world.
CHAPLAIN. The Bible says: the Lord will provide.
MOTHER COURAGE. You should rub them dry, I said!
        [*They clean the knives in silence. Suddenly* KATTRIN
                runs sobbing behind the wagon.]
YVETTE (*comes running in*). They won't do it. I warned you. One
    Eye was going to drop it then and there. There's no point, he said.
    He said the drums would roll any second now and that's the sign
    a verdict has been pronounced. I offered a hundred and fifty, he
    didn't even shrug his shoulders. I could hardly get him to stay
    there while I came to you.
MOTHER COURAGE. Tell him I'll pay two hundred. Run!
        [YVETTE *runs.* MOTHER COURAGE *sits, silent. The*
            CHAPLAIN *has stopped doing the glasses.*]
    I believe—I've haggled too long.
        [*In the distance, a roll of drums. The* CHAPLAIN *stands*
        up and walks toward the rear. MOTHER COURAGE *re-*
        mains seated. It grows dark. It gets light again.
            MOTHER COURAGE *has not moved.*]
YVETTE (*appears, pale*). Now you've done it—with your haggling.
    You can keep the wagon now. He got eleven bullets, that's what.
    I don't know why I still bother about you, you don't deserve it, but
    I just happened to learn they don't think the cashbox is really in the
    river. They suspect it's here, they think you have something to do
    with him. I think they mean to bring him here to see if you'll give
    yourself away when you see him. You'd better not know him or
    we're in for it. And I'd better tell you straight, they're just behind
    me. Shall I keep Kattrin away?
                [MOTHER COURAGE *shakes her head.*]
Does she know? Maybe she never heard the drums or didn't understand.

MOTHER COURAGE. She knows. Bring her.

> [YVETTE *brings* KATTRIN, *who walks over to her mother and stands by her.* MOTHER COURAGE *takes her hand. Two men come on with a stretcher; there is a sheet on it and something underneath. Beside them, the* SERGEANT. *They put the stretcher down.*]

SERGEANT. Here's a man we don't know the name of. But he has to be registered to keep the records straight. He bought a meal from you. Look at him, see if you know him.

> [*He pulls back the sheet.*]

Do you know him?

> [MOTHER COURAGE *shakes her head.*]

What? You never saw him before he took that meal?

> [MOTHER COURAGE *shakes her head.*]

Lift him up. Throw him on the junk heap. He has no one that knows him.   [*They carry him off.*]

Scene 4

Mother Courage sings "The Song of the Great Capitulation."

[*Outside an officer's tent,* MOTHER COURAGE *waits. A*
SCRIVENER *looks out of the tent.*]

SCRIVENER. I know you. You had a Protestant paymaster with you,
he was hiding with you. Better make no complaint.

MOTHER COURAGE. I will too! I'm innocent and if I give up it'll look
like I have a bad conscience. They cut everything in my wagon to
ribbons with their sabres and then claimed a fine of five thalers for
nothing and less than nothing.

SCRIVENER. For your own good, keep your trap shut. We haven't
many canteens, so we let you stay in business, especially if you've
a bad conscience and have to pay a fine now and then.

MOTHER COURAGE. I'm going to lodge a complaint.

SCRIVENER. As you wish. Wait here till the captain has time.
[*Withdraws into the tent.*]

YOUNG SOLDIER (*comes storming in*). Bugger the captain! Where *is*
the son of a bitch? Swiping my reward, spending it on brandy for
his whores, I'll rip his belly open!

OLDER SOLDIER (*coming after him*). Shut your hole, you'll wind up in
the stocks.

YOUNG SOLDIER. Come out, you thief, I'll make lamb chops out of you!
I was the only one in the squad who swam the river and *he* grabs
my money, I can't even buy myself a beer. Come on out! And let
me slice you up!

OLDER SOLDIER. Holy Christ, he'll destroy himself!

YOUNG SOLDIER. Let me go or I'll run *you* down too. This thing has got to be settled!

OLDER SOLDIER. Saved the colonel's horse and didn't get the reward. He's young, he hasn't been at it long.

MOTHER COURAGE. Let him go. He doesn't have to be chained, he's not a dog. Very reasonable to want a reward. Why else should he want to shine?

YOUNG SOLDIER. He's in there pouring it down! You're all chickens. I've done something special, I want the reward!

MOTHER COURAGE. Young man, don't scream at *me,* I have my own troubles. And go easy on your voice, you may need it when the Captain comes. The Captain'll come and you'll be hoarse and can't make a sound, so he'll have to deny himself the pleasure of sticking you in the stocks till you pass out. The screamers don't scream long, only half an hour, after which they have to be sung to sleep, they're all in.

YOUNG SOLDIER. I'm not all in, and sleep's out of the question. I'm hungry. They're making their bread out of acorns and hemp-seed, and not even much of that. He's whoring on my money, and I'm hungry. I'll murder him!

MOTHER COURAGE. I understand: you're hungry. Last year your Commander ordered you people out of the streets and into the fields. So the crops got trampled down. I could have got ten gilders for boots, if anyone'd had ten gilders, and if I'd had any boots. He didn't expect to be around this year, but he is, and there's famine. I understand: you're angry.

YOUNG SOLDIER. It's no use you talking. I won't stand for injustice!

MOTHER COURAGE. You're quite right. But how long? How long won't you stand for injustice? One hour? Or two? You haven't asked yourself that, have you? And yet it's the main thing. It's pure misery to sit in the stocks. Especially if you leave it till then to decide you do stand for injustice.

YOUNG SOLDIER. I don't know why I listen to you. Bugger that captain! Where is he?

MOTHER COURAGE. You listen because you know I'm right. Your rage has calmed down already. It was a short one and you'd need a long one. But where would you find it?

YOUNG SOLDIER. Are you trying to say it's not right to ask for the money?

MOTHER COURAGE. Just the opposite. I only say, your rage won't last. You'll get nowhere with it, it's a pity. If your rage was a long one, I'd urge you on. Slice him up, I'd advise you. But what's the use if you *don't* slice him up because you can feel your tail between your legs? You stand there and the captain lets you have it.

OLDER SOLDIER. You're quite right, he's mad.

YOUNG SOLDIER. All right, we'll see whether I slice him up or not.
[*Draws his sword.*]
When he comes out, I slice him up!
SCRIVENER (*looking out*). The captain will be out in a minute.
[*In the tone of military command.*]
Be seated!
[*The* YOUNG SOLDIER *sits.*]
MOTHER COURAGE. And he *is* seated. What did I tell you? You are
seated. They know us through and through. They know how they
must work it. Be seated! And we sit. And in sitting there's no revolt.
Better not stand up again—not the way you did before—don't stand
up again. And don't be embarrassed in front of me, I'm no better,
not a scrap. We don't stick our necks out, do we, and why not? It
wouldn't be good for business. Let me tell you about the great
capitulation.

[*She sings* "The Song of the Great Capitulation."]

Long, long ago, a green beginner
   I thought myself a special case.
(None of your ordinary, run of the mill girls, with my looks and
   my talent and my love of the higher things!)
I picked a hair out of my dinner
   And put the waiter in his place.
(All or nothing. Anyway, never the second best. I am the master
   of my fate. I'll take no orders from no one.)
Then a little bird whispers!
   The bird says: "Wait a year or so
   And marching with the band you'll go
   Keeping in step, now fast, now slow,
   And piping out your little spiel.
   Then one day the battalions wheel
   And you go down upon your knees
   To God Almighty if you please!"

My friend, before that year was over
   I'd learned to drink their cup of tea.
(Two children round your neck and the price of bread and what
   all!)
When they were through with me, moreover,
   They had me where they wanted me.
(You must get well in with people. If you scratch my back, I'll
   scratch yours. Never stick your neck out!)
Then a little bird whispered!
   The bird says: "Scarce a year or so

And marching with the band she'd go
Keeping in step, now fast, now slow,
And piping out her little spiel.
Then one day the battalions wheel
And she goes down upon her knees
To God Almighty if you please!"

Our plans are big, our hopes colossal.
   We hitch our wagon to a star.
(Where there's a will, there's a way. You can't hold a good man
   down.)
"We can lift mountains," says the apostle.
   And yet: how heavy one cigar!
(You must cut your coat according to your cloth.)
That little bird whispers!
   The bird says: "Wait a year or so
   And marching with the band we go
   Keeping in step, now fast, now slow,
   And piping out our little spiel.
   Then one day the battalions wheel
   And we go down upon our knees
   To God Almighty if you please!"

MOTHER COURAGE. And so I think you should stay here with your
sword drawn if you're set on it and your anger is big enough. You
have good cause, I admit. But if your anger is a short one, you'd
better go.

YOUNG SOLDIER. Oh, shove it up!

    [*He stumbles off, the other soldier following him.*]

SCRIVENER (*sticks his head out*). The captain is here. You can lodge
your complaint.

MOTHER COURAGE. I've thought better of it. I'm not complaining.

    [*Exit. The* SCRIVENER *looks after her, shaking his head.*]

Scene 5

Two years have passed. The war covers wider and wider territory. Forever on the move the little wagon crosses Poland, Moravia, Bavaria, Italy, and again Bavaria. 1631. Tilly's victory at Magdeburg costs Mother Courage four officer shirts.

[*The wagon stands in a war-ruined village. Faint military music from the distance. Two soldiers are being served at a counter by* KATTRIN *and* MOTHER COURAGE. *One of them has a woman's fur coat about his shoulders.*]

MOTHER COURAGE. What, you can't pay? No money, no brandy! They can play victory marches, they should pay their men.

FIRST SOLDIER. I want my brandy! I arrived too late for plunder. The Chief allowed one hour to plunder the town, it's a swindle. He's not inhuman, he says. So I suppose they bought him off.

CHAPLAIN (*staggering in*). There are more in the farmhouse. A family of peasants. Help me someone. I need linen!

[*The* SECOND SOLDIER *goes with him.* KATTRIN *is getting very excited. She tries to get her mother to bring linen out.*]

MOTHER COURAGE. I have none. I sold all my bandages to the regiment. I'm not tearing up my officer's shirts for these people.

CHAPLAIN (*calling over his shoulder*). I said I need linen!

MOTHER COURAGE (*stopping* KATTRIN *from entering the wagon*). Not a thing! They have nothing and they pay nothing!

CHAPLAIN (*to a woman he is carrying in*). Why did you stay out there in the line of fire?

WOMAN. Our farm—

MOTHER COURAGE. Think they'd ever let go of *anything*? And now I'm supposed to pay. Well, I won't!

FIRST SOLDIER. They're Protestants, why should they be Protestants?

MOTHER COURAGE. Protestant, Catholic, what do *they* care? Their farm's gone, that's what.

SECOND SOLDIER. They're not Protestants anyway, they're Catholics.

FIRST SOLDIER. In a bombardment we can't pick and choose.

PEASANT (*brought on by* CHAPLAIN). My arm's gone.

CHAPLAIN. Where's that linen?

> [*All look at Mother Courage who doesn't budge.*]

MOTHER COURAGE. I can't give you any. With all I have to pay out— taxes, duties, bribes . . .

> [KATTRIN *takes up a board and threatens her mother
> with it, emitting gurgling sounds.*]

Are you out of your mind? Put that board down or I'll fetch you one, you lunatic! I'm giving nothing, I daren't, I have myself to think of.

> [*The* CHAPLAIN *lifts her bodily off the steps of the
> wagon and sets her down on the ground. He takes out
> shirts from the wagon and tears them in strips.*]

My shirts, my officer's shirts!

> [*From the house comes the cry of a child in pain.*]

PEASANT. The child's still in there!

> [KATTRIN *runs in.*]

CHAPLAIN (*to the woman*). Stay where you are. She's getting it for you.

MOTHER COURAGE. Hold her back, the roof may fall in!

CHAPLAIN. I'm not going back in there!

MOTHER COURAGE (*pulled in both directions at once*). Go easy on my expensive linen.

> [*The* SECOND SOLDIER *holds her back.*]

> [KATTRIN *brings a baby out of the ruins.*]

MOTHER COURAGE. Another baby to drag around, you must be pleased with yourself. Give it to its mother this minute! Or do I have to fight you again for hours till I get it from you? Are you deaf?

> [*To the* SECOND SOLDIER.]

Don't stand around gawking, go back there and tell 'em to stop that music, I can see their victory without it. I have nothing but losses from your victory!

CHAPLAIN (*bandaging*). The blood's coming through.

> [KATTRIN *is rocking the child and half-humming a
> lullaby.*]

MOTHER COURAGE. There she sits, happy as a lark in all this misery. Give the baby back, the mother is coming to!

[*She sees the* FIRST SOLDIER. *He had been handling the drinks, and is now trying to make off with the bottle.*]

God's blood! You beast! You want another victory, do you? Then pay for it!

FIRST SOLDIER. I have nothing.

MOTHER COURAGE (*snatching the fur coat back*). Then leave this coat, it's stolen goods anyhow.

CHAPLAIN. There's still someone in there.

Scene 6

Before the City of Ingolstadt in Bavaria Mother Courage is present at the funeral of the fallen commander, Tilly. Conversations take place about war heroes and the duration of the war. The chaplain complains that his talents are lying fallow and Kattrin gets the red boots. The year is 1632.

[*The inside of a canteen tent. The inner side of a counter at the rear. Rain. In the distance, drums and funeral music. The* CHAPLAIN *and the* REGIMENTAL CLERK *are playing checkers.* MOTHER COURAGE *and her* DAUGHTER *are taking inventory.*]

CHAPLAIN. The funeral procession is just starting out.

MOTHER COURAGE. Pity about the Chief—twenty-two pairs of socks—getting killed that way. They say it was an accident. There was a fog over the fields that morning, and the fog was to blame. The Chief called up another regiment, told 'em to fight to the death, rode back again, missed his way in the fog, went forward instead of back, and ran smack into a bullet in the thick of the battle—only four lanterns left.

[*A whistle from the rear. She goes to the counter. To a soldier.*]

It's a disgrace the way you're all skipping your Commander's funeral!

[*She pours a drink.*]

SCRIVENER. They shouldn't have handed the money out before the funeral. Now the men are all getting drunk instead of going to it.

CHAPLAIN (*to the* SCRIVENER). Don't you have to be there?

SCRIVENER. I stayed away because of the rain.

MOTHER COURAGE. It's different for you, the rain might spoil your uniform. I hear they wanted to ring the bells for his funeral, which is natural, but it came out that the churches had been shot up by his orders, so the poor Commander won't be hearing any bells when they lower him in his grave. Instead, they will fire off three shots so the occasion won't be *too* sober—sixteen leather belts.

VOICE FROM THE COUNTER. Service! One brandy!

MOTHER COURAGE. Your money first. No, you *can't* come inside the tent, not with those boots on. You can drink outside, rain or no rain. I only let officers in here.

[*To* SCRIVENER.]

The Chief had his troubles lately, I hear. There was unrest in the Second Regiment because he didn't pay 'em but said it was a war of religion and they must fight it free of charge.

[*Funeral March. All look towards the rear.*]

CHAPLAIN. Now they're filing past the body.

MOTHER COURAGE. I feel sorry for a commander or an emperor like that—when he might have had something special in mind, something they'd talk about in times to come, something they'd raise a statue to him for. The conquest of the world now, *that's* a goal for a commander, he couldn't do better than *that,* could he? . . . Lord, worms have got into the biscuits. . . . In short he works his hands to the bone and then it's all spoiled by the common riffraff that only wants a jug of beer or a bit of company, not the higher things in life. The finest plans have always been spoiled by the littleness of them that should carry them out. Even emperors can't do it all by themselves. They count on support from their soldiers and the people round about. Am I right?

CHAPLAIN (*laughing*). You're right, Mother Courage, till you come to the soldiers. They do what they can. Those chaps outside, for example, drinking their brandy in the rain, I'd trust 'em to fight a hundred years, one war after another, two at a time if necessary. And I wasn't trained as a Commander.

MOTHER COURAGE. . . . Seventeen leather belts . . . Then you don't think the war might end?

CHAPLAIN. Because a Commander's dead? Don't be childish, they're sixpence a dozen. There are always heroes.

MOTHER COURAGE. Well, I wasn't asking just for the sake of argument. I was wondering if I should buy up a lot of supplies. They happen to be cheap just now. But if the war ended, I might just as well throw them away.

CHAPLAIN. I realize you are serious, Mother Courage. Well, there's always been people going around saying someday the war will end. I say, you can't be sure the war will *ever* end. Of course it may have to pause occasionally—for breath, as it were—it can even meet with an accident—nothing on this earth is perfect—a war of which we could say it left nothing to be desired will probably never exist. A war can come to a sudden halt—from unforeseen causes—you can't think of everything—a little oversight, and the war's in the hole, and someone's got to pull it out again! The someone is the Emperor or the King or the Pope. They're such friends in need, the war has really nothing to worry about, it can look forward to a prosperous future.

[*A* SOLDIER *sings at the counter.*]

One schnapps, mine host, be quick, make haste!
A soldier's got no time to waste:
He must be shooting, shooting, shooting,
His Kaiser's enemies unrooting!
Make it a double. This is a holiday.

MOTHER COURAGE. If I was sure you're right . . .

CHAPLAIN. Think it out for yourself: how *could* the war end?

SOLDIER.

Two breasts, my girl, be quick, make haste!
A soldier's got no time to waste:
He must be hating, hating, hating,
He cannot keep his Kaiser waiting!

SCRIVENER (*suddenly*). What about peace? Yes, peace. I'm from Bohemia. I'd like to get home once in a while.

CHAPLAIN. Oh, you would, would you? Dear old peace! What happens to the hole when the cheese is gone?

SOLDIER (*off stage*).

Your blessing, priest, be quick, make haste!
A soldier's got no time to waste:
He must be dying, dying, dying,
His Kaiser's greatness glorifying!

SCRIVENER. In the long run you can't live without peace!

CHAPLAIN. Well, I'd say there's peace even in war, war has its islands of peace. For war satisfies *all* needs, even those of peace, yes, they're provided for, or the war couldn't keep going. In war—as in the very thick of peace—you can empty your bowels, and between one battle and the next there's always a beer, and even on the march you can take a nap—on your elbow maybe, in a gutter—something can always be managed. Of course you can't play cards during an attack, but neither can you while plowing the fields in peacetime; it's when the victory's won that there are possibilities. You have your leg shot off, and at first you raise quite an outcry as if it *was* something, but soon you calm down or take a swig of brandy, and you end up hopping around, and the war is none the worse for your little misadventure. And can't you be fruitful and multiply in the thick of slaughter—behind a barn or somewhere? Nothing can keep you from it very long in any event. And so the war has your offspring and can carry on. War is like love, it always finds a way. Why *should* it end?

[KATTRIN *has stopped working. She stares at the* CHAPLAIN.]

MOTHER COURAGE. Then I *will* buy those supplies, I'll rely on you.

[KATTRIN *suddenly bangs a basket of glasses down on the ground and runs out.* MOTHER COURAGE *laughs.*]

Kattrin! Lord, Kattrin's still going to wait for peace. I promised her she'll get a husband—when it's peace.

[*Runs after her.*]

SCRIVENER (*standing up*). I win. You were talking. You pay.

MOTHER COURAGE (*returning with* KATTRIN). Be sensible, the war'll go on a bit longer, and we'll make a bit more money, then peace'll be all the nicer. Now you go into the town, it's not ten minutes' walk, and bring the things from the Golden Lion, just the dearer ones, we can get the rest later in the wagon. It's all arranged, the clerk will go with you, most of the soldiers are at the Commander's funeral, nothing can happen to you. Do a good job, don't lose anything, Kattrin, think of your trousseau!

[KATTRIN *ties a cloth round her head and leaves with the* SCRIVENER.]

CHAPLAIN. You don't mind her going with Scrivener?

MOTHER COURAGE. She's not so pretty anyone would want to ruin her.

CHAPLAIN. The way you run your business and always come through is highly commendable, Mother Courage—I see how you got your name.

MOTHER COURAGE. The poor need courage. They're lost, that's why. That they even get up in the morning is something—in *their* plight. Or that they plow a field—in war time. Even their bringing children into the world shows they have courage, for they have no prospects. They have to hang each other one by one and slaughter each other in the lump, so if they want to look each other in the face once in a while, well, it takes courage. That they put up with an Emperor and a Pope, that takes an unnatural amount of courage, for *they* cost you your life.

[*She sits, takes a small pipe from her pocket and smokes it.*]

You might chop me a bit of firewood.

CHAPLAIN (*reluctantly taking his coat off and preparing to chop wood*). Properly speaking, I'm a pastor of souls, not a woodcutter.

MOTHER COURAGE. But I don't have a soul. And I do need wood.

CHAPLAIN. What's that little pipe you've got there?

MOTHER COURAGE. Just a pipe.

CHAPLAIN. I think it's a very particular pipe.

MOTHER COURAGE. Oh?

CHAPLAIN. The cook's pipe in fact. The cook from the Oxenstiern Regiment.

MOTHER COURAGE. If you know, why beat about the bush?

CHAPLAIN. Because I don't know if you've been *aware* that's what you've been smoking. It was possible you just rummaged among your belongings and your fingers just lit on a pipe and you just took it. In pure absentmindedness.

MOTHER COURAGE. How do you know that's not it?

CHAPLAIN. It isn't. You *are* aware of it.

[*He brings the ax down on the block with a crash.*]

MOTHER COURAGE. What if I was?

CHAPLAIN. I must give you a warning, Mother Courage, it's my duty. You are unlikely ever again to see the gentleman but that's no pity, you're in luck. Mother Courage, he did not impress me as trustworthy. On the contrary.

MOTHER COURAGE. Really? He was such a nice man.

CHAPLAIN. Well! So that's what you call a nice man. I do not.

[*The ax falls again.*]

Far be it from me to wish him ill, but I cannot—cannot—describe him as nice. No, no, he's a Don Juan, a cunning Don Juan. Just look at that pipe if you don't believe me. You must admit it tells all.

MOTHER COURAGE. I see nothing special in it. It's been, um, used.

CHAPLAIN. It's bitten half-way through! He's a man of great violence! It is the pipe of a man of great violence, you can see *that* if you've any judgment left!

[*He deals the block a tremendous blow.*]

MOTHER COURAGE. Don't bite my chopping block halfway through!

CHAPLAIN. I told you I had no training as a woodcutter. The care of souls was my field. Around here my gifts and capabilities are grossly misused. In physical labor my god-given talents find no—um—adequate expression—which is a sin. You haven't heard me preach. Why, I can put such spirit into a regiment with a single sermon that the enemy's a mere flock of sheep to them and their own lives no more than smelly old shoes to be thrown away at the thought of final victory! God has given me the gift of tongues. I can preach you out of your senses!

MOTHER COURAGE. I need my senses, what would I do without them?

CHAPLAIN. Mother Courage, I have often thought that—under a veil of plain speech—you conceal a heart. You are human, you need warmth.

MOTHER COURAGE. The best way of warming this tent is to chop plenty of firewood.

CHAPLAIN. You're changing the subject. Seriously, my dear Courage, I
sometimes ask myself how it would be if our relationship should be
somewhat more firmly cemented. I mean, now the wind of war has
whirled us so strangely together.

MOTHER COURAGE. The cement's pretty firm already. I cook your meals.
And you lend a hand—at chopping firewood, for instance.

CHAPLAIN (going over to her, gesturing with the ax). You know what
I mean by a close relationship. It has nothing to do with eating and
woodcutting and such base necessities. Let your heart speak!

MOTHER COURAGE. Don't come at me like that with your ax, that'd be
too close a relationship!

CHAPLAIN. This is no laughing matter, I am in earnest. I've thought it all
over.

MOTHER COURAGE. Dear Chaplain, be a sensible fellow. I like you, and
I don't want to heap coals of fire on your head. All I'm after is to
bring me and my children through in that wagon. It isn't just mine,
the wagon, and anyway I've no mind to start having a private life.
At the moment I'm taking quite a risk buying these things when the
Commander's fallen and there's all this talk of peace. Where would
you go, if I was ruined? See? You don't even know. Now chop some
firewood and it'll be warm of an evening, which is quite a lot in times
like these. What was that?

[She stands up. KATTRIN enters, breathless, with a
wound across the eye and forehead. She is dragging
all sorts of articles, parcels, leather goods, a drum,
etc.]

MOTHER COURAGE. What is it, were you attacked? On the way back?
She was attacked on the way back! I'll bet it was that soldier who got
drunk on my liquor. I should never have let you go. Dump all that
stuff! It's not bad, the wound is only a flesh wound. I'll bandage it
for you, it'll be all healed up in a week. They're worse than animals.

[She bandages the wound.]

CHAPLAIN. I reproach them with nothing. At home they never did these
shameful things. The men who start the wars are responsible, they
bring out the worst in people.

MOTHER COURAGE. Didn't the Scrivener walk you back home? That's
because you're a respectable girl, he thought they'd leave you alone.
The wound's not at all deep, it will never show. There: all bandaged
up. Now, I've got something for you, rest easy. I secret. I've been
holding it, you'll see.

[She digs Yvette's red boots out of a bag.]

Well, what do you see? You always wanted them. Now you have
them. Put them on quick, before I'm sorry I let you have them. (She
helps her to put the boots on.) It will never show, though it wouldn't
bother me if it did. The fate of the ones they like is the worst. They

drag them around with them till they're through. A girl they don't care for they leave alone. I've seen so many girls, pretty as they come in the beginning, then all of a sudden they looked a fright—enough to scare a wolf. They can't even go behind a tree on the street without having something to fear from it. They lead a frightful life. Like with trees: the tall, straight ones are cut down for roof timber, and the crooked ones can enjoy life. So this wound here is really a piece of luck. The boots have kept well, I cleaned them good before I put them away.

[KATTRIN *leaves the boots and creeps into the wagon.*]

CHAPLAIN (*when she's gone*). I hope she won't be disfigured?

MOTHER COURAGE. There'll be a scar. She needn't wait for peace now.

CHAPLAIN. She didn't let them get any of the stuff away from her.

MOTHER COURAGE. Maybe I shouldn't have made such a point of it. If only I ever knew what went on inside her head. One time she stayed out all night, once in all the years. I could never get out of her what happened, I racked my brains for quite a while.

[*She picks up the things* KATTRIN *spilled and sorts them angrily.*]

This is war. A nice source of income, I must say!

[*Cannon shots.*]

CHAPLAIN. Now they're lowering the Commander in his grave! A historic moment.

MOTHER COURAGE. It's a historic moment to me when they hit my daughter over the eye. She's all but finished now, she'll never get a husband, and she's so mad about children! Even her dumbness comes from the war. A soldier stuck something in her mouth when she was little. I'll not see Swiss Cheese again, and where my Eilif is the Good Lord knows. Curse the war!

Scene 7

Mother Courage at the height of her business career.

[*A highway. The* CHAPLAIN, MOTHER COURAGE, *and her daughter* KATTRIN *pull the wagon, and new wares are hanging from it.* MOTHER COURAGE *wears a necklace: a chain of silver coins.*]

MOTHER COURAGE. I won't let you spoil my war for me. Destroys the weak, does it? Well, what does peace do for 'em, huh? War feeds its people better.

[*She sings*]

If war don't suit your disposition
When victory comes you will be dead.
War is a business proposition:
Not with cream-cheese but steel and lead.

And staying in one place won't help either. Those who stay home are the first to go.

[*She sings.*]

Too many seek a bed to sleep in:
Each ditch is taken, and each cave,
And he who digs a hole to creep in
Finds he has dug an early grave.
And many a man spends many a minute
In hurrying toward some resting place.
You wonder, when at last he's in it,
Just why the fellow forced the pace.

[*The wagon proceeds.*]

Scene 8

1632. In this same year Gustavus Adolphus fell in the battle of Lützen. The peace threatens Mother Courage with ruin. Her brave son performs one heroic deed too many and comes to a shameful end.

[*A camp. A summer morning. In front of the wagon, an old woman and her son. The son is dragging a large bag of bedding.*]

MOTHER COURAGE (*from inside the wagon*). Must you come at the crack of dawn?

YOUNG MAN. We've been walking all night, twenty miles it was, we have to be back today.

MOTHER COURAGE (*still inside*). What do I want with bed feathers? People don't even have houses.

YOUNG MAN. At least wait till you see 'em.

OLD WOMAN. Nothing doing here either, let's go.

YOUNG MAN. And let 'em sign away the roof over our heads for taxes? Maybe she'll pay three gilders if you throw in that bracelet.

[*Bells start ringing.*]

You hear, mother?

VOICES (*from the rear*). It's peace! The King of Sweden's been killed!

MOTHER COURAGE (*sticking her head out of the wagon. She hasn't done her hair yet*). Bells! What are the bells for, middle of the week?

CHAPLAIN (*crawling out from under the wagon*). What's that they're shouting?

YOUNG MAN. It's peace.

CHAPLAIN. Peace?

MOTHER COURAGE. Don't tell me peace has broken out—when I've just gone and bought all these supplies!

CHAPLAIN (*calling, toward the rear*). Is it peace?

VOICE (*from a distance*). They say the war stopped three weeks ago, I've only just heard.

CHAPLAIN (*to* MOTHER COURAGE). Or why would they ring the bells?

VOICE. A great crowd of Lutherans have just arrived with wagons— they brought the news.

YOUNG MAN. It's peace, mother.

[*The* OLD WOMAN *collapses.*]

What's the matter?

MOTHER COURAGE (*back in the wagon*). Kattrin, it's peace! Put on your black dress, we're going to church, we owe it to Swiss Cheese! Can it be true?

YOUNG MAN. The people here say so too, the war's over. Can you stand up?

[*The* OLD WOMAN *stands up, dazed.*]

I'll get the harness shop going again now, I promise you. Everything'll be all right, father will get his bed back. . . . Can you walk?

[*To the* CHAPLAIN.]

She felt sick, it was the news. She didn't believe there'd ever be peace again. Father always said there would. We're going home.

[*They leave.*]

MOTHER COURAGE (*off*). Give her some brandy.

CHAPLAIN. They've left already.

MOTHER COURAGE (*still off*). What's going on in the camp over there?

CHAPLAIN. They're all getting together, I think I'll go over. Shall I put my pastor's clothes on again?

MOTHER COURAGE. Better get the exact news first, and not risk being taken for the Antichrist. I'm glad about the peace even though I'm ruined. At least I've got two of my children through the war. Now I'll see my Eilif again.

CHAPLAIN. And who may this be coming down from the camp? Well, if it isn't our Swedish Commander's cook!

COOK (*somewhat bedraggled, carrying a bundle*). Who's here? The Chaplain!

CHAPLAIN. Mother Courage, a visitor!

[MOTHER COURAGE *clambers out.*]

COOK. Well, I promised I'd come over for a brief conversation as soon as I had time. I didn't forget your brandy, Mrs. Fierling.

MOTHER COURAGE. Jesus, the Commander's cook! After all these years! Where is Eilif, my eldest?

COOK. Isn't he here yet? He went on ahead yesterday, he was on his way over.

CHAPLAIN. I *will* put my pastor's clothes on. I'll be back.

[*He goes behind the wagon.*]

MOTHER COURAGE. He may be here any minute then.

[*Calls toward the wagon.*]

Kattrin, Eilif's coming! Bring a glass of brandy for the cook, Kattrin!

[KATTRIN *doesn't come.*]

Pull your hair over it and have done. Mr. Lamb is no stranger.

[*She gets the brandy herself.*]

She won't come out. Peace is nothing to her, it was too long coming. They hit her right over the eye. You can hardly see it now. But she thinks people stare at her.

COOK. Ah yes, war!

[*He and* MOTHER COURAGE *sit.*]

MOTHER COURAGE. Cook, you come at a bad time: I'm ruined.

COOK. What? That's terrible!

MOTHER COURAGE. The peace has broken my neck. On the Chaplain's advice I've gone and bought a lot of supplies. Now everybody's leaving and I'm holding the baby.

COOK. How could you listen to the Chaplain? If I'd had time—but the Catholics were too quick for me—I'd have warned you against him. He's a windbag. Well, so now he's the big man round here!

MOTHER COURAGE. He's been doing the dishes for me and helping with the wagon.

COOK. With the wagon—him! And I'll bet he's told you a few of his jokes. He has a most unhealthy attitude to women. I tried to influence him but it was no good. He isn't sound.

MOTHER COURAGE. Are you sound?

COOK. If I'm nothing else, I'm sound. Your health!

MOTHER COURAGE. Sound! Only one person around here was ever sound, and I never had to slave as I did then. He sold the blankets off the children's beds in the spring, and he found my harmonica unchristian. You aren't recommending yourself if you *admit* you're sound.

COOK. You fight tooth and nail, don't you? I like that.

MOTHER COURAGE. Don't tell me you've been dreaming of my teeth and nails.

COOK. Well, here we sit, while the bells of peace do ring, and you pouring your famous brandy as only you know how!

MOTHER COURAGE. I don't think much of the bells of peace at the moment. I don't see how they can hand out all this pay that's in arrears. And then where shall I be with my famous brandy? Have you all been paid?

COOK (*hesitating*). Not exactly. That's why we disbanded. In the circumstances, I thought, why stay? For the time being, I'll look up a couple of friends. So here I sit—with you.

MOTHER COURAGE. In other words, you're broke.

COOK (*annoyed by the bells*). It's about time they stopped that racket! I'd like to set myself up in some business. I'm fed up with being their cook. I'm supposed to make do with tree roots and shoe leather, and then they throw the hot soup in my face. Being a cook nowadays is a dog's life. I'd sooner do war service, but of course it's peace now.

[*As the* CHAPLAIN *turns up, wearing his old costume.*]

We'll talk it over later.

CHAPLAIN. The coat's pretty good. Just a few moth holes.

COOK. I don't know why you take the trouble. You won't find another job. Who could you incite now to earn an honorable wage or risk his life for a cause? Besides I have a bone to pick with you.

CHAPLAIN. Have you?

COOK. I have. You advised a lady to buy superfluous goods on the pretext that the war would never end.

CHAPLAIN (*hotly*). I'd like to know what business it is of yours?

COOK. It's unprincipled behavior! How can you give unwanted advice? And interfere with the conduct of other people's businesses?

CHAPLAIN. Who's interfering now, I'd like to know?

[*To* MOTHER COURAGE.]

I had no idea you were such a close friend of this gentleman and had to account to him for everything.

MOTHER COURAGE. Now don't get excited. The Cook's giving his personal opinion. You can't deny your war was a frost.

CHAPLAIN. You mustn't take the name of peace in vain, Courage. Remember, you're a hyena of the battlefield!

MOTHER COURAGE. A what?

COOK. If you insult my girl friend, you'll have to reckon with me!

CHAPLAIN. I am *not* speaking to you, your intentions are only too transparent!

[*To* MOTHER COURAGE.]

But when I see *you* take peace between finger and thumb like a snotty old hanky, my humanity rebels! It shows that you want war, not peace, for what you get out of it. But don't forget the proverb: he who sups with the devil must use a long spoon!

MOTHER COURAGE. Remember what one fox said to another that was caught in a trap? "If you stay there, you're just asking for trouble!" There isn't much love lost between me and the war. And when it comes to calling me a hyena, you and I part company.

CHAPLAIN. Then why all this grumbling about the peace just as everyone's heaving a sigh of relief? Is it just for the junk in your wagon?

MOTHER COURAGE. My goods are not junk. I live off them. *You've* been living off them.

CHAPLAIN. You live off war. Exactly.

COOK (*to the* CHAPLAIN). As a grown man, you should know better than to go around advising people.

[*To* MOTHER COURAGE.]

Now, in your situation you'd be wise to get rid of certain goods at once—before the prices sink to nothing. Get ready and get going, there isn't a moment to lose!

MOTHER COURAGE. That's sensible advice, I think I'll take it.

CHAPLAIN. Because the Cook says so.

MOTHER COURAGE. Why didn't *you* say so? He's right, I must get to the market.

[*She climbs into the wagon.*]

COOK. One up for me, Chaplain. You have no presence of mind. You should have said, "*I* gave you advice? Why, I was just talking politics!" And you shouldn't take me on as a rival. Cockfights are not becoming to your cloth.

CHAPLAIN. If you don't shut your trap, I'll murder you, cloth or no cloth!

COOK (*taking his boots off and unwinding the wrappings on his feet*). If you hadn't degenerated into a godless tramp, you could easily get yourself a parsonage, now it's peace. Cooks won't be needed, there's nothing to cook, but there's still plenty to believe, and people are prepared to go right on believing it.

CHAPLAIN. Mr. Lamb, please don't drive me out! Since I became a tramp, I'm a somewhat better man. I couldn't preach to 'em any more.

[YVETTE POTTIER *enters, decked out in black, with a stick. She is much older, fatter, and heavily powdered. Behind her, a servant.*]

YVETTE. Hullo, everybody! Is this Mother Courage's establishment?

CHAPLAIN. Quite right. And with whom have we the pleasure?

YVETTE. I am Madame Colonel Starhemberg, good people. Where's Mother Courage?

CHAPLAIN (*calling to the wagon*). Madame Colonel Starhemberg wants to speak with you!

MOTHER COURAGE (*from inside*). Coming!

YVETTE (*calling*). It's Yvette!

MOTHER COURAGE (*inside*). Yvette!

YVETTE. Just to see how you're getting on!

[*As the* COOK *turns round in horror.*]

Peter!

COOK. Yvette!

YVETTE. Of all things! How did *you* get here?

COOK. On a cart.

CHAPLAIN. Well! You know each other? Intimately?

YVETTE. Not half.

[*Scrutinizing the* COOK.]

You're fat.

COOK. For that matter, *you're* no beanpole.

YVETTE. Anyway, nice meeting you, tramp. Now I can tell you what I think of you.

CHAPLAIN. Do so, tell him all, but wait till Mother Courage comes out.

COOK. Now don't make a scene . . .

MOTHER COURAGE (*comes out, laden with goods*). Yvette!

[*They embrace.*]

But why are you in mourning?

YVETTE. Doesn't it suit me? My husband, the colonel, died several years ago.

MOTHER COURAGE. The old fellow that nearly bought my wagon?

YVETTE. His older brother.

MOTHER COURAGE. So you're not doing badly. Good to see one person who got somewhere in the war.

YVETTE. I've had my ups and downs.

MOTHER COURAGE. Don't let's speak ill of Colonels. They make money like hay.

CHAPLAIN (*to the* COOK). If I were you, I'd put my shoes on again.

[*To* YVETTE.]

You promised to give us your opinion of this gentleman.

COOK. Now, Yvette, don't make a stink!

MOTHER COURAGE. He's a friend of mine, Yvette.

YVETTE. He's—Peter Piper, that's who.

MOTHER COURAGE. What!?

COOK. Cut the nicknames. My name's Lamb.

MOTHER COURAGE (*laughing*). Peter Piper? Who turned the women's heads? And I've been keeping your pipe for you.

CHAPLAIN. And smoking it.

YVETTE. Lucky I can warn you against him. He's a bad lot. You won't find a worse on the whole coast of Flanders. He got more girls in trouble than . . .

COOK. That's a long time ago, it isn't true any more.

YVETTE. Stand up when you talk to a lady! Oh, how I loved that man! And all the time he was having a little bowlegged brunette. He got *her* in trouble too, of course.

COOK. I seem to have brought *you* luck!

YVETTE. Shut your trap, you hoary ruin! And you take care, Mother Courage, this type is still dangerous even in decay!

MOTHER COURAGE (*to* YVETTE). Come with me, I must get rid of this stuff before the prices fall.

YVETTE (*concentrating on* COOK). Miserable cur!

MOTHER COURAGE. Maybe you can help me at army headquarters, you have contacts.

YVETTE. Damnable whore hunter!

MOTHER COURAGE (*shouting into the wagon*). Kattrin, church is all off, I'm going to market!

YVETTE. Inveterate seducer!

MOTHER COURAGE (*still to* KATTRIN). When Eilif comes, give him something to drink!

YVETTE. That a man of *his* ilk should have been able to turn me from the straight and narrow! I have only my own star to thank that I rose nonetheless to the heights! But I've put an end to your tricks, Peter Piper, and one day—in a better life than this—the Lord God will reward me! Come, Mother Courage!

[*Leaves with* MOTHER COURAGE.]

CHAPLAIN. As our text this morning let us take the saying, the mills of God grind slowly. And you complain of my jokes!

COOK. I never have any luck. I'll be frank, I was hoping for a good hot dinner, I'm starving. And now they'll be talking about me, and she'll get a completely wrong picture. I think I should go before she comes back.

CHAPLAIN. I think so too.

COOK. Chaplain, peace makes me sick. Mankind must perish by fire and sword, we're born and bred in sin! Oh, how I wish I was roasting a great fat capon for the Commander—God knows where *he's* got to—with mustard sauce and those little yellow carrots . . .

CHAPLAIN. Red cabbage—with capon, red cabbage.

COOK. You're right. But he always wanted yellow carrots.

CHAPLAIN. He never understood a thing.

COOK. You always put plenty away.

CHAPLAIN. Under protest.

COOK. Anyway, you must admit, those were the days.

CHAPLAIN. Yes, that I might admit.

COOK. Now you've called her a hyena, there's not much future for you here either. What are you staring at?

CHAPLAIN. It's Eilif!

[*Followed by two soldiers with halberds,* EILIF *enters. His hands are fettered. He is white as chalk.*]
What's happened to you?

EILIF. Where's mother?

CHAPLAIN. Gone to town.

EILIF. They said she was here. I was allowed a last visit.

COOK (*to the soldiers*). Where are you taking him?

SOLDIER. For a ride.

[*The other soldier makes the gesture of throat cutting.*]

CHAPLAIN. What has he done?

SOLDIER. He broke in on a peasant. The wife is dead.

CHAPLAIN. Eilif, how could you?

EILIF. It's no different. It's what I did before.

COOK. That was in wartime.

EILIF. Shut your hole. Can I sit down till she comes?

SOLDIER. No.

CHAPLAIN. It's true. In war time they honored him for it. He sat at the Commander's right hand. It was bravery. Couldn't we speak with the provost?

SOLDIER. What's the use? Stealing cattle from a peasant, what's brave about that?

COOK. It was just stupid.

EILIF. If I'd been stupid, I'd have starved, clever dick.

COOK. So you were bright and paid for it.

CHAPLAIN. At least we must bring Kattrin out.

EILIF. Let her alone. Just give me some brandy.

SOLDIER. No.

CHAPLAIN. What shall we tell your mother?

EILIF. Tell her it was no different. Tell her it was the same. Oh, tell her nothing. [*The soldiers take him away.*]

CHAPLAIN. I'll come with you, I'll . . .

EILIF. I don't need a priest!

CHAPLAIN. You don't know—yet.

[*Follows him.*]

COOK (*calling after him*). I'll have to tell her, she'll want to see him!

CHAPLAIN. Better tell her nothing. Or maybe just that he was here, and he'll return, maybe tomorrow. Meantime I'll be back and can break the news.

[*Leaves quickly. The* COOK *looks after him, shakes his head, then walks uneasily around. Finally, he approaches the wagon.*]

COOK. Hi! Won't you come out? You want to sneak away from the peace, don't you? Well, so do I! I'm the Swedish Commander's cook, remember me? I was wondering if you've got anything to eat in there—while we're waiting for your mother. I wouldn't mind a bit of bacon—or even bread—just to pass the time.

[*He looks in.*]

She's got a blanket over her head.

[*The thunder of cannon.*]

MOTHER COURAGE (*running, out of breath, still carrying the goods*). Cook, the peace is over, the war's on again, has been for three days! I didn't get rid of this stuff after all, thank God! There's a shooting match in the town already—with the Lutherans. We must get away with the wagon. Pack, Kattrin! What's on *your* mind? Something the matter?

COOK. Nothing.

MOTHER COURAGE. But there is. I see it in your face.

COOK. Because the war's on again, most likely. May it last till tomorrow evening, so I can get something in my belly!

MOTHER COURAGE. You're not telling me.

COOK. Eilif was here. Only he had to go away again.

MOTHER COURAGE. He was here? Then we'll see him on the march. I'll be with our side this time. How'd he look?

COOK. The same.

MOTHER COURAGE. He'll *never* change. And the war couldn't get *him,* he's bright. Help me with the packing.

[*She starts it.*]

Did he tell you anything? Is he well in with the captain? Did he tell you about his heroic deeds?

COOK (*darkly*). He's done one of them again.

MOTHER COURAGE. Tell me about it later.

[KATTRIN *appears.*]

Kattrin, the peace is all through, we're on the move again.

[*To the* COOK.]

What *is* biting you?

COOK. I'll enlist.

MOTHER COURAGE. A good idea. Where's the Chaplain?

COOK. In the town. With Eilif.

MOTHER COURAGE. Stay with us a while, Lamb, I need a bit of help.

COOK. This matter of Yvette . . .

MOTHER COURAGE. Hasn't done you any harm at all in my eyes. Just the opposite. Where there's smoke, there's fire, they say. You'll come?

COOK. I may as well.

MOTHER COURAGE. The twelfth regiment's under way. Into harness with you! Maybe I'll see Eilif before the day is out, just think! That's what I like best. Well, it wasn't such a long peace, we can't grumble. Let's go!

[*The* COOK *and* KATTRIN *are in harness.*]

[MOTHER COURAGE *sings.*]

Up hill, down dale, past dome and steeple,
    My wagon always moves ahead.
The war can care for all its people
    So long as there is steel and lead.
Though steel and lead are stout supporters
    A war needs human beings too.
Report today to your headquarters!
    If it's to last, this war needs you!
        Christians, awake! The winter's gone!
        The snows depart, the dead sleep on.
        And though you may not long survive
        Get out of bed and look alive!

Scene 9

The great war of religion has lasted sixteen years and Germany has lost half its inhabitants. Those who are spared in battle die by plague. Over once blooming countryside hunger rages. Towns are burned down. Wolves prowl the empty streets. In the autumn of 1634 we find Mother Courage in the Fichtelge-birge not far from the road the Swedish army is taking. Winter has come early and is hard. Business is bad. Only begging remains. The cook receives a letter from Utrecht and is sent packing.

[*In front of a half-ruined parsonage. Early winter.*
A grey morning. Gusts of wind. MOTHER COURAGE
and the COOK *at the wagon in shabby clothes.*]

COOK. There are no lights on. No one's up.

MOTHER COURAGE. But it's a parsonage. The parson'll have to leave his feather bed and ring the bells. Then he'll have some hot soup.

COOK. Where'll he get it from? The whole village is starving.

MOTHER COURAGE. The house is lived in. There was a dog barking.

COOK. If the parson has anything, he'll stick to it.

MOTHER COURAGE. Maybe if we sang him something . . .

COOK. I've had enough.

[*Suddenly.*]

I didn't tell you, a letter came from Utrecht. My mother's died of cholera, the inn is mine. There's the letter, if you don't believe me. I'll show it to you, though my aunt's railing about me and my ups and downs is none of your business.

MOTHER COURAGE (*reading*). Lamb, I'm tired of wandering, too. I feel like a butcher's dog taking meat to my customers and getting none myself. I've nothing more to sell and people have nothing to pay with. In Saxony someone tried to saddle me with a chestful of books in return for two eggs. And in Württemberg they would have let me have their plough for a bag of salt. Nothing grows any more, only thorn bushes. I hear that in Pomerania the villagers have been eating their younger children. Nuns have been caught committing robbery.

COOK. The world's dying out.

MOTHER COURAGE. Sometimes I see myself driving through hell with this wagon and selling brimstone. And sometimes I'm driving through heaven handing out provisions to wandering souls! If only we could find a place where there's no shooting, me and my children—what's left of 'em—we might rest a while.

COOK. We could open this inn together. Think about it, Courage. *My* mind's made up. With or without you, I'm leaving for Utrecht. And today too.

MOTHER COURAGE. I must talk to Kattrin, it's a little bit sudden, and I don't like to make my decisions in the cold on an empty stomach.

[KATTRIN *emerges from the wagon.*]

Kattrin, I've something to tell you. The cook and I want to go to Utrecht, he's been left an inn. You'd be able to stay put and get to know some people. Many a man'd be prepared to take on a girl with a position. Looks aren't everything. I wouldn't mind it. I get on well with the Cook. I'll say this for him: he has a head for business. We'd be sure of our dinner, that would be all right, wouldn't it? You'd have your own bed, what do you think of *that?* In the long run, this is no life, on the road. You might be killed any time. You're already lousy. And we must decide now, because otherwise we go north with the Swedes. They must be over there somewhere.

[*She points to the left.*]

I think we'll decide to go, Kattrin.

COOK. Anna, I must have a word with you alone.

MOTHER COURAGE. Go back inside, Kattrin.

[KATTRIN *does so.*]

COOK. I'm interrupting because there's a misunderstanding, Anna. I thought I wouldn't have to say it right out, but I see I must. If you're bringing *her,* it's all off. Do we understand each other?

[KATTRIN *has her head out of the back of the wagon*
and is listening.]

MOTHER COURAGE. You mean I leave Kattrin behind?

COOK. What do you think? There's no room in the inn, it isn't one of those places with three counters. If the two of us look lively we can earn a living, but three's too many. Let Kattrin keep your wagon.

MOTHER COURAGE. I was thinking we might find her a husband in Utrecht.

COOK. Don't make me laugh. With that scar? And old as she is? And dumb?

MOTHER COURAGE. Not so loud!

COOK. Loud or soft, what is, is. That's another reason I can't have her in the inn. Customers don't like having something like that always before their eyes. You can't blame them.

MOTHER COURAGE. Shut up. I told you not to talk so loud.

COOK. There's a light in the parsonage, we can sing now!

MOTHER COURAGE. Cook, how could she pull the wagon by herself? The war frightens her. She can't bear it. She has terrible dreams. I hear her groan at night, especially after battles. What she sees in her dreams I don't know. She suffers from pity. The other day I found a hedgehog with her that we'd run over.

COOK. The inn's too small.

[*Calling.*]

Worthy Sir, menials, and all within! We now present the song of Solomon, Julius Caesar, and other great souls who came to no good, so you can see we're law-abiding folk too, and have a hard time getting by, especially in winter.

[*He sings:* "The Song of the Great Souls of This Earth."]

You've heard of wise old Solomon
    You know his history.
He thought so little of this earth
He cursed the hour of his birth
    Declaring: all is vanity.
How very wise was Solomon!
    But ere night came and day did go
This fact was clear to everyone:
    It was his wisdom that had brought him low.
Better for you if you have none.

For the virtues are dangerous in this world, as our fine song tells. You're better off without, you have a nice life, breakfast included—some good hot soup maybe . . . I'm an example of a man who's not had any, and I'd like some, I'm a soldier, but what good did my bravery do me in all those battles? None at all. I might just as well have wet my pants like a poltroon and stayed home. For why?

And Julius Caesar, who was brave,
    You saw what came of him.
He sat like God on an altar-piece
    And yet they tore him limb from limb
While his prestige did still increase!
"Et tu, Brute, I am undone!"
    And ere night came and day did go

This fact was clear to everyone:
    It was his bravery that brought him low
Better for you if you have none.
              [Under his breath.]
They don't even look out.
              [Aloud.]
Worthy Sir, menials, and all within! You should say, no, courage isn't the thing to fill a man's belly, try honesty, that should be worth a dinner, at any rate it must have *some* effect. Let's see.

You all know honest Socrates
    Who always spoke the truth.
They owed him thanks for that, you'd think,
Yet they put hemlock in his drink
    And swore that he was bad for youth.
How honest was the people's son!
    But ere night came and day did go
This fact was clear to everyone:
    It was his honesty that brought him low.
Better for you if you have none.

Yes, we're told to be unselfish and share what we have, but what if we have nothing? And those who do share it don't have an easy time either, for what's left when you've finished sharing? Unselfishness is a very rare virtue—it doesn't pay.

Unselfish Martin could not bear
    His fellow creature's woes.
    He met a beggar in the snows
And gave him half his cloak to wear:
    So both of them fell down and froze.
What an unselfish paragon!
    But ere night came and day did go
This fact was clear to everyone:
    It was unselfishness that brought him low.
Better for you if you have none.

That's how it is with us. We're law-abiding folk, we keep to ourselves, don't steal, don't kill, don't burn the place down. And in this way we sink lower and lower and the song proves true and there's no soup going. And if we were different, if we were thieves and killers, maybe we could eat our fill! For virtues bring no reward, only vices. Such is the world, need it be so?

God's Ten Commandments we have kept
    And acted as we should.
    It has not done us any good.
O you who sit beside a fire
Please help us now: our need is dire!
Strict godliness we've always shown
    But ere night came and day did go

This fact was clear to everyone:
It was our godliness that brought us low.
Better for you if you have none!

VOICES (*from above*). You there! Come up! There's some soup here
for you!

MOTHER COURAGE. Lamb, I couldn't swallow a thing. I don't say what
you said is unreasonable, but was it your last word? We've always
understood each other.

COOK. Yes, Anna. Think it over.

MOTHER COURAGE. There's nothing to think over. I'm not leaving her
here.

COOK. You're going to be silly, but what can I do? I'm not inhuman,
it's just that the inn's a small one. And now we must go up, or it'll
be nothing doing here too, and we've been singing in the cold to no
avail.

MOTHER COURAGE. I'll fetch Kattrin.

COOK. Better stick something in your pocket for her. If there are three
of us, they'll get a shock.

[*Exeunt.*]

[KATTRIN *clambers out of the wagon with a bundle.*
She makes sure they're both gone. Then, on a wagon
wheel, she lays out a skirt of her mother's and a pair
of the COOK's *trousers side by side and easy to see.*
She has just finished, and has picked up her bundle,
when MOTHER COURAGE *returns.*]

MOTHER COURAGE (*with a plate of soup*). Kattrin! Stay where you
are, Kattrin! Where do you think you're going with that bundle?
[*She examines the bundle.*]

She's packed her things. Were you listening? I told him there was
nothing doing, he can *have* Utrecht and his lousy inn, what would
we want with a lousy inn?
[*She sees the skirt and trousers.*]

Oh, you're a stupid girl, Kattrin, what if I'd seen that and you gone?
[*She takes hold of* KATTRIN, *who's trying to leave.*]

And don't think I've sent him packing on your account. It was the
wagon. You can't part us, I'm too used to it, *you* didn't come into
it, it was the wagon. Now we're leaving, and we'll put the cook's
things here where he'll find 'em, the stupid man.
[*She clambers up and throws a couple of things down*
to go with the trousers.]

There! He's sacked! The last man I'll take into *this* business! Now
let's be going, you and me. Get into harness. This winter'll pass—
like all the others.
[*They harness themselves to the wagon, turn it*
around, and start out. A gust of wind. Enter the
COOK, *still chewing. He sees his things.*]

Scene 10

During the whole of 1635 Mother Courage and Kattrin pull the wagon along the roads of central Germany in the wake of the ever more ragged armies.

[*On the highway,* MOTHER COURAGE *and* KATTRIN *are pulling the wagon. They come to a prosperous farmhouse. Someone inside is singing.*]

"The Song of Shelter"

THE VOICE.

In March a tree we planted
   To make the garden gay.
In June we were enchanted:
A lovely rose was blooming
The balmy air perfuming!
   Blest of the gods are they
   Who have a garden gay!
In June we were enchanted.

When snow falls helter-skelter
   And loudly blows the storm
Our farmhouse gives us shelter.
The winter's in a hurry
But we've no cause to worry.
   Cosy are we and warm
   Though loudly blows the storm
Our farmhouse gives us shelter.

[MOTHER COURAGE *and* KATTRIN *have stopped to listen. Then they start out again.*]

Scene 11

January, 1636. Catholic troops threaten the Protestant town of Halle. The stone begins to speak. Mother Courage loses her daughter and journeys onwards alone. The war is not yet near its end.

[*The wagon, very far gone now, stands near a farm-house with a straw roof. It is night. Out of the wood come a* LIEUTENANT *and* THREE SOLDIERS *in full armor.*]

LIEUTENANT. And there mustn't be a sound. If anyone yells, cut him down.

FIRST SOLDIER. But we'll have to knock—if we want a guide.

LIEUTENANT. Knocking's a natural noise, it's all right, could be a cow hitting the wall of the cowshed.

[*The* SOLDIERS *knock at the farmhouse door. An old peasant woman opens. A hand is clapped over her mouth. Two soldiers enter.*]

MAN'S VOICE. What is it?

[*The* SOLDIERS *bring out an old peasant and his son.*]

LIEUTENANT (*pointing to the wagon on which* KATTRIN *has appeared*). There's one.

[*A soldier pulls her out.*]

Is this everybody that lives here?

PEASANTS (*alternating*). That's our son. And that's a girl that can't talk. Her mother's in town buying up stocks because the shopkeepers are running away and selling cheap. They're canteen people.

LIEUTENANT. I'm warning you. Keep quiet. One sound and we'll crack you one with a pike. And I need someone to show us the path to the town.

> [*Points to the* YOUNG PEASANT.]

You! Come here!

YOUNG PEASANT. I don't know any path!

SECOND SOLDIER (*grinning*). He don't know any path!

YOUNG PEASANT. I don't help Catholics.

LIEUTENANT (*to* SECOND SOLDIER). Let him feel your pike in his side.

YOUNG PEASANT (*forced to his knees, the pike at his throat*). I'd rather die!

SECOND SOLDIER (*again mimicking*). He'd rather die!

FIRST SOLDIER. I know how to change his mind.

> [*Walks over to the cowshed.*]

Two cows and a bull. Listen, you. If you aren't going to be reasonable, I'll sabre your cattle.

YOUNG PEASANT. Not the cattle!

PEASANT WOMAN (*weeping*). Spare the cattle, captain, or we'll starve!

LIEUTENANT. If he must be pigheaded!

FIRST SOLDIER. I think I'll start with the bull.

YOUNG PEASANT (*to the old one*). Do I have to?

> [*The* OLDER ONE *nods.*]

I'll do it.

PEASANT WOMAN. Thank you, thank you, captain, for sparing us, for ever and ever. Amen.

> [*The old man stops her going on thanking him.*]

FIRST SOLDIER. I knew the bull came first all right!

> [*Led by the* YOUNG PEASANT, *the* LIEUTENANT *and the* SOLDIERS *go on their way.*]

OLD PEASANT. I wish we knew what it was. Nothing good, I suppose.

PEASANT WOMAN. Maybe they're just scouts. What are you doing?

OLD PEASANT (*setting a ladder against the roof and climbing up*). I'm seeing if they're alone.

> [*On the roof.*]

Things are moving—all over. I can see armor. And a cannon. There must be more than a regiment. God have mercy on the town and all within!

PEASANT WOMAN. Are there lights in the town?

OLD PEASANT. No, they're all asleep.

> [*He climbs down.*]

There'll be an attack, and they'll all be slaughtered in their beds.

PEASANT WOMAN. The watchman'll give warning.

OLD PEASANT. They must have killed the watchman in the tower on the hill or he'd have sounded his horn before this.

PEASANT WOMAN. If there were more of us . . .

OLD PEASANT. But being that we're alone with that cripple . . .

PEASANT WOMAN. There's nothing we can do, is there?

OLD PEASANT. Nothing.

PEASANT WOMAN. We can't get down there. In the dark.

OLD PEASANT. The whole hillside's swarming with 'em.

PEASANT WOMAN. We could give a sign?

OLD PEASANT. And be cut down for it?

PEASANT WOMAN. No, there's nothing we can do.

[*To* KATTRIN.]

Pray, poor thing, pray! There's nothing we can do to stop this blood-
shed, so even if you can't talk, at least pray! He hears, if no one
else does. I'll help you.

[*All kneel,* KATTRIN *behind.*]

Our Father, which art in Heaven, hear our prayer, let not the town
perish with all that lie therein asleep and fearing nothing. Wake
them, that they rise and go to the walls and see the foe that comes
with fire and sword in the night down the hill and across the fields.
[*Back to* KATTRIN.] God protect our mother and make the watchman
not sleep but wake ere it's too late. And save our son-in-law too,
O God, he's there with his four children, let them not perish, they're
innocent, they know nothing [*to* KATTRIN, *who groans*], one of
them's not two years old, the eldest is seven.

[KATTRIN *rises, troubled.*]

Heavenly Father, hear us, only Thou canst help us or we die, for
we are weak and have no sword nor nothing; we cannot thrust our
own strength but only Thine, O Lord; we are in Thy hands, our
cattle, our farm, and the town too, we're all in Thy hands, and the
foe is nigh unto the walls with all his power.

[KATTRIN *unperceived, has crept off to the wagon,*
has taken something out of it, put it under her apron,
and has climbed up the ladder to the roof.]

Be mindful of the children in danger, especially the little ones, be
mindful of the old folk who cannot move, and of all Christian souls,
O Lord.

OLD PEASANT. And forgive us our trespasses as we forgive them that
trespass against us. Amen.

[*Sitting on the roof,* KATTRIN *takes a drum from un-*
der her apron, and starts to beat it.]

PEASANT WOMAN. Heavens, what's she doing?

OLD PEASANT. She's out of her mind!

PEASANT WOMAN. Bring her down, quick!

[*The* OLD PEASANT *runs to the ladder but* KATTRIN
pulls it up on the roof.]

She'll get us in trouble.

OLD PEASANT. Stop it this minute, you silly cripple!

PEASANT WOMAN. The soldiers'll come!

OLD PEASANT (*looking for stones*). I'll stone you!

PEASANT WOMAN. Have you no pity, have you no heart? We have relations there too, four grandchildren, but there's nothing we can do. If they find us now, it's the end, they'll stab us to death!

[KATTRIN *is staring into the far distance, toward the town. She goes on drumming.*]

PEASANT WOMAN (*to the* PEASANT). I told you not to let that riffraff in your farm. What do *they* care if we lose our cattle?

LIEUTENANT (*running back with* SOLDIERS *and* YOUNG PEASANT). I'll cut you all to bits!

PEASANT WOMAN. We're innocent, sir, there's nothing we can do. She did it, a stranger!

LIEUTENANT. Where's the ladder?

OLD PEASANT. On the roof.

LIEUTENANT (*calling*). Throw down the drum. I order you!

[KATTRIN *goes on drumming.*]

You're all in this, but you won't live to tell the tale.

OLD PEASANT. They've been cutting down fir trees around here. If we bring a tall enough trunk we can knock her off the roof . . .

FIRST SOLDIER (*to the* LIEUTENANT). I beg leave to make a suggestion.

[*He whispers something to the* LIEUTENANT, *who nods.*]

Listen, you! We have an idea—for your own good. Come down and go with us to the town. Show us your mother and we'll spare her.

[KATTRIN *replies and goes on drumming.*]

LIEUTENANT (*pushing him away*). She doesn't trust you, no wonder with your face.

[*He calls up to* KATTRIN.]

Hey, you! Suppose I give you my word? I'm an officer, my word's my bond!

[KATTRIN *drums louder.*]

Nothing is sacred to her.

YOUNG PEASANT. Sir, it's not just because of her mother!

FIRST SOLDIER. This can't go on, they'll hear it in the town as sure as hell.

LIEUTENANT. We must make another noise with something. Louder than that drum. What can we make a noise with?

FIRST SOLDIER. But we mustn't make a noise!

LIEUTENANT. A harmless noise, fool, a peacetime noise!

OLD PEASANT. I could start chopping wood.

LIEUTENANT. That's it!

[*The* PEASANT *brings his ax and chops away.*]

Chop! Chop harder! Chop for your life! [KATTRIN *has been listening, beating her drum less hard. Very upset, and peering around, She now goes on drumming.*] It's not enough.

[*To* FIRST SOLDIER.]

You chop too!

OLD PEASANT. I've only one ax. [*He stops chopping.*]

LIEUTENANT. We must set fire to the farm. Smoke her out.

OLD PEASANT. That's no good, Captain, when they see fire from the town, they'll know everything.

[*During the drumming* KATTRIN *has been listening again. Now she laughs.*]

LIEUTENANT. She's laughing at us, that's too much, I'll have her guts if it's the last thing I do. Bring a musket!

[*Two* SOLDIERS *off.* KATTRIN *goes on drumming.*]

PEASANT WOMAN. I have it, Captain. That's their wagon over there, Captain. If we smash that, she'll stop. It's all they have, Captain.

LIEUTENANT (*to the* YOUNG PEASANT). Smash it!

[*Calling.*]

If you don't stop that noise, we'll smash your wagon!

[*The* YOUNG PEASANT *deals the wagon a couple of feeble blows with a board.*]

PEASANT WOMAN (*to* KATTRIN). Stop, you little beast!

[KATTRIN *stares at the wagon and pauses. Noises of distress come out of her. But she goes on drumming.*]

LIEUTENANT. Where are those sons of bitches with that gun?

FIRST SOLDIER. They can't have heard anything in the town or we'd hear their cannon.

LIEUTENANT (*calling*). They don't hear you. And now we're going to shoot you. I'll give you one more chance: throw down that drum!

YOUNG PEASANT (*dropping the board, screaming to* KATTRIN). Don't stop now! Or they're all done for. Go on, go on, go on . . .

[*The* SOLDIER *knocks him down and beats him with his pike.* KATTRIN *starts crying but goes on drumming.*]

PEASANT WOMAN. Not in the back, you're killing him!

[*The* SOLDIERS *arrive with the musket.*]

SECOND SOLDIER. The Colonel's foaming at the mouth. We'll be court-martialed.

LIEUTENANT. Set it up! Set it up!

[*Calling while the musket is set up on forks.*]

Once for all: stop that drumming!

[*Still crying,* KATTRIN *is drumming as hard as she can.*]

[*The* SOLDIERS *fire.* KATTRIN *is hit. She gives the drum another feeble beat or two, then slowly collapses.*]

LIEUTENANT. That's an end to the noise.

[*But the last beats of the drum are lost in the din of cannon from the town. Mingled with the thunder of cannon, alarm bells are heard in the distance.*]

FIRST SOLDIER. She did it.

Scene 12

[*Toward morning. The drums and pipes of troops on the march, receding. In front of the wagon* MOTHER COURAGE *sits by* KATTRIN'S *body. The peasants of the last scene are standing near.*]

PEASANTS. You must leave, ma'am. There's only one regiment to go. You can never get away by yourself.

MOTHER COURAGE. Maybe she's fallen asleep.

[*She sings.*]

Lullay, lullay, what's that in the hay?
The neighbor's babes cry but mine are gay.
The neighbor's babes are dressed in dirt:
Your silks were cut from an angel's skirt.
They are all starving: you have a cake;
If it's too stale, you need but speak.
Lullay, lullay, what's rustling there?
One lad fell in Poland. The other is where?

You shouldn't have told her about the children.

PEASANTS. If you hadn't gone off to the town to get your cut, maybe it wouldn't have happened.

MOTHER COURAGE. She's asleep now.

PEASANTS. She's not asleep, it's time you realized. She's through. You must get away. There are wolves in these parts. And the bandits are worse.

MOTHER COURAGE. That's right.

[*She goes and fetches a piece of cloth from the wagon to cover the body.*]

PEASANTS. Have you no one now? Someone you can go to?

MOTHER COURAGE. There's one. My Eilif.

PEASANTS (*while* COURAGE *covers the body*). Leave *her* to us. We'll give her a proper burial. You needn't worry.

MOTHER COURAGE. Here's money for the expenses.

[*She pays the peasant. The* PEASANT *and his son shake her hand and carry* KATTRIN *away.*]

PEASANT WOMAN (*also taking her hand, and bowing, as she goes away*). Hurry!

MOTHER COURAGE (*harnessing herself to the wagon*). I hope I can pull the wagon by myself. Yes, I'll manage, there's not much in it now. I must start up again in business.

[*Another regiment passes at the rear with pipe and drum.*]

MOTHER COURAGE. Hey! Take me with you!

[*She starts pulling the wagon. Soldiers are heard singing.*]

Dangers, surprises, devastations—
    The war takes hold and will not quit.
But though it last three generations
    We shall get nothing out of it.
Starvation, filth, and cold enslave us.
    The army robs us of our pay.
Only a miracle can save us
    And miracles have had their day.
        Christians, awake! The winter's gone!
        The snows depart. The dead sleep on.
        And though you may not long survive
        Get out of bed and look alive!

TRANSLATOR'S NOTES TO MOTHER COURAGE

When I first translated *Mother Courage,* I worked from a copy of the play as printed in the *Versuche* series. It was marked up by a member of the staff of the Berlin Ensemble: I made the cuts indicated and put in the penciled additions. The translation appeared in *The Modern Theatre,* Volume 2, 1955, Doubleday Anchor Books.

Next I made a somewhat shorter stage version with new lyrics, which Darius Milhaud set to music. This version was published in *Seven Plays* by Bertolt Brecht, 1961.

The present text, commissioned by Methuen & Co. for their collected Brecht, is the only one of my three versions which is complete. The basis of this version is, in general, the text in the *Versuche,* but I have frequently consulted the text in the *Stücke* too.

The few words in my translation for which no equivalent will be found in either the Versuche or the Stücke I took from the Berlin Ensemble copy mentioned above; and Brecht has recorded them permanently in the Notes to the special Modell edition published by Henschel in East Berlin, 1958.

. To the list of helpers acknowledged in former editions of the English *Mother Courage,* I should like to add the names of two who helped with this new effort: Miss Jill Booty and Dr. Hugo Schmidt.

The music for the lyrics here printed, which is by Darius Milhaud, has not yet (early 1962) been made available to producers. A score by Paul Dessau has been used in all authorized English-language productions. A piano reduction of Dessau's songs will be found in the Doubleday Anchor edition of *Mother Courage* with English words to fit. Some of these songs are to be found, sung by Germaine Montero, on a 12-inch disc (VKS-9022) distributed in the United States by Vanguard Records. The East-German records of some of the *Mother Courage* songs, performed by the original Berlin Ensemble cast, have usually been available from Deutsche Schallplatten, Deutscher Buch Export, Leninstrasse 16, Leipzig C.1, Germany. There is an East-German movie of the play which has not yet been generally released, and there is a British TV-film of the Bentley version which has not been shown outside Britain.

Mother Courage was first produced in 1941 in Zurich and since the Berlin Ensemble production (1949) has been performed in many countries. The Bentley version alone has been professionally produced in Dublin, London (TV only), Cleveland, and San Francisco. Pictures of each scene in the Berlin Ensemble production are provided in *Courage-Modell 1949,* published by the Henschel Verlag in East Berlin, along with Brecht's own scene-by-scene analysis of the play.

Eric Bentley

QUESTIONS

SCENE 1

1. The play opens with two recruiters discussing the advantages of war over peace. What is the major advantage? Does the attribution of this value to war link war with certain other social and political philosophies?

2. In the course of Scene 1 a number of traditional moral values, such as courage and patriotism, are brought under discussion indirectly. Do the Fierlings and the recruiters fulfill our usual moral expectations? Is "morality" perhaps redefined in this scene?

3. What is the meaning of everyone's drawing a black cross from the helmet? Is death brought into the first scene in other ways?

4. Do you see any significance in the manner in which the recruiter gets Eilif? Consider Eilif's actions as well as Mother Courage's.

SCENE 2

5. What devices does Brecht use in this scene to introduce religion into the play? How do men in general use religion?

6. What effect is achieved by having Eilif sing the first two stanzas of "The Fishwife and the Soldier," and Mother Courage sing the third?

7. How would you describe the "world" of the play? Out of what components has Brecht constructed it?

8. While the commander and Eilif discuss the "glories of war" in the front of the tent, Mother Courage and the cook bargain over a capon in the back. Two ways of life are thus juxtaposed. Find other places and other ways in which Brecht manages this same kind of juxtaposition.

SCENE 3

9. Consider carefully the things Mother Courage does and says and describe her basic "motive."

10. Why does this motive bring her into conflict with her world? How is the conflict realized dramatically?

11. Mother Courage's wagon is the one prop continually on stage. What does it represent? In answering this question take into account not only what the wagon looks like but the changes it undergoes and the observations that are made about it.

12. The third scene centers on a few props: a cashbox, a pair of red boots, a fancy hat, and a flag. What do these objects have in common, and why are they all dangerous to their possessors?

13. On several occasions Kattrin's muteness has serious consequences. What point do you think Brecht is making?

14. How does Brecht manage to make us sympathize with Mother Courage even when her haggling over price costs the life of Swiss Cheese and when she denies that she recognizes his corpse? Is the word "courage" taking on a new meaning?

SCENE 4

15. What understanding of justice is dramatized by the incident of the young soldier?

16. Who are the "they" of Mother Courage's song, "The Great Capitulation"? Are there any characters in the play who can be identified with "they"?

SCENE 5

17. Sound effects are as much a part of the scene as objects. What function does the victory march played in the background serve in this scene?

18. Do you see any progression in the first five episodes of the play? Any regression?

SCENE 6

19. Is the Chaplain's statement that the war "can look forward to a prosperous future" and his view that war is the natural state of man successfully dramatized? That is, is the Chaplain's *idea* translated into theatrical terms?

20. *Mother Courage* was written in 1939 when Brecht was an exile from Hitler's Germany. Can you see any reason for setting the play in the religious wars of the seventeenth century? Why not dramatize the same ideas in contemporary terms?

21. What is the meaning of Kattrin's longing for children? What does the attack on her tell us about the nature of war?

22. What comment does the attack on Kattrin make on the "jolly" picture of war the Chaplain has presented at the beginning of this episode?

SCENE 7

23. Mother Courage's song faces directly and states succinctly the frightening facts of life as the play presents them. What response to the facts does Mother Courage suggest in her song? Would you describe her as sentimental? brutal? cynical? despairing?

SCENE 8

24. What point is Brecht making by having Eilif executed in peacetime for the same kind of act that won him great praise during wartime? Is Brecht defending Eilif? Is he presenting him in a favorable light?

25. How is the relationship between war and the business of earning a living established in this scene? Has Brecht drawn this parallel in other ways in the play?

SCENE 9

26. Brecht argued that he was interested in presenting in his plays human character as it is shaped by the conditions of the time, by the society and the world. How has Mother Courage been shaped by her time? Is she, however, entirely a product of social conditions, conforming entirely to the necessities the times force on her?

27. Is the effect of this scene with its "Song of the Wise and the Good" to persuade us that all virtue is a disaster for its possessor?

SCENE 10

28. Does "The Song of Shelter" offer any genuine alternative for man, any escape from pulling the wagon from battlefield to battlefield?

SCENE 11

29. What three virtues or human qualities do Mother Courage's three children represent? Does Mother Courage share in these virtues or does she lack them?
30. Are we meant to despise the peasants who will destroy a town to save their cattle? How does Brecht make their situation understandable?

SCENE 12

31. Is Mother Courage able to live without illusions?
32. *Mother Courage* has been played most successfully on a revolving stage. At the end Mother Courage moves off pulling her wagon in one direction while the stage revolves in the opposite direction. In what ways is this an appropriate statement in visual terms of the play as a whole? If you were the director, would you have the wagon and stage move at the same speed, have the wagon move faster, or have the stage move faster? Why?
33. Should the song end as Mother Courage and her wagon exit from the stage, or should it continue after all movement on stage has ceased and the lights have darkened?

The World in Expressionistic Drama

The scenes used in the previous section as examples of the ways in which playwrights construct their dramatic worlds are all realistic; that is, these scenes portray nothing that we might not see in real life. Interior settings such as that of *Hedda Gabler* may be more commonplace, more familiar, than the bare, blasted heath on which Macbeth encounters the witches, but the latter is certainly not outside the range of what can be seen in nature. (Even the witches are realistic if you believe in witches.) But Shakespeare shows less concern for reproducing the familiar and unremarkable than does a modern playwright like Ibsen, and his scenes, his images of the world, tend to slip away from the strictly realistic toward the expressionistic; he is less concerned with making his stage world resemble everyday reality and more concerned with creating visual and verbal images that fully reveal the nature of the world. For example, in *Timon of Athens* he sets the first half of the play in the house of the wealthy Timon, who loves all mankind and overwhelms his friends and acquaintances with gifts and feasting. When Timon discovers that his friends are false and that his own wealth is exhausted, he turns into as great an enemy of mankind as he was once its friend, and he departs from the city into a desert where nature is grudging and brutal. There is nothing unrealistic about a great house or a desert—they can be seen every day—but it is quite clear from the way in which Shakespeare has juxtaposed these two places that he is not so concerned with presenting realistic scenes as he is with finding appropriate images for two types of worlds existing side by side—the rich and prosperous social setting, which man creates for himself, and the harsh, isolated world of barren, hostile nature.

Brecht's methods for creating the world in *Mother Courage* are closer to Shakespeare's than to Ibsen's. While it is true that wagons, cannons, soldiers, battlefields, cookshacks, and cashboxes are all drawn from the real world, it is nonetheless startling to find our world represented as a continuous battlefield on which man must contrive to stay alive. Brecht's scenes are realistic enough in one sense—they do show aspects of what can be seen in reality—but they are unrealistic or expressionistic ultimately, since they portray the world as a never-ending war, which is not the *literal* truth.

A number of modern dramatists have carried this technique a step further and have created scenes that bear little resemblance to what can be seen on earth. Nevertheless, they register accurately and forcefully the nature of our environment as man apprehends it with his mind, not his senses. In Arthur Miller's *Death of a Salesman* realism and expressionism are mixed; the salesman, Willy Loman, is crushed down by the weight of the world in which he lives. The set of the play represents this graphically by placing his house between two towering apartment buildings, which lean menacingly—in a structurally impossible manner—over it and block the sunlight. The flimsiness of Willy's hope is made visible by the construction of his house. While the walls of the apartment houses seem to be solid, the walls of the Loman house consist of flimsy, open framework; the furnishings —like the salesman's achievements—are few: a brass bed, a refrigerator, a silver trophy, and a few sticks of furniture. Other modern dramatists have made good use of similar sets to suggest the insubstantiality, the dream-like quality, of the material goods that man believes so solid and permanent. For example, in Thornton Wilder's *The Skin of Our Teeth*, a play celebrating man's indomitable will to survive and affirming those human virtues that make life worth living, the play centers in a house made of simple painted flats, which are knocked down the moment disaster strikes, and restored the moment things improve. Our worldly goods, the play seems to say, are no more substantial than these canvas frames out of which this stage house is constructed. Human qualities are alone real and permanent.

The use of expressionistic devices to portray the world is as old as the theater. In one of the earliest tragedies, Aeschylus' *Prometheus Bound*, produced in Athens about 460 B.C., the hero Prometheus is chained to a rock in the center of the stage throughout the play. He has been placed there by Zeus because he defied the god and brought fire to man, who, Zeus fears, may with the new power of fire challenge the rule of the gods. If one believes literally in the Greek gods, this is a "realistic" enough explanation of events, but the rock and the chains are principally a dramatic device for showing a "hard" world that resists and punishes any attempt to control and utilize for human purposes the gigantic powers—"gods" in Aeschylus' terms—of the universe. (In our time we seem to be fixed and bound in an unexpected way by the realities consequent on our attempts to use the power of the atom.) Medieval drama was even more openly expressionistic. In medieval plays the entire Christian world was often laid out schematically on the "stage"—often a town square—with no concern for the fact that this scene violated normal understanding of time and space. On one side was the mouth of Hell, on the other the mountain of Paradise and the Garden of Eden. In between was the field where Cain strikes Abel, Mount Ararat where the ark of Noah grounds, and Calvary where Christ dies, all represented symbolically and all in front of the still visible buildings of the town where, Christians believe, the sins and sufferings, the just acts and rewards dramatized in the Bible were daily re-enacted in contemporary costumes and accents.

Expressionistic scenes are not, therefore, an unfamiliar dramatic technique for picturing the world; they are rather exaggerated uses of familiar techniques. A realistic author like Ibsen constructs a scene that is familiar in the extreme: a dark, sedate middle-class room; and a modern stage designer is likely to make this set seem all the more real by providing it with solid walls that do not rattle when a door is slammed, with oil lamps that actually light, and with a stove that really burns. But however real the scene may appear, it is still an illusion, and its function in the play is not to reproduce a real room but to symbolize visually and to define the bourgeois social world. It is an image, a metaphor, not a photograph of reality. The scene works this same way in the most extreme forms of expressionism, only all pretense of faithfulness to literal reality is abandoned. In Fernando Arrabal's *The Automobile Graveyard* the set of the play is a hotel constructed of old, abandoned, rusting automobiles, complete with a valet and a prostitute who kisses everyone good night. In *Waiting for Godot* the natural world is reduced to a bare stage with one stunted tree, and the social world of rich and poor, owner and laborer, is represented by one vulgar, well-dressed man leading a ragged idiot along on a rope. When the rich man sits down to a lunch of chicken, he tosses the bones to the idiot, who gratefully gnaws them. As strange and unacceptable as such "worlds" may seem to us, there is no difficulty in comprehending their meaning. In fact, it is a great deal easier to see how *The Automobile Graveyard* defines the world as grotesque luxury living in the ugly waste created by an industrial society, than it is to see how the scene of *Hedda Gabler* defines middle-class society. We are likely to take the scene of the realistic play for granted, comfortably accepting it as no more than a picture of the everyday world; but the expressionistic dramatist will not allow us to ignore the meaning of his scene. He insists upon it, and some familiarity with expressionistic drama will make us more alert and more sensitive to the worlds of realistic drama. Both use scenes for the same purpose: to represent the world as the dramatist apprehends it.

THE FALL OF
THE CITY

BY

ARCHIBALD MACLEISH

Archibald MacLeish (born 1892) is better known as a poet than as
a playwright, but during the 1930's he wrote a number of verse plays
for stage and radio, and recently one of his plays, *J.B.*, a dramatic
adaptation of the story of Job, was a great success on Broadway. *The
Fall of the City* was first produced on radio in 1937, at a time when
it was apparent that freedom stood in danger from dictatorships and
from the indecision of the democracies. But the play is as pertinent
now as then because it dramatizes the internal weaknesses and fears
that always beset a free and prosperous people.

Because *The Fall of the City* is a radio play, it illustrates very well
an important point discussed in the section on the world of the play.
All dramatists rely heavily on language to fill out the dramatic worlds
that are first presented in the scenery and sets. But the radio dramatist
cannot use scenery to present his world; therefore he is forced to make
the words alone create his dramatic world. As a result this dramatic
technique becomes more obvious in a radio play like *The Fall of the
City,* and MacLeish's skillful exploitation of the ways in which worlds
may be constructed from words offers insights into the less obvious
ways dramatists like Brecht and Ibsen use the same techniques.

In the other plays in this volume the dramatic worlds have been constructed out of carefully selected, realistic details, but in *The Fall of
the City,* MacLeish constructs his world from expressionistic scenes
and events created by language—a city that is still in the Stone Age but

has radio, a woman who rises from the tomb to prophesy, and a hollow, mechanical figure, a compound of the Spanish conquistador and the German soldier, striding relentlessly across continents. All of these expressionistic images are used to focus our attention on the dangers and terrors that surround man, and to express the world as men sense it in times of the breaking of nations.

VOICE OF THE STUDIO DIRECTOR (*orotund and professional*). Ladies
and gentlemen:
This broadcast comes to you from the city
Listeners over the curving air have heard
From furthest-off frontiers of foreign hours—
Mountain Time: Ocean Time: of the islands:
Of waters after the islands—some of them waking
Where noon here is the night there: some
Where noon is the first few stars they see or the last one.

For three days the world has watched this city—
Not for the common occasions of brutal crime
Or the usual violence of one sort or another
Or coronations of kings or popular festivals:
No: for stranger and disturbing reasons—
The resurrection from death and the tomb of a dead woman.

Each day for three days there has come
To the door of her tomb at noon a woman buried!

The terror that stands at the shoulder of our time
Touches the cheek with this: the flesh winces.
There have been other omens in other cities
But never of this sort and never so credible.

In a time like ours seemings and portents signify.
Ours is a generation when dogs howl and the
Skin crawls on the skull with its beast's foreboding.
All men now alive with us have feared.
We have smelled the wind in the street that changes weather.

We have seen the familiar room grow unfamiliar:
The order of numbers alter: the expectation
Cheat the expectant eye. The appearance defaults with us.

Here in this city the wall of the time cracks.

We take you now to the great square of this city. . . .
    [*The shuffle and hum of a vast patient crowd gradu-
        ally rises: swells: fills the background.*]
VOICE OF THE ANNOUNCER (*matter-of-fact*). We are here on the central
    plaza.
We are well off to the eastward edge.
There is a kind of terrace over the crowd here.
It is precisely four minutes to twelve.
The crowd is enormous: there might be ten thousand:
There might be more: the whole square is faces.
Opposite over the roofs are the mountains.
It is quite clear: there are birds circling.
We think they are kites by the look: they are very high. . . .

The tomb is off to the right somewhere—
We can't see for the great crowd.
Close to us here are the cabinet ministers:
They stand on a raised platform with awnings.
The farmers' wives are squatting on the stones:
Their children have fallen asleep on their shoulders.
The heat is harsh: the light dazzles like metal.
It dazes the air as the clang of a gong does. . . .

News travels in this nation:
There are people here from away off—
Horse-raisers out of the country with brooks in it:
Herders of cattle from up where the snow stays—
The kind that cook for themselves mostly:
They look at the girls with their eyes hard
And a hard grin and their teeth showing. . . .

It is one minute to twelve now:
There is still no sign: they are still waiting:
No one doubts that she will come:
No one doubts that she will speak too:
Three times she has not spoken.
    [*The murmur of the crowd changes—not louder but
        more intense: higher.*]

THE VOICE OF THE ANNOUNCER (*low but with increasing excitement*).
    Now it is twelve: now they are rising:
    Now the whole plaza is rising:
    Fathers are lifting their small children:
    The plumed fans on the platform are motionless. . . .

    There is no sound but the shuffle of shoe leather. . . .

    Now even the shoes are still. . . .

    We can hear the hawks: it is quiet as that now. . . .

    It is strange to see such throngs so silent. . . .

    Nothing yet: nothing has happened. . . .

    Wait! There's a stir here to the right of us:
    They're turning their heads: the crowd turns:
    The cabinet ministers lean from their balcony:
    There's no sound: only the turning. . . .
        [*A woman's voice comes over the silence of the
        crowd: it is a weak voice but penetrating: it speaks
                slowly and as though with difficulty.*]
THE VOICE OF THE DEAD WOMAN. First the waters rose with no
    wind. . . .
THE VOICE OF THE ANNOUNCER (*whispering*). Listen: that is she! She's
    speaking!
THE VOICE OF THE DEAD WOMAN. Then the stones of the temple kindled
    Without flame or tinder of maize-leaves. . . .
THE VOICE OF THE ANNOUNCER (*whispering*). They see her beyond us:
    the crowd sees her. . . .
THE VOICE OF THE DEAD WOMAN. Then there were cries in the night
    haze:
    Words in a once-heard tongue: the air
    Rustling above us as at dawn with herons.

    Now it is I who must bring fear:
    I who am four days dead: the tears
    Still unshed for me—all of them: I
    For whom a child still calls at nightfall.

    Death is young in me to fear!
    My dress is kept still in the press in my bedchamber:
    No one has broken the dish of the dead woman.

Nevertheless I must speak painfully:
I am to stand here in the sun and speak:
   [*There is a pause. Then her voice comes again loud,
      mechanical, speaking as by rote.*]

The city of masterless men
Will take a master.
There will be shouting then:
Blood after!
   [*The crowd stirs. Her voice goes on weak and slow
      as before.*]

Do not ask what it means: I do not know:
Only sorrow and no hope for it.
THE VOICE OF THE ANNOUNCER. She has gone. . . . No, they are still
   looking.
THE VOICE OF THE DEAD WOMAN. It is hard to return from the time
   past. I have come
In the dream we must learn to dream where the crumbling of
Time like the ash from a burnt string has
Stopped for me. For you the thread still burns:
You take the feathery ash upon your fingers.
You bring yourselves from the time past as it pleases you.

It is hard to return to the old nearness . . .

Harder to go again. . . .
THE VOICE OF THE ANNOUNCER. She is gone.
   We know because the crowd is closing.
   All we can see is the crowd closing.
   We hear the releasing of held breath—
   The weight shifting: the lifting of shoe leather.
   The stillness is broken as surface of water is broken—
   The sound circling from in outward.
                  [*The murmur of the crowd rises.*]
   Small wonder they feel fear.
   Before the murders of the famous kings—
   Before imperial cities burned and fell—
   The dead were said to show themselves and speak.
   When dead men came disaster came. Presentiments
   That let the living on their beds sleep on
   Woke dead men out of death and gave them voices.
   All ancient men in every nation knew this.
A VOICE OVER THE CROWD. Masterless men . . .

A VOICE OVER THE CROWD. When shall it be . . .
A VOICE OVER THE CROWD. Masterless men
     Will take a master . . .
A VOICE OVER THE CROWD. What has she said to us . . .
A VOICE OVER THE CROWD. When shall it be . . .
A VOICE OVER THE CROWD. Masterless men
     Will take a master.
     Blood after . . .
A VOICE OVER THE CROWD. What has she said to us . . .
VOICES TOGETHER. Blood after!
          [*The voices run together into the excited roar of the
               crowd. The* ANNOUNCER'S *voice is loud over it.*]
THE VOICE OF THE ANNOUNCER. They are milling around us like cattle
     that smell death.
     The whole square is whirling and turning and shouting.
     One of the ministers raises his arms on the platform.
     No one is listening: now they are sounding drums:
     Trying to quiet them likely: No! No!
     Something is happening: there in the far corner:
     A runner: a messenger: staggering: people are helping him:
     People are calling: he comes through the crowd: they are quieter.
     Only those on the far edge are still shouting:
     Listen! He's here by the ministers now! He is speaking. . . .
THE VOICE OF THE MESSENGER. There has come the conqueror!
     I am to tell you.
     I have raced over sea land:
     I have run over cane land:
     I have climbed over cone land.
     It was laid on my shoulders
     By shall and by shan't
     That standing by day
     And staying by night
     Were not for my lot
     Till I came to the sight of you.
     Now I have come.

     Be warned of this conqueror!
     This one is dangerous!
     Word has out-oared him.
     East over sea-cross has
     All taken—
     Every country.
     No men are free there.
     Ears overhear them.
     Their words are their murderers.

Judged before judgment
Tried after trial
They die as do animals:—
Offer their throats
As the goat to her slaughterer.
Terror has taught them this!

Now he is here!

He was violent in his vessel:
He was steering in her stern:
He was watching in her waist:
He was peering in her prow:
And he dragged her up
Nine lengths
Till her keel lodged
On this nation.

Now he is here
Waylaying and night-lying.
If they hide before dark
He comes before sunup.
Where hunger is eaten
There he sits down:
Where fear sleeps
There he arises.

I tell you beware of him!
All doors are dangers.
The warders of wealth
Will admit him by stealth.
The lovers of men
Will invite him as friend.
The drinkers of blood
Will drum him in suddenly.
Hope will unlatch to him:
Hopelessness open.

I say and say truly
To all men in honesty
Such is this conqueror!
Shame is his people.
Lickers of spittle
Their lives are unspeakable:
Their dying indecent.

Be well warned!
He comes to you slightly
Slanting and sprinting
Hinting and shadowing:
Sly is his hiding:—
A hard lot:
A late rider:

Watch! I have said to you!
THE VOICE OF THE ANNOUNCER. They are leading him out: his legs give:
Now he is gone in the crowd: they are silent:
No one has spoken since his speaking:

They stand still circling the ministers.
No one has spoken or called out:—
There is no stir at all nor movement:
Even the farthest have stood patiently:
They wait trusting the old men:
They wait faithfully trusting the answer.
Now the huddle on the platform opens:
A minister turns to them raising his two arms. . . .
THE VOICE OF THE ORATOR. Freemen of this nation!
The persuasion of your wills against your wisdom is not dreamed
of.
We offer themes for your consideration.

What is the surest defender of liberty?
Is it not liberty?
A free people resists by freedom:
Not locks! Not blockhouses!

The future is a mirror where the past
Marches to meet itself. Go armed toward arms!
Peaceful toward peace! Free and with music toward freedom!
Face tomorrow with knives and tomorrow's a knife-blade.
Murder your foe and your foe will be murder!—
Even your friends suspected of false-speaking:
Hands on the door at night and the floor boards squeaking.

Those who win by the spear are the spear-toters.
And what do they win? Spears! What else is there?
If their hands let go they have nothing to hold by.
They are no more free than a paralytic propped against a tree is.

With the armored man the arm is upheld by the weapon:
The man is worn by the knife.

Once depend on iron for your freedom and your
Freedom's iron!
Once overcome your resisters with force and your
Force will resist you!—
You will never be free of force.
Never of arms unarmed
Will the father return home:
The lover to her loved:
The mature man to his fruit orchard
Walking at peace in that beauty—
The years of his trees to assure him.

Force is a greater enemy than this conqueror—
A treacherous weapon.

Nevertheless my friends there *is* a weapon!
Weakness conquers!

Against chainlessness who breaks?
Against wall-lessness who vaults?
Against forcelessness who forces?

Against the feather of the thistle
Is blunted sharpest metal.
No edge cuts seed-fluff.

This conqueror unresisted
Will conquer no longer: a posturer
Beating his blows upon burdocks—
Shifting his guard against shadows.
Snickers will sound among road-menders:
Titters be stifled by laundresses:
Coarse guffaws among chambermaids.
Reddened with rage he will roar.
He will sweat in his uniform foolishly.
He will disappear: no one hear of him!

There *is* a weapon my friends.
Scorn conquers!

THE VOICE OF THE ANNOUNCER (*the* ORATOR'S *voice unintelligible under
        it*). I wish you could all see this as we do—
    The whole plaza full of these people—
    Their colorful garments—the harsh sunlight—
    The water-sellers swinging enormous gourds—
    The orator there on the stone platform—
    The temple behind him: the high pyramid—
    The hawks overhead in the sky teetering
    Slow to the windward: swift to the down-wind—
    The houses blind with the blank sun on them. . . .
THE VOICE OF THE ORATOR. There is a weapon.
    Reason and truth are that weapon.

    Let this conqueror come!
    Show him no hindrance!
    Suffer his flag and his drum!
    Words . . . win!
THE VOICE OF THE ANNOUNCER. There's the shout now: he's done:
    He's climbing down: a great speech:
    They're all smiling and pressing around him:
    The women are squatting in full sunlight:
    They're opening packages: bread we'd say by the look—
    Yes: bread: bread wrapped between corn leaves:
    They're squatting to eat: they're quite contented and happy:
    Women are calling their men from the sunny stones:
    There are flutes sounding away off:
    We can't see for the shifting and moving—
    Yes: there are flutes in the cool shadow:
    Children are dancing in intricate figures.
            [*A drum and flute are heard under the voice.*]
    Even a few old men are dancing.
    You'd say they'd never feared to see them dancing.
    A great speech! really great!
    Men forget these truths in passion:
    They oppose the oppressors with blind blows:
    They make of their towns tombs: of their roofs burials:
    They build memorial ruins to liberty:
    But liberty is not built from ruins:
    Only in peace is the work excellent. . . .

    That's odd! The music has stopped. There's something—
    It's a man there on the far side: he's pointing:
    He seems to be pointing back through the farthest street:
    The people are twisting and rising: bread in their fists. . . .
    We can't see what it is. . . . Wait! . . . it's a messenger.

It must be a messenger. Yes. It's a message—another.
Here he is at the turn of the street trotting:
His neck's back at the nape: he looks tired:
He winds through the crowd with his mouth open: laboring:
People are offering water: he pushes away from them:
Now he has come to the stone steps: to the ministers:
Stand by: we're edging in. . . .
  [*There are sounds of people close by: coughs: mur-
    murs. The* ANNOUNCER'S *voice is lowered.*]
Listen: he's leaning on the stone: he's speaking.
THE VOICE OF THE MESSENGER. There has come . . . the Con-
 queror. . . .

I am to tell you . . .

I have run over corn land:
I have climbed over cone land:
I have crossed over mountains. . . .

It was laid on my shoulders
By shall and by shan't
That standing by day
And staying by night
Were not for my lot
Till I came to the sight of you. . . .

Now I have come.

I bear word:
Beware of this conqueror!

The fame of his story
Like flame in the winter-grass
Widens before him.
Beached on our shore
With the dawn over shoulder
The lawns were still cold
When he came to the sheep meadows:—
Sun could not keep with him
So was he forward.
Fame is his sword.

No man opposing him
Still grows his glory.
He needs neither foeman nor

Thickset of blows to
Gather his victories—
Nor a foe's match
To earn him his battles.

He brings his own enemy!

He baggages with him
His closet antagonist—
His private opposer.
He's setting him up
At every road corner—
A figure of horror
With blood for his color:
Fist for his hand:
Reek where he stands:
Hate for his heat:
Sneers for his mouth:
Clouts for his clothes:
Oaths if he speak:—
And he's knocking him down
In every town square
Till hair's on his blade
And blood's all about
Like dust in a drouth
And the people are shouting
Flowers him flinging
Music him singing
And bringing him gold
And holding his heels
And feeling his thighs
Till their eyes start
And their hearts swell
And they're telling his praises
Like lays of the heroes
And chiefs of antiquity.

Such are his victories!
So does he come:
So he approaches. . . .
                [*A whisper rustles through the crowd.*]

No man to conquer
Yet as a conqueror

Marches he forward. . . .
> [*The whisper is louder.*]

Stands in your mountains. . . .
> [*A murmur of voices.*]

Soon to descend on you!
> [*A swelling roar.*]

THE VOICE OF THE ANNOUNCER. That touched them! That frightened
   them!
   Some of them point to the east hills:
   Some of them mock at the ministers: 'Freedom!'
   'Freedom for what? To die in a rat trap?'
   They're frantic with anger and plain fear.
   They're sold out they say. You can hear them.
   'Down with the government! Down with the orators!
   'Down with liberal learned minds!
   'Down with the mouths and the loose tongues in them!
   'Down with the lazy lot! They've sold us!
   'We're sold out! Talking has done for us!' . . .
   They're boiling around us like mullet that smell shark.
   We can't move for the mob: they're crazy with terror. . . .
A LOUD VOICE (*distant*). God-lovers!
   Think of your gods!

   Earth-masters!
   Taste your disasters!

   Men!
   Remember!
THE VOICE OF THE ANNOUNCER. There's a voice over the crowd some-
   where.
   They hear it: they're quieting down. . . . It's the priests!
   We see them now: it's the priests on the pyramid!
   There might be ten of them: black with their hair tangled.
   The smoke of their fire is flat in the quick wind:
   They stand in the thick of the smoke by the stone of the victims:
   Their knives catch in the steep sun: they are shouting:
   Listen!—
VOICES OF THE PRIESTS. Turn to your gods rememberers!
A SINGLE VOICE. Let the world be saved by surrendering the world:
   Not otherwise shall it be saved.
VOICES OF THE PRIESTS. Turn to your gods rememberers!

A SINGLE VOICE. Let evil be overcome by the coming over of evil:
>   Your hearts shall be elsewhere.

VOICES OF THE PRIESTS. Turn to your gods rememberers!

VOICES OF THE PRIESTS (*antiphonally*). Turn to your gods!
>   The conqueror cannot take you!

>   Turn to your gods!
>   The narrow dark will keep you!

>   Turn to your gods!
>   In god's house is no breaking!

>   Turn to your gods!
>   In god's silences sleep is!

>   Lay up your will with the gods!
>   Stone cannot still you!

>   Lay up your mind with the gods!
>   Blade cannot blind you!

>   Lay up your heart with the gods!
>   Danger departs from you!

THE VOICE OF THE ANNOUNCER. It's a wonderful thing to see this crowd
>   responding.
>   Even the simplest citizens feel the emotion.
>   There's hardly a sound now in the square. It's wonderful:
>   Really impressive: the priests there on the pyramid:
>   The smoke blowing: the bright sun: the faces—

A SINGLE VOICE. In the day of confusion of reason when all is delusion:
>   In the day of the tyrants of tongues when the truth is for hire:
>   In the day of deceit when ends meet:
>   Turn to your gods!
>   In the day of division of nations when hope is derision:
>   In the day of the supping of hate when the soul is corrupted:
>   In the day of despair when the heart's bare:
>   Turn to your gods!

> [*A slow drum beat.*]

THE VOICE OF THE ANNOUNCER. A kind of dance is beginning: a serpent
>   of people:
>   A current of people coiling and curling through people:
>   A circling of people through people like water through water. . . .

CHANTING VOICES (*to the drums*). Out of the stir of the sun
>   Out of the shout of the thunder

Out of the hush of the star . . .
Withdraw the heart.

THE VOICE OF THE ANNOUNCER (*the chant and drums under*). A very
young girl is leading them:
They have torn the shawl from her bare breast:
They are giving her flowers: her mouth laughs:
Her eyes are not laughing. . . .

CHANTING VOICES. Leave now the lovely air
To the sword and the sword-wearer—
Leave to the marksman the mark—
Withdraw the heart.

THE VOICE OF THE ANNOUNCER (*the chant and drums louder*). She's
coming . . . the drums pound . . . the crowd
Shrieks . . . she's reaching the temple . . . she's climbing
it. . . .
Others are following: five: ten . . .
Hundreds are following . . . crowding the stairway. . . .
She's almost there . . . her flowers have fallen . . .
She looks back . . . the priests are surrounding her. . . .
[*The drums suddenly stop: there is an instant's silence:
then an angry shout from the crowd.*]

THE VOICE OF THE ANNOUNCER. Wait! Wait! Something has happened!
One of the ministers: one of the oldest:
The general: the one in the feathered coat:—
He's driving them down with the staff of a banner:
He's climbed after them driving them down:
There's shouting and yelling enough but they're going:
He's telling them off too: you can hear him—

A DEEP VOICE (*chatter of the crowd under it*). Men! Old men! Listen!
Twist your necks on your nape bones!
The knife will wait in the fist for you.
There is a time for everything—
Time to be thinking of heaven:
Time of your own skins!

Cock your eyes to the windward!

Do you see smoke on those mountains?
The smoke is the smoke of towns.
And who makes it? The conqueror!
And where will he march now? Onward!
The heel of the future descends on you!

THE VOICE OF THE ANNOUNCER. He has them now: even the priests
have seen it:
They're all looking away here to the east.

There's smoke too: filling the valleys: like thunderheads! . . .
THE VOICE OF THE GENERAL. You are foolish old men.

You ought to be flogged for your foolishness.
Your grandfathers died to be free
And you—you juggle with freedom!
Do you think you're free by a law
Like the falling of apples in autumn?

You thought you were safe in your liberties!
You thought you could always quibble!
You can't! You take my word for it.
Freedom's the rarest bird!
You risk your neck to snare it—
It's gone while your eyeballs stare!

Those who'd lodge with a tyrant
Thinking to feed at his fire
And leave him again when they're fed are
Plain fools or were bred to it—
Brood of the servile races
Born with the hang-dog face. . . .
THE VOICE OF THE ANNOUNCER. They're all pointing and pushing to-
    gether:
    The women are shouldering baskets: bread: children. . . .
    They smell smoke in the air: they smell terror. . . .
THE VOICE OF THE GENERAL (*louder over the increasing sound*). There's
    nothing in this world worse—
Empty belly or purse or the
Pitiful hunger of children—
Than doing the Strong Man's will!

The free will fight for their freedom.
They're free men first. They feed
Meager or fat but as free men.
Everything else comes after—
Food: roof: craft—
Even the sky and the light of it!
        [*The voices of the crowd rise to a tumult of sounds
                —drums: shouts: cries.*]
THE VOICE OF THE ANNOUNCER. The sun is yellow with smoke . . .
    the town's burning. . . .
    The war's at the broken bridge. . . .
THE VOICE OF THE GENERAL (*shouting*). You! Are you free? Will you
    fight?

There are still inches for fighting!

There is still a niche in the streets!

You can stand on the stairs and meet him!

You can hold in the dark of a hall!

You can die!

   —or your children will crawl for it!

THE VOICE OF THE ANNOUNCER (*over the tumult*). They won't listen.
They're shouting and screaming and circling.
The square is full of deserters with more coming.
Every street from the bridge is full of deserters.
They're rolling in with the smoke blowing behind them.
The plaza's choked with the smoke and the struggling of stragglers.
They're climbing the platform: driving the ministers: shouting—
One speaks and another:

THE VOICES OF CITIZENS. The city is doomed!

                        There's no holding it!

Let the conqueror have it! It's his!

The age is his! It's his century!

Our institutions are obsolete.
He marches a mile while we sit in a meeting.

Opinions and talk!
Deliberative walks beneath the ivy and the creepers!

The age demands a made-up mind.
The conqueror's mind is decided on everything.

His doubt comes after the deed or never.

He knows what he wants for his want's what he knows.
He's gone before they say he's going.
He's come before you've barred your house.

He's one man: we are but thousands!

Who can defend us from one man?

Bury your arms! Break your standards!

Give him the town while the town stands!
THE VOICE OF THE ANNOUNCER. They're throwing their arms away: their
    bows are in bonfires.
The plaza is littered with torn plumes: spear-handles. . . .
THE VOICES OF CITIZENS. Masterless men! . . .

Masterless men
Must take a master! . . .

Order must master us! . . .

Freedom's for fools:
Force is the certainty!

Freedom has eaten our strength and corrupted our virtues!

Men must be ruled!

Fools must be mastered!

Rigor and fast
Will restore us our dignity!

Chains will be liberty!
THE VOICE OF THE ANNOUNCER. The last defenders are coming: they
    whirl from the streets like
Wild leaves on a wind: the square scatters them.
Now they are fewer—ten together or five:
They come with their heads turned: their eyes back.

Now there are none. The street's empty—in shadow.
The crowd is retreating—watching the empty street:
The shouts die.

The voices are silent.

                  They're watching. . . .

They stand in the slant of the sunlight silent and watching.
The silence after the drums echoes the drum beat.

Now there's a sound. They see him. They must see him!
They're shading their eyes from the sun: there's a rustle of whis-
    pering:
We can't see for the glare of it. . . . Yes! . . . Yes! . . .

He's there in the end of the street in the shadow. We see him!
He looks huge—a head taller than anyone:
Broad as a brass door: a hard hero:
Heavy of heel on the brick: clanking with metal:
The helm closed on his head: the eyeholes hollow.

He's coming! . . .
                    He's clear of the shadow! . . .
                                        The sun takes him.

They cover their faces with fingers. They cower before him.
They fall: they sprawl on the stone. He's alone where he's walk-
    ing.
He marches with rattle of metal. He tramples his shadow.
He mounts by the pyramid—stamps on the stairway—turns—
His arm rises—his visor is opening. . . .
    [*There is an instant's breathless silence: then the
    voice of the Announcer low—almost a whisper.*]

                            There's no one! . . .
There's no one at all! . . .
                    No one! . . .
                            The helmet is hollow!
The metal is empty! The armor is empty! I tell you
There's no one at all there: there's only the metal:
The barrel of metal: the bundle of armor. It's empty!

The push of a stiff pole at the nipple would topple it.

They don't see! They lie on the paving. They lie in the
Burnt spears: the ashes of arrows. They lie there . . .
They don't see or they won't see. They are silent. . . .

The people invent their oppressors: they wish to believe in them.
They wish to be free of their freedom: released from their lib-
    erty:—
The long labor of liberty ended!
                        They lie there!
    [*There is a whisper of sound. The announcer's voice
    is louder.*]

Look! It's his arm! It is rising! His arm's rising!
They're watching his arm as it rises. They stir. They cry.
They cry out. They are shouting. They're shouting with happiness.
Listen! They're shouting like troops in a victory. Listen—

'The city of masterless men has found a master!'

You'd say it was they were the conquerors: they that had conquered.

A ROAR OF VOICES. The city of masterless men has found a master!

The city has fallen!

The city has fallen!

THE VOICE OF THE ANNOUNCER (*flat*). The city has fallen. . . .

QUESTIONS

1. What are the "terrors" of our time of which the Studio Director
    speaks?

2. In his introduction to the first edition of *The Fall of the City,* Mac-
    Leish argues that radio is the most rewarding medium for the poetic
    dramatist to work in because it restores the primacy of the word.
    Everything is created by language alone, not by sets, costumes, and
    actors. How are words used at the beginning of the play to create
    a world? Could the play be improved by stage production? What
    effects are created by language that could not be staged?

3. What is the meaning of using a dead woman to announce the future?

4. Who are the masterless men?

5. What kind of evidence can be produced from the play to show that
    the title refers to no one specific city but to several cities? What
    meaning does the word "city" come to have during the course of the
    play? If a number of cities are amalgamated, or collapsed into one
    another, in what way does this fact affect the meaning of the play?

6. Under what conditions does the Conqueror come?

7. What course of action does the Orator advise? What are his reasons?

8. What does the news of the second messenger tell us about the Orator's
    advice?

9. Discuss the significance of the fact that the crowd and the announcer
    are enthusiastic after each new course of action is presented. Con-
    sider too that after each man has given his counsel the Conqueror
    is reported to be closer.

10. Account for the figure of the Conqueror. What do his armor, his
    manner of walking, and his hollowness mean?

PLOT

"FOR FAITH AND PHILOSOPHY ARE AIR, BUT EVENTS ARE BRASS. AMIDST HIS GRAY PHILOSOPHIZINGS, LIFE BREAKS UPON A MAN LIKE A MORNING."
(Herman Melville, *Pierre.*)

In these lines Melville expresses the sense of life that is fundamental to the drama: that actions have consequences, that life is always in movement, and that the meaning of being only becomes apparent in events. Ophelia's plaintive cry in *Hamlet*, "Lord, we know what we are, but know not what we may be," expresses poignantly the painful knowledge that only in events can we truly discover ourselves. This view is not, of course, peculiar to the drama; most forms of history, the theory of evolution, and philosophical dialectic, assume that life can be defined not by fine analysis of the single static object, but only by observation of the changes through which creation moves. The primacy of movement in the drama is reflected in all basic dramatic terms. The verbs "to act" and "to perform" mean not only "to pretend" but also "to do something." "Drama" derives from a Greek root, the verb *dran,* meaning "to do" or "to act." "Play" comes from the Old English *plegan,* which means in one of its senses "to strive." "Protagonist" and "antagonist," the technical names for the chief character and his opponent, mean literally "the first struggler" (i.e., the principal character) and "the struggler against." The over-all term for the movement in a play is, of course, the *plot,* and, though the word originally had no connection with the concept of action, in modern English it may be used as a verb meaning "to plan to achieve something." With this sense of the word we can begin our discussion of the complex nature of *plot.*

First we must look for the origins of the forces that set the play in motion. The prime mover is usually some tendency inherent in one or both of the two constituents of drama already discussed: in the world of the play or in the characters. When the world of the play—the environment—has an important role, it will show a definite direction, a tendency to complete a pattern. In Shakespeare's *Antony and Cleopatra*, Octavius Caesar describes the world's tendency as a constant ebbing and flowing movement, a ceaseless process of recurring change in which all life is caught up, going "to and back . . . to rot itself with motion." This tendency is at work in everything in the play: men, love, friendship, marriage, empire, and favor, all move, change, dissolve, and ultimately become as "indistinct as water is in water." The pressure of the world here is like the action of the sea upon the beach, consistent only in the destruction of existing shapes and the replacement of them with new shapes, which in their turn are washed away. The world of *Mother Courage* has a similar direction, though its changes are more brutal. Here the nature of the world leads toward an extinction of life, a slowing down of all moving things—the beat of a heart or the wheels of Mother Courage's wagon. The great world outside the doors of the Tesman house in *Hedda Gabler* lacks the single tendency of the worlds of *Antony and Cleopatra* and *Mother Courage*. Its vitality is random, a surging power, which at one moment throws up a mountain range and at another brings a flower to bloom, which brings death to one person and life to another.

It requires some care to discern the direction in which the world of a play is moving, for the actions in which its nature becomes manifest are not always conspicuous, and we often "sense" its presence before we know it. In *Mother Courage* the efforts necessary to move the wagon suggest—for we do not actually see it—the enormous resistance of the world to all movement. And in *Hedda Gabler* the clutter of furniture on stage, which makes free movement difficult, suggests that the social world the furniture represents is crowding in on life, channeling it into restrained and awkward movements. These single effects are not, fortunately, isolated expressions of the world's pressure; they join with other effects to form a larger, more definite pattern, which we must seek out. But the first step is to look closely at individual movements, or countermovements—for resistance to a force moving in one direction constitutes another force—which express the nature of the world. We can expect to find the world's motive expressed in such events as a storm at sea or the swing of a clock's pendulum, in the shape taken by a battle, and in the activities of those characters who do not move of their own volition. Whenever movement is not directed by the human will—in the splashing of rain on a window or in the gradual decay of a body—the world has traced its passage in matter.

John Synge's *Riders to the Sea* is set inside a fisherman's hut on an Atlantic island; throughout the play the roar of the nearby sea can be heard, rising and falling, as it smashes against the rocks of the coast and eats away at the land. During the play news is brought to the hut of a succession of broken boats and drowned men; eventually the smashed body of the last man in the house is carried in wrapped in a sail, dripping with water from the sea in which he has just drowned. The sea, which represents the world, during the play comes to have a monstrous, malevolent life of its own and a will to smash and engulf all that is human and has shape.

In *Riders to the Sea* the principal motive force is the world, but in most plays it is the characters with their motives that are the obvious prime movers. No matter how complex a dramatic character may be, all his nature is usually condensed into one or two fundamental desires toward which he moves. Mother Courage strives to protect her family and her life; this basic motive is visible in her shabby wagon stocked, somehow, with shoddy goods, which she doggedly keeps moving across the stage by putting her children and herself between the shafts. Her feeling for life and her tough courage, which endure despite many defeats, also ring in her song.

> Christians, awake! The winter's gone!
> The snows depart, the dead sleep on.
> And though you may not long survive,
> Get out of bed and look alive!

A character seems always to reach out, trying to realize in his actions and in his speeches the effect that it is his nature to want and to strive for. We become aware of Hedda's desire to be free from involvement, to remain her own possessor, by even such trivial events as her pulling herself out of Miss Tesman's embrace in Act I, saying at the same time, "Oh! Let me go." The same determination appears in her refusal to admit that she is pregnant and in her denial that her husband has any "opportunities" to see her unclothed. Later on her attempts to defy restraint become more obvious and wilder as she urges Lövborg to debauchery and suicide to realize her own longing for an absolute, nihilistic freedom, and as she kills herself to escape Judge Brack.

We have spoken so far as though the identification of a character's basic motive were a simple matter. In fact, a great deal of close attention to everything the character does is required to identify motive, because each new speech, each gesture, in some way qualifies his motive. Often we can hope for only an approximation of the fundamental motive of a given character. In the greatest drama, such as

Sophocles' *Oedipus the King* and Shakespeare's *Hamlet,* the playwright seems to have caught what we might call *the human motive:* the urgent need to perform some peculiarly human act, to realize in space and time some value that lies at the very root of the creature man and distinguishes him from the rest of creation. The perpetual fascination of these plays suggests that such is the case, but while we may "feel" that *the* fundamental human motive is successfully dramatized, it remains extraordinarily difficult to say with exactitude what it is. However, in the play that follows, Sophocles' *Antigone,* the basic motives, though ultimately quite subtle, stand out with a good deal of clarity.

A character's motive is first expressed in a variety of seemingly irrelevant and unimportant details—a comment on the weather, a decision about entertaining, a reaction to an embrace or to the sunshine pouring into a room. The author usually concentrates a number of these details at the beginning of a play, so that in the first scene or two we begin to get the "feel" of the characters and to identify their motives. This section of the play is usually called the *exposition.* (For a fuller definition of this and other technical terms used in this chapter see the glossary.)

By definition a motive is the force that moves a person to seek the satisfaction of some need. (Hunger is the motive forcing us to go out and seek food.) A dramatic motive forces the character into the world where he can realize the goal his motive directs him toward. Hedda Gabler tries to control and destroy Eilert Lövborg; Mother Courage tries to keep her family together and her wagon moving. But as soon as this movement toward realization begins it encounters an opposing force, and *conflict* results. (The part of the play in which the conflict occurs and is developed is known as the *complication.*) The law that every body moving in one direction is opposed by a force exerted in another direction is as fundamental to the drama as it is to physics. That is to say, all drama turns on a conflict of some kind. If the character is complex, the opposing forces may be internal. Hedda Gabler is torn by her conflicting fear of scandal and her desire to live without restraint. Or the force opposing a character's realization of his motive may come from another character, whose own motive causes him to move in a contrary direction. Hedda's desire to control Lövborg meets the counter desire of Mrs. Elvsted, who wishes to protect him. Or the conflict may be between a character and the world, as Mother Courage's desire to protect herself and her children sets her in opposition to a world whose tendency is to bring life to a stop.

This is only an outline of the many possibilities for conflict that the dramatist can exploit in order to generate the forward movement of his play. In the greatest drama, conflicts usually occur on several levels and each conflict mirrors the others. In *Hedda Gabler*, for example, we are first aware of a conflict within the character of Hedda herself, between her excessive desire for respectability and her equally fierce desire for freedom. This same struggle is projected outward in Hedda's efforts to control and use Eilert Lövborg. By listening to his tales about his wild life, by engaging in a carefully controlled flirtation with him, and by sending him out to commit violent acts, she achieves her freedom by proxy. Hedda is actually engaged in conflict with nearly every character in the play—with her husband, his aunt, and Judge Brack; they represent some repression of the free play of instinct, while she struggles for freedom from restraint. The same conflict appears in her struggle with society, represented by her house, by Judge Brack, and by the family into which she has married. She is also at odds with the long historical process—her husband's special subject, which bores her profoundly, but which has resulted in the civilization now represented by Tesman and Judge Brack. The play then is not one but a series of internal and external conflicts between two basic principles of life: freedom vs. suppression, anarchy vs. order, self vs. society.

To recapitulate: the basic forces at work within a play seek fulfillment, and as they do they come into conflict. Out of this conflict, or, more accurately, out of a series of conflicts, the plot emerges. It is necessary at this point to define just what we mean by plot, and this is a most difficult question, about which there is still no general agreement. Perhaps the most helpful way of approaching the problem is to distinguish plot from the motives of the characters and the pressure of the dramatic world in which they move. A character strives in one direction to achieve some particular goal, but his movements are deflected by some other force or forces, such as another character, or society, or the nature of reality, or some countering motive within himself. The plot grows out of these *conflicts,* and we can think of it as a linear progression produced by, but differing in direction from, two or more forces moving in different directions:

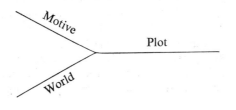

In some plays, of course, the character's motive and the plot are the same, or nearly the same. Everyman sets out to find someone who will accompany him into the grave (i.e., he seeks a power that will save his soul), and after several disappointments he finds Good Works, who goes with him to the place of judgment. What Everyman tries to do is in fact accomplished; the character's motive and the plot are nearly identical. In a naturalistic play the direction in which the world moves will correspond to the plot. August Strindberg's *The Father,* for example, presents a world in which the stronger, more ruthless, and least complex survive by destroying the weaker, who are unfit for some reason to endure the inevitable battle to the death. This struggle is dramatized as a conflict between an intelligent, moral, and idealistic man and his cunning, self-satisfied, and relentless wife for control over their daughter. "The survival of the fittest" is the law that governs this world, and the end is inevitable: the wife keeps the daughter and arranges to have her husband declared insane. He is carried off in a straitjacket still screaming protests, but his opposition to the world has not veered it from its inevitable course. The world makes the plot here; events can only conform to the world's pre-established pattern. Character has little influence on the plot of any play that gives dramatic form to a closed system of belief. Plot in plays of this type will manifest the unimpeded operation of some natural or moral law.

The majority of plays, however, show man's destiny as more mysterious and more dependent on human action. In plays where man helps determine his own fate, the plot is likely to be the result of complex interacting factors, and it will be difficult to separate plot from what the characters are trying to do. The point to remember is that *plot is what actually happens.* The distinction is easy to make in some types of comedy; the fool tries to show that he is a learned man, but succeeds only in showing again and again that he is a fool. The plot here consists of a series of incidents all of which reveal the character to be a fool. But let us take a more complicated case. Hedda Gabler is in conflict with a restraining social world. She reaches out for freedom from all bonds and seems to be successful in her attempts: she refuses to have anything to do with Tesman's family or his career; she controls Mrs. Elvsted; she sends Lövborg out to a drunken party; and she persuades him to commit suicide in what seems to her a truly glorious manner. When she appears to be trapped by Judge Brack, she escapes his control by killing herself. But this is really a description of the way things *seem* to be going, the way Hedda herself understands the progression of events. At the end of the play Lövborg does not die gloriously like an ancient Viking hero or the Greek celebrant in Bacchic rites with vine leaves in his hair, as Hedda had planned, but in a sordid accident in the local bawdyhouse, shot not cleanly through the heart but through the bowels. This brutal, sordid business is the real end toward which Hedda's acts have led. It reveals what she has really been building all the time and forces us to see that her every act has not been the noble, romantic movement toward freedom and joy that Hedda has thought, but a step toward confusion and death. The end reveals the nature of all that has led up to that end. The point at which a character discovers that the effect of his actions has been contrary to what he intended and thought he was achieving was called *the reversal* by Aristotle. Reversal is now usually described as a form of *dramatic irony*.

An even more frightful irony awaits Hedda than Lövborg's grubby death. She has hoped to gain through him that freedom which she longs for, an escape from the boring, restrictive middle-class society of Tesman. Because of her nearly pathological fear of scandal, she dares not seize this freedom for herself, but she hopes to achieve it vicariously through the actions of Lövborg. Actually, the opposite results. Judge Brack recognizes her pistol and uses his knowledge to blackmail her. She is, she says, now "subject" to his "will" and "demands. A slave, a slave then!" Her actions have led not to the freedom she sought, but to slavery. She then kills herself to remain free. But still the irony rings through her act, for the course of action she undertakes to grasp "life" —true life as opposed to the slow stagnation of the Tesman household —leads in fact to death.

Irony based on this kind of exact reversal of intent is not uncommon in great tragedy. Oedipus leaves Corinth to free himself from the prediction of the oracle that he will kill his father and marry his mother, but each step he takes toward escape leads him nearer to the fulfillment of the oracle. Othello sets out to kill Desdemona as a judge executing justice on a criminal, but he ends by discovering that he is a criminal guilty of a ghastly crime, and is forced to judge and execute himself.

Having distinguished the general nature of the plot as the *actual events of a play*, we can now discuss the constituent parts of a plot and the ways in which these are related. Ordinarily, a description of the events that make up a plot will include only the major occurrences. Hedda Gabler returns from her wedding trip, is visited by Mrs. Elvsted who tells her what has happened to Eilert Lövborg. Hedda then meets Lövborg and persuades him to go to Judge Brack's party. Lövborg loses the manuscript of his new book, Tesman finds it, and Hedda burns it. She then persuades Lövborg to kill himself, but he dies in an unpleasant accident, and Judge Brack, knowing of Hedda's implication, tries to control her by threatening scandal. She shoots herself in order to escape. Describing the plot in this way amounts to no more than telling the *story* of the play and provides little or no insight into its meaning. We only recount the obvious.

If plot is to be a useful tool for dramatic analysis, we must refine our definition. We can begin by sharpening the meaning of the word "events." When we recount the *story,* the only events dealt with are the largest, the grossest of happenings. But is not Hedda's reaction to Miss Tesman's bonnet just as much an "event" as her suicide? A plot is actually constructed of a great many events, some ordinary and apparently trivial, others more unusual and obviously critical; if the play is artistically made, every event has meaning. We must accustom ourselves to thinking of the plot as the totality of events, not as a few crucial occurrences surrounded by a number of unimportant, expository details, if we are to understand plot in its most significant sense: a *continuous movement* in a certain direction. This movement in a great play is as much present, though muted, in a movement about a room, the drawing of a shade, the theft of a pair of red boots, as it is in more spectacular events, such as the burning of a manuscript or the destruction of a town. The larger events, the kind we select when telling the story, are the culmination of the smaller events that have preceded them. Firing the pistol at Judge Brack and burning Lövborg's manuscript are crucial events in *Hedda Gabler*—anyone telling the story will probably include them—but these spectacularly destructive acts gain full meaning only when we realize that they serve to focus a number of Hedda's less obviously destructive acts, such as refusing to admit that she is pregnant, treating her husband and his aunt cruelly, rejecting the flowers, and insisting that Tesman's precarious financial and professional affairs are none of her concern.

Plot properly understood, then, includes not only the major events, but *all* the actions and occurrences of the play. Ordinarily, a dramatist plots his play so that a number of these minor events *build up* to an explosive scene in which an obviously crucial event occurs. Ibsen is predictably regular in his use of this plot pattern. The movement in each of the four acts of *Hedda Gabler* builds from quiet, ordinary events at the beginning to some spectacular decision or violent action at the end. Just as each act moves from calm to *crisis,* so the crises of the four acts, taken together, form an ascending scale in which the crisis of each new act is more violent than that of the last, with the *climax* of the play, Hedda's suicide, coming at the very end. One school of dramatic criticism explains this pattern, which is a fairly common one, as the release and tightening of tension necessary to keep the spectator interested. It may do this, but its most important function is to give concrete form to the playwright's sense of the characteristic movement of the affairs of men: long, slow periods in which apparently nothing happens suddenly culminate in a burst of action, which releases the energy built up previously, just as the lightning releases in a flash a slowly accumulated electrical charge.

We must always pay close attention to the particular manner in which scenes of comparative rest and scenes of direct action are spaced, for this is one of the playwright's principal devices for giving form to his sense of the rhythm of life. In some plays—Chekhov's, for example—the body of the work consists of what appear to be trivial happenings. Nothing important seems to happen during the entire play until the end when the powers that have been collecting underneath the surface explode in one violent act. Some modern dramatists have attempted to recreate *only* the dull sameness of lives that *never* reach a climax. In Samuel Beckett's *Waiting for Godot,* for example, the two characters who are waiting for someone to appear when the play begins are still waiting at the end. In *Mother Courage,* however, the brief intervals of comparative peace simply emphasize the fact that life is one crisis after another. Clearly, the plots that Ibsen, Chekhov, Beckett, and Brecht constructed have quite different "rhythms," and these rhythms are a fundamental part of the meaning of the plays. No one rhythm is inherently superior to the others—though Ibsen's is the most traditional. Each reproduces the playwright's estimate of the basic rhythm of life. We can judge its effectiveness only by observing how well it is realized and how well it supports the vision of life created by the other details of the play.

Now that we have extended our definition of plot to cover *all* of the events of the play and have taken into account plot rhythm, we must examine the causal relationship between the events that comprise plot. To describe a plot accurately, it is not enough to recount the events *chronologically;* it is necessary to explain how the events are related. E. M. Forster in his *Aspects of the Novel* says that "The King died and then the Queen died" is a *story,* but that "The King died and then the Queen died of grief" is a plot. In other words, according to Forster, plot requires a cause and effect relationship between events. This common view goes back to the *Poetics,* in which Aristotle wrote that a well-constructed tragic plot "must neither begin nor end at haphazard" but must be a whole.

A whole is that which has a beginning, a middle, and an end. A beginning is that which does not itself follow anything by causal necessity, but after which something naturally is or comes to be. An end, on the contrary, is that which itself naturally follows some other thing, either by necessity, or as a rule, but has nothing following it. A middle is that which follows something, as some other thing follows it.

Most tragic drama has this cause-and-effect progression. Among the plays in this volume *Hedda Gabler* provides us with a perfect example. Because Hedda wants to send Lövborg out as her agent to live for her, to "be a free man," she says, "for all his days," she must first break up his relationship with Mrs. Elvsted, who acts as a restraining, civilizing force on the wild Lövborg. Once Hedda has set her plan in motion, she follows it relentlessly, and each succeeding step—Lövborg's drunkenness, the loss of his manuscript, Hedda's giving him the pistol, his death, and hers—follows inevitably from what has gone before, and not one of the steps could have occurred without the event that preceded it. We may speak therefore of a chain of cause and effect.

The use of such Aristotelian terms as "probable" and "necessary" to describe the relationship of the events that form plot is likely, however, to be in some ways misleading. To say that one event must necessarily follow another in a play is to suggest that this particular sequence is as inevitable as is that which follows the introduction of two parts of hydrogen to one part of oxygen at a particular temperature and pressure. In the latter case only one result is possible, but in a play any event may have a variety of possible consequences. *Hedda Gabler* could end in a number of ways. Instead of shooting herself she might be killed by Tesman; Lövborg might return to kill her before killing himself; or she might kill Judge Brack and be executed for the crime. Speculations of this kind are idle, of course, but they serve to make the point that the *exact* outcome of an event is not as predictable in the drama, or in human life, as it would be in nature. However, no ending is really possible for *Hedda Gabler* that does not involve the death of the protagonist, and Ibsen's choice, suicide, is the most proper form for her death to take because Hedda, by her cruelty to others, her rejection of life, has been "killing herself" piece by piece throughout the play. Her ultimate death by suicide may then be said to be a "probable or necessary" consequence of her previous actions because it reveals fully the nature of her consistent refusal to participate in life. In any probable or necessary sequence, the dramatist is free to choose the particular events he creates, but each event must open up the implications of the preceding events.

No matter what variations are made in this plot pattern, it remains essentially a cause-and-effect progression in which every event in the play results from the initial act; given *that* act, the cause-and-effect type of plot requires that *this* event must follow. But it would be a mistake to assume, as Forster and most critics have, that the cause-and-effect relationship is the only true plot pattern. It is—the only claim Aristotle makes for it in the *Poetics*—the most suitable plot for tragedy. Tragedy assumes a world in which man makes a choice and abides by the inevitable consequences of that choice. Hedda Gabler puts the matter more simply: "They say, as you make your bed, so you must lie." Tragic life is an iron chain of causation in which the characters can never escape the consequences of their acts, which are usually performed in ignorance of what their results will be. Comedy shows life from a different perspective and therefore makes use of a different type of plot. In comedy character is neither so constant nor so important that it can determine the course of events. Men make foolish mistakes in comedy, and for a time it looks as if these mistakes will be fatal, but at the opportune moment some stroke of good luck occurs and all is well. A will is discovered revealing that the poor young man who loves the wealthy girl is really wellborn and incredibly rich; a wealthy uncle, hitherto not heard from, returns to the country at the right moment to reward the virtuous nephew and punish the wicked one; or the wife and child, whom the tyrant thought he had killed in his jealousy twenty years before, miraculously turn out to have been saved. The world of comedy is filled with good fortune and unexpected surprise; therefore the comic plot shows sudden changes and effects that have no causes, at least no cause in what has gone before in the play. The introduction of some person from outside the play or the use of some fortuitous happening to resolve the plot is known as a *deus ex machina,* literally "the god from the machine," referring to the occasional practice in the Greek theater of lowering a god onto the stage from a machine to settle the issues of the play.

The point to be made is that there is no one "right" kind of plot, no type of relationship between events that is inherently superior to all other types. The dramatist connects the events that make up the play in the manner that will best reflect the relationship between events in the world as he understands it. Brecht's *Mother Courage,* for example, has an *episodic plot,* which is usually said, following Aristotle, to be an inferior type of plot arrangement. The more traditional plot arrangement is one in which X causes Y and Y leads inevitably to Z. The plot of *Mother Courage* might be described as X, X, X, since no necessary relationship exists between events. The play consists of a series of scenes each of which displays the same forces in conflict, the brutal world and the sharp-witted Mother Courage trying to preserve life and family. The scenes are related *thematically,* each one presenting a variation on the central theme of the play, but it cannot be said that the situation in Scene 10 is the result of what Mother Courage did in Scene 1. It might be argued that the plot develops, that it moves toward a climax, for the world grinds Mother Courage down—though it never defeats her—robbing her of one child after another until all are gone. But there is no climax in the ordinary sense, for there is no real change: at the end of the play as at the beginning the two ancient antagonists, the world and Mother Courage, destruction and creation, are left locked in a battle that will never cease. In this play the episodic plot is not a failure but a great success, for it shows consistently and perfectly Brecht's view of a world where there is no longer any necessary connection between events, only the certainty that the war in Sweden will occur again in Germany, in Poland, in Bohemia, that the army will always want the young men, that the rapist will always be waiting for the daughter, and that the wagon will always be hard to pull. The more traditional cause-and-effect plot with its pattern of exposition, conflict, and climax, could not render Brecht's concept of the world as a place where the same struggle is always beginning again and where men are not responsible for the situations in which they find themselves.

Having examined the nature of the plot, we must now consider the question of the number of plots possible in a play. Aristotle laid down the rule (and the classicists have maintained it until this day), that the action of a tragedy must be unified, that it cannot consist of episodes or parts "which follow one another without any probable or necessary connection." This has traditionally been interpreted to mean that all the events in a play must contribute to one central plot, that the dramatist must present one story, and one story only. But during the Renaissance the English playwrights frequently built their plays around a *double plot:* two or more plots, which crossed one another only rarely or not at all. In Robert Green's *Friar Bacon and Friar Bungay,* for example, there are two quite distinct plots, one involving the romantic loves of Margaret, "the fair maid of Fressingham," and the other dealing with the magical exploits of Roger Bacon and his apprentice, Friar Bungay. Margaret and Bacon never meet and do not shape in any way one another's destiny. It would at first appear that Greene wanted to provide a mixed fare of love and magic to satisfy the varied interests of his audience, but a closer look at the play reveals that Greene is suggesting that both beauty and magic—or the learning that magic represents—are related, god-given powers, which must be used with care and for proper purposes.

Shakespeare's double plots are never so separated. For example, the plot involving Gloucester and his two sons is a distinct plot in *King Lear,* running parallel to the plot of Lear and his three daughters. But Gloucester is one of Lear's nobles; he encounters the King at several points on their respective journeys, and at one point he risks his life to save him. The double, or multiple, plot is managed in the same way in *I Henry IV.* Here three plots are distinguishable: the first dealing with Falstaff and the Boarshead Tavern, a second centering on King Henry and the palace at Westminster, and a third involving Hotspur in his northern castle. The characters in each plot are intensely aware of what is going on in the other plots, and at the conclusion of the play the characters from the three plots join at the great battle of Shrewsbury where Hotspur is killed. By strict standards *I Henry IV* is not a well-constructed play, for the three plot lines are distinguishable throughout the play, and this means that the action is not one and unified. But does it mean this? When we look closely at these three plots we discover that Shakespeare has paralleled them in a remarkable fashion. A plot to rob some travelers planned in the Boarshead Tavern is paralleled by a plot to steal a kingdom planned in the palace. A stately council scene at Westminster is followed by a mock council in the alehouse. The preparations for a battle in which chivalric knights anticipate winning great honor is followed by a cynical preparation for the same battle in which an officer commissioned to draft a company of soldiers takes bribes to release the well-to-do and able, enlisting only the dregs of the population with the cynical comment that they will fill a ditch as well as their betters.

What Shakespeare and other Elizabethan playwrights discovered was a new kind of plot unity, not the Aristotelian unity of a single chain of "probable or necessary" events, but a unity based on the principle of *parallelism.* Different kinds of people do the same things, plot a theft, prepare for war, hold a council. The single plot is duplicated and distributed to all levels of society.

The values derived from this type of plot construction will depend on the skill and the interests of the particular playwright, but it will be useful to outline a few of the major possibilities. First of all, the double plot has a potential for making universal the image of life presented in the play by extending its range of reference. The duplication of the same problems and the same patterns of events on two or more social levels suggests that these particular problems and patterns are common to all humanity rather than peculiar to one person at one time. The double plot also allows the playwright to provide a perspective on his plots or to suggest a complicated attitude toward them. To juxtapose a plot to overthrow a king with a plot to hold up some travelers on the highway is to suggest that the difference between usurpation and armed robbery is not so great as we might think, that the difference is one of degree, not of kind. But comments of this nature always work in both directions. If Falstaff's cynically realistic comments about the nature of war mock Hotspur's romanticism, then Hotspur's idealism, courage, and energy force us to question Falstaff's military "prudence," his reduction of all life to a whole skin and a full belly.

The most obvious form of the double plot disappeared from the stage about the middle of the seventeenth century, but in one way or another the double plot has always been and still is a standard dramatic technique, although the different strands may no longer stand out so clearly as the three plot lines of *I Henry IV*. *Hedda Gabler* appears to be a play plotted according to the Aristotelian formula: one plot line only, and that consisting of a necessary or probable series of events. But though they intertwine, it is still possible to discern several plots moving through the play. Mrs. Elvsted is trapped, as Hedda is, in a marriage of convenience. She married Sheriff Elvsted because he needed a housekeeper and she had no other place to go; Hedda, getting too old to play the belle any longer and with no other offers, marries Tesman, who also was moved not by love but by her beauty and the opportunity to marry someone from a family that was socially superior to his own. Both women hate the domestic cages in which they are placed, but both face scandal if they leave. Both see in Lövborg a man who transcends their dreary circumstances. But here, because of their differing natures, their paths (plots) divide. Mrs. Elvsted first nourishes the creative instincts in Lövborg, restores him to normal life, and, finally, courageously leaves her home to follow and protect him. Hedda, motivated by her conflicting fear of scandal and her fascination with absolute freedom, first encourages Lövborg and then refuses to take him as a lover; after he leaves and ruins himself, she recaptures him and sends him out to drunkenness and death. It might appear that Hedda has triumphed and Mrs. Elvsted has lost; actually, the endings of the two plots force a different judgment. Mrs. Elvsted, though she has lost Lövborg, remains creative, for she still has his manuscript, which will permit her, with Tesman's aid, to reconstruct "the future of civilization." Hedda loses Lövborg, her freedom, her husband, and finally her life. Since her way has been the way of death, it leads to death. Mrs. Elvsted's way has been the way of creation and it leads to creation. Dissimilar natures faced with similar circumstances have achieved different results, and the plot of Mrs. Elvsted provides a perspective on the plot of Hedda.

Since both characters are involved in one central plot turning on the struggle for Eilert Lövborg, it may be technically correct to consider the play as having only a single plot. But it is often useful for critical purposes to think of each major character as having a separate plot and to investigate the similarities and differences of these plots. Mother Courage and her three children face the same problems and, acting on different values, come to different conclusions. Her three children die: Eilif through valor, Swiss Cheese through honesty, and Kattrin through idealism; while resourcefulness, cunning, and pertinacity keep their mother alive. But can we conclude from these facts that the plot unambiguously demonstrates the superiority of Mother Courage's values and actions? Brecht would disagree violently, but does not Kattrin's dying to save the people of a town, and particularly its children, suggest that there are values more important than survival? The play really leaves us with an unanswerable question: Who has met this brutal world of war and struggle most successfully: the dead girl or the old woman staggering on, pulling her wagon to another battlefield?

It may be a simple enough matter to see *what really happens* in *Hedda Gabler*—a woman destroys herself by cutting her ties with the world and with the rest of humanity—but in plays like *Mother Courage* the plots often lead not to a flat definition of the meaning of a particular course of action, but to a sharply etched image of an abiding human problem that defies any easy solution. Are the bodies of Romeo and Juliet lying together in the gloomy tomb of the Capulets an image of triumph or defeat? Have they won a battle with life and made their love eternal? Or are they merely the pitiful victims of their own impetuousness and of the hatred that surrounds them? The play poses the question rather than answers it, suggesting that life, at least tragic life, is always double in nature, always a mystery, and that what we gain in one way we must pay for in another.

In summary: a plot is composed of a series of related events. These events are initiated by the characters trying to realize their motives, or by the world pressing in the direction which it is its nature to move in, or by some interaction of these forces. What happens in the play happens to the characters and to the world, and is manifested in their changed conditions and situations. But the dramatic focus is not finally on the characters or the world; it is on "what happens," on the plot, on the fundamental pattern of movement and change, which is given substantial form by the events of the play. What the dramatist imitates, as Aristotle pointed out, is "action," and the plot is his primary mode of imitation. Everything in a play exists to give form to the plot, and the plot in turn represents, or imitates, what a dramatist conceives as the recurring movement of life, and particularly human life, in time.

ANTIGONE

BY

SOPHOCLES

In *Antigone* plot stands out as a distinct element of construction, quite separate from the characters and the world of the play. The major characters, Antigone and Creon, are surely and definitely, if not elaborately, drawn, and their motives are sharply defined. The play also has a vivid setting: the center of the city of Thebes, which has just been attacked by a fierce and determined army. During the course of the action the body of the leader of that army lies unburied in the sun just outside the gates, a fact that no one in the play can forget. But despite the clarity and economy with which the characters and the world are constructed, and the ways in which they help to shape events, the dramatic focus is not on them.

It used to be common for critics to argue that *Antigone* is a poorly constructed play because the heroine disappears halfway through the action, and we hear of her only by report after that time. Such an argument makes sense only if one believes the play to be a study of the character of Antigone, which it is not. If one argues that it is a character study of Creon, then one is faced with the difficulty that he emerges as the central figure only after Antigone has been sent to her death. Had Sophocles been interested in providing a dramatic study of a particular type of character, he would have focused his play on that character from beginning to end, as Ibsen concentrated his play on Hedda Gabler. A careful reading of *Antigone* shows that neither Antigone nor Creon singly is the true subject, but that the play is designed to show a pattern of events, a pattern that emerges in the life of Antigone *and* in the life of Creon, as well as in the lives of the brothers Eteocles and Polyneices and a number of other figures mentioned, chiefly by the Chorus, during the course of the action. Choose one good to the exclusion of another—and it seems to be the nature of great men to do so—the play shows, and *this* will inevitably happen. *This* is the plot of the play, and the play is shaped in all of its parts to reveal and define this plot.

Sophocles (496–406 B.C.) lived in the great age of Athens. He grew up in the brightness of the day that dawned with the Athenian defeat of the Persians at Marathon and Salamis, and he died before his city was finally defeated by Sparta and her allies. During his lifetime the Athenians brought to perfection not only a political and artistic ideal, but an ideal of character, an *ethos*. The key term in the Greeks' new definition of man was *harmony*, a balance and adjustment of thought and action that led to proportionate expression of man's many faculties and abilities. The ideal man was philosopher, artist, soldier, and politician because all of these activities expressed him, and because in each he could shape himself and his world to that harmonious balance of form which eliminated all violent exaggeration and disordered enthusiasm. It is against this ideal of completeness, of proportion, and of control—in short, of wisdom—that the characters of Antigone and Creon and their ultimate fate must be seen.

But *Antigone* is not a "problem play." That is, it does not merely show us wrong conduct and provide a forceful object lesson in what happens when men become "unbalanced" and pursue one value to the exclusion of other equally necessary values. Instead, it suggests that it is in the very nature of men—at least of heroes—to choose this course, even though they know better; and, furthermore, that political and social situations regularly occur that require a choice of one value because other values directly conflict with it.

Antigone was presented at the annual festival of Dionysius (March–April) around the year 442 B.C. A description of the Greek theater and of the occasion of Greek dramatic productions appears in the glossary.

PERSONS REPRESENTED

ANTIGONE
ISMENE
EURYDICE
CREON

HAIMON
TEIRESIAS
A SENTRY
A MESSENGER

CHORUS

Scene: *Before the palace of Creon, King of Thebes. A central double door, and two lateral doors. A platform extends the length of the façade, and from this platform three steps lead down into the "orchestra," or chorus-ground.* Time: *dawn of the day after the repulse of the Argive army from the assault on Thebes.*

The Antigone of Sophocles: An English Version by Dudley Fitts and Robert Fitzgerald, copyright 1939 by Harcourt, Brace & World, Inc. and reprinted with their permission.

Prologue

[ANTIGONE *and* ISMENE *enter from the central door of the Palace.*]

ANTIGONE. Ismene, dear sister,
　　You would think that we had already suffered enough
　　For the curse on Oedipus:
　　I cannot imagine any grief
　　That you and I have not gone through. And now—
　　Have they told you of the new decree of our King Creon?
ISMENE. I have heard nothing: I know
　　That two sisters lost two brothers, a double death
　　In a single hour; and I know that the Argive army
　　Fled in the night; but beyond this, nothing.
ANTIGONE. I thought so. And that is why I wanted you
　　To come out here with me. There is something we must do.
ISMENE. Why do you speak so strangely?
ANTIGONE. Listen, Ismene:
　　Creon buried our brother Eteocles
　　With military honors, gave him a soldier's funeral,
　　And it was right that he should; but Polyneices,
　　Who fought as bravely and died as miserably,—
　　They say that Creon has sworn
　　No one shall bury him, no one mourn for him,
　　But his body must lie in the fields, a sweet treasure
　　For carrion birds to find as they search for food.
　　That is what they say, and our good Creon is coming here
　　To announce it publicly; and the penalty—
　　Stoning to death in the public square!
　　　　　　　　　　　　　　　　There it is,
　　And now you can prove what you are:
　　A true sister, or a traitor to your family.

ISMENE. Antigone, you are mad! What could I possibly do?
ANTIGONE. You must decide whether you will help me or not.
ISMENE. I do not understand you. Help you in what?
ANTIGONE. Ismene, I am going to bury him. Will you come?
ISMENE. Bury him! You have just said the new law forbids it.
ANTIGONE. He is my brother. And he is your brother, too.
ISMENE. But think of the danger! Think what Creon will do!
ANTIGONE. Creon is not strong enough to stand in my way.
ISMENE. Ah sister!
    Oedipus died, everyone hating him
    For what his own search brought to light, his eyes
    Ripped out by his own hand; and Iocaste died,
    His mother and wife at once: she twisted the cords
    That strangled her life; and our two brothers died,
    Each killed by the other's sword. And we are left:
    But oh, Antigone,
    Think how much more terrible than these
    Our own death would be if we should go against Creon
    And do what he has forbidden! We are only women,
    We cannot fight with men, Antigone!
    The law is strong, we must give in to the law
    In this thing, and in worse. I beg the Dead
    To forgive me, but I am helpless: I must yield
    To those in authority. And I think it is dangerous business
    To be always meddling.
ANTIGONE.   If that is what you think,
    I should not want you, even if you asked to come.
    You have made your choice, you can be what you want to be.
    But I will bury him; and if I must die,
    I say that this crime is holy: I shall lie down
    With him in death, and I shall be as dear
    To him as he to me.
             It is the dead,
    Not the living, who make the longest demands:
    We die for ever . . .
           You may do as you like,
    Since apparently the laws of the gods mean nothing to you.
ISMENE. They mean a great deal to me; but I have no strength
    To break laws that were made for the public good.
ANTIGONE. That must be your excuse, I suppose. But as for me,
    I will bury the brother I love.
ISMENE.   Antigone,
    I am so afraid for you!
ANTIGONE.   You need not be:
    You have yourself to consider, after all.

ISMENE. But no one must hear of this, you must tell no one!
   I will keep it a secret, I promise!
ANTIGONE.   Oh tell it! Tell everyone!
   Think how they'll hate you when it all comes out
   If they learn that you knew about it all the time!
ISMENE. So fiery! You should be cold with fear.
ANTIGONE. Perhaps. But I am doing only what I must.
ISMENE. But can you do it? I say that you cannot.
ANTIGONE. Very well: when my strength gives out, I shall do no more.
ISMENE. Impossible things should not be tried at all.
ANTIGONE. Go away, Ismene:
   I shall be hating you soon, and the dead will too,
   For your words are hateful. Leave me my foolish plan:
   I am not afraid of the danger; if it means death,
   It will not be the worst of deaths—death without honor.
ISMENE. Go then, if you feel that you must.
   You are unwise,
   But a loyal friend indeed to those who love you.

                    [*Exit into the Palace.* ANTIGONE *goes off, L.*]
                    [*Enter the* CHORUS.]

Párados

STROPHE 1

CHORUS. Now the long blade of the sun, lying
    Level east to west, touches with glory
    Thebes of the Seven Gates. Open, unlidded
    Eye of golden day! O marching light
    Across the eddy and rush of Dirce's stream,
    Striking the white shields of the enemy
    Thrown headlong backward from the blaze of morning!
CHORAGOS. Polyneices their commander
    Roused them with windy phrases,
    He the wild eagle screaming
    Insults above our land,
    His wings their shields of snow,
    His crest their marshalled helms.

ANTISTROPHE 1

CHORUS. Against our seven gates in a yawning ring
    The famished spears came onward in the night;
    But before his jaws were sated with our blood,
    Or pinefire took the garland of our towers,
    He was thrown back; and as he turned, great Thebes—
    No tender victim for his noisy power—
    Rose like a dragon behind him, shouting war.
CHORAGOS. For God hates utterly
    The bray of bragging tongues;
    And when he beheld their smiling,
    Their swagger of golden helms,
    The frown of his thunder blasted
    Their first man from our walls.

STROPHE 2

CHORUS. We heard his shout of triumph high in the air
      Turn to a scream; far out in a flaming arc
      He fell with his windy torch, and the earth struck him.
      And others storming in fury no less than his
      Found shock of death in the dusty joy of battle.
CHORAGOS. Seven captains at seven gates
      Yielded their clanging arms to the god
      That bends the battle-line and breaks it.
      These two only, brothers in blood,
      Face to face in matchless rage,
      Mirroring each the other's death,
      Clashed in long combat.

ANTISTROPHE 2

CHORUS. But now in the beautiful morning of victory
      Let Thebes of the many chariots sing for joy!
      With hearts for dancing we'll take leave of war:
      Our temples shall be sweet with hymns of praise,
      And the long night shall echo with our chorus.

Scene I

CHORAGOS. But now at last our new King is coming:
　　Creon of Thebes, Menoikeus' son.
　　In this auspicious dawn of his reign
　　What are the new complexities
　　That shifting Fate has woven for him?
　　What is his counsel? Why has he summoned
　　The old men to hear him?
　　　　[*Enter* CREON *from the Palace, C. He addresses the*
　　　　　　CHORUS *from the top step.*]
CREON. Gentlemen: I have the honor to inform you that our Ship
　　of State, which recent storms have threatened to destroy, has
　　come safely to harbor at last, guided by the merciful wisdom
　　of Heaven. I have summoned you here this morning because I
　　know that I can depend upon you: your devotion to King
　　Laïos was absolute; you never hesitated in your duty to our
　　late ruler Oedipus; and when Oedipus died, your loyalty was
　　transferred to his children. Unfortunately, as you know, his
　　two sons, the princes Eteocles and Polyneices, have killed each
　　other in battle; and I, as the next in blood, have succeeded to
　　the full power of the throne.
　　I am aware, of course, that no Ruler can expect complete loyalty
　　from his subjects until he has been tested in office. Neverthe-
　　less, I say to you at the very outset that I have nothing but
　　contempt for the kind of Governor who is afraid, for what-
　　ever reason, to follow the course that he knows is best for the
　　State; and as for the man who sets private friendship above
　　the public welfare,—I have no use for him, either. I call God
　　to witness that if I saw my country headed for ruin, I should
　　not be afraid to speak out plainly; and I need hardly remind
　　you that I would never have any dealings with an enemy of

the people. No one values friendship more highly than I; but
we must remember that friends made at the risk of wrecking
our Ship are not real friends at all.

These are my principles, at any rate, and that is why I have made
the following decision concerning the sons of Oedipus: Eteocles,
who died as a man should die, fighting for his country, is to
be buried with full military honors, with all the ceremony that
is usual when the greatest heroes die; but his brother Polyneices,
who broke his exile to come back with fire and sword against
his native city and the shrines of his fathers' gods, whose one
idea was to spill the blood of his blood and sell his own people
into slavery—Polyneices, I say, is to have no burial: no man
is to touch him or say the least prayer for him; he shall lie on
the plain, unburied; and the birds and the scavenging dogs can
do with him whatever they like.

This is my command, and you can see the wisdom behind it. As
long as I am King, no traitor is going to be honored with the
loyal man. But whoever shows by word and deed that he is
on the side of the State,—he shall have my respect while he is
living, and my reverence when he is dead.

CHORAGOS. If that is your will, Creon son of Menoikeus,
    You have the right to enforce it: we are yours.
CREON. That is my will. Take care that you do your part.
CHORAGOS. We are old men: let the younger ones carry it out.
CREON. I do not mean that: the sentries have been appointed.
CHORAGOS. Then what is it that you would have us do?
CREON. You will give no support to whoever breaks this law.
CHORAGOS. Only a crazy man is in love with death!
CREON. And death it is; yet money talks, and the wisest
    Have sometimes been known to count a few coins too many.
                    [Enter SENTRY from L.]
SENTRY. I'll not say that I'm out of breath from running, King, be-
    cause every time I stopped to think about what I have to tell
    you, I felt like going back. And all the time a voice kept saying,
    "You fool, don't you know you're walking straight into trou-
    ble?"; and then another voice: "Yes, but if you let somebody
    else get the news to Creon first, it will be even worse than that
    for you!" But good sense won out, at least I hope it was good
    sense, and here I am with a story that makes no sense at all; but
    I'll tell it anyhow, because, as they say, what's going to happen's
    going to happen, and—
CREON. Come to the point. What have you to say?
SENTRY. I did not do it. I did not see who did it. You must not punish
    me for what someone else has done.

CREON. A comprehensive defense! More effective, perhaps,
 If I knew its purpose. Come: what is it?
SENTRY. A dreadful thing . . . I don't know how to put it—
CREON. Out with it!
SENTRY.   Well, then;
 The dead man—
     Polyneices—
   [*Pause. The* SENTRY *is overcome, fumbles for words.*
      CREON *waits impassively.*]
        out there—
          someone,—
 New dust on the slimy flesh!
     [*Pause. No sign from* CREON.]
 Someone has given it burial that way, and
 Gone . . .
   [*Long pause.* CREON *finally speaks with deadly con-*
       trol:]
CREON. And the man who dared do this?
SENTRY.   I swear I
 Do not know! You must believe me!
         Listen:
 The ground was dry, not a sign of digging, no,
 Not a wheeltrack in the dust, no trace of anyone.
 It was when they relieved us this morning: and one of them,
 The corporal, pointed to it.
       There it was,
 The strangest—
    Look:
 The body, just mounded over with light dust: you see?
 Not buried really, but as if they'd covered it
 Just enough for the ghost's peace. And no sign
 Of dogs or any wild animal that had been there.

 And then what a scene there was! Every man of us
 Accusing the other: we all proved the other man did it,
 We all had proof that we could not have done it.
 We were ready to take hot iron in our hands,
 Walk through fire, swear by all the gods,
 It was not I!
 I do not know who it was, but it was not I!
   [CREON'S *rage has been mounting steadily, but the*
     SENTRY *is too intent upon his story to notice it.*]
 And then, when this came to nothing, someone said
 A thing that silenced us and made us stare

Down at the ground: you had to be told the news,
And one of us had to do it! We threw the dice,
And the bad luck fell to me. So here I am,
No happier to be here than you are to have me:
Nobody likes the man who brings bad news.

CHORAGOS. I have been wondering, King: can it be that the gods have
  done this?

[*Furiously*]

CREON. Stop!
    Must you doddering wrecks
  Go out of your heads entirely? "The gods!"
  Intolerable!
  The gods favor this corpse? Why? How had he served them?
  Tried to loot their temples, burn their images,
  Yes, and the whole State, and its laws with it!
  Is it your senile opinion that the gods love to honor bad men?
  A pious thought!—
                    No, from the very beginning
  There have been those who have whispered together,
  Stiff-necked anarchists, putting their heads together,
  Scheming against me in alleys. These are the men,
  And they have bribed my own guard to do this thing.

[*Sententiously*]

Money!
There's nothing in the world so demoralizing as money.
Down go your cities,
Homes gone, men gone, honest hearts corrupted,
Crookedness of all kinds, and all for money!

[*To* SENTRY]

                                But you—!
I swear by God and by the throne of God,
The man who has done this thing shall pay for it!
Find that man, bring him here to me, or your death
Will be the least of your problems: I'll string you up
Alive, and there will be certain ways to make you
Discover your employer before you die;
And the process may teach you a lesson you seem to have missed:
The dearest profit is sometimes all too dear:
That depends on the source. Do you understand me?
A fortune won is often misfortune.

SENTRY. King, may I speak?

CREON.   Your very voice distresses me.

SENTRY. Are you sure that it is my voice, and not your conscience?

CREON. By God, he wants to analyze me now!

SENTRY. It is not what I say, but what has been done, that hurts you.
CREON. You talk too much.
SENTRY.   Maybe; but I've done nothing.
CREON. Sold your soul for some silver: that's all you've done.
SENTRY. How dreadful it is when the right judge judges wrong!
CREON. Your figures of speech
    May entertain you now; but unless you bring me the man,
    You will get little profit from them in the end.
                        [*Exit* CREON *into the Palace.*]
SENTRY. "Bring me the man"—!
    I'd like nothing better than bringing him the man!
    But bring him or not, you have seen the last of me here.
    At any rate, I am safe!   [*Exit* SENTRY.]

Ode I

CHORUS. Numberless are the world's wonders, but none
    More wonderful than man; the stormgray sea
    Yields to his prows, the huge crests bear him high;
    Earth, holy and inexhaustible, is graven
    With shining furrows where his plows have gone
    Year after year, the timeless labor of stallions.

The lightboned birds and beasts that cling to cover,
The lithe fish lighting their reaches of dim water,
All are taken, tamed in the net of his mind;
The lion on the hill, the wild horse windy-maned,
Resign to him; and his blunt yoke has broken
The sultry shoulders of the mountain bull.

Words also, and thought as rapid as air,
He fashions to his good use; statecraft is his,
And his the skill that deflects the arrows of snow,
The spears of winter rain: from every wind
He has made himself secure—from all but one:
In the late wind of death he cannot stand.

O clear intelligence, force beyond all measure!
O fate of man, working both good and evil!
When the laws are kept, how proudly his city stands!
When the laws are broken, what of his city then?
Never may the anárchic man find rest at my hearth,
Never be it said that my thoughts are his thoughts.

Scene 2

[*Re-enter* SENTRY *leading* ANTIGONE.]
CHORAGOS. What does this mean? Surely this captive woman
    Is the Princess, Antigone. Why should she be taken?
SENTRY. Here is the one who did it! We caught her
    In the very act of burying him.—Where is Creon?
CHORAGOS. Just coming from the house.
                      [*Enter* CREON, *C.*]
CREON.   What has happened?
    Why have you come back so soon?
                  [*Expansively*]
SENTRY.   O King,
    A man should never be too sure of anything: I would have sworn
    That you'd not see me here again: your anger
    Frightened me so, and the things you threatened me with;
    But how could I tell then
    That I'd be able to solve the case so soon?

    No dice-throwing this time: I was only too glad to come!

    Here is this woman. She is the guilty one:
    We found her trying to bury him.
    Take her, then; question her; judge her as you will.
    I am through with the whole thing now, and glád óf it.
CREON. But this is Antigone! Why have you brought her here?
SENTRY. She was burying him, I tell you!
                  [*Severely*]
CREON.   Is this the truth?
SENTRY. I saw her with my own eyes. Can I say more?
CREON. The details: come, tell me quickly!
SENTRY.   It was like this:
    After those terrible threats of yours, King,

We went back and brushed the dust away from the body.
The flesh was soft by now, and stinking,
So we sat on a hill to windward and kept guard.
No napping this time! We kept each other awake.
But nothing happened until the white round sun
Whirled in the center of the round sky over us:
Then, suddenly,
A storm of dust roared up from the earth, and the sky
Went out, the plain vanished with all its trees
In the stinging dark. We closed our eyes and endured it.
The whirlwind lasted a long time, but it passed;
And then we looked, and there was Antigone!
I have seen
A mother bird come back to a stripped nest, heard
Her crying bitterly a broken note or two
For the young ones stolen. Just so, when this girl
Found the bare corpse, and all her love's work wasted,
She wept, and cried on heaven to damn the hands
That had done this thing.

                    And then she brought more dust
And sprinkled wine three times for her brother's ghost.

We ran and took her at once. She was not afraid,
Not even when we charged her with what she had done.
She denied nothing.

             And this was a comfort to me,
And some uneasiness: for it is a good thing
To escape from death, but it is no great pleasure
To bring death to a friend.

                Yet I always say
There is nothing so comfortable as your own safe skin!

               [*Slowly, dangerously*]

CREON. And you, Antigone,
    You with your head hanging,—do you confess this thing?
ANTIGONE. I do. I deny nothing.

            [*To* SENTRY:]

CREON.   You may go.   [*Exit* SENTRY.]

            [*To* ANTIGONE:]

Tell me, tell me briefly:
    Had you heard my proclamation touching this matter?
ANTIGONE. It was public. Could I help hearing it?
CREON. And yet you dared defy the law.
ANTGIONE.   I dared.
    It was not God's proclamation. That final Justice
    That rules the world below makes no such laws.

Your edict, King, was strong,
But all your strength is weakness itself against
The immortal unrecorded laws of God.
They are not merely now: they were, and shall be,
Operative for ever, beyond man utterly.

I knew I must die, even without your decree:
I am only mortal. And if I must die
Now, before it is my time to die,
Surely this is no hardship: can anyone
Living, as I live, with evil all about me,
Think Death less than a friend? This death of mine
Is of no importance; but if I had left my brother
Lying in death unburied, I should have suffered.
Now I do not.
               You smile at me. Ah Creon,
Think me a fool, if you like; but it may well be
That a fool convicts me of folly.

CHORAGOS. Like father, like daughter: both headstrong, deaf to reason!
    She has never learned to yield.

CREON.   She has much to learn.
    The inflexible heart breaks first, the toughest iron
Cracks first, and the wildest horses bend their necks
At the pull of the smallest curb.
                    Pride? In a slave?
This girl is guilty of a double insolence,
Breaking the given laws and boasting of it.
Who is the man here,
She or I, if this crime goes unpunished?
Sister's child, or more than sister's child,
Or closer yet in blood—she and her sister
Win bitter death for this!
                [*To servants:*]
                Go, some of you,
Arrest Ismene. I accuse her equally.
Bring her: you will find her sniffling in the house there.

Her mind's a traitor: crimes kept in the dark
Cry for light, and the guardian brain shudders;
But how much worse than this
Is brazen boasting of barefaced anarchy!

ANTIGONE. Creon, what more do you want than my death?

CREON.   Nothing.
    That gives me everything.

ANTIGONE.   Then I beg you: kill me.

This talking is a great weariness: your words
Are distasteful to me, and I am sure that mine
Seem so to you. And yet they should not seem so:
I should have praise and honor for what I have done.
All these men here would praise me
Were their lips not frozen shut with fear of you.
                    [*Bitterly*]
Ah the good fortune of kings,
    Licensed to say and do whatever they please!
CREON. You are alone here in that opinion.
ANTIGONE. No, they are with me. But they keep their tongues in leash.
CREON. Maybe. But you are guilty, and they are not.
ANTIGONE. There is no guilt in reverence for the dead.
CREON. But Eteocles—was he not your brother too?
ANTIGONE. My brother too.
CREON.   And you insult his memory?
                    [*Softly*]
ANTIGONE. The dead man would not say that I insult it.
CREON. He would: for you honor a traitor as much as him.
ANTIGONE. His own brother, traitor or not, and equal in blood.
CREON. He made war on his country. Eteocles defended it.
ANTIGONE. Nevertheless, there are honors due all the dead.
CREON. But not the same for the wicked as for the just.
ANTIGONE. Ah Creon, Creon,
    Which of us can say what the gods hold wicked?
CREON. An enemy is an enemy, even dead.
ANTIGONE. It is my nature to join in love, not hate.
                    [*Finally losing patience*]
CREON. Go join them, then; if you must have your love,
    Find it in hell!
CHORAGOS. But see, Ismene comes:
                    [*Enter* ISMENE, *guarded.*]
    Those tears are sisterly, the cloud
    That shadows her eyes rains down gentle sorrow.
CREON. You too, Ismene,
    Snake in my ordered house, sucking my blood
    Stealthily—and all the time I never knew
    That these two sisters were aiming at my throne!
                                                Ismene,
    Do you confess your share in this crime, or deny it?
    Answer me.
ISMENE. Yes, if she will let me say so. I am guilty.
                    [*Coldly*]
ANTIGONE. No, Ismene. You have no right to say so.
    You would not help me, and I will not have you help me.

ISMENE. But now I know what you meant; and I am here
> To join you, to take my share of punishment.
ANTIGONE. The dead man and the gods who rule the dead
> Know whose act this was. Words are not friends.
ISMENE. Do you refuse me, Antigone? I want to die with you:
> I too have a duty that I must discharge to the dead.
ANTIGONE. You shall not lessen my death by sharing it.
ISMENE. What do I care for life when you are dead?
ANTIGONE. Ask Creon. You're always hanging on his opinions.
ISMENE. You are laughing at me. Why, Antigone?
ANTIGONE. It's a joyless laughter, Ismene.
ISMENE.   But can I do nothing?
ANTIGONE. Yes. Save yourself. I shall not envy you.
> There are those who will praise you; I shall have honor, too.
ISMENE. But we are equally guilty!
ANTIGONE.   No more, Ismene.
> You are alive, but I belong to Death.
> > [*To the* CHORUS:]
CREON. Gentlemen, I beg you to observe these girls:
> One has just now lost her mind; the other,
> It seems, has never had a mind at all.
ISMENE. Grief teaches the steadiest minds to waver, King.
CREON. Yours certainly did, when you assumed guilt with the guilty!
ISMENE. But how could I go on living without her?
CREON.   You are.
> She is already dead.
ISMENE.   But your own son's bride!
CREON. There are places enough for him to push his plow.
> I want no wicked women for my sons!
ISMENE. O dearest Haimon, how your father wrongs you!
CREON. I've had enough of your childish talk of marriage!
CHORAGOS. Do you really intend to steal this girl from your son?
CREON. No; Death will do that for me.
CHORAGOS.   Then she must die?
> > [*Ironically*]
CREON. You dazzle me.
> > —But enough of this talk!
> > [*To* GUARDS:]
> You, there, take them away and guard them well:
> For they are but women, and even brave men run
> When they see Death coming.
> > [*Exeunt* ISMENE, ANTIGONE, *and* GUARDS.]

Ode 2

CHORUS. Fortunate is the man who has never tasted God's vengeance!
Where once the anger of heaven has struck, that house is shaken
For ever: damnation rises behind each child
Like a wave cresting out of the black northeast,
When the long darkness under sea roars up
And bursts drumming death upon the windwhipped sand.

ANTISTROPHE 1

I have seen this gathering sorrow from time long past
Loom upon Oedipus' children: generation from generation
Takes the compulsive rage of the enemy god.
So lately this last flower of Oedipus' line
Drank the sunlight! but now a passionate word
And a handful of dust have closed up all its beauty.

STROPHE 2

What mortal arrogance
Transcends the wrath of Zeus?
Sleep cannot lull him, nor the effortless long months
Of the timeless gods: but he is young for ever,
And his house is the shining day of high Olympos.
All that is and shall be,
And all the past, is his.
No pride on earth is free of the curse of heaven.

ANTISTROPHE 2

The straying dreams of men
May bring them ghosts of joy:

But as they drowse, the waking embers burn them;
Or they walk with fíxed éyes, as blind men walk.
But the ancient wisdom speaks for our own time:
Fate works most for woe
With Folly's fairest show.
Man's little pleasure is the spring of sorrow.

Scene 3

CHORAGOS. But here is Haimon, King, the last of all your sons.
Is it grief for Antigone that brings him here,
And bitterness as being robbed of his bride?
[*Enter* HAIMON.]
CREON. We shall soon see, and no need of diviners.

—Son,
You have heard my final judgment on that girl:
Have you come here hating me, or have you come
With deference and with love, whatever I do?
HAIMON. I am your son, father. You are my guide.
You make things clear for me, and I obey you.
No marriage means more to me than your continuing wisdom.
CREON. Good. That is the way to behave: subordinate
Everything else, my son, to your father's will.
This is what a man prays for, that he may get
Sons attentive and dutiful in his house,
Each one hating his father's enemies,
Honoring his father's friends. But if his sons
Fail him, if they turn out unprofitably,
What has he fathered but trouble for himself
And amusement for the malicious?

So you are right
Not to lose your head over this woman.
Your pleasure with her would soon grow cold, Haimon,
And then you'd have a hellcat in bed and elsewhere.
Let her find her husband in Hell!
Of all the people in this city, only she
Has had contempt for my law and broken it.

Do you want me to show myself weak before the people?
Or to break my sworn word? No, and I will not.
The woman dies.
I suppose she'll plead "family ties." Well, let her.
If I permit my own family to rebel,
How shall I earn the world's obedience?
Show me the man who keeps his house in hand,
He's fit for public authority.
                              I'll have no dealings
With law-breakers, critics of the government:
Whoever is chosen to govern should be obeyed—
Must be obeyed, in all things, great and small,
Just and unjust! O Haimon,
The man who knows how to obey, and that man only,
Knows how to give commands when the time comes.
You can depend on him, no matter how fast
The spears come: he's a good soldier, he'll stick it out.

Anarchy, anarchy! Show me a greater evil!
This is why cities tumble and the great houses rain down,
This is what scatters armies!

No, no: good lives are made so by discipline.
We keep the laws then, and the lawmakers,
And no woman shall seduce us. If we must lose,
Let's lose to a man, at least! Is a woman stronger than we?
CHORAGOS. Unless time has rusted my wits,
    What you say, King, is said with point and dignity.
                    [*Boyishly earnest*]
HAIMON. Father:
    Reason is God's crowning gift to man, and you are right
    To warn me against losing mine. I cannot say—
    I hope that I shall never want to say!—that you
    Have reasoned badly. Yet there are other men
    Who can reason, too; and their opinions might be helpful.
    You are not in a position to know everything
    That people say or do, or what they feel:
    Your temper terrifies them—everyone
    Will tell you only what you like to hear.
    But I, at any rate, can listen; and I have heard them
    Muttering and whispering in the dark about this girl.
    They say no woman has ever, so unreasonably,
    Died so shameful a death for a generous act:
    "She covered her brother's body. Is this indecent?

She kept him from dogs and vultures. Is this a crime?
Death?—She should have all the honor that we can give her!"

This is the way they talk out there in the city.

You must believe me:
Nothing is closer to me than your happiness.
What could be closer? Must not any son
Value his father's fortune as his father does his?
I beg you, do not be unchangeable:
Do not believe that you alone can be right.
The man who thinks that,
The man who maintains that only he has the power
To reason correctly, the gift to speak, the soul—
A man like that, when you know him, turns out empty.

It is not reason never to yield to reason!

In flood time you can see how some trees bend,
And because they bend, even their twigs are safe,
While stubborn trees are torn up, roots and all.
And the same thing happens in sailing:
Make your sheet fast, never slacken,—and over you go,
Head over heels and under: and there's your voyage.
Forget you are angry! Let yourself be moved!
I know I am young; but please let me say this:
The ideal condition
Would be, I admit, that men should be right by instinct;
But since we are all too likely to go astray,
The reasonable thing is to learn from those who can teach.
CHORAGOS. You will do well to listen to him, King,
     If what he says is sensible. And you, Haimon,
     Must listen to your father.—Both speak well.
CREON. You consider it right for a man of my years and experience
     To go to school to a boy?
HAIMON.   It is not right
     If I am wrong. But if I am young, and right,
     What does my age matter?
CREON. You think it right to stand up for an anarchist?
HAIMON. Not at all. I pay no respect to criminals.
CREON. Then she is not a criminal?
HAIMON. The City would deny it, to a man.
CREON. And the City proposes to teach me how to rule?
HAIMON. Ah. Who is it that's talking like a boy now?
CREON. My voice is the one voice giving orders in this City!

HAIMON. It is no City if it takes orders from one voice.
CREON. The State is the King!
HAIMON.   Yes, if the State is a desert.
                    [*Pause*]
CREON. This boy, it seems, has sold out to a woman.
HAIMON. If you are a woman: my concern is only for you.
CREON. So? Your "concern"! In a public brawl with your father!
HAIMON. How about you, in a public brawl with justice?
CREON. With justice, when all that I do is within my rights?
HAIMON. You have no right to trample on God's right.
                    [*Completely out of control*]
CREON. Fool, adolescent fool! Taken in by a woman!
HAIMON. You'll never see me taken in by anything vile.
CREON. Every word you say is for her!
                    [*Quietly, darkly*]
HAIMON.   And for you.
     And for me. And for the gods under the earth.
CREON. You'll never marry her while she lives.
HAIMON. Then she must die.—But her death will cause another.
CREON. Another?
     Have you lost your senses? Is this an open threat?
HAIMON. There is no threat in speaking to emptiness.
CREON. I swear you'll regret this superior tone of yours!
     You are the empty one!
HAIMON.   If you were not my father,
     I'd say you were perverse.
CREON. You girlstruck fool, don't play at words with me!
HAIMON. I am sorry. You prefer silence.
CREON.   Now, by God—!
     I swear, by all the gods in heaven above us,
     You'll watch it, I swear you shall!
                    [*To the* SERVANTS:]
                          Bring her out!
     Bring the woman out! Let her die before his eyes!
     Here, this instant, with her bridegroom beside her!
HAIMON. Not here, no; she will not die here, King.
     And you will never see my face again.
     Go on raving as long as you've a friend to endure you.
                                        [*Exit* HAIMON.]
CHORAGOS. Gone, gone.
     Creon, a young man in a rage is dangerous!
CREON. Let him do, or dream to do, more than a man can.
     He shall not save these girls from death.
CHORAGOS.   These girls?
     You have sentenced them both?

CREON.   No, you are right.
I will not kill the one whose hands are clean.
CHORAGOS. But Antigone?

[*Somberly*]
CREON.   I will carry her far away
Out there in the wilderness, and lock her
Living in a vault of stone. She shall have food,
As the custom is, to absolve the State of her death.
And there let her pray to the gods of hell:
They are her only gods:
Perhaps they will show her an escape from death,
Or she may learn,
                        though late,
That piety shown the dead is pity in vain.   [*Exit* CREON.]

Ode 3

CHORUS. Love, unconquerable
   Waster of rich men, keeper
   Of warm lights and all-night vigil
   In the soft face of a girl:
   Sea-wanderer, forest-visitor!
   Even the pure Immortals cannot escape you,
   And mortal man, in his one day's dusk,
   Trembles before your glory.

   Surely you swerve upon ruin
   The just man's consenting heart,
   As here you have made bright anger
   Strike between father and son—
   And none has conquered but Love!
   A girl's glánce wórking the will of heaven:
   Pleasure to her alone who mocks us,
   Merciless Aphrodite.

Scene 4

[*As* ANTIGONE *enters guarded.*]

CHORAGOS. But I can no longer stand in awe of this,
　　Nor, seeing what I see, keep back my tears.
　　Here is Antigone, passing to that chamber
　　Where all find sleep at last.

STROPHE 1

ANTIGONE. Look upon me, friends, and pity me
　　Turning back at the night's edge to say
　　Good-by to the sun that shines for me no longer;
　　Now sleepy Death
　　Summons me down to Acheron, that cold shore:
　　There is no bridesong there, nor any music.
CHORUS. Yet not unpraised, not without a kind of honor,
　　You walk at last into the underworld;
　　Untouched by sickness, broken by no sword.
　　What woman has ever found your way to death?

ANTISTROPHE 1

ANTIGONE. How often I have heard the story of Niobe,
　　Tantalos' wretched daughter, how the stone
　　Clung fast about her, ivy-close: and they say
　　The rain falls endlessly
　　And sifting soft snow; her tears are never done.
　　I feel the loneliness of her death in mine.
CHORUS. But she was born of heaven, and you
　　Are woman, woman-born. If her death is yours,
　　A mortal woman's, is this not for you
　　Glory in our world and in the world beyond?

STROPHE 2

ANTIGONE. You laugh at me. Ah, friends, friends,
　　Can you not wait until I am dead? O Thebes,
　　O men many-charioted, in love with Fortune,
　　Dear springs of Dirce, sacred Theban grove,
　　Be witnesses for me, denied all pity,
　　Unjustly judged! and think a word of love
　　For her whose path turns
　　Under dark earth, where there are no more tears.
CHORUS. You have passed beyond human daring and come at last
　　Into a place of stone where Justice sits.
　　I cannot tell
　　What shape of your father's guilt appears in this.

ANTISTROPHE 2

ANTIGONE. You have touched it at last: that bridal bed
　　Unspeakable, horror of son and mother mingling:
　　Their crime, infection of all our family!
　　O Oedipus, father and brother!
　　Your marriage strikes from the grave to murder mine.
　　I have been a stranger here in my own land:
　　All my life
　　The blasphemy of my birth has followed me.
CHORUS. Reverence is a virtue, but strength
　　Lives in established law: that must prevail.
　　You have made your choice,
　　Your death is the doing of your conscious hand.

EPODE

ANTIGONE. Then let me go, since all your words are bitter,
　　And the very light of the sun is cold to me.
　　Lead me to my vigil, where I must have
　　Neither love nor lamentation; no song, but silence.
　　　　　　[CREON interrupts impatiently.]
CREON. If dirges and planned lamentations could put off death,
　　Men would be singing for ever.
　　　　　　[To the SERVANTS:]
　　　　　　　　　Take her, go!
　　You know your orders: take her to the vault
　　And leave her alone there. And if she lives or dies,
　　That's her affair, not ours: our hands are clean.
ANTIGONE. O tomb, vaulted bride-bed in eternal rock,
　　Soon I shall be with my own again
　　Where Persephone welcomes the thin ghosts underground:

And I shall see my father again, and you, mother,
And dearest Polyneices—
                              dearest indeed
To me, since it was my hand
That washed him clean and poured the ritual wine:
And my reward is death before my time!

And yet, as men's hearts know, I have done no wrong,
I have not sinned before God. Or if I have,
I shall know the truth in death. But if the guilt
Lies upon Creon who judged me, then, I pray,
May his punishment equal my own.

CHORAGOS.   O passionate heart,
     Unyielding, tormented still by the same winds!
CREON. Her guards shall have good cause to regret their delaying.
ANTIGONE. Ah! That voice is like the voice of death!
CREON. I can give you no reason to think you are mistaken.
ANTIGONE. Thebes, and you my fathers' gods,
     And rules of Thebes, you see me now, the last
     Unhappy daughter of a line of kings,
     Your kings, led away to death. You will remember
     What things I suffer, and at what men's hands,
     Because I would not transgress the laws of heaven.
               [*To the* GUARDS, *simply*:]
     Come: let us wait no longer.

                              [*Exit* ANTIGONE, *L., guarded.*]

Ode 4

STROPHE 1

CHORUS. All Danae's beauty was locked away
    In a brazen cell where the sunlight could not come:
    A small room, still as any grave, enclosed her.
    Yet she was a princess too,
    And Zeus in a rain of gold poured love upon her.
    O child, child,
    No power in wealth or war
    Or tough sea-blackened ships
    Can prevail against untiring Destiny!

ANTISTROPHE 1

And Dryas' son also, that furious king,
    Bore the god's prisoning anger for his pride:
    Sealed up by Dionysos in deaf stone,
    His madness died among echoes.
    So at the last he learned what dreadful power
    His tongue had mocked:
    For he had profaned the revels,
    And fired the wrath of the nine
    Implacable Sisters that love the sound of the flute.

STROPHE 2

And old men tell a half-remembered tale
    Of horror done where a dark ledge splits the sea
    And a double surf beats on the gráy shóres:
    How a king's new woman, sick
    With hatred for the queen he had imprisoned,
    Ripped out his two sons' eyes with her bloody hands

While grinning Ares watched the shuttle plunge
Four times: four blind wounds crying for revenge,

ANTISTROPHE 2

Crying, tears and blood mingled.—Piteously born,
Those sons whose mother was of heavenly birth!
Her father was the god of the North Wind
And she was cradled by gales,
She raced with young colts on the glittering hills
And walked untrammeled in the open light:
But in her marriage deathless Fate found means
To build a tomb like yours for all her joy.

Scene 5

[Enter blind TEIRESIAS, *led by a boy. The opening speeches of* TEIRESIAS *should be in singsong contrast to the realistic lines of* CREON.*]*

TEIRESIAS. This is the way the blind man comes, Princes, Princes,
  Lock-step, two heads lit by the eyes of one.

CREON. What new thing have you to tell us, old Teiresias?

TEIRESIAS. I have much to tell you: listen to the prophet, Creon.

CREON. I am not aware that I have ever failed to listen.

TEIRESIAS. Then you have done wisely, King, and ruled well.

CREON. I admit my debt to you. But what have you to say?

TEIRESIAS. This, Creon: you stand once more on the edge of fate.

CREON. What do you mean? Your words are a kind of dread.

TEIRESIAS. Listen, Creon:
  I was sitting in my chair of augury, at the place
  Where the birds gather about me. They were all a-chatter,
  As is their habit, when suddenly I heard
  A strange note in their jangling, a scream, a
  Whirring fury; I knew that they were fighting,
  Tearing each other, dying
  In a whirlwind of wings clashing. And I was afraid.
  I began the rites of burnt-offering at the altar,
  But Hephaistos failed me: instead of bright flame,
  There was only the sputtering slime of the fat thigh-flesh
  Melting: the entrails dissolved in gray smoke,
  The bare bone burst from the welter. And no blaze!

  This was a sign from heaven. My boy described it,
  Seeing for me as I see for others.

  I tell you, Creon, you yourself have brought
  This new calamity upon us. Our hearths and altars

Are stained with the corruption of dogs and carrion birds
That glut themselves on the corpse of Oedipus' son.
The gods are deaf when we pray to them, their fire
Recoils from our offering, their birds of omen
Have no cry of comfort, for they are gorged
With the thick blood of the dead.
                       O my son,
These are no trifles! Think: all men make mistakes,
But a good man yields when he knows his course is wrong,
And repairs the evil. The only crime is pride.

Give in to the dead man, then: do not fight with a corpse—
What glory is it to kill a man who is dead?
Think, I beg you:
It is for your own good that I speak as I do.
You should be able to yield for your own good.

CREON. It seems that prophets have made me their especial province.
    All my life long
    I have been a kind of butt for the dull arrows
    Of doddering fortune-tellers!
                      No, Teiresias:
    If your birds—if the great eagles of God himself
    Should carry him stinking bit by bit to heaven,
    I would not yield. I am not afraid of pollution:
    No man can defile the gods.
                  Do what you will,
    Go into business, make money, speculate
    In India gold or that synthetic gold from Sardis,
    Get rich otherwise than by my consent to bury him.
    Teiresias, it is a sorry thing when a wise man
    Sells his wisdom, lets out his words for hire!
TEIRESIAS. Ah Creon! Is there no man left in the world—
CREON. To do what?—Come, let's have the aphorism!
TEIRESIAS. No man who knows that wisdom outweighs any wealth?
CREON. As surely as bribes are baser than any baseness.
TEIRESIAS. You are sick, Creon! You are deathly sick!
CREON. As you say: it is not my place to challenge a prophet.
TEIRESIAS. Yet you have said my prophecy is for sale.
CREON. The generation of prophets has always loved gold.
TEIRESIAS. The generation of kings has always loved brass.
CREON. You forget yourself! You are speaking to your King.
TEIRESIAS. I know it. You are a king because of me.
CREON. You have a certain skill; but you have sold out.
TEIRESIAS. King, you will drive me to words that—

CREON.   Say them, say them!
     Only remember: I will not pay you for them.
TEIRESIAS. No, you will find them too costly.
CREON.   No doubt. Speak:
     Whatever you say, you will not change my will.
TEIRESIAS. Then take this, and take it to heart!
     The time is not far off when you shall pay back
     Corpse for corpse, flesh of your own flesh.
     You have thrust the child of this world into living night,
     You have kept from the gods below the child that is theirs:
     The one in a grave before her death, the other,
     Dead, denied the grave. This is your crime:
     And the Furies and the dark gods of Hell
     Are swift with terrible punishment for you.

     Do you want to buy me now, Creon?
                           Not many days,
     And your house will be full of men and women weeping,
     And curses will be hurled at you from far
     Cities grieving for sons unburied, left to rot
     Before the walls of Thebes.

     These are my arrows, Creon: they are all for you.

               [*To* BOY:]
     But come, child: lead me home.
     Let him waste his fine anger upon younger men.
     Maybe he will learn at last
     To control a wiser tongue in a better head.   [*Exit* TEIRESIAS.]
CHORAGOS. The old man has gone, King, but his words
     Remain to plague us. I am old, too,
     But I cannot remember that he was ever false.
CREON. That is true. . . . It troubles me.
     Oh it is hard to give in! but it is worse
     To risk everything for stubborn pride.
CHORAGOS. Creon: take my advice.
CREON.   What shall I do?
CHORAGOS. Go quickly: free Antigone from her vault
     And build a tomb for the body of Polyneices.
CREON. You would have me do this?
CHORAGOS.   Creon, yes!
     And it must be done at once: God moves
     Swiftly to cancel the folly of stubborn men.
CREON. It is hard to deny the heart! But I
     Will do it: I will not fight with destiny.

CHORAGOS. You must go yourself, you cannot leave it to others.
CREON. I will go.
    —Bring axes, servants:
Come with me to the tomb. I buried her, I
Will set her free.
     Oh quickly!
My mind misgives—
The laws of the gods are mighty, and a man must serve them
To the last day of his life!   [*Exit* CREON.]

Paean

CHORAGOS. God of many names
CHORUS.   O Iacchos
                                                    son
   of Kadmeian Sémele
              O born of the Thunder!
   Guardian of the West
             Regent
   of Eleusis' plain
           O Prince of maenad Thebes
   and the Dragon Field by rippling Ismenos:

CHORAGOS. God of many names
CHORUS.   the flame of torches
   flares on our hills
         the nymphs of Iacchos
   dance at the spring of Castalia:

   from the vine-close mountain
            come ah come in ivy:
   Evohé evohé! sings through the streets of Thebes

CHORAGOS. God of many names
CHORUS.   Iacchos of Thebes
   heavenly Child
         of Sémele bride of the Thunderer!
   The shadow of plague is upon us:
            come

with clement feet
                    oh come from Parnasos
    down the long slopes
                    across the lamenting water

ANTISTROPHE 2

CHORAGOS. Io Fire! Chorister of the throbbing stars!
    O purest among the voices of the night!
    Thou son of God, blaze for us!
CHORUS. Come with choric rapture of circling Maenads
    Who cry *Io Iacche!*
                    God of many names!

Éxodos

[*Enter* MESSENGER, *L.*]

MESSENGER. Men of the line of Kadmos, you who live
    Near Amphion's citadel:
                     I cannot say
    Of any condition of human life "This is fixed,
    This is clearly good, or bad." Fate raises up,
    And Fate casts down the happy and unhappy alike:
    No man can foretell his Fate.
                     Take the case of Creon:
    Creon was happy once, as I count happiness:
    Victorious in battle, sole governor of the land,
    Fortunate father of children nobly born.
    And now it has all gone from him! Who can say
    That a man is still alive when his life's joy fails?
    He is a walking dead man. Grant him rich,
    Let him live like a king in his great house:
    If his pleasure is gone, I would not give
    So much as the shadow of smoke for all he owns.
CHORAGOS. Your words hint at sorrow: what is your news for us?
MESSENGER. They are dead. The living are guilty of their death.
CHORAGOS. Who is guilty? Who is dead? Speak!
MESSENGER.   Haimon.
    Haimon is dead; and the hand that killed him
    Is his own hand.
CHORAGOS.   His father's? or his own?
MESSENGER. His own, driven mad by the murder his father had done.
CHORAGOS. Teiresias, Teiresias, how clearly you saw it all!
MESSENGER. This is my news: you must draw what conclusions you can
    from it.

CHORAGOS. But look: Eurydice, our Queen:
    Has she overheard us?

                [*Enter* EURYDICE *from the Palace, C.*]

EURYDICE. I have heard something, friends:
    As I was unlocking the gate of Pallas' shrine,
    For I needed her help today, I heard a voice
    Telling of some new sorrow. And I fainted
    There at the temple with all my maidens about me.
    But speak again: whatever it is, I can bear it:
    Grief and I are no strangers.

MESSENGER.   Dearest Lady,
    I will tell you plainly all that I have seen.
    I shall not try to comfort you: what is the use,
    Since comfort could lie only in what is not true?
    The truth is always best.

                    I went with Creon
    To the outer plain where Polyneices was lying,
    No friend to pity him, his body shredded by dogs.
    We made our prayers in that place to Hecate
    And Pluto, that they would be merciful. And we bathed
    The corpse with holy water, and we brought
    Fresh-broken branches to burn what was left of it,
    And upon the urn we heaped up a towering barrow
    Of the earth of his own land.

                  When we were done, we ran
    To the vault where Antigone lay on her couch of stone.
    One of the servants had gone ahead,
    And while he was yet far off he heard a voice
    Grieving within the chamber, and he came back
    And told Creon. And as the King went closer,
    The air was full of wailing, the words lost,
    And he begged us to make all haste. "Am I a prophet?"
    He said, weeping, "And must I walk this road,
    The saddest of all that I have gone before?
    My son's voice calls me on. Oh quickly, quickly!
    Look through the crevice there, and tell me
    If it is Haimon, or some deception of the gods!"
    We obeyed; and in the cavern's farthest corner
    We saw her lying:
    She had made a noose of her fine linen veil
    And hanged herself. Haimon lay beside her,
    His arms about her waist, lamenting her,
    His love lost under ground, crying out
    That his father had stolen her away from him.
    When Creon saw him the tears rushed to his eyes

And he called to him: "What have you done, child? Speak to me.
What are you thinking that makes your eyes so strange?
O my son, my son, I come to you on my knees!"
But Haimon spat in his face. He said not a word,
Staring—
               And suddenly drew his sword
And lunged. Creon shrank back, the blade missed; and the boy,
Desperate against himself, drove it half its length
Into his own side, and fell. And as he died
He gathered Antigone close in his arms again,
Choking, his blood bright red on her white cheek.
And now he lies dead with the dead, and she is his
At last, his bride in the houses of the dead.
                      [*Exit* EURYDICE *into the Palace.*]

CHORAGOS. She has left us without a word. What can this mean?
MESSENGER. It troubles me, too; yet she knows what is best,
    Her grief is too great for public lamentation,
    And doubtless she has gone to her chamber to weep
    For her dead son, leading her maidens in his dirge.
CHORAGOS. It may be so: but I fear this deep silence
                  [*Pause*]
MESSENGER. I will see what she is doing. I will go in.
                [*Exit* MESSENGER *into the Palace.*]
     [*Enter* CREON *with attendants, bearing* HAIMON'S
               body.]

CHORAGOS. But here is the King himself: oh look at him,
    Bearing his own damnation in his arms.
CREON. Nothing you say can touch me any more.
    My own blind heart has brought me
    From darkness to final darkness. Here you see
    The father murdering, the murdered son—
    And all my civic wisdom!

    Haimon my son, so young, so young to die,
    I was the fool, not you; and you died for me.
CHORAGOS. That is the truth; but you were late in learning it.
CREON. This truth is hard to bear. Surely a god
    Has crushed me beneath the hugest weight of heaven.
    And driven me headlong a barbaric way
    To trample out the thing I held most dear.

    The pains that men will take to come to pain!
            [*Enter* MESSENGER *from the Palace.*]
MESSENGER. The burden you carry in your hands is heavy,
    But it is not all: you will find more in your house.

CREON. What burden worse than this shall I find there?
MESSENGER. The Queen is dead.
CREON. O port of death, deaf world,
　　　Is there no pity for me? And you, Angel of evil,
　　　I was dead, and your words are death again.
　　　Is it true, boy? Can it be true?
　　　Is my wife dead? Has death bred death?
MESSENGER. You can see for yourself.
　　　　　[*The doors are opened, and the body of* EURYDICE *is
　　　　　　　　disclosed within.*]
CREON. Oh pity!
　　　All true, all true, and more than I can bear!
　　　O my wife, my son!
MESSENGER. She stood before the altar, and her heart
　　　Welcomed the knife her own hand guided,
　　　And a great cry burst from her lips for Megareus dead,
　　　And for Haimon dead, her sons; and her last breath
　　　Was a curse for their father, the murderer of her sons.
　　　And she fell, and the dark flowed in through her closing eyes
CREON. O God, I am sick with fear.
　　　Are there no swords here? Has no one a blow for me?
MESSENGER. Her curse is upon you for the deaths of both.
CREON. It is right that it should be. I alone am guilty.
　　　I know it, and I say it. Lead me in,
　　　Quickly, friends.
　　　I have neither life nor substance. Lead me in.
CHORAGOS. You are right, if there can be right in so much wrong.
　　　The briefest way is best in a world of sorrow.
CREON. Let it come,
　　　Let death come quickly, and be kind to me.
　　　I would not ever see the sun again.
CHORAGOS. All that will come when it will; but we, meanwhile,
　　　Have much to do. Leave the future to itself.
CREON. All my heart was in that prayer!
CHORAGOS. Then do not pray any more: the sky is deaf.
CREON. Lead me away. I have been rash and foolish.
　　　I have killed my son and my wife.
　　　I look for comfort; my comfort lies here dead.
　　　Whatever my hands have touched has come to nothing.
　　　Fate has brought all my pride to a thought of dust.
　　　　　[*As* CREON *is being led into the house, the* CHORAGOS
　　　　　　advances and speaks directly to the audience.]
CHORAGOS. There is no happiness where there is no wisdom;
　　　No wisdom but in submission to the gods.
　　　Big words are always punished,
　　　And proud men in old age learn to be wise.

TRANSLATOR'S COMMENTARY

Et quod propriè dicitur in idiomate Picardorum horrescit apud Burgundos, immò apud Gallicos viciniores; quanto igitur magis accidet hoc apud linguas diversas! Quapropter quod bene factum est in unâ linguâ non est possibile ut transferatur in aliam secundum ejus proprietatem quam habuerit in priori.

ROGER BACON

I. In the Commentary appended to our version of Euripides' *Alcestis* we wrote: "Our object was to make the *Alcestis* clear and credible in English. Since it is a poem, it had to be made clear as a poem; and since it is a play, it had to be made credible as a play. We set for ourselves no fixed rules of translation or of dramatic verse: often we found the best English equivalent in a literalness which extended to the texture and rhythm of the Greek phrasing; at other times we were forced to a more or less free paraphrase in order to achieve effects which the Greek conveyed in ways impossible to English. Consequently, this version of the *Alcestis* is not a 'translation' in the classroom sense of the word. The careful reader, comparing our text with the original, will discover alterations, suppressions, expansions—a word, perhaps, drawn out into a phrase, or a phrase condensed to a word: a way of saying things that is admittedly not Euripidean, if by Euripidean one means a translation *ad verbum expressa* of Euripides' poem. In defense we can say only that our purpose was to reach—and, if possible, to render precisely—the emotional and sensible meaning in every speech in the play; we could not follow the Greek word for word, where to do so would have been weak and therefore false." We have been guided by the same principles in making this version of the *Antigone*.

II. We have made cuts only when it seemed absolutely necessary. The most notable excision is that of a passage of sixteen lines beginning with 904 (Antigone's long speech near the end of Scene 4), which has been bracketed as spurious, either in whole or in part, by the best critics. Aristotle quotes two verses from it, which proves, as Professor Jebb points out, that if it is an interpolation it must have been made soon after Sophocles' death, possibly by his son Iophon. However that may be, it is dismal stuff. Antigone is made to interrupt her lamentation by a series of limping verses whose sense is as discordant as their sound. We quote the Oxford Translation, the style of which is for once wholly adequate to the occasion:

And yet, in the opinion of those who have just sentiments, I honoured you [Polyneices] aright. For neither, though I had been the mother of children, nor though my husband dying, had mouldered away, would I have undertaken this toil against the will of the citizens. On account of what law do I say this? There would have been another husband for me if the first died, and if I lost my child there would have been another from another man! but my father and my mother being laid in the grave, it is impossible a brother should ever be born to me. On the principle of such a law, having preferred you, my brother, to all other considerations, I seemed to Creon to commit a sin, and to dare what was dreadful. And now, seizing me by force, he thus leads me away, having never enjoyed the nuptial bed, nor heard the nuptial lay, nor having gained the lot of marriage, nor of rearing my children; but thus I, an unhappy woman, deserted by my friends, go, while alive, to the cavern of the dead.

There are other excisions of less importance. Perhaps the discussion of one of them will serve to explain them all. Near the end of the *Éxodos,* Creon is told of his wife's suicide. The Messenger has five very graphic lines describing Eurydice's suicide, to which Creon responds with an outburst of dread and grief; yet two lines later, as if he had not heard the first time, he is asking the Messenger how Eurydice died. The Messenger replies that she stabbed herself to the heart. There is no evidence that the question and reply are interpolations: on the contrary, they serve the definite purpose of filling out the iambic interlude between two lyric strophes; but in a modern version which does not attempt to reproduce the strophic structure of this *Kommós* they merely clog the dialogue. Therefore we have skipped them; and the occasional suppression of short passages throughout the play is based upon similar considerations.

III. In a like manner, we have not hesitated to use free paraphrase when a literal rendering of the Greek would result in obscurity. Again, the discussion of a specific instance may illuminate the whole question.

After Antigone has been led away to death, the Chorus, taking a hint from her having compared her own fate to that of Niobe, proceeds to elaborate the stories of mythological persons who have suffered similar punishment. The Fourth Ode cites Danaë, Lycurgos, the son of Dryas, and Cleopatra, the daughter of Boreas and wife of the Thracian king Phineus. Only Danaë is mentioned by name; the others are allusively identified. The difficulty arises from the allusive method. Sophocles' audience would be certain to recognize the allusions, but that is not true of ours. To what extent can we depend upon the audience's recognition in a day when, to quote Mr. I. A. Richards, "we can no longer refer with any confidence to any episode in the Bible, or to any nursery tale or any piece of mythology"? We can assume that the story of Danaë is still current; but Lycurgos is forgotten now, and the sordid Phineus-Cleopatra-Eidothea affair no longer stirs so much as an echo. Nevertheless, Sophocles devotes two of his four strophes to this Cleopatra, and he does it in so oblique a manner that 'translation' is out of the question. We have therefore rendered these strophes with such slight additions to the Greek sense as might convey an equivalent suggestion of fable to a modern audience.

IV. The Chorus is composed, says the Scholiast, of "certain old men of Thebes": leading citizens ("O men many-charioted, in love with Fortune") to whom Creon addresses his fatal decree, and from whom he later takes advice. Sophocles' Chorus numbered fifteen, including the Choragos, or Leader; its function was to chant the Odes and, in the person of the Choragos, to participate in the action. In a version designed for the modern stage certain changes are inevitable. It cannot be urged too strongly that the words of the Odes must be intelligible to the audience; and they are almost certain not to be intelligible if they are chanted in unison by so large a group, with or without musical accompaniment. It is suggested, then, that in producing this play no attempt be made to follow the ancient choric method. There should be no dancing. The *Párodos,* for example, should be a solemn but almost unnoticeable evolution of moving or still patterns accompanied by a drum-beat whose rhythm may be derived from the cadence of the Ode itself. The lines given to the Chorus in the Odes should probably be spoken by single voices. The only accompaniment should be percussion: we follow Allan Sly's score of the *Alcestis* in suggesting a large side drum from which the snares have been removed, to be struck with two felt-headed tympani sticks, one hard, one soft.

V. A careful production might make successful use of masks. They should be of the Benda type used in the production of O'Neill's *The Great God Brown:* lifelike, closely fitting the contours of the face, and valuable only as they give the effect of immobility to character. On no account should there be any attempt to reproduce the Greek mask, which was larger than life size and served a function non-existent on the modern stage—the amplification of voice and mood for projection to the distant seats of the outdoor theater.

If masks are used at all, they might well be allotted only to those characters who are somewhat depersonalized by official position or discipline: Creon, Teiresias, the Chorus and Choragos, possibly the Messenger. By this rule, Antigone has no mask; neither has Ismene, Haimon, nor Eurydice. If Creon is masked, we see no objection, in art or feeling, to the symbolic removal of his mask before he returns with the dead body of his son.

QUESTIONS

PROLOGUE

1. What is Antigone's expressed purpose in the Prologue? How does Sophocles use a contrasting character here to emphasize her determination to achieve her end?
2. Usually the expressed purpose of a dramatic character is only the objective form manifesting a more basic motive. Is it possible to discover from Antigone's lines what her basic motive is here?

PÁRODOS

3. The relationship of the Chorus to the action in Greek tragedy is complicated, but the first step in understanding this relationship is to ask how the subject they discuss and their attitude toward it bear on the characters and actions of the preceding scene. What is the connection here between the exultant description of the destruction of Polyneices and his army and the scene between Antigone and Ismene?
4. What does Antigone's "family tree" tell us about her nature and her prospects?

SCENE 1

5. How would you describe Creon's speech? Do his values accord with his manner of speaking?
6. A character reveals a good deal of himself in the motives he consistently attributes to others. What is Creon's repeated explanation of the actions of others? How does this fit in with the other details of his character?
7. What function, other than to bring the news of Polyneices' burial, does the messenger serve? Consider the meaning of the manner in which he was chosen to carry the message to Creon.
8. By the end of Scene 1 the conflict of Antigone and Creon has occurred and the initial action has been taken. Re-examine Antigone and Creon and try to state what general principles, or values, are represented by the two characters, and why a conflict between them is inevitable. What enduring human problem is imaged in this conflict?

ODE 1

9. What attitude toward Man is expressed in the Ode? Is Man simple or complex?
10. In this ode the prime mover seems to be the human will alone. Does the "world" have any effect on the course of events in the play?

SCENE 2

11. When Antigone returns to bury Polyneices, her movements are for a time covered by a whirlwind. Is this merely a realistic detail that makes plausible Antigone's ability to reach the body undetected, or is there some relationship between her and the whirlwind?
12. Both Antigone and Creon present themselves as the selfless defenders of "the law." What evidence in this scene suggests that they both have additional motives?

ODE 2

13. The Chorus is made up of the elderly men of Thebes who move and speak as a group, except when the Chorus Leader speaks for all of them. Can you see any relationship between these facts and the explanation they give in this Ode for the disaster that has struck Antigone?

SCENE 3

14. In one sense the word "necessary" in Aristotle's prescription for the tragic plot as a chain of "necessary or probable" events means the inevitable unfolding of the full significance of taking a particular stand or committing a particular act. Can the disruption of the marriage plans be seen as such an elaboration of Antigone's original decision to bury the body of Polyneices and Creon's determination to leave it unburied?
15. What is Creon's view of women? Is there any significance in the sex of the two major characters? Would it do just as well to make Antigone a man?

ODE 3

16. Can you trace in the first three odes a progression in the attitude of the Chorus toward the events to which they are spectators?

SCENE 4

17. Why does Antigone say, "You laugh at me" to the Chorus after they have tried to console her by describing the glory of her death? Has her attitude changed in the interval between this scene and her last appearance?
18. Is the Chorus right when they tell Antigone, "Your death is the doing

of your conscious hand"? Pay particular attention to the word "conscious."

19. Do the arrangements Creon makes for Antigone's death tell us anything about her nature? That is, does the *scene* of her death suit her nature as Hedda Gabler's does?

ODE 4

20. In what way do the tragic tales referred to by the Chorus in this ode constitute abbreviated *double* plots? Do all these stories parallel Antigone's situation, or do some of them serve as contrasts? (For identification of the persons referred to here see Section III of the Translator's Commentary.)

SCENE 5

21. What course of action does Teiresias recommend and why does Creon refuse to accept it at first? What causes him to change his mind?

22. What does the fact that the seer is blind contribute to the meaning of what he says? Look back at the people Creon has encountered and see if they have anything in common.

PAEAN

23. Why should the Chorus invoke the god at this moment when Creon has gone to free Antigone and all should be well?

ÉXODOS

24. The messenger reporting the disasters in Creon's house says, "Fate raises up, and Fate casts down the happy and unhappy alike. . . ." For him, then, the plot of *Antigone* reveals the movements of Fortune's wheel: whoever rises and becomes great must expect to fall as the wheel turns. Does the play, however, allow us to accept such an interpretation? Is Fate the prime mover in the plot or does the action grow from other causes? Could these causes be called "Fate" also?

25. At the end of the play Creon says, "I alone am guilty," and accepts full responsibility for all the deaths. Is he correct in his self-accusation, or is the matter more complicated?

26. Throughout the play the Chorus and Teiresias have recommended that Antigone and Creon abandon their extreme positions and follow a middle course. Such action would have prevented disaster, but does anything in the play suggest that it was ever a genuine possibility?

27. Antigone's major effort was "to cover the body of Polyneices," and Creon's major effort was "to keep the body uncovered." Taking these two contrary actions as metaphors, can you see how the motives expressed in each action are present in all that is said and done in the play?

Plot on the Psychological Level

Maurice Maeterlinck, in his *The Tragedy of Daily Life,* says:

I have come to believe that an old man seated in his armchair, waiting quietly under the lamplight, listening without knowing it to all the eternal laws which reign about his house, interpreting without understanding it all that there is in the silence of doors and windows . . . I have come to believe that this motionless old man lived really a more profound, human, and universal life than the lover who strangles his mistress, the captain who gains a victory, or the husband who "avenges his honor."

In this passage, and in his plays, the Belgian dramatist turns away from objective, physical action—strangling a mistress, winning a victory—and focuses attention on subjective, psychological action—listening, interpreting. For Maeterlinck and for a great many modern dramatists, the most meaningful action occurs in the mind of man, not out in the visible, audible world of bodies, objects, and voices. W. B. Yeats puts the same idea into specifically dramatic terms: "After all, is not the greatest play not the play that gives the sensation of an external reality but the play in which there is the greatest abundance of life itself, of the reality that is in our minds?"

But even if Maeterlinck and Yeats are right in claiming that true life is located within the mind, how can the movement of this life, its plot, be represented in the play, a form which by its very nature requires that everything be objectified in a physical set, in audible words, in visible movements, in clothing, and in bodies? A novelist would have no difficulty at all in presenting the thoughts of "an old man seated in his armchair, waiting quietly under the lamplight," but a play which consisted of only a man sitting motionless in a chair would convey next to nothing. The characters in a play, like real men, must find objective forms for what they wish to express. The ways in which mental conditions can be objectified are discussed in the section on character. But there character is largely treated as if it were unchanging, as if a character continued throughout a play with exactly the same motives and exactly the same attitudes. In some plays this is nearly the case. Hedda Gabler has the same values and is trying to do the same thing at the beginning and at the end of the play. Nevertheless it is impossible to think of her mind as static; her motives remain the same, but she passes through a series of moods and mental states. On the other hand, Antigone and Creon, though they cannot escape the consequences of the train of action they set in motion with their initial acts, undergo radical changes of character during the course of the play. Since some dramatists try to show a psychological as well as an objective reality, and since the minds of their characters move from one condition to another, we can speak of *psychological plots* and try to describe their dynamics.

Most major playwrights have been concerned, though not as exclusively as Maeterlinck and Yeats were, to find a way to present on the stage the mental life of at least their major characters, and to record the changes in their minds. *Macbeth,* for example, has a striking objective plot composed of great battles, the murder of a king, the disruption of a kingdom, and the violent deaths of the usurper and his queen. Below this objective plot, and parallel to it, runs the psychological plot, the chain of mental "events" or conditions in Macbeth's mind. In the depths of his being he is first courageous, simple, and loyal; he passes on to nervous indecision as ambition leads him to kill the king and loyalty and reverence for human life cause him to recoil from the act; he nearly turns into a maniac as fear breaks his "single state of man" and he begins to see visions; he hardens as he becomes accustomed to the business of killing all who threaten his rule; and, finally, just before he dies fighting like an enraged animal, he changes to a walking ghost, a man for whom life has lost all meaning and has become no more than "sound and fury, signifying nothing." The plot of Macbeth's mind as he changes from a loyal and straightforward subject to an empty husk is as important to the play as what happens in the kingdom of Scotland. However, the subjective and objective plots of *Macbeth* are not unrelated; they mirror one another in such a way that the events of one reflect the events of the other. As the first, half-formed thoughts of ambition take shape in Macbeth's mind, they take shape physically in the form of witches who suddenly appear on the heath. As he destroys the ruling principles of loyalty and reverence for life in himself, so he kills his king. The hand and the heart go together. As his mind progresses from disorder to joylessness and hope-lessness, so the country he rules is thrown into turmoil and becomes finally a wasteland. But the events of the physical plot do not exist here, as they would in an expressionistic play, merely to give objective form to Macbeth's mental processes. Scotland and the mind of Mac-beth are equally real, and they parallel one another because the same principles are at work with the same effects in both. The forces that destroy a kingdom also destroy the little kingdom, man, in Shake-speare's coherent view of existence.

Few playwrights have coordinated their physical and psychological plots so perfectly as Shakespeare did, but as a rule the objective plot does double duty at least in plays that have a psychological dimension. It records the changes that take place in the objective world and in the material condition of man, and it provides a rough parallel to what is taking place in the minds of the central characters. Once the fact is established that the objective plot reflects the subjective plot, we can begin to examine the way the subjective or psychological plot functions. It is composed and structured in the same manner as the external plot. Just as conflict results in the external, objective world from the collision of opposing forces, so certain forces within a person can cause internal, or mental, conflict. Hedda Gabler is both fascinated by freedom and afraid of it. Hamlet is torn by a longing to retire from the world to escape the struggle with evil and an equally powerful longing to be active and to bring about the needed changes in Den-mark. Macbeth is torn between his ambition and his loyalty. The con-flict causing psychological changes need not, however, be entirely in-ternal. A change of mind may be brought about by a character's realization of what he has done, or not done, in the objective world. Creon's major change of mind occurs, for example, when he realizes that his course of action has destroyed his son and his wife. Once the conflict has begun, the psychological plot, made up of a series of mental events, is underway. We must watch for the way these mental events are related, just as we would in an objective plot, and we must look for the way in which changes come about.

For example, the way changes occur in the psychological plots of *Macbeth* and *Antigone* differs considerably. Macbeth's progress from one mental state to another is a gradual and continuous movement to-ward a climax: the absolute emptiness expressed in the speech be-ginning, "Tomorrow, and tomorrow . . ." Antigone shifts abruptly. She appears, during the first part of the play, to be absolute for death and completely without fear; suddenly, when she is condemned to be buried alive, the full significance of what she has done comes home to her. She prevents herself from becoming an hysterical girl at this point, but she is nonetheless radically changed. Sharp intrusions of truth, prepared for but coming suddenly, are called *recognitions*. If a character recognizes that the truth is quite the opposite of what he has previously believed to be the case, we have a *reversal*. Oedipus, for example, discovers that by his intelligence and skill he has fulfilled rather than evaded the oracular prophecy that he would kill his father and marry his mother. The reversal occurs when he learns these facts and is forced to see that he is not the greatest of men, but the weakest and most pitiable.

Psychological plots can be arranged in as many ways as physical plots. The events of Macbeth's mind are connected in a cause-and-effect pattern: because his ambition overcomes his care for human life, his own life becomes meaningless to him. Mother Courage does not undergo any development or change, except that her hope is perhaps dimmer by the end of the play. Her toughness, her common sense, her wit, and her courage are permanent parts of her mental makeup and can only be qualified or destroyed by death. Probably no psychological plot has so distressed the critics as the familiar comic plot in which a character who has been consistently single-minded suddenly and without warning changes. This psychological version of the *deus ex machina* is frequent in love comedy: a man and a woman (Beatrice and Benedick in Shakespeare's *Much Ado About Nothing,* for example) who have previously hated one another discover in a flash that they love one another. Shakespeare presents an elaborate form of this same change of mind in *A Midsummer Night's Dream*: the four lovers in the forest get incredibly mixed up as Puck's magic potion causes them to love where once they had hated. Such changes are often explained as mere devices used by the author to tie up his play, without regard for credibility; but surely these psychological shifts, particularly when they involve love, are just as credible, as lifelike, as the relentless pattern along which Macbeth's mind moves. We all know that love is close to hate, and we can accept also what Shakespeare tells us in *A Midsummer Night's Dream,* that sudden love is a magical quality in man which transforms what was once hated into something desirable and lovely. We must try to approach psychological plots as well as physical plots without preconceptions about how the playwright ought to portray the workings of human nature. In his depiction of the process of mental change he offers an image of the dynamics of the human mind, and we are likely to miss his point completely if we fail to take his plot seriously.

THE STRONGER

BY

AUGUST STRINDBERG

August Strindberg (1849–1912), the foremost Swedish dramatist, was one of the great originators of the modern theater. While the other great Scandinavian dramatist of the nineteenth century. Henrik Ibsen, developed and perfected the beautifully machined realistic play to present the interaction of man and society, Strindberg constantly experimented with dramatic forms ranging from the extreme naturalism of a play like *The Father* to the equally extreme surrealism of a play like *The Ghost Sonata*. He moved restlessly from one dramatic style to another in search of a theatrical idiom that could convey the subject which most interested him—man's intense, explosive passions and his strange, unexplored inner life. *The Stronger* (1889), though extremely short, is one of his most successful attempts to find a way to dramatize in the realistic mode the workings of the mind.

CHARACTERS

MRS. X, *actress, married*

MISS Y, *actress, unmarried*

A WAITRESS

Scene: A corner of a ladies' café (in Stockholm in the 1880's). Two small wrought-iron tables, a red plush settee and a few chairs.

MISS Y. *is sitting with a half-empty bottle of beer on the table before her, reading an illustrated weekly which from time to time she exchanges for another.*

MRS. X. *enters, wearing a winter hat and coat and carrying a decorative Japanese basket.*

MRS. X. Why, Millie, my dear, how are you? Sitting here all alone on Christmas Eve like some poor bachelor.

> [MISS Y. *looks up from her magazine, nods, and continues to read.*]

MRS. X. You know it makes me feel really sad to see you. Alone. Alone in a café and on Christmas Eve of all times. It makes me feel as sad as when once in Paris I saw a wedding party at a restaurant. The bride was reading a comic paper and the bridegroom playing billiards with the witnesses. Ah me, I said to myself, with such a beginning how will it go, and how will it end? He was playing billiards on his wedding day! And she, you were going to say, was reading a comic paper on hers. But that's not quite the same.

> [*A* WAITRESS *brings a cup of chocolate to* MRS. X. *and goes out.*]

MRS. X. Do you know, Amelia, I really believe now you would have done better to stick to him. Don't forget I was the first who told you to forgive him. Do you remember? Then you would be married now

and have a home. Think how happy you were that Christmas when
you stayed with your fiancé's people in the country. How warmly
you spoke of domestic happiness! You really quite longed to be
out of the theatre. Yes, Amelia dear, home is best—next best to
the stage, and as for children—but you couldn't know anything
about that.

> [MISS Y.'s *expression is disdainful.* MRS. X. *sips a few
> spoonfuls of chocolate, then opens her basket and
> displays some Christmas presents.*]

MRS. X. Now you must see what I have bought for my little chicks.
[*Takes out a doll.*] Look at this. That's for Liza. Do you see how
she can roll her eyes and turn her head. Isn't she lovely? And here's
a toy pistol for Maja. [*She loads the pistol and shoots it at* MISS Y.
who appears frightened.]

MRS. X. Were you scared? Did you think I was going to shoot you?
Really, I didn't think you'd believe that of me. Now if *you* were to
shoot *me* it wouldn't be so surprising, for after all I did get in your
way, and I know you never forget it—although I was entirely innocent. You still think I intrigued to get you out of the Grand
Theatre, but I didn't. I didn't, however much you think I did. Well,
it's no good talking, you will believe it was me . . . [*Takes out
a pair of embroidered slippers.*] And these are for my old man, with
tulips on them that I embroidered myself. As a matter of fact I
hate tulips, but he has to have tulips on everything.

> [MISS Y. *looks up, irony and curiosity in her face.*]

MRS. X. [*putting one hand in each slipper*]. Look what small feet Bob
has, hasn't he? And you ought to see the charming way he walks—
you've never seen him in slippers, have you?

> [MISS Y. *laughs.*]

MRS. X. Look, I'll show you. [*She makes the slippers walk across the
table, and* MISS Y. *laughs again.*]

MRS. X. But when he gets angry, look, he stamps his foot like this.
"Those damn girls who can never learn how to make coffee! Blast!
That silly idiot hasn't trimmed the lamp properly!" Then there's a
draught under the door and his feet get cold. "Hell, it's freezing,
and the damn fools can't even keep the stove going!" [*She rubs
the sole of one slipper against the instep of the other.* MISS Y. *roars
with laughter.*]

MRS. X. And then he comes home and has to hunt for his slippers,
which Mary has pushed under the bureau . . . Well, perhaps it's
not right to make fun of one's husband like this. He's sweet anyhow, and a good, dear husband. You ought to have had a husband
like him, Amelia. What are you laughing at? What is it? Eh? And,
you see, I know he is faithful to me. Yes, I know it. He told me
himself—what *are* you giggling at?—that while I was on tour in

Norway that horrible Frederica came and tried to seduce him. Can you imagine anything more abominable? [*Pause.*] I'd have scratched her eyes out if she had come around while I was at home. [*Pause.*] I'm glad Bob told me about it himself, so I didn't just hear it from gossip. [*Pause.*] And as a matter of fact, Frederica wasn't the only one. I can't think why, but all the women in the Company seem to be crazy about my husband. They must think his position gives him some say in who is engaged at the Theatre. Perhaps you have run after him yourself? I don't trust you very far, but I know he has never been attracted by you, and you always seemed to have some sort of grudge against him, or so I felt. [*Pause. They look at one another guardedly.*]

MRS. X. Do come and spend Christmas Eve with us tonight, Amelia— just to show that you're not offended with us, or anyhow not with me. I don't know why, but it seems specially unpleasant not to be friends with you. Perhaps it's because I did get in your way that time . . . [*slowly*] or—I don't know—really, I don't know at all why it is.

[*Pause.* MISS Y. *gazes curiously at* MRS. X.]

MRS. X. [*thoughtfully*]. It was so strange when we were getting to know one another. Do you know, when we first met, I was frightened of you, so frightened I didn't dare let you out of my sight. I arranged all my goings and comings to be near you. I dared not be your enemy, so I became your friend. But when you came to our home, I always had an uneasy feeling, because I saw my husband didn't like you, and that irritated me—like when a dress doesn't fit. I did all I could to make him be nice to you, but it was no good— until you went and got engaged. Then you became such tremendous friends that at first it looked as if you only dared show your real feelings then—when you were safe. And then, let me see, how was it after that? I wasn't jealous—that's queer. And I remember at the christening, when you were the godmother, I told him to kiss you. He did, and you were so upset . . . As a matter of fact I didn't notice that then . . . I didn't think about it afterwards either . . . I've never thought about it—until *now!* [*Rises abruptly.*] Why don't you say something? You haven't said a word all this time. You've just let me go on talking. You have sat there with your eyes drawing all these thoughts out of me—they were there in me like silk in a cocoon—thoughts . . . Mistaken thoughts? Let me think. Why did you break off your engagement? Why did you never come to our house after that? Why don't you want to come to us tonight?

[MISS Y. *makes a motion, as if about to speak.*]

MRS. X. No. You don't need to say anything, for now I see it all. That was why—and why—and why. Yes. Yes, that's why it was. Yes, yes, all the pieces fit together now. That's it. I won't sit at the same

table as you. [*Moves her things to the other table.*] That's why I
have to embroider tulips, which I loathe, on his slippers—because
you liked tulips. [*Throws the slippers on the floor.*] That's why we
have to spend the summer on the lake—because you couldn't bear
the seaside. That's why my son had to be called Eskil—because it
was your father's name. That's why I had to wear your colours,
read your books, eat the dishes you liked, drink your drinks—your
chocolate, for instance. That's why—oh my God, it's terrible to
think of, terrible! Everything, everything came to me from you—
even your passions. Your soul bored into mine like a worm into an
apple, and ate and ate and burrowed and burrowed, till nothing
was left but the skin and a little black mould. I wanted to fly from
you, but I couldn't. You were there like a snake, your black eyes
fascinating me. When I spread my wings, they only dragged me
down. I lay in the water with my feet tied together, and the harder
I worked my arms, the deeper I sank—down, down, till I reached
the bottom, where you lay in waiting like a giant crab to catch me
in your claws—and now here I am. Oh how I hate you! I hate you,
I hate you! And you just go on sitting there, silent, calm, indifferent,
not caring whether the moon is new or full, if it's Christmas or New
Year, if other people are happy or unhappy. You don't know how
to hate or to love. You just sit there without moving—like a cat
at a mouse hole. You can't drag your prey out, you can't chase it,
but you can outstay it. Here you sit in your corner—you know they
call it the rattrap after you—reading the papers to see if anyone's
ruined or wretched or been thrown out of the Company. Here you
sit sizing up your victims and weighing your chances—like a pilot
his shipwrecks for the salvage. [*Pause.*] Poor Amelia! Do you know,
I couldn't be more sorry for you. I know you are miserable, miserable like some wounded creature, and vicious because you are
wounded. I can't be angry with you. I should like to be, but after
all you are the small one—and as for your affair with Bob, that
doesn't worry me in the least. Why should it matter to me? And
if you, or somebody else taught me to drink chocolate, what's the
difference? [*Drinks a spoonful. Smugly.*] Chocolate is very wholesome anyhow. And if I learnt from you how to dress, *tant mieux!*—
that only gave me a stronger hold over my husband, and you have
lost what I gained. Yes, to judge from various signs, I think you
have now lost him. Of course, you meant me to walk out, as you
once did, and which you're now regretting. But I won't do that,
you may be sure. One shouldn't be narrow-minded, you know. And
why should nobody else want what I have? [*Pause.*] Perhaps, my
dear, taking everything into consideration, at this moment it is I
who am the stronger. You never got anything from me, you just
gave away—from yourself. And now, like the thief in the night,
when you woke up I had what you had lost. Why was it then that

MEANING

The term *meaning* appears throughout the first three sections of this book and has already been defined implicitly. An explicit definition is more difficult because the word seems to invite circular definitions such as "meaning *means* to mean." It will therefore be useful to focus our discussion in this section on some of the ways in which a play "means." Perhaps it will be helpful to think of the alternate ways in which the question "What does a play mean?" can be phrased: "What kind of knowledge does a play provide?" "What use does a play have?" "In what sense is a play true?" Each of these questions really provides a definition of meaning: to provide knowledge, to be useful, to be true. But these words are nearly as ambiguous as "meaning" itself, and we shall have to be more specific.

Many plays may be said to lack any important meaning. Most musical comedies, the standard television dramas, and all plays generally lumped together as *entertainments* have as their primary purpose the amusement of the audience. Such entertainments try to provide as much of what is immediately pleasing as possible—pretty girls, elaborate sets, marvelous machines, amusing clowns, and heartwarming sentiments. We watch them (we seldom read them) only to pass a pleasant evening and to escape our own lives for a brief time. The general moral or theme, if there is one at all, is something banal like "love conquers all," or "virtue is more important than gold in the long run." (There are cynical banalities as well as optimistic ones: "a corrupt society is responsible for all crime," or "men are always selfish.") Because these moral lessons are not grounded deeply in the characters or in the actions, and because their real implications are never explored, they gratify a simple appetite for uncomplicated and undemanding truisms. Nothing is more relaxing after struggling with the complexities of life than to be told that life is really all very simple and straightforward.

At the next level are plays whose whole "meaning" is to give dramatic life to some *specific* person, historical event, or social condition. *Sunrise at Campobello* dramatizes Franklin Roosevelt's struggle to overcome the crippling effects of polio; *Hatful of Rain* makes clear the problems and agonies of the drug addict; *The Far Country* re-creates Freud's treatment of the mentally sick and his first formulations of the principles of psychoanalysis; *Justice* deals with the workings of the English legal system. Such plays are not to be scorned as inferior substitutes for history, biography, or objective reporting. They do not merely make their subjects more vivid by acting them out before us; they actually convey additional information, which other more "factual" treatments of the same subject are likely to omit. Instead of telling us, as a newspaper report might, that so many people are drug addicts, that a large percentage of addicts take up the habit because they are unable to cope with personal problems, and that the habit leads to crime, suffering, and death in a certain number of cases, a play about drug addiction, such as *Hatful of Rain,* will in addition to providing factual information attempt to show us the "human facts." What does it mean to a real person, not an abstract statistic, to be unable to deal with life? What degradation does he suffer to satisfy his need for drugs? What breakdown of character results? Usually such plays contain either an implicit or explicit moral judgment and suggest some attitude or course of action that will help eliminate the problem. The general term for plays that dramatize specific personal or social situations and suggest a remedy is *problem play*. The "meaning" of such plays is the problem they present and the solution they propose. Interesting as they may be, problem plays fall short of greatness because their meaning has limited application. They deal with *particular* men and *particular* situations, not with *man* and *the human condition*.

Plays that are great literature continue to entertain and to render in dramatic terms specific lives and social conditions. *Antigone* is a thrilling play by any standards. It contains enough violence and suspense to satisfy the crudest appetite, and it presents the crucial events in the life of a specific, though fictional, woman. It also dramatizes indirectly a social problem of a particular time: the dilemma of Athens in the middle of the fifth century B.C. when she had grown to a great power in the Greek world and was discovering that practical politics do not always square with morality. Thus it would be possible by giving it only a partial reading to conclude that the play is an exciting entertainment, pitiful scenes in which lovers are separated, suspenseful conflicts between a young girl and a proud tyrant, and unusual punishments and cruel deaths. Or it could be read, inadequately, as a problem play dealing with the Athenian political situation, which recommends a compromise between absolute nationalism and absolute morality, between the laws of men and the laws of the gods. But *Antigone* is more than an entertainment or a problem play; it is a dramatic presentation of at least one aspect of the human condition as it always was and always will be. The demands of kings and the demands of the gods always seem to be at variance, just as the human body and the human spirit always seem to tug in opposite directions. Creon and Antigone are the voices of these eternal opposites, and their story illustrates the consequences, the *meaning,* of choosing to follow exclusively one value or the other. The play, then, while it also presents a specific social and political problem in an entertaining manner, has a universal meaning. If we were asked to state the ultimate meaning of *Antigone,* it could only be stated in some such universal terms as these: "The human condition is one in which every good is strangely in conflict with some other good, and while it is necessary to choose one good and act upon it, this choice is always infinitely painful and destructive for the men involved." Any reading of the play, whether this one or another, will probably state in abstract language some general truth about the human condition.

Since this is true, it appears that the greatest kind of drama has two dimensions simultaneously. It is specific in that it deals not with abstractions but with particulars—a particular character, a definite setting, an action located in a specific time and place—and it is universal in that its specific parts are arranged to show a crucial and enduring human situation. Much of the pleasure of a great play comes from the vividness with which specific characters taking part in definite events are embodied on the stage. That mankind is infinitely durable and quick-witted even in the most desperate circumstances is a truism that is not likely to arouse much interest or enthusiasm, but Mother Courage providing for her children by pulling her wagon from town to town to sell her wares to the soldiers is extremely moving. A sermon about our need for other people is not nearly so compelling as seeing a particular woman, Hedda Gabler, refusing to acknowledge that she is pregnant, handling her pistols, shutting out the sunlight, treating her family in a politely savage manner, and pacing back and forth between the walls of her dark, encumbered room. How mean-

ingless a philosophical discussion about the conflict of duty to the
state and moral duty seems compared with watching Antigone and
Creon hurl words at one another! The fact that the characters and
the other details of a drama are not real in an absolute sense does
not prevent the dramatist from giving us the illusion of intense, actual
life. Dramatic characters may be merely collections of traits, embodi-
ments of a few ideas expressed in a few actions and words, but they
often seem to have a heightened, intensified vitality.

Here is one way in which a play "means." It creates existence on
the most immediate and personal level, and it deals with the solid facts
of life: the emotions of love and hate, the terror of death, the conviction of pride, the persistence of living things. In this sense the
meaning of Romeo's love or Hamlet's despair is the fullness, the
power, the truth with which they are realized in words and acts. "A
poem," says Archibald MacLeish in "Ars Poetica," "should not mean
but be." But fully realized "being," the dramatist has always insisted, is
one kind of meaning. Philosophy, science, theology, statistics—these all
make statements about reality in abstract terms such as the good, the
true, the one, or the norm; but the arts, drama included, make their
statements in specific terms: Hamlet, Claudius, Elsinore, the Ghost, the
stabbing of Polonius. Meaning in the drama must grow out of particular events, must be built on the facts of human nature, and must show
a man living and experiencing the world immediately and intensely.

As we have seen, however, great drama also has a universal meaning. Antigone is not only a strong-willed human who obeys the laws
of the gods, rather than the law of the ruler of Thebes, and buries
Polyneices, but she is also the representative image of the power of the
human spirit, which disdains practicalities and refuses compromises.
What in a play permits us to extend its meaning from a powerful
creation of a unique experience to a picture of general human nature,
as true for us as for those who saw its first performance?

First of all, a play's universality of meaning depends to some extent on the kind of experience portrayed and on the power and
accuracy with which it is brought to life. If the drama creates a convincing image of some primary human situation or attitude—love, for
example, or the difficulty of communication with other people, loneliness and fear of death, the conflict of fate and free will, or the relationship of man and woman—then its bearing on all men will be
apparent. The audience will recognize itself in whatever figures the
dramatist uses because its members have experienced, in some degree,
the same passions, hopes, and conflicts to which the actors give voice

and body. It was once believed that only a great action like the struggle for a kingdom, involving great heroes such as kings and queens, could serve as the subjects of great drama. We now know that it is not the apparent grandeur of the play's subject that bestows importance on it, but the fact that it depicts powerfully and truthfully some eternal aspect of the human condition. A salesman can face the same overwhelming questions and the same terrors that the Prince of Denmark can—though the fact that he is a salesman, not a prince, suggests that he will have less success in answering his questions and that his failure or his achievement will have less impact on the world at large. We must always remember that it is not the apparent subject matter, but the accurate and vivid presentation of some crucial human problem that enlarges the play's range of meaning. Thus the action of a woman trying to give a successful garden party may be very important because it embodies a characteristic human attempt to create by means of tact, graciousness, and planning, an ordered and mutually satisfying relationship between human beings; while a play about the fall of kingdoms in which such subjects as free will, honor, and death are openly and frequently discussed may be no more than philosophical "horse opera." Hamlet sums up very nicely the necessity for presenting "true" images of man on stage.

The purpose of playing . . . was and is to hold as 'twere the mirror up to Nature—to show Virtue her own feature, scorn her own image, and the very age and body of the time his form and pressure. Now this overdone or come tardy off, though it make the unskillful laugh, cannot but make the judicious grieve . . . oh, there be players . . . that neither having the accent of Christians nor the gait of Christian, pagan, nor man, have so strutted and bellowed that I have thought some of Nature's journeymen had made men, and not made them well, they imitated humanity so abominably.

In earlier discussions of character, world, and plot, another answer to the question of how a play acquires universal meaning was stated implicitly a number of times. In the discussion of each of these elements of drama we noted a number of particulars. A dramatic character, we said, is made up of a number of distinct details: way of dressing, physical characteristics, traits of speech, recurrent use of certain images, way of acting. But in trying to understand the whole character we examined each detail to see what it had in common with the other details. We tried to locate the center of the character, the essential being. The term that best describes that essence in the drama is *motive,* the basic act that the character is trying to perform, which is expressed in each of the details. The critical term used to describe this relation of one detail to another is *structure,* and the presence of structure is one of the distinguishing marks of the play that is also literature.

As we read a play of the first rank we gradually become aware of emerging patterns; we begin to sense the relationship between apparently diverse events. Characters come into focus as we see that each is not a collection of disparate traits, but a unity in which clothing, physical appearance, peculiarities of speech, movements, gestures, and dominant interests all help make up the essential pattern. The furniture on the stage, the arrangement of the props, the decor, the references to a world just beyond the stage coalesce to suggest some one force or recurring conflict. We discover a central power moving through the plays as we observe that events have a characteristic direction, that apparently trivial events manifest the same struggle between the same forces as do the obviously crucial confrontations, and that again and again the same order of consequence results from the same kind of cause. Ultimately, if we read the play well, it becomes apparent that all the components—characters, world, and plot—are not only unified within themselves but comprise a total unity: a coherent image of man and his world in movement.

As we become aware that the parts of a play are closely related to each other, we begin to understand its universal implications. Everything Hedda Gabler does manifests what we have called a drive toward freedom, an attempt to escape all restraints. This drive always encounters an opposing power in some form, which seeks to enclose her and limit her actions. Thus it becomes obvious that this particular woman in this particular setting is but one instance (a late nineteenth-century version) of a universal struggle between man's desire to be absolutely, anarchically free and the bonds imposed on him by his own nature, by other people, and by social arrangements.

By structuring the parts of the play, the dramatist transforms his particular rendering of life into a statement of a universal. In one sense this universal is the "meaning" of the play. A statement of the "meaning" in this sense, however, is no substitute for the play. Our task as critics is not to boil the play down to a general statement about life. While it is necessary to search for the ultimate unity of the play, and while some brief statement of the nature of that unity will be critically useful, no such statement does justice to the full meaning of the play. To say that *Hedda Gabler* is a dramatization of the struggle between freedom and restraint, or that *Mother Courage* shows the determination and magnificence of humanity in a hostile world, or that *Antigone* reveals the inevitable conflict of body and spirit or of individual and political morality, is not really to state adequately what these plays mean. To be understandable, to be fully *meaningful*, these statements require a full knowledge of all the specific details in the plays, for these details are necessary qualifications and refinements—the modifiers and subordinate clauses, as it were—of the general idea. Antigone's haughtiness, her scorn for weaker people such as her sister Ismene, and her monumental certainty that she alone is right are all as integral to Sophocles' dramatic definition of man's tragic situation as is the general idea that emerges from the particulars of the play: that life is a conflict between equally necessary moral and practical values. We cannot, therefore, discard either the specific details or the central idea of the play in seeking its meaning, for each depends on the other for its full meaning; or, rather, meaning grows from an interaction of detail and general theme. The great dramatists work with severe economy, wasting neither word nor gesture; if what they have to say about life could be reduced to some such simple phrases as those given above, there would be no point in writing plays. A single sentence would suffice.

The dramatist may extend the universal implications of his image of life in several ways. All of these may be regarded as aspects of structure, but it will be helpful to examine a few of them separately. In the discussion of plot, we noticed that the device of the double, or multiple, plot tends to expand the meaning of the play. If we observe the same events, the same problems, the same human actions, occurring in more than one life, in more than one place, the implication is that this is not a unique but a common pattern of life. W. B. Yeats referred to this effect as the "emotion of multitude" and illustrated it in this way:

The Shakespearean drama gets the emotion of multitude out of the subplot which copies the main plot, much as a shadow upon the wall copies one's body in the firelight. We think of *King Lear* less as the history of one man and his sorrows than as the history of a whole evil time. Lear's shadow is in Gloster, who also has ungrateful children, and the mind goes on imagining other shadows, shadow beyond shadow till it has pictured the world.

Except for the Elizabethans, few dramatists have felt free to construct two or three distinct plots in a single play, but modified double plots, used to suggest the universal validity of the action, have been a fairly constant feature of Western drama. In the modern theater the dramatist often weaves two or more plots into one, as MacLeish does in *The Fall of the City,* where the imagery suggests that the action is at once the descent of the Vikings on peaceful lands, the conquest of Mexico by Cortez, and Hitler's attacks on the European democracies. Any historical drama also collapses two plots together, though we are scarcely aware that the process is taking place. Bernard Shaw's *Saint Joan,* for example, dramatizes the career of Joan of Arc. But the Joan of the play speaks in the accents of twentieth-century England. She discusses such matters as nationalism, religion, and feminine rights in the sprightly manner of a good Fabian Socialist like Bernard Shaw. The play is not, then, just the story of the historical Joan, nor that of a twentieth-century liberal: it is both, and by implication a continuing pattern in life. One of the most interesting plays of modern times, Thornton Wilder's *The Skin of Our Teeth,* contains many plots collapsed into one. On the surface, the play is a drawing-room comedy, which deals with a busy husband who returns from work in New York every day to a typical middle-class home and family in the suburbs. The members of the family, their activities, ways of speaking, and problems are so familiar that they are little more than theatrical clichés. But Mr. Antrobus' job in the city turns out to be inventing such things as the wheel, the alphabet, and the ordinal numbers. The problems he faces at home turn out to be such cataclysms as the advance of the glaciers, the deluge, and an apocalyptic world war. His son who throws rocks at other boys is at once Henry Antrobus and Cain. This interweaving of plots from different periods in the history of the human race shows that the problems faced by modern man in trying to earn a living and raise a family are only less striking versions of the same problems faced by man in the past in trying to combat the threat of extinction by hostile forces. The same virtues are required in a modern New Jersey suburb as in an ice-age cave to meet these challenges successfully.

It should perhaps be added that any stage production of a play which uses costumes of another age than those specified—*Julius Caesar* done in black shirts with all the trappings of Mussolini's Italy, for example—provides a variety of the double plot. In such cases, of course, the additional plot is the director's, not the playwright's, and its effectiveness will depend on how well it suits the original meaning of the play. Often we become aware, in a rather curious way, of second plots running through a play, which are not referred to in the text and are not consciously intended by the author to be present.

While the names of characters and the surface details of great plays
differ widely, their characters and plots often seem to fall into one
of several basic patterns. Thus, in all tragedy, no matter when or
where it was written, the heroes will be somewhat the same type of
men who ask the same kind of questions of the world, who pass
through something like the same patterns of experience, and who end
in similar states. As we view a play in which the tragic pattern emerges,
we are inevitably forced to reflect that the human experience being
acted out before us is not unique but rather a recreation in different
voices and in a different setting of a most ancient passage. To see
Hamlet is to remember Achilles on the battlefield before Troy, Oedipus
in the square at Thebes, and even Willy Loman, the salesman, trying
to plant seeds in the shadows cast by two tall apartment buildings.
To some extent, then, our ability to get the fullest meaning from a
great play depends on our ability to recognize its resemblance to other
plays. Each tragedy evokes all other tragedies, and each comedy in
some ways is founded on all other comedies. Since the author of
Hamlet had never read or seen Sophocles' plays, it can be argued that
this parallel to *Oedipus the King* was no part of his intention and
therefore is not a legitimate addition to the meaning of the play. But
it can be argued in return that in one way or another Shakespeare
was aware of the tragic pattern in human experience, though not of
all its individual expressions in art, and that he shaped *Hamlet* to this
pattern. It therefore recalls, quite properly, our memories of other
tragedies. At any rate, it is an undeniable fact that our reading and
understanding of literature is cumulative: we see more meaning in
Antigone, Hedda Gabler, and *Mother Courage* when we are able to
compare them.

There are other techniques for widening the range of meaning by
placing the immediate dramatic event in an expanded context. A mere
touch is often enough to suggest that the action before us is not
"separated . . . from all but itself." In *Antigone* the name of Antigone's father, Oedipus, is mentioned naturally enough on several
occasions, and at one point the Chorus draws an analogy between
present and past difficulties in the Theban royal family. This is all,
but it is enough to tell us that Antigone is motivated in somewhat
the same way her father was and that she is following the same tragic
path. In *Mother Courage* a song on the wisdom of Solomon, the bravery of Caesar, the honesty of Socrates, and the charity of St. Martin
tells us that great virtue is a misfortune, which has in every case led

to disaster. Exalted as these men are compared with the homely characters in *Mother Courage,* their lives serve as grim parallels to the
fates of the heroic Eilif, the honest Swiss Cheese, and the charitable
Kattrin.

So far we have discussed how playwrights enrich the meaning of
their plays by expanding the human context of their main action, the
central plot of the play. But dramatists, and particularly poetic dramatists, are frequently interested in extending the meaning of their action beyond the range of the human. For instance, in Shakespeare's
The Winter's Tale, the literal action of the play consists of a sequence
of events in which a king, because of unwarranted jealousy, destroys
his growing family, breaks off an old friendship, and disrupts the order
of his kingdom. When he learns of his mistake and repents, his children and his wife are dead, or so he believes. But sixteen years later
his daughter and her mother are miraculously returned to him, and
the ancient friendship is renewed by the marriage of his daughter to
the son of his old friend. At several points during the course of this
plot, the characters and their activities are compared to the changes
of the seasons, to domestic animals such as the sheep, and to fruits
and flowers. This sustained development of one theme of imagery is
known as an *imagery pattern,* and in this play it is arranged in such
a way that the seasons of the year and the changes in nature parallel
the human events of the primary plot. The King's destruction of his
family, his kingdom, and his peace of mind is linked by imagery with
winter; the rescue of the daughter and her growth to womanhood are
compared to the events of spring; the restoration of the King and the
marriage of the daughter become the fruition of summer. The round
of the seasons with their attendant growth and death of natural things
forms in this way a second plot, and through its imagery the play
suggests that the life of the natural and human worlds are identical.
All creation passes through the same cycle.

Shakespeare's plays regularly show this type of secondary plot constructed by means of imagery patterns. When Macbeth enters on his
course of murder and tyranny, the imagery tells us that he leaves the
light behind and passes into darker and darker night. His acts are like
the extinction of sunlight and the coming of darkness, confusion, and
terror over the earth. Use of this particular pattern implies, of course,
that as the sun will inevitably return when the earth rotates, so the
tyrant will be destroyed and the kingdom restored. The pattern of
light and darkness is established chiefly by the language. Here is Lady
Macbeth's invocation to night when she plans the murder of Duncan:

> Come, thick night,
> And pall thee in the dunnest smoke of Hell,
> That my keen knife see not the wound it makes,
> Nor Heaven peep through the blanket of the dark
> To cry "Hold, hold!"

But the darkness pattern emerges or expands into the scene of the play as well. Day fades and darkness falls as Duncan arrives at the castle of Macbeth. The murder is done in the deepest hour of the night and is discovered as the night moves toward day again. Banquo is murdered in darkness; Lady Macbeth sleepwalks in the night, unable to forget her crimes; day comes again to the world as Macbeth is killed.

In realistic prose drama, because the playwright attempts to make his dialogue approximate daily speech, metaphor is not used as freely as in poetic drama—though traces of it always remain—and *scenic metaphor* or the *symbol* is used more heavily. For example, in Ibsen's *The Wild Duck* a family who have failed to meet life successfully retreat to a make-believe world where each member can escape the intrusions of reality and pretend that everything is as he would like it to be. Instead of using verbal imagery to extend their "withdrawal" to other areas of life, Ibsen constructs a series of symbolic parallels. In the attic of their house, these lost people create an imaginary wild forest in which they can pretend to be mighty hunters. This mock forest is populated with small, harmless animals, as ineffective as the people who put them there. The prize is a wild duck, which when wounded by a hunter dived to the bottom of a lake and locked itself in the weeds, until it was brought up by the hunter's dog. The family earns its living by taking photographic portraits, but these portraits have to be touched up carefully to conceal blemishes and create illusions of beauty before they are acceptable to the customers. Symbolism may be used in such a way that it forms a continuing pattern, as in *The Wild Duck,* or it may be used to create one brief, sharp effect. Tennessee Williams regularly makes use of symbolism in this second way. At the opening of *A Streetcar Named Desire,* Stanley Kowalski returning home from work throws a package of dripping, red meat to his wife waiting on the steps. The symbol, which suggests that Stanley is a cave man returning with the meat killed on the day's hunt, provides an illuminating parallel to the brutal, direct, primitive manner in which Stanley lives in twentieth-century New Orleans.

These are a few of the dramatist's major techniques for expanding the meaning of his image of life and making it universal. Double plot, perspective, analogue, symbol, and image pattern are all different aspects of what we generally term imagery. This word is ordinarily used in a limited sense to refer to comparisons in which one thing is said to be *like* another thing—"The Chair she sat in, *like* a burnished throne, Glowed on the marble"—or in which one thing is said *to be* another thing—"I have measured out my life with coffee spoons." In these examples of simile and metaphor (two varieties of imagery) meaning is achieved by yoking one thing with some other thing that it resembles or with which, according to the poetic statement, it is identical. The dramatist uses this same process, more elaborately when he establishes meaning by paralleling his main action with imagery patterns, extended symbols, and multiple plots. Ultimately, the artifice of the entire play may itself profitably be considered a complex image; every serious dramatist is saying in effect, "Life is like this play."

Two fundamentals emerge from our brief discussion of the drama, and if you can make them basic to your way of thinking about the drama, you will find that the details and complexities of any given play will be readily understandable. First, a good play presents the playwright's vision of what life is. From this it follows that every part of an artistically successful play is significant, and we cannot pass over any detail—the coloring of a character's hair, the placement of a piece of furniture, the most seemingly casual remark or gesture—as mere realistic stuffing. The irrelevant is omitted; only the relevant is present. Second, insofar as a play is a work of art, all its parts are related. When we ask the significance of any one part, we must ask how it is related to the other parts. We must discover not only how the components of a character form a unity, but how that character is related to the scene in which he is placed and to the other characters around him. The key to reading *any* play is to think of it not as photography or as life, but as art, as a heightened and structured image of man and his world in movement.

KING HENRY IV,
PART I

BY

WILLIAM SHAKESPEARE

The crucial period of English history for the Elizabethans was the long series of revolutions, internal wars, and struggles for power that followed the deposition of Richard II in 1399 and continued until 1485, when Henry VII assumed the crown. The period was crucial, the Elizabethans believed, because, like our own Civil War, it defined the national character and dramatized the basic issues and problems of their time. Stated in its most simple terms, these issues turned on the conflict of authority and freedom. The Elizabethans inherited from the Middle Ages the concept of an ordered, hierarchical world in which everyone was supposed to accept for better or worse the position in society to which he was born and to fulfill the duties belonging to his station. The king was God's deputy on earth and charged with the welfare of his subjects, and the subjects in turn owed absolute loyalty to the king; the husband ruled his household with justice and wisdom, and in return his children and wife rendered him honor and obedience; the young gave deference to the old, the subject obeyed the law, and all men controlled their unruly passions with their reason. The result was, ideally, a peaceful, orderly society and a prosperous kingdom.

Opposing this attractive ideal of a well-ordered society was the equally, if not more, attractive Renaissance belief in the greatness of the individual and the necessity for allowing him, no matter to what station he was born, to realize his full potential. In politics he might achieve the heights of power and at the same time make the state more efficient and glorious; in war he might rise to become the very name of honor and make for himself a reputation that would endure forever; in learning he might discover the secrets of the universe and gather all knowledge to himself; in commerce he might achieve the wealth and power of Croesus; and in pleasure he might seek out the greatest joys and turn life into an endless, painless delight. It is important to remember that both freedom and order were equally attractive to the Elizabethan mind, and that just as the nation was pulled apart by this opposition of ideals, so the single individual was subject to the same divisive forces.

The long wars between the houses of York and Lancaster in the fifteenth century may not have been in fact anything more than the squabbling of a group of dangerously powerful nobles, but the Elizabethans thought that these wars showed the working out in history of a struggle between the ideals of freedom and order—ideals which, whatever the outcome of the wars may have been, were still the crucial facts of politics, morality, religion, and psychology in the England of 1597, when *I Henry IV* was probably written. Shakespeare had already in *Richard II* dramatized the reign of that weak king, who was the legitimate heir of his grandfather, Edward III. Richard's rule was shown as a disaster for England, and he was defeated, deposed, and murdered by Henry Bolingbroke, Duke of Lancaster, the King Henry of the present play. Henry, though he too was a grandson of Edward III, had no legitimate claim to the throne; the sources of his authority, however much he might try to disguise the fact, were his own political skill, his courage, his daring, and his ruthless strength. He was, however, an able and efficient king, and *I Henry IV* shows him struggling valiantly to maintain peace in his kingdom and to control the disorder that he had released when he seized power. Shakespeare continued his dramatization of this period in two later plays, *II Henry IV* and *Henry V*. He already had treated in earlier plays, the three parts of *Henry VI* and *Richard III,* the end of the period that led to the establishment of the Tudor kings. Elizabeth I, the reigning queen at the time *I Henry IV* was written, was the last of the Tudors.

Given the problem of dealing with two or more ways of life, each of which appears to be equally valid, the dramatist comes face to face with a particularly striking question of "meaning." After he has realized as fully as he can in the characters the opposing ideals of freedom and order, he must go on to work out dramatically the significance of these ideals: Where do they lead? What are they like? How do they resemble and differ from one another? What variant forms do they take? From what sources do they derive? In what ways are they characteristic not only of an age but of all time? What can be revealed about them by viewing them from several perspectives? Shakespeare was grappling in *I Henry IV* with a number of questions vital to his age, and he believed that the answers lay locked in the sparse facts of the political history of the fifteenth century. His work as a dramatist was to bring these facts to life on the stage and to bring out the meaning implicit in them. To do so he used nearly every technique available to the playwright, and as a result *I Henry IV* is not only one of the great plays of the world but almost a textbook lesson in ways of discovering meaning in the theater.

DRAMATIS PERSONAE

KING HENRY *the Fourth*

HENRY, *Prince of Wales* }
JOHN *of Lancaster* } *sons to the King*

EARL OF WESTMORELAND

SIR WALTER BLUNT

THOMAS PERCY, *Earl of Worcester*

HENRY PERCY, *Earl of Northumberland*

HENRY PERCY, *surnamed* HOTSPUR, *his son*

EDMUND MORTIMER, *Earl of March*

RICHARD SCROOP, *Archbishop of York*

ARCHIBALD, *Earl of Douglas*

OWEN GLENDOWER

SIR RICHARD VERNON

SIR JOHN FALSTAFF

SIR MICHAEL, *a friend to the Archbishop of York*

POINS

GADSHILL

PETO

BARDOLPH

LADY PERCY, *wife to Hotspur and sister to Mortimer*

LADY MORTIMER, *daughter to Glendower and wife to Mortimer*

MISTRESS QUICKLY, *hostess of a tavern in Eastcheap*

LORDS, OFFICERS, SHERIFF, VINTNER, CHAMBERLAIN, DRAWERS, *two* CARRIERS, TRAVELERS, *and* ATTENDANTS

SCENE——*England and Wales.*

From Shakespeare: The Complete Works edited by G. B. Harrison, copyright 1948, 1952 by Harcourt, Brace & World, Inc. and reprinted with their permission. Line numbers do not represent the actual lineation of this edition but are keyed to the Globe Shakespeare to provide for easy cross reference to other editions of the play.

ACT I

Scene 1 ⚬ᢓ *London. The palace.*

[*Enter* KING HENRY, LORD JOHN OF LANCASTER, *the* EARL OF WESTMORELAND, SIR WALTER BLUNT, *and others.*]

KING. So shaken as we are, so wan with care,
    Find we° a time for frighted peace to pant,
    And breathe short-winded accents of new broils
    To be commenced in stronds° afar remote.
    No more the thirsty entrance of this soil   5
    Shall daub her lips with her own children's blood.
    No more shall trenching war° channel her fields,
    Nor bruise her flowerets° with the armèd hoofs
    Of hostile paces. Those opposèd eyes,
    Which, like the meteors° of a troubled heaven,   10
    All of one nature, of one substance bred,
    Did lately meet in the intestine shock°
    And furious close° of civil butchery,
    Shall now, in mutual well-beseeming° ranks,
    March all one way, and be no more opposed   15
    Against acquaintance, kindred, and allies.
    The edge of war, like an ill-sheathèd knife,
    No more shall cut his master. Therefore, friends,
    As far as to the sepulcher of Christ,
    Whose soldier now, under whose blessèd cross   20
    We are impressèd° and engaged to fight,
    Forthwith a power of English shall we levy,
    Whose arms were molded in their mothers' womb

  Act I, Sc. 1: 2. Find we: let us find. **4. stronds:** strands, shores. **7. trenching war:** trench warfare. **8. flowerets:** little flowers. **10. meteors:** comets or shooting stars, regarded as terrifying omens. **12. intestine shock:** clash of civil war. **13. close:** hand-to-hand battle. **14. well-beseeming:** seemly. **21. impressed:** enlisted.

To chase these pagans in those holy fields
Over whose acres walked those blessed feet   25
Which fourteen hundred years ago were nailed
For our advantage on the bitter cross.
But this our purpose now is twelvemonth old,
And bootless 'tis to tell you we will go.
Therefore we meet not now.° Then let me hear   30
Of you, my gentle cousin° Westmoreland,
What yesternight our Council did decree
In forwarding this dear expedience.°
WESTMORELAND. My liege, this haste was hot in question,°
And many limits of the charge° set down   35
But yesternight, when all athwart° there came
A post° from Wales loaden° with heavy news,
Whose worst was that the noble Mortimer,
Leading the men of Herefordshire to fight
Against the irregular° and wild Glendower,   40
Was by the rude hands of that Welshman taken,
A thousand of his people butchered.
Upon whose dead corpse there was such misuse,
Such beastly shameless transformation,
By those Welshwomen done as may not be   45
Without much shame retold or spoken of.
KING. It seems then that the tidings of this broil
Brake off our business for the Holy Land.
WESTMORELAND. This matched with other did, my gracious lord;
For more uneven° and unwelcome news   50
Came from the north and thus it did import:
On Holyrood Day,° the gallant Hotspur there,
Young Harry Percy, and brave Archibald,
That ever valiant and approvèd° Scot,
At Holmedon° met,   55
Where they did spend a sad and bloody hour,
As by discharge of their artillery,
And shape of likelihood,° the news was told.

29–30. bootless . . . now: i.e., there is no need to tell you of my decision,
which has long been made. Our present meeting is to consider the details.
bootless: vain.   31. cousin: kinsman, used of any near relation.   33. dear
expedience: urgent enterprise, dear to me.   34. hot in question: under eager
discussion.   35. limits . . . charge: estimates of the cost.   36. athwart:
cutting across.   37. post: messenger. loaden: laden.   40. irregular: unruly.
50. uneven: rough.   52. Holyrood Day: September 14.   54. approved:
tried.   55. Holmedon: in Northumberland, near the Scottish border.   58.
shape of likelihood: what was likely to happen.

For he that brought them, in the very heat
And pride of their contention° did take horse,   60
Uncertain of the issue° any way.
KING. Here is a dear, a true industrious friend,
    Sir Walter Blunt, new-lighted from his horse,
    Stained with the variation of each soil
    Betwixt that Holmedon and this seat of ours,   65
    And he had brought us smooth and welcome news.
    The Earl of Douglas is discomfited.
    Ten thousand bold Scots, two and twenty knights,
    Balked° in their own blood did Sir Walter see
    On Holmedon's plains. Of prisoners, Hotspur took   70
    Mordake the Earl of Fife, and eldest son
    To beaten Douglas; and the Earl of Athol,
    Of Murray, Angus, and Menteith.
    And is not this an honorable spoil?
    A gallant prize? Ha, Cousin, is it not?   75
WESTMORELAND. In faith,
    It is a conquest for a prince to boast of.
KING. Yea, there thou makest me sad and makest me sin
    In envy that my Lord Northumberland
    Should be the father to so blest a son—   80
    A son who is the theme of honor's tongue,
    Amongst a grove, the very straightest plant,
    Who is sweet Fortune's minion° and her pride—
    Whilst I, by looking on the praise of him,
    See riot and dishonor stain the brow   85
    Of my young Harry. Oh, that it could be proved
    That some night-tripping fairy° had exchanged
    In cradle clothes our children where they lay,
    And called mine Percy, his Plantagenet!
    Then would I have his Harry, and he mine.   90
    But let him from my thoughts. What think you, Coz,°
    Of this young Percy's° pride? The prisoners
    Which he in this adventure hath surprised
    To his own use he keeps, and sends me word
    I shall have none but Mordake Earl of Fife.   95
WESTMORELAND. This is his uncle's teaching. This is Worcester,

---

60. pride . . . contention: height of battle.   **61. issue:** result.   **69. Balked:** laid in ridges.   **83. minion:** darling.   **87. night-tripping fairy:** a fairy coming by night. The fairies, so some believed, used sometimes to steal a beautiful child and to leave a changeling in its place.   **91. Coz:** cousin.   **92. young Percy:** Shakespeare depicts Hotspur as a rash youth of about the same age as Prince Hal. Actually at the battle of Shrewsbury (1403) the Prince was barely 14 years old and Percy was 39.

Malevolent° to you in all aspécts,
Which makes him prune° himself, and bristle up
The crest of youth against your dignity.
KING. But I have sent for him to answer this,   100
And for this cause awhile we must neglect
Our holy purpose to Jerusalem.
Cousin, on Wednesday next our Council we
Will hold at Windsor. So inform the lords,
But come yourself with speed to us again,   105
For more is to be said and to be done
Than out of anger° can be uttered.
WESTMORELAND. I will, my liege.   [*Exeunt.*]

Scene 2 ⤳ *London. An apartment of the Prince's.*

[*Enter the* PRINCE OF WALES *and* FALSTAFF.]
FALSTAFF. Now, Hal, what time of day is it, lad?
PRINCE. Thou art so fat-witted, with drinking of old sack° and
   unbuttoning thee after supper and sleeping upon benches
   after noon, that thou hast forgotten to demand that truly
   which thou wouldst truly know. What a devil hast thou to do   5
   with the time of day? Unless hours were cups of sack, and
   minutes capons, and clocks the tongues of bawds, and dials
   the signs of leaping houses,° and the blessed sun himself a
   fair hot wench in flame-colored taffeta,° I see no reason why
   thou shouldst be so superfluous to demand the time of the
   day.   13
FALSTAFF. Indeed, you come near me now, Hal; for we that take
   purses go by the moon and the seven stars, and not by Phoebus,° he, "that wandering knight so fair." And I prithee,
   sweet wag, when thou art King, as, God save thy Grace—

97. **Malevolent:** boding evil, like a planet that brings disaster.   98. **prune:**
preen, like a hawk in good condition trimming its feathers.   107. **out of**
anger: from an angry heart.
   Sc. 2: 3. **sack:** dry white Spanish wine.   10. **leaping houses:** brothels.
11–12. **flame-colored taffeta:** bright red silk—the color flaunted by harlots.
16. **Phoebus:** the sun, with a pun on the Knight of the Sun, hero of a
chivalric romance.

Majesty I should say, for grace thou wilt have none——   20

PRINCE. What, none?

FALSTAFF. No, by my troth,° not so much as will serve to be prologue to an egg and butter.   24

PRINCE. Well, how then? Come, roundly, roundly.

FALSTAFF. Marry, then, sweet wag, when thou art King, let not us
that are squires of the night's body be called thieves of the
day's beauty.° Let us be Diana's foresters,° gentlemen of the
shade, minions of the moon. And let men say we be men of
good government,° being governed, as the sea is, by our noble and chaste mistress the moon, under whose countenance
we steal.   33

PRINCE. Thou sayest well, and it holds well too; for the fortune of
us that are the moon's men doth ebb and flow like the sea,
being governed, as the sea is, by the moon. As for proof,
now—a purse of gold most resolutely snatched on Monday
night and most dissolutely spent on Tuesday morning; got   40
with swearing "Lay by"° and spent with crying "Bring in"°
—now in as low an ebb as the foot of the ladder,° and by
and by in as high a flow as the ridge of the gallows.

FALSTAFF. By the Lord, thou sayest true, lad. And is not my hostess of the tavern a most sweet wench?   46

PRINCE. As the honey of Hybla,° my old lad of the castle.° And
is not a buff jerkin° a most sweet robe of durance?°

FALSTAFF. How now, how now, mad wag! What, in thy quips°
and thy quiddities?° What a plague have I to do with a buff
jerkin?   52

PRINCE. Why, what a pox have I to do with my hostess of the tavern?

FALSTAFF. Well, thou has called her to a reckoning many a time
and oft.

PRINCE. Did I ever call for thee to pay thy part?

FALSTAFF. No. I'll give thee thy due, thou hast paid all there.   60

PRINCE. Yea, and elsewhere, so far as my coin would stretch. And
where it would not, I have used my credit.

22. troth: truth.   **27–28. let . . . beauty:** i.e., do not let us who are gentlemen of the dark (i.e., highwaymen) be called *thieves of the day's beauty*
(i.e., loafers)—with a pun on "beauty" and "booty."   **28–29. Diana's
foresters:** thieves who rob by night. *Diana:* the moon.   **30–31. good government:** well-behaved.   **41. Lay by:** i.e., "stick 'em up."   **42. Bring in:**
i.e., the drink.   **43. ladder:** from which a condemned man was thrust off
the gallows into space.   **47. Hybla:** in Sicily, famous for its honey.   **47–48.
old . . . castle:** roisterer, with a pun on Falstaff's original name of Old-
castle.   **48. buff jerkin:** leather coat worn by the sheriff's sergeant.   **49.
robe of durance:** coat that endures (wears well) and that takes you to
durance (prison).   **51. quips:** wisecracks. **quiddities:** quibbles.

FALSTAFF. Yea, and so used it that, were it not here apparent that   64
    thou art heir° apparent—— But I prithee, sweet wag, shall
    there be gallows standing in England when thou art King?
    And resolution° thus fobbed° as it is with the rusty curb of
    old Father Antic° the law? Do not thou, when thou art King,
    hang a thief.   70
PRINCE. No, thou shalt.
FALSTAFF. Shall I? Oh, rare! By the Lord, I'll be a brave judge.
PRINCE. Thou judgest false already. I mean thou shalt have the
    hanging of the thieves and so become a rare hangman.   76
FALSTAFF. Well, Hal, well, and in some sort it jumps° with my
    humor° as well as waiting in the court, I can tell you.
PRINCE. For obtaining of suits?   80
FALSTAFF. Yea, for obtaining of suits,° whereof the hangman°
    hath no lean wardrobe. 'Sblood,° I am as melancholy as a
    gib-cat° or a lugged bear.°
PRINCE. Or an old lion, or a lover's lute.   84
FALSTAFF. Yea, or the drone of a Lincolnshire bagpipe.
PRINCE. What sayest thou to a hare,° or the melancholy of Moor-
    ditch?°   88
FALSTAFF. Thou hast the most unsavory similes, and art indeed
    the most comparative,° rascaliest, sweet young Prince. But,
    Hal, I prithee trouble me no more with vanity. I would to
    God thou and I knew where a commodity° of good names
    were to be bought. An old lord of the Council rated° me the   94
    other day in the street about you, sir, but I marked him not;
    and yet he talked very wisely, but I regarded him not; and
    yet he talked wisely, and in the street too.
PRINCE. Thou didst well, for wisdom cries out in the streets, and
    no man regards it.°   100
FALSTAFF. Oh, thou hast damnable iteration,° and art indeed able
    to corrupt a saint. Thou hast done much harm upon me,
    Hal. God forgive thee for it! Before I knew thee, Hal, I
    knew nothing; and now am I, if a man should speak truly,

64–65. here . . . heir: a pun, *heir* being pronounced as "hair." **67. resolu-**
tion: a stout heart. **68. fobbed:** fubbed, cheated. **69. Father Antic:** i.e.,
Daddy Buffoon. **77. jumps:** agrees. **78. humor:** whim. **81. obtaining of**
suits: with a pun on *suit*—"petitions to the sovereign for favor" and "clothes."
82. hangman: The clothes of the executed were the hangman's perquisite.
'Sblood: by God's blood. **83. gib-cat:** tomcat. **lugged bear:** bear torn by
the dogs in the sport of bear-baiting. **87. hare:** regarded as a melancholy
creature. **88. melancholy of Moorditch:** Moorditch was one of the open
sewers of the City of London, proverbial for its stink. **90. comparative:**
quick at making comparisons. **93. commodity:** parcel. **94. rated:** rebuked.
99–100. wisdom . . . it: quoted loosely from Proverbs 1:20–24. **101.**
iteration: ability to quote.

little better than one of the wicked. I must give over this life,
and I will give it over. By the Lord, an° I do not, I am a vil-   107
lain. I'll be damned for never a king's son in Christendom.

PRINCE. Where shall we take a purse tomorrow, Jack?   111

FALSTAFF. 'Zounds,° where thou wilt, lad. I'll make one. An I do
not, call me villain and baffle° me.

PRINCE. I see a good amendment of life in thee—from praying to
purse-taking.

FALSTAFF. Why, Hal, 'tis my vocation, Hal. 'Tis no sin for a man   117
to labor in his vocation. [*Enter* POINS.] Poins! Now shall we
know if Gadshill have set a match.° Oh, if men were to be
saved by merit, what hole in Hell were hot enough for him?
This is the most omnipotent villain that ever cried "Stand"
to a true man.

PRINCE. Good morrow, Ned.   123

POINS. Good morrow, sweet Hal. What says Monsieur Remorse?
What says Sir John Sack and Sugar? Jack! How agrees the
Devil and thee about thy soul, that thou soldest him on Good
Friday last for a cup of Madeira and a cold capon's leg?°   129

PRINCE. Sir John stands to his word, the Devil shall have his bargain, for he was never yet a breaker of proverbs.° He will
give the Devil his due.

POINS. Then art thou damned for keeping thy word with the Devil.   135

PRINCE. Else he had been damned for cozening° the Devil.

POINS. But, my lads, my lads, tomorrow morning, by four o'clock,
early at Gadshill!° There are pilgrims going to Canterbury   139
with rich offerings,° and traders riding to London with fat
purses. I have vizards° for you all, you have horses for yourselves. Gadshill lies tonight in Rochester. I have bespoke°   144
supper tomorrow night in Eastcheap. We may do it as secure
as sleep. If you will go, I will stuff your purses full of crowns.
If you will not, tarry at home and be hanged.

FALSTAFF. Hear ye, Yedward,° if I tarry at home and go not, I'll
hang you for going.   150

POINS. You will, chops?

FALSTAFF. Hal, wilt thou make one?

---

107. an: if.   **112. 'Zounds:** by God's Wounds.   **113. baffle:** disgrace.   **119.
set a match:** "framed a holdup."   **128–29. Good . . . leg:** Good Friday
being the Church's most solemn fast day, to drink Madeira and eat chicken
was a damnable sin.   **131–32. breaker of proverbs:** one to prove proverbs
false.   **136. cozening:** cheating.   **139. Gadshill:** near Rochester in Kent.
Some slight confusion is caused as the same name is used for one of the
gang. See l. 118, and II.1. 36–106.   **140–41. rich offerings:** i.e., for the
shrine of Saint Thomas à Becket at Canterbury.   **142. vizards:** masks.   **144.
bespoke:** ordered.   **149. Yedward:** a form of Edward, Poins's first name.

PRINCE. Who, I rob? I a thief? Not I, by my faith.

FALSTAFF. There's neither honesty, manhood, nor good fellowship in thee, nor thou camest not of the blood royal, if thou darest not stand for ten shillings.°

PRINCE. Well then, once in my days I'll be a madcap.   160

FALSTAFF. Why, that's well said.

PRINCE. Well, come what will, I'll tarry at home.

FALSTAFF. By the Lord, I'll be a traitor then, when thou art King.   165

PRINCE. I care not.

POINS. Sir John, I prithee, leave the Prince and me alone. I will lay him down such reasons for this adventure that he shall go.   169

FALSTAFF. Well, God give thee the spirit of persuasion and him the ears of profiting, that what thou speakest may move and what he hears may be believed,° that the true Prince may, for recreation sake, prove a false thief; for the poor abuses of the time want countenance.° Farewell. You shall find me in Eastcheap.   176

PRINCE. Farewell, thou latter spring!° Farewell, Allhallown summer!°   [Exit FALSTAFF.]

POINS. Now, my good sweet honey lord, ride with us tomorrow. I have a jest to execute that I cannot manage alone. Falstaff,   180 Bardolph, Peto, and Gadshill shall rob those men that we have already waylaid. Yourself and I will not be there, and when they have the booty, if you and I do not rob them, cut this head off from my shoulders.

PRINCE. How shall we part with them in setting forth?   188

POINS. Why, we will set forth before or after them, and appoint them a place of meeting, wherein it is at our pleasure to fail, and then will they adventure upon the exploit themselves; which they shall have no sooner achieved but we'll set upon them.   194

PRINCE. Yea, but 'tis like that they will know us by our horses, by our habits,° and by every other appointment,° to be ourselves.

POINS. Tut! Our horses they shall not see, I'll tie them in the wood. Our vizards we will change after we leave them. And, sirrah, I have cases of buckram° for the nonce,° to immask our noted outward garments.   202

PRINCE. Yea, but I doubt they will be too hard for us.

157–58. blood . . . shillings: pun on *royal,* a coin worth 10*s*.   **170–72. God . . . believed:** Falstaff constantly drops into the pious jargon of professional preachers.   **174–75. want countenance:** need encouragement.   **177. latter spring:** late spring; i.e., green autumn.   **178. Allhallown summer:** Indian summer. Allhallown (All Saints' Day) is on November 1.   **196. habits:** clothes.   **197. appointment:** accouterment.   **200–01. cases of buckram:** overalls of coarse linen.   **201. nonce:** occasion.

POINS. Well, for two of them, I know them to be as true-bred
    cowards as ever turned back; and for the third, if he fight
    longer than he sees reason,° I'll forswear arms. The virtue of   208
    this jest will be the incomprehensible lies that this same fat
    rogue will tell us when we meet at supper—how thirty, at
    least, he fought with; what wards,° what blows, what ex-
    tremities he endured. And in the reproof° of this lies the jest.   213
PRINCE. Well, I'll go with thee. Provide us all things necessary
    and meet me tomorrow night in Eastcheap. There I'll sup.
    Farewell.
POINS. Farewell, my lord.   [*Exit.*]
PRINCE. I know you all,° and will a while uphold°
    The unyoked humor° of your idleness.
    Yet herein will I imitate the sun,   220
    Who doth permit the base contagious° clouds
    To smother up his beauty from the world,
    That, when he please again to be himself,
    Being wanted, he may be more wondered at
    By breaking through the foul and ugly mists   225
    Of vapors that did seem to strangle him.
    If all the year were playing holidays,
    To sport would be as tedious as to work.
    But when they seldom come, they wished-for come,
    And nothing pleaseth but rare accidents.   230
    So, when this loose behavior I throw off
    And pay the debt I never promisèd,
    By how much better than my word I am,
    By so much shall I falsify men's hopes.
    And like bright metal on a sullen° ground,   235
    My reformation, glittering o'er my fault,
    Shall show more goodly and attract more eyes
    Than that which hath no foil° to set it off.
    I'll so offend, to make offense a skill,°
    Redeeming time° when men think least I will.   [*Exit.*]   240

207–08. **fight . . . reason:** This is Falstaff's avowed rule of life. See later
V.4.120.   **211. wards:** defense. See II.4.215.   **212. reproof:** rebuttal.   **218.
I . . . all:** This soliloquy is important for the understanding of the Prince's
later treatment of Falstaff and the gang. **uphold:** tolerate.   **219. unyoked
humor:** unrestrained behavior.   **221. contagious:** poisonous.   **235. sullen:**
dull.   **238. foil:** lit., tin foil set behind a jewel to give it sparkle.   **239. skill:**
art.   **240. Redeeming time:** making up for the time I have lost.

Scene 3 ⬤ *London. The palace.*

[*Enter the* KING, NORTHUMBERLAND, WORCESTER,
HOTSPUR, SIR WALTER BLUNT, *with others.*]

KING. My blood hath been too cold and temperate,
    Unapt to stir at these indignities,
    And you have found me;° for accordingly
    You tread upon my patience. But be sure
    I will from henceforth rather be myself,°   5
    Mighty and to be feared, than my condition,°
    Which hath been smooth as oil, soft as young down,
    And therefore lost that title of respect°
    Which the proud soul ne'er pays but to the proud.
WORCESTER. Our house, my sovereign liege, little deserves   10
    The scourge of greatness to be used on it,
    And that same greatness too which our own hands
    Have holp° to make so portly.°
NORTHUMBERLAND. My lord——
KING. Worcester, get thee gone, for I do see   15
    Danger and disobedience in thine eye.
    O sir, your presence is too bold and peremptory,
    And Majesty might never yet endure
    The moody frontier of a servant brow.°
    You have good leave to leave us.° When we need   20
    Your use and counsel, we shall send for you.

                      [*Exit* WORCESTER.]
  [*To* NORTHUMBERLAND] You were about to speak.
NORTHUMBERLAND.   Yea, my good lord.
    Those prisoners in your Highness' name demanded,°
    Which Harry Percy here at Holmedon took,

Sc. 3: 3. found me: found me out. **5. myself:** i.e., King. **6. than my condition:** than my naturally mild disposition. **8. title of respect:** claim to be respected. **13. holp:** helped. **portly:** magnificent. **19. moody . . . brow:** frowning look on a servant's brow. **20. leave . . . us:** a polite phrase of dismissal. **23. prisoners . . . demanded:** In earlier times a prisoner became the property of his captor, who released him on payment of a ransom according to his rank and wealth.

Were, as he says, not with such strength denied   25
As is delivered to your Majesty.
Either envy,° therefore, or misprision°
Is guilty of this fault, and not my son.
HOTSPUR. My liege, I did deny no prisoners.
But I remember, when the fight was done,   30
When I was dry with rage and éxtreme toil,
Breathless and faint, leaning upon my sword,
Came there a certain lord, neat, and trimly dressed,
Fresh as a bridegroom, and his chin new-reaped°
Showed like a stubble land at harvest home.   35
He was perfumèd like a milliner,
And 'twixt his finger and his thumb he held
A pouncet box,° which ever and anon
He gave his nose and took 't away again;
Who therewith angry, when it next came there,   40
Took it in snuff.° And still he smiled and talked,
And as the soldiers bore dead bodies by,
He called them untaught knaves, unmannerly,
To bring a slovenly unhandsome corse°
Betwixt the wind and his nobility.   45
With many holiday and lady terms°
He questioned me, amongst the rest, demanded
My prisoners in your Majesty's behalf.
I then, all smarting with my wounds being cold,
To be so pestered with a popinjay,°   50
Out of my grief° and my impatience
Answered neglectingly I know not what,
He should, or he should not; for he made me mad
To see him shine so brisk, and smell so sweet,
And talk so like a waiting gentlewoman°   55
Of guns and drums and wounds—God save the mark!—°
And telling me the sovereign'st° thing on earth
Was parmaceti° for an inward bruise;
And that it was great pity, so it was,

27. **envy:** malice—of Hotspur's enemies. **misprision:** misunderstanding. **34. chin new-reaped:** beard closely cut. **38. pouncet box:** small box containing perfume, which the fastidious sniffed to counteract foul smells. **41. Took . . . snuff:** sniffed, with a pun on the idiomatic meaning "resented." **44. corse:** corpse. **46. holiday . . . terms:** fancy phrases, as opposed to "working-day" or plain English. **50. popinjay:** parrot. **51. grief:** smart (of my wounds). **55. waiting gentlewoman:** lady in waiting, the essence of fancy femininity. **56. God . . . mark:** an impatient apology for a coarse remark. **57. sovereign'st:** most excellent. **58. parmaceti:** spermaceti, a fatty substance found in the whale and used as an ointment.

This villainous saltpeter should be digged   60
Out of the bowels of the harmless earth,
Which many a good tall° fellow had destroyed
So cowardly; and but for these vile guns,
He would himself have been a soldier.
This bald unjointed chat° of his, my lord,   65
I answered indirectly, as I said.
And I beseech you, let not his report
Come current° for an accusation
Betwixt my love and your high Majesty.
BLUNT. The circumstance considered, good my lord,   70
Whate'er Lord Harry Percy then had said
To such a person and in such a place,
At such a time, with all the rest retold,
May reasonably die and never rise
To do him wrong, or any way impeach°   75
What then he said, so he unsay it now.
KING. Why, yet° he doth deny his prisoners,
But with proviso° and exception,
That we at our own charge shall ransom straight
His brother-in-law, the foolish Mortimer,   80
Who, on my soul, hath willfully betrayed
The lives of those that he did lead to fight
Against that great magician,° damned Glendower,
Whose daughter, as we hear, the Earl of March
Hath lately married. Shall our coffers, then,   85
Be emptied to redeem a traitor home?
Shall we buy treason, and indent° with fears,
When they have lost and forfeited themselves?
No, on the barren mountains let him starve.
For I shall never hold that man my friend
Whose tongue shall ask me for one penny cost   90
To ransom home revolted Mortimer.
HOTSPUR. Revolted Mortimer!
He never did fall off,° my sovereign liege,
But by the chance of war. To prove that true   95
Needs no more but one tongue for all those wounds,
Those mouthèd° wounds, which valiantly he took
When on the gentle Severn's sedgy° bank,
In single opposition, hand to hand,

62. tall: brave.   **65. bald . . . chat:** slight disconnected chatter.   **68. Come current:** be regarded as valid.   **75. impeach:** accuse, call in question.   **77. yet:** still, after all.   **78. proviso:** stipulation.   **83. magician:** See III.1.36–49.   **87. indent:** make an agreement.   **94. fall off:** desert.   **97. mouthed:** looking like a mouth.   **98. sedgy:** reedy.

He did confound° the best part of an hour   100
In changing hardiment° with great Glendower.
Three times they breathed and three times did they drink,
Upon agreement, of swift Severn's flood;
Who then, affrighted with their bloody looks,
Ran fearfully among the trembling reeds,   105
And hid his crisp head in the hollow bank
Bloodstainèd with these valiant combatants.
Never did base and rotten policy°
Color her working° with such deadly wounds;
Nor never could the noble Mortimer   110
Receive so many, and all willingly.
Then let not him be slandered with revolt.
KING. Thou dost belie him,° Percy, thou dost belie him.
He never did encounter with Glendower.
I tell thee,   115
He durst as well have met the Devil alone
As Owen Glendower for an enemy.
Art thou not ashamed? But, sirrah,° henceforth
Let me not hear you speak of Mortimer.
Send me your prisoners with the speediest means,   120
Or you shall hear in such a kind from me
As will displease you. My Lord Northumberland,
We license your departure with your son.
Send us your prisoners, or you will hear of it.
                    [*Exeunt* KING HENRY, BLUNT, *and train.*]
HOTSPUR. An if the Devil come and roar for them,   125
I will not send them. I will after straight
And tell him so, for I will ease my heart,
Albeit I make a hazard° of my head.
NORTHUMBERLAND. What, drunk with choler?° Stay and pause
          awhile.
Here comes your uncle.
                    [*Re-enter* WORCESTER.]
HOTSPUR.   Speak of Mortimer!   130
'Zounds, I will speak of him, and let my soul
Want mercy if I do not join with him.
Yea, on his part I'll empty all these veins,
And shed my dear blood drop by drop in the dust,
But I will lift the downtrod Mortimer   135
As high in the air as this unthankful King,

100. confound: consume.   101. changing hardiment: exchanging blows.
108. policy: cunning.   109. Color . . . working: disguise its real intention.
113. belie him: lie about him.   118. sirrah: a form of address used to an
inferior, here deliberately insulting.   128. hazard: risk.   129. choler: wrath.

    As this ingrate and cankered° Bolingbroke.
NORTHUMBERLAND. Brother, the King hath made your nephew
        mad.
WORCESTER. Who struck this heat up after I was gone?
HOTSPUR. He will, forsooth, have all my prisoners.   140
        And when I urged the ransom once again
        Of my wife's brother, then his cheek looked pale,
        And on my face he turned an eye of death,
        Trembling even at the name of Mortimer.
WORCESTER. I cannot blame him. Was not he proclaimed   145
        By Richard that dead is the next of blood?
NORTHUMBERLAND. He was, I heard the proclamation.
        And then it was when the unhappy King—
        Whose wrongs in us God pardon!°—did set forth
        Upon his Irish expedition,
        From whence he intercepted° did return   150
        To be deposed and shortly° murderèd.
WORCESTER. And for whose death we in the world's wide mouth
        Live scandalized and foully spoken of.
HOTSPUR. But, soft, I pray you. Did King Richard then   155
        Proclaim my brother° Edmund Mortimer
        Heir to the crown?
NORTHUMBERLAND.   He did, myself did hear it.
HOTSPUR. Nay, then I cannot blame his cousin King,
        That wished him on the barren mountains starve.
        But shall it be that you, that set the crown   160
        Upon the head of this forgetful man,
        And for his sake wear the detested blot
        Of murderous subornation,° shall it be
        That you a world of curses undergo,
        Being the agents, or base second means,°   165
        The cords, the ladder, or the hangman rather?
        Oh, pardon me that I descend so low,
        To show the line° and the predicament°
        Wherein you range° under this subtle King.
        Shall it for shame be spoken in these days,   170
        Or fill up chronicles in time to come,
        That men of your nobility and power

---

137. cankered: malignant.   149. Whose . . . pardon: may God forgive the
wrongs committed by us against him.   151. intercepted: being hindered.
152. shortly: in a short time.   156. brother: brother-in-law.   162–63. wear
. . . subornation: wear the mark of shame as accessories to murder. subornation: procuring someone to commit a crime.   165. second means: assistants.
168. line: disgrace. predicament: class, category.   169. range: rank.

Did gage° them both in an unjust behalf,
As both of you—God pardon it!—have done,
To put down Richard, that sweet lovely rose,   175
And plant this thorn, this canker,° Bolingbroke?
And shall it in more shame be further spoken,
That you are fooled, discarded, and shook off
By him for whom these shames ye underwent?
No, yet time serves wherein you may redeem   180
Your banished honors, and restore yourselves
Into the good thoughts of the world again,
Revenge the jeering and disdained° contempt
Of this proud King, who studies day and night
To answer all the debt he owes to you   185
Even with the bloody payment of your deaths.
Therefore, I say——
WORCESTER.   Peace, Cousin, say no more.
And now I will unclasp a secret book,
And to your quick-conceiving° discontents
I'll read you matter deep and dangerous,   190
As full of peril and adventurous spirit
As to o'erwalk a current roaring loud
On the unsteadfast footing of a spear.°
HOTSPUR. If he fall in, good night! Or sink or swim.
Send danger from the east unto the west,   195
So honor cross it from the north to south,
And let them grapple, Oh, the blood more stirs
To rouse a lion than to start a hare!
NORTHUMBERLAND. Imagination of some great exploit.
Drives him beyond the bounds of patience.°   200
HOTSPUR. By Heaven, methinks it were an easy leap,
To pluck bright honor from the pale-faced moon,
Or dive into the bottom of the deep,
Where fathom line could never touch the ground,
And pluck up drownèd honor by the locks,   205
So he that doth redeem her thence might wear
Without corrival° all her dignities.
But out upon this half-faced fellowship!°
WORCESTER. He apprehends a world of figures here,°

173. gage: pledge, engage. 176. canker: wild rose, contrasted with the
garden rose. 183. disdained: disdainful. 189. quick-conceiving: quick-
witted. 193. unsteadfast . . . spear: with a spear as unsteady bridge.
200. patience: self-control. 207. corrival: partner. 208. half-faced fellowship: starving partnership; i.e., sharing of honor which is insufficient for two
to share. 209. apprehends . . . here: i.e., he is entirely carried away by his
imagination. figures: shapes, fantasies.

But not the form of what he should attend.   210
Good Cousin, give me audience for a while.
HOTSPUR. I cry you mercy.
WORCESTER.   Those same noble Scots
That are your prisoners——
HOTSPUR.   I'll keep them all.
By God, he shall not have a Scot of them.
No, if a Scot would save his soul, he shall not.   215
I'll keep them, by this hand.
WORCESTER.   You start away
And lend no ear unto my purposes.
Those prisoners you shall keep.
HOTSPUR.   Nay, I will, that's flat.
He said he would not ransom Mortimer,
Forbade my tongue to speak of Mortimer.   220
But I will find him when he lies asleep,
And in his ear I'll holloa "Mortimer!"
Nay,
I'll have a starling° shall he taught to speak
Nothing but "Mortimer," and give it him,   225
To keep his anger still in motion.
WORCESTER. Hear you, Cousin, a word.
HOTSPUR. All studies here I solemnly defy,
Save how to gall° and pinch this Bolingbroke.
And that same sword-and-buckler° Prince of Wales,   230
But that I think his father loves him not
And would be glad he met with some mischance,
I would have him poisoned with a pot of ale.
WORCESTER. Farewell, kinsman. I'll talk to you
When you are better tempered to attend.   235
NORTHUMBERLAND. Why, what a wasp-stung and impatient fool
Art thou to break into this woman's mood,
Tying thine ear to no tongue but thine own!
HOTSPUR. Why, look you, I am whipped and scourged with rods,
Nettled,° and stung with pismires,° when I hear   240
Of this vile politician,° Bolingbroke.
In Richard's time—what do you call the place?—
A plague upon it, it is in Gloucestershire,
'Twas where the madcap Duke his uncle kept,
His uncle York, where I first bowed my knee   245
Unto this king of smiles, this Bolingbroke—

224. starling: The starling, like the jackdaw and the parrot, can be taught to
mimic sound. 229. gall: make sore. 230. sword-and-buckler: swash-
buckler. 240. Nettled: whipped with nettles. pismires: ants. 241. politician: schemer.

'Sblood!—
When you and he came back from Ravenspurgh.
NORTHUMBERLAND. At Berkeley Castle.°
                                                       250
HOTSPUR. You say true.
    Why, what a candy deal° of courtesy
    This fawning greyhound then did proffer me!
    Look, "when his infant fortune came to age,"
    And "gentle Harry Percy," and "kind Cousin."
    Oh, the devil take such cozeners! God forgive me!   255
    Good Uncle, tell your tale, I have done.
WORCESTER. Nay, if you have not, to it again.
    We will stay° your leisure.
HOTSPUR.   I have done, i' faith.
WORCESTER. Then once more to your Scottish prisoners.
    Deliver them up without their ransom straight,   260
    And make the Douglas' son your only mean°
    For powers° in Scotland; which, for divers reasons
    Which I shall send you written, be assured
    Will easily be granted. [*To* NORTHUMBERLAND] You, my lord,
    Your son in Scotland being thus employed,   265
    Shall secretly into the bosom creep
    Of that same noble prelate, well beloved,
    The Archbishop.
HOTSPUR. Of York, is it not?   270
WORCESTER. True, who bears hard°
    His brother's death at Bristol, the Lord Scroop.
    I speak not this in estimation,°
    As what I think might be, but what I know
    Is ruminated,° plotted, and set down,
    And only stays but to behold the face   275
    Of that occasion that shall bring it on.
HOTSPUR. I smell it. Upon my life, it will do well.
NORTHUMBERLAND. Before the game is afoot, thou still° let'st
    slip.°
HOTSPUR. Why, it cannot choose but be a noble plot.
    And then the power of Scotland and of York,   280
    To join with Mortimer, ha?
WORCESTER.   And so they shall.
HOTSPUR. In faith, it is exceedingly well aimed.

---

249. **Berkeley Castle:** For this episode see *Rich II*, II.3.41–50. **251. candy deal:** deal of candy; i.e., hypocritical. **258. stay:** await. **261. mean:** means. **262. powers:** forces, armies. **270. bears hard:** takes hardly. **272. in estimation:** as a guess. **274. ruminated:** considered. **278. still:** continuously. **let'st slip:** let loose the greyhound.

WORCESTER. And 'tis no little reason bids us speed,
    To save our heads by raising of a head;°
    For, bear ourselves as even as we can,°   285
    The King will always think him in our debt,
    And think we think ourselves unsatisfied,
    Till he hath found a time to pay us home.
    And see already how he doth begin
    To make us strangers to his looks of love.   290
HOTSPUR. He does, he does. We'll be revenged on him.
WORCESTER. Cousin, farewell. No further go in this
    Than I by letters shall direct your course.
    When time is ripe, which will be suddenly,
    I'll steal to Glendower and Lord Mortimer,   295
    Where you and Douglas and our powers at once,
    As I will fashion° it, shall happily meet,
    To bear our fortunes in our own strong arms,
    Which now we hold at much uncertainty.
NORTHUMBERLAND. Farewell, good Brother. We shall thrive, I
    trust.   300
HOTSPUR. Uncle, adieu. Oh, let the hours be short
    Till fields and blows and groans applaud our sport! [*Exeunt.*]

---

284. head: armed force.   **285. bear . . . can:** however discreetly we may
behave.   **297. fashion:** contrive.

ACT II

Scene 1 ✒ *Rochester. An innyard.*

[*Enter a* CARRIER *with a lantern in his hand.*]

FIRST CARRIER. High-ho! An it be not four by the day, I'll be
hanged. Charles's Wain° is over the new chimney, and yet
our horse not packed.° What, ostler!

OSTLER. [*Within*] Anon, anon.

FIRST CARRIER. I prithee, Tom, beat° Cut's° saddle, put a few   6
flocks° in the point.° Poor jade,° is wrung° in the withers°
out of all cess.°

[*Enter another* CARRIER.]

SECOND CARRIER. Peas and beans are as dank here as a dog, and
that is the next way to give poor jades the bots.° This house   10
is turned upside down since Robin Ostler died.

FIRST CARRIER. Poor fellow, never joyed since the price of oats
rose. It was the death of him.

SECOND CARRIER. I think this be the most villainous house in all
London road for fleas. I am stung like a tench.°   16

FIRST CARRIER. Like a tench! By the mass, there is ne'er a king
Christen° could be better bit than I have been since the first
cock.   20

SECOND CARRIER. Why, they will allow us ne'er a jordan,° and
then we leak in your chimney, and your chamber lye° breeds
fleas like a loach.

Act II, Sc. 1: 2. **Charles's Wain:** Charles's Wagon, the constellation of
the Great Bear, called also the Great Dipper. 4. **horse . . . packed:**
Carriers at this time used pack horses for transport. 6. **beat:** i.e., to make
the padding more even. **Cut:** name of a horse with a docked tail. 7. **flocks:**
tufts of wool. **point:** pommel. **jade:** horse in poor condition. **wrung:** galled.
8. **withers:** point of the shoulder. **out . . . cess:** excessively. 10. **bots:**
worms. 16. **tench:** The tench and the loach (fresh-water fish) are sometimes infested with a form of louse. 19. **Christen:** Christian. 21. **jordan:**
chamber pot. 23. **chamber lye:** urine. Elizabethan sanitary arrangements
and domestic habits were crude.

FIRST CARRIER. What, ostler! Come away and be hanged! Come
    away.   25
SECOND CARRIER. I have a gammon of bacon° and two razes° of
    ginger, to be delivered as far as Charing Cross.
FIRST CARRIER. God's body! The turkeys in my pannier° are quite   28
    starved. What, ostler! A plague on thee! Hast thou never an
    eye in thy head? Canst not hear? An 'twere not as good
    deed as drink to break the pate on thee, I am a very villain.
    Come, and be hanged! Hast no faith in thee?   35
                  [*Enter* GADSHILL.]
GADSHILL. Good morrow, carriers. What's o'clock?
FIRST CARRIER. I think it be two o'clock.
GADSHILL. I prithee lend me thy lantern, to see my gelding in the
    stable.
FIRST CARRIER. Nay, by God, soft,° I know a trick worth two of   40
    that, i' faith.
GADSHILL. I pray thee, lend me thine.
SECOND CARRIER. Aye, when? Canst tell?° Lend me thy lantern,
    quoth he? Marry, I'll see thee hanged first.
GADSHILL. Sirrah carrier, what time do you mean to come to
    London?
                                         46
SECOND CARRIER. Time enough to go to bed with a candle, I war-
    rant thee. Come, Neighbor Mugs, we'll call up the gentle-
    men. They will along with company, for they have great
    charge.°   [*Exuent* CARRIERS.]
GADSHILL. What ho! Chamberlain!°   52
CHAMBERLAIN. [*Within*] At hand, quoth pickpurse.
GADSHILL. That's even as fair as—at hand, quoth the chamber-
    lain; for thou variest no more from picking of purses than
    giving direction doth from laboring. Thou layest the plot°   57
    how.
                [*Enter* CHAMBERLAIN.]
CHAMBERLAIN. Good morrow, Master Gadshill. It holds current
    that I told you yesternight. There's a franklin° in the wild°
    of Kent hath brought three hundred marks° with him in
    gold. I heard him tell it to one of his company last night at
    supper—a kind of auditor, one that hath abundance of

---

26. gammon of bacon: cured ham. **razes:** roots.   **28. pannier:** basket.   **40. soft:** go easy.   **43. Canst tell:** i.e., "says you!"   **51. great charge:** much money.   **52. Chamberlain:** man in charge of the bedrooms at an inn.   **57. layest . . . plot:** It was a common complaint that the chamberlains of inns were in league with highwaymen.   **60. franklin:** rich farmer. **wild:** weald; the hilly district in Kent and adjoining counties.   **61. mark:** 13*s* 4*d* ($\frac{2}{3}$ of a pound).

charge too, God knows what. They are up already, and call
for eggs and butter. They will away presently.   66
GADSHILL. Sirrah, if they meet not with Saint Nicholas' clerks,°
I'll give thee this neck.
CHAMBERLAIN. No, I'll none of it. I pray thee, keep that for the
hangman, for I know thou worshipest Saint Nicholas as
truly as a man of falsehood may.   72
GADSHILL. What talkest thou to me of the hangman? If I hang, I'll
make a fat pair of gallows; for if I hang, old Sir John hangs
with me, and thou knowest he is no starveling. Tut! There are
other Trojans° that thou dreamest not of, the which for sport   76
sake are content to do the profession some grace; that would,
if matters should be looked into, for their own credit sake,
make all whole. I am joined with no foot landrakers,° no   81
long-staff sixpenny strikers,° none of these mad mustachio
purple-hued maltworms;° but with nobility and tranquility,
burgomasters and great oneyers,° such as can hold in,° such   84
as will strike sooner than speak, and speak sooner than drink,
and drink sooner than pray. And yet, 'zounds, I lie; for they
pray continually to their saint, the commonwealth; or rather,
not pray to her, but prey on her, for they ride up and down
on her and make her their boots.°   91
CHAMBERLAIN. What, the commonwealth their boots? Will she
hold out water in foul way?
GADSHILL. She will, she will—justice hath liquored° her. We steal
as in a castle, cocksure. We have the receipt° of fern seed,°
we walk invisible.   96
CHAMBERLAIN. Nay, by my faith, I think you are more beholding
to the night than to fern seed for your walking invisible.
GADSHILL. Give me thy hand. Thou shalt have a share in our pur-
chase,° as I am a true man.   101
CHAMBERLAIN. Nay, rather let me have it, as you are a false thief.
GADSHILL. Go to. "Homo" is a common name to all men. Bid the
ostler bring my gelding out of the stable. Farewell, you
muddy° knave.   [Exeunt.]   106

67–68. Saint Nicholas' clerks: thieves, Saint Nicholas being their patron
saint. 76. Trojans: good lads. 81. foot landrakers: roving footpads; i.e.,
thieves so poor that they go on foot. long-staff . . . strikers: robbers who
use a long staff and will hold a man up for a pittance. 82–83. mustachio
. . . maltworms: red-faced tipplers with great mustaches. 84. oneyers:
ones. hold in: keep their mouths shut. 91. boots: booty. The chamberlain
caps his remark with a pun on leather boots. 94. liquored: greased. 96.
receipt: directions for using, recipe. fern seed: The seed of the fern is so
small that it was said to be invisible, and if found on Saint John's Day,
to confer invisibility on the finder. 101. purchase: in thieves' language,
plunder. 106. muddy: muddleheaded.

Scene 2 ◈ℰ *The highway, near Gadshill.*

[*Enter* PRINCE HENRY *and* POINS.]

POINS. Come, shelter, shelter. I have removed Falstaff's horse, and he frets like a gummed velvet.°

PRINCE. Stand close.

[*Enter* FALSTAFF.]

FALSTAFF. Poins! Poins, and be hanged! Poins!

PRINCE. Peace, ye fat-kidneyed rascal! What a brawling dost thou keep!   5

FALSTAFF. Where's Poins, Hal?

PRINCE. He is walked up to the top of the hill. I'll go seek him.   9

FALSTAFF. I am accursed to rob in that thief's company. The rascal hath removed my horse, and tied him I know not where. If I travel but four foot by the squier° further afoot, I shall break my wind. Well, I doubt not but to die a fair death for all this, if I 'scape hanging for killing that rogue. I have forsworn° his company hourly any time this two and   16 twenty years, and yet I am bewitched with the rogue's company. If the rascal have not given me medicines° to make me love him, I'll be hanged; it could not be else, I have drunk medicines. Poins! Hal! A plague upon you both! Bardolph!   21 Peto! I'll starve ere I'll rob a foot further. An 'twere not as good a deed as drink, to turn true man and to leave these rogues, I am the veriest varlet° that ever chewed with a tooth.   25 Eight yards of uneven ground is threescore and ten miles afoot with me, and the stony-hearted villains know it well enough. A plague upon it when thieves cannot be true one to another! [*They whistle.*] Whew! A plague upon you all! Give   30 me my horse, you rogues, give me my horse, and be hanged!

PRINCE. Peace, ye fat-guts! Lie down, lay thine ear close to the ground and list if thou canst hear the tread of travelers.   35

FALSTAFF. Have you any levers to lift me up again, being down? 'Sblood, I'll not bear mine own flesh so far afoot again for

---

Sc. 2: 2. **gummed velvet:** Cheap velvet (as well as taffeta) was sometimes treated with gum to give it stiffening, but it frayed sooner. **13. squier:** square, rule. **16. forsworn:** sworn off. **19. medicines:** love potions. **25. varlet:** knave.

all the coin in thy father's exchequer. What a plague mean
ye to colt° me thus?

PRINCE. Thou liest. Thou art not colted, thou art uncolted.   42

FALSTAFF. I prithee, good Prince Hal, help me to my horse, good
king's son.

PRINCE. Out, ye rogue! Shall I be your ostler?

FALSTAFF. Go hang thyself in thine own heir-apparent garters! If
I be ta'en, I'll peach for this. An I have not ballads° made   48
on you all and sung to filthy tunes, let a cup of sack be my
poison. When a jest is so forward, and afoot too! I hate it.

[*Enter* GADSHILL, BARDOLPH *and* PETO *with him.*]

GADSHILL. Stand.

FALSTAFF. So I do, against my will.

POINS. Oh, 'tis our setter.° I know his voice. Bardolph, what
news?   54

BARDOLPH. Case° ye, case ye, on with your vizards. There's
money of the King's coming down the hill, 'tis going to the
King's exchequer.

FALSTAFF. You lie, ye rogue, 'tis going to the King's tavern.

GADSHILL. There's enough to make us all.   60

FALSTAFF. To be hanged.

PRINCE. Sirs, you four shall front them in the narrow lane, Ned
Poins and I will walk lower. If they 'scape from your encounter, then they light on us.

PETO. How many be there of them?   66

GADSHILL. Some eight or ten.

FALSTAFF. 'Zounds, will they not rob us?

PRINCE. What, a coward, Sir John Paunch?

FALSTAFF. Indeed I am not John of Gaunt, your grandfather, but
yet no coward, Hal.   71

PRINCE. Well, we leave that to the proof.

POINS. Sirrah Jack, thy horse stands behind the hedge. When thou
needest him, there thou shalt find him. Farewell, and stand
fast.   75

FALSTAFF. Now cannot I strike him, if I should be hanged.

PRINCE. Ned, where are our disguises?

POINS. Here, hard by. Stand close.   [*Exeunt* PRINCE *and* POINS.]

FALSTAFF. Now, my masters, happy man be his dole,° say I.
Every man to his business.   81

[*Enter the* TRAVELERS.]

---

40. colt: trick.   **48. ballads:** low popular songs.   **53. setter:** the accomplice
who brings in the victim.   **55. Case:** mask.   **80. happy . . . dole:** i.e., here's
luck; lit., may the lucky man have his reward.

FIRST TRAVELER. Come, neighbor. The boy shall lead our horses
   down the hill. We'll walk afoot awhile, and ease our legs.
THIEVES. Stand!
TRAVELERS. Jesus bless us!   86
FALSTAFF. Strike, down with them, cut the villains' throats! Ah,
   whoreson° caterpillars,° bacon-fed knaves! They hate us
   youth. Down with them, fleece them.
TRAVELERS. Oh, we are undone, both we and ours forever!   92
FALSTAFF. Hang ye, gorbellied° knaves, are ye undone? No, ye
   fat chuffs,° I would your store were here!° On, bacons,° on!
   What, ye knaves! Young men must live. You are grand jurors,° are ye? We'll jure ye, 'faith.   97
                [*Here they rob them and bind them. Exeunt.*]
          [*Re-enter* PRINCE HENRY *and* POINS *disguised.*]
PRINCE. The thieves have bound the true men. Now could thou
   and I rob the thieves and go merrily to London, it would be
   argument° for a week, laughter for a month, and a good jest
   forever.
POINS. Stand close. I hear them coming.   103
              [*Enter the* THIEVES *again.*]
FALSTAFF. Come, my masters, let us share, and then to horse
   before day. An the Prince and Poins be not two arrant°
   cowards, there's no equity stirring.° There's no more valor
   in that Poins than in a wild duck.   108
PRINCE. Your money!
POINS. Villains! [*As they are sharing, the* PRINCE *and* POINS *set
   upon them; they all run away; and* FALSTAFF, *after a blow or
   two, runs away too, leaving the booty behind them.*]
PRINCE. Got with much ease. Now merrily to horse.
   The thieves are all scattered and possessed with fear
   So strongly that they dare not meet each other.
   Each takes his fellow for an officer.
   Away, good Ned. Falstaff sweats to death,   115
   And lards the lean earth as he walks along.
   Were't not for laughing, I should pity him.
POINS. How the rogue roared!   [*Exeunt.*]

---

88. whoreson: bastard. **caterpillars:** parasites on the public. **93. gor-
bellied:** big-bellied. **94. chuffs:** mean misers. **were here:** i.e., in your bellies.
95. bacons: fat pigs. **96. grand jurors:** i.e., men of highest respectability.
101. argument: matter for talk. **106. arrant:** complete. **no . . . stirring:**
no sound judgment in the world.

Scene 3 ✌ *Warkworth Castle.*

[*Enter* HOTSPUR *alone, reading a letter.*]

HOTSPUR. "But, for mine own part, my lord, I could be well contented to be there, in respect of the love I bear your house."
He could be contented. Why is he not, then? In respect of the
love he bears our house. He shows in this he loves his own
barn better than he loves our house. Let me see some more.   5
"The purpose you undertake is dangerous"—why, that's certain. 'Tis dangerous to take a cold, to sleep, to drink; but I tell
you, my lord fool, out of this nettle danger we pluck this
flower safety. "The purpose you undertake is dangerous; the
friends you have named uncertain; the time itself unsorted;°   11
and your whole plot too light for the counterpoise of so great
an opposition." Say you so, say you so? I say unto you again,
you are a shallow cowardly hind,° and you lie. What a lack-   16
brain is this! By the Lord, our plot is a good plot as ever was
laid, our friends true and constant—a good plot, good friends,
and full of expectation. An excellent plot, very good friends.
What a frosty-spirited rogue is this! Why, my Lord of York°   21
commends the plot and the general course of the action.
'Zounds, an I were now by this rascal, I could brain him with
his lady's fan. Is there not my father, my uncle, and myself?
Lord Edmund Mortimer, my Lord of York, and Owen Glen-   25
dower? Is there not besides the Douglas? Have I not all their
letters to meet me in arms by the ninth of the next month?
And are they not some of them set forward already? What a
pagan rascal is this, an infidel! Ha! You shall see now in   30
very sincerity of fear and cold heart, will he to the King, and
day open all our proceedings. Oh, I could divide myself, and
go to buffets,° for moving° such a dish of skim milk with so
honorable an action! Hang him! Let him tell the King. We   35
are prepared. I will set forward tonight.

Sc. 3: **11. unsorted:** ill-chosen. **16. hind:** female deer, the essence of
timidity. **21. Lord of York:** Richard Scroop, Archbishop of York. **34. go
to buffets:** come to blows. **moving:** trying to move.

[*Enter* LADY PERCY.] How now, Kate! I must leave you within
these two hours.

LADY PERCY. O my good lord, why are you thus alone?   40
For what offense have I this fortnight been
A banished woman from my Harry's bed?
Tell me, sweet lord, what is't that takes from thee
Thy stomach,° pleasure, and thy golden sleep?
Why dost thou bend thine eyes upon the earth,   45
And start so often when thou sit'st alone?
Why hast thou lost the fresh blood in thy cheeks,
And given my treasures° and my rights of thee
To thick-eyed° musing and cursed melancholy?
In thy faint slumbers I by thee have watched,   50
And heard thee murmur tales of iron wars,
Speak terms of manage° to thy bounding steed,
Cry "Courage! To the field!" And thou hast talked
Of sallies and retires,° of trenches, tents,
Of palisadoes,° frontiers,° parapets,   55
Of basilisks, of cannon, culverin,°
Of prisoners' ransom, and of soldiers slain,
And all the currents° of a heady° fight.
Thy spirit within thee hath been so at war
And thus hath so bestirred thee in thy sleep   60
That beads of sweat have stood upon thy brow,
Like bubbles in a late disturbèd stream.
And in thy face strange motions have appeared,
Such as we see when men restrain their breath
On some great sudden hest.° Oh, what portènts are these?   65
Some heavy business hath my lord in hand,
And I must know it, else he loves me not.

HOTSPUR. What ho! [*Enter* SERVANT.] Is Gilliams with the packet
gone?

SERVANT. He is, my lord, an hour ago.

HOTSPUR. Hath Butler brought those horses from the sheriff?   70

SERVANT. One horse, my lord, he brought even now.

HOTSPUR. What horse? A roan, a crop-ear,° is it not?

44. stomach: appetite. **48. treasures:** i.e., that ought to be mine. **49.
thick-eyed:** dull-sighted, because he sees nothing. **52. manage:** horsemanship. **54. sallies . . . retires:** raids and retreats. **55. palisadoes:** defen-
sive protection of pointed stakes. **frontiers:** barricades, **56. basilisks . . .
culverin:** the heavier pieces of artillery. The basilisk was of 5-inch caliber
and fired a shot of 15½ lbs., the cannon of 8-inch caliber with a 60-lb. shot,
the culverin of 5½-inch caliber with a 17-lb. shot. Shakespeare is thinking
of Elizabethan ordnance rather than the cannon used in 1400. **58. currents:** courses, rapid movement. **heady:** fierce. **65. hest:** command, action.
72. crop-ear: with short ears.

SERVANT. It is, my lord.
HOTSPUR.   That roan shall be my throne.
    Well, I will back him straight. Oh, Esperance!°
    Bid Butler lead him forth into the park.   [*Exit* SERVANT.]   75
LADY PERCY. But hear you, my lord.
HOTSPUR. What say'st thou, my lady?
LADY PERCY. What is it carries you away?
HOTSPUR. Why, my horse, my love, my horse.
LADY PERCY. Out, you mad-headed ape!   80
    A weasel hath not such a deal of spleen°
    As you are tossed with. In faith,
    I'll know your business, Harry, that I will.
    I fear my brother Mortimer doth stir
    About his title, and hath sent for you   85
    To line° his enterprise. But if you go——
HOTSPUR. So far afoot, I shall be weary, love.
LADY PERCY. Come, come, you paraquito,° answer me
    Directly unto this question that I ask.
    In faith, I'll break thy little finger, Harry,   90
    An if thou wilt not tell me all things true.
HOTSPUR. Away,
    Away, you trifler! Love! I love thee not,
    I care not for thee, Kate. This is no world
    To play with mammets° and to tilt with lips.°   95
    We must have bloody noses and cracked crowns,
    And pass them current° too. God's me, my horse!
    What say'st thou, Kate? What wouldst thou have with me?
LADY PERCY. Do you not love me? Do you not, indeed?
    Well, do not, then, for since you love me not,   100
    I will not love myself. Do you not love me?
    Nay, tell me if you speak in jest or no.
HOTSPUR. Come, wilt thou see me ride?
    And when I am o' horseback, I will swear
    I love thee infinitely. But hark you, Kate,   105
    I must not have you henceforth question me
    Whither I go, nor reason whereabout.
    Whither I must, I must. And to conclude,
    This evening must I leave you, gentle Kate.
    I know you wise, but yet no farther wise   110
    Than Harry Percy's wife. Constant you are,
    But yet a woman. And for secrecy,

---

74. Esperance: hope—the battle cry of the Percies. **81.** spleen: anger,
passion. **86.** line: strengthen. **88.** paraquito: parrot. **95.** mammets: dolls.
tilt . . . lips: kiss. **97.** current: with a pun on *cracked crowns;* i.e., broken
heads, and crown pieces, cracked and so not current.

No lady closer, for I well believe
Thou wilt not utter what thou dost not know,
And so far will I trust thee, gentle Kate.   115
LADY PERCY. How! So far?
HOTSPUR. Not an inch further. But hark you, Kate,
Whither I go, thither shall you go too;
Today will I set forth, tomorrow you.
Will this content you, Kate?
LADY PERCY.   It must of force.   [*Exeunt.*]   120

Scene 4 ⟋ *The Boar's Head Tavern in Eastcheap.*

[*Enter the* PRINCE, *and* POINS.]

PRINCE. Ned, prithee come out of that fat° room, and lend me
thy hand to laugh a little.
POINS. Where hast been, Hal?
PRINCE. With three or four loggerheads° amongst three or four-
score hogsheads.° I have sounded the very base string of hu-   5
mility.° Sirrah, I am sworn brother to a leash° of drawers,
and can call them all by their Christen names, as Tom, Dick,
and Francis. They take it already upon their salvation that
though I be but Prince of Wales, yet I am the king of courtesy; and tell me flatly I am no proud Jack, like Falstaff, but
a Corinthian,° a lad of mettle, a good boy, by the Lord, so   12
they call me, and when I am King of England, I shall command all the good lads in Eastcheap. They call drinking
deep, dyeing scarlet, and when you breathe in your watering,° they cry "hem!"° and bid you play it off.° To conclude,   17
I am so good a proficient in one quarter of an hour that I
can drink with any tinker in his own language during my
life. I tell thee, Ned, thou hast lost much honor that thou

Sc. 4: 1. fat: stuffy. 4. loggerheads: blockheads. 5. hogsheads: casks.
5–6. sounded . . . humility: i.e., have sunk to the lowest depth. 7. leash:
set of three, properly used of a *leash* of greyhounds. 12. Corinthian: a
gay lad. 16. watering: drinking. 17. cry "hem": one of those exclamations made by topers, like "Here's how." play it off: get it down.

wert not with me in this action. But, sweet Ned—to sweeten
which name of Ned, I give thee this pennyworth of sugar,
clapped even now into my hand by an underskinker,° one   25
that never spake other English in his life than "Eight shillings and sixpence," and "You are welcome," with this shrill
addition, "Anon,° anon, sir! Score° a pint of bastard° in the   29
Half-Moon,"° or so. But, Ned, to drive away the time till
Falstaff come, I prithee do thou stand in some by-room while
I question my puny° drawer to what end he gave me the sugar. And do thou never leave calling "Francis," that his tale
to me may be nothing but "Anon." Step aside, and I'll show
thee a precedent.°   36

POINS. Francis!
PRINCE. Thou art perfect.
POINS. Francis!   [*Exit* POINS.]
                    [*Enter* FRANCIS.]
FRANCIS. Anon, anon, sir. Look down into the Pomgarnet,° Ralph.   42
PRINCE. Come hither, Francis.
FRANCIS. My lord?
PRINCE. How long hast thou to serve, Francis?°
FRANCIS. Forsooth, five years, and as much as to——
POINS. [*Within*] Francis!
FRANCIS. Anon, anon, sir.   49
PRINCE. Five year! By'r Lady, a long lease for the clinking of
     pewter. But, Francis, darest thou be so valiant as to play the
     coward with thy indenture° and show it a fair pair of heels
     and run from it?
FRANCIS. Oh, Lord, sir, I'll be sworn upon all the books in England
     I could find in my heart.°   56
POINS. [*Within*] Francis!
FRANCIS. Anon, sir.
PRINCE. How old art thou, Francis?
FRANCIS. Let me see—about Michaelmas next I shall be——   61
POINS. [*Within*] Francis!
FRANCIS. Anon, sir. Pray stay a little, my lord.
PRINCE. Nay, but hark you, Francis. For the sugar thou gavest

25. underskinker: assistant bartender. 28. Anon: at once or by and by,
the drawer's cry, "Coming, sir." 29. Score: chalk up, the method of re-
cording a debt for drink still used in English public houses. bastard: a
sweet white wine. Half-Moon: Each room in an inn or a tavern had its
own name. 32. puny: freshman. 36. precedent: specimen. 42. Pomgarnet: Pomegranate—another room. 45. How . . . Francis: i.e., how many
years of your apprenticeship still remain. As Francis has only served two
of his seven years, he is sixteen. 53. indenture: agreement of apprenticeship. 56. could . . . heart: i.e., very willingly.

me, 'twas a pennyworth, was't not?   66

FRANCIS. Oh, Lord, I would it had been two!

PRINCE. I will give thee for it a thousand pound. Ask me when
thou wilt, and thou shalt have it.   70

POINS. [*Within*] Francis!

FRANCIS. Anon, anon.

PRINCE. Anon, Francis? No, Francis, but tomorrow, Francis; or,
Francis, o' Thursday; or indeed, Francis, when thou wilt.
But Francis!

FRANCIS. My lord?   76

PRINCE. Wilt thou rob this leathern-jerkin, crystal-button, not-
pated, agate-ring, puke-stocking, caddis-garter, smooth-
tongue, Spanish-pouch——°   80

FRANCIS. Oh, Lord, sir, who do you mean?

PRINCE. Why, then, your brown bastard is your only drink, for
look you, Francis, your white canvas doublet will sully. In
Barbary,° sir, it cannot come to so much.   86

FRANCIS. What, sir?

POINS. [*Within*] Francis!

PRINCE. Away, you rogue! Dost thou not hear them call? [*Here
they both call him; the* DRAWER *stands amazed, not knowing
which way to go.*]

[*Enter* VINTNER.]

VINTNER. What, standest thou still, and hearest such a calling? Look
to the guests within. [*Exit* FRANCIS.] My lord, old Sir John,
with half-a-dozen more, are at the door. Shall I let them in?   94

PRINCE. Let them alone awhile, and then open the door. [*Exit*
VINTNER.] Poins!

[*Re-enter* POINS.]

POINS. Anon, anon, sir.

PRINCE. Sirrah, Falstaff and the rest of the thieves are at the door.
Shall we be merry?   99

POINS. As merry as crickets, my lad. But hark ye, what cunning
match° have you made with this jest of the drawer? Come,
what's the issue?°

PRINCE. I am now of all humors° that have showed themselves hu-   104
mors since the old days of Goodman Adam to the pupilage°

77–80. **leathern-jerkin . . . Spanish-pouch:** This list gives the outward
characteristics of a prosperous innkeeper: leather coat (*jerkin*) with crystal
buttons, close-cropped head (*not-pated*), large ring, gray (*puke*) stockings,
worsted (*caddis*) garters, a *smooth tongue,* and a *pouch* of *Spanish* leather.
84. **Barbary:** in North Africa—but the Prince's words have passed beyond
location. 101. **what . . . match:** what is the game. 103. **issue:** result.
104. **of . . . humors:** i.e., will match my mood with any man's. 106.
pupilage: boyhood.

of this present twelve o'clock at midnight.
[*Re-enter* FRANCIS.] What's o'clock, Francis?   108
FRANCIS. Anon, anon, sir.   [*Exit.*]
PRINCE. That ever this fellow should have fewer words than a
parrot, and yet the son of a woman! His industry is upstairs
and downstairs, his eloquence the parcel° of a reckoning. I   113
am not yet of Percy's mind, the Hotspur of the North, he
that kills me some six or seven dozen of Scots at a breakfast,
washes his hands, and says to his wife, "Fie upon this quiet
life! I want work." "O my sweet Harry," says she, "how
many hast thou killed today?" "Give my roan horse a
drench,"° says he, and answers "Some fourteen" an hour   119
after—"a trifle, a trifle." I prithee call in Falstaff. I'll play
Percy, and that damned brawn° shall play Dame Mortimer
his wife. "Rivo!"° says the drunkard. Call in ribs, call in   124
tallow.
            [*Enter* FALSTAFF, GADSHILL, BARDOLPH, *and* PETO;
                    FRANCIS *following with wine.*]
POINS. Welcome, Jack. Where hast thou been?
FALSTAFF. A plague of all cowards, I say, and a vengeance too!
Marry, and amen! Give me a cup of sack, boy. Ere I lead
this life long, I'll sew netherstocks° and mend them and foot   129
them too. A plague of all cowards! Give me a cup of sack,
rogue. Is there no virtue extant?°   [*He drinks.*]
PRINCE. Didst thou never see Titan° kiss a dish of butter? Pitiful-
hearted Titan, that melted° at the sweet tale of the sun's! If 134
thou didst, then behold that compound.
FALSTAFF. You rogue, here's lime° in this sack too. There is nothing but roguery to be found in villainous man. Yet a coward
is worse than a cup of sack with lime in it. A villainous coward! Go thy ways, old Jack, die when thou wilt. If manhood, 140
good manhood, be not forgot upon the face of the earth,
then am I a shotten° herring. There live not three good men
unhanged in England, and one of them is fat, and grows old.
God help the while!° A bad world, I say. I would I were a   145
weaver, I could sing psalms° or anything. A plague of all
cowards, I say still.

113. parcel: items.   119. drench: purge.   112. brawn: fat pig.   124. Rivo:
another drinkers' exclamation. See l. 17.   129. netherstocks: stockings, at
this time cut out of material and sewed, not knitted.   132. virtue extant:
manhood in existence.   133. Titan: the sun.   134. that melted: i.e., the
butter.   137. lime: used to adulterate wine by giving it a better color and
taste.   143. shotten: without its roe.   145. God . . . while: God help these
times.   146–47. weaver . . . psalms: Weavers, mostly Puritan refugees
from the Netherlands, were noted psalm singers.

PRINCE. How now, woolsack! What mutter you?

FALSTAFF. A king's son! If I do not beat thee out of thy kingdom
with a dagger of lath,° and drive all thy subjects afore thee   151
like a flock of wild geese, I'll never wear hair on my face
more. You Prince of Wales!

PRINCE. Why, you whoreson round man, what's the matter?

FALSTAFF. Are you not a coward? Answer me to that. And Poins
there?

POINS. 'Zounds, ye fat paunch, an ye call me coward, by the
Lord, I'll stab thee.   160

FALSTAFF. I call thee coward! I'll see thee damned ere I call thee
coward. But I would give a thousand pound I could run as
fast as thou canst. You are straight enough in the shoulders,
you care not who sees your back. Call you that backing of
your friends? A plague upon such backing! Give me them
that will face me. Give me a cup of sack. I am a rogue if I
drunk today.   169

PRINCE. O villain! Thy lips are scarce wiped since thou drunkest
last.

FALSTAFF. All's one for that. [*He drinks.*] A plague of all cowards, still say I.

PRINCE. What's the matter?   174

FALSTAFF. What's the matter! There be four of us here have ta'en
a thousand pound this day morning.

PRINCE. Where is it, Jack? Where is it?

FALSTAFF. Where is it! Taken from us it is—a hundred upon poor
four of us.   180

PRINCE. What, a hundred, man?

FALSTAFF. I am a rogue if I were not at half-sword° with a dozen
of them two hours together. I have 'scaped by miracle. I am
eight times thrust through the doublet,° four through the   185
hose;° my buckler° cut through and through; my sword
hacked like a handsaw—*ecce signum!*° I never dealt° better
since I was a man. All would not do. A plague of all cowards! Let them speak. If they speak more or less than
truth, they are villains and the sons of darkness.   191

PRINCE. Speak, sirs, how was it?

GADSHILL. We four set upon some dozen——

FALSTAFF. Sixteen at least, my lord.

GADSHILL. And bound them.   195

PETO. No, no, they were not bound.

151. dagger of lath: wooden dagger. 182. at half-sword: within half a
sword's length. A cautious fighter kept at greater distance. 185. doublet:
coat. hose: breeches. buckler: small shield. 187. ecce signum: behold
the sign. dealt: fought.

FALSTAFF. You rogue, they were bound, every man of them, or I
     am a Jew else, an Ebrew° Jew.

GADSHILL. As we were sharing, some six or seven fresh men set
     upon us——   200

FALSTAFF. And unbound the rest, and then come in the other.

PRINCE. What, fought you with them all?   203

FALSTAFF. All! I know not what you call all, but if I fought not
     with fifty of them, I am a bunch of radish. If there were not
     two or three and fifty upon poor old Jack, then am I no two-
     legged creature.

PRINCE. Pray God you have not murdered some of them.   210

FALSTAFF. Nay, that's past praying for. I have peppered two of
     them—two I am sure I have paid,° two rogues in buckram
     suits. I tell thee what, Hal, if I tell thee a lie, spit in my face,
     call me horse.° Thou knowest my old ward.° Here I lay, and   215
     thus I bore my point. Four rogues in buckram let drive at
     me——

PRINCE. What, four? Thou saidst but two even now.

FALSTAFF. Four, Hal, I told thee four.

POINS. Aye, aye, he said four.

FALSTAFF. These four came all afront, and mainly° thrust at me.   222
     I made me no more ado, but took all their seven points in
     my target, thus.

PRINCE. Seven? Why, there were but four even now.

FALSTAFF. In buckram?

POINS. Aye, four, in buckram suits.

FALSTAFF. Seven, by these hilts,° or I am a villain else.   229

PRINCE. Prithee let him alone. We shall have more anon.

FALSTAFF. Dost thou hear me, Hal?

PRINCE. Aye, and mark thee too, Jack.   234

FALSTAFF. Do so, for it is worth the listening to. These nine in
     buckram that I told thee of——

PRINCE. So, two more already.

FALSTAFF. Their points being broken——

POINS. Down fell their hose.°   239

FALSTAFF. Began to give me ground. But I followed me close,
     came in foot and hand, and with a thought seven of the
     eleven I paid.

PRINCE. Oh, monstrous! Eleven buckram men grown out of two!   244

FALSTAFF. But, as the Devil would have it, three misbegotten

198. Ebrew: Hebrew.   212. paid: paid home, done for.   214. horse: Like
the ass, the horse was regarded as stupid.   215. ward: stance, position of
guard. Here Falstaff re-enacts his heroic exploit.   222. mainly: violently.
229. hilts: sword hilt.   238–39. Their . . . hose: The Prince puns on the
other meaning of *points*, laces tying the hose to the doublet.

knaves in Kendal green° came at my back and let drive at
me; for it was so dark, Hal, that thou couldst not see thy
hand.

PRINCE. These lies are like their father that begets them—gross as
a mountain, open, palpable. Why, thou clay-brained guts,
thou knotty-pated° fool, thou whoreson, obscene, greasy tal-   252
low catch——°

FALSTAFF. What, art thou mad? Art thou mad? Is not the truth
truth?

PRINCE. Why, how couldst thou know these men in Kendal green
when it was so dark thou couldst not see thy hand? Come,
tell us your reason. What sayest thou to this?   259

POINS. Come, your reason, Jack, your reason.

FALSTAFF. What, upon compulsion? 'Zounds, an I were at the
strappado, or all the racks° in the world, I would not tell
you on compulsion. Give your reason on compulsion! If reasons were as plentiful as blackberries, I would give no man a   264
reason upon compulsion, I.

PRINCE. I'll be no longer guilty of this sin—this sanguine° coward, this bed-presser, this horseback-breaker, this huge hill of
flesh——

FALSTAFF. 'Sblood, you starveling,° you elf skin,° you dried neat's   270
tongue,° you bull's pizzle,° you stockfish!° Oh, for breath to
utter what is like thee! You tailor's yard, you sheath, you
bow case, you vile standing tuck——°   274

PRINCE. Well, breathe a while, and then to it again, and when
thou hast tired thyself in base comparisons, hear me speak
but this.

POINS. Mark, Jack.   278

---

246. Kendal green: cloth made (originally at Kendal in Westmoreland) of
the poorest-quality wool, and used by woodmen and servants. **252. knotty-
pated:** blockhead. **253. tallow catch:** the word is variously emended and
interpreted. Johnson suggested "keech"—a lump of fat prepared by the
butcher for the candlemaker. A *tallow catch* would naturally be "a thing
for catching tallow"; i.e., the rim on the candlestick which, when piled up
with the drippings of wax, is no bad image for Falstaff. **262. strappado
. . . racks:** forms of torture. See Additional Note 3, p. 199. **268. sanguine:**
one suffering from an excess of the sanguine humor, of which the outward
symptoms were a red face and an optimistic temperament. **270. you
starveling:** Falstaff, being thoroughly roused, retorts with a string of images
expressing the thinness of the Prince. **elf skin:** sometimes emended to eel-
skin, but probably it meant snakeskin, which, as Oberon observed, was
"Weed wide enough to wrap a fairy in." (*MND*, II.1.256.) **271. neat's
tongue:** ox tongue, **bull's pizzle:** This portion of the bull's anatomy was
dried and used as a whip. **272. stockfish:** dried codfish. **274. standing
tuck:** a rapier stuck in the ground.

PRINCE. We two saw you four set on four and bound them, and
    were masters of their wealth. Mark now, how a plain tale
    shall put you down. Then did we two set on you four; and,
    with a word, outfaced you from your prize, and have it, yea,
    and can show it you here in the house. And, Falstaff, you
    carried your guts away as nimbly, with as quick dexterity,   285
    and roared for mercy, and still run and roared, as ever I
    heard bull calf. What a slave art thou, to hack thy sword
    as thou hast done, and then say it was in fight! What trick,
    what device, what starting hole,° canst thou now find out
    to hide thee from this open and apparent shame?   292
POINS. Come, let's hear Jack. What trick hast thou now?
FALSTAFF. By the Lord, I knew ye as well as he that made ye.
    Why, hear you, my masters. Was it for me to kill the heir
    apparent? Should I turn upon the true Prince? Why, thou
    knowest I am as valiant as Hercules. But beware instinct, the
    lion will not touch the true prince.° Instinct is a great mat-   299
    ter, I was now a coward on instinct. I shall think the better
    of myself and thee during my life, I for a valiant lion, and
    thou for a true Prince. But, by the Lord, lads, I am glad you
    have the money. Hostess, clap to the doors. Watch tonight,
    pray tomorrow. Gallants, lads, boys, hearts of gold, all the   305
    titles of good fellowship come to you! What, shall we be
    merry? Shall we have a play extempore?
PRINCE. Content, and the argument° shall be thy running away.   311
FALSTAFF. Ah, no more of that, Hal, an thou lovest me!
                    [*Enter* HOSTESS.]
HOSTESS. O Jesu, my lord the Prince!
PRINCE. How now, my lady the hostess! What sayest thou to me?   316
HOSTESS. Marry, my lord, there is a nobleman of the Court at
    door would speak with you. He says he comes from your fa-
    ther.
PRINCE. Give him as much as will make him a royal man,° and
    send him back again to my mother.
FALSTAFF. What manner of man is he?   323
HOSTESS. An old man.
FALSTAFF. What doth gravity out of his bed at midnight? Shall I
    give him his answer?
PRINCE. Prithee do, Jack.
FALSTAFF. Faith, and I'll send him packing.   [*Exit.*]

290–91. starting hole: a hole into which a rabbit bolts for safety. 298–99.
lion . . . prince: This was very generally believed. 310. argument: plot.
321–22. as . . . man: i.e., 3s 4d, which is the difference between a *royal*
(10s) and a noble (6s 8d). It is a sign of Prince Hal's low behavior that
he should make such jokes about a nobleman of the Court.

PRINCE. Now, sirs. By'r Lady, you fought fair; so did you, Peto;
so did you, Bardolph. You are lions too, you ran away upon
instinct, you will not touch the true prince—no, fie!   332

BARDOLPH. Faith, I ran when I saw others run.

PRINCE. Faith, tell me now in earnest, how came Falstaff's sword
so hacked?

PETO. Why, he hacked it with his dagger, and said he would swear
truth out of England but he would make you believe it was
done in fight, and persuaded us to do the like.   339

BARDOLPH. Yea, and to tickle our noses with speargrass to make
them bleed, and then to beslubber° our garments with it and
swear it was the blood of true men. I did that I did not
this seven year before, I blushed to hear his monstrous devices.   344

PRINCE. O villain, thou stolest a cup of sack eighteen years ago,
and wert taken with the manner,° and ever since thou hast
blushed° extempore. Thou hadst fire and sword on thy side,
and yet thou rannest away. What instinct hadst thou for
it?   350

BARDOLPH. My lord, do you see these meteors? Do you behold
these exhalations?°

PRINCE. I do.

BARDOLPH. What think you they portend?

PRINCE. Hot livers and cold purses.   355

BARDOLPH. Choler,° my lord, if rightly taken.

PRINCE. No, if rightly taken, halter.

[Re-enter FALSTAFF.] Here comes lean Jack, here comes
barebone. How now, my sweet creature of bombast!° How   360
long is't ago, Jack, since thou sawest thine own knee?

FALSTAFF. My own knee! When I was about thy years, Hal, I was
not an eagle's talon in the waist, I could have crept into any
alderman's thumb ring.° A plague of sighing and grief! It   364
blows a man up like a bladder. There's villainous news
abroad. Here was Sir John Bracy from your father; you
must to the Court in the morning. That same mad fellow
of the North, Percy, and he of Wales, that gave Amamon° the   369

341. beslubber: smear.   346. with . . . manner: in the act.   347. blushed:
For Bardolph's permanent blush see III.3.27–55 and *Hen V*, III.6.108.
351–52. meteors . . . exhalations: Bardolph indicates his own fiery face
which, he claims, is proof that he is a man of wrath. exhalations: meteors.
356. Choler: anger; pronounced in the same way as "collar," and so puns
on the two words are common.   360. bombast: cotton batting, used to stuff
garments to make them appear baggy.   364. thumb ring: large seal ring,
especially common on the thumbs of businessmen.   369. Amamon: the
name of a fiend.

bastinado° and made Lucifer cuckold,° and swore the Devil
his true liegeman° upon the cross of a Welsh hook—what a
plague call you him?

POINS. O, Glendower.°   373

FALSTAFF. Owen, Owen, the same. And his son-in-law Mortimer,
  and old Northumberland, and that sprightly Scot of Scots,
  Douglas, that runs o' horseback up a hill perpendicular——

PRINCE. He that rides at high speed and with his pistol kills a
  sparrow flying.   380

FALSTAFF. You have hit it.

PRINCE. So did he never the sparrow.

FALSTAFF. Well, that rascal hath good mettle° in him. He will not
  run.   384

PRINCE. Why, what a rascal art thou then, to praise him so for
  running!

FALSTAFF. O' horseback, ye cuckoo, but afoot he will not budge
  a foot.

PRINCE. Yes, Jack, upon instinct.

FALSTAFF. I grant ye, upon instinct. Well, he is there too, and one
  Mordake, and a thousand bluecaps° more. Worcester is   391
  stolen away tonight; thy father's beard is turned white with
  the news. You may buy land now as cheap as stinking mack-
  erel.   395

PRINCE. Why, then, it is like, if there come a hot June and this
  civil buffeting hold, we shall buy maidenheads as they buy
  hobnails, by the hundreds.

FALSTAFF. By the mass, lad, thou sayest true; it is like we shall
  have good trading that way. But tell me, Hal, art not thou
  horrible afeard? Thou being heir apparent, could the world
  pick thee out three such enemies again as that fiend Douglas,
  that spirit Percy, and that devil Glendower? Art thou not
  horribly afraid? Doth not thy blood thrill at it?   407

PRINCE. Not a whit, i' faith. I lack some of thy instinct.

FALSTAFF. Well, thou wilt be horribly chid tomorrow when thou
  comest to thy father. If thou love me, practice an answer.   412

PRINCE. Do thou stand for° my father, and examine me upon the
  particulars of my life.

FALSTAFF. Shall I? Content. This chair shall be my state,° this
  dagger my scepter, and this cushion my crown.

PRINCE. Thy state is taken for a joined stool,° thy golden scepter 418

370. **bastinado:** thrashing. **cuckold:** a man deceived by his wife. **371.
liegeman:** subject. **373. O, Glendower:** probably Shakespeare wrote *O* in
his manuscript as abbreviation for Owen, which the printer mistook for an
exclamation. **383. mettle:** matter, material. **391. bluecaps:** Scots. **413.
stand for:** represent. **416. state:** throne. **418. joined stool:** wooden stool
made by a joiner.

for a leaden° dagger, and thy precious rich crown for a pitiful bald crown!

FALSTAFF. Well, an the fire of grace be not quite out of thee, now
shalt thou be moved. Give me a cup of sack to make my
eyes look red, that it may be thought I have wept; for I
must speak in passion, and I will do it in King Cambyses'°   426
vein.

PRINCE. Well, here is my leg.°

FALSTAFF. And here is my speech. Stand aside, nobility.

HOSTESS. Oh Jesu, this is excellent sport, i' faith!

FALSTAFF. Weep° not, sweet queen, for trickling tears are vain.

HOSTESS. Oh, the father,° know how he holds his countenance!°   431

FALSTAFF. For God's sake, lords, convey my tristful° queen,
For tears do stop the floodgates of her eyes.

HOSTESS. Oh Jesu, he doth it as like one of these harlotry play-
ers° as ever I see!   437

FALSTAFF. Peace, good pint pot; peace, good ticklebrain. Harry, I
do not only marvel where thou spendest thy time, but also
how thou art accompanied.° For though the camomile,° the
more it is trodden on, the faster it grows, yet youth, the more
it is wasted, the sooner it wears. That thou art my son, I have
partly thy mother's word, partly my own opinion, but chiefly
a villainous trick° of thine eye, and a foolish hanging of thy   445
nether° lip, that doth warrant° me. If then thou be son to
me, here lies the point; why, being son to me, art thou so
pointed at? Shall the blessed sun of heaven prove a micher°   450
and eat blackberries? A question not to be asked. Shall the
son of England prove a thief and take purses? A question to
be asked. There is a thing, Harry, which thou hast often
heard of, and it is known to many in our land by the name
of pitch. This pitch, as ancient writers do report, doth defile;   455
so doth the company thou keepest. For, Harry, now I do not

---

419. leaden: blunt.   **426. King Cambyses':** the chief character in an early
drama which still survives; it is a marvelous specimen of ridiculous rant.
427. my leg: my curtsy.   **430–35: Weep . . . eyes:** Falstaff begins in the
artificial style of earlier plays, of the kind still being acted by the rival
company at the Rose.   **431. Oh . . . father:** by God the Father. **holds . . .
countenance:** keeps a straight face.   **434. tristful:** sad, a poetical word.
437. harlotry players: worthless players. As the Admiral's Men were the only
other company then playing in London, the parody of their heavy style was
obvious.   **440. how . . . accompanied:** what company you keep.   **441. For
. . . camomile:** The whole of this passage is a parody of the elaborate style
of Lyly's *Euphues*. The *camomile* is a small creeping aromatic plant with a
flower like a daisy.   **445. trick:** habit.   **446. nether:** lower.   **447. warrant:**
guarantee.   **450. micher:** a truant.

speak to thee in drink but in tears, not in pleasure but in passion, not in words only, but in woes also. And yet there is a
virtuous man whom I have often noted in thy company, but
I know not his name.   461

PRINCE. What manner of man, an it like your Majesty?

FALSTAFF. A goodly portly° man, i' faith, and a corpulent; of a
cheerful look, a pleasing eye, and a most noble carriage. And,
as I think, his age some fifty, or, by'r Lady, inclining to
threescore. And now I remember me, his name is Falstaff. If
that man should be lewdly given, he deceiveth me, for,
Harry, I see virtue in his looks. If then the tree may be   470
known by the fruit, as the fruit by the tree, then, peremp-
torily° I speak it, there is virtue in that Falstaff. Him keep
with, the rest banish. And tell me now, thou naughty varlet,
tell me, where hast thou been this month?   475

PRINCE. Dost thou speak like a king? Do thou stand for me, and
I'll play my father.

FALSTAFF. Depose me? If thou dost it half so gravely, so majes-
tically, both in word and matter, hang me up by the heels
for a rabbit-sucker° or a poulter's° hare.   481

PRINCE. Well, here I am set.

FALSTAFF. And here I stand. Judge, my masters.

PRINCE. Now, Harry, whence come you?

FALSTAFF. My noble lord, from Eastcheap.

PRINCE. The complaints I hear of thee are grievous.

FALSTAFF. 'Sblood, my lord, they are false. Nay, I'll tickle ye°
for a young Prince, i' faith.   489

PRINCE. Swearest thou, ungracious° boy? Henceforth ne'er look
on me. Thou art violently carried away from grace. There is
a devil haunts thee in the likeness of an old fat man, a tun°
of man is thy companion. Why dost thou converse with that
trunk of humors,° that bolting hutch° of beastliness, that   495
swollen parcel of dropsies, that huge bombard° of sack, that
stuffed cloak bag° of guts, that roasted Manningtree° ox
with the pudding in his belly, that reverend vice,° that gray
iniquity, that father ruffian, that vanity in years? Wherein is 500

---

464. portly: dignified.   **472. peremptorily:** conclusively.   **481. rabbit-sucker:**
young rabbit. **poulter:** poulterer.   **489. I'll . . . ye:** I'll show you how to
do it.   **490. ungracious:** graceless.   **493. tun:** large barrel.   **494–95. trunk
of humors:** great collection of diseases.   **495. bolting hutch:** round bin into
which flour was sifted.   **496. bombard:** large leather jug.   **497. cloak bag:**
for carrying cloaks, "kit bag."   **498. Manningtree:** a town in Essex where
there was a famous cattle market. At fairs it was often a custom to roast
an ox whole.   **499. vice:** the Devil in the old Morality Plays.

he good, but to taste sack and drink it? Wherein neat and
cleanly,° but to carve a capon and eat it? Wherein cunning,°
but in craft? Wherein crafty,° but in villainy? Wherein villainous, but in all things? Wherein worthy, but in nothing?   505
FALSTAFF. I would your Grace would take me with you.° Whom
means your Grace?
PRINCE. That villainous abominable misleader of youth, Falstaff,
that old white-bearded Satan.
FALSTAFF. My lord, the man I know.   510
PRINCE. I know thou dost.
FALSTAFF. But to say I know more harm in him than in myself
were to say more than I know. That he is old, the more the
pity, his white hairs do witness it; but that he is, saving your
reverence, a whoremaster, that I utterly deny. If sack and   515
sugar be a fault, God help the wicked! If to be old and merry
be a sin, then many an old host that I know is damned. If
to be fat be to be hated, then Pharaoh's lean kine are to be
loved. No, my good lord. Banish Peto, banish Bardolph,   520
banish Poins. But for sweet Jack Falstaff, kind Jack Falstaff,
true Jack Falstaff, valiant Jack Falstaff, and therefore more
valiant, being, as he is, old Jack Falstaff, banish not him thy
Harry's company, banish not him thy Harry's company.   525
Banish plump Jack, and banish all the world.
PRINCE. I do, I will.

> [*A knocking heard. Exeunt* HOSTESS, FRANCIS,
> *and* BARDOLPH.]
> [*Re-enter* BARDOLPH, *running.*]

BARDOLPH. Oh, my lord, my lord! The sheriff with a most monstrous watch° is at the door.   530
FALSTAFF. Out, ye rogue! Play out the play. I have much to say in
the behalf of that Falstaff.

> [*Re-enter the* HOSTESS.]

HOSTESS. Oh Jesu, my lord, my lord!—
PRINCE. Heigh, heigh! The Devil rides upon a fiddlestick.° What's
the matter?   535
HOSTESS. The sheriff and all the watch are at the door. They are
come to search the house. Shall I let them in?
FALSTAFF. Dost thou hear, Hal? Never call a true piece of gold a
counterfeit. Thou art essentially mad, without seeming so.   541
PRINCE. And thou a natural coward, without instinct.

---

502. **cleanly:** clever.   503. **cunning:** skillful.   **crafty:** a craftsman.   **506–07.**
take . . . you: explain yourself.   530. **watch:** citizen police force.   **534–35.**
Devil . . . fiddlestick: what's all the fuss about?

FALSTAFF. I deny your major.° If you will deny the sheriff, so;
    if not, let him enter. If I become not a cart° as well as an-
    other man, a plague on my bringing up! I hope I shall as
    soon be strangled with a halter as another.   548
PRINCE. Go, hide thee behind the arras,° the rest walk up above.
    Now, my masters, for a true face and good conscience.
FALSTAFF. Both which I have had; but their date is out,° and there-
    fore I'll hide me.   553
PRINCE. Call in the sheriff.
          [*Exeunt all except the* PRINCE *and* PETO.]
          [*Enter* SHERIFF *and the* CARRIER.]
    Now, Master Sheriff, what is your will with me?
SHERIFF. First, pardon me, my lord. A hue and cry°
    Hath followed certain men unto this house.
PRINCE. What men?
SHERIFF. One of them is well known, my gracious lord,
    A gross fat man.
CARRIER.   As fat as butter.   560
PRINCE. The man, I do assure you, is not here,
    For I myself at this time have employed him.
    And sheriff, I will engage my word to thee
    That I will, by tomorrow dinnertime,
    Send him to answer thee, or any man,   565
    For anything he shall be charged withal.
    And so let me entreat you leave the house.
SHERIFF. I will, my lord. There are two gentlemen
    Have in this robbery lost three hundred marks.
PRINCE. It may be so. If he have robbed these men,   570
    He shall be answerable. And so farewell
SHERIFF. Good night, my noble lord.
PRINCE. I think it is good morrow, is it not?
SHERIFF. Indeed, my lord, I think it be two o'clock.
          [*Exeunt* SHERIFF *and* CARRIER.]
PRINCE. This oily rascal is known as well as Paul's.° Go, call him 576
    forth.
PETO. Falstaff!—Fast asleep behind the arras, and snorting like a
    horse.

544. I . . . major: I deny your major premise, i.e., the main argument on
which your conclusion is based; a phrase used in academic arguments. Falstaff puns also on "mayor." "Major" and "mayor" were pronounced alike.
546. cart: which will take him to execution. **549. arras:** curtain. **552. date
is out:** time is expired. **556. hue . . . cry:** when a crime was discovered
everyone took a hand in aiding justice. A "hue and cry" was raised, and
the whole parish pursued the criminal. **576. Paul's:** St. Paul's Church,
the most conspicuous building in London.

PRINCE. Hark how hard he fetches breath. Search his pockets. [*He searcheth his pockets, and findeth certain papers.*] What hast thou found?   582

PETO. Nothing but papers, my lord.

PRINCE. Let's see what they be. Read them.

PETO. [*Reads.*]

"Item, A capon,									2s. 2d.
Item, Sauce,									4d.
Item, Sack, two gallons,							5s. 8d.
Item, Anchovies and sack after supper,			2s. 6d.
Item, Bread ,									ob.°"

PRINCE. Oh, monstrous! But one halfpenny-worth of bread to this   591
intolerable deal of sack! What there is else, keep close, we'll
read it at more advantage. There let him sleep till day. I'll to
the Court in the morning. We must all to the wars, and thy
place shall be honorable. I'll procure this fat rogue a charge
of foot,° and I know his death will be a march of twelvescore.° The money shall be paid back again with advantage.°   598
Be with me betimes in the morning. And so good morrow,
Peto.

PETO. Good morrow, good my lord.   [*Exeunt.*]

---

590. ob: one halfpenny.   597. charge of foot: commission as commander of a company of infantry.   598. twelvescore: i.e., paces. The pace was 60 inches.   599. advantage: interest.

ACT III

Scene 1 ⚜ *Bangor. The* ARCHDEACON'S *house.*

[*Enter* HOTSPUR, WORCESTER, MORTIMER,
and GLENDOWER.]

MORTIMER. These promises are fair, the parties sure,
    And our induction° full of prosperous hope.
HOTSPUR. Lord Mortimer, and Cousin Glendower,
    Will you sit down?
    And Uncle Worcester. A plague upon it!   5
    I have forgot the map.
GLENDOWER.   No, here it is.
    Sit, Cousin Percy. Sit, good Cousin Hotspur,
    For by that name as oft as Lancaster
    Doth speak of you, his cheek looks pale, and with
    A rising sigh he wisheth you in Heaven.   10
HOTSPUR. And you in Hell, as oft as he hears Owen Glendower
    spoke of.
GLENDOWER. I cannot blame him. At my nativity°
    The front° of heaven was full of fiery shapes,
    Of burning cressets;° and at my birth   15
    The frame and huge foundation of the earth
    Shaked like a coward.
HOTSPUR. Why, so it would have done at the same season if your
    mother's cat had but kittened, though yourself had never
    been born.   20
GLENDOWER. I say the earth did shake when I was born.
HOTSPUR. And I say the earth was not of my mind
    If you suppose as fearing you it shook.

  Act III, Sc. 1: **2. induction:** opening.   **12. nativity:** moment of birth.
14. front: forehead.   **15. burning cressets:** stars blazing like beacons.

GLENDOWER. The heavens were all on fire, the earth did tremble.
HOTSPUR. Oh, then the earth shook to see the heavens on fire,   25
    And not in fear of your nativity.
    Diseasèd nature oftentimes breaks forth
    In strange eruptions; oft the teeming° earth
    Is with a kind of colic pinched and vexed
    By the imprisoning of unruly wind   30
    Within her womb; which, for enlargement striving,
    Shakes the old beldam° earth and topples down
    Steeples and moss-grown towers. At your birth
    Our grandam earth, having this distemperature,°
    In passion° shook.
GLENDOWER.   Cousin,° of many men   35
    I do not bear these crossings.° Give me leave
    To tell you once again that at my birth
    The front of heaven was full of fiery shapes,
    The goats ran from the mountains, and the herds
    Were strangely clamorous to the frighted fields.   40
    These signs have marked me extraordinary,
    And all the courses of my life do show
    I am not in the roll of common men.
    Where is he living, clipped in° with the sea
    That chides° the banks of England, Scotland, Wales,   45
    Which calls me pupil,° or hath read to me?°
    And bring him out that is but woman's son
    Can trace° me in the tedious ways of art,°
    And hold me pace° in deep experiments.
HOTSPUR. I think there's no man speaks better Welsh.   50
    I'll to dinner.
MORTIMER. Peace, Cousin Percy, you will make him mad.
GLENDOWER. I can call spirits from the vasty deep.
HOTSPUR. Why, so can I, or so can any man;
    But will they come when you do call for them?   55
GLENDOWER. Why, I can teach you, Cousin, to command
    The Devil.
HOTSPUR. And I can teach thee, Coz, to shame the Devil°

---

28. teeming: pregnant. This theory of earthquakes—that they were caused
by the expulsion of wind from within the earth—was generally believed.
32. beldam: grandmother.   **34. distemperature:** disorder.   **35. passion:** agitation. **Cousin:** kinsman; used of any relation. Hotspur is remotely related
to Glendower through Lady Percy.   **36. crossings:** opposition.   **44. clipped
in:** encircled.   **45. chides:** roars against.   **46. calls me pupil:** i.e., is my
master. **hath . . . me:** has been my tutor.   **48. trace:** follow. **tedious . . .
art:** difficult course of magic.   **49. hold me pace:** keep pace with me.   **58.
shame . . . Devil:** because he is the father of lies.

By telling truth. Tell truth, and shame the Devil.
If thou have power to raise him, bring him hither,   60
    And I'll be sworn I have power to shame him hence.
    Oh, while you live, tell truth, and shame the Devil!
MORTIMER. Come, come, no more of this unprofitable chat.
GLENDOWER. Three times hath Henry Bolingbroke made head°
    Against my power. Thrice from the banks of Wye   65
    And sandy-bottomed Severn have I sent him
    Bootless° home and weather-beaten back.
HOTSPUR. Home without boots, and in foul weather too!
    How 'scapes he agues,° in the Devil's name?
GLENDOWER. Come, here's the map. Shall we divide our right   70
    According to our threefold order° ta'en?
MORTIMER. The Archdeacon hath divided it
    Into three limits° very equally.
    England, from Trent and Severn hitherto,
    By south and east is to my part assigned.   75
    All westward, Wales beyond the Severn shore,
    And all the fertile land within that bound,
    To Owen Glendower. And, dear Coz, to you
    The remnant northward, lying off from Trent.
    And our indentures tripartite° are drawn;   80
    Which being sealèd interchangeably,°
    A business that this night may execute,
    Tomorrow, Cousin Percy, you and I
    And my good Lord of Worcester will set forth
    To meet your father and the Scottish power,   85
    As is appointed us, at Shrewsbury.
    My father° Glendower is not ready yet,
    Nor shall we need his help these fourteen days.
    Within that space you may have drawn together
    Your tenants, friends, and neighboring gentlemen.   90
GLENDOWER. A shorter time shall send me to you, lords.
    And in my conduct shall your ladies come,
    From whom you now must steal and take no leave;
    For there will be a world of water shed
    Upon the parting of your wives and you.   95
HOTSPUR. Methinks my moiety,° north from Burton here,
    In quantity equals not one of yours.

64. made head: advanced. 67. Bootless: profitless. 69. agues: fever.
71. our . . . order: agreement made between us three. 73. limits: divi-
sions. 80. indentures tripartite: legal agreement among three parties. 81.
sealed interchangeably: each party sealing each copy of the agreement.
87. father: i.e., father-in-law. 96. moiety: share.

See how this river comes me cranking in,°
And cuts me from the best of all my land
A huge half-moon, a monstrous cantle° out.   100
I'll have the current in this place dammed up,
And here the smug° and silver Trent shall run
In a new channel, fair and evenly.
It shall not wind with such a deep indent,°
To rob me of so rich a bottom° here.   105

GLENDOWER. Not wind? It shall, it must. You see it doth.

MORTIMER. Yea, but
Mark how he bears his course, and runs me up
With like advantage on the other side,
Gelding the opposèd continent° as much   110
As on the other side it takes from you.

WORCESTER. Yea, but a little charge° will trench him here
And on this north side win this cape of land,
And then he runs straight and even.

HOTSPUR. I'll have it so. A little charge will do it.   115

GLENDOWER. I'll not have it altered.

HOTSPUR.   Will not you?

GLENDOWER. No, nor you shall not.

HOTSPUR.   Who shall say me nay?

GLENDOWER. Why, that will I.

HOTSPUR. Let me not understand you, then. Speak it in Welsh.   120

GLENDOWER. I can speak English, lord, as well as you;
For I was trained up in the English Court,
Where, being but young, I framèd to the harp
Many an English ditty lovely well,
And gave the tongue a helpful ornament,°   125
A virtue that was never seen in you.

HOTSPUR. Marry,°
And I am glad of it with all my heart.
I had rather be a kitten and cry mew
Than one of these same meter balladmongers.°   130
I had rather hear a brazen canstick turned,°
Or a dry wheel grate on the axletree;
And that would set my teeth nothing on edge,
Nothing so much as mincing poetry.

---

98. me . . . in: comes winding into my part. 100. cantle: slice. 102.
smug: smooth. 104. indent: indentation. 105. bottom: valley. 110. opposed continent: opposite bank. 112. charge: cost. 125. helpful ornament: i.e., musical accompaniment. 127. Marry: Mary, by the Virgin.
130. meter balladmongers: doggerel rhymesters. 131. brazen . . . turned:
brass candlestick being cut out on the lathe.

'Tis like the forced gait of a shuffling nag.   135
GLENDOWER. Come, you shall have Trent turned.
HOTSPUR. I do not care. I'll give thrice so much land
    To any well-deserving friend.
    But in the way of bargain, mark ye me,
    I'll cavil° on the ninth part of a hair.   140
    Are the indentures drawn? Shall we be gone?
GLENDOWER. The moon shines fair, you may away by night.
    I'll haste the writer, and withal
    Break with° your wives of your departure hence.
    I am afraid my daughter will run mad,   145
    So much she doteth on her Mortimer.   [*Exit.*]
MORTIMER. Fie, Cousin Percy! How you cross my father!
HOTSPUR. I cannot choose. Sometime he angers me
    With telling me of the moldwarp° and the ant,
    Of the dreamer Merlin° and his prophecies,   150
    And° of a dragon and a finless fish,
    A clip-winged griffin° and a molten raven,
    A couching lion and a ramping° cat,
    And such a deal of skimble-skamble° stuff
    As puts me from my faith. I tell you what—   155
    He held me last night at least nine hours
    In reckoning up the several° devils' names
    That were his lackeys. I cried "hum," and "well, go to,"
    But marked him not a word. Oh, he is as tedious
    As a tired horse, a railing wife,   160
    Worse than a smoky house. I had rather live
    With cheese and garlic in a windmill, far,
    Than feed on cates° and have him talk to me
    In any summerhouse° in Christendom.
MORTIMER. In faith, he is a worthy gentleman,   165
    Exceedingly well read, and profited
    In strange concealments;° valiant as a lion,
    And wondrous affable, and as bountiful
    As mines of India. Shall I tell you, Cousin?

140. cavil: raise objections.   144. Break with: break the news to.   149. mold-
warp: mole.   150. Merlin: the old magician at King Arthur's Court. As
the Welsh were (more or less) descendants of Arthur's British countrymen,
Merlin's prophecies would appeal to Glendower.   151–53. And . . . cat:
These beasts occur as symbols in ancient prophecies. griffin: fabulous
beast—half lion, half eagle.   153. ramping: on its hind legs.   154. skimble-
skamble: rambling.   157. several: separate, different.   163. cates: delica-
cies.   164. summerhouse: country house.   166–67. profited . . . conceal-
ments: expert in strange mysteries.

He holds your temper° in a high respect,   170
And curbs himself even of his natural scope
When you come 'cross his humor; faith, he does.
I warrant you that man is not alive
Might so have tempted him as you have done
Without the taste of danger and reproof.   175
But do not use it oft, let me entreat you.
WORCESTER. In faith, my lord, you are too willful-blame;°
    And since your coming hither have done enough
    To put him quite beside his patience.
    You must needs learn, lord, to amend this fault.   180
    Though sometimes it show greatness, courage, blood—
    And that's the dearest° grace it renders you—
    Yet oftentimes it doth present harsh rage,
    Defect of manners, want of government,°
    Pride, haughtiness, opinion,° and disdain;   185
    The least of which haunting a nobleman
    Loseth men's hearts, and leaves behind a stain
    Upon the beauty of all parts besides,
    Beguiling° them of commendation.
HOTSPUR. Well, I am schooled. Good manners be your speed!°   190
    Here come our wives, and let us take our leave.
            [Re-enter GLENDOWER with the LADIES.]
MORTIMER. This is the deadly spite° that angers me—
    My wife can speak no English, I no Welsh.
GLENDOWER. My daughter weeps. She will not part with you.
    She'll be a soldier too, she'll to the wars.   195
MORTIMER. Good Father, tell her that she and my aunt Percy
    Shall follow in your conduct speedily.
            [GLENDOWER speaks to LADY MORTIMER in Welsh,
                    and she answers him in the same.]
GLENDOWER. She is desperate here, a peevish self-willed harlotry,°
    one that no persuasion can do good upon.
            [LADY MORTIMER speaks in Welsh.]
MORTIMER. I understand thy looks. That pretty Welsh°   200
    Which thou pour'st down from these swelling heavens°
    I am too perfect in; and but for shame,
    In such a parley° should I answer thee.
            [LADY MORTIMER speaks again in Welsh.]

170. temper: character.   177. willful-blame: to be blamed for willfulness.
182. dearest: most valuable.   184. government: self-control.   185. opinion:
conceit.   189. Beguiling: causing to lose.   190. Good . . . speed: may
good manners bring you luck.   192. spite: vexation.   199. harlotry: silly
girl.   201. pretty Welsh: i.e., tears.   202. swelling heavens: i.e., eyes full
of tears.   204. parley: manner of speech.

I understand thy kisses and thou mine,   205
And that's a feeling disputation.°
But I will never be a truant, love,
Till I have learned thy language; for thy tongue
Makes Welsh as sweet as ditties highly penned,
Sung by a fair queen in a summer's bower,   210
With ravishing division,° to her lute.

GLENDOWER. Nay, if you melt, then will she run mad.
         [LADY MORTIMER *speaks again in Welsh*.]

MORTIMER. Oh, I am ignorance itself in this!

GLENDOWER. She bids you on the wanton° rushes° lay you down
  And rest your gentle head upon her lap,   215
  And she will sing the song that pleaseth you
  And on your eyelids crown the god of sleep,
  Charming your blood with pleasing heaviness,°
  Making such difference 'twixt wake and sleep
  As is the difference betwixt day and night   220
  The hour before the heavenly-harnessed team°
  Begins his golden progress in the east.

MORTIMER. With all my heart I'll sit and hear her sing.
  By that time will our book,° I think, be drawn.

GLENDOWER. Do so,   225
  And those musicians that shall play to you
  Hang in the air a thousand leagues from hence,
  And straight they shall be here. Sit, and attend.

HOTSPUR. Come, Kate, thou art perfect in lying down.
  Come, quick, quick, that I may lay my head in thy lap.   231

LADY PERCY. Go, ye giddy goose.   [*The music plays.*]

HOTSPUR. Now I perceive the Devil understands Welsh,
  And 'tis no marvel he is so humorous.°
  By'r Lady, he is a good musician.   235

LADY PERCY. Then should you be nothing but musical, for you are
  altogether governed by humors. Lie still, ye thief, and hear
  the lady sing in Welsh.

HOTSPUR. I had rather hear Lady, my brach,° howl in Irish.   240

LADY PERCY. Wouldst thou have thy head broken?

HOTSPUR. No.

LADY PERCY. Then be still.

HOTSPUR. Neither—'tis a woman's fault.   245

LADY PERCY. Now God help thee!

---

206. feeling disputation: conversation by touch. **211. division:** melody.
214. wanton: luxuriant. **rushes:** used to cover floors. **218. heaviness:** drow-
siness. **221. team:** i.e., the horses of the sun. **224. book:** agreement.
234. humorous: full of whims. **240. brach:** bitch.

HOTSPUR. To the Welsh lady's bed.

LADY PERCY. What's that?

HOTSPUR. Peace! She sings.

        [*Here* LADY MORTIMER *sings a Welsh song.*]

    Come, Kate, I'll have your song too.   250

LADY PERCY. Not mine, in good sooth.°

HOTSPUR. Not yours, in good sooth! Heart! You swear like a com-
    fit-maker's° wife. "Not you, in good sooth," and "as true as I
    live," and "as God shall mend me," and "as sure as day,"   255
    And givest such sarcenet surety for thy oaths°
    As if thou never walk'st further than Finsbury.°
    Swear me, Kate, like a lady as thou art,
    A good mouth-filling oath, and leave "in sooth"
    And such protest of pepper gingerbread°   260
    To velvet guards° and Sunday citizens.°
    Come, sing.

LADY PERCY. I will not sing.

HOTSPUR. 'Tis the next way to turn tailor,° or be redbreast
    teacher.° An the indentures be drawn, I'll away within these   265
    two hours, and so come in when ye will.   [*Exit.*]

GLENDOWER. Come, come, Lord Mortimer, you are as slow
    As hot Lord Percy is on fire to go.
    By this our book is drawn. We'll but seal,   270
    And then to horse immediately.

MORTIMER.   With all my heart. [*Exeunt.*]

---

251. sooth: truth. **253. comfitmaker:** candymaker. **256. sarcenet . . .
oaths:** you swear by such soft things. *sarcenet:* fine silk. **257. Finsbury:**
Finsbury fields, whither London citizens took their Sunday-afternoon walk.
260. pepper gingerbread: a very mild form of heat. **261. velvet guards:**
literally bands of velvet used to ornament a gown (and still used on the
gown of a Ph.D.). **Sunday citizens:** citizens in their Sunday best. **264. turn
tailor:** Tailors (before the invention of the sewing machine) used to sing at
their work as they sat cross-legged. **265. redbreast teacher:** one who teaches
caged birds to sing. The little English robin was highly valued as a song-
bird.

Scene 2 ✑ *London. The palace.*

[*Enter the* KING, PRINCE OF WALES, *and others.*]

KING. Lords, give us leave. The Prince of Wales and I
 Must have some private conference. But be near at hand,
 For we shall presently have need of you.   [*Exeunt* LORDS.]
 I know not whether God will have it so,
 For some displeasing service I have done,   5
 That, in his secret doom,° out of my blood°
 He'll breed revengement and a scourge for me;
 But thou dost in thy passages of life
 Make me believe that thou art only marked
 For the hot vengeance and the rod of Heaven   10
 To punish my mistreadings. Tell me else,
 Could such inordinate° and low desires,
 Such poor, such bare, such lewd,° such mean attempts,
 Such barren pleasures, rude society,
 As thou art matched withal and grafted to,   15
 Accompany the greatness of thy blood,
 And hold their level with thy princely heart?
PRINCE. So please your Majesty, I would I could
 Quit° all offences with as clear excuse
 As well as I am doubtless I can purge   20
 Myself of many I am charged withal.
 Yet such extenuation let me beg
 As, in reproof° of many tales devised,
 Which oft the ear of greatness needs must hear,
 By smiling pickthanks° and base newsmongers,   25
 I may for some things true wherein my youth
 Hath faulty wandered and irregular
 Find pardon on my true submission.
KING. God pardon thee! Yet let me wonder, Harry,
 At thy affections, which do hold a wing   30
 Quite from the flight° of all thy ancestors.

Sc. 2: 6. **doom:** judgment. **out . . . blood:** through one of my children.
12. **inordinate:** intemperate. 13. **lewd:** low. 19. **Quit:** acquit myself of.
23. **reproof:** rebuttal. 25. **pickthanks:** men who curry favor by telling tales.
30–31. **affections . . . flight:** desires, natural inclinations . . . fly a different
course.

Thy place in Council thou hast rudely lost,
Which by thy younger brother is supplied,
And art almost an alien to the hearts
Of all the Court and princes of my blood.   35
The hope and expectation of thy time°
Is ruined, and the soul of every man
Prophetically doth forethink thy fall.
Had I so lavish of my presence been,
So common-hackneyed° in the eyes of men,   40
So stale and cheap to vulgar company,
Opinion,° that did help me to the crown,
Had still kept loyal to possession,°
And left me in reputeless banishment,
A fellow of no mark nor likelihood.   45
By being seldom seen, I could not stir
But like a comet I was wondered at,
That men would tell their children "This is he."
Others would say, "Where, which is Bolingbroke?"
And then I stole all courtesy from Heaven,   50
And dressed myself in such humility
That I did pluck allegiance from men's hearts,
Loud shouts and salutations from their mouths,
Even in the presence of the crowned King.
Thus did I keep my person fresh and new,   55
My presence, like a robe pontifical,°
Ne'er seen but wondered at. And so my state,
Seldom but sumptuous, showed like a feast,
And won by rareness such solemnity.
The skipping° King, he ambled up and down,   60
With shallow jesters and rash bavin° wits,
Soon kindled and soon burnt; carded° his state,
Mingled his royalty with capering fools,
Had his great name profanèd with their scorns,
And gave his countenance, against his name,°   65
To laugh at gibing° boys and stand the push°
Of every beardless vain comparative,°
Grew a companion to the common streets,

36. time: lifetime.   40. common-hackneyed: at every man's call. A hackney
is a hired horse.   42. Opinion: popular opinion.   43. loyal to possession:
loyal to the possessor; i.e., Richard II.   56. robe pontifical: a bishop's robe.
60. skipping: frivolous.   61. bavin: brushwood for kindling, worthless and
easily broken.   62. carded: adulterated.   65. against . . . name: contrary
to the interest of his reputation.   66. gibing: mocking. stand . . . push:
endure the sallies of.   67. beardless . . . comparative: every boy who cared
to make jokes at his expense.

Enfeoffed° himself to popularity,°
That, being daily swallowed by men's eyes,   70
They surfeited with honey and began
To loathe the taste of sweetness, whereof a little
More than a little is by much too much.
So when he had occasion to be seen,
He was but as the cuckoo is in June,°   75
Heard, not regarded; seen, but with such eyes
As, sick and blunted with community,°
Afford no extraordinary gaze,
Such as is bent on sunlike majesty
When it shines seldom in admiring eyes;   80
But rather drowsed and hung their eyelids down,
Slept in his face° and rendered such aspèct°
As cloudy° men use to their adversaries,
Being with his presence glutted, gorged, and full.
And in that very line,° Harry, standest thou;   85
For thou hast lost thy princely privilege
With vile participation.° Not an eye
But is aweary of thy common sight,
Save mine, which hath desired to see thee more,
Which now doth that I would not have it do—   90
Make blind itself with foolish tenderness.
PRINCE. I shall hereafter, my thrice gracious lord,
  Be more myself.
KING.   For all the world
  As thou art to this hour° was Richard then
  When I from France set foot at Ravenspurgh,   95
  And even as I was then is Percy now.
  Now, by my scepter and my soul to boot,
  He hath more worthy interest to the state
  Than thou the shadow of succession;°
  For of no right,° nor color like to right,   100
  He doth fill fields with harness° in the realm,
  Turns head against the lion's armèd jaws,
  And being no more in debt to years than thou,°

69. Enfeoffed: conveyed, made himself over to. popularity: low company,
common people. 75. cuckoo . . . June: The cuckoo is a migrant bird, with
a monotonous cry of "cuck-oo, cuck-oo," which first appears in April and
disappears in July. The note of the first cuckoo is welcomed as a sign of
spring, but has become tedious by June. 77. community: that which is
common. 82. in . . . face: in his presence—a gross insult. aspect: look.
83. cloudy: sullen. 85. line: class. 87. vile participation: mixing with low
company. 94. to . . . hour: up to now. 99. shadow of succession: shad-
owy right of succession. 100. of no right: with no right. 101. harness:
armor. 103. no . . . thou: See I.1.92, n.

Leads ancient lords and reverend bishops on
To bloody battles and to bruising arms.   105
What never-dying honor hath he got
Against renownèd Douglas!—whose high deeds,
Whose hot incursions° and great name in arms
Holds from all soldiers chief majority
And military title capital°   110
Through all the kingdoms that acknowledge Christ.
Thrice hath this Hotspur, Mars in swathling° clothes,
This infant warrior, in his enterprises
Discomfited great Douglas, ta'en him once,
Enlarged him, and made a friend of him,   115
To fill the mouth of deep defiance up°
And shake the peace and safety of our throne.
And what say you to this? Percy, Northumberland,
The Archbishop's Grace of York, Douglas, Mortimer,
Capitulate° against us and are up.   120
But wherefore do I tell these news to thee?
Why, Harry, do I tell thee of my foes,
Which art my near'st and dearest enemy?
Thou that art like enough through vassal° fear,
Base inclination, and the start of spleen°   125
To fight against me under Percy's pay,
To dog his heels and curtsy at his frowns,
To show how much thou art degenerate.
PRINCE. Do not think so, you shall not find it so.
And God forgive them that so much have swayed   130
Your Majesty's good thoughts away from me!
I will redeem all this on Percy's head,
And in the closing of some glorious day
Be bold to tell you that I am your son;
When I will wear a garment all of blood,   135
And stain my favors° in a bloody mask
Which, washed away, shall scour my shame with it.
And that shall be the day, whene'er it lights,
That this same child of honor and renown,
This gallant Hotspur, this all-praisèd knight,   140
And your unthought-of Harry chance to meet.
For every honor sitting on his helm,

---

108. **incursions:** raids.   109–10. **Holds . . . capital:** keeps from all other
soldiers the claim to be considered the greatest.   112. **swathling:** swaddling.
116. **To . . . up:** so that defiance may speak with a loud mouth.   120.
Capitulate: make agreement.   124. **vassal:** slavish.   125. **start of spleen:**
impulse of bad temper.   136. **favors:** features, face.

Would they were multitudes, and on my head
My shames redoubled! For the time will come
That I shall make this Northern youth exchange   145
His glorious deeds for my indignities.
Percy is but my factor,° good my lord,
To engross° up glorious deeds on my behalf.
And I will call him to so strict account
That he shall render every glory up—   150
Yea, even the slightest worship° of his time—
Or I will tear the reckoning from his heart.
This, in the name of God, I promise here.
The which if He be pleased I shall perform,
I do beseech your Majesty may salve°   155
The long-grown wounds of my intemperance.
If not, the end of life cancels all bands,°
And I will die a hundred thousand deaths
Ere break the smallest parcel° of this vow.
KING. A hundred thousand rebels die in this.   160
    Thou shalt have charge and sovereign trust herein.
    [*Enter* BLUNT.] How now, good Blunt? Thy looks are full of
        speed.
BLUNT. So hath the business that I come to speak of.
    Lord Mortimer of Scotland hath sent word
    That Douglas and the English rebels met   165
    The eleventh of this month at Shrewsbury.
    A mighty and a fearful head° they are,
    If promises be kept on every hand,
    As ever offered foul play in a state.
KING. The Earl of Westmoreland set forth today,   170
    With him my son, Lord John of Lancaster;
    For this advértisement is five days old.
    On Wednesday next, Harry, you shall set forward,
    On Thursday we ourselves will march. Our meeting
    Is Bridgenorth. And, Harry, you shall march   175
    Through Gloucestershire, by which account,
    Our business valued,° some twelve days hence
    Our general forces at Bridgenorth shall meet.
    Our hands are full of business. Let's away.
    Advantage feeds him fat° while men delay.   [*Exeunt.*]   180

---

147. factor: agent, buyer.   **148. engross:** buy up wholesale.   **151. worship:**
honor.   **155. salve:** heal.   **157. bands:** bonds, debts.   **159. parcel:** portion.
167. head: force.   **177. Our . . . valued:** considering how much we have to
do.   **180. Advantage . . . fat:** advantage makes the most of his opportunities.

Scene 3 ⌘ *Boar's Head Tavern in Eastcheap.*

[*Enter* FALSTAFF *and* BARDOLPH.]

FALSTAFF. Bardolph, am I not fallen away vilely since this last
action?° Do I not bate?° Do I not dwindle? Why, my skin
hangs about me like an old lady's loose gown, I am withered
like an old applejohn.° Well, I'll repent, and that suddenly,   4
while I am in some liking.° I shall be out of heart° shortly,
and then I shall have no strength to repent. An I have not
forgotten what the inside of a church is made of, I am a pep-
percorn, a brewer's horse°—the inside of a church! Company, villainous company, hath been the spoil of me.   11

BARDOLPH. Sir John, you are so fretful you cannot live long.

FALSTAFF. Why, there is it. Come sing me a bawdy song, make me
merry. I was as virtuously given as a gentleman need to be
—virtuous enough; swore little; diced not above seven times
a week; went to a bawdyhouse not above once in a quarter
—of an hour; paid money that I borrowed, three or four   20
times; lived well, and in good compass.° And now I live out
of all order, out of all compass.

BARDOLPH. Why, you are so fat, Sir John, that you must needs
be out of all compass, out of all reasonable compass, Sir
John.   26

FALSTAFF. Do thou amend thy face, and I'll amend my life. Thou
art our admiral,° thou bearest the lantern in the poop,° but
'tis in the nose of thee. Thou art the Knight of the Burning
Lamp.   30

BARDOLPH. Why, Sir John, my face does you no harm.

FALSTAFF. No, I'll be sworn, I make as good use of it as many a
man doth of a death's-head° or a memento mori.° I never

Sc. 3: **2. last action:** i.e., the Gadshill affair. **bate:** grow thin.   **4. applejohn:** withered apple, long kept.   **6. in . . . liking:** in good condition. **out
of heart:** have no heart for it.   **9. brewer's horse:** i.e., old and decrepit.   **21.
compass:** (lit., circumference) limits, with a pun on Falstaff's girth.   **28.
admiral:** the admiral's ship, which led the way and carried a lighted lantern
by night so that the fleet should keep together.   **29. poop:** stern.   **34.
death's-head:** skull.   **34–35. memento mori:** reminder of death.

see thy face but I think upon Hell-fire and Dives° that lived   36
in purple, for there he is in his robes, burning, burning. If
thou wert anyway given to virtue, I would swear by thy face;
my oath should be "By this fire, that's God's angel."° But
thou art altogether given over, and wert indeed, but for the   40
light in thy face, the son of utter darkness. When thou rannest up Gadshill in the night to catch my horse, if I did not
think thou hadst been an ignis fatuus° or a ball of wildfire,°
there's no purchase in money. Oh, thou art a perpetual tri-   45
umph,° an everlasting bonfire light! Thou hast saved me a
thousand marks in links° and torches, walking with thee in
the night betwixt tavern and tavern. But the sack that thou
hast drunk me would have bought me lights as good cheap
at the dearest chandler's° in Europe. I have maintained that   52
salamander° of yours with fire any time this two and thirty
years, God reward me for it!

BARDOLPH. 'Sblood, I would my face were in your belly!

FALSTAFF. God-a-mercy! So should I be sure to be heartburned.
[*Enter* HOSTESS.] How now, Dame Partlet the hen!° Have
you inquired yet who picked my pocket?   61

HOSTESS. Why, Sir John, what do you think, Sir John? Do you
think I keep thieves in my house? I have searched, I have inquired, so has my husband, man by man, boy by boy, servant by servant. The tithe° of a hair was never lost in my   66
house before.

FALSTAFF. Ye lie, hostess. Bardolph was shaved° and lost many a
hair, and I'll be sworn my pocket was picked. Go to, you are
a woman, go.   70

HOSTESS. Who, I? No, I defy thee. God's light, I was never called
so in mine own house before!

FALSTAFF. Go to, I know you well enough.

HOSTESS. No, Sir John, you do not know me, Sir John. I know
you, Sir John. You owe me money, Sir John, and now you   75
pick a quarrel to beguile me of it. I bought you a dozen of
shirts to your back.

FALSTAFF. Dowlas,° filthy dowlas. I have given them away to

---

36. Dives: the rich man in the parable of Dives and Lazarus. See Luke
16:19–31. **39. By . . . angel:** a parody of a line in Chapman's *Blind
Beggar of Alexandria,* a recent and popular play at the Rose Theater. **44.
ignis fatuus:** will-o'-the-wisp. **wildfire:** firework. **46. triumph:** rejoicing,
celebrated with torches and bonfires. **47. links:** torches used to light the
way on a dark night. **52. chandler:** seller of candles. **54. salamander:** a
kind of lizard, believed to enjoy fire. **59–60. Dame . . . hen:** the wife of
Chanticleer the cock in the story of Reynard the Fox. **66. tithe:** tenth part.
68. shaved: caught venereal disease. **78. Dowlas:** coarse linen.

bakers' wives, and they have made bolters° of them.   80

HOSTESS. Now, as I am a true woman, holland° of eight shillings
an ell.° You owe money here besides, Sir John, for your diet
and by-drinkings,° and money lent you, four and twenty
pound.   86

FALSTAFF. He had his part of it. Let him pay.

HOSTESS. He? Alas, he is poor, he hath nothing.

FALSTAFF. How! Poor? Look upon his face—what call you rich?
Let them coin his nose, let them coin his cheeks. I'll not pay   90
a denier.° What, will you make a younker° of me? Shall I
not take mine ease in mine inn but I shall have my pocket
picked? I have lost a seal ring of my grandfather's worth
forty mark.   95

HOSTESS. Oh Jesu, I have heard the Prince tell him, I know not
how oft, that that ring was copper!°

FALSTAFF. How! The Prince is a Jack,° a sneak-cup.° 'Sblood, an
he were here, I would cudgel him like a dog if he would say
so.   101

    [Enter the PRINCE *and* PETO, *marching, and* FALSTAFF
      meets them playing on his truncheon like a fife.]

How now, lad! Is the wind in that door, i' faith?
Must we all march?

BARDOLPH. Yea, two and two, Newgate fashion.°   105

HOSTESS. My lord, I pray you hear me.

PRINCE. What sayest thou, Mistress Quickly? How doth thy husband? I love him well, he is an honest man.

HOSTESS. Good my lord, hear me.

FALSTAFF. Prithee let her alone, and list to me.   110

PRINCE. What sayest thou, Jack?

FALSTAFF. The other night I fell asleep here behind the arras, and
had my pocket picked. This house is turned bawdyhouse;
they pick pockets.

PRINCE. What didst thou lose, Jack?   115

FALSTAFF. Wilt thou believe me, Hal? Three or four bonds of
forty pound apiece, and a seal ring of my grandfather's.

PRINCE. A trifle, some eightpenny matter.

HOSTESS. So I told him, my lord, and I said I heard your Grace   120
say so. And, my lord, he speaks most vilely of you, like a

---

80. bolters: sieves for sifting flour from bran.   **82. holland:** fine linen.   **83. ell:** 45 inches.   **85. by-drinking:** drinks between meals.   **91. denier:** the smallest English coin, worth 1/10d.   **92. younker:** "sucker."   **97. copper:** copper-gilt was the cheapest kind of imitation gold.   **99. Jack:** knave. **sneak-cup:** one who steals cups from taverns, the lowest kind of theft.   **104. Newgate fashion:** i.e., like the chain gang. **Newgate:** the London prison for felons.

foul-mouthed man as he is, and said he would cudgel° you.

PRINCE. What! He did not!

HOSTESS. There's neither faith, truth, nor womanhood in me else.   126

FALSTAFF. There's no more faith in thee than in a stewed prune, nor no more truth in thee than in a drawn fox,° and for womanhood, Maid Marian may be the deputy's wife of the ward to thee.° Go, you thing, go.   131

HOSTESS. Say, what thing? What thing?

FALSTAFF. What thing! Why, a thing to thank God on.

HOSTESS. I am no thing to thank God on, I would thou shouldst   135 know it. I am an honest man's wife. And, setting thy knight-hood aside, thou art a knave to call me so.

FALSTAFF. Setting thy womanhood aside, thou art a beast to say otherwise.   140

HOSTESS. Say, what beast, thou knave, thou?

FALSTAFF. What beast! Why, an otter.

PRINCE. An otter, Sir John! Why an otter?

FALSTAFF. Why, she's neither fish nor flesh. A man knows not where to have her.   145

HOSTESS. Thou art an unjust man in saying so. Thou or any man knows where to have me, thou knave, thou!

PRINCE. Thou sayest true, hostess, and he slanders thee most grossly.   150

HOSTESS. So he doth you, my lord, and said this other day you ought° him a thousand pound.

PRINCE. Sirrah, do I owe you a thousand pound?

FALSTAFF. A thousand pound, Hal! A million! Thy love is worth   155 a million. Thou owest me thy love.

HOSTESS. Nay, my lord, he called you Jack, and said he would cudgel you.

FALSTAFF. Did I, Bardolph?   160

BARDOLPH. Indeed, Sir John, you said so.

FALSTAFF. Yea, if he said° my ring was copper.

PRINCE. I say 'tis copper.° Darest thou be as good as thy word now?   164

FALSTAFF. Why, Hal, thou knowest, as thou art but man, I dare;

123. cudgel: beat. 129. drawn fox: fox driven out from cover, and so cunning. 129–30. Maid . . . thee: Maid Marian, the woman in Robin Hood's gang, was a character in a morris dance. She was played by a man as lumpish and awkward. The wife of the deputy of the ward was likely to give herself airs of dignity. Falstaff means "you are more lumpish than Maid Marian compared with a most stately matron." 152. ought: owed. 162. if he said: Touchstone (in As You Like It, V.5.100–08) has much to say on the virtue of "if" as a means of making a safe threat. 163. I . . . copper: Here Falstaff gets the "lie direct."

but as thou art Prince, I fear thee as I fear the roaring of the lion's whelp.

PRINCE. And why not as the lion?

FALSTAFF. The King himself is to be feared as the lion. Dost thou
think I'll fear thee as I fear thy father? Nay, an I do, I pray   170
God my girdle break.

PRINCE. Oh, if it should, how would thy guts fall about thy knees!
But, sirrah, there's no room for faith, truth, nor honesty in
this bosom of thine; it is all filled up with guts and midriff.
Charge an honest woman with picking thy pocket! Why,
thou whoreson, impudent, embossed° rascal, if there were   177
anything in thy pocket but tavern reckonings, memorandums
of bawdyhouses, and one poor pennyworth of sugar candy to
make thee long-winded, if thy pocket were enriched with any
other injuries° but these, I am a villain. And yet you will
stand to it, you will not pocket up wrong. Art thou not
ashamed?   184

FALSTAFF. Dost thou hear, Hal? Thou knowest in the state of innocency Adam fell, and what should poor Jack Falstaff do
in the days of villainy?° Thou seest I have more flesh than
another man, and therefore more frailty. You confess, then,
you picked my pocket?   190

PRINCE. It appears so by the story.

FALSTAFF. Hostess, I forgive thee. Go, make ready breakfast.
Love thy husband, look to thy servants, cherish thy guests.
Thou shalt find me tractable° to any honest reason. Thou
seest I am pacified still.° Nay, prithee be gone. [Exit HOST-   196
ESS.] Now, Hal, to the news at Court. For the robbery, lad,
how is that answered?

PRINCE. Oh, my sweet beef,° I must still be good angel to thee.
The money is paid back again.   200

FALSTAFF. Oh, I do not like that paying back. 'Tis a double labor.

PRINCE. I am good friends with my father, and may do anything.

FALSTAFF. Rob me the exchequer the first thing thou doest, and
do it with unwashed hands° too.   206

BARDOLPH. Do, my lord.

PRINCE. I have procured thee, Jack, a charge of foot.

FALSTAFF. I would it had been of horse. Where shall I find one
that can steal well? Oh for a fine thief, of the age of two and
twenty or thereabouts! I am heinously° unprovided. Well,   212

---

177. embossed: swollen.   181–82. pocket . . . injuries: a pun on the phrase
"to pocket up injuries."   187. days of villainy: these wicked times.   194.
tractable: agreeable.   196. still: always.   199. beef: ox.   206. unwashed
hands: without stopping to wash your hands.   212. heinously: atrociously.

God be thanked for these rebels, they offend none but the
virtuous. I laud them, I praise them.

PRINCE. Bardolph!

BARDOLPH. My lord?

PRINCE. Go bear this letter to Lord John of Lancaster, to my
brother John; this to my Lord of Westmoreland. [*Exit* BAR-   220
DOLPH.] Go, Peto, to horse, to horse, for thou and I have
thirty miles to ride yet ere dinnertime. [*Exit* PETO.] Jack,
meet me tomorrow in the Temple Hall at two o'clock in the
afternoon.
There shalt thou know thy charge, and there receive
Money and order for their furniture.°   226
The land is burning, Percy stands on high,
And either we or they must lower lie.   [*Exit.*]

FALSTAFF. Rare words! Brave world! Hostess, my breakfast, come!
Oh, I could wish this tavern were my drum!   [*Exit.*]

226. furniture: equipment.

ACT IV

Scene 1 ⚜ *The rebel camp near Shrewsbury.*

        [*Enter* HOTSPUR, WORCESTER, *and* DOUGLAS.]

HOTSPUR. Well said, my noble Scot. If speaking truth
  In this fine age were not thought flattery,
  Such attribution° should the Douglas have
  As not a soldier of this season's stamp°
  Should go so general current through the world.   5
  By God, I cannot flatter, I do defy
  The tongues of soothers;° but a braver place
  In my heart's love hath no man than yourself.
  Nay, task me to my word.° Approve° me, lord.
DOUGLAS. Thou art the king of honor.   10
  No man so potent breathes upon the ground
  But I will beard° him.
HOTSPUR.   Do so, and 'tis well.
            [*Enter a* MESSENGER *with letters.*]
  What letters hast thou there?—I can but thank you.
MESSENGER. These letters come from your father.
HOTSPUR. Letters from him! Why comes he not himself?   15
MESSENGER. He cannot come, my lord, he is grievous sick.
HOTSPUR. 'Zounds! How has he the leisure to be sick
  In such a justling° time? Who leads his power?
  Under whose government come they along?
MESSENGER. His letters bear his mind, not I, my lord.   20
WORCESTER. I prithee tell me, doth he keep his bed?

    Act IV, Sc. 1: 3. attribution: citation of merits.   **4. season's stamp:** of this
year's minting. The idea is that Douglas is like a new coin, acceptable
(*current*) everywhere as valuable.   **7. soothers:** flatterers.   **9. task . . .
word:** cause me to make my word good. **Approve:** put to the proof.   **12.
beard:** dare; lit., pull by the beard.   **18. justling:** jostling, disturbed.

MESSENGER. He did, my lord, four days ere I set forth,
  And at the time of my departure thence
  He was much feared by his physicians.
WORCESTER. I would the state of time had first been whole° 25
  Ere he by sickness had been visited.
  His health was never better worth° than now.
HOTSPUR. Sick now! Droop now! This sickness doth infect
  The very lifeblood of our enterprise.
  'Tis catching hither, even to our camp. 30
  He writes me here that inward sickness—
  And that his friends by deputation° could not
  So soon be drawn,° nor did he think it meet
  To lay so dangerous and dear° a trust
  On any soul removed but on his own. 35
  Yet doth he give us bold advértisement°
  That with our small conjunction° we should on,
  To see how fortune is disposed to us;
  For, as he writes, there is no quailing now,
  Because the King is certainly possessed° 40
  Of all our purposes. What say you to it?
WORCESTER. Your father's sickness is a maim to us.
HOTSPUR. A perilous gash, a very limb lopped off.
  And yet, in faith, it is not; his present want°
  Seems more than we shall find it. Were it good 45
  To set° the exact° wealth of all our states
  All at one cast?° To set so rich a main°
  On the nice hazard° of one doubtful hour?
  It were not good, for therein should we read
  The very bottom and the soul of hope, 50
  The very list,° the very utmost bound°
  Of all our fortunes.
DOUGLAS.   Faith, and so we should,
  Where now remains a sweet reversion.°
  We may boldly spend upon the hope of what
  Is to come in. 55

---

25. I . . . whole: I wish the times themselves had first been healthy. 27.
better worth: worth more. 32. deputation: deputy; i.e., he could not send
anyone else. 33. drawn: drawn together. 34. dear: important. 36. ad-
vertisement: advice. 37. conjunction: forces that have joined. 40. possessed: informed. 44. his . . . want: the need of him at this present time.
46. set: hazard. exact: entire. 47. cast: throw of the dice. main: stake. 48.
nice hazard: delicate chance. 51. list: limit. bound: boundary. 53. reversion: portion yet to come.

A comfort of retirement° lives in this.

HOTSPUR. A rendezvous, a home to fly unto,
    If that the Devil and mischance look big°
    Upon the maidenhead of our affairs.

WORCESTER. But yet I would your father had been here.   60
    The quality and hair° of our attempt
    Brooks no division. It will be thought
    By some, that know not why he is away,
    That wisdom, loyalty, and mere dislike
    Of our proceedings kept the Earl from hence.   65
    And think how such an apprehension
    May turn the tide of fearful faction,°
    And breed a kind of question in our cause;
    For well you know we of the offering° side
    Must keep aloof from strict arbitrament,°   70
    And stop all sight holes, every loop from whence
    The eye of reason may pry in upon us.
    This absence of your father's draws° a curtain
    That shows the ignorant a kind of fear
    Before not dreamed of.

HOTSPUR.   You strain too far.   75
    I rather of his absence make this use.
    It lends a luster and more great opinion,
    A larger dare to our great enterprise,
    Than if the Earl were here; for men must think
    If we without his help can make a head°   80
    To push against a kingdom, with his help
    We shall o'erturn it topsy-turvy down.
    Yet all goes well, yet all our joints are whole.

DOUGLAS. As heart can think. There is not such a word
    Spoke of in Scotland as this term of fear.   85

                [*Enter* SIR RICHARD VERNON.]

HOTSPUR. My cousin Vernon! Welcome, by my soul.

VERNON. Pray God my news be worth a welcome, lord.
    The Earl of Westmoreland, seven thousand strong,
    Is marching hitherward; with him Prince John.

HOTSPUR. No harm. What more?

VERNON.   And further, I have learned,   90
    The King himself in person is set forth,

---

56. comfort of retirement: a place to which we can retire for comfort. 58.
look big: threaten. 61. hair: nature. 67. fearful faction: timid rebellion.
69. offering: challenging. 70. strict arbitrament: exact judgment. 73.
draws: draws back. 80. make a head: raise an army. See I.3.284.

Or hitherward intended speedily,
With strong and mighty preparation.
HOTSPUR. He shall be welcome too. Where is his son,
The nimble-footed madcap Prince of Wales,   95
And his comrades, that daffed° the world aside
And bid it pass?°
VERNON.   All furnished,° all in arms;
All plumed like estridges that with the wind
Bated like eagles having lately bathed;°
Glittering in golden coats, like images;°   100
As full of spirit as the month of May,
And gorgeous as the sun at midsummer;
Wanton° as youthful goats, wild as young bulls.
I saw young Harry, with his beaver° on,
His cuisses° on his thighs, gallantly armed,   105
Rise from the ground like feathered Mercury,°
And vaulted with such ease into his seat
As if an angel dropped down from the clouds
To turn and wind a fiery Pegasus,°
And witch° the world with noble horsemanship.   110
HOTSPUR. No more, no more. Worse than the sun in March,
This praise doth nourish agues. Let them come.
They come like sacrifices in their trim,°
And to the fire-eyed maid of smoky war
All hot and bleeding will we offer them.   115
The mailèd Mars° shall on his altar sit
Up to the ears in blood. I am on fire
To hear this rich reprisal° is so nigh
And yet not ours. Come, let me taste my horse,
Who is to bear me like a thunderbolt   120
Against the bosom of the Prince of Wales.
Harry to Harry shall, hot horse to horse,
Meet and ne'er part till one drop down a corse.

---

96. daffed: waved.   97. bid it pass: cried "let the world pass"; i.e., "who cares a damn?" furnished: in full armor.   97–99. All . . . bathed: These lines are much annotated. As they stand they mean: "All wearing plumes like ostriches that flap their wings (*bate*) in the wind like eagles that have lately bathed." But the comparison seems hardly apt. Either a line has been omitted after *wind*, or *with* is a misprint of some such verb as "wing."   100. images: i.e., of the saints in a Catholic church.   103. Wanton: lusty.   104. beaver: visor of the helmet.   105. cuisses: thigh pieces.   106. feathered Mercury: Mercury, the messenger of the gods, wore winged sandals.   109. Pegasus: Perseus's winged horse.   110. witch: bewitch.   113. in . . . trim: dressed up.   116. mailed Mars: the god of war in his armor.   118. reprisal: prize.

Oh that Glendower were come!
VERNON.   There is more news.
I learned in Worcester, as I rode along,   125
He cannot draw his power this fourteen days.
DOUGLAS. That's the worst tidings that I hear of yet.
WORCESTER. Aye, by my faith, that bears a frosty sound.
HOTSPUR. What may the King's whole battle° reach unto?
VERNON. To thirty thousand.
HOTSPUR.   Forty let it be.   130
My father and Glendower being both away,
The powers of us may serve so great a day.
Come, let us take a muster speedily.
Doomsday is near. Die all, die merrily.
DOUGLAS. Talk not of dying. I am out of° fear   135
Of death or death's hand for this one half-year.   [*Exeunt.*]

Scene 2 ⚜ *A public road near Coventry.*

[*Enter* FALSTAFF *and* BARDOLPH.]
FALSTAFF. Bardolph, get thee before to Coventry, fill me a bottle
     of sack. Our soldiers shall march through, we'll to Sutton
     Co'fil'° tonight.
BARDOLPH. Will you give me money, Captain?
FALSTAFF. Lay out,° lay out.   5
BARDOLPH. This bottle makes an angel.°
FALSTAFF. An if it do, take it for thy labor. And if it make twenty,
     take them all, I'll answer the coinage.° Bid my Lieutenant
     Peto meet me at town's end.   10
BARDOLPH. I will, Captain. Farewell.   [*Exit.*]
FALSTAFF. If I be not ashamed of my soldiers,° I am a soused

129. battle: main army.   135. out of: free from.
   Sc. 2: 3. Sutton Co'fil': Sutton Coldfield, a town in Warwickshire.   5.
Lay out: pay for it.   6. makes an angel: comes to an angel (10s) which you
owe me.   7–9. take . . . coinage: Falstaff deliberately misunderstands Bardolph's "make"—"if the bottle will make angels, I'll guarantee the coins."
12. If . . . soldiers: Falstaff (see following to l. 52) was typical of many
dishonest captains in the 1590's. His methods of levying recruits are further
shown in *II Hen IV*, III.2.

gurnet.° I have misused the King's press° damnably. I have
got, in exchange of a hundred and fifty soldiers, three hundred and odd pounds. I press me none but good household-   15
ers, yeomen's° sons; inquire me out contracted bachelors,°
such as had been asked twice on the banns; such a commod-
ity° of warm slaves as had as lieve° hear the Devil as a drum;
such as fear the report of a caliver° worse than a struck fowl   20
or a hurt wild duck. I pressed me none but such toasts-and-
butter, with hearts in their bellies no bigger than pins' heads,
and they have bought out their services. And now my whole
charge consists of ancients, corporals, lieutenants, gentlemen   25
of companies,° slaves as ragged as Lazarus in the painted
cloth° where the glutton's dogs licked his sores; and such as
indeed were never soldiers, but discarded unjust servingmen,° younger sons to younger brothers,° revolted tapsters,   31
and ostlers trade-fallen;° the cankers of a calm world and a
long peace, ten times more dishonorable ragged than an old-
faced ancient. And such have I to fill up the rooms of them
that have bought out their services that you would think that
I had a hundred and fifty tattered prodigals lately come from
swine-keeping, from eating draff and husks.° A mad fellow°   39
met me on the way and told me I had unloaded all the gib-
bets° and pressed the dead bodies. No eye hath seen such
scarecrows. I'll not march through Coventry with them,
that's flat. Nay, and the villains march wide betwixt the legs,
as if they had gyves° on, for indeed I had the most of them   44
out of prison. There's but a shirt and a half in all my com-

13. soused gurnet: pickled gurnet (sea fish with a large head). King's press:
the right to conscript soldiers granted by the King's commission. 16.
yeomen: wealthy farmers. 17. contracted bachelors: bachelors engaged to
be married in a short time. 19. commodity: parcel. lieve: soon. 20. caliver:
lighter form of musket or harquebus, used by the infantry. 25–26. charge
. . . companies: Falstaff has picked up a selection of veterans of various
ranks. ancients: ensigns, second lieutenants. gentlemen of companies: gentlemen of good family who served in the ranks of the companies of noblemen.
27. Lazarus . . . cloth: In taverns and less wealthy houses painted cloths
showing scenes from Scripture and classical legend were hung on the walls
instead of the more costly tapestry. 31. servingmen: servants from some
great household. younger . . . brothers: young gentlemen who had no hope
of an allowance or a legacy. 32. ostlers trade-fallen: unemployed grooms.
39. draff . . . husks: offal and husks, like the Prodigal Son in the parable
who "would fain have filled his belly with the husks that the swine did eat"
(Luke, 15:11–32). mad fellow: wit. 40. unloaded . . . gibbets: The bodies
of executed felons were often hung up in iron cages near the scene of the
crime until they rotted. 44. gyves: fetters on the legs.

pany; and the half-shirt is two napkins tacked together and thrown over the shoulders like a herald's coat° without sleeves; and the shirt, to say the truth, stolen from my host at St. Alban's, or the red-nose innkeeper of Daventry. But that's all one. They'll find linen enough on every hedge.° 51

[*Enter the* PRINCE *and* WESTMORELAND.]

PRINCE. How now, blown° Jack! How now, quilt!

FALSTAFF. What, Hal! How now, mad wag! What a devil dost thou in Warwickshire? My good Lord of Westmoreland, I cry you mercy. I thought your honor had already been at Shrewsbury. 59

WESTMORELAND. Faith, Sir John, 'tis more than time that I were there, and you too; but my powers are there already. The King, I can tell you, looks for us all. We must away all night.

FALSTAFF. Tut, never fear me. I am as vigilant as a cat to steal cream. 65

PRINCE. I think to steal cream indeed, for thy theft hath already made thee butter. But tell me, Jack, whose fellows are these that come after?

FALSTAFF. Mine, Hal, mine.

PRINCE. I did never see such pitiful rascals. 70

FALSTAFF. Tut, tut, good enough to toss,° food for powder, food for powder. They'll fill a pit as well as better. Tush, man, mortal men, mortal men.

WESTMORELAND. Aye, but, Sir John, methinks they are exceeding poor and bare, too beggarly. 75

FALSTAFF. Faith, for their poverty, I know not where they had that; and for their bareness, I am sure they never learned that of me.

PRINCE. No, I'll be sworn, unless you call three fingers° on the ribs bare. But, sirrah, make haste. Percy is already in the field. 81

FALSTAFF. What, is the King encamped?

WESTMORELAND. He is, Sir John. I fear we shall stay too long.

FALSTAFF. Well,

To the latter end of a fray and the beginning of a feast 85
Fits a dull fighter and a keen guest.   [*Exeunt.*]

---

48. herald's coat: a sleeveless coat embroidered with the royal coat of arms. **41–52. linen . . . hedge:** The washing was laid on the hedges to dry and air. **53. blown:** inflated. **71. good . . . toss:** i.e., on pikes; "good enough for cannon fodder." **79–80. three fingers:** i.e., three fingers' thickness of fat.

Scene 3 🙡 *The rebel camp near Shrewsbury.*

[*Enter* HOTSPUR, WORCESTER, DOUGLAS, *and* VERNON.]

HOTSPUR. We'll fight with him tonight.

WORCESTER.   It may not be.

DOUGLAS. You give him then advantage.

VERNON.   Not a whit.

HOTSPUR. Why say you so? Looks he not for supply?°

VERNON. So do we.

HOTSPUR.   His is certain, ours is doubtful.

WORCESTER. Good Cousin, be advised, stir not tonight.   5

VERNON. Do not, my lord.

DOUGLAS.   You do not counsel well.
    You speak it out of fear and cold heart.

VERNON. Do me no slander, Douglas. By my life,
    And I dare well maintain it with my life,
    If well-respected° honor bid me on,   10
    I hold as little counsel with weak fear
    As you, my lord, or any Scot that this day lives.
    Let it be seen tomorrow in the battle
    Which of us fears.

DOUGLAS.   Yea, or tonight.

VERNON.   Content.

HOTSPUR. Tonight, say I.   15

VERNON. Come, come, it may not be. I wonder much,
    Being men of such great leading° as you are,
    That you foresee not what impediments
    Drag back our expedition.° Certain horse°
    Of my cousin Vernon's are not yet come up.   20
    Your uncle Worcester's horse came but today,
    And now their pride and mettle° is asleep,
    Their courage with hard labor tame and dull,
    That not a horse is half of himself.

Sc. 3: 3. supply: reinforcements.   **10. well-respected:** well-considered (not foolhardy).   **17. leading:** experience in leadership.   **19. expedition:** haste. **horse:** cavalry.   **22. mettle:** ardor.

HOTSPUR. So are the horses of the enemy   25
    In general, journey-bated° and brought low.
    The better part of ours are full of rest.
WORCESTER. The number of the King exceedeth ours.
    For God's sake, Cousin, stay till all come in.
                        [The trumpet sounds a parley.]
                [Enter SIR WALTER BLUNT.]
BLUNT. I come with gracious offers from the King,   30
    If you vouchsafe me hearing and respect.
HOTSPUR. Welcome, Sir Walter Blunt, and would to God
    You were of our determination!°
    Some of us love you well, and even those some
    Envy your great deservings and good name   35
    Because you are not of our quality,°
    But stand against us like an enemy.
BLUNT. And God defend° but still I should stand so
    So long as out of limit and true rule
    You stand against anointed Majesty.   40
    But to my charge.° The King hath sent to know
    The nature of your griefs, and whereupon
    You conjure from the breast of civil peace
    Such bold hostility, teaching his duteous land
    Audacious cruelty. If that the King   45
    Have any way your good deserts forgot,
    Which he confesseth to be manifold,
    He bids you name your griefs, and with all speed
    You shall have your desires with interest,
    And pardon absolute for yourself and these   50
    Herein misled by your suggestion.°
HOTSPUR. The King is kind, and well we know the King
    Knows at what time to promise, when to pay.
    My father and my uncle and myself
    Did give him that same royalty he wears.   55
    And when he was not six and twenty strong,
    Sick in the world's regard,° wretched and low,
    A poor unminded outlaw sneaking home,
    My father gave him welcome to the shore.
    And when he heard him swear and vow to God   60
    He came but to be Duke of Lancaster,
    To sue his livery° and beg his peace

---

26. journey-bated: tired by the journey. **33. determination:** mind. **36. quality:** fellowship, party. **38. defend:** forbid. **41. my change:** what I have been instructed (*charged*) to say. **51. suggestion:** temptation. **57. Sick . . . regard:** poorly regarded by the world. **62. sue . . . livery:** claim his inheritance.

With tears of innocency and terms of zeal,°
My father, in kind heart and pity moved,
Swore him assistance, and performed it too.   65
Now when the lords and barons of the realm
Perceived Northumberland did lean to him,
The more and less came in with cap and knee—
Met him in boroughs, cities, villages,
Attended him on bridges, stood in lanes,   70
Laid gifts before him, proffered him their oaths,
Gave him their heirs as pages, followed him
Even at the heels in golden° multitudes.
He presently, as greatness knows itself,
Steps me a little higher than his vow   75
Made to my father while his blood was poor,
Upon the naked shore at Ravenspurgh;
And now, forsooth, takes on him to reform
Some certain edicts and some strait° decrees
That lie too heavy on the commonwealth,   80
Cries out upon abuses, seems to weep
Over his country's wrongs. And by this face,
This seeming brow of justice, did he win
The hearts of all that he did angle for—
Proceeded further, cut me off the heads   85
Of all the favorites that the absent King
In deputation° left behind him here
When he was personal° in the Irish war.
BLUNT. Tut, I came not to hear this.
HOTSPUR.   Then to the point.
In short time after, he deposed the King,   90
Soon after that, deprived him of his life.
And in the neck° of that, tasked° the whole state.
To make that worse, suffered his kinsman March,
Who is, if every owner were well placed,
Indeed his king, to be engaged° in Wales,   95
There without ransom to lie forfeited;
Disgraced me in my happy victories,
Sought to entrap me by intelligence;°
Rated° mine uncle from the Council board,
In rage dismissed my father from the Court;   100
Broke oath on oath, committed wrong on wrong;

63. terms of zeal: protestations of loyalty.   **73. golden:** wearing their richest clothes.   **79. strait:** strict.   **87. In deputation:** as his deputies.   **88. was personal:** went in person.   **92. in . . . neck:** on top of. **tasked:** taxed.   **95. engaged:** held as pledge, hostage.   **98. intelligence:** spies.   **99. Rated:** dismissed with abuse.

And in conclusion drove us to seek out
This head of safety,° and withal to pry
Into his title, the which we find
Too indirect° for long continuance.   105
BLUNT. Shall I return this answer to the King?
HOTSPUR. Not so, Sir Walter. We'll withdraw a while.
Go to the King, and let there be impawned°
Some surety for a safe return again,
And in the morning early shall mine uncle   110
Bring him our purposes. And so farewell.
BLUNT. I would you would accept of grace and love.
HOTSPUR. And maybe so we shall.
BLUNT.   ·   Pray God you do.   [*Exeunt.*]

Scene 4 ᴇᴢ *York. The* ARCHBISHOP'S *palace.*

[*Enter the* ARCHBISHOP OF YORK *and* SIR MICHAEL.°]
ARCHBISHOP. Hie, good Sir Michael, bear this sealèd brief°
With wingèd haste to the Lord Marshal,
This to my cousin Scroop, and all the rest
To whom they are directed. If you knew
How much they do import, you would make haste.   5
SIR MICHAEL. My good lord,
I guess their tenor.°
ARCHBISHOP.   Like enough you do.
Tomorrow, good Sir Michael, is a day
Wherein the fortune of ten thousand men
Must abide the touch;° for, sir, at Shrewsbury,   10
As I am truly given to understand,
The King with mighty and quick-raisèd power
Meets with Lord Harry. And I fear, Sir Michael—
What with the sickness of Northumberland,

---

103. **head of safety:** armed force to keep us safe.   **105. indirect:** not in the
straight line of descent.   **108. impawned:** kept as hostage.
Sc. 4: s.d., **Sir Michael:** He has not been identified, presumably a priest or
knight in the Archbishop's service.   **1. brief:** letter.   **7. tenor:** import.   **10.**
bide . . . touch: be put to the test.

Whose power was in the first proportion,°   15
And what with Owen Glendower's absence thence,
Who with them was a rated sinew° too
And comes not in, o'er-ruled by prophecies—
I fear the power of Percy is too weak
To wage an instant° trial with the King.   20
SIR MICHAEL. Why, my good lord, you need not fear.
    There is Douglas and Lord Mortimer.
ARCHBISHOP. No, Mortimer is not there.
SIR MICHAEL. But there is Mordake, Vernon, Lord Harry Percy,
    And there is my Lord of Worcester and a head   25
    Of gallant warriors, noble gentlemen.
ARCHBISHOP. And so there is. But yet the King hath drawn
    The special head° of all the land together—
    The Prince of Wales, Lord John of Lancaster,
    The noble Westmoreland and warlike Blunt,   30
    And many mo° corrivals° and dear men
    Of estimation° and command in arms.
SIR MICHAEL. Doubt not, my lord, they shall be well opposed.
ARCHBISHOP. I hope no less, yet needful 'tis to fear,
    And, to prevent° the worst, Sir Michael, speed.   35
    For if Lord Percy thrive not ere the King
    Dismiss his power, he means to visit us,°
    For he hath heard of our confederacy,°
    And 'tis but wisdom to make strong against him.
    Therefore make haste. I must go write again   40
    To other friends. And so farewell, Sir Michael.   [*Exeunt.*]

---

15. in . . . proportion: the largest part.   17. rated sinew: strength highly
valued.   20. instant: immediate.   28. special head: crack troops, "shock
troops."   31. mo: more. corrivals: supporters.   31–32. dear . . . estimation:
men highly regarded.   35. prevent: forestall.   37. visit us: come our way.
38. confederacy: conspiracy.

ACT V

Scene 1 ☙ *The* KING'S *camp near Shrewsbury.*

[*Enter the* KING, PRINCE OF WALES, LORD JOHN OF
LANCASTER, SIR WALTER BLUNT, *and* FALSTAFF.°]

KING. How bloodily the sun begins to peer
    Above yon busky° hill! The day looks pale
    At his distemperature.°
PRINCE.   The southern wind
    Doth play the trumpet° to his purposes,
    And by his hollow whistling in the leaves
    Foretells a tempest and a blustering day.   5
KING. Then with the losers let it sympathize,
    For nothing can seem foul to those that win.
        [*The trumpet sounds. Enter* WORCESTER *and* VERNON.]
    How now, my Lord of Worcester! 'Tis not well
    That you and I should meet upon such terms   10
    As now we meet. You have deceived our trust,
    And made us doff our easy robes of peace
    To crush our old limbs in ungentle steel.
    This is not well, my lord, this is not well.
    What say you to it? Will you again unknit
    This churlish knot° of all-abhorrèd war?   15
    And move in that obedient orb° again
    Where you did give a fair and natural light,

And be no more an exhalèd meteor,°
A prodigy of fear,° and a portent   20
Of broachèd° mischief to the unborn times?
WORCESTER. Hear me, my liege.
      For mine own part, I could be well content
      To entertain the lag end of my life
      With quiet hours, for I do protest   25
      I have not sought the day of this dislike.
KING. You have not sought it! How comes it, then?
FALSTAFF. Rebellion lay in his way, and he found it.
PRINCE. Peace, chewet,° peace!
WORCESTER. It pleased your Majesty to turn your looks   30
      Of favor from myself and all our house.
      And yet I must remember° you, my lord,
      We were the first and dearest of your friends.
      For you my staff of office° did I break
      In Richard's time, and posted° day and night   35
      To meet you on the way, and kiss your hand,
      When yet you were in place and in account
      Nothing so strong and fortunate as I.
      It was myself, my brother, and his son
      That brought you home, and boldly did outdare   40
      The dangers of the time. You swore to us,
      And you did swear that oath at Doncaster,
      That you did nothing purpose 'gainst the state,
      Nor claim no further than your new-fall'n right,°
      The seat of Gaunt, Dukedom of Lancaster.   45
      To this we swore our aid. But in short space
      It rained down fortune showering on your head;
      And such a flood of greatness fell on you,
      What with our help, what with the absent King,
      What with the injuries of a wanton° time,   50
      The seeming sufferances° that you had borne,
      And the contrarious winds that held the King
      So long in his unlucky Irish wars
      That all in England did repute him dead.
      And from this swarm of fair advantages   55
      You took occasion to be quickly wooed

19. **exhaled meteor:** meteor created of vapor drawn up by the sun. 20.
prodigy of fear: a fearful sign of disaster. 21. **broached:** set loose; lit.,
tapped (like a cask). 29. **chewet:** jackdaw. 32. **remember:** remind. 34.
staff of office: See *Rich II,* II.3.26–28. 35. **posted:** rode hastily. 44. **new-fall'n right:** inheritance which had recently come. 50. **wanton:** wild. 51.
sufferances: injuries.

To gripe° the general sway° into your hand;
Forgot your oath to us at Doncaster;
And being fed by us you used us so
As that ungentle gull,° the cuckoo's bird,°   60
Useth the sparrow—did oppress our nest;
Grew by our feeding to so great a bulk
That even our love durst not come near your sight
For fear of swallowing, but with nimble wing
We were enforced, for safety sake, to fly   65
Out of your sight and raise this present head.
Whereby we stand opposèd by such means
As you yourself have forged against yourself,
By unkind usage, dangerous countenance,°
And violation of all faith and troth°   70
Sworn to us in your younger enterprise.

KING. These things indeed you have articulate,°
Proclaimed at market crosses, read in churches,
To face° the garment of rebellion
With some fine color that may please the eye   75
Of fickle changelings° and poor discontents,
Which gape and rub the elbow at the news
Of hurly-burly innovation.°
And never yet did insurrection want
Such water colors to impaint his cause,   80
Nor moody beggars, starving for a time
Of pell-mell havoc° and confusion.

PRINCE. In both your armies there is many a soul
Shall pay full dearly for this encounter
If once they join in trial. Tell your nephew,   85
The Prince of Wales doth join with all the world
In praise of Henry Percy. By my hopes,
This present enterprise set off his head,°
I do not think a braver gentleman,
More active-valiant or more valiant-young,   90
More daring or more bold, is now alive
To grace this latter age with noble deeds.
For my part, I may speak it to my shame,
I have a truant been to chivalry,°

---

57. **gripe:** grip. **general sway:** rule of the whole state.   60. **gull:** nestling.
cuckoo's bird: The cuckoo lays its eggs in the nests of smaller birds. When
the young cuckoo is hatched, it pushes the other nestlings out of the nest.
69. **dangerous countenance:** threatening looks.   70. **troth:** truth.   72. **articulate:** drawn up in schedules.   74. **face:** trim.   76. **changelings:** turncoats.
78. **hurly-burly innovation:** confusion and revolution.   82. **havoc:** slaughter.
88. **set . . . head:** being excepted.   94. **chivalry:** knightly deeds.

And so I hear he doth account me too.   95
Yet this before my father's majesty—
I am content that he shall take the odds°
Of his great name and estimation,
And will, to save the blood on either side,
Try fortune with him in a single fight.   100

KING. And, Prince of Wales, so dare we venture thee,
Albeit considerations infinite
Do make against it. No, good Worcester, no,
We love our people well, even those we love
That are misled upon your cousin's part.   105
And, will they take the offer of our grace,
Both he and they and you—yea, every man—
Shall be my friend again and I'll be his.
So tell your cousin, and bring me word
What he will do. But if he will not yield,   110
Rebuke and dread correction wait on us°
And they shall do their office. So, be gone.
We will not now be troubled with reply.
We offer fair, take it advisedly.
                              [*Exeunt* WORCESTER *and* VERNON.]

PRINCE. It will not be accepted, on my life.   115
The Douglas and the Hotspur both together
Are confident against the world in arms.

KING. Hence, therefore, every leader to his charge,°
For on their answer will we set on them.
And God befriend us as our cause is just!   120
             [*Exeunt all but the* PRINCE OF WALES *and* FALSTAFF.]

FALSTAFF. Hal, if thou see me down in the battle, and bestride me
   so, 'tis a point of friendship.

PRINCE. Nothing but a colossus° can do thee that friendship. Say
   thy prayers, and farewell.

FALSTAFF. I would 'twere bedtime, Hal, and all well.   125

PRINCE. Why, thou owest God a death.   [*Exit.*]

FALSTAFF. 'Tis not due yet, I would be loath to pay Him before
   his day. What need I be so forward with him that calls not
   on me? Well, 'tis no matter. Honor pricks me on.° Yea, but   131
   how if honor prick me off° when I come on? How then? Can
   honor set to° a leg? No. Or an arm? No. Or take away the

---

97. take . . . odds: have the advantage.   **111. wait on us:** are our servants.
118. charge: command.   **123. colossus:** a huge bronze statue which in
ancient times straddled the harbor of Rhodes.   **131. Honor . . . on:** honor
spurs me forward to heroism.   **131–32. prick me off:** mark me down on the
casualty list.   **132–33. set to:** mend.

grief of a wound? No. Honor hath no skill in surgery, then?
No. What is honor? A word. What is in that word honor?
What is that honor? Air. A trim° reckoning! Who hath it?   137
He that died o' Wednesday. Doth he feel it? No. Doth he
hear it? No. 'Tis insensible, then? Yea, to the dead. But will
it not live with the living? No. Why? Detraction° will not
suffer it. Therefore I'll none of it. Honor is a mere scutcheon.° And so ends my catechism.   [*Exit.*]   143

Scene 2 ᴈ᠍ᠷ *The rebel camp.*

[*Enter* WORCESTER *and* VERNON.]

WORCESTER. Oh, no, my nephew must not know, Sir Richard,
    The liberal and kind offer of the King.
VERNON. 'Twere best he did.
WORCESTER.   Then are we all undone.
    It is not possible, it cannot be
    The King should keep his word in loving us.   5
    He will suspect us still, and find a time
    To punish this offense in other faults.
    Suspicion all our lives shall be stuck full of eyes;
    For treason is but trusted like the fox,
    Who, ne'er so tame, so cherished and locked up,   10
    Will have a wild trick° of his ancestors.
    Look how we can, or° sad or merrily,
    Interpretation will misquote° our looks,
    And we shall feed like oxen at a stall,
    The better cherished, still the nearer death.   15
    My nephew's trespass may be well forgot.
    It hath the excuse of youth and heat of blood,
    And an adopted name of privilege,°
    A harebrained Hotspur, governed by a spleen.°

137. trim: neat.   141. Detraction: slander.   143. scutcheon: coat of arms,
painted on boards or cloth, carried in the funeral of a gentleman and afterward hung up in the church.
    Sc. 2: 11. wild trick: wild habits.   12. or: either.   13. Interpretation . . .
misquote: men will deliberately misinterpret.   18. adopted . . . privilege:
his nickname Hotspur will be his excuse.   19. spleen: impetuosity.

All his offenses live upon my head   20
And on his father's. We did train° him on,
And, his corruption being ta'en from us,
We, as the spring of all, shall pay for all.
Therefore, good Cousin, let not Harry know,
In any case, the offer of the King.   25

VERNON. Deiiver° what you will, I'll say 'tis so.
     Here comes your cousin.
                    [*Enter* HOTSPUR *and* DOUGLAS.]

HOTSPUR. My uncle is returned.
     Deliver up° my Lord of Westmoreland.
     Uncle, what news?   30

WORCESTER. The King will bid you battle presently.°

DOUGLAS. Defy him by the Lord of Westmoreland.

HOTSPUR. Lord Douglas, go you and tell him so.

DOUGLAS. Marry, and shall, and very willingly.   [*Exit.*]

WORCESTER. There is no seeming mercy in the King.   35

HOTSPUR. Did you beg any? God forbid!

WORCESTER. I told him gently of our grievances,
     Of his oath-breaking, which he mended thus,
     By now forswearing° that he is forsworn.
     He calls us rebels, traitors, and will scourge   40
     With haughty arms this hateful name in us.
                    [*Re-enter* DOUGLAS.]

DOUGLAS. Arm, gentlemen, to arms! For I have thrown
     A brave defiance in King Henry's teeth—
     And Westmoreland, that was engaged,° did bear it—
     Which cannot choose but bring him quickly on.   45

WORCESTER. The Prince of Wales stepped forth before the King
     And, Nephew, challenged you to single fight.

HOTSPUR. Oh, would the quarrel lay upon our heads,
     And that no man might draw short breath° today
     But I and Harry Monmouth! Tell me, tell me,   50
     How showed his tasking?° Seem'd it in contempt?

VERNON. No, by my soul. I never in my life
     Did hear a challenge urged° more modestly,
     Unless a brother should a brother dare
     To gentle exercise and proof of arms.   55
     He gave you all the duties of° a man,

---

21. train: lure.   **26. Deliver:** report.   **29. Deliver up:** release. Westmoreland
had been hostage for Worcester's safe return.   **31. presently:** immediately.
39. forswearing: falsely denying an oath.   **44. engaged:** pledged as hostage.
49. draw . . . breath: i.e., in fighting.   **51. tasking:** challenge.   **53. urged:**
put forward.   **56. duties of:** respect due to.

Trimmed up your praises with a princely tongue,
Spoke your deservings like a chronicle,
Making you ever better than his praise
By still dispraising praise valued with you.°   60
And, which became him like a prince indeed,
He made a blushing cital° of himself,
And chid his truant youth with such a grace
As if he mastered there a double spirit
Of teaching and of learning instantly.   65
There did he pause. But let me tell the world,
If he outlive the envy° of this day,
England did never owe° so sweet a hope,
So much misconstrued in his wantonness.
HOTSPUR. Cousin, I think thou art enamored   70
    On his follies. Never did I hear
    Of any prince so wild a libertine.
    But be he as he will, yet once ere night
    I will embrace him with a soldier's arm,
    That he shall shrink under my courtesy.   75
    Arm, arm with speed. And, fellows, soldiers, friends,
    Better consider what you have to do
    Than I, that have not well the gift of tongue,
    Can lift your blood up with persuasion.
              [*Enter a* MESSENGER.]
MESSENGER. My lord, here are letters for you.   80
HOTSPUR. I cannot read them now.
    O gentlemen, the time of life is short!
    To spend that shortness basely were too long
    If life did ride upon a dial's point,°
    Still° ending at the arrival of an hour.   85
    An if we live, we live to tread on kings;
    If die, brave death when princes die with us!
    Now, for our consciences, the arms are fair
    When the intent° of bearing them is just.
              [*Enter another* MESSENGER.]
MESSENGER. My lord, prepare. The King comes on apace.   90
HOTSPUR. I thank him, that he cuts me from my tale,
    For I profess not talking, only this—
    Let each man do his best. And here draw I
    A sword whose temper° I intend to stain

---

60. By . . . you: by continuously saying that your praise was undervalued.
62. cital: recital.   **68. envy:** malice.   **69. owe:** own.   **84. dial's point:** hand
of a clock.   **85. Still:** always.   **89. intent:** cause.   **94. temper:** lit., hardness,
quality.

With the best blood that I can meet withal   95
In the adventure of this perilous day.
Now, Esperance! Percy! and set on.
Sound all the lofty instruments of war,
And by that music let us all embrace;
For, heaven to earth, some of us never shall   100
A second time do such a courtesy.
    [*The trumpets sound. They embrace, and exeunt.*]

Scene 3 ✒ *Plain between the camps.*

   [*The* KING *enters with his power. Alarum to the*
   battle.° Then enter DOUGLAS *and* SIR WALTER BLUNT.]
BLUNT. What is thy name, that in the battle thus
  Thou crossest me? What honor dost thou seek
  Upon my head?
DOUGLAS.   Know then, my name is Douglas,
  And I do haunt thee in the battle thus
  Because some tell me that thou art a King.   5
BLUNT. They tell thee true.
DOUGLAS. The Lord of Stafford dear today hath bought
  Thy likeness; for instead of thee, King Harry,°
  This sword hath ended him. So shall it thee
  Unless thou yield thee as my prisoner.   10
BLUNT. I was not born a yielder, thou proud Scot,
  And thou shalt find a King that will revenge
  Lord Stafford's death.
    [*They fight.* DOUGLAS *kills* BLUNT. *Enter* HOTSPUR.]
HOTSPUR. O Douglas, hadst thou fought at Holmedon thus,
  I never had triumphed upon a Scot.   15
DOUGLAS. All's done, all's won. Here breathless lies the King.
HOTSPUR. Where?
DOUGLAS. Here.
HOTSPUR. This, Douglas? No. I know this face full well.
  A gallant knight he was, his name was Blunt,   20

Sc. 3: s.d., **Alarum . . . battle:** battle noises.   **8. thee . . . Harry:** Blunt
is wearing the King's coat of arms and not his own, and so is mistaken by
Douglas for the King.

Semblably furnished° like the King himself.

DOUGLAS. A fool go with thy soul° whither it goes!
    A borrowed title hast thou bought too dear.
    Why didst thou tell me that thou wert a king?
HOTSPUR. The King hath many marching in his coats.°   25
DOUGLAS. Now, by my sword, I will kill all his coats.
    I'll murder all his wardrobe, piece by piece,
    Until I meet the King.
HOTSPUR.   Up, and away!
    Our soldiers stand full fairly for the day.°   [*Exeunt.*]
                [*Alarum. Enter* FALSTAFF, *alone.*]

FALSTAFF. Though I could 'scape shot-free° at London, I fear the   30
    shot here. Here's no scoring but upon the pate. Soft! Who
    are you? Sir Walter Blunt. There's honor for you! Here's
    no vanity!° I am as hot as molten lead, and as heavy too.
    God keep lead out of me! I need no more weight than mine
    own bowels. I have led my ragamuffins where they are pep-   36
    pered.° There's not three of my hundred and fifty left alive,
    and they are for the town's end, to beg during life. But who
    comes here?   40
                [*Enter the* PRINCE.]

PRINCE. What, stand'st thou idle here? Lend me thy sword.
    Many a nobleman lies stark and stiff
    Under the hoofs of vaunting enemies
    Whose deaths are yet unrevenged. I prithee lend me thy
        sword.
FALSTAFF. O Hal, I prithee give me leave to breathe a while. Turk
    Gregory° never did such deeds in arms as I have done this   46
    day. I have paid Percy, I have made him sure.
PRINCE. He is, indeed, and living to kill thee. I prithee lend me thy
    sword.
FALSTAFF. Nay, before God, Hal, if Percy be alive, thou get'st not   51
    my sword. But take my pistol, if thou wilt.
PRINCE. Give it me. What, is it in the case?
FALSTAFF. Aye, Hal, 'tis hot, 'tis hot. There's that will sack a city.   56
            [*The* PRINCE *draws it out, and finds it to be a bottle of sack.*]

---

21. **Semblably furnished:** wearing similar armor. 22. **A . . . soul:** a proverbial phrase, "you foolish soul." 25. **coats:** coats of arms. 29. **full . . .
day:** i.e., are full of fight. 30. **shot-free:** without paying the *shot* (the
tavern bill) which had been scored up against him. 33. **no vanity:** spoken
ironically. "Who said honor was not a vain thing?" 36–37. **where . . .
peppered:** Falstaff's heroism has a base motive. Until the army is remustered
he will pocket the pay of his dead soldiers. 46. **Turk Gregory:** Pope Gregory
VII, who had a reputation for ferocity. The Turk was proverbial for cruelty.

PRINCE. What, is it a time to jest and dally now?
> [*He throws the bottle at him. Exit.*]

FALSTAFF. Well, if Percy be alive, I'll pierce° him. If he do come
in my way, so. If he do not, if I come in his willingly, let him
make a carbonado° of me. I like not such grinning honor as   61
Sir Walter hath. Give me life, which if I can save, so; if not,
honor comes unlooked-for, and there's an end.   [*Exit.*]

Scene 4 ❧ *Another part of the field.*

> [*Alarum. Excursions.° Enter the* KING, *the* PRINCE,
> LORD JOHN OF LANCASTER, *and* EARL OF
> WESTMORELAND.]

KING. I prithee
Harry, withdraw thyself, thou bleed'st too much.
Lord John of Lancaster, go you with him.

LANCASTER. Not I, my lord, unless I did bleed too.

PRINCE. I beseech your Majesty, make up,°   5
Lest your retirement do amaze° your friends.

KING. I will do so.
My Lord of Westmoreland, lead him to his tent.

WESTMORELAND. Come, my lord, I'll lead you to your tent.

PRINCE. Lead me, my lord? I do not need your help.   10
And God forbid a shallow scratch should drive
The Prince of Wales from such a field as this,
Where stained° nobility lies trodden on
And rebels' arms triumph in massacres!

LANCASTER. We breathe° too long. Come, Cousin Westmoreland,   15
Our duty this way lies. For God's sake, come.
> [*Exeunt* PRINCE JOHN *and* WESTMORELAND.]

PRINCE. By God, thou hast deceived me, Lancaster,
I did not think thee lord of such a spirit.
Before, I loved thee as a brother, John,

---

59. pierce: pronounced "perse," a pun on "Percy."   **61. carbonado:** piece of
meat slashed for broiling.
    Sc. 4: s.d., Excursions: noises to indicate rapid movements in battle.   **5.
make up:** go up to the front line.   **6. amaze:** fill with dismay.   **13. stained:**
bloodstained.   **15. breathe:** rest.

But now I do respect thee as my soul.   20
KING. I saw him hold Lord Percy at the point
    With lustier maintenance than I did look for
    Of such an ungrown warrior.
PRINCE.   Oh, this boy
    Lends mettle° to us all!   [*Exit.*]

              [*Enter* DOUGLAS.]

DOUGLAS. Another King! They grow like Hydra's heads.°   25
    I am the Douglas, fatal to all those
    That wear those colors on them. What art thou,
    That counterfeit'st the person of a king?
KING. The King himself, who, Douglas, grieves at heart
    So many of his shadows° thou hast met   30
    And not the very King. I have two boys
    Seek Percy and thyself about the field.
    But, seeing thou fall'st on me so luckily,
    I will assay° thee. So defend thyself.
DOUGLAS. I fear thou art another counterfeit,   35
    And yet, in faith, thou bear'st thee like a king.
    But mine I am sure thou art, whoe'er thou be,
    And thus I win thee.

        [*They fight; the* KING *being in danger, re-enter*
                  PRINCE OF WALES.]

PRINCE. Hold up thy head, vile Scot, or thou art like
    Never to hold it up again! The spirits   40
    Of valiant Shirley, Stafford, Blunt,° are in my arms.
    It is the Prince of Wales that threatens thee,
    Who never promiseth but he means to pay.

            [*They fight:* DOUGLAS *flies.*]

    Cheerly, my lord. How fares your Grace?
    Sir Nicholas Gawsey hath for succor sent,   45
    And so hath Clifton. I'll to Clifton straight.
KING. Stay, and breathe a while.
    Thou hast redeemed thy lost opinion,°
    And showed thou makest some tender° of my life,
    In this fair rescue thou hast brought to me.   50
PRINCE. Oh God! They did me too much injury
    That ever said I hearkened for° your death.

---

24. mettle: courage.   **25. Hydra's heads:** Hydra was a many-headed monster
slain by Hercules. As soon as one head was cut off, two others grew in its
place.   **30. shadows:** imitations.   **34. assay:** challenge.   **41. Shirley . . .
Blunt:** who have all fallen in the battle.   **48. opinion:** reputation.   **49.
makest . . . tender:** hast some regard for.   **52. hearkened for:** desired.

If it were so, I might have let alone
The insulting° hand of Douglas over you,
Which would have been as speedy in your end   55
As all the poisonous portions in the world,
And saved the treacherous labor of your son.
KING. Make up to Clifton. I'll to Sir Nicholas Gawsey.   [*Exit.*]
                    [*Enter* HOTSPUR.]
HOTSPUR. If I mistake not, thou art Harry Monmouth.
PRINCE. Thou speak'st as if I would deny my name.   60
HOTSPUR. My name is Harry Percy.
PRINCE.   Why, then I see
    A very valiant rebel of the name.
    I am the Prince of Wales. And think not, Percy,
    To share with me in glory any more.
    Two stars keep not their motion in one sphere,   65
    Nor can one England brook a double reign
    Of Harry Percy and the Prince of Wales.
HOTSPUR. Nor shall it, Harry, for the hour is come
    To end the one of us. And would to God
    Thy name in arms were now as great as mine!   70
PRINCE. I'll make it greater ere I part from thee,
    And all the budding honors on thy crest
    I'll crop, to make a garland for my head.
HOTSPUR. I can no longer brook thy vanities.   [*They fight.*]
                    [*Enter* FALSTAFF.]
FALSTAFF. Well said, Hal! To it, Hal! Nay, you shall find no boy's   75
    play here, I can tell you.
        [*Re-enter* DOUGLAS; *he fights with* FALSTAFF, *who falls
        down as if he were dead, and exit* DOUGLAS, HOTSPUR
                    is wounded, and falls.]
HOTSPUR. O Harry, thou hast robbed me of my youth!
    I better brook the loss of brittle life
    Than those proud titles thou hast won of me.
    They wound my thoughts worse than thy sword my flesh.   80
    But thought's the slave of life, and life Time's fool,
    And Time, that takes survèy of all the world,
    Must have a stop.° Oh, I could prophesy,
    But that the earthy and cold hand of death
    Lies on my tongue. No, Percy, thou art dust,   85
    And food for——   [*Dies.*]

54. insulting: triumphing. 81–83. thought's . . . stop: thought can only
exist while there is life, but life is treated like a fool by Time, and Time
itself will end—a thought in one form or another constantly recurring in
Shakespeare's plays.

PRINCE. For worms, brave Percy. Fare thee well, great heart!
    Ill-weaved ambition, how much art thou shrunk!
    When that this body did contain a spirit,
    A kingdom for it was too small a bound,°   90
    But now two paces of the vilest earth
    Is room enough. This earth that bears thee dead
    Bears not alive so stout a gentleman.
    If thou wert sensible° of courtesy,
    I should not make so dear a show of zeal.°   95
    But let my favors° hide thy mangled face,
    And, even in thy behalf, I'll thank myself
    For doing these fair rites of tenderness.
    Adieu, and take thy praise with thee to Heaven!
    Thy ignominy sleep with thee in the grave,   100
    But not remembered in thy epitaph!
                    [*He spieth* FALSTAFF *on the ground.*]
    What, old acquaintance! Could not all this flesh
    Keep in a little life? Poor Jack, farewell!
    I could have better spared a better man.
    Oh, I should have a heavy miss of thee   105
    If I were much in love with vanity!°
    Death hath not struck so fat a deer today,
    Though many dearer, in this bloody fray.
    Emboweled° will I see thee by and by.
    Till then in blood by noble Percy lie.   [*Exit.*]   110
FALSTAFF. [*Rising up*] Emboweled! If thou embowel me today,
    I'll give you leave to powder° me and eat me too tomorrow.
    'Sblood, 'twas time to counterfeit, or that hot termagant°
    Scot had paid me scot and lot° too. Counterfeit? I lie, I am   115
    no counterfeit. To die is to be a counterfeit, for he is but the
    counterfeit of a man who hath not the life of a man. But to
    counterfeit dying when a man thereby liveth is to be no coun-
    terfeit, but the true and perfect image of life indeed. The
    better part of valor is discretion, in the which better part I   120
    have saved my life. 'Zounds, I am afraid of this gunpowder
    Percy, though he be dead. How if he should counterfeit too,
    and rise? By my faith, I am afraid he would prove the better   125

90. bound: boundary.   94. sensible: able to feel.   95. show of zeal: mark of
respect.   96. favors: scarf or handkerchief given to a knight by his lady.
106. vanity: folly.   109. Emboweled: disemboweled. He carries on the
metaphor and pun of deer (l. 107), for the last act in the hunt was the disem-
boweling of the slain deer.   112. powder: pickle.   114. termagant: ferocious.
114–15. paid . . . lot: paid all dues.

counterfeit. Therefore I'll make him sure. Yea, and I'll swear
I killed him. Why may he not rise as well as I? Nothing con-
futes me but eyes, and nobody sees me. Therefore, sirrah
[*Stabbing him*], with a new wound in your thigh, come you   130
along with me.   [*Takes up* HOTSPUR *on his back.*]
    [*Re-enter the* PRINCE OF WALES *and* LORD JOHN
               OF LANCASTER.]
PRINCE. Come, Brother John, full bravely hast thou fleshed
  Thy maiden sword.°
LANCASTER.   But, soft! Whom have we here?
  Did you not tell me this fat man was dead?   135
PRINCE. I did, I saw him dead,
  Breathless and bleeding on the ground. Art thou alive?
  Or is it fantasy° that plays upon our eyesight?
  I prithee, speak, we will not trust our eyes
  Without our ears. Thou art not what thou seem'st.   140
FALSTAFF. No, that's certain. I am not a double° man. But if I be
  not Jack Falstaff, then am I a Jack. There is Percy [*Throw-
  ing the body down*]. If your father will do me any honor,
  so; if not, let him kill the next Percy himself. I look to be
  either earl or duke, I can assure you.   146
PRINCE. Why, Percy I killed myself, and saw thee dead.
FALSTAFF. Didst thou? Lord, Lord, how this world is given to
  lying! I grant you I was down and out of breath, and so was
  he. But we rose both at an instant, and fought a long hour by   150
  Shrewsbury clock. If I may be believed, so; if not, let them
  that should reward valor bear the sin upon their own heads.
  I'll take it upon my death, I gave him this wound in the
  thigh. If the man were alive, and would deny it, 'zounds, I   155
  would make him eat a piece of my sword.
LANCASTER. This is the strangest tale that ever I heard.
PRINCE. This is the strangest fellow, Brother John.
  Come, bring your luggage nobly on your back.   160
  For my part, if a lie may do thee grace,
  I'll gild it with the happiest terms° I have.
                      [*A retreat is sounded.*]
  The trumpet sounds retreat,° the day is ours.
  Come, Brother, let us to the highest° of the field,
  To see what friends are living, who are dead.   165
        [*Exeunt* PRINCE OF WALES *and* LANCASTER.]

133–34. fleshed . . . sword: you have fought bravely in your first action.
138. fantasy: imagination, illusion.   141. double: i.e., a double of myself.
162. happiest terms: best phrases.   163. trumpet . . . retreat: i.e., to recall
the troops from the pursuit.   164. highest: i.e., ground.

FALSTAFF. I'll follow, as they say, for reward. He that rewards
me, God reward him! If I do grow great, I'll grow less; for
I'll purge, and leave sack, and live cleanly as a nobleman
should do.   [*Exit.*]

Scene 5 ⌘ *Another part of the field.*

[*The trumpets sound. Enter the* KING, PRINCE OF WALES,
LORD JOHN OF LANCASTER, EARL OF WESTMORELAND,
            with WORCESTER *and* VERNON *prisoners.*]
KING. Thus ever did rebellion find rebuke.
    Ill-spirited° Worcester! Did not we send grace,
    Pardon, and terms of love to all of you?
    And wouldst thou turn our offers contrary,
    Misuse the tenor of thy kinsman's trust?   5
    Three knights upon our party slain today,
    A noble Earl and many a creature else
    Had been alive this hour
    If like a Christian thou hadst truly borne
    Betwixt our armies true intelligence.   10
WORCESTER. What I have done my safety urged me to.
    And I embrace this fortune patiently,
    Since not to be avoided it falls on me.
KING. Bear Worcester to the death, and Vernon too.
    Other offenders we will pause upon.   15
                    [*Exeunt* WORCESTER *and* VERNON, *guarded.*]
    How goes the field?
PRINCE. The noble Scot, Lord Douglas, when he saw
    The fortune of the day quite turned from him,
    The noble Percy slain, and all his men
    Upon the foot of fear, fled with the rest;   20
    And falling from a hill, he was so bruised
    That the pursuers took him. At my tent
    The Douglas is, and I beseech your Grace
    I may dispose of him.
KING.   With all my heart.
PRINCE. Then, Brother John of Lancaster, to you   25

Sc. 5: 2. **Ill-spirited:** evil-spirited.

This honorable bounty shall belong.
Go to the Douglas, and deliver him
Up to his pleasure, ransomless and free.
His valor shown upon our crests today
Hath taught us how to cherish such high deeds   30
Even in the bosom of our adversaries.
LANCASTER. I thank your Grace for this high courtesy,
        Which I shall give away immediately.
KING. Then this remains, that we divide our power.
        You, Son John, and my cousin Westmoreland   35
        Toward York shall bend you with your dearest° speed,
        To meet Northumberland and the prelate Scroop,
        Who, as we hear, are busily in arms.
        Myself and you, Son Harry, will toward Wales,
        To fight with Glendower and the Earl of March.   40
        Rebellion in this land shall lose his sway,
        Meeting the check° of such another day.
        And since this business so fair is done,
        Let us not leave till all our own be won.   [*Exeunt.*]

36. dearest: best.   42. Meeting . . . check: incurring such a disaster.

QUESTIONS

NOTE: In approaching the difficult problem of the "meaning" of *I Henry IV* it will be most helpful if you first read through the play quickly and then return for a closer second reading. The first three questions are designed to be answered after the first reading. The remaining questions should be consulted during the course of the second, more deliberate reading.

1. *Henry IV* has long been a favorite in the theater, largely because of Falstaff. On the basis of a quick reading, describe the kinds of entertainment the play provides. How do you account for those sections of the play that do not, by your standards, provide entertainment?

2. While the historical events dramatized in *I Henry IV* occurred nearly 200 years before the play was written, they have a very clear relevance to the latter years of Elizabeth's reign when England was again concerned with the problems of succession to the throne, rebellion, and civil disorder. Taking the play for a moment as a dramatized sermon on the nature of rebellion, what political lesson does the play teach and how is this lesson made memorable?

3. Consider the following facts that emerge in the play and decide how they may qualify the view that the play provides a *simple* lesson in political morality: King Henry is himself a usurper who took the

throne from his cousin Richard II by force; the King never gives a convincing reason for his failure to ransom Mortimer; Hotspur, for all his weaknesses, is the most honest and courageous character in the play; Falstaff, though loyal to the regime in power, is as much a rebel against the established morality as the Percies are against the established political rule.

ACT I

4. Look carefully at all three scenes in Act I and see how often disorder is either referred to or is acted out before us. ("Disorder" here means only some disarrangement of normal and proper functioning.) On how many levels of society are matters topsy-turvy?

5. Taking for the moment King Henry, Falstaff, and Hotspur as the chief characters of the play, look at their speeches and actions carefully and see if you can discover the principal purpose of each. How do their ways of achieving their purposes differ? Can one nevertheless perceive an essential likeness in them, some quality that makes them all men who belong in the same world?

6. Does Hal's political strategy, as explained in the concluding speech of Scene 2, seem sound? Is it convincing? How does it change our opinion of him? Knowing why he keeps company with Falstaff, can we see his true attitudes running through his earlier punning exchanges with Falstaff?

7. Hotspur speaks (I.3.201–07) of redeeming lost honor so that he may "wear without corrival all her dignities." In what ways does this speech suggest something unattractive about this otherwise heroic figure? Can you find speeches in which the other major characters similarly give themselves away?

8. What activity is common to each of the three component scenes of Act I? What is the effect of placing the Boar's Head Tavern scene between the two scenes in Westminster Palace?

9. Looking back over your answers to these questions on Act I, discuss the manner in which Shakespeare has enlarged, or made universal, the problem of order. Has he suggested what the causes of disorder in the world are?

10. What makes it impossible to see the ordered society and the ordered man as absolute, unqualified goods, while rejecting all forms of disorder as equally unqualified evils? Have we moved beyond the simplicity of the problem play?

ACT II

11. Some critics have charged that the first scene in this act, the innyard at Rochester, is superfluous. Can you justify the details here as an extension of the world of the play? In what ways is the situation at

the inn like the situations in the Palace and in the Boar's Head Tavern?

12. There has been much discussion about whether Falstaff is or is not a coward. On the basis of the events in this act, what do you think?

13. How does Shakespeare make clear in Scene 3 Hotspur's impetuosity, his haste? How would you direct him to move on stage in this scene?

14. What do Hotspur's dreams, his attitudes toward his wife, his statement about action and the world tell us about his nature?

15. The joke that Hal plays on Francis the drawer in Scene 4 seems almost pointless now, even a piece of wanton cruelty. Actually, the type of waiter that Francis represents is still familiar, the kind who calls out that he will be there at once ("anon, anon, sir"), but never stirs. In order to understand how this fits into the structure of the play it is necessary to be aware of the "time theme" which runs through everything that is said. Go back through the first two acts and pick out all the references to time, including such apparently trivial remarks as Gadshill's question to the first Carrier, "What's o'clock?" Do not be too literal in understanding "time" but look for indirect references in such phrases as Hotspur's, "This evening must I leave you." When you have collected these references try to (1) state what it is that time represents in this play, (2) distinguish the attitudes of the major characters toward time, and (3) see how basically different attitudes toward time are summed up in the joke on Francis.

16. The question of whether or not Falstaff is self-conscious has always intrigued readers. Is he the good-natured, self-indulgent rogue he seems to be, easily made the butt of Hal and Poins's joke; or is he simply playing this part for the fun of the game, aware all the time of the figure he cuts and laughing secretly at those who are laughing at him? Is it possible on the basis of what he says here and elsewhere to decide this question?

17. The device known as *foreshadowing* hints or warns of what is to come later. In Scene 4 we have several examples of this device, beginning with the appearance of the noble messenger from the King, whom Falstaff sends packing. This message from the King represents, of course, the call of duty to Hal, a call he will eventually have to answer. Pick out several other events in this scene that foreshadow future happenings. Of what value is foreshadowing to the dramatist?

18. By now it is apparent that disorder, depicted in many ways and on many levels, is the subject of *I Henry IV*. Can the "mock king" scene be considered a summary image of this theme of disorder? In answering this question look closely at Falstaff's parody of the King's speech and compare it with the formal tones of King Henry at the opening of the play. Is it a fair approximation?

19. What is the significance of Hal's "deposing" Falstaff and playing the King himself?

ACT III

20. Glendower believes that he is "not in the common roll of men," that signs have marked him "extraordinary." Might the same be said of all the major characters? Each of them is pre-eminent in one field of "action," and all together might make one "complete man." What virtue does each represent?

21. What subjects in this first scene of Act III does Hotspur express opinions on? How do these opinions help to characterize him? What would you say is his greatest failing as a man and a politician, and how does this scene make the weakness clear? Can the weakness be seen at the same time as the greatness?

22. If the King is right at the beginning of Scene 2 in his suspicion that God is punishing his former "misreadings" (i.e., his seizure of the throne from Richard) in the "inordinate" way of life chosen by the Prince of Wales, does the punishment accord with the original sin?

23. Henry's acknowledgment of guilt in the opening lines of Scene 2 complicates his character enormously. Look back at his earlier speeches and see if in the light of this a duality of motive is discernible.

24. Was Henry's seizure of the throne a carefully calculated move, shrewdly managed? Are he and Hal really so different?

25. What does the way King Henry makes his battle plan at the end of Scene 2 tell us about his relationship to time? Contrast this approach to time with Hotspur's at the end of Scene 1 and with Falstaff's at the end of Scene 3.

26. In Scene 3 Falstaff refuses to pay a debt that he owes Mistress Quickly. This refusal to pay an honest debt stands in obvious contrast to Hal's acceptance of his debt to his father and his country in the preceding scene. (Look at Scene 2 for instances of debt imagery.) These are but two instances of a theme of indebtedness and promises and refusals to pay that runs through the play. Look back through the first three acts for uses of imagery of debt and allied terms suggesting financial transactions, e.g., Hotspur speaks of "redeeming" honor. (You will find it helpful to begin by looking at I.3.285–90 and III.2.132, 144–52.)

27. What does the use of this "mercantile" imagery tell us about the way men in this disordered kingdom conceive of their relationships to other men and to their world? Is there some other obviously better way of understanding human relationships than as a "lender-borrower" arrangement? Does the play offer examples or statements of this other way of ordering life?

ACT IV

28. Is Hotspur's battle plan typical of him, an expression of his basic character?

29. Examine Sir Harry Vernon's description of the Prince of Wales and his companions (IV.1.97–110), paying particular attention to the metaphors he uses. What values do they have; what do they tell us about Hal? Could the same points be made in realistic prose drama?

30. Analyze in the same manner Hotspur's answer to Vernon's description. Does the imagery suggest that the man embodies supernatural forces?

31. Compare Falstaff's attitude toward war and his preparations for it with those of the brave captains in the preceding scenes. Up to this point, despite a few serious comments, it has been possible to dismiss Falstaff as an amiable buffoon whose view of life has no relevance in a serious world such as this one. Why do his views suddenly seem worth more careful consideration?

32. By now it is obvious that *I Henry IV* is built on the basis of three distinct plots. Review the first four acts and distinguish these plots. Does each plot originate in a particular place? Is there some locality where each plot centers? What methods has Shakespeare used to tie the plots together? How do the three plots function together to create the meaning of the play?

33. Is there any justice in Hotspur's answer to Blunt in Scene 3 about why the rebels have taken up arms? On the other hand, is there any reason to doubt the honesty of the King's offer to redress grievances?

ACT V

34. In the exchange between Worcester and King Henry in the first scene, is either entirely wrong or right? What is the effect of presenting two opposing points of view and providing no certainty about which is true and which is false? Even if you conclude that Henry is honest here, are the fears Worcester voices at the beginning of Scene 2 unfounded?

35. Can we conclude that Worcester is merely a villain because he does not tell Hotspur of Henry's offer? Is it inevitable, considering his nature, that Hotspur should be managed by men like Worcester?

36. In what ways does the battle scene restate in visual terms the central themes of the play?

37. Considered in one way the device of dressing many men in the King's arms is typical Bolingbroke cleverness; does it suggest something else about the nature of kingship?

38. How does Hotspur's dying speech gather together the meanings of "time" that have run through the play and sum up the relationship of man and time?

39. Hal is the only man in the play who has moved easily from one plot to another—from the tavern, to the palace, to the battlefield; some critics have suggested that the true plot of the play is the education of a prince for his duties as king. Is his education in any way symbolized by the position he occupies on stage between the dead body of Hotspur and the supposedly dead Falstaff?

40. Why is it "dramatically right" for Falstaff to come to life after seeming to be dead?

41. What is the meaning of Falstaff's carrying off the dead Hotspur and claiming him as his victim?

42. At the end of the play is it possible to say with any surety that the approach to life embodied in any one of the three plots is superior to the other two?

PART II

❧

PLAYS
FOR
FURTHER READING

THE CHERRY ORCHARD

BY

ANTON CHEKHOV

The plays of Anton Chekhov (1860–1904) are likely at first glance to seem trivial, pointless, plotless—the chronicle of futile people, more than slightly mad. In fact, the plays seem at first "undramatic." This effect is largely intentional, for Chekhov wanted to write plays in which, as he said, he "let the things that happen on stage be as complex and yet as simple as they are in life. For instance, people are having a meal at the table, just having a meal, but at the same time their happiness is being created, or their lives are being smashed up." *The Cherry Orchard,* first produced in 1904, was Chekhov's greatest achievement in staging these simple, seemingly unimportant events. His earlier plays—*Ivanov* (1887), *The Seagull* (1896), *Uncle Vanya* (1899), and *The Three Sisters* (1901)—all show "men and life as they are," not "on stilts," but each culminates in violence, involving in every case the firing of a gun. Chekhov could boast, however, that "there is not a shot" in *The Cherry Orchard* and point out that it is not "a tragedy of blood," but a "tragedy of life's trivialities."

Chekhov was the chronicler of the breakup of a way of life, of a society that had lost its ability to act effectively because it had lost the answer to basic questions like those posed by a character in *The Three Sisters*: Why do cranes fly? Why are children born? Why do stars shine in the sky? Specifically, the social group whose aimless wanderings Chekhov dramatizes is the Russian upper class of the late nineteenth and early twentieth century. But the impact of his plays on people of all nations suggests that Chekhov catches not just the hopelessness of one moment of history, but the general loss in our century of answers to crucial questions. "Look out there," says one of his characters, "it's snowing. What's the meaning of that?" Many people could provide a scientific description of snow, but most would find it difficult to state the "meaning" of a snowstorm.

Chekhov's charming, melancholic people have lost their bearings because by knowing too much they have come to understand too little. They still care desperately about finding a meaning in their lives, a purpose and a relation to the world around them, and though they always fail, they still have in a curious, ironic way that tragic nobility which Wallace Stevens once defined as "a violence from within that protects from a violence without; it is imagination pressing back against the pressure of reality." Chekhov's characters don't know what they seek or where to seek it, but they do seek.

Perhaps the greatest achievement of *The Cherry Orchard* is the way Chekhov keeps before us the inner lives of his characters. Even in translation, every word spoken seems the echo of a reality deep within. The characters seem transient inhabitants of the world outside themselves. And yet this outer world is always sharply defined and ever present. There are always crops to gather, mortgages to pay, and orchards to be tended. Above all else this outer reality is the progress of time in which bills and lives inevitably come due. *The Cherry Orchard* begins in the spring, and after that no one notices the time of year; but when the play closes, fall is there and the frosts are beginning.

CHARACTERS

MADAME RANEVSKY (LYUBOV ANDREYEVNA), *the owner of the Cherry Orchard*

ANYA, *her daughter, aged* 17

VARYA, *her adopted daughter, aged* 24

GAEV, LEONID ANDREYEVITCH, *brother of Madame Ranevsky*

LOPAHIN, YERMOLAY ALEXEYEVITCH, *a Merchant*

TROFIMOV, PYOTR SERGEYEVITCH, *a Student*

SEMYONOV-PISHTCHIK, *a Landowner*

CHARLOTTA IVANOVNA, *a Governess*

EPIHODOV, SEMYON PANTALEYEVITCH, *a Clerk*

DUNYASHA, *a Maid*

FIRS, *an old Valet, aged* 87

YASHA, *a young Valet*

A VAGRANT A POST-OFFICE CLERK

THE STATION MASTER VISITORS, SERVANTS

The action takes place on the estate of Madame Ranevsky.

The Cherry Orchard by Anton Chekhov, translated by Constance Garnett. Reprinted by permission of Chatto & Windus Ltd. and by the estate of Constance Garnett.

ACT I

Scene: A room, which has always been called the nursery. One of the doors leads into ANYA'S *room. Dawn, sun rises during the scene. May, the cherry trees in flower, but it is cold in the garden with the frost of early morning. Windows closed.*

[*Enter* DUNYASHA *with a candle and* LOPAHIN *with a book in his hand.*]

LOPAHIN. The train's in, thank God. What time is it?

DUNYASHA. Nearly two o'clock (*puts out the candle*). It's daylight already.

LOPAHIN. The train's late! Two hours, at least (*yawns and stretches*). I'm a pretty one; what a fool I've been. Came here on purpose to meet them at the station and dropped asleep. . . . Dozed off as I sat in the chair. It's annoying. . . . You might have waked me.

DUNYASHA. I thought you had gone (*listens*). There, I do believe they're coming!

LOPAHIN (*listens*). No, what with the luggage and one thing and another (*a pause*). Lyubov Andreyevna has been abroad five years; I don't know what she is like now. . . . She's a splendid woman. A good-natured, kind-hearted woman. I remember when I was a lad of fifteen, my poor father—he used to keep a little shop here in the village in those days—gave me a punch in the face with his fist and made my nose bleed. We were in the yard here, I forget what we'd come about—he had had a drop. Lyubov Andreyevna—I can see her now—she was a slim young girl then—took me to wash my face, and then brought me into this very room, into the nursery. "Don't cry, little peasant," says she, "it will be well in time for your wedding day" . . . (*a pause*). Little peasant. . . .

My father was a peasant, it's true, but here am I in a white waist-coat and brown shoes, like a pig in a bun shop. Yes, I'm a rich man, but for all my money, come to think, a peasant I was, and a peasant I am (*turns over the pages of the book*). I've been reading this book and I can't make head or tail of it. I fell asleep over it (*a pause*).

DUNYASHA. The dogs have been awake all night, they feel that the mistress is coming.

LOPAHIN. Why, what's the matter with you, Dunyasha?

DUNYASHA. My hands are all of a tremble. I feel as though I should faint.

LOPAHIN. You're a spoilt soft creature, Dunyasha. And dressed like a lady too, and your hair done up. That's not the thing. One must know one's place.

> [*Enter* EPIHODOV *with a nosegay; he wears a pea jacket and highly polished creaking topboots; he drops the nosegay as he comes in.*]

EPIHODOV (*picking up the nosegay*). Here! the gardener's sent this, says you're to put it in the dining room (*gives* DUNYASHA *the nosegay*).

LOPAHIN. And bring me some kvass.

DUNYASHA. I will (*goes out*).

EPIHODOV. It's chilly this morning, three degrees of frost, though the cherries are all in flower. I can't say much for our climate (*sighs*). I can't. Our climate is not often propitious to the occasion. Yermolay Alexeyevitch, permit me to call your attention to the fact that I purchased myself a pair of boots the day before yesterday, and they creak, I venture to assure you, so that there's no tolerating them. What ought I to grease them with?

LOPAHIN. Oh, shut up! Don't bother me.

EPIHODOV. Every day some misfortune befalls me. I don't complain. I'm used to it, and I wear a smiling face.

> [DUNYASHA *comes in, hands* LOPAHIN *the kvass.*]

EPIHODOV. I am going (*stumbles against a chair, which falls over*). There! (*as though triumphant*). There you see now, excuse the expression, an accident like that among others. . . . It's positively remarkable (*goes out*).

DUNYASHA. Do you know, Yermolay Alexeyevitch, I must confess, Epihodov has made me a proposal.

LOPAHIN. Ah!

DUNYASHA. I'm sure I don't know. . . . He's a harmless fellow, but sometimes when he begins talking, there's no making anything of it. It's all very fine and expressive, only there's no understanding it. I've a sort of liking for him too. He loves me to distraction. He's

an unfortunate man; every day there's something. They tease him
about it—two and twenty misfortunes they call him.

LOPAHIN (*listening*). There! I do believe they're coming.

DUNYASHA. They are coming! What's the matter with me? . . . I'm
cold all over.

LOPAHIN. They really are coming. Let's go and meet them. Will she
know me? It's five years since I saw her.

DUNYASHA (*in a flutter*). I shall drop this very minute. . . . Ah, I
shall drop.

> [*There is a sound of two carriages driving up to the
> house.* LOPAHIN *and* DUNYASHA *go out quickly. The
> stage is left empty. A noise is heard in the adjoining
> rooms.* FIRS, *who has driven to meet* MADAME RANEV-
> SKY, *crosses the stage hurriedly leaning on a stick.
> He is wearing old-fashioned livery and a high hat.
> He says something to himself, but not a word can be
> distinguished. The noise behind the scenes goes on
> increasing. A voice: "Come, let's go in here." Enter*
> LYUBOV ANDREYEVNA, ANYA, *and* CHARLOTTA IVAN-
> OVNA *with a pet dog on a chain, all in travelling
> dresses.* VARYA *in an outdoor coat with a kerchief
> over her head,* GAEV, SEMYONOV-PISHTCHIK, LOPAHIN,
> DUNYASHA *with bag and parasol, servants with other
> articles. All walk across the room.*]

ANYA. Let's come in here. Do you remember what room this is,
mamma?

LYUBOV (*joyfully, through her tears*). The nursery!

VARYA. How cold it is, my hands are numb. (*To* LYUBOV ANDREYEVNA)
Your rooms, the white room and the lavender one, are just the
same as ever, mamma.

LYUBOV. My nursery, dear delightful room. . . . I used to sleep here
when I was little . . . (*cries*). And here I am, like a little child . . .
(*kisses her brother and* VARYA, *and then her brother again*). Varya's
just the same as ever, like a nun. And I knew Dunyasha (*kisses*
DUNYASHA).

GAEV. The train was two hours late. What do you think of that? Is
that the way to do things?

CHARLOTTA (*to* PISHTCHIK). My dog eats nuts, too.

PISHTCHIK (*wonderingly*). Fancy that!

> [*They all go out except* ANYA *and* DUNYASHA.]

DUNYASHA. We've been expecting you so long (*takes* ANYA'S *hat and
coat*).

ANYA. I haven't slept for four nights on the journey. I feel dreadfully
cold.

DUNYASHA. You set out in Lent, there was snow and frost, and now?

My darling! (*laughs and kisses her*). I *have* missed you, my precious, my joy. I must tell you . . . I can't put it off a minute. . . .

ANYA (*wearily*). What now?

DUNYASHA. Epihodov, the clerk, made me a proposal just after Easter.

ANYA. It's always the same thing with you . . . (*straightening her hair*). I've lost all my hairpins . . . (*she is staggering from exhaustion*).

DUNYASHA. I don't know what to think, really. He does love me, he does love me so!

ANYA (*looking towards her door, tenderly*). My own room, my windows just as though I had never gone away. I'm home! Tomorrow morning I shall get up and run into the garden. . . . Oh, if I could get to sleep! I haven't slept all the journey, I was so anxious and worried.

DUNYASHA. Pyotr Sergeyevitch came the day before yesterday.

ANYA (*joyfully*). Petya!

DUNYASHA. He's asleep in the bathhouse, he has settled in there. I'm afraid of being in their way, says he. (*Glancing at her watch*) I was to have waked him, but Varvara Mihalovna told me not to. Don't you wake him, says she.

[*Enter* VARYA *with a bunch of keys at her waist.*]

VARYA. Dunyasha, coffee and make haste. . . . Mamma's asking for coffee.

DUNYASHA. This very minute (*goes out*).

VARYA. Well, thank God, you've come. You're home again (*petting her*). My little darling has come back! My precious beauty has come back again!

ANYA. I have had a time of it!

VARYA. I can fancy.

ANYA. We set off in Holy Week—it was so cold then, and all the way Charlotta would talk and show off her tricks. What did you want to burden me with Charlotta for?

VARYA. You couldn't have travelled all alone, darling. At seventeen!

ANYA. We got to Paris at last, it was cold there—snow. I speak French shockingly. Mamma lives on the fifth floor, I went up to her and there were a lot of French people, ladies, an old priest with a book. The place smelt of tobacco and so comfortless. I felt sorry, oh! so sorry for mamma all at once, I put my arms round her neck, and hugged her and wouldn't let her go. Mamma was as kind as she could be, and she cried. . . .

VARYA (*through her tears*). Don't speak of it, don't speak of it!

ANYA. She had sold her villa at Mentone, she had nothing left, nothing. I hadn't a farthing left either, we only just had enough to get here. And mamma doesn't understand! When we had dinner at the stations, she always ordered the most expensive things and gave the waiters a whole rouble. Charlotta's just the same. Yasha too must have the same as we do; it's simply awful. You know Yasha is mamma's valet now, we brought him here with us.

VARYA. Yes, I've seen the young rascal.

ANYA. Well, tell me—have you paid the arrears on the mortgage?

VARYA. How could we get the money?

ANYA. Oh, dear! Oh, dear!

VARYA. In August the place will be sold.

ANYA. My goodness!

LOPAHIN (*peeps in at the door and moos like a cow*). Moo! (*disappears*).

VARYA (*weeping*). There, that's what I could do to him (*shakes her fist*).

ANYA (embracing VARYA, *softly*). Varya, has he made you an offer? (VARYA *shakes her head*). Why, but he loves you. Why is it you don't come to an understanding? What are you waiting for?

VARYA. I believe that there never will be anything between us. He has a lot to do, he has no time for me . . . and takes no notice of me. Bless the man, it makes me miserable to see him. . . . Everyone's talking of our being married, everyone's congratulating me, and all the while there's really nothing in it; it's all like a dream. (*In another tone*) You have a new brooch like a bee.

ANYA (*mournfully*). Mamma bought it. (*Goes into her own room and in a lighthearted childish tone*) And you know, in Paris I went up in a balloon!

VARYA. My darling's home again! My pretty is home again!

[DUNYASHA *returns with the coffee pot and is making the coffee.*]

VARYA (*standing at the door*). All day long, darling, as I go about looking after the house, I keep dreaming all the time. If only we could marry you to a rich man, then I should feel more at rest. Then I would go off by myself on a pilgrimage to Kiev, to Moscow . . . and so I would spend my life going from one holy place to another. . . . I would go on and on. . . . What bliss!

ANYA. The birds are singing in the garden. What time is it?

VARYA. It must be nearly three. It's time you were asleep, darling (*going into* ANYA'S *room*). What bliss!

[YASHA *enters with a rug and a travelling bag.*]

YASHA (*crosses the stage, mincingly*). May one come in here, pray?

DUNYASHA. I shouldn't have known you, Yasha. How you have changed abroad.

YASHA. H'm! . . . And who are you?

DUNYASHA. When you went away, I was that high (*shows distance from floor*). Dunyasha, Fyodor's daughter. . . . You don't remember me!

YASHA. H'm! . . . You're a peach! (*Looks round and embraces her:
she shrieks and drops a saucer.* YASHA *goes out hastily.*)

VARYA (*in the doorway, in a tone of vexation*). What now?

DUNYASHA (*through her tears*). I have broken a saucer.

VARYA. Well, that brings good luck.

ANYA (*coming out of her room*). We ought to prepare mamma: Petya
is here.

VARYA. I told them not to wake him.

ANYA (*dreamily*). It's six years since father died. Then only a month
later little brother Grisha was drowned in the river, such a pretty
boy he was, only seven. It was more than mamma could bear, so she
went away, went away without looking back (*shuddering*). . . .
How well I understand her, if only she knew! (*a pause*) And Petya
Trofimov was Grisha's tutor, he may remind her.

> [*Enter* FIRS: *he is wearing a pea jacket and a white
> waistcoat.*]

FIRS (*goes up to the coffee pot, anxiously*). The mistress will be served
here (*puts on white gloves*). Is the coffee ready? (*Sternly to* DUN-
YASHA) Girl! Where's the cream?

DUNYASHA. Ah, mercy on us! (*goes out quickly*).

FIRS (*fussing round the coffee pot*). Ech! you good-for-nothing! (*Muttering to himself*) Come back from Paris. And the old master used
to go to Paris too . . . horses all the way (*laughs*).

VARYA. What is it, Firs?

FIRS. What is your pleasure? (*Gleefully*) My lady has come home! I
have lived to see her again! Now I can die (*weeps with joy*).

> [*Enter* LYUBOV ANDREYEVNA, GAEV *and* SEMYONOV-
> PISHTCHIK; *the latter is in a short-waisted full coat of
> fine cloth, and full trousers.* GAEV, *as he comes in,
> makes a gesture with his arms and his whole body, as
> though he were playing billiards.*]

LYUBOV. How does it go? Let me remember. Cannon off the red!

GAEV. That's it—in off the white! Why, once, sister, we used to sleep
together in this very room, and now I'm fifty-one, strange as it seems.

LOPAHIN. Yes, time flies.

GAEV. What do you say?

LOPAHIN. Time, I say, flies.

GAEV. What a smell of patchouli!

ANYA. I'm going to bed. Good night, mamma (*kisses her mother*).

LYUBOV. My precious darling (*kisses her hands*). Are you glad to be
home? I can't believe it.

ANYA. Good night, uncle.

GAEV (*kissing her face and hands*). God bless you! How like you are
to your mother! (*To his sister*) At her age you were just the same,
Lyuba.

[ANYA *shakes hands with* LOPAHIN *and* PISHTCHIK,
then goes out, shutting the door after her.]

LYUBOV. She's quite worn out.

PISHTCHIK. Aye, it's a long journey, to be sure.

VARYA (*to* LOPAHIN *and* PISHTCHIK). Well, gentlemen? It's three o'clock
and time to say good-by.

LYUBOV (*laughs*). You're just the same as ever, Varya (*draws her to
her and kisses her*). I'll just drink my coffee and then we will all go
and rest. (FIRS *puts a cushion under her feet.*) Thanks, friend. I
am so fond of coffee, I drink it day and night. Thanks, dear old man
(*kisses* FIRS).

VARYA. I'll just see whether all the things have been brought in (*goes
out*).

LYUBOV. Can it really be me sitting here? (*laughs*). I want to dance
about and clap my hands. (*Covers her face with her hands*) And I
could drop asleep in a moment! God knows I love my country, I
love it tenderly; I couldn't look out of the window in the train, I kept
crying so. (*Through her tears*) But I must drink my coffee, though.
Thank you, Firs, thanks, dear old man. I'm so glad to find you still
alive.

FIRS. The day before yesterday.

GAEV. He's rather deaf.

LOPAHIN. I have to set off for Harkov directly, at five o'clock. . . . It
is annoying! I wanted to have a look at you, and a little talk. . . .
You are just as splendid as ever.

PISHTCHIK (*breathing heavily*). Handsomer, indeed. . . . Dressed in
Parisian style . . . completely bowled me over.

LOPAHIN. Your brother, Leonid Andreyevitch here, is always saying
that I'm a low-born knave, that I'm a money grubber, but I don't
care one straw for that. Let him talk. Only I do want you to believe
in me as you used to. I do want your wonderful tender eyes to look
at me as they used to in the old days. Merciful God! My father was
a serf of your father and of your grandfather, but you—you—did so
much for me once, that I've forgotten all that; I love you as though
you were my kin . . . more than my kin.

LYUBOV. I can't sit still, I simply can't . . . (*jumps up and walks
about in violent agitation*). This happiness is too much for me. . . .
You may laugh at me, I know I'm silly. . . . My own bookcase
(*kisses the bookcase*). My little table.

GAEV. Nurse died while you were away.

LYUBOV (*sits down and drinks coffee*). Yes, the Kingdom of Heaven
be hers! You wrote me of her death.

GAEV. And Anastasy is dead. Squinting Petruchka has left me and is in
service now with the police captain in the town (*takes a box of
caramels out of his pocket and sucks one*).

PISHTCHIK. My daughter, Dashenka, wishes to be remembered to you.

LOPAHIN. I want to tell you something very pleasant and cheering (*glancing at his watch*). I'm going directly . . . there's no time to say much . . . well, I can say it in a couple of words. I needn't tell you your cherry orchard is to be sold to pay your debts; the 22nd of August is the date fixed for the sale; but don't you worry, dearest lady, you may sleep in peace, there is a way of saving it. . . . This is what I propose. I beg your attention! Your estate is not twenty miles from the town, the railway runs close by it, and if the cherry orchard and the land along the river bank were cut up into building plots and then let on lease for summer villas, you would make an income of at least 25,000 roubles a year out of it.

GAEV. That's all rot, if you'll excuse me.

LYUBOV. I don't quite understand you, Yermolay Alexeyevitch.

LOPAHIN. You will get a rent of at least 25 roubles a year for a three-acre plot from summer visitors, and if you say the word now, I'll bet you what you like there won't be one square foot of ground vacant by the autumn, all the plots will be taken up. I congratulate you; in fact, you are saved. It's a perfect situation with that deep river. Only, of course, it must be cleared—all the old buildings, for example, must be removed, this house too, which is really good for nothing and the old cherry orchard must be cut down.

LYUBOV. Cut down? My dear fellow, forgive me, but you don't know what you are talking about. If there is one thing interesting—remarkable indeed—in the whole province, it's just our cherry orchard.

LOPAHIN. The only thing remarkable about the orchard is that it's a very large one. There's a crop of cherries every alternate year, and then there's nothing to be done with them, no one buys them.

GAEV. This orchard is mentioned in the "Encyclopædia."

LOPAHIN (*glancing at his watch*). If we don't decide on something and don't take some steps, on the 22nd of August the cherry orchard and the whole estate too will be sold by auction. Make up your minds! There is no other way of saving it, I'll take my oath on that. No, No!

FIRS. In old days, forty or fifty years ago, they used to dry the cherries, soak them, pickle them, make jam too, and they used——

GAEV. Be quiet, Firs.

FIRS. And they used to send the preserved cherries to Moscow and to Harkov by the wagon-load. That brought the money in! And the preserved cherries in those days were soft and juicy, sweet and fragrant. . . . They knew the way to do them then. . . .

LYUBOV. And where is the recipe now?

FIRS. It's forgotten. Nobody remembers it.

PISHTCHIK (*to* LYUBOV ANDREYEVNA). What's it like in Paris? Did you eat frogs there?

LYUBOV. Oh, I ate crocodiles.

PISHTCHIK. Fancy that now!

LOPAHIN. There used to be only the gentlefolks and the peasants in the country, but now there are these summer visitors. All the towns, even the small ones, are surrounded nowadays by these summer villas. And one may say for sure, that in another twenty years there'll be many more of these people and that they'll be everywhere. At present the summer visitor only drinks tea in his verandah, but maybe he'll take to working his bit of land too, and then your cherry orchard would become happy, rich and prosperous. . . .

GAEV (*indignant*). What rot!

[*Enter* VARYA *and* YASHA.]

VARYA. There are two telegrams for you, mamma (*takes out keys and opens an old-fashioned bookcase with a loud crack*). Here they are.

LYUBOV. From Paris (*tears the telegrams, without reading them*). I have done with Paris.

GAEV. Do you know, Lyuba, how old that bookcase is? Last week I pulled out the bottom drawer and there I found the date branded on it. The bookcase was made just a hundred years ago. What do you say to that? We might have celebrated its jubilee. Though it's an in-animate object, still it is a *book* case.

PISHTCHIK (*amazed*). A hundred years! Fancy that now.

GAEV. Yes. . . . It is a thing . . . (*feeling the bookcase*). Dear, honoured, bookcase! Hail to thee who for more than a hundred years hast served the pure ideals of good and justice; thy silent call to fruitful labour has never flagged in those hundred years, main-taining (*in tears*) in the generations of man, courage and faith in a brighter future and fostering in us ideals of good and social con-sciousness (*a pause*).

LOPAHIN. Yes. . . .

LYUBOV. You are just the same as ever, Leonid.

GAEV (*a little embarrassed*). Cannon off the right into the pocket!

LOPAHIN (*looking at his watch*). Well, it's time I was off.

YASHA (*handing* LYUBOV ANDREYEVNA *medicine*). Perhaps you will take your pills now.

PISHTCHIK. You shouldn't take medicines, my dear madam . . . they do no harm and no good. Give them here . . . honoured lady (*takes the pillbox, pours the pills into the hollow of his hand, blows on them, puts them in his mouth and drinks off some kvass*). There!

LYUBOV (*in alarm*). Why, you must be out of your mind!

PISHTCHIK. I have taken all the pills.

LOPAHIN. What a glutton! (*All laugh.*)

FIRS. His honour stayed with us in Easter week, ate a gallon and a half of cucumbers . . . (*mutters*).

LYUBOV. What is he saying?

VARYA. He has taken to muttering like that for the last three years. We are used to it.

YASHA. His declining years!

> [CHARLOTTA IVANOVNA, *a very thin, lanky figure in a white dress with a lorgnette in her belt, walks across the stage.*]

LOPAHIN. I beg your pardon, Charlotta Ivanovna, I have not had time to greet you (*tries to kiss her hand*).

CHARLOTTA (*pulling away her hand*). If I let you kiss my hand, you'll be wanting to kiss my elbow, and then my shoulder.

LOPAHIN. I've no luck today! (*All laugh.*) Charlotta Ivanovna, show us some tricks!

LYUBOV. Charlotta, do show us some tricks!

CHARLOTTA. I don't want to. I'm sleepy (*goes out*).

LOPAHIN. In three weeks' time we shall meet again (*kisses LYUBOV ANDREYEVNA'S hand*). Good-by till then—I must go. (*To GAEV*) Good-by. (*Kisses PISHTCHIK*) Good-by. (*Gives his hand to VARYA, then to FIRS and YASHA*) I don't want to go. (*To LYUBOV ANDRE-YEVNA*) If you think over my plan for the villas and make up your mind, then let me know; I will lend you 50,000 roubles. Think of it seriously.

VARYA (*angrily*). Well, do go, for goodness sake.

LOPAHIN. I'm going, I'm going (*goes out*).

GAEV. Low-born knave! I beg pardon, though . . . Varya is going to marry him, he's Varya's fiancé.

VARYA. Don't talk nonsense, uncle.

LYUBOV. Well, Varya, I shall be delighted. He's a good man.

PISHTCHIK. He is, one must acknowledge, a most worthy man. And my Dashenka . . . says too that . . . she says . . . various things (*snores, but at once wakes up*). But all the same, honoured lady, could you oblige me . . . with a loan of 240 roubles . . . to pay the interest on my mortgage tomorrow?

VARYA (*dismayed*). No, no.

LYUBOV. I really haven't any money.

PISHTCHIK. It will turn up (*laughs*). I never lose hope. I thought every-thing was over, I was a ruined man, and lo and behold—the railway passed through my land and . . . they paid me for it. And some-thing else will turn up again, if not today, then tomorrow . . . Dashenka'll win two hundred thousand . . . she's got a lottery ticket.

LYUBOV. Well, we've finished our coffee, we can go to bed.

FIRS (*brushes GAEV, reprovingly*). You have got on the wrong trousers again! What am I to do with you?

VARYA (*softly*). Anya's asleep. (*Softly opens the window*) Now the sun's risen, it's not a bit cold. Look, mamma, what exquisite trees! My goodness! And the air! The starlings are singing!

GAEV (*opens another window*). The orchard is all white. You've not forgotten it, Lyuba? That long avenue that runs straight, straight as an arrow, how it shines on a moonlight night. You remember? You've not forgotten?

LYUBOV (*looking out of the window into the garden*). Oh, my childhood, my innocence! It was in this nursery I used to sleep, from here I looked out into the orchard, happiness waked with me every morning and in those days the orchard was just the same, nothing has changed (*laughs with delight*). All, all white! Oh, my orchard! After the dark gloomy autumn, and the cold winter; you are young again, and full of happiness, the heavenly angels have never left you. . . . If I could cast off the burden that weighs on my heart, if I could forget the past!

GAEV. H'm! and the orchard will be sold to pay our debts; it seems strange. . . .

LYUBOV. See, our mother walking . . . all in white, down the avenue! (*Laughs with delight.*) It is she!

GAEV. Where?

VARYA. Oh, don't, mamma!

LYUBOV. There is no one. It was my fancy. On the right there, by the path to the arbor, there is a white tree bending like a woman. . . .

[*Enter* TROFIMOV *wearing a shabby student's uniform and spectacles.*]

LYUBOV. What a ravishing orchard! White masses of blossom, blue sky. . . .

TROFIMOV. Lyubov Andreyevna! (*She looks round at him.*) I will just pay my respects to you and then leave you at once (*kisses her hand warmly*). I was told to wait until morning, but I hadn't the patience to wait any longer. . . .

[LYUBOV ANDREYEVNA *looks at him in perplexity.*]

VARYA (*through her tears*). This is Petya Trofimov.

TROFIMOV. Petya Trofimov, who was your Grisha's tutor. . . . Can I have changed so much?

[LYUBOV ANDREYEVNA *embraces him and weeps quietly.*]

GAEV (*in confusion*). There, there, Lyuba.

VARYA (*crying*). I told you, Petya, to wait till tomorrow.

LYUBOV. My Grisha . . . my boy . . . Grisha . . . my son!

VARYA. We can't help it, mamma, it is God's will.

TROFIMOV (*softly through his tears*). There . . . there.

LYUBOV (*weeping quietly*). My boy was lost . . . drowned. Why? Oh, why, dear Petya? (*More quietly*) Anya is asleep in there, and I'm talking loudly . . . making this noise. . . . But, Petya? Why have you grown so ugly? Why do you look so old?

TROFIMOV. A peasant woman in the train called me a mangy-looking gentleman.

LYUBOV. You were quite a boy then, a pretty little student, and now your hair's thin—and spectacles. Are you really a student still? (*Goes towards the door.*)

TROFIMOV. I seem likely to be a perpetual student.

LYUBOV (*kisses her brother, then* VARYA). Well, go to bed. . . . You are older too, Leonid.

PISHTCHIK (*follows her*). I suppose it's time we were asleep. . . . Ugh! my gout. I'm staying the night! Lyubov Andreyevna, my dear soul, if you could . . . tomorrow morning . . . 240 roubles.

GAEV. That's always his story.

PISHTCHIK. 240 roubles . . . to pay the interest on my mortgage.

LYUBOV. My dear man, I have no money.

PISHTCHIK. I'll pay it back, my dear . . . a trifling sum.

LYUBOV. Oh, well. Leonid will give it you. . . . You give him the money, Leonid.

GAEV. Me give it him! Let him wait till he gets it!

LYUBOV. It can't be helped, give it him. He needs it. He'll pay it back.

[LYUBOV ANDREYEVNA, TROFIMOV, PISHTCHIK *and* FIRS *go out.* GAEV, VARYA *and* YASHA *remain.*]

GAEV. Sister hasn't got out of the habit of flinging away her money. (*To* YASHA) Get away, my good fellow, you smell of the hen house.

YASHA (*with a grin*). And you, Leonid Andreyevitch, are just the same as ever.

GAEV. What's that? (*To* VARYA) What did he say?

VARYA (*to* YASHA). Your mother has come from the village; she has been sitting in the servants' room since yesterday, waiting to see you.

YASHA. Oh, bother her!

VARYA. For shame!

YASHA. What's the hurry? She might just as well have come tomorrow (*goes out*).

VARYA. Mamma's just the same as ever, she hasn't changed a bit. If she had her own way, she'd give away everything.

GAEV. Yes (*a pause*). If a great many remedies are suggested for some disease, it means that the disease is incurable. I keep thinking and racking my brains; I have many schemes, a great many, and that really means none. If we could only come in for a legacy from somebody, or marry our Anya to a very rich man, or we might go to Yaroslavl and try our luck with our old aunt, the Countess. She's very, very rich, you know.

VARYA (*weeps*). If God would help us.

GAEV. Don't blubber. Aunt's very rich, but she doesn't like us. First, sister married a lawyer instead of a nobleman. . . .

[ANYA *appears in the doorway.*]

GAEV. And then her conduct, one can't call it virtuous. She is good, and kind, and nice, and I love her, but, however one allows for extenuating circumstances, there's no denying that she's an immoral woman. One feels it in her slightest gesture.

VARYA (*in a whisper*). Anya's in the doorway.

GAEV. What do you say? (*a pause*). It's queer, there seems to be something wrong with my right eye. I don't see as well as I did. And on Thursday when I was in the district Court . . .

[*Enter* ANYA.]

VARYA. Why aren't you asleep, Anya?

ANYA. I can't get to sleep.

GAEV. My pet (*kisses* ANYA's *face and hands*). My child (*weeps*). You are not my niece, you are my angel, you are everything to me. Believe me, believe . . .

ANYA. I believe you, uncle. Everyone loves you and respects you . . . but, uncle dear, you must be silent . . . simply be silent. What were you saying just now about my mother, about your own sister? What made you say that?

GAEV. Yes, yes . . . (*puts his hand over his face*). Really, that was awful! My God, save me! And today I made a speech to the bookcase . . . so stupid! And only when I had finished, I saw how stupid it was.

VARYA. It's true, uncle, you ought to keep quiet. Don't talk, that's all.

ANYA. If you could keep from talking, it would make things easier for you, too.

GAEV. I won't speak (*kisses* ANYA's *and* VARYA's *hands*). I'll be silent. Only this is about business. On Thursday I was in the district Court; well, there was a large party of us there and we began talking of one thing and another, and this and that, and do you know, I believe that it will be possible to raise a loan on an I.O.U. to pay the arrears on the mortgage.

VARYA. If the Lord would help us!

GAEV. I'm going on Tuesday; I'll talk of it again. (*To* VARYA) Don't blubber. (*To* ANYA) Your mamma will talk to Lopahin; of course, he won't refuse her. And as soon as you're rested you shall go to Yaroslavl to the Countess, your great-aunt. So we shall all set to work in three directions at once, and the business is done. We shall pay off arrears, I'm convinced of it (*puts a caramel in his mouth*). I swear on my honour, I swear by anything you like, the estate shan't be sold (*excitedly*). By my own happiness, I swear it! Here's my hand on it, call me the basest, vilest of men, if I let it come to an auction! Upon my soul I swear it!

ANYA (*her equanimity has returned, she is quite happy*). How good you are, uncle, and how clever! (*Embraces her uncle.*) I'm at peace now! Quite at peace! I'm happy!

[*Enter* FIRS.]

FIRS (*reproachfully*). Leonid Andreyevitch, have you no fear of God? when are you going to bed?

GAEV. Directly, directly. You can go, Firs. I'll . . . yes, I will undress myself. Come, children, by-by. We'll go into details tomorrow, but now go to bed (*kisses* ANYA *and* VARYA). I'm a man of the eighties. They run down that period, but still I can say I have had to suffer not a little for my convictions in my life. It's not for nothing that the peasant loves me. One must know the peasant! One must know how . . .

ANYA. At it again, uncle!

VARYA. Uncle dear, you'd better be quiet!

FIRS (*angrily*). Leonid Andreyevitch!

GAEV. I'm coming. I'm coming. Go to bed. Potted the shot—there's a shot for you! A beauty! (*Goes out,* FIRS *hobbling after him.*)

ANYA. My mind's at rest now. I don't want to go to Yaroslavl, I don't like my great-aunt, but still my mind's at rest. Thanks to uncle (*sits down*).

VARYA. We must go to bed. I'm going. Something unpleasant happened while you were away. In the old servants' quarters there are only the old servants, as you know—Efimyushka, Polya and Yevstigney —and Karp too. They began letting stray people in to spend the night—I said nothing. But all at once I heard they had been spreading a report that I gave them nothing but pease pudding to eat. Out of stinginess, you know. . . . And it was all Yevstigney's doing. . . . Very well, I said to myself. . . . If that's how it is, I thought, wait a bit. I sent for Yevstigney . . . (*yawns*). He comes. . . . "How's this, Yevstigney," I said, "you could be such a fool as to? . . ." (*Looking at* ANYA) Anitchka! (*a pause*). She's asleep (*puts her arm round* ANYA). Come to bed . . . come along! (*leads her*). My darling has fallen asleep! Come . . . (*They go.*)

[*Far away beyond the orchard a shepherd plays on
a pipe.* TROFIMOV *crosses the stage and, seeing* VARYA
and ANYA, *stands still.*]

VARYA. 'Sh! asleep, asleep. Come, my own.

ANYA (*softly, half asleep*). I'm so tired. Still those bells. Uncle . . . dear . . . mamma and uncle. . . .

VARYA. Come, my own, come along.

[*They go into* ANYA'S *room.*]

TROFIMOV (*tenderly*). My sunshine! My spring.

ACT II

꤮ Scene: *The open country. An old shrine, long abandoned and fallen out of the perpendicular; near it a well, large stones that have apparently once been tombstones, and an old garden seat. The road to* GAEV'S *house is seen. On one side rise dark poplars; and there the cherry orchard begins. In the distance a row of telegraph poles and far, far away on the horizon there is faintly outlined a great town, only visible in very fine clear weather. It is near sunset.* CHARLOTTA, YASHA *and* DUNYASHA *are sitting on the seat.* EPIHODOV *is standing near, playing something mournful on a guitar. All sit plunged in thought.* CHARLOTTA *wears an old forage cap; she has taken a gun from her shoulder and is tightening the buckle on the strap.*

CHARLOTTA (*musingly*). I haven't a real passport of my own, and I don't know how old I am, and I always feel that I'm a young thing. When I was a little girl, my father and mother used to travel about to fairs and give performances—very good ones. And I used to dance *salto-mortale* and all sorts of things. And when papa and mamma died, a German lady took me and had me educated. And so I grew up and became a governess. But where I came from, and who I am, I don't know. . . . Who my parents were, very likely they weren't married . . . I don't know (*takes a cucumber out of her pocket and eats*). I know nothing at all (*a pause*). One wants to talk and has no one to talk to . . . I have nobody.

EPIHODOV (*plays on the guitar and sings*). "What care I for the noisy world! What care I for friends or foes!" How agreeable it is to play on the mandolin!

DUNYASHA. That's a guitar, not a mandolin (*looks in a hand mirror and powders herself*).

EPIHODOV. To a man mad with love, it's a mandolin. (*Sings*) "Where her heart but aglow with love's mutual flame." (YASHA *joins in.*)

CHARLOTTA. How shockingly these people sing! Foo! Like jackals!

DUNYASHA (*to* YASHA). What happiness, though, to visit foreign lands.

YASHA. Ah, yes! I rather agree with you there (*yawns, then lights a cigar*).

EPIHODOV. That's comprehensible. In foreign lands everything has long since reached full complexion.

YASHA. That's so, of course.

EPIHODOV. I'm a cultivated man, I read remarkable books of all sorts, but I can never make out the tendency I am myself precisely inclined for, whether to live or to shoot myself, speaking precisely, but nevertheless I always carry a revolver. Here it is . . . (*shows revolver*).

CHARLOTTA. I've had enough, and now I'm going (*puts on the gun*). Epihodov, you're a very clever fellow, and a very terrible one too, all the women must be wild about you. Br-r-r! (*goes*) These clever fellows are all so stupid; there's not a creature for me to speak to. . . . Always alone, alone, nobody belonging to me . . . and who I am, and why I'm on earth, I don't know (*walks away slowly*).

EPIHODOV. Speaking precisely, not touching upon other subjects, I'm bound to admit about myself, that destiny behaves mercilessly to me, as a storm to a little boat. If, let us suppose, I am mistaken, then why did I wake up this morning, to quote an example, and look round, and there on my chest was a spider of fearful magnitude . . . like this (*shows with both hands*). And then I take up a jug of kvass, to quench my thirst, and in it there is something in the highest degree unseemly of the nature of a cockroach (*a pause*). Have you read Buckle? (*a pause*). I am desirous of troubling you, Dunyasha, with a couple of words.

DUNYASHA. Well, speak.

EPIHODOV. I should be desirous to speak with you alone (*sighs*).

DUNYASHA (*embarrassed*). Well—only bring me my mantle first. It's by the cupboard. It's rather damp here.

EPIHODOV. Certainly. I will fetch it. Now I know what I must do with my revolver (*takes guitar and goes off playing on it*).

YASHA. Two and twenty misfortunes! Between ourselves, he's a fool (*yawns*).

DUNYASHA. God grant he doesn't shoot himself! (*a pause*) I am so nervous, I'm always in a flutter. I was a little girl when I was taken into our lady's house, and now I have quite grown out of peasant ways, and my hands are white, as white as a lady's. I'm such a delicate, sensitive creature, I'm afraid of everything. I'm so frightened. And if you deceive me, Yasha, I don't know what will become of my nerves.

YASHA (*kisses her*). You're a peach! Of course a girl must never forget herself; what I dislike more than anything is a girl being flighty in her behavior.

DUNYASHA. I'm passionately in love with you, Yasha; you are a man of culture—you can give your opinion about anything (*a pause*).

YASHA (*yawns*). Yes, that's so. My opinion is this: if a girl loves anyone, that means that she has no principles (*a pause*). It's pleasant smoking a cigar in the open air (*listens*). Someone's coming this way . . . it's the gentlefolk (DUNYASHA *embraces him impulsively*). Go home, as though you had been to the river to bathe; go by that path, or else they'll meet you and suppose I have made an appointment with you here. That I can't endure.

DUNYASHA (*coughing softly*). The cigar has made my head ache . . . (*goes off*).

[YASHA *remains sitting near the shrine. Enter* LYUBOV
ANDREYEVNA, GAEV *and* LOPAHIN.]

LOPAHIN. You must make up your mind once for all—there's no time to lose. It's quite a simple question, you know. Will you consent to letting the land for building or not? One word in answer: Yes or no? Only one word!

LYUBOV. Who is smoking such horrible cigars here? (*sits down*).

GAEV. Now the railway line has been brought near, it's made things very convenient (*sits down*). Here we have been over and lunched in town. Cannon off the white! I should like to go home and have a game.

LYUBOV. You have plenty of time.

LOPAHIN. Only one word! (*Beseechingly*). Give me an answer!

GAEV (*yawning*). What do you say?

LYUBOV (*looks in her purse*). I had quite a lot of money here yesterday, and there's scarcely any left today. My poor Varya feeds us all on milk soup for the sake of economy; the old folks in the kitchen get nothing but pease pudding, while I waste my money in a senseless way (*drops purse, scattering gold pieces*). There, they have all fallen out! (*annoyed*)

YASHA. Allow me, I'll soon pick them up (*collects the coins*).

LYUBOV. Pray do, Yasha. And what did I go off to the town to lunch for? Your restaurant's a wretched place with its music and the tablecloth smelling of soap. . . . Why drink so much, Leonid? And eat so much? And talk so much? Today you talked a great deal again in the restaurant, and all so inappropriately. About the era of the 'seventies, about the decadents. And to whom? Talking to waiters about decadents!

LOPAHIN. Yes.

GAEV (*waving his hand*). I'm incorrigible; that's evident. (*Irritably to* YASHA) Why is it you keep fidgeting about in front of us!

YASHA (*laughs*). I can't help laughing when I hear your voice.

GAEV (*to his sister*). Either I or he . . .

LYUBOV. Get along! Go away, Yasha.

YASHA (*gives* LYUBOV ANDREYEVNA *her purse*). Directly (*hardly able to suppress his laughter*). This minute . . . (*goes off*).

LOPAHIN. Deriganov, the millionaire, means to buy your estate. They say he is coming to the sale himself.

LYUBOV. Where did you hear that?

LOPAHIN. That's what they say in town.

GAEV. Our aunt in Yaroslavl has promised to send help; but when, and how much she will send, we don't know.

LOPAHIN. How much will she send? A hundred thousand? Two hundred?

LYUBOV. Oh, well! . . . Ten or fifteen thousand, and we must be thankful to get that.

LOPAHIN. Forgive me, but such reckless people as you are—such queer, unbusinesslike people—I never met in my life. One tells you in plain Russian your estate is going to be sold, and you seem not to understand it.

LYUBOV. What are we to do? Tell us what to do.

LOPAHIN. I do tell you every day. Every day I say the same thing. You absolutely must let the cherry orchard and the land on building leases; and do it at once, as quick as may be—the auction's close upon us! Do understand! Once make up your mind to build villas, and you can raise as much money as you like, and then you are saved.

LYUBOV. Villas and summer visitors—forgive me saying so—it's so vulgar.

GAEV. There I perfectly agree with you.

LOPAHIN. I shall sob, or scream, or fall into a fit. I can't stand it! You drive me mad! (*To* GAEV) You're an old woman!

GAEV. What do you say?

LOPAHIN. An old woman! (*Gets up to go.*)

LYUBOV (*in dismay*). No, don't go! Do stay, my dear friend! Perhaps we shall think of something.

LOPAHIN. What is there to think of?

LYUBOV. Don't go, I entreat you! With you here it's more cheerful, anyway (*a pause*). I keep expecting something, as though the house were going to fall about our ears.

GAEV (*in profound dejection*). Potted the white! It fails—a kiss.

LYUBOV. We have been great sinners. . . .

LOPAHIN. You have no sins to repent of.

GAEV (*puts a caramel in his mouth*). They say I've eaten up my property in caramels (*laughs*).

LYUBOV. Oh, my sins! I've always thrown my money away recklessly like a lunatic. I married a man who made nothing but debts. My husband died of champagne—he drank dreadfully. To my misery I loved another man, and immediately—it was my first punishment— the blow fell upon me, here, in the river . . . my boy was drowned and I went abroad—went away for ever, never to return, not to see that river again . . . I shut my eyes, and fled, distracted, and *he* after me . . . pitilessly, brutally. I bought a villa at Mentone, for *he* fell ill there, and for three years I had no rest day or night. His illness wore me out, my soul was dried up. And last year, when my villa was sold to pay my debts, I went to Paris and there he robbed me of everything and abandoned me for another woman; and I tried to poison myself. . . . So stupid, so shameful! . . . And suddenly I felt a yearning for Russia, for my country, for my little girl . . . (*dries her tears*). Lord, Lord, be merciful! Forgive my sins! Do not chastise me more! (*Takes a telegram out of her pocket*) I got this today from Paris. He implores forgiveness, entreats me to return (*tears up the telegram*). I fancy there is music somewhere (*listens*).

GAEV. That's our famous Jewish orchestra. You remember, four violins, a flute and a double bass.

LYUBOV. That still in existence? We ought to send for them one evening, and give a dance.

LOPAHIN (*listens*). I can't hear. . . . (*Hums softly*) "For money the Germans will turn a Russian into a Frenchman." (*Laughs*) I did see such a piece at the theatre yesterday! It was funny!

LYUBOV. And most likely there was nothing funny in it. You shouldn't look at plays, you should look at yourself a little oftener. How grey your lives are! How much nonsense you talk.

LOPAHIN. That's true. One may say honestly, we live a fool's life (*pause*). My father was a peasant, an idiot; he knew nothing and taught me nothing, only beat me when he was drunk, and always with his stick. In reality I am just such another blockhead and idiot. I've learnt nothing properly. I write a wretched hand. I write so that I feel ashamed before folks, like a pig.

LYUBOV. You ought to get married, my dear fellow.

LOPAHIN. Yes . . . that's true.

LYUBOV. You should marry our Varya, she's a good girl.

LOPAHIN. Yes.

LYUBOV. She's a good-natured girl, she's busy all day long, and what's more, she loves you. And you have liked her for ever so long.

LOPAHIN. Well? I'm not against it. . . . She's a good girl (*pause*).

GAEV. I've been offered a place in the bank: 6,000 roubles a year. Did you know?

LYUBOV. You would never do for that! You must stay as you are.

[*Enter* FIRS *with overcoat.*]

FIRS. Put it on, sir, it's damp.

GAEV (*putting it on*). You bother me, old fellow.

FIRS. You can't go on like this. You went away in the morning without leaving word (*looks him over*).

LYUBOV. You look older, Firs!

FIRS. What is your pleasure?

LOPAHIN. You look older, she said.

FIRS. I've had a long life. They were arranging my wedding before your papa was born . . . (*laughs*). I was the head footman before the emancipation came. I wouldn't consent to be set free then; I stayed on with the old master . . . (*a pause*). I remember what rejoicings they made and didn't know themselves what they were rejoicing over.

LOPAHIN. Those were fine old times. There was flogging anyway.

FIRS (*not hearing*). To be sure! The peasants knew their place, and the masters knew theirs; but now they're all at sixes and sevens, there's no making it out.

GAEV. Hold your tongue, Firs. I must go to town tomorrow. I have been promised an introduction to a general, who might let us have a loan.

LOPAHIN. You won't bring that off. And you won't pay your arrears, you may rest assured of that.

LYUBOV. That's all his nonsense. There is no such general.

[*Enter* TROFIMOV, ANYA *and* VARYA.]

GAEV. Here come our girls.

ANYA. There's mamma on the seat.

LYUBOV (*tenderly*). Come here, come along. My darlings! (*Embraces* ANYA *and* VARYA.) If you only knew how I love you both. Sit beside me, there, like that. (*All sit down.*)

LOPAHIN. Our perpetual student is always with the young ladies.

TROFIMOV. That's not your business.

LOPAHIN. He'll soon be fifty, and he's still a student.

TROFIMOV. Drop your idiotic jokes.

LOPAHIN. Why are you so cross, you queer fish?

TROFIMOV. Oh, don't persist!

LOPAHIN (*laughs*). Allow me to ask you what's your idea of me?

TROFIMOV. I'll tell you my idea of you, Yermolay Alexeyevitch: you are a rich man, you'll soon be a millionaire. Well, just as in the economy of nature a wild beast is of use, who devours everything that comes in his way, so you too have your use.

[*All laugh.*]

VARYA. Better tell us something about the planets, Petya.

LYUBOV. No, let us go on with the conversation we had yesterday.

TROFIMOV. What was it about?

GAEV. About pride.

TROFIMOV. We had a long conversation yesterday, but we came to no conclusion. In pride, in your sense of it, there is something mystical. Perhaps you are right from your point of view; but if one looks at it simply, without subtlety, what sort of pride can there be, what sense is there in it, if man in his physiological formation is very imperfect, if in the immense majority of cases he is coarse, dull-witted, profoundly unhappy? One must give up glorification of self. One should work, and nothing else.

GAEV. One must die in any case.

TROFIMOV. Who knows? And what does it mean—dying? Perhaps man has a hundred senses, and only the five we know are lost at death, while the other ninety-five remain alive.

LYUBOV. How clever you are, Petya!

LOPAHIN (*ironically*). Fearfully clever!

TROFIMOV. Humanity progresses, perfecting its powers. Everything that is beyond its ken now will one day become familiar and comprehensible; only we must work, we must with all our powers aid the seeker after truth. Here among us in Russia the workers are few in number as yet. The vast majority of the intellectual people I know, seek nothing, do nothing, are not fit as yet for work of any kind. They call themselves intellectual, but they treat their servants as inferiors, behave to the peasants as though they were animals, learn little, read nothing seriously, do practically nothing, only talk about science and know very little about art. They are all serious people, they all have severe faces, they all talk of weighty matters and air their theories, and yet the vast majority of us—ninety-nine per cent. —live like savages, at the least thing fly to blows and abuse, eat piggishly, sleep in filth and stuffiness, bugs everywhere, stench and damp and moral impurity. And it's clear all our fine talk is only to divert our attention and other people's. Show me where to find the crèches there's so much talk about, and the reading rooms? They only exist in novels: in real life there are none of them. There is nothing but filth and vulgarity and Asiatic apathy. I fear and dislike very serious faces. I'm afraid of serious conversations. We should do better to be silent.

LOPAHIN. You know, I get up at five o'clock in the morning, and I work from morning to night; and I've money, my own and other people's, always passing through my hands, and I see what people are made of all round me. One has only to begin to do anything to see how few honest, decent people there are. Sometimes when I lie awake at night, I think: "Oh! Lord, thou hast given us immense forests, boundless plains, the widest horizons, and living here we ourselves ought really to be giants."

LYUBOV. You ask for giants! They are no good except in storybooks; in real life they frighten us.

[EPIHODOV *advances in the background, playing on the guitar.*]

LYUBOV (*dreamily*). There goes Epihodov.

ANYA (*dreamily*). There goes Epihodov.

GAEV. The sun has set, my friends.

TROFIMOV. Yes.

GAEV (*not loudly, but, as it were, declaiming*). O nature, divine nature, thou art bright with eternal luster, beautiful and indifferent! Thou, whom we call mother, thou dost unite within thee life and death! Thou dost give life and dost destroy!

VARYA (*in a tone of supplication*). Uncle!

ANYA. Uncle, you are at it again!

TROFIMOV. You'd much better be cannoning off the red!

GAEV. I'll hold my tongue, I will.

[*All sit plunged in thought. Perfect stillness. The only thing audible is the muttering of* FIRS. *Suddenly there is a sound in the distance, as it were from the sky— the sound of a breaking harp string, mournfully dying away.*]

LYUBOV. What is that?

LOPAHIN. I don't know. Somewhere far away a bucket fallen and broken in the pits. But somewhere very far away.

GAEV. It might be a bird of some sort—such as a heron.

TROFIMOV. Or an owl.

LYUBOV (*shudders*). I don't know why, but it's horrid (*a pause*).

FIRS. It was the same before the calamity—the owl hooted and the samovar hissed all the time.

GAEV. Before what calamity?

FIRS. Before the emancipation (*a pause*).

LYUBOV. Come, my friends, let us be going; evening is falling. (*To* ANYA) There are tears in your eyes. What is it, darling? (*Embraces her.*)

ANYA. Nothing, mamma; it's nothing.

TROFIMOV. There is somebody coming.

[*The wayfarer appears in a shabby white forage cap and an overcoat; he is slightly drunk.*]

WAYFARER. Allow me to inquire, can I get to the station this way?

GAEV. Yes. Go along that road.

WAYFARER. I thank you most feelingly (*coughing*). The weather is superb. (*Declaims*) My brother, my suffering brother! . . . Come out to the Volga! Whose groan do you hear? . . . (*To* VARYA) Mademoiselle, vouchsafe a hungry Russian thirty kopeks.

[VARYA *utters a shriek of alarm.*]

LOPAHIN (*angrily*). There's a right and a wrong way of doing everything!

LYUBOV (*hurriedly*). Here, take this (*looks in her purse*). I've no silver. No matter—here's gold for you.

WAYFARER. I thank you most feelingly! (*goes off*).

[*Laughter.*]

VARYA (*frightened*). I'm going home—I'm going . . . Oh, mamma, the servants have nothing to eat, and you gave him gold!

LYUBOV. There's no doing anything with me. I'm so silly! When we get home, I'll give you all I possess. Yermolay Alexeyevitch, you will lend me some more . . . !

LOPAHIN. I will.

LYUBOV. Come, friends, it's time to be going. And Varya, we have made a match of it for you. I congratulate you.

VARYA (*through her tears*). Mamma, that's not a joking matter.

LOPAHIN. "Ophelia, get thee to a nunnery!"

GAEV. My hands are trembling; it's a long while since I had a game of billiards.

LOPAHIN. "Ophelia! Nymph, in thy orisons be all my sins remember'd."

LYUBOV. Come, it will soon be suppertime.

VARYA. How he frightened me! My heart's simply throbbing.

LOPAHIN. Let me remind you, ladies and gentlemen: on the 22nd of August the cherry orchard will be sold. Think about that! Think about it!

[*All go off, except* TROFIMOV *and* ANYA.]

ANYA (*laughing*). I'm grateful to the wayfarer! He frightened Varya and we are left alone.

TROFIMOV. Varya's afraid we shall fall in love with each other, and for days together she won't leave us. With her narrow brain she can't grasp that we are above love. To eliminate the petty and transitory which hinders us from being free and happy—that is the aim and meaning of our life. Forward! We go forward irresistibly towards the bright star that shines yonder in the distance. Forward! Do not lag behind, friends.

ANYA (*claps her hands*). How well you speak! (*a pause*). It is divine here today.

TROFIMOV. Yes, it's glorious weather.

ANYA. Somehow, Petya, you've made me so that I don't love the cherry orchard as I used to. I used to love it so dearly. I used to think that there was no spot on earth like our garden.

TROFIMOV. All Russia is our garden. The earth is great and beautiful— there are many beautiful places in it (*a pause*). Think only, Anya, your grandfather, and great-grandfather, and all your ancestors were slave owners—the owners of living souls—and from every cherry in the orchard, from every leaf, from every trunk there are human creatures looking at you. Cannot you hear their voices? Oh, it is awful! Your orchard is a fearful thing, and when in the evening or at night one walks about the orchard, the old bark on the trees glimmers dimly in the dusk, and the old cherry trees seem to be dreaming of centuries gone by and tortured by fearful visions. Yes! We are at least two hundred years behind, we have really gained nothing yet, we have no definite attitude to the past, we do nothing but theorize or complain of depression or drink vodka. It is clear that to begin to live in the present we must first expiate our past, we must break with it; and we can expiate it only by suffering, by extraordinary unceasing labour. Understand that, Anya.

ANYA. The house we live in has long ceased to be our own, and I shall leave it, I give you my word.

TROFIMOV. If you have the house keys, fling them into the well and go away. Be free as the wind.

ANYA (*in ecstasy*). How beautifully you said that!

TROFIMOV. Believe me, Anya, believe me! I am not thirty yet, I am young, I am still a student, but I have gone through so much already! As soon as winter comes I am hungry, sick, careworn, poor as a beggar, and what ups and downs of fortune have I not known! And my soul was always, every minute, day and night, full of inexplicable forebodings. I have a foreboding of happiness, Anya. I see glimpses of it already.

ANYA (*pensively*). The moon is rising.

[EPIHODOV *is heard playing still the same mournful song on the guitar. The moon rises. Somewhere near the poplars* VARYA *is looking for* ANYA *and calling "Anya! where are you?"*]

TROFIMOV. Yes, the moon is rising (*a pause*). Here is happiness—here it comes! It is coming nearer and nearer; already I can hear its footsteps. And if we never see it—if we may never know it—what does it matter? Others will see it after us.

VARYA'S VOICE. Anya! Where are you?

TROFIMOV. That Varya again! (*Angrily*) It's revolting!

ANYA. Well, let's go down to the river. It's lovely there.

TROFIMOV. Yes, let's go. (*They go.*)

VARYA'S VOICE. Anya! Anya!

ACT III

⌐§ Scene: *A drawing room divided by an arch from a larger drawing room. A chandelier burning. The Jewish orchestra, the same that was mentioned in Act II, is heard playing in the anteroom. It is evening. In the larger drawing room they are dancing the grand chain. The voice of* SEMYONOV-PISHTCHIK: *"Promenade à une paire!" Then enter the drawing room in couples first* PISHTCHIK *and* CHARLOTTA IVANOVNA, *then* TROFIMOV *and* LYUBOV ANDREYEVNA, *thirdly* ANYA *with the Post Office Clerk, fourthly* VARYA *with the Station Master, and other guests.* VARYA *is quietly weeping and wiping away her tears as she dances. In the last couple is* DUNYASHA. *They move across the drawing room.* PISHTCHIK *shouts:* "Grand rond, balancez!" *and* "Les Cavaliers à genou et remerciez vos dames."

[FIRS *in a swallow-tail coat brings in seltzer water on a tray.*]
[PISHTCHIK *and* TROFIMOV *enter the drawing room.*]

PISHTCHIK. I am a full-blooded man; I have already had two strokes. Dancing's hard work for me, but as they say, if you're in the pack, you must bark with the rest. I'm as strong, I may say, as a horse. My parent, who would have his joke—may the Kingdom of Heaven be his!—used to say about our origin that the ancient stock of the Semyonov-Pishtchiks was derived from the very horse that Caligula made a member of the senate (*sits down*). But I've no money, that's where the mischief is. A hungry dog believes in nothing but meat . . . (*snores, but at once wakes up*). That's like me . . . I can think of nothing but money.

TROFIMOV. There really is something horsy about your appearance.

PISHTCHIK. Well . . . a horse is a fine beast . . . a horse can be sold.

[*There is the sound of billiards being played in an adjoining room.* VARYA *appears in the arch leading to the larger drawing room.*]

TROFIMOV (*teasing*). Madame Lopahin! Madame Lopahin!

VARYA (*angrily*). Mangy-looking gentleman!

TROFIMOV. Yes, I am a mangy-looking gentleman, and I'm proud of it!

VARYA (*pondering bitterly*). Here we have hired musicians and nothing to pay them! (*Goes out.*)

TROFIMOV (*to* PISHTCHIK). If the energy you have wasted during your lifetime in trying to find the money to pay your interest, had gone to something else, you might in the end have turned the world upside down.

PISHTCHIK. Nietzsche, the philosopher, a very great and celebrated man . . . of enormous intellect . . . says in his works, that one can make forged bank notes.

TROFIMOV. Why, have you read Nietzsche?

PISHTCHIK. What next . . . Dashenka told me. . . . And now I am in such a position, I might just as well forge bank notes. The day after tomorrow I must pay 310 roubles—130 I have procured (*feels in his pockets, in alarm*). The money's gone! I have lost my money! (*Through his tears*) Where's the money? (*Gleefully*) Why, here it is behind the lining. . . . It has made me hot all over.

[*Enter* LYUBOV ANDREYEVNA *and* CHARLOTTA IVAN-OVNA.]

LYUBOV (*hums the Lezginka*). Why is Leonid so long? What can he be doing in town? (*To* DUNYASHA) Offer the musicians some tea.

TROFIMOV. The sale hasn't taken place, most likely.

LYUBOV. It's the wrong time to have the orchestra, and the wrong time to give a dance. Well, never mind (*sits down and hums softly*).

CHARLOTTA (*gives* PISHTCHIK *a pack of cards*). Here's a pack of cards. Think of any card you like.

PISHTCHIK. I've thought of one.

CHARLOTTA. Shuffle the pack now. That's right. Give it here, my dear Mr. Pishtchik. Ein, zwei, drei—now look, it's in your breast pocket.

PISHTCHIK (*taking a card out of his breast pocket*). The eight of spades! Perfectly right! (*Wonderingly*) Fancy that now!

CHARLOTTA (*holding pack of cards in her hands, to* TROFIMOV). Tell me quickly which is the top card.

TROFIMOV. Well, the queen of spades.

CHARLOTTA. It is! (*To* PISHTCHIK) Well, which card is uppermost?

PISHTCHIK. The ace of hearts.

CHARLOTTA. It is! (*claps her hands, pack of cards disappears*). Ah! what lovely weather it is today!

[*A mysterious feminine voice which seems coming out of the floor answers her.* "Oh, yes, it's magnificent weather, madam."]

CHARLOTTA. You are my perfect ideal.

VOICE. And I greatly admire you too, madam.

STATION MASTER (*applauding*). The lady ventriloquist—bravo!

PISHTCHIK (*wonderingly*). Fancy that now! Most enchanting Charlotta Ivanovna. I'm simply in love with you.

CHARLOTTA. In love? (*Shrugging shoulders*) What do you know of love, guter Mensch, aber schlechter Musikant.

TROFIMOV (*pats* PISHTCHIK *on the shoulder*). You dear old horse. . . .

CHARLOTTA. Attention, please! Another trick! (*takes a traveling rug from a chair*). Here's a very good rug; I want to sell it (*shaking it out*). Doesn't anyone want to buy it?

PISHTCHIK (*wonderingly*). Fancy that!

CHARLOTTA. Ein, zwei, drei! (*quickly picks up rug she has dropped; behind the rug stands* ANYA; *she makes a curtsey, runs to her mother, embraces her and runs back into the larger drawing room amidst general enthusiasm.*)

LYUBOV (*applauds*). Bravo! Bravo!

CHARLOTTA. Now again! Ein, zwei, drei! (*lifts up the rug; behind the rug stands* VARYA, *bowing*).

PISHTCHIK (*wonderingly*). Fancy that now!

CHARLOTTA. That's the end (*throws the rug at* PISHTCHIK, *makes a curtsey, runs into the larger drawing room*).

PISHTCHIK (*hurries after her*). Mischievous creature! Fancy! (*Goes out.*)

LYUBOV. And still Leonid doesn't come. I can't understand what he's doing in the town so long! Why, everything must be over by now. The estate is sold, or the sale has not taken place. Why keep us so long in suspense?

VARYA (*trying to console her*). Uncle's bought it. I feel sure of that.

TROFIMOV (*ironically*). Oh, yes!

VARYA. Great-aunt sent him an authorization to buy it in her name, and transfer the debt. She's doing it for Anya's sake, and I'm sure God will be merciful. Uncle will buy it.

LYUBOV. My aunt in Yaroslavl sent fifteen thousand to buy the estate in her name, she doesn't trust us—but that's not enough even to pay the arrears (*hides her face in her hands*). My fate is being sealed today, my fate . . .

TROFIMOV (*teasing* VARYA). Madame Lopahin.

VARYA (*angrily*). Perpetual student! Twice already you've been sent down from the University.

LYUBOV. Why are you angry, Varya? He's teasing you about Lopahin. Well, what of that? Marry Lopahin if you like, he's a good man, and interesting; if you don't want to, don't! Nobody compels you, darling.

VARYA. I must tell you plainly, mamma, I look at the matter seriously; he's a good man, I like him.

LYUBOV. Well, marry him. I can't see what you're waiting for.

VARYA. Mamma. I can't make him an offer myself. For the last two years, everyone's been talking to me about him. Everyone talks; but he says nothing or else makes a joke. I see what it means. He's growing rich, he's absorbed in business, he has no thoughts for me. If I had money, were it ever so little, if I had only a hundred roubles, I'd throw everything up and go far away. I would go into a nunnery.

TROFIMOV. What bliss!

VARYA (to TROFIMOV). A student ought to have sense! (*In a soft tone with tears*) How ugly you've grown, Petya! How old you look! (*To* LYUBOV ANDREYEVNA, *no longer crying*) But I can't do without work, mamma; I must have something to do every minute.

[*Enter* YASHA.]

YASHA (*hardly restraining his laughter*). Epihodov has broken a billiard cue! (*Goes out.*)

VARYA. What is Epihodov doing here? Who gave him leave to play billiards? I can't make these people out (*goes out*).

LYUBOV. Don't tease her, Petya. You see she has grief enough without that.

TROFIMOV. She is so very officious, meddling in what's not her business. All the summer she's given Anya and me no peace. She's afraid of a love affair between us. What's it to do with her? Besides, I have given no grounds for it. Such triviality is not in my line. We are above love!

LYUBOV. And I suppose I am beneath love. (*Very uneasily*) Why is it Leonid's not here? If only I could know whether the estate is sold or not! It seems such an incredible calamity that I really don't know what to think. I am distracted . . . I shall scream in a minute . . . I shall do something stupid. Save me, Petya, tell me something, talk to me!

TROFIMOV. What does it matter whether the estate is sold today or not? That's all done with long ago. There's no turning back, the path is overgrown. Don't worry yourself, dear Lyubov Andreyevna. You mustn't deceive yourself; for once in your life you must face the truth!

LYUBOV. What truth? You see where the truth lies, but I seem to have lost my sight, I see nothing. You settle every great problem so boldly, but tell me, my dear boy, isn't it because you're young—because you haven't yet understood one of your problems through suffering? You look forward boldly, and isn't it that you don't see and don't expect anything dreadful because life is still hidden from your young eyes? You're bolder, more honest, deeper than we are, but think, be just a little magnanimous, have pity on me. I was born here, you know, my father and mother lived here, my grandfather lived here, I love this house. I can't conceive of life without the cherry orchard, and if it really must be sold, then sell me with the orchard (*embraces* TROFI-MOV, *kisses him on the forehead*). My boy was drowned here (*weeps*). Pity me, my dear kind fellow.

TROFIMOV. You know I feel for you with all my heart.

LYUBOV. But that should have been said differently, so differently (*takes out her handkerchief, telegram falls on the floor*). My heart is so heavy today. It's so noisy here my soul is quivering at every sound, I'm shuddering all over, but I can't go away; I'm afraid to be quiet and alone. Don't be hard on me, Petya . . . I love you as though you were one of ourselves. I would gladly let you marry Anya—I swear I would—only, my dear boy, you must take your degree, you do nothing—you're simply tossed by fate from place to place. That's so strange. It is, isn't it? And you must do something with your beard to make it grow somehow (*laughs*). You look so funny!

TROFIMOV (*picks up the telegram*). I've no wish to be a beauty.

LYUBOV. That's a telegram from Paris. I get one every day. One yesterday and one today. That savage creature is ill again, he's in trouble again. He begs forgiveness, beseeches me to go, and really I ought to go to Paris to see him. You look shocked, Petya. What am I to do, my dear boy, what am I to do? He is ill, he is alone and unhappy, and who'll look after him, who'll keep him from doing the wrong thing, who'll give him his medicine at the right time? And why hide it or be silent? I love him, that's clear. I love him! I love him! He's a millstone about my neck, I'm going to the bottom with him, but I love that stone and can't live without it (*presses* TROFIMOV's *hand*). Don't think ill of me, Petya, don't tell me anything, don't tell me . . .

TROFIMOV (*through his tears*). For God's sake forgive my frankness: why, he robbed you!

LYUBOV. No! No! No! You mustn't speak like that (*covers her ears*).

TROFIMOV. He is a wretch! You're the only person that doesn't know it! He's a worthless creature! A despicable wretch!

LYUBOV (*getting angry, but speaking with restraint*). You're twenty-six or twenty-seven years old, but you're still a schoolboy.

TROFIMOV. Possibly.

LYUBOV. You should be a man at your age! You should understand what love means! And you ought to be in love yourself. You ought to fall in love! (*Angrily*) Yes, yes, and it's not purity in you, you're simply a prude, a comic fool, a freak.

TROFIMOV (*in horror*). The things she's saying!

LYUBOV. I am above love! You're not above love, but simply as our Firs here says, "You are a good-for-nothing." At your age not to have a mistress!

TROFIMOV (*in horror*). This is awful! The things she is saying! (*goes rapidly into the larger drawing room clutching his head*). This is awful! I can't stand it! I'm going. (*Goes off, but at once returns.*) All is over between us! (*Goes off into the anteroom.*)

LYUBOV (*shouts after him*). Petya! Wait a minute! You funny creature! I was joking! Petya! (*There is a sound of somebody running quickly downstairs and suddenly falling with a crash.* ANYA *and* VARYA *scream, but there is a sound of laughter at once.*)

LYUBOV. What has happened?

[ANYA *runs in.*]

ANYA (*laughing*). Petya's fallen downstairs! (*Runs out.*)

LYUBOV. What a queer fellow that Petya is!

[*The Station Master stands in the middle of the larger room and reads "The Magdalene," by Alexey Tolstoy. They listen to him, but before he has recited many lines strains of a waltz are heard from the anteroom and the reading is broken off. All dance.* TROFIMOV, ANYA, VARYA *and* LYUBOV ANDREYEVNA *come in from the anteroom.*]

LYUBOV. Come, Petya—come, pure heart! I beg your pardon. Let's have a dance! (*dances with* PETYA).

[ANYA *and* VARYA *dance.* FIRS *comes in, puts his stick down near the side door.* YASHA *also comes into the drawing room and looks on at the dancing.*]

YASHA. What is it, old man?

FIRS. I don't feel well. In old days we used to have generals, barons and admirals dancing at our balls, and now we send for the post office clerk and the station master and even they're not overanxious to come. I am getting feeble. The old master, the grandfather, used to give sealing wax for all complaints. I have been taking sealing wax for twenty years or more. Perhaps that's what's kept me alive.

YASHA. You bore me, old man! (*yawns*) It's time you were done with.

FIRS. Ach, you're a good-for-nothing! (*mutters*)

[TROFIMOV *and* LYUBOV ANDREYEVNA *dance in larger room and then on to the stage.*]

LYUBOV. *Merci.* I'll sit down a little (*sits down*). I'm tired.

[*Enter* ANYA.]

ANYA (*excitedly*). There's a man in the kitchen has been saying that the cherry orchard's been sold today.

LYUBOV. Sold to whom?

ANYA. He didn't say to whom. He's gone away.

[*She dances with* TROFIMOV, *and they go off into the larger room.*]

YASHA. There was an old man gossiping there, a stranger.

FIRS. Leonid Andreyevitch isn't here yet, he hasn't come back. He has his light overcoat on, *demi-saison*, he'll catch cold for sure. Ach! Foolish young things!

LYUBOV. I feel as though I should die. Go, Yasha, find out to whom it has been sold.

YASHA. But he went away long ago, the old chap (*laughs*).

LYUBOV (*with slight vexation*). What are you laughing at? What are you pleased at?

YASHA. Epihodov is so funny. He's a silly fellow, two and twenty misfortunes.

LYUBOV. Firs, if the estate is sold, where will you go?

FIRS. Where you bid me, there I'll go.

LYUBOV. Why do you look like that? Are you ill? You ought to be in bed.

FIRS. Yes (*ironically*). Me go to bed and who's to wait here? Who's to see to things without me? I'm the only one in all the house.

YASHA (*to* LYUBOV ANDREYEVNA). Lyubov Andreyevna, permit me to make a request of you; if you go back to Paris again, be so kind as to take me with you. It's positively impossible for me to stay here (*looking about him; in an undertone*). There's no need to say it, you see for yourself—an uncivilized country, the people have no morals, and then the dullness! The food in the kitchen's abominable, and then Firs runs after one muttering all sorts of unsuitable words. Take me with you, please do!

[*Enter* PISHTCHIK.]

PISHTCHIK. Allow me to ask you for a waltz, my dear lady. (LYUBOV ANDREYEVNA *goes with him*.) Enchanting lady, I really must borrow of you just 180 roubles (*dances*), only 180 roubles. (*They pass into the larger room*.)

YASHA (*hums softly*). "Knowest thou my soul's emotion."

[*In the larger drawing room, a figure in a gray top hat and in check trousers is gesticulating and jumping about. Shouts of* "Bravo, Charlotta Ivanovna."]

DUNYASHA (*she has stopped to powder herself*). My young lady tells me to dance. There are plenty of gentlemen, and too few ladies, but dancing makes me giddy and makes my heart beat. Firs, the post office clerk said something to me just now that quite took my breath away.

[*Music becomes more subdued.*]

FIRS. What did he say to you?

DUNYASHA. He said I was like a flower.

YASHA (*yawns*). What ignorance! (*Goes out.*)

DUNYASHA. Like a flower. I am a girl of such delicate feelings, I am awfully fond of soft speeches.

FIRS. Your head's being turned.

[*Enter* EPIHODOV.]

EPIHODOV. You have no desire to see me, Dunyasha. I might be an insect (*sighs*). Ah! life!

DUNYASHA. What is it you want?

EPIHODOV. Undoubtedly you may be right (*sighs*). But of course, if one looks at it from that point of view, if I may so express myself, you have, excuse my plain speaking, reduced me to a complete state of mind. I know my destiny. Every day some misfortune befalls me and I have long ago grown accustomed to it, so that I look upon my fate with a smile. You gave me your word, and though I——

DUNYASHA. Let us have a talk later, I entreat you, but now leave me in peace, for I am lost in reverie (*plays with her fan*).

EPIHODOV. I have a misfortune every day, and if I may venture to express myself, I merely smile at it, I even laugh.

[VARYA *enters from the larger drawing room.*]

VARYA. You still have not gone, Epihodov. What a disrespectful creature you are, really! (*To* DUNYASHA) Go along, Dunyasha! (*To* EPIHODOV) First you play billiards and break the cue, then you go wandering about the drawing room like a visitor!

EPIHODOV. You really cannot, if I may so express myself, call me to account like this.

VARYA. I'm not calling you to account, I'm speaking to you. You do nothing but wander from place to place and don't do your work. We keep you as a counting-house clerk, but what use you are I can't say.

EPIHODOV (*offended*). Whether I work or whether I walk, whether I eat or whether I play billiards, is a matter to be judged by persons of understanding and my elders.

VARYA. You dare to tell me that! (*Firing up*) You dare! You mean to say I've no understanding. Begone from here! This minute!

EPIHODOV (*intimidated*). I beg you to express yourself with delicacy.

VARYA (*beside herself with anger*). This moment! get out! away! (*He goes towards the door, she following him.*) Two and twenty misfortunes! Take yourself off! Don't let me set eyes on you! (EPIHODOV *has gone out, behind the door his voice,* "I shall lodge a complaint against you.") What! You're coming back? (*Snatches up the stick* FIRS *has put down near the door.*) Come! Come! Come! I'll show you! What! You're coming? Then take that! (*She swings the stick, at the very moment that* LOPAHIN *comes in.*)

LOPAHIN. Very much obliged to you!

VARYA (*angrily and ironically*). I beg your pardon!

LOPAHIN. Not at all! I humbly thank you for your kind reception!

VARYA. No need of thanks for it. (*Moves away, then looks round and asks softly*) I haven't hurt you?

LOPAHIN. Oh, no! Not at all! There's an immense bump coming up, though!

VOICES FROM LARGER ROOM. Lopahin has come! Yermolay Alexeye-vitch!

PISHTCHIK. What do I see and hear? (*Kisses* LOPAHIN.) There's a whiff of cognac about you, my dear soul, and we're making merry here too!

[*Enter* LYUBOV ANDREYEVNA.]

LYUBOV. Is it you, Yermolay Alexeyevitch? Why have you been so long? Where's Leonid?

LOPAHIN. Leonid Andreyevitch arrived with me. He is coming.

LYUBOV (*in agitation*). Well! Well! Was there a sale? Speak!

LOPAHIN (*embarrassed, afraid of betraying his joy*). The sale was over at four o'clock. We missed our train—had to wait till half-past nine. (*Sighing heavily*) Ugh! I feel a little giddy.

[*Enter* GAEV. *In his right hand he has purchases, with his left hand he is wiping away his tears.*]

LYUBOV. Well, Leonid? What news? (*Impatiently, with tears*) Make haste, for God's sake!

GAEV (*makes her no answer, simply waves his hand. To* FIRS, *weeping*) Here, take them; there's anchovies, Kertch herrings. I have eaten nothing all day. What I have been through! (*Door into the billiard room is open. There is heard a knocking of balls and the voice of* YASHA *saying "Eighty-seven."* GAEV'S *expression changes, he leaves off weeping*). I am fearfully tired. Firs, come and help me change my things (*goes to his own room across the larger drawing room*).

PISHTCHIK. How about the sale? Tell us, do!

LYUBOV. Is the cherry orchard sold?

LOPAHIN. It is sold.

LYUBOV. Who has bought it?

LOPAHIN. I have bought it. (*A pause.* LYUBOV *is crushed; she would fall down if she were not standing near a chair and table.*)

[VARYA *takes keys from her waistband, flings them on the floor in middle of drawing room and goes out.*]

LOPAHIN. I have bought it! Wait a bit, ladies and gentlemen, pray. My head's a bit muddled, I can't speak (*laughs*). We came to the auction. Deriganov was there already. Leonid Andreyevitch only had 15,000 and Deriganov bid 30,000, besides the arrears, straight off. I saw how the land lay. I bid against him. I bid 40,000, he bid 45,000, I said 55, and so he went on, adding 5 thousands and I adding 10. Well . . . So it ended. I bid 90, and it was knocked down to me. Now the cherry orchard's mine! Mine! (*chuckles*) My God, the cherry orchard's mine! Tell me that I'm drunk, that I'm out of my mind, that it's all a dream (*stamps with his feet*).

Don't laugh at me! If my father and my grandfather could rise from their graves and see all that has happened! How their Yermolay, ignorant, beaten Yermolay, who used to run about barefoot in winter, how that very Yermolay has bought the finest estate in the world! I have bought the estate where my father and grandfather were slaves, where they weren't even admitted into the kitchen. I am asleep, I am dreaming! It is all fancy, it is the work of your imagination plunged in the darkness of ignorance (*picks up keys, smiling fondly*). She threw away the keys; she means to show she's not the housewife now (*jingles the keys*). Well, no matter. (*The orchestra is heard tuning up.*) Hey, musicians! Play! I want to hear you. Come, all of you, and look how Yermolay Lopahin will take the axe to the cherry orchard, how the trees will fall to the ground! We will build houses on it and our grandsons and great-grandsons will see a new life springing up there. Music! Play up!

[*Music begins to play.* LYUBOV ANDREYEVNA *has sunk into a chair and is weeping bitterly.*]

LOPAHIN (*reproachfully*). Why, why didn't you listen to me? My poor friend! Dear lady, there's no turning back now. (*With tears*) Oh, if all this could be over, oh, if our miserable disjointed life could somehow soon be changed!

PISHTCHIK (*takes him by the arm, in an undertone*). She's weeping, let us go and leave her alone. Come (*takes him by the arm and leads him into the larger drawing room*).

LOPAHIN. What's that? Musicians, play up! All must be as I wish it. (*With irony*) Here comes the new master, the owner of the cherry orchard! (*Accidentally tips over a little table, almost upsetting the candelabra.*) I can pay for everything! (*Goes out with* PISHTCHIK. *No one remains on the stage or in the larger drawing room except* LYUBOV, *who sits huddled up, weeping bitterly. The music plays softly.* ANYA *and* TROFIMOV *come in quickly.* ANYA *goes up to her mother and falls on her knees before her.* TROFIMOV *stands at the entrance to the larger drawing room.*)

ANYA. Mamma! Mamma, you're crying, dear, kind, good mamma! My precious! I love you! I bless you! The cherry orchard is sold, it is gone, that's true, that's true! But don't weep, mamma! Life is still before you, you have still your good, pure heart! Let us go, let us go, darling, away from here! We will make a new garden, more splendid than this one; you will see it, you will understand. And joy, quiet, deep joy, will sink into your soul like the sun at evening! And you will smile, mamma! Come, darling, let us go!

ACT IV

Scene: *Same as in First Act. There are neither curtains on the windows nor pictures on the walls: only a little furniture remains piled up in a corner as if for sale. There is a sense of desolation; near the outer door and in the background of the scene are packed trunks, travelling bags, etc. On the left the door is open, and from here the voices of* VARYA *and* ANYA *are audible.* LOPAHIN *is standing waiting.* YASHA *is holding a tray with glasses full of champagne. In front of the stage* EPIHODOV *is tying up a box. In the background behind the scene a hum of talk from the peasants who have come to say good-by. The voice of* GAEV: *"Thanks, brothers, thanks!"*

YASHA. The peasants have come to say good-by. In my opinion, Yermolay Alexeyevitch, the peasants are good-natured, but they don't know much about things.

> [*The hum of talk dies away. Enter across front of stage* LYUBOV ANDREYEVNA *and* GAEV. *She is not weeping, but is pale; her face is quivering—she cannot speak.*]

GAEV. You gave them your purse, Lyuba. That won't do—that won't do!

LYUBOV. I couldn't help it! I couldn't help it!

> [*Both go out.*]

LOPAHIN (*in the doorway, calls after them*). You will take a glass at parting? Please do. I didn't think to bring any from the town, and at the station I could only get one bottle. Please take a glass (*a pause*). What? You don't care for any? (*Comes away from the door*) If I'd known, I wouldn't have bought it. Well, and I'm not going to drink it. (YASHA *carefully sets the tray down on a chair.*) You have a glass, Yasha, anyway.

YASHA. Good luck to the travelers, and luck to those that stay behind! (*drinks*) This champagne isn't the real thing, I can assure you.

LOPAHIN. It cost eight roubles the bottle (*a pause*). It's devilish cold here.

YASHA. They haven't heated the stove today—it's all the same since we're going (*laughs*).

LOPAHIN. What are you laughing for?

YASHA. For pleasure.

LOPAHIN. Though it's October, it's as still and sunny as though it were summer. It's just right for building! (*Looks at his watch; says in doorway*) Take note, ladies and gentlemen, the train goes in forty-seven minutes; so you ought to start for the station in twenty minutes. You must hurry up!

[TROFIMOV *comes in from out of doors wearing a greatcoat.*]

TROFIMOV. I think it must be time to start, the horses are ready. The devil only knows what's become of my galoshes; they're lost. (*In the doorway*) Anya! My galoshes aren't here. I can't find them.

LOPAHIN. And I'm getting off to Harkov. I am going in the same train with you. I'm spending all the winter at Harkov. I've been wasting all my time gossiping with you and fretting with no work to do. I can't get on without work. I don't know what to do with my hands, they flap about so queerly, as if they didn't belong to me.

TROFIMOV. Well, we're just going away, and you will take up your profitable labours again.

LOPAHIN. Do take a glass.

TROFIMOV. No, thanks.

LOPAHIN. Then you're going to Moscow now?

TROFIMOV. Yes. I shall see them as far as the town, and tomorrow I shall go on to Moscow.

LOPAHIN. Yes, I daresay, the professors aren't giving any lectures, they're waiting for your arrival.

TROFIMOV. That's not your business.

LOPAHIN. How many years have you been at the University?

TROFIMOV. Do think of something newer than that—that's stale and flat (*hunts for galoshes*). You know we shall most likely never see each other again, so let me give you one piece of advice at parting: don't wave your arms about—get out of the habit. And another thing, building villas, reckoning up that the summer visitors will in time become independent farmers—reckoning like that, that's not the thing to do either. After all, I am fond of you: you have fine delicate fingers like an artist, you've a fine delicate soul.

LOPAHIN (*embraces him*). Good-by, my dear fellow. Thanks for every-thing. Let me give you money for the journey, if you need it.

TROFIMOV. What for? I don't need it.

LOPAHIN. Why, you haven't got a halfpenny.

TROFIMOV. Yes, I have, thank you. I got some money for a translation. Here it is in my pocket, (*anxiously*) but where can my galoshes be!

VARYA (*from the next room*). Take the nasty things! (*Flings a pair of galoshes on to the stage.*)

TROFIMOV. Why are you so cross, Varya? h'm! . . . but those aren't my galoshes.

LOPAHIN. I sowed three thousand acres with poppies in the spring, and now I have cleared forty thousand profit. And when my poppies were in flower, wasn't it a picture! So here, as I say, I made forty thousand, and I'm offering you a loan because I can afford to. Why turn up your nose? I am a peasant—I speak bluntly.

TROFIMOV. Your father was a peasant, mine was a chemist—and that proves absolutely nothing whatever. (LOPAHIN *takes out his pocket-book.*) Stop that—stop that. If you were to offer me two hundred thousand I wouldn't take it. I am an independent man, and every-thing that all of you, rich and poor alike, prize so highly and hold so dear, hasn't the slightest power over me—it's like so much fluff fluttering in the air. I can get on without you. I can pass by you. I am strong and proud. Humanity is advancing towards the highest truth, the highest happiness, which is possible on earth, and I am in the front ranks.

LOPAHIN. Will you get there?

TROFIMOV. I shall get there (*a pause*). I shall get there, or I shall show others the way to get there.

> [*In the distance is heard the stroke of an axe on a tree.*]

LOPAHIN. Good-by, my dear fellow; it's time to be off. We turn up our noses at one another, but life is passing all the while. When I am working hard without resting, then my mind is more at ease, and it seems to me as though I too know what I exist for; but how many people there are in Russia, my dear boy, who exist, one doesn't know what for. Well, it doesn't matter. That's not what keeps things spinning. They tell me Leonid Andreyevitch has taken a situation. He is going to be a clerk at the bank—6,000 roubles a year. Only, of course, he won't stick to it—he's too lazy.

ANYA (*in the doorway*). Mamma begs you not to let them chop down the orchard until she's gone.

TROFIMOV. Yes, really, you might have the tact (*walks out across the front of the stage*).

LOPAHIN. I'll see to it! I'll see to it! Stupid fellows! (*Goes out after him.*)

ANYA. Has Firs been taken to the hospital?

YASHA. I told them this morning. No doubt they have taken him.

ANYA (*to* EPIHODOV, *who passes across the drawing room*). Semyon Pantaleyevitch, inquire, please, if Firs has been taken to the hospital.

YASHA (*in a tone of offense*). I told Yegor this morning—why ask a dozen times?

EPIHODOV. Firs is advanced in years. It's my conclusive opinion no treatment would do him good; it's time he was gathered to his fathers. And I can only envy him (*puts a trunk down on a cardboard hatbox and crushes it*). There, now, of course—I knew it would be so.

YASHA (*jeeringly*). Two and twenty misfortunes!

VARYA (*through the door*). Has Firs been taken to the hospital?

ANYA. Yes.

VARYA. Why wasn't the note for the doctor taken too?

ANYA (*from the adjoining room*). Where's Yasha? Tell him his mother's come to say good-by to him.

YASHA (*waves his hand*). They put me out of all patience! (DUNYASHA *has all this time been busy about the luggage. Now, when* YASHA *is left alone, she goes up to him*).

DUNYASHA. You might just give me one look, Yasha. You're going away. You're leaving me (*weeps and throws herself on his neck*).

YASHA. What are you crying for? (*drinks the champagne*). In six days I shall be in Paris again. Tomorrow we shall get into the express train and roll away in a flash. I can scarcely believe it! *Vive la France!* It doesn't suit me here—it's not the life for me; there's no doing anything. I have seen enough of the ignorance here. I have had enough of it (*drinks champagne*). What are you crying for? Behave yourself properly, and then you won't cry.

DUNYASHA (*powders her face, looking in a pocket mirror*). Do send me a letter from Paris. You know how I loved you, Yasha—how I loved you! I am a tender creature, Yasha.

YASHA. Here they are coming!

[*Busies himself about the trunks, humming softly.*
Enter LYUBOV ANDREYEVNA, GAEV, ANYA *and* CHAR-
LOTTA IVANOVNA.]

GAEV. We ought to be off. There's not much time now (*looking at* YASHA). What a smell of herrings!

LYUBOV. In ten minutes we must get into the carriage (*casts a look about the room*). Farewell, dear house, dear old home of our fathers! Winter will pass and spring will come, and then you will be no more; they will tear you down! How much those walls have seen! (*Kisses her daughter passionately.*) My treasure, how bright you look! Your eyes are sparkling like diamonds! Are you glad? Very glad?

ANYA. Very glad! A new life is beginning, mamma.

GAEV. Yes, really, everything is all right now. Before the cherry orchard was sold, we were all worried and wretched, but afterwards, when once the question was settled conclusively, irrevocably, we all felt calm and even cheerful. I am a bank clerk now—I am a financier—cannon off the red. And you, Lyuba, after all, you are looking better; there's no question of that.

LYUBOV. Yes. My nerves are better, that's true. (*Her hat and coat are handed to her.*) I'm sleeping well. Carry out my things, Yasha. It's time. (*To* ANYA) My darling, we shall soon see each other again. I am going to Paris. I can live there on the money your Yaroslavl auntie sent us to buy the estate with—hurrah for auntie!—but that money won't last long.

ANYA. You'll come back soon, mamma, won't you? I'll be working up for my examination in the high school, and when I have passed that, I shall set to work and be a help to you. We will read all sorts of things together, mamma, won't we? (*Kisses her mother's hands.*) We will read in the autumn evenings. We'll read lots of books, and a new wonderful world will open out before us (*dreamily*). Mamma, come soon.

LYUBOV. I shall come, my precious treasure (*embraces her*).

[*Enter* LOPAHIN. CHARLOTTA *softly hums a song.*]

GAEV. Charlotta's happy; she's singing!

CHARLOTTA (*picks up a bundle like a swaddled baby*). By, by, my baby. (*A baby is heard crying: "Ooah! ooah!"*) Hush, hush, my pretty boy! (*Ooah! ooah!*) Poor little thing! (*Throws the bundle back.*) You must please find me a situation. I can't go on like this.

LOPAHIN. We'll find you one, Charlotta Ivanovna. Don't you worry yourself.

GAEV. Everyone's leaving us. Varya's going away. We have become of no use all at once.

CHARLOTTA. There's nowhere for me to be in the town. I must go away. (*Hums*) What care I . . .

[*Enter* PISHTCHIK.]

LOPAHIN. The freak of nature!

PISHTCHIK (*gasping*). Oh! . . . let me get my breath. . . . I'm worn out . . . my most honoured . . . Give me some water.

GAEV. Want some money, I suppose? Your humble servant! I'll go out of the way of temptation (*goes out*).

PISHTCHIK. It's a long while since I have been to see you . . . dearest lady. (*To* LOPAHIN) You are here . . . glad to see you . . . a man of immense intellect . . . take . . . here (*gives* LOPAHIN) 400 roubles. That leaves me owing 840.

LOPAHIN (*shrugging his shoulders in amazement*). It's like a dream. Where did you get it?

PISHTCHIK. Wait a bit . . . I'm hot . . . a most extraordinary occurrence! Some Englishmen came along and found in my land some sort of white clay. (*To* LYUBOV ANDREYEVNA) And 400 for you . . . most lovely . . . wonderful (*gives money*). The rest later (*sips water*). A young man in the train was telling me just now that a great philosopher advises jumping off a housetop. "Jump!" says he; "the whole gist of the problem lies in that." (*Wonderingly*) Fancy that, now! Water, please!

LOPAHIN. What Englishmen?

PISHTCHIK. I have made over to them the rights to dig the clay for twenty-four years . . . and now, excuse me . . . I can't stay . . . I must be trotting on. I'm going to Znoikovo . . . to Kardamanovo. . . . I'm in debt all round (*sips*). . . . To your very good health! . . . I'll come in on Thursday.

LYUBOV. We are just off to the town, and tomorrow I start for abroad.

PISHTCHIK. What! (*In agitation*) Why to the town? Oh, I see the furniture . . . the boxes. No matter . . . (*through his tears*) . . . no matter . . . men of enormous intellect . . . these Englishmen. . . . Never mind . . . be happy. God will succor you . . . no matter . . . everything in this world must have an end (*kisses* LYUBOV ANDREYEVNA'S *hand*). If the rumour reaches you that my end has come, think of this . . . old horse, and say: "There once was such a man in the world . . . Semyonov-Pishtchik . . . the Kingdom of Heaven be his!" . . . most extraordinary weather . . . yes. (*Goes out in violent agitation, but as once returns and says in the doorway*) Dashenka wishes to be remembered to you (*goes out*).

LYUBOV. Now we can start. I leave with two cares in my heart. The first is leaving Firs ill. (*Looking at her watch*) We have still five minutes.

ANYA. Mamma, Firs has been taken to the hospital. Yasha sent him off this morning.

LYUBOV. My other anxiety is Varya. She is used to getting up early and working; and now, without work, she's like a fish out of water. She is thin and pale, and she's crying, poor dear! (*a pause*) You are well aware, Yermolay Alexeyevitch, I dreamed of marrying her to you, and everything seemed to show that you would get married (*whispers to* ANYA *and motions to* CHARLOTTA *and both go out*). She loves you—she suits you. And I don't know—I don't know why it is you seem, as it were, to avoid each other. I can't understand it!

LOPAHIN. I don't understand it myself, I confess. It's queer somehow, altogether. If there's still time, I'm ready now at once. Let's settle it straight off, and go ahead; but without you, I feel I shan't make her an offer.

LYUBOV. That's excellent. Why, a single moment's all that's necessary. I'll call her at once.

LOPAHIN. And there's champagne all ready too (*looking into the glasses*). Empty! Someone's emptied them already. (YASHA *coughs.*) I call that greedy.

LYUBOV (*eagerly*). Capital! We will go out. Yasha, *allez!* I'll call her in. (*At the door*) Varya, leave all that; come here. Come along! (*goes out with* YASHA).

LOPAHIN (*looking at his watch*). Yes.

> [*A pause. Behind the door, smothered laughter and
> whispering, and, at last, enter* VARYA.]

VARYA (*looking a long while over the things*). It is strange, I can't find it anywhere.

LOPAHIN. What are you looking for?

VARYA. I packed it myself, and I can't remember (*a pause*).

LOPAHIN. Where are you going now, Varvara Mihailova?

VARYA. I? To the Ragulins. I have arranged to go to them to look after the house—as a housekeeper.

LOPAHIN. That's in Yashnovo? It'll be seventy miles away (*a pause*). So this is the end of life in this house!

VARYA (*looking among the things*). Where is it? Perhaps I put it in the trunk. Yes, life in this house is over—there will be no more of it.

LOPAHIN. And I'm just off to Harkov—by this next train. I've a lot of business there. I'm leaving Epihodov here, and I've taken him on.

VARYA. Really!

LOPAHIN. This time last year we had snow already, if you remember; but now it's so fine and sunny. Though it's cold, to be sure—three degrees of frost.

VARYA. I haven't looked (*a pause*). And besides, our thermometer's broken (*a pause*).

> [*Voice at the door from the yard:* "Yermolay Alex-
> eyevitch!"]

LOPAHIN (*as though he had long been expecting this summons*). This minute!

> [LOPAHIN *goes out quickly.* VARYA *sitting on the floor
> and laying her head on a bag full of clothes, sobs
> quietly. The door opens.* LYUBOV ANDREYEVNA *comes
> in cautiously.*]

LYUBOV. Well? (*a pause*) We must be going.

VARYA (*has wiped her eyes and is no longer crying*). Yes, mamma, it's time to start. I shall have time to get to the Ragulins today, if only you're not late for the train.

LYUBOV (*in the doorway*). Anya, put your things on.

> [*Enter* ANYA, *then* GAEV *and* CHARLOTTA IVANOVNA.

GAEV *has on a warm coat with a hood. Servants and cabmen come in.* EPIHODOV *bustles about the luggage.*]

LYUBOV. Now we can start on our travels.

ANYA (*joyfully*). On our travels!

GAEV. My friends—my dear, my precious friends! Leaving this house forever, can I be silent? Can I refrain from giving utterance at leave-taking to those emotions which now flood all my being?

ANYA (*supplicatingly*). Uncle!

VARYA. Uncle, you mustn't!

GAEV (*dejectedly*). Cannon and into the pocket . . . I'll be quiet. . . .
[*Enter* TROFIMOV *and afterwards* LOPAHIN.]

TROFIMOV. Well, ladies and gentlemen, we must start.

LOPAHIN. Epihodov, my coat!

LYUBOV. I'll stay just one minute. It seems as though I have never seen before what the walls, what the ceilings in this house were like, and now I look at them with greediness, with such tender love.

GAEV. I remember when I was six years old sitting in that window on Trinity Day watching my father going to church.

LYUBOV. Have all the things been taken?

LOPAHIN. I think all. (*Putting on overcoat, to* EPIHODOV) You, Epihodov, mind you see everything is right.

EPIHODOV (*in a husky voice*). Don't you trouble, Yermolay Alexeyevitch.

LOPAHIN. Why, what's wrong with your voice?

EPIHODOV. I've just had a drink of water, and I choked over something.

YASHA (*contemptuously*). The ignorance!

LYUBOV. We are going—and not a soul will be left here.

LOPAHIN. Not till the spring.

VARVA (*pulls a parasol out of a bundle, as though about to hit someone with it.* LOPAHIN *makes a gesture as though alarmed*). What is it? I didn't mean anything.

TROFIMOV. Ladies and gentlemen, let us get into the carriage. It's time. The train will be in directly.

VARYA. Petya, here they are, your galoshes, by that box. (*With tears*) And what dirty old things they are!

TROFIMOV (*putting on his galoshes*). Let us go, friends!

GAEV (*greatly agitated, afraid of weeping*). The train—the station! Double balk, ah!

LYUBOV. Let us go!

LOPAHIN. Are we all here? (*Locks the side door on left.*) The things are all here. We must lock up. Let us go!

ANYA. Good-by, home! Good-by to the old life!

TROFIMOV. Welcome to the new life!

[TROFIMOV *goes out with* ANYA. VARYA *looks round
the room and goes out slowly.* YASHA *and* CHARLOTTA
IVANOVNA, *with her dog, go out.*]

LOPAHIN. Till the spring, then! Come, friends, till we meet! (*Goes out.*)
[LYUBOV ANDREYEVNA *and* GAEV *remain alone. As
though they had been waiting for this, they throw
themselves on each other's necks, and break into
subdued smothered sobbing, afraid of being over-
heard.*]

GAEV (*in despair*). Sister, my sister!

LYUBOV. Oh, my orchard!—my sweet, beautiful orchard! My life, my
youth, my happiness, good-by! good-by!

VOICE OF ANYA (*calling gaily*). Mamma!

VOICE OF TROFIMOV (*gaily, excitedly*). Aa—oo!

LYUBOV. One last look at the walls, at the windows. My dear mother
loved to walk about this room.

GAEV. Sister, sister!

VOICE OF ANYA. Mamma!

VOICE OF TROFIMOV. Aa—oo!

LYUBOV. We are coming. (*They go out.*)
[*The stage is empty. There is the sound of the doors
being locked up, then of the carriages driving away.
There is silence. In the stillness there is the dull stroke
of an axe in a tree, clanging with a mournful lonely
sound. Footsteps are heard.* FIRS *appears in the doorway on the right. He is dressed as always—in a pea
jacket and white waistcoat with slippers on his feet.
He is ill.*]

FIRS (*goes up to the doors, and tries the handles*). Locked! They have
gone . . . (*sits down on sofa*). They have forgotten me. . . .
Never mind . . . I'll sit here a bit. . . . I'll be bound Leonid
Andreyevitch hasn't put his fur coat on and has gone off in his thin
overcoat (*sighs anxiously*). I didn't see after him. . . . These young
people . . . (*mutters something that can't be distinguished*). Life
has slipped by as though I hadn't lived. (*Lies down*) I'll lie down a
bit. . . . There's no strength in you, nothing left you—all gone!
Ech! I'm good for nothing (*lies motionless*).
[*A sound is heard that seems to come from the sky,
like a breaking harp string, dying away mournfully.
All is still again, and there is heard nothing but the
strokes of the axe far away in the orchard.*]

QUESTIONS

1. The play begins with a series of trivial acts such as missing a train, dropping some flowers, and bumping into a chair. What do these actions, and others like them, tell us about the characters and their ability to deal with life?
2. Do the things they say correspond with their actions?
3. Ordinarily, dramatic dialogue proceeds with the different characters commenting on or developing a single subject—the topic of conversation. This is not Chekhov's way, however. Describe the manner in which his dialogue works.
4. How does this peculiar type of dialogue make real, or bring into being, the inner life of the characters?
5. Is the deaf Firs an appropriate servant for this family?
6. Would an apple orchard or a wild wood be equally effective as a symbol of the society of which these people are a part?
7. Once the characters and the orchard are identified as different forms of the same society, what information provided about the orchard tells us something about the people who own it?

8. How is the larger world, the reality existing outside the orchard, brought into being? What is its nature?
9. The family has gathered around itself a number of friends and retainers such as Trofimov, Lopahin, and Charlotta. Do these people tell us anything about the family to which they have attached themselves?
10. Do the occupations of each of these people suggest anything about the makeup of society—about its source of energy and direction?
11. In the plays you have read so far the chief characters always have a definite motive; they want to do something desperately and their whole being is directed toward that end. Can this be said of the characters in *The Cherry Orchard*? If so, must their motives be distinguished from the usual kind of dramatic motive?
12. Most of the characters are fond of philosophizing, and in their rambling discourses they say a good deal about their understanding of life. Do they explain in these speeches what is missing in their lives? what has happened to their vitality and drive?
13. How do the characters attempt to explain the "breaking harp string" heard in the distance? Are their explanations sufficient?
14. Is Lyubov really the sinner she believes herself to be? Does sin account for her present situation?

ACT III

15. How does the play express the movement of time? Do the characters understand time correctly? Consider their tendency to reminisce.

16. How many love affairs are in the play? Take into account those that are only mentioned. What do these loves have in common?

17. Does the play contain any representatives of a "new order"? Are they encouraging omens for the future?

18. Look carefully at all the actions at the party. Would the meaning of events here and the nature of the characters still be evident if the scene were "mimed," that is, acted out without words?

19. After answering the above question look at the speeches of the characters and see how (a) they support the actions, and (b) they extend their meaning. Could the language be eliminated without loss?

20. Does the destruction of the orchard to make room for a "housing development" suggest that *The Cherry Orchard* is not only presenting the lives of a number of people but also describing a well-known historical and social change? What other evidence of this historical movement does the play offer?

ACT IV

21. What significance does the sound of the axe striking the trees have? In answering this question consider the peculiar nature of this sound.

22. There is a good deal of talk in the departure scene about beginning a new and more successful life of work and love. How is it made clear that these hopes are vain?

23. Does the abandonment of Firs at the end of the play force us to take these people somewhat more seriously? This is the last event of the play, the revelation of plot. Looking back on the play, can we say that what is shown here in striking form has really been occurring all along?

24. The final scene is made up of an image and a sound: an old man lying on a couch in a chilling house and the thud of an axe biting into a cherry tree. Are the dying man and the dying orchard connected in any way?

25. Did the family *intend* to leave Firs behind? Is this characteristic? Was the orchard "left behind" for the same reasons?

26. Chekhov sometimes referred to *The Cherry Orchard* as a tragedy, but on the title page he calls it a comedy. Can you see why he might be confused? Is it comedy or tragedy?

THE TIME OF YOUR LIFE

BY

WILLIAM SAROYAN

"In the time of your life, live." This line from the epigraph William Saroyan (born 1908) provides for *The Time of Your Life* (1939) expresses perfectly the comic approach to experience dramatized in such plays of his as *My Heart's in the Highlands* (1939), *Love's Old Sweet Song* (1940), and *Hello Out There* (1942). Saroyan's characters inhabit the same bleak, frightening world that Chekhov's do, and they, like Chekhov's moribund aristocrats, have lost contact with the powers outside themselves—the kind of contact that Antigone feels with the moral laws of the universe, that Creon feels with the Theban state, or that Henry IV feels with the great principle of universal order. In Chekhov's and Saroyan's plays there is, as the Arab says in *The Time of Your Life,* "no foundation," no certainty that personal existence and history are moving toward an end that justifies human suffering. Faced with this grim reality, Chekhov's characters and their society disintegrate. But Saroyan's characters—largely outcasts from society—struggle to assert, and largely do achieve, purely human values, values that have no justification outside man himself: life is good; nature is enjoyable; love and artistic creation are valuable expressions of self; man can feel sympathy for man; death can be qualified if not defeated.

Saroyan began writing his plays toward the end of the great depression of the thirties and on the eve of the Second World War, when the historical scene offered very little encouragement to man. The plays were immediately acclaimed; *The Time of Your Life* won both the Pulitzer Prize—which Saroyan refused without explanation—and the Drama Critics' Award in the same year, 1939. In the years after the war the reputation of the plays faded, and they were seldom performed. Perhaps when the world seems to be going along fairly well, audiences are not so concerned with bedrock values and simple meanings. Recently there have been signs of a Saroyan revival. Hitler is gone, but no one reading the play today will have any difficulty imagining the grim headlines in the newspapers Joe buys, glances at, and discards, to return to what really interests him—people. But, however much Saroyan's popularity may wax and wane as the world situation fluctuates, *The Time of Your Life* will remain one of the very few great American comedies.

THE PEOPLE

JOE, *a young loafer with money and a good heart*

TOM, *his admirer, disciple, errand boy, stooge, and friend*

KITTY DUVAL, *a young woman with memories*

NICK, *owner of Nick's Pacific Street Saloon, Restaurant, and Entertainment Palace*

ARAB, *an Eastern philosopher and harmonica-player*

KIT CARSON, *an old Indian-fighter*

MCCARTHY, *an intelligent and well-read longshoreman*

KRUPP, *his boyhood friend, a water-front cop who hates his job but doesn't know what else to do instead*

HARRY, *a natural-born hoofer who wants to make people laugh but can't*

WESLEY, *a colored boy who plays a mean and melancholy boogie-woogie piano*

DUDLEY, *a young man in love*

ELSIE, *a nurse, the girl he loves*

LORENE, *an unattractive woman*

MARY L., *an unhappy woman of quality and great beauty*

WILLIE, *a marble-game maniac*

BLICK, *a heel*

MA, *Nick's mother*

A KILLER

HER SIDE KICK

A COP

ANOTHER COP

A SAILOR

A SOCIETY GENTLEMAN

A SOCIETY LADY

THE DRUNKARD

THE NEWSBOY

ANNA, *Nick's daughter*

THE PLACE: *Nick's Pacific Street Saloon, Restaurant, and Entertainment Palace at the foot of Embarcadero, in San Francisco. A suggestion of Room 21 at The New York Hotel, upstairs, around the corner.*

THE TIME: *Afternoon and night of a day in October 1939.*

In the time of your life, live—so that in that good time there shall be no ugliness or death for yourself or for any life your life touches. Seek goodness everywhere, and when it is found, bring it out of its hiding place and let it be free and unashamed. Place in matter and in flesh the least of the values, for these are the things that hold death and must pass away. Discover in all things that which shines and is beyond corruption. Encourage virtue in whatever heart it may have been driven into secrecy and sorrow by the shame and terror of the world. Ignore the obvious, for it is unworthy of the clear eye and the kindly heart. Be the inferior of no man, nor of any man be the superior. Remember that every man is a variation of yourself. No man's guilt is not yours, nor is any man's innocence a thing apart. Despise evil and ungodliness, but not men of ungodliness or evil. These, understand. Have no shame in being kindly and gentle, but if the time comes in the time of your life to kill, kill and have no regret. In the time of your life, live—so that in that wondrous time you shall not add to the misery and sorrow of the world, but shall smile to the infinite delight and mystery of it.

ACT I

🦢 Scene: *Nick's is an American place: a San Francisco water-front honky-tonk. At a table,* JOE: *always calm, always quiet, always thinking, always eager, always bored, always superior. His expensive clothes are casually and youthfully worn and give him an almost boyish appearance. He is thinking. Behind the bar,* NICK: *a big redheaded young Italian-American with an enormous naked woman tattooed in red on the inside of his right arm. He is studying* The Racing Form.

The ARAB, *at his place at the end of the bar. He is a lean old man with a rather ferocious old-country mustache, with the ends twisted up. Between the thumb and forefinger of his left hand is the Mohammedan tattoo indicating that he has been to Mecca. He is sipping a glass of beer.*

It is about eleven-thirty in the morning. SAM *is sweeping out. We see only his back. He disappears into the kitchen. The* SAILOR *at the bar finishes his drink and leaves, moving thoughtfully, as though he were trying very hard to discover how to live. The* NEWSBOY *comes in.*

NEWSBOY (*cheerfully*). Good morning, everybody. (*No answer. To* NICK.) Paper, mister? (NICK *shakes his head, no. The* NEWSBOY *goes to* JOE.) Paper, mister?

[JOE *shakes his head, no. The* NEWSBOY *walks away, counting papers.*]

JOE (*noticing him*). How many you got?

NEWSBOY. Five.

[JOE *gives him a quarter, takes all the papers, glances at the headlines with irritation, throws them away. The* NEWSBOY *watches carefully, then goes.*]

ARAB (*picks up a paper, looks at the headlines, shakes his head as if*

rejecting everything else a man might say about the world). No
foundation. All the way down the line.

> [*The* DRUNK *comes in. Walks to the telephone, looks
> for a nickel in the chute, sits down at* JOE'S *table.*
> NICK *takes the* DRUNK *out. The* DRUNK *returns.*]

DRUNK (*champion of the Bill of Rights*). This is a free country, ain't
it?

> [WILLIE, *the marble-game maniac, explodes through
> the swinging doors and lifts the forefinger of his
> right hand comically, indicating one beer. He is a
> very young man, not more than twenty. He is wear-
> ing heavy shoes, a pair of old and dirty corduroys, a
> light-green turtle-neck jersey with a large letter F on
> the chest, an oversize two-button tweed coat, and a
> green hat, with the brim up.* NICK *sets out a glass of
> beer for him, he drinks it, straightens up vigorously,
> saying "Aaah," makes a solemn face, gives* NICK *a
> one-finger salute of adieu, and begins to leave, re-
> freshed and restored in spirit. He walks by the marble
> game, halts suddenly, turns, studies the contraption,
> gestures as if to say, "Oh no." Turns to go, stops, re-
> turns to the machine, studies it, takes a handful of
> small coins out of his pants pocket, lifts a nickel, in-
> dicates with a gesture, One game, no more. Puts the
> nickel in the slot, pushes in the slide, making an in-
> teresting noise.*]

NICK. You can't beat that machine.

WILLIE. Oh yeah?

> [*The marbles fall, roll, and take their place. He
> pushes down the lever, placing one marble in posi-
> tion. Takes a very deep breath, walks in a small cir-
> cle, excited at the beginning of great drama. Stands
> straight and pious before the contest. Himself vs. the
> machine. Willie vs. Destiny. His skill and daring vs.
> the cunning and trickery of the novelty industry of
> America, and the whole challenging world. He is the
> last of the American pioneers, with nothing more to
> fight but the machine, with no other reward than
> lights going on and off, and six nickels for one. Be-
> fore him is the last champion, the machine. He is the
> last challenger, the young man with nothing to do in
> the world.* WILLIE *grips the knob delicately, studies
> the situation carefully, draws the knob back, holds it
> a moment, and then releases it. The first marble rolls
> out among the hazards, and the contest is on. At the*]

> very beginning of the play "The Missouri Waltz" is
> coming from the phonograph. The music ends here.]
>   This is the signal for the beginning of the play.
> [JOE suddenly comes out of his reverie. He whistles
> the way people do who are calling a cab that's about
> a block away, only he does it quietly. WILLIE turns
> around, but JOE gestures for him to return to his
> work. NICK looks up from The Racing Form.]

JOE (calling). Tom. (To himself.) Where the hell is he, every time I
need him? (He looks around calmly: the nickel-in-the-slot phonograph in the corner; the open public telephone; the stage; the marble
game; the bar; and so on. He calls again, this time very loud.) Hey,
Tom.

NICK (with morning irritation). What do you want?

JOE (without thinking). I want the boy to get me a watermelon, that's
what I want. What do you want? Money, or love, or fame, or what?
You won't get them studying The Racing Form.

NICK. I like to keep abreast of the times.

> [TOM comes hurrying in. He is a great big man of
> about thirty or so who appears to be much younger
> because of the childlike expression of his face: hand-
> some, dumb, innocent, troubled, and a little be-
> wildered by everything. He is obviously adult in years,
> but it seems as if by all rights he should still be a boy.
> He is defensive as clumsy, self-conscious, overgrown
> boys are. He is wearing a flashy cheap suit. JOE leans
> back and studies him with casual disapproval. TOM
> slackens his pace and becomes clumsy and embar-
> rassed, waiting for the bawling-out he's pretty sure
> he's going to get.]

JOE (objectively, severely, but a little amused). Who saved your life?

TOM (sincerely). You did, Joe. Thanks.

JOE (interested). How'd I do it?

TOM (confused). What?

JOE (even more interested). How'd I do it?

TOM. Joe, you know how you did it.

JOE (softly). I want you to answer me. How'd I save your life? I've
forgotten.

TOM (remembering, with a big sorrowful smile). You made me eat all
that chicken soup three years ago when I was sick and hungry.

JOE (fascinated). Chicken soup?

TOM (eagerly). Yeah.

JOE. Three years? Is it that long?

TOM (delighted to have the information). Yeah, sure. 1937. 1938.
1939. This is 1939, Joe.

JOE (*amused*). Never mind what year it is. Tell me the whole story.

TOM. You took me to the doctor. You gave me money for food and clothes, and paid my room rent. Aw, Joe, you know all the different things you did.

> [JOE *nods, turning away from* TOM *after each question.*]

JOE. You in good health now?

TOM. Yeah, Joe.

JOE. You got clothes?

TOM. Yeah, Joe.

JOE. You eat three times a day. Sometimes four?

TOM. Yeah, Joe. Sometimes five.

JOE. You got a place to sleep?

TOM. Yeah, Joe.

> [JOE *nods. Pauses. Studies* TOM *carefully.*]

JOE. Then where the hell have you been?

TOM (*humbly*). Joe, I was out in the street listening to the boys. They're talking about the trouble down here on the water front.

JOE (*sharply*). I want you to be around when I need you.

TOM (*pleased that the bawling-out is over*). I won't do it again. Joe, one guy out there says there's got to be a revolution before anything will ever be all right.

JOE (*impatient*). I know all about it. Now, here. Take this money. Go up to the Emporium. You know where the Emporium is?

TOM. Yeah, sure, Joe.

JOE. All right. Take the elevator and go up to the fourth floor. Walk around to the back, to the toy department. Buy me a couple of dollars' worth of toys and bring them here.

TOM (*amazed*). Toys? What *kind* of toys, Joe?

JOE. Any kind of toys. Little ones that I can put on this table.

TOM. What do you want toys for, Joe?

JOE (*mildly angry*). *What?*

TOM. All right, all right. You don't have to get sore at *everything*. What'll people think, a big guy like me buying toys?

JOE. *What people?*

TOM. Aw, Joe, you're always making me do crazy things for you, and *I'm* the guy that gets embarrassed. You just sit in this place and make me do all the dirty work.

JOE (*looking away*). Do what I tell you.

TOM. O.K., but I wish I knew *why*. (*He makes to go.*)

JOE. Wait a minute. Here's a nickel. Put it in the phonograph. Number seven. I want to hear that waltz again.

TOM. Boy, I'm glad *I* don't have to stay and listen to it. Joe, what do you hear in that song anyway? We listen to that song ten times a

day. Why can't we hear number six, or two, or nine? There are a
lot of other numbers.

JOE (*emphatically*). Put the nickel in the phonograph. (*Pause.*) Sit
down and wait till the music's over. Then go get me some toys.

TOM. O.K. O.K.

JOE (*loudly*). Never mind being a martyr about it, either. The cause
isn't worth it.

> [TOM *puts the nickel into the machine, with a ritual
> of impatient and efficient movement which plainly
> shows his lack of sympathy or enthusiasm. His man-
> ner also reveals, however, that his lack of sympathy
> is spurious and exaggerated. Actually, he is fascinated
> by the music, but is so confused by it that he pre-
> tends he dislikes it.*
>
> *The music begins. It is another variation of "The
> Missouri Waltz," played dreamily and softly, with
> perfect orchestral form, and with a theme of weeping
> in the horns repeated a number of times. At first* TOM
> *listens with something close to irritation, since he
> can't understand what is so attractive in the music to*
> JOE, *and what is so painful and confusing in it to
> himself. Very soon, however, he is carried away by
> the melancholy story of grief and nostalgia of the
> song. He stands, troubled by the poetry and confu-
> sion in himself.*
>
> [JOE, *on the other hand, listens as if he were not
> listening, indifferent and unmoved. What he's inter-
> ested in is* TOM. *He turns and glances at* TOM.
>
> [KITTY DUVAL, *who lives in a room in the New
> York Hotel, around the corner, comes beyond the
> swinging doors quietly, and walks slowly to the bar,
> her reality and rhythm a perfect accompaniment to
> the sorrowful American music, which is her music,
> as it is* TOM'S. *Which the world drove out of her,
> putting in its place brokenness and all manner of
> spiritually crippled forms. She seems to understand
> this, and is angry. Angry with herself, full of hate for
> the poor world, and full of pity and contempt for its
> tragic, unbelievable, confounded people. She is a
> small, powerful girl, with that kind of delicate and
> rugged beauty which no circumstance of evil or ugly
> reality can destroy. This beauty is that element of the
> immortal which is in the seed of good and common
> people, and which is kept alive in some of the female
> of our kind, no matter how accidentally or pointlessly*

they may have entered the world. KITTY DUVAL *is somebody. There is an angry purity, and a fierce pride, in her. In her stance, and way of walking, there is grace and arrogance.* JOE *recognizes her as a great person immediately. She goes to the bar.*]

KITTY. Beer.

[NICK *places a glass of beer before her mechanically. She swallows half the drink, and listens to the music again.* TOM *turns and sees her. He becomes dead to everything in the world but her. He stands like a lump, fascinated and undone by his almost religious adoration for her.* JOE *notices* TOM.]

JOE (*gently*). Tom. (TOM *begins to move toward the bar, where* KITTY *is standing. Loudly.*) Tom. (TOM *halts, then turns, and* JOE *motions to him to come over to the table.* TOM *goes over. Quietly.*) Have you got everything straight?

TOM (*out of the world*). What?

JOE. What do you mean, what? I just gave you some instructions.

TOM (*pathetically*). What do you want, Joe?

JOE. I want you to come to your senses.

[*He stands up quietly and knocks* TOM'S *hat off.*
TOM *picks up his hat quickly.*]

TOM. I got it, Joe. I got it. The Emporium. Fourth floor. In the back. The toy department. Two dollars' worth of toys. That you can put on a table.

KITTY (*to herself*). Who the hell is he to push a big man like that around?

JOE. I'll expect you back in a half hour. Don't get sidetracked anywhere. Just do what I tell you.

TOM (*pleading*). Joe? Can't I bet four bits on a horse race? There's a long shot—Precious Time—that's going to win by ten lengths. I got to have money.

[JOE *points to the street.* TOM *goes out.* NICK *is combing his hair, looking in the mirror.*]

NICK. I thought you wanted him to get you a watermelon.

JOE. I forgot. (*He watches* KITTY *a moment. To* KITTY, *clearly, slowly, with great compassion.*) What's the dream?

KITTY (*moving to* JOE, *coming to*). What?

JOE (*holding the dream for her*). What's the dream, *now?*

KITTY (*coming still closer*). What dream?

JOE. What dream! The dream you're dreaming.

NICK. Suppose he did bring you a watermelon? What the hell would you do with it?

JOE (*irritated*). I'd put it on this table. I'd look at it. Then I'd eat it. What do you *think* I'd do with it, sell it for a profit?

NICK. How should I know what *you'd* do with *anything?* What I'd like to know is, where do you get your money from? What work do you do?

JOE (*looking at* KITTY). Bring us a bottle of champagne.

KITTY. Champagne?

JOE (*simply*). Would you rather have something else?

KITTY. What's the big idea?

JOE. I thought you might like some champagne. I myself am very fond of it.

KITTY. Yeah, but what's the big idea? You can't push *me* around.

JOE (*gently but severely*). It's not in my nature to be unkind to another human being. I have only contempt for wit. Otherwise I might say something obvious, therefore cruel, and perhaps untrue.

KITTY. You be careful what you think about me.

JOE (*slowly, not looking at her*). I have only the noblest thoughts for both your person and your spirit.

NICK (*having listened carefully and not being able to make it out*). What are you talking about?

KITTY. You shut up. You——

JOE. He owns this place. He's an important man. All kinds of people come to him looking for work. Comedians. Singers. Dancers.

KITTY. I don't care. He can't call me names.

NICK. All right, sister.

KITTY (*furiously*). Don't you dare call me names. I used to be in burlesque.

NICK. If you were ever in burlesque, I used to be Charlie Chaplin.

KITTY (*angry and a little pathetic*). I *was* in burlesque. I played the burlesque circuit from coast to coast. I've had flowers sent to me by European royalty. I've had dinner with young men of wealth and social position.

NICK. You're dreaming.

KITTY (*to* JOE). *I was in burlesque.* Kitty Duval. That was my name. Life-size photographs of me in costume in front of burlesque theaters all over the country.

JOE (*gently, coaxingly*). I believe you. Have some champagne.

NICK (*going to the table with champagne bottle and glasses*). There he goes again.

JOE. Miss Duval?

KITTY (*sincerely, going over*). That's not my *real* name. That's my *stage* name.

JOE. I'll call you by your stage name.

NICK (*pouring*). All right, sister, make up your mind. Are you going to have champagne with him, or not?

JOE. Pour the lady some wine.

NICK. O.K., Professor. Why you come to this joint instead of one of the high-class dumps uptown is more than I can understand. Why don't you have champagne at the St. Francis? Why don't you drink with a lady?

KITTY (*furiously*). Don't you call me names—you dentist.

JOE. Dentist?

NICK (*amazed, loudly*). What kind of cussing is that? (*Pause. Looking at* KITTY, *then at* JOE, *bewildered*.) This guy doesn't belong here. The only reason I've got champagne is because *he* keeps ordering it all the time. (*To* KITTY.) Don't think you're the only one he drinks champagne with. He drinks with *all* of them. (*Pause.*) He's crazy. Or something.

JOE (*confidentially*). Nick, I think you're going to be all right in a couple of centuries.

NICK. I'm sorry, I don't understand your English.

> [JOE *lifts his glass.* KITTY *slowly lifts hers, not quite*
> *sure of what's going on.*]

JOE (*sincerely*). To the spirit, Kitty Duval.

KITTY (*beginning to understand, and very grateful, looking at him*). Thank you.

> [*They drink.*]

JOE (*calling*). Nick.

NICK. Yeah?

JOE. Would you mind putting a nickel in the machine again? Number——

NICK. Seven. I know. I know. I don't mind at all, your Highness, although, personally, I'm not a lover of music. (*Going to the machine.*) As a matter of fact I think Tchaikowsky was a dope.

JOE. Tchaikowsky? Where'd you ever hear of Tchaikowsky?

NICK. He was a dope.

JOE. Yeah. Why?

NICK. They talked about him on the radio one Sunday morning. He was a sucker. He let a woman drive him crazy.

JOE. I see.

NICK. I stood behind that bar listening to the goddamn stuff and cried like a baby. *None but the lonely heart!* He was a dope.

JOE. What made you cry?

NICK. What?

JOE (*sternly*). What made you cry, Nick?

NICK (*angry with himself*). I don't know.

JOE. I've been underestimating you, Nick. Play number seven.

NICK. They get everybody worked up. They give everybody stuff they shouldn't have.

> [NICK *puts the nickel into the machine and the waltz*
> *begins again. He listens to the music, then studies*
> The Racing Form.]

KITTY (*to herself, dreaming*). I like champagne, and everything that goes with it. Big houses with big porches, and big rooms with big windows, and big lawns, and big trees, and flowers growing everywhere, and big shepherd dogs sleeping in the shade.

NICK. I'm going next door to Frankie's to make a bet. I'll be right back.

JOE. Make one for me.

NICK (*going to* JOE). Who do you like?

JOE (*giving him money*). Precious Time.

NICK. *Ten dollars? Across the board?*

JOE. No. On the nose.

NICK. O.K. (*He goes.*)

> [DUDLEY R. BOSTWICK, *as he calls himself, breaks through the swinging doors, and practically flings himself upon the open telephone beside the phonograph.*
>
> [DUDLEY *is a young man of about twenty-four or twenty-five, ordinary and yet extraordinary. He is smallish, as the saying is, neatly dressed in bargain clothes, overworked and irritated by the routine and dullness and monotony of his life, apparently nobody and nothing, but in reality a great personality. The swindled young man. Educated, but without the least real understanding. A brave, dumb, salmon-spirit struggling for life in weary, stupefied flesh, dueling ferociously with a banal mind which has been only irritated by what it has been taught. He is a great personality because, against all these handicaps, what he wants is simple and basic: a woman. This urgent and violent need, common yet miraculous enough in itself, considering the unhappy environment of the animal, is the force which elevates him from nothingness to greatness. A ridiculous greatness, but in the nature of things beautiful to behold. All that he has been taught, and everything he believes, is phony, and yet he himself is real, almost super-real, because of this indestructible force in himself. His face is ridiculous. His personal rhythm is tense and jittery. His speech is shrill and violent. His gestures are wild. His ego is disjointed and epileptic. And yet deeply he possesses the same wholeness of spirit, and directness of energy, that is in all species of animals. There is little innate or cultivated spirit in him, but there is no absence of innocent animal force. He is a young man who has*

*been taught that he has a chance, as a person, and
believes it. As a matter of fact, he hasn't a chance
in the world, and should have been told by somebody, or should not have had his natural and valuable ignorance spoiled by education, ruining an
otherwise perfectly good and charming member of
the human race.*

*[At the telephone he immediately begins to dial
furiously, hesitates, changes his mind, stops dialing,
hangs up furiously, and suddenly begins again.*

*[Not more than half a minute after the firecracker
arrival of* DUDLEY R. BOSTWICK, *occurs the polka-
and-waltz arrival of* HARRY.

*[*HARRY *is another story. He comes in timidly,
turning about uncertainly, awkward, out of place
everywhere, embarrassed and encumbered by the
contemporary costume, sick at heart, but determined
to fit in somewhere. His arrival constitutes a dance.
His clothes don't fit. The pants are a little too large.
The coat, which doesn't match, is also a little too
large, and loose. He is a dumb young fellow, but
he has ideas. A philosophy, in fact. His philosophy
is simple and beautiful. The world is sorrowful. The
world needs laughter.* HARRY *is funny. The world
needs* HARRY. HARRY *will make the world laugh. He
has probably had a year or two of high school.
He has also listened to the boys at the poolroom.
He's looking for* NICK. *He goes to the* ARAB, *and
says, "Are you Nick?" The* ARAB *shakes his head.
He stands at the bar, waiting. He waits very busily.]*

HARRY (*as* NICK *returns*). You Nick?

NICK (*very loudly*). I am Nick.

HARRY (*acting*). Can you use a great comedian?

NICK (*behind the bar*). Who, for instance?

HARRY (*almost angry*). Me.

NICK. You? What's funny about you?

> *[*DUDLEY, *at the telephone, is dialing. Because of
> some defect in the apparatus the dialing is very loud.]*

DUDLEY. Hello. Sunset 7349? May I speak to Miss Elsie Mandelspiegel?
(*Pause.*)

HARRY (*with spirit and noise, dancing*). I dance and do gags and stuff.

NICK. In costume? Or are you wearing your costume?

DUDLEY. All I need is a cigar.

KITTY (*continuing the dream of grace*). I'd walk out of the house,
and stand on the porch, and look at the trees, and smell the flowers,

and run across the lawn, and lie down under a tree, and read a
book. (*Pause.*) A book of poems, maybe.

DUDLEY (*very, very clearly*). Elsie Mandelspiegel. (*Impatiently.*) She
has a room on the fourth floor. She's a nurse at the Southern Pacific
Hospital. Elsie Mandelspiegel. She works at night. Elsie. Yes.

> [*He begins waiting again.* WESLEY, *a colored boy,*
> *comes to the bar and stands near* HARRY, *waiting.*]

NICK. Beer?

WESLEY. No, sir. I'd like to talk to you.

NICK (*to* HARRY). All right. Get funny.

HARRY (*getting funny, an altogether different person, an actor with
great energy, both in power of voice, and in force and speed of
physical gesture*). Now I'm standing on the corner of Third and
Market. I'm looking around. I'm figuring it out. There it is. Right
in front of me. The whole city. The whole world. People going by.
They're going somewhere. I don't know where, but they're going.
I ain't going *anywhere*. Where the hell can you go? I'm figuring
it out. All right, I'm a citizen. A fat guy bumps his stomach into
the face of an old lady. They were in a hurry. Fat and old. *They
bumped.* Boom. I don't know. It may mean war. *War.* Germany.
England. Russia. I don't know for sure. (*Loudly, dramatically, he
salutes, about-faces, presents arms, aims, and fires.*) WAAAAAR.

> [*He blows a call to arms.* NICK *gets sick of this, in-*
> *dicates with a gesture that* HARRY *should hold it,*
> *and goes to* WESLEY.]

NICK. What's on your mind?

WESLEY (*confused*). Well——

NICK. Come on. Speak up. Are you hungry, or what?

WESLEY. Honest to God, I ain't hungry. All I want is a job. I don't
want no charity.

NICK. Well, what can you do, and how good are you?

WESLEY. I can run errands, clean up, wash dishes, anything.

DUDLEY (*on the telephone, very eagerly*). Elsie? Elsie, this is Dudley.
Elsie, I'll jump in the bay if you don't marry me. Life isn't worth
living without you. I can't sleep. I can't think of anything but you.
All the time. Day and night and night and day. Elsie, I love you. I
love you. What? (*Burning up.*) Is this Sunset 7-3-4-9? (*Pause.*)
7943? (*Calmly, while* WILLIE *begins making a small racket.*) Well,
what's *your* name? *Lorene?* Lorene Smith? I thought you were
Elsie Mandelspiegel. What? Dudley. Yeah. Dudley R. Bostwick.
Yeah. R. It stands for Raoul, but I never spell it out. I'm pleased
to meet *you*, too. What? There's a lot of noise around here. (WILLIE
stops hitting the marble game.) Where am I? At Nick's, on Pacific
Street. I work at the S. P. I told them I was sick and they gave me

the afternoon off. Wait a minute. I'll ask them. I'd like to meet *you*, too. Sure. I'll ask them. (*Turns around to* NICK.) What's this address?

NICK. Number 3 Pacific Street, you cad.

DUDLEY. Cad? You don't know how I've been suffering on account of Elsie. I take things too ceremoniously. I've got to be more lackadaisical. (*Into telephone.*) Hello, Elenore? I mean Lorene. It's Number 3 Pacific Street. Yeah. Sure. I'll wait for you. How'll you know me? You'll *know* me. I'll recognize *you*. Good-by, now. (*He hangs up.*)

HARRY (*continuing his monologue, with gestures, movements, and so on*). I'm standing there. I didn't do anything to anybody. Why should *I* be a soldier? (*Sincerely, insanely.*) BOOOOOOOOOOM. *WAR!* O.K .War. *I* retreat. *I* hate war. *I* move to Sacramento.

NICK (*shouting*). All right, comedian. Lay off a minute.

HARRY (*brokenhearted, going to* WILLIE). Nobody's got a sense of humor any more. The world's dying for comedy like never before, but nobody knows how to *laugh*.

NICK (*to* WESLEY). Do you belong to the union?

WESLEY. What union?

NICK. For the love of Mike, where've you been? Don't you know you can't come into a place and ask for a job and get one and go to work, just like that. You've got to belong to one of the unions.

WESLEY. I didn't know. I got to have a job. Real soon.

NICK. Well, you've got to belong to a union.

WESLEY. I don't want any favors. All I want is a chance to earn a living.

NICK. Go on into the kitchen and tell Sam to give you some lunch.

WESLEY. Honest, I ain't hungry.

DUDLEY (*shouting*). What I've gone through for Elsie.

HARRY. I've got all kinds of funny ideas in my head to help make the world happy again.

NICK (*holding* WESLEY). No, he isn't hungry.

[WESLEY *almost faints from hunger.* NICK *catches him just in time. The* ARAB *and* NICK *go off with* WESLEY *into the kitchen.*]

HARRY (*to* WILLIE). See if you think this is funny. It's my own idea. I created this dance myself. It comes after the monologue.

[HARRY *begins to dance.* WILLIE *watches a moment, and then goes back to the game. It's a goofy dance, which* HARRY *does with great sorrow, but much energy.*]

DUDLEY. Elsie. Aw, gee, Elsie. What the hell do I want to see Lorene Smith for? Some girl I don't know.

[JOE *and* KITTY *have been drinking in silence. There
is no sound now except the soft-shoe shuffling of*
HARRY *the comedian.*]

JOE. What's the dream now, Kitty Duval?

KITTY (*dreaming the words and pictures*). I dream of home. Christ,
I always dream of home. I've no *home*. I've no place. But I always
dream of all of us together again. We had a farm in Ohio. There
was nothing good about it. It was always sad. There was always
trouble. But I always dream about it as if I could go back and
Papa would be there and Mamma and Louie and my little brother
Stephen and my sister Mary. I'm Polish. Duval! My name isn't
Duval, it's Koranovsky. Katerina Koranovsky. We lost everything.
The house, the farm, the trees, the horses, the cows, the chickens.
Papa died. He was old. He was thirteen years older than Mamma.
We moved to Chicago. We tried to work. We tried to stay together.
Louie got in trouble. The fellows he was with killed him for some-
thing. I don't know what. Stephen ran away from home. Seventeen
years old. I don't know where he is. Then Mamma died. (*Pause.*)
What's the dream? I dream of home.

[NICK *comes out of the kitchen with* WESLEY.]

NICK. Here. Sit down here and rest. That'll hold you for a *while*. Why
didn't you tell me you were hungry? You all right now?

WESLEY (*sitting down in the chair at the piano*). Yes, I am. Thank
you. I didn't know I was *that* hungry.

NICK. Fine. (*To* HARRY, *who is dancing.*) Hey. What the hell do you
think you're doing?

HARRY (*stopping*). That's my own idea. I'm a natural-born dancer and
comedian.

[WESLEY *begins slowly, one note, one chord, at a
time, to play the piano.*]

NICK. You're no good. Why don't you try some other kind of work?
Why don't you get a job in a store, selling something? What do
you want to be a comedian for?

HARRY. I've got something for the world and they haven't got sense
enough to let me give it to them. Nobody knows me.

DUDLEY. Elsie. Now I'm waiting for some dame I've never seen before.
Lorene Smith. Never saw her in my life. Just happened to get the
wrong number. She turns on the personality and I'm a cooked
Indian. Give me a beer, please.

HARRY. Nick, you've got to see my act. It's the greatest thing of its
kind in America. All I want is a chance. No salary to begin. Let
me try it out tonight. If I don't wow 'em, O.K., I'll go home. If
vaudeville wasn't dead, a guy like me would have a chance.

NICK. You're not funny. You're a sad young punk. What the hell do
you want to try to be funny for? You'll break everybody's heart.

What's there for you to be funny about? You've been poor all your life, haven't you?

HARRY. I've been poor all right, but don't forget that some things count more than some other things.

NICK. What counts more, for instance, than what else, for instance?

HARRY. Talent, for instance, counts more than money, for instance, that's what, and I've got talent. I get new ideas night and day. Everything comes natural to me. I've got style, but it'll take me a little time to round it out. That's all.

> [*By now* WESLEY *is playing something of his own which is very good and out of the world. He plays about half a minute, after which* HARRY *begins to dance.*]

NICK (*watching*). I run the lousiest dive in Frisco, and a guy arrives and makes me stock up with champagne. The streetwalkers come in and holler at me that they're ladies. Talent comes in and begs me for a chance to show itself. Even society people come here once in a while. I don't know what for. Maybe it's liquor. Maybe it's the location. Maybe it's my personality. Maybe it's the crazy personality of the joint. The old honky-tonk. (*Pause.*) Maybe they can't feel at home anywhere else.

> [*By now* WESLEY *is really playing, and* HARRY *is going through a new routine.* DUDLEY *grows sadder and sadder.*]

KITTY. Please dance with me.

JOE (*loudly*). I never learned to dance.

KITTY. Anybody can dance. Just hold me in your arms.

JOE. I'm very fond of you. I'm *sorry*. I *can't* dance. I wish to God I could.

KITTY. Oh, please.

JOE. Forgive me. I'd like to very much.

> [KITTY *dances alone.* TOM *comes in with a package. He sees* KITTY *and goes gaga again. He comes out of the trance and puts the bundle on the table in front of* JOE.]

JOE (*taking the package*). What'd you get?

TOM. Two dollars' worth of toys. That's what you sent me for. The girl asked me what I wanted with toys. I didn't know what to tell her. (*He stares at* KITTY, *then back at* JOE.) Joe? I've got to have some money. After all you've done for me, I'll do anything in the world for you, but, Joe, you got to give me some money once in a while.

JOE. What do you want it for?

> [TOM *turns and stares at* KITTY *dancing.*]

JOE (*noticing*). Sure. Here. Here's five. (*Shouting.*) Can you dance?

TOM (*proudly*). I got second prize at the Palomar in Sacramento five years ago.

JOE (*loudly, opening the package*). O.K., dance with her.

TOM. You mean *her?*

JOE (*loudly*). I mean Kitty Duval, the burlesque queen. I mean the queen of the world burlesque. Dance with her. She wants to dance.

TOM (*worshipping the name Kitty Duval, helplessly*). Joe, can I tell you something?

JOE (*he brings out a toy and winds it*). You don't have to. I know. You love her. You *really* love her. I'm not blind. I know. But take care of yourself. Don't get sick that way again.

NICK (*looking at and listening to* WESLEY *with amazement*). Comes in here and wants to be a dishwasher. Faints from hunger. And then sits down and plays better than Heifetz.

JOE. Heifetz plays the violin.

NICK. All right, don't get careful. He's good, ain't he?

TOM (*to* KITTY). Kitty.

JOE (*he lets the toy go, loudly*). Don't *talk*. Just *dance*.

> [TOM *and* KITTY *dance.* NICK *is at the bar, watching everything.* HARRY *is dancing.* DUDLEY *is grieving into his beer.* LORENE SMITH, *about thirty-seven, very overbearing and funny-looking, comes to the bar.*]

NICK. What'll it be, lady?

LORENE (*looking about and scaring all the young men*). I'm looking for the young man I talked to on the telephone. Dudley R. Bostwick.

DUDLEY (*jumping, running to her, stopping, shocked*). Dudley R. (*Slowly.*) Bostwick? Oh yeah. He left here ten minutes ago. You mean Dudley Bostwick, that poor man on crutches?

LORENE. Crutches?

DUDLEY. Yeah. Dudley Bostwick. That's what he *said* his name was. He said to tell you not to wait.

LORENE. Well. (*She begins to go, turns around.*) Are you sure *you're* not Dudley Bostwick?

DUDLEY. Who—me? (*Grandly.*) My name is Roger Tenefrancia. I'm a French Canadian. I never saw the poor fellow before.

LORENE. It seems to me your voice is like the voice I heard over the telephone.

DUDLEY. A coincidence. An accident. A quirk of fate. One of those things. Dismiss the thought. That poor cripple hobbled out of here ten minutes ago.

LORENE. He said he was going to commit suicide. I only wanted to be of help. (*She goes.*)

DUDLEY. Be of help? What kind of help could she be of? (DUDLEY *runs to the telephone in the corner.*) Gee whiz, Elsie. Gee whiz.

I'll never leave you again. (*He turns the pages of a little address book.*) Why do I always forget the number? I've tried to get her on the phone a hundred times this week and I still forget the number. She won't come to the phone, but I keep trying anyway. She's out. She's not in. She's working. I get the wrong number. Everything goes haywire. I can't sleep. (*Defiantly.*) She'll come to the phone one of these days. If there's anything to true love at all, she'll come to the phone. Sunset 7349.

> [*He dials the number as* JOE *goes on studying the
> toys. They are one big mechanical toy, whistles, and
> a music box.* JOE *blows into the whistles, quickly,
> by way of getting casually acquainted with them.*
> TOM *and* KITTY *stop dancing.* TOM *stares at her.*]

DUDLEY. Hello. Is this Sunset 7349? May I speak to Elsie? Yes. (*Emphatically, and bitterly.*) No, this is *not* Dudley Bostwick. This is Roger Tenefrancia of Montreal, Canada. I'm a childhood friend of Miss Mandelspiegel. We went to kindergarten together. (*His hand over the phone.*) God damn it. (*Into the phone.*) Yes. I'll wait, thank you.

TOM. I love you.

> [TOM *embraces her. They go.* JOE *watches. Goes
> back to the toy.*]

JOE. Where's that longshoreman, McCarthy?

NICK. He'll be around.

JOE. What do you think he'll have to say today?

NICK. Plenty, as usual. I'm going next door to see who won that third race at Laurel.

JOE. Precious Time won it.

NICK. That's what you think. (*He goes.*)

JOE (*to himself*). A horse named McCarthy is running in the sixth race today.

DUDLEY (*on the phone*). Hello. Hello, Elsie? Elsie? (*His voice weakens, also his limbs.*) My God. She's come to the phone. Elsie, I'm at Nick's on Pacific Street. You've got to come here and talk to me. Hello. Hello, Elsie? (*Amazed.*) Did she hang up? Or was I disconnected? (*He hangs up and goes to the bar.*)

> [WESLEY *is still playing the piano.* HARRY *is still
> dancing.* JOE *has wound up the big mechanical toy
> and is watching it work.* NICK *returns.*]

NICK (*watching the toy*). Say. That's some gadget.

JOE. How much did I win?

NICK. How do you know you *won?*

JOE. Don't be silly. He said Precious Time was going to win by ten lengths, didn't he? He's in love, isn't he?

NICK. O.K. I don't know why, but Precious Time won. You got eighty
for ten. How do you do it?

JOE (*roaring*). Faith. Faith. How'd he win?

NICK. By a nose. Look him up in *The Racing Form*. The slowest, the
cheapest, the worst horse in the race, and the worst jockey. What's
the matter with my luck?

JOE. How much did you lose?

NICK. Fifty cents.

JOE. You should never gamble.

NICK. Why not?

JOE. You always bet fifty cents. You've got no more faith than a flea,
that's why.

HARRY (*shouting*). How do you like this, Nick? (*He is really busy
now, all legs and arms.*)

NICK (*turning and watching*). Not bad. Hang around. You can wait
table. (*To* WESLEY.) Hey. Wesley. Can you play that again tonight?

WESLEY (*turning, but still playing the piano*). I don't know for sure,
Mr. Nick. I can play *something*.

NICK. Good. *You* hang around, too. (*He goes behind the bar.*)

> [*The atmosphere is now one of warm, natural, Amer-
> ican ease; every man innocent and good; each doing
> what he believes he should do, or what he must do.
> There is deep American naïveté and faith in the be-
> havior of each person. No one is competing with
> anyone else. No one hates anyone else. Every man is
> living, and letting live. Each man is following his
> destiny as he feels it should be followed; or is aban-
> doning it as he feels it must, by now, be abandoned;
> or is forgetting it for the moment as he feels he should
> forget it. Although everyone is dead serious, there is
> unmistakable smiling and humor in the scene; a sense
> of the human body and spirit emerging from the
> world-imposed state of stress and fretfulness, fear and
> awkwardness, to the more natural state of casualness
> and grace. Each person belongs to the environment,
> in his own person, as himself:* WESLEY *is playing bet-
> ter than ever.* HARRY *is hoofing better than ever.* NICK
> is behind the bar shining glasses.* JOE *is smiling at the
> toy and studying it.* DUDLEY, *although still troubled,
> is at least calm now and full of melancholy poise.*
> WILLIE, *at the marble game, is happy. The* ARAB *is
> deep in his memories, where he wants to be.*

> [*Into this scene and atmosphere comes* BLICK.
> BLICK *is the sort of human being you dislike at sight.
> He is no different from anybody else physically. His*

*face is an ordinary face. There is nothing obviously
wrong with him, and yet you know that it is impossible, even by the most generous expansion of understanding, to accept him as a human being. He is the
strong man without strength—strong only among the
weak—the weakling who uses force on the weaker.*
BLICK *enters casually, as if he were a customer, and
immediately* HARRY *begins slowing down.*]

BLICK (*oily, and with mock friendliness*). Hello, Nick.

NICK (*stopping his work and leaning across the bar*). What do you
want to come here for? You're too big a man for a little honky-tonk.

BLICK (*flattered*). Now, Nick.

NICK. Important people never come here. *Here.* Have a drink. (*Whisky
bottle.*)

BLICK. Thanks, I don't drink.

NICK (*drinking the drink himself*). Well, why don't you?

BLICK. I have responsibilities.

NICK. You're head of the lousy Vice Squad. There's no vice here.

BLICK (*sharply*). Streetwalkers are working out of this place.

NICK (*angry*). What do you want?

BLICK (*loudly*). I just want you to know that it's got to *stop.*

[*The music stops. The mechanical toy runs down.
There is absolute silence, and a strange fearfulness
and disharmony in the atmosphere now.* HARRY
doesn't know what to do with his hands or feet. WES-
LEY'S *arms hang at his sides.* JOE *quietly pushes the
toy to one side of the table, eager to study what is
happening.* WILLIE *stops playing the marble game,
turns around, and begins to wait.* DUDLEY *straightens
up very, very vigorously, as if to say: "Nothing can
scare me. I know love is the only thing." The* ARAB *is
the same as ever, but watchful.* NICK *is arrogantly
aloof. There is a moment of this silence and tension,
as though* BLICK *were waiting for everybody to acknowledge his presence. He is obviously flattered by
the acknowledgment of* HARRY, DUDLEY, WESLEY,
and WILLIE, *but a little irritated by* NICK'S *aloofness
and unfriendliness.*]

NICK. Don't look at me. I can't tell a streetwalker from a lady. You
married?

BLICK. You're not asking *me* questions. *I'm* telling *you.*

NICK (*interrupting*). You're a man of about forty-five or so. You
ought to know better.

BLICK (*angry*). Streetwalkers are working out of this place.

NICK (*beginning to shout*). Now don't start any trouble with me. People come here to drink and loaf around. I don't care who they are.

BLICK. Well, I do. Any more of it, and I'll have your joint closed.

NICK (*very casually, without ill will*). Listen. I've got no use for you, or anybody like you. You're out to change the world from something bad to something worse. Something like yourself.

BLICK (*furious pause, and contempt*). I'll be back tonight. (*He begins to go.*)

NICK (*very angry but very calm*). Do yourself a big favor and don't come back tonight. Send somebody else. I don't like your personality

BLICK (*casually, but with contempt*). Don't break any laws. I don't like yours, either. (*He looks the place over, and goes.*)

> [*There is a moment of silence. Then* WILLIE *turns and puts a new nickel in the slot and starts a new game.* WESLEY *turns to the piano and rather falteringly begins to play. His heart really isn't in it.* HARRY *walks about, unable to dance.* DUDLEY *lapses into his customary melancholy, at a table.* NICK *whistles a little, suddenly stops.* JOE *winds the toy.*]

JOE (*comically*). Nick. You going to kill that man?

NICK. I'm disgusted.

JOE. Yeah? Why?

NICK. Why should I get worked up over a guy like that? Why should I hate *him*. He's nothing. He's nobody. He's a mouse. But every time he comes into this place I get burned up. He doesn't want to drink. He doesn't want to sit down. He doesn't want to take things easy. Tell me one thing?

JOE. Do my best.

NICK. What's a punk like *that* want to go out and try to change the world for?

JOE (*amazed*). Does *he* want to change the world, too?

NICK (*irritated*). You know what I mean. What's he want to bother people for? He's *sick*.

JOE (*almost to himself, reflecting on the fact that* BLICK *too wants to change the world*). I guess he wants to change the world at that.

NICK. So I go to work and hate him.

JOE. It's not him, Nick. It's everything.

NICK. Yeah, I *know*. But I've still got no use for him. He's no good. You know what I mean? He hurts little people. (*Confused.*) One of the girls tried to commit suicide on account of him. (*Furiously.*) I'll break his head if he hurts anybody around here. This is *my* joint. (*Afterthought.*) Or anybody's *feelings*, either.

JOE. He may not be so bad, deep down underneath.

NICK. I know all about him. He's no good.

> [*During this talk* WESLEY *has really begun to play the piano, the toy is rattling again, and little by little*

HARRY *has begun to dance.* NICK *has come around the
bar, and now, very much like a child—forgetting all
his anger—is watching the toy work. He begins to
smile at everything: turns and listens to* WESLEY;
watches HARRY; *nods at the* ARAB; *shakes his head at*
DUDLEY; *and gestures amiably about* WILLIE. *It's his
joint all right. It's a good, low-down, honky-tonk
American place that lets people alone.*]

NICK. I've got a good joint. There's nothing wrong here. Hey. Comedian. Stick to the dancing tonight. I think you're O.K. Wesley? Do
some more of that tonight. That's fine!

HARRY. Thanks, Nick. Gosh, I'm on my way at last. (*On the telephone.*) Hello, Ma? Is that you, Ma? Harry. I got the job. (*He
hangs up and walks around, smiling.*)

NICK (*watching the toy all this time*). Say, that really is something.
What is that, anyway?

[MARY L. *comes in.*]

JOE (*holding it toward* NICK, *and* MARY L.). Nick, this is a toy. A con-
traption devised by the cunning of man to drive boredom, or grief,
or anger out of children. A noble gadget. A gadget, I might say, infinitely nobler than any other I can think of at the moment. (*Everybody gathers around* JOE'S *table to look at the toy. The toy stops
working.* JOE *winds the music box. Lifts a whistle, blows it, making
a very strange, funny and sorrowful sound.*) Delightful. Tragic, but
delightful.

[WESLEY *plays the music-box theme on the piano.*
MARY L. *takes a table.*]

NICK. Joe. That girl, Kitty. What's she mean, calling me a dentist? I
wouldn't hurt anybody, let alone a tooth.

[NICK *goes to* MARY L.'s *table.* HARRY *imitates the toy.
Dances. The piano music comes up, the light dims
slowly, while the piano solo continues.*]

ACT II

⌗ Scene: *An hour later. All the people who were at Nick's when the curtain came down are still there.* JOE *at his table, quietly shuffling and turning a deck of cards, and at the same time watching the face of the woman, and looking at the initials on her handbag, as though they were the symbols of the lost glory of the world. The woman, in turn, very casually regards* JOE *occasionally. Or rather senses him; has sensed him in fact the whole hour. She is mildly tight on beer, and* JOE *himself is tight, but as always completely under control, simply sharper. The others are about, at tables, and so on.*

JOE. Is it Madge—Laubowitz?

MARY. Is what *what?*

JOE. Is the name Mabel Lepescu?

MARY. What name?

JOE. The name the initials M. L. stand for. The initials on your bag.

MARY. No.

JOE (*after a long pause, thinking deeply what the name might be, turning a card, looking into the beautiful face of the woman*). Margie Longworthy?

MARY (*all this is very natural and sincere, no comedy on the part of the people involved: they are both solemn, being drunk*). No.

JOE (*his voice higher-pitched, as though he were growing a little alarmed*). Midge Laurie? (MARY *shakes her head.*) My initials are J. T.

MARY (*pause*). John?

JOE. No. (*Pause.*) Martha Lancaster?

MARY. No. (*Slight pause.*) Joseph?

JOE. Well, not exactly. That's my first name, but everybody calls me

Joe. The last name is the tough one. I'll help you a little. I'm Irish. (*Pause.*) Is it just plain Mary?

MARY. Yes, it is. I'm Irish, too. At least on my father's side. English on my mother's side.

JOE. I'm Irish on both sides. Mary's one of my favorite names. I guess that's why I didn't think of it. I met a girl in Mexico City named Mary once. She was an American from Philadelphia. She got married there. In Mexico City, I mean. While I was *there*. We were in love, too. At least *I* was. You never know about anyone else. They were engaged, you see, and her mother was with her, so they went through with it. Must have been six or seven years ago. She's probably got three or four children by this time.

MARY. Are you still in love with her?

JOE. Well—no. To tell you the truth, I'm not sure. I guess I am. I didn't even know she was engaged until a couple of days before they got married. I thought *I* was going to marry her. I kept thinking all the time about the kind of kids we would be likely to have. My favorite was the third one. The first two were fine. Handsome and fine and intelligent, but that third one was different. Dumb and goofy-looking. I liked *him* a lot. When she told me she was going to be married, I didn't feel so bad about the first two, it was that dumb one.

MARY (*after a pause of some few seconds*). What do you do?

JOE. Do? To tell you the truth, nothing.

MARY. Do you always drink a great deal?

JOE (*scientifically*). Not *always*. Only when I'm awake. I sleep seven or eight hours every night, you know.

MARY. How nice. I mean to drink when you're awake.

JOE (*thoughtfully*). It's a privilege.

MARY. Do you really *like* to drink?

JOE (*positively*). As much as I like to *breathe*.

MARY (*beautifully*). Why?

JOE (*dramatically*). Why do I like to drink? (*Pause.*) Because I don't like to be gypped. Because I don't like to be dead most of the time and just a little alive every once in a long while. (*Pause.*) If I don't drink, I become fascinated by unimportant things—like everybody else. I get busy. Do things. All kinds of little stupid things, for all kinds of little stupid reasons. Proud, selfish, *ordinary* things. I've done them. Now I don't do anything. *I live all the time.* Then I go to sleep. (*Pause.*)

MARY. Do you sleep well?

JOE (*taking it for granted*). Of course.

MARY (*quietly, almost with tenderness*). What are your plans?

JOE (*loudly, but also tenderly*). Plans? I haven't *got* any. *I just get up.*

MARY (*beginning to understand everything*). Oh yes. Yes, of course.

[DUDLEY *puts a nickel in the phonograph.*]

JOE (*thoughtfully*). Why do I drink? (*Pause, while he thinks about it. The thinking appears to be profound and complex, and has the effect of giving his face a very comical and naïve expression.*) That question calls for a pretty complicated answer. (*He smiles abstractly.*)

MARY. Oh, I didn't mean——

JOE (*swiftly, gallantly*). No. No. I *insist.* I *know* why. It's just a matter of finding words. Little ones.

MARY. It really doesn't matter.

JOE (*seriously*). Oh yes it does. (*Clinically.*) Now, why do I drink? (*Scientifically.*) No. Why does *anybody* drink? (*Working it out.*) Every day has twenty-four hours.

MARY (*sadly, but brightly*). Yes, that's true.

JOE. Twenty-four hours. Out of the twenty-four hours at *least* twenty-three and a half are—my God, I don't know why—dull, dead, boring, empty, and murderous. Minutes on the clock, *not time of living.* It doesn't make any difference who you are or what you do, twenty-three and a half hours of the twenty-four are spent *waiting.*

MARY. Waiting?

JOE (*gesturing, loudly*). And the more you wait, the less there is to wait *for.*

MARY (*attentively, beautifully his student*). Oh?

JOE (*continuing*). That goes on for days and days, and weeks and months and years and years, and the first thing you know *all* the years are dead. All the minutes are dead. You yourself are dead. There's nothing to wait for any more. Nothing except *minutes* on the *clock.* No time of life. Nothing but minutes, and idiocy. Beautiful, bright, intelligent idiocy. (*Pause.*) Does that answer your question?

MARY (*earnestly*). I'm afraid it does. Thank you. You shouldn't have gone to all the trouble.

JOE. No trouble at all. (*Pause.*) You have children?

MARY. Yes. Two. A son and a daughter.

JOE (*delighted*). How swell. Do they look like you?

MARY. Yes.

JOE. Then why are you sad?

MARY. I was always sad. It's just that after I was married I was allowed to drink.

JOE (*eagerly*). Who are you waiting for?

MARY. No one.

JOE (*smiling*). I'm not waiting for anybody, either.

MARY. My husband, of course.

JOE. Oh, sure.

MARY. He's a lawyer.

JOE (*standing, leaning on the table*). He's a great guy. I like him. I'm very fond of him.

MARY (*listening*). You have responsibilities?

JOE (*loudly*). *One*, and *thousands*. As a matter of fact, I feel responsible to everybody. At least to everybody I meet. I've been trying for three years to find out if it's possible to live what I think is a civilized life. I mean a life that can't hurt any other life.

MARY. You're famous?

JOE. Very. Utterly unknown, but very famous. Would you like to dance?

MARY. All right.

JOE (*loudly*). I'm sorry. I don't dance. I didn't think you'd like to.

MARY. To tell you the truth, I don't like to dance at all.

JOE (*proudly. Commentator*). I can hardly walk.

MARY. You mean you're tight?

JOE (*smiling*). *No.* I mean *all* the time.

MARY (*looking at him closely*). Were you ever in Paris?

JOE. In 1929, and again in 1934.

MARY. What month of 1934?

JOE. Most of April, all of May, and a little of June.

MARY. I was there in November and December that year.

JOE. We were there almost at the same time. You were married?

MARY. Engaged. (*They are silent a moment, looking at one another. Quietly and with great charm.*) Are you *really* in love with me?

JOE. Yes.

MARY. Is it the champagne?

JOE. Yes. Partly, at least. (*He sits down.*)

MARY. If you don't see me again, will you be very unhappy?

JOE. Very.

MARY (*getting up*). I'm so pleased. (*JOE is deeply grieved that she is going. In fact, he is almost panic-stricken about it, getting up in a way that is full of furious sorrow and regret.*) I must go now. Please don't get up. (*JOE is up, staring at her with amazement.*) Good-by.

JOE (*simply*). Good-by.

> [*The woman stands looking at him a moment, then turns and goes.* JOE *stands staring after her for a long time. Just as he is slowly sitting down again, the* NEWSBOY *enters, and goes to* JOE'S *table.*]

NEWSBOY. Paper, mister?

JOE. How many you got this time?

NEWSBOY. Eleven.

> [JOE *buys them all, looks at the lousy headlines, throws them away. The* NEWSBOY *looks at* JOE, *amazed. He walks over to* NICK *at the bar.*]

NEWSBOY (*troubled*). Hey, mister, do you own this place?

NICK (*casually but emphatically*). I own this place.

NEWSBOY. Can you use a great lyric tenor?

NICK (*almost to himself*). Great lyric tenor? (*Loudly.*) Who?

NEWSBOY (*loud and the least bit angry*). Me. I'm getting too big to sell papers. I don't want to holler headlines all the time. I want to *sing*. You can use a great lyric tenor, can't you?

NICK. What's lyric about you?

NEWSBOY (*voice high-pitched, confused*). My voice.

NICK. Oh. (*Slight pause, giving in.*) All right, then—sing!

> [*The* NEWSBOY *breaks into swift and beautiful song:*
> "*When Irish Eyes Are Smiling.*" NICK *and* JOE *listen*
> *carefully,* NICK *with wonder,* JOE *with amazement*
> *and delight.*]

NEWSBOY (*singing*).

> When Irish eyes are smiling,
> Sure 'tis like a morn in spring.
> In the lilt of Irish laughter,
> You can hear the angels sing.
> When Irish hearts are happy,
> All the world seems bright and gay.
> But when Irish eyes are smiling——

NICK (*loudly, swiftly*). Are you Irish?

NEWSBOY (*speaking swiftly, loudly, a little impatient with the irrelevant question*). No. I'm Greek. (*He finishes the song, singing louder than ever.*)

> Sure they steal your heart away.

> [*He turns to* NICK *dramatically, like a vaudeville*
> *singer begging his audience for applause.* NICK *studies*
> *the boy eagerly.* JOE *gets to his feet, and leans toward*
> *the boy and* NICK.]

NICK. Not bad. Let me hear you again about a year from now.

NEWSBOY (*thrilled*). Honest?

NICK. Yeah. Along about November seventh, 1940.

NEWSBOY (*happier than ever before in his life, running over to* JOE). Did you hear it too, mister?

JOE. Yes, and it's great. What part of Greece?

NEWSBOY. Salonica. Gosh, mister. Thanks.

JOE. Don't wait a year. Come back with some papers a little later. You're a great singer.

NEWSBOY (*thrilled and excited*). Aw, thanks, mister. So long. (*Running, to* NICK.) Thanks, mister.

> [*He runs out.* JOE *and* NICK *look at the swinging*
> *doors.* JOE *sits down.* NICK *laughs.*]

NICK. Joe, people are so wonderful. Look at that kid.

JOE. Of course they're wonderful. Every one of them is wonderful.

[MC CARTHY *and* KRUPP *come in, talking.* MC CARTHY
*is a big man in work clothes, which make him seem
very young. He is wearing black jeans, and a blue
workman's shirt. No tie. No hat. He has broad
shoulders, a lean intelligent face, thick black hair. In
his right back pocket is the longshoreman's hook. His
arms are long and hairy. His sleeves are rolled up to
just below his elbows. He is a casual man, easy-going
in movement, sharp in perception, swift in appreciation of charm or innocence or comedy, and gentle in
spirit. His speech is clear and full of warmth. His
voice is powerful, but modulated. He enjoys the
world, in spite of the mess it is, and he is fond of
people, in spite of the mess they are.* KRUPP *is not
quite as tall or broad-shouldered as* MC CARTHY. *He
is physically encumbered by his uniform, club, pistol,
belt, and cap. And he is plainly not at home in the
role of policeman. His movement is stiff and unin-
tentionally pompous. He is a naïve man, essentially
good. His understanding is less than* MC CARTHY'S, *but
he is honest and he doesn't try to bluff.*]

KRUPP. You don't understand what I mean. Hi-ya, Joe.

JOE. Hello, Krupp.

MC CARTHY. Hi-ya, Joe.

JOE. Hello, McCarthy.

KRUPP. Two beers, Nick. (*To* MC CARTHY.) All I do is carry out orders,
carry out orders. I don't know what the idea is behind the order.
Who it's for, or who it's against, or why. All I do is carry it out.

[NICK *gives them beer.*]

MC CARTHY. You don't read enough.

KRUPP. I do read. I read the *Examiner* every morning. The *Call-Bulletin*
every night.

MC CARTHY. And carry out orders. What are the orders now?

KRUPP. To keep the peace down here on the water front.

MC CARTHY. Keep it for who? (*To* JOE.) Right?

JOE (*sorrowfully*). Right.

KRUPP. How do I know for who? The peace. Just keep it.

MC CARTHY. It's got to be kept for somebody. Who would you suspect
it's kept for?

KRUPP. For citizens!

MC CARTHY. I'm a citizen!

KRUPP. All right, I'm keeping it for you.

MC CARTHY. By hitting me over the head with a club? (*To* JOE.) Right?

JOE (*meiancholy, with remembrance*). I don't know.

KRUPP. Mac, you know I never hit you over the head with a club.

MC CARTHY. But you will if you're on duty at the time and happen to stand on the opposite side of myself, on duty.

KRUPP. We went to Mission High together. We were always good friends. The only time we ever fought was that time over Alma Haggerty. Did *you* marry Alma Haggerty? (*To* JOE.) Right?

JOE. Everything's right.

MC CARTHY. No. Did you? (*To* JOE.) Joe, are you with me or against me?

JOE. I'm with everybody. One at a time.

KRUPP. No. And that's just what I mean.

MC CARTHY. You mean neither one of us is going to marry the thing we're fighting for?

KRUPP. *I don't even know what it is.*

MC CARTHY. You don't read enough, I tell you.

KRUPP. Mac, you don't know what you're fighting for, either.

MC CARTHY. It's so simple it's fantastic.

KRUPP. All right, what are you fighting for?

MC CARTHY. For the rights of the inferior. Right?

JOE. Something like that.

KRUPP. The who?

MC CARTHY. The inferior. The world full of Mahoneys who haven't got what it takes to make monkeys out of everybody else, near by. The men who were created equal. Remember?

KRUPP. Mac, you're not inferior.

MC CARTHY. I'm a longshoreman. And an idealist. I'm a man with too much brawn to be an intellectual, exclusively. I married a small, sensitive, cultured woman so that my kids would be sissies instead of suckers. A strong man with any sensibility has no choice in this world but to be a heel, or a *worker*. I haven't the heart to be a heel, so I'm a worker. I've got a son in high school who's already thinking of being a writer.

KRUPP. I wanted to be a writer once.

JOE. Wonderful. (*He puts down the paper, looks at* KRUPP *and* MC-CARTHY.)

MC CARTHY. They *all* wanted to be writers. Every maniac in the world that ever brought about the murder of people through war started out in an attic or a basement writing poetry. It stank. So they got even by becoming important heels. And it's still going on.

KRUPP. Is it really, Joe?

JOE. Look at today's paper.

MC CARTHY. Right now on Telegraph Hill is some punk who is trying to be Shakespeare. Ten years from now he'll be a Senator. Or a communist.

KRUPP. Somebody ought to do something about it.

MC CARTHY (*mischievously, with laughter in his voice*). The thing to do is to have more magazines. Hundreds of them. *Thousands.* Print everything they write, so they'll believe they're immortal. That way keep them from going haywire.

KRUPP. Mac, you ought to be a writer yourself.

MC CARTHY. I hate the tribe. They're mischief-makers. Right?

JOE (*swiftly*). Everything's right. Right and wrong.

KRUPP. Then why do you read?

MC CARTHY (*laughing*). It's relaxing. It's soothing. (*Pause.*) The lousiest people born into the world are writers. Language is all right. It's the people who use language that are lousy. (*The* ARAB *has moved a little closer, and is listening carefully. To the* ARAB.) What do you think, brother?

ARAB (*after making many faces, thinking very deeply*). No foundation. All the way down the line. What. What-not. Nothing. I go walk and look at sky. (*He goes.*)

KRUPP. What? What-not? (*To* JOE.) What's that mean?

JOE (*slowly, thinking, remembering*). What? What-not? That means this side, that side. Inhale, exhale. What: birth. What-not: death. The inevitable, the astounding, the magnificent seed of growth and decay in all things. Beginning, and end. That man, in his own way, is a prophet. He is one who, with the help of *beer,* is able to reach that state of deep understanding in which what and what-not, the reasonable and the unreasonable, are *one.*

MC CARTHY. Right.

KRUPP. If you can understand that kind of talk, how can you be a long-shoreman?

MC CARTHY. I come from a long line of McCarthys who never married or slept with anything but the most powerful and quarrelsome flesh. (*He drinks beer.*)

KRUPP. I could listen to you two guys for hours, but I'll be damned if I know what the hell you're talking about.

MC CARTHY. The consequence is that all the McCarthys are too great and too strong to be heroes. Only the weak and unsure perform the heroic. They've *got* to. The more heroes you have, the worse the history of the world becomes. Right?

JOE. Go outside and look at it.

KRUPP. You sure can philos—philosoph—— Boy, you can talk.

MC CARTHY. I wouldn't talk this way to anyone but a man in uniform, and a man who couldn't understand a word of what I was saying. The party I'm speaking of, my friend, is *YOU.*

[*The phone rings.* HARRY *gets up from his table suddenly and begins a new dance.*]

KRUPP (*noticing him, with great authority*). Here. Here. What do you think you're doing?

HARRY (*stopping*). I just got an idea for a new dance. I'm trying it out. Nick. Nick, the phone's ringing.

KRUPP (*to* MC CARTHY). Has he got a right to do that?

MC CARTHY. The living have danced from the beginning of time. I might even say the dance and the life have moved along together, until now we have—— (*To* HARRY.) Go into your dance, son, and show us what we have.

HARRY. I haven't got it worked out *completely* yet, but it starts out like this. (*He dances.*)

NICK (*on the phone*). Nick's Pacific Street Restaurant, Saloon, and Entertainment Palace. Good afternoon. Nick speaking. (*Listens.*) Who? (*Turns around.*) Is there a Dudley Bostwick in the joint?

> [DUDLEY *jumps to his feet and goes to the phone.*]

DUDLEY (*on the phone*). Hello. Elsie? (*Listens.*) You're coming down? (*Elated. To the saloon.*) She's coming down. (*Pause.*) No. I won't drink. Aw, gosh, Elsie.

> [*He hangs up, looks about him strangely, as if he were just born, walks around touching things, putting chairs in place, and so on.*]

MC CARTHY (*to* HARRY). Splendid. Splendid.

HARRY. Then I go into this little routine. (*He demonstrates.*)

KRUPP. Is that good, Mac?

MC CARTHY. It's awful, but it's honest and ambitious, like everything else in this great country.

HARRY. Then I work along into this. (*He demonstrates.*) And *this* is where I *really* get going. (*He finishes the dance.*)

MC CARTHY. Excellent. A most satisfying demonstration of the present state of the American body and soul. Son, you're a genius.

HARRY (*delighted, shaking hands with* MC CARTHY). I go on in front of an audience for the first time in my life tonight.

MC CARTHY. They'll be delighted. Where'd you learn to dance?

HARRY. Never took a lesson in my life. I'm a natural-born dancer. And *comedian*, too.

MC CARTHY (*astounded*). You can make people *laugh*?

HARRY (*dumbly*). I can be funny, but they won't laugh.

MC CARTHY. That's odd. Why not?

HARRY. I don't know. They just won't laugh.

MC CARTHY. Would you care to be funny now?

HARRY. I'd like to try out a new monologue I've been thinking about.

MC CARTHY. Please do. I promise you if it's funny I shall *roar* with laughter.

HARRY. This is it. (*Goes into the act, with much energy.*) I'm up at Sharkey's on Turk Street. It's a quarter to nine, daylight-saving. Wednesday, the eleventh. What I've got is a headache and a 1918 nickel. What I *want* is a cup of coffee. If I buy a cup of coffee with

the nickel, I've got to walk home. I've got an eight-ball problem.
George the Greek is shooting a game of snooker with Pedro the
Filipino. I'm in rags. They're wearing thirty-five dollar suits, made to
order. I haven't got a cigarette. They're smoking Bobby Burns
panatelas. I'm thinking it over, like I always do. George the Greek is
in a tough spot. If I buy a cup of coffee, I'll want another cup. What
happens? My *ear* aches! My ear. George the Greek takes the cue.
Chalks it. Studies the table. Touches the cue ball delicately. Tick.
What happens? He makes the three-ball! What do I do? I get confused. *I go out and buy a morning paper.* What the hell do I want
with a morning paper? What I *want* is a cup of coffee, and a good
used car. I go out and buy a morning paper. Thursday, the twelfth.
Maybe the headline's about *me.* I take a quick look. *No. The headline is not about me.* It's about Hitler. Seven thousand miles away.
I'm here. Who the hell is Hitler? Who's behind the eight-ball? I turn
around. *Everybody's behind the eight-ball!*

> [*Pause.* KRUPP *moves toward* HARRY *as if to make an
> important arrest.* HARRY *moves to the swinging doors.*
> MC CARTHY *stops* KRUPP.]

MC CARTHY (*to* HARRY). It's the funniest thing I've ever heard. Or *seen,*
for that matter.

HARRY (*coming back to* MC CARTHY). Then why don't you laugh?

MC CARTHY. I don't know, *yet.*

HARRY. I'm always getting funny ideas that nobody will laugh at.

MC CARTHY (*thoughtfully*). It may be that you've stumbled headlong
into a new kind of comedy.

HARRY. Well, what good is it if it doesn't make anybody laugh?

MC CARTHY. There are *kinds* of laughter, son. I must say, in all truth,
that I *am* laughing, although not *out loud.*

HARRY. I want to *hear* people laugh. *Out loud.* That's why I keep thinking of funny things to say.

MC CARTHY. Well. They may catch on in time. Let's go, Krupp. So
long, Joe.

> [MC CARTHY *and* KRUPP *go.*]

JOE. So long. (*After a moment's pause.*) Hey, Nick.

NICK. Yeah.

JOE. Bet McCarthy in the last race.

NICK. You're crazy. That horse is a double-crossing, no-good——

JOE. Bet everything you've got on McCarthy.

NICK. I'm not betting a nickel on him. You bet everything you've got on
McCarthy.

JOE. I don't need money.

NICK. What makes you think McCarthy's going to win?

JOE. McCarthy's name's McCarthy, isn't it?

NICK. Yeah. So what?

JOE. The *horse* named McCarthy is going to win, *that's all*. Today.

NICK. Why?

JOE. You do what I tell you and everything will be all right.

NICK. McCarthy likes to talk, that's all. (*Pause.*) Where's Tom?

JOE. He'll be around. He'll be miserable, but he'll be around. Five or ten minutes more.

NICK. You don't believe that Kitty, do you? About being in burlesque?

JOE (*very clearly*). I believe dreams sooner than statistics.

NICK (*remembering*). She sure is somebody. Called me a dentist.

> [TOM, *turning about, confused, troubled, comes in,
> and hurries to* JOE'S *table.*]

JOE. What's the matter?

TOM. Here's your five, Joe. I'm in trouble again.

JOE. If it's not organic, it'll cure itself. If it is organic, science will cure it. What is it, organic or nonorganic?

TOM. Joe, I don't know—— (*He seems to be completely broken-down.*)

JOE. What's eating you? I want you to go on an errand for me.

TOM. It's Kitty.

JOE. What about her?

TOM. She's up in her room, crying.

JOE. Crying?

TOM. Yeah, she's been crying for over an hour. I been talking to her all this time, but she won't stop.

JOE. What's she crying about?

TOM. I don't know. I couldn't understand anything. She kept crying and telling me about a big house and collie dogs all around and flowers and one of her brothers's dead and the other one lost somewhere. Joe, I can't stand Kitty crying.

JOE. You want to marry the girl?

TOM (*nodding*). Yeah.

JOE (*curious and sincere*). Why?

TOM. I don't know why, exactly, Joe. (*Pause.*) Joe, I don't like to think of Kitty out in the streets. I guess I love her, that's all.

JOE. She's a nice girl.

TOM. She's like an angel. She's not like those other streetwalkers.

JOE (*swiftly*). Here. Take all this money and run next door to Frankie's and bet it on the nose of McCarthy.

TOM (*swiftly*). All this money, Joe? McCarthy?

JOE. Yeah. Hurry.

TOM (*going*). Ah, Joe. If McCarthy wins we'll be rich.

JOE. Get going, will you?

> [TOM *runs out and nearly knocks over the* ARAB
> *coming back in.* NICK *fills him a beer without a word.*]

ARAB. No foundation, anywhere. Whole world. No foundation. All the way down the line.

NICK (*angry*). McCarthy! Just because you got a little lucky this morning, you have to go to work and throw away eighty bucks.

JOE. He wants to marry her.

NICK. Suppose she doesn't want to marry *him?*

JOE (*amazed*). Oh yeah. (*Thinking.*) Now, why wouldn't she want to marry a nice guy like Tom?

NICK. She's been in burlesque. She's had flowers sent to her by European royalty. She's dined with young men of quality and social position. She's above Tom.

[TOM *comes running in.*]

TOM (*disgusted*). They were running when I got there. Frankie wouldn't take the bet. McCarthy didn't get a call till the stretch. I thought we were going to save all this money. Then McCarthy won by *two* lengths.

JOE. What'd he pay, fifteen to one?

TOM. Better, but Frankie wouldn't take the bet.

NICK (*throwing a dish towel across the room*). Well, for the love of Mike.

JOE. Give me the money.

TOM (*giving back the money*). We would have had about a thousand five hundred dollars.

JOE (*bored, casually, inventing*). Go up to Schwabacher-Frey and get me the biggest Rand McNally map of the nations of Europe they've got. On your way back stop at one of the pawnshops on Third Street and buy me a good revolver and some cartridges.

TOM. She's up in her room crying, Joe.

JOE. Go get me those things.

NICK. What are you going to do, study the map and then go out and shoot somebody?

JOE. I want to read the names of some European towns and rivers and valleys and mountains.

NICK. What do you want with the revolver?

JOE. I want to study it. I'm interested in things. Here's twenty dollars, Tom. Now go get them things.

TOM. A big map of Europe. And a revolver.

JOE. Get a good one. Tell the man you don't know anything about firearms and you're trusting him not to fool you. Don't pay more than ten dollars.

TOM. Joe, you got something on your mind. Don't go fool with a revolver.

JOE. Be sure it's a good one.

TOM. Joe.

JOE (*irritated*). What, Tom?

TOM. Joe, what do you send me out for crazy things for all the time?

JOE (*angry*). They're not crazy, Tom. Now get going.

TOM. What about Kitty, Joe?

JOE. Let her cry. It'll do her good.

TOM. If she comes in here while I'm gone, talk to her, will you, Joe? Tell her about me.

JOE. O.K. Get going. Don't load that gun. Just buy it and bring it here.

TOM (*going*). You won't catch me loading any gun.

JOE. Wait a minute. Take these toys away.

TOM. Where'll I take them?

JOE. Give them to some kid. (*Pause.*) No. Take them up to Kitty. Toys stopped me from crying once. That's the reason I had you buy them. I wanted to see if I could find out *why* they stopped me from crying. I remember they seemed awfully stupid at the time.

TOM. Shall I, Joe? Take them up to Kitty? Do you think they'd stop *her* from crying?

JOE. They might. You get curious about the way they work and you forget whatever it is you're remembering that's making you cry. That's what they're for.

TOM. Yeah. Sure. The girl at the store asked me what I wanted with toys. I'll take them up to Kitty. (*Tragically.*) She's like a little girl. (*He goes.*)

WESLEY. Mr. Nick, can I play the piano again?

NICK. Sure. Practice all you like—until I tell you to stop.

WESLEY. You going to pay me for playing the piano?

NICK. Sure. I'll give you enough to get by on.

WESLEY (*amazed and delighted*). Get money for playing the piano?
> [*He goes to the piano and begins to play quietly.*
> HARRY *goes up on the little stage and listens to the music. After a while he begins a soft-shoe dance.*]

NICK. What were you crying about?

JOE. My mother.

NICK. What about her?

JOE. She was dead. I stopped crying when they gave me the toys.
> [NICK'S MOTHER, *a little old woman of sixty or so, dressed plainly in black, her face shining, comes in briskly, chattering loudly in Italian, gesturing.* NICK *is delighted to see her.*]

NICK'S MOTHER (*in Italian*). Everything all right, Nickie?

NICK (*in Italian*). Sure, Mamma.
> [NICK'S MOTHER *leaves as gaily and as noisily as she came, after half a minute of loud Italian family talk.*]

JOE. Who was that?

NICK (*to* JOE, *proudly and a little sadly*). My mother. (*Still looking at the swinging doors.*)

JOE. What'd she say?

NICK. Nothing. Just wanted to see me. (*Pause.*) What do you want with that gun?

JOE. I study things, Nick.

> [*An old man who looks as if he might have been Kit Carson at one time walks in importantly, moves about, and finally stands at* JOE'S *table.*]

KIT CARSON. Murphy's the name. Just an old trapper. Mind if I sit down?

JOE. Be delighted. What'll you drink?

KIT CARSON (*sitting down*). Beer. Same as I've been drinking. And thanks.

JOE (*to* NICK). Glass of beer, Nick.

> [NICK *brings the beer to the table,* KIT CARSON *swallows it in one swig, wipes his big white mustache with the back of his right hand.*]

KIT CARSON (*moving in*). I don't suppose you ever fell in love with a midget weighing thirty-nine pounds?

JOE (*studying the man*). Can't say I have, but have another beer.

KIT CARSON (*intimately*). Thanks, thanks. Down in Gallup, twenty-years ago. Fellow by the name of Rufus Jenkins came to town with six white horses and two black ones. Said he wanted a man to break the horses for him because his left leg was wood and he couldn't do it. Had a meeting at Parker's Mercantile Store and finally came to blows, me and Henry Walpal. Bashed his head with a brass cuspidor and ran away to Mexico, but he didn't die.

Couldn't speak a word. Took up with a cattle-breeder named Diego, educated in California. Spoke the language better than you and me. Said, "Your job, Murph, is to feed them prize bulls." I said, "Fine, what'll I feed them?" He said, "Hay, lettuce, salt, beer, and aspirin." Came to blows two days later over an accordion he claimed I stole. I had *borrowed* it. During the fight I busted it over his head; ruined one of the finest accordions I ever saw. Grabbed a horse and rode back across the border. Texas. Got to talking with a fellow who looked honest. Turned out to be a Ranger who was looking for me.

JOE. Yeah. You were saying, a thirty-nine-pound midget.

KIT CARSON. Will I ever forget that lady? Will I ever get over that Amazon of small proportions?

JOE. Will you?

KIT CARSON. If I live to be sixty.

JOE. Sixty? You look more than sixty now.

KIT CARSON. That's trouble showing in my face. Trouble and complications. I was fifty-eight three months ago.

JOE. That accounts for it, then. Go ahead, tell me more.

KIT CARSON. Told the Texas Ranger my name was Rothstein, mining engineer from Pennsylvania, looking for something worth while. Mentioned two places in Houston. Nearly lost an eye early one morning, going down the stairs. Ran into a six-footer with an iron claw where his right hand was supposed to be. Said, "You broke up my home." Told him I was a stranger in Houston. The girls gathered at the top of the stairs to see a fight. Seven of them. Six feet and an iron claw. That's bad on the nerves. Kicked him in the mouth when he swung for my head with the claw. Would have lost an eye except for quick thinking. He rolled into the gutter and pulled a gun. Fired seven times. I was back upstairs. Left the place an hour later, dressed in silk and feathers, with a hat swung around over my face. Saw him standing on the corner, waiting. Said, "Care for a wiggle?" Said he didn't. I went on down the street and left town. I don't suppose you ever had to put a dress on to save your skin, did you?

JOE. No, and I never fell in love with a midget weighing thirty-nine pounds. Have another beer?

KIT CARSON. Thanks. (*Swallows a glass of beer.*) Ever try to herd cattle on a bicycle?

JOE. No. I never got around to that.

KIT CARSON. Left Houston with sixty cents in my pocket, gift of a girl named Lucinda. Walked fourteen miles in fourteen hours. Big house with barb wire all around, and big dogs. One thing I never could get around. Walked past the gate, anyway, from hunger and thirst. Dogs jumped up and came for me. Walked right into them, growing older every second. Went up to the door and knocked. Big Negress opened the door, closed it quick. Said, "On your way, white trash." Knocked again. Said, "On your way." Again. "On your way." Again. This time the old man himself opened the door, ninety, if he was a day. Sawed-off shotgun, too. Said, "I ain't looking for trouble, Father. I'm hungry and thirsty, name's Cavanaugh." Took me in and made mint juleps for the two of us. Said, "Living here alone, Father?" Said, "Drink and ask no questions. Maybe I am and maybe I ain't. You saw the lady. Draw your own conclusions." I'd heard of that, but didn't wink out of tact. If I told you that old Southern gentleman was my grandfather, you wouldn't believe me, would you?

JOE. I might.

KIT CARSON. Well, it so happens he wasn't. Would have been romantic if he had been, though.

JOE. Where did you herd cattle on a bicycle?

KIT CARSON. Toledo, Ohio, 1918.

JOE. Toledo, Ohio? They don't herd cattle in Toledo.

KIT CARSON. They don't any more. They did in 1918. One fellow did, leastaways. Bookkeeper named Sam Gold. Straight from the East Side, New York. Sombrero, lariats, Bull Durham, two head of cattle and two bicycles. Called his place The Gold Bar Ranch, two acres, just outside the city limits. That was the year of the war, you'll remember.

JOE. Yeah, I remember, but how about herding them two cows on a bicycle? How'd you do it?

KIT CARSON. Easiest thing in the world. Rode no hands. Had to, otherwise couldn't lasso the cows. Worked for Sam Gold till the cows ran away. Bicycles scared them. They went into Toledo. Never saw hide nor hair of them again. Advertised in every paper, but never got them back. Broke his heart. Sold both bikes and returned to New York. Took four aces from a deck of red cards and walked to town. Poker. Fellow in the game named Chuck Collins, liked to gamble. Told him with a smile I didn't suppose he'd care to bet a hundred dollars I wouldn't hold four aces the next hand. Called it. My cards were red on the blank side. The other cards were blue. Plumb forgot all about it. Showed him four aces. Ace of spades, ace of clubs, ace of diamonds, ace of hearts. I'll remember them four cards if I live to be sixty. Would have been killed on the spot except for the hurricane that year.

JOE. Hurricane?

KIT CARSON. You haven't forgotten the Toledo hurricane of 1918, have you?

JOE. No. There was no hurricane in Toledo in 1918, or any other year.

KIT CARSON. For the love of God, then what do you suppose that commotion was? And how come I came to in Chicago, dream-walking down State Street?

JOE. I guess they scared you.

KIT CARSON. No, that wasn't it. You go back to the papers of November 1918 and I think you'll find there was a hurricane in Toledo. I remember sitting on the roof of a two-story house, floating northwest.

JOE (*seriously*). Northwest?

KIT CARSON. Now, son, don't tell me *you* don't believe me, either?

JOE (*Pause. Very seriously, energetically and sharply*). Of course I believe you. Living is an art. It's not bookkeeping. It takes a lot of rehearsing for a man to get to be himself.

KIT CARSON (*thoughtfully, smiling, and amazed*). You're the first man I've ever met who believes me.

JOE (*seriously*). Have another beer.

> [TOM *comes in with the Rand McNally book, the*
> *revolver, and the box of cartridges.* KIT *goes to the*
> *bar.*]

JOE (*to* TOM). Did you give her the toys?

TOM. Yeah, I gave them to her.

JOE. Did she stop crying?

TOM. No. She started crying harder than ever.

JOE. That's funny. I wonder why.

TOM. Joe, if I was a minute earlier, Frankie would have taken the bet and now we'd have about a thousand five hundred dollars. How much of it would you have given me, Joe?

JOE. If she'd marry you—*all* of it.

TOM. Would you, Joe?

JOE (*opening the packages, examining the book first, and the revolver next*). Sure. In this realm there's only one subject and you're it. It's my duty to see that my subject is happy.

TOM. Joe, do you think we'll ever have eighty dollars for a race sometime again when there's a fifteen-to-one shot that we like, weather good, track fast, they get off to a good start, our horse doesn't get a call till the stretch, we think we're going to lose all that money, and then it wins, by a nose?

JOE. I didn't quite get that.

TOM. You know what I mean.

JOE. You mean the impossible. No, Tom, we won't. We were just a little late, that's all.

TOM. We might, Joe.

JOE. It's not likely.

TOM. Then how am I ever going to make enough money to marry her?

JOE. I don't know, Tom. Maybe you aren't.

TOM. Joe, I got to marry Kitty. (*Shaking his head.*) You ought to see the crazy room she lives in.

JOE. What kind of a room is it?

TOM. It's little. It crowds you in. It's bad, Joe. Kitty don't belong in a place like that.

JOE. You want to take her away from there?

TOM. Yeah. I want her to live in a house where there's room enough to live. Kitty ought to have a garden, or something.

JOE. You want to take care of her?

TOM. Yeah, sure, Joe. I ought to take care of somebody good that makes me feel like *I'm* somebody.

JOE. That means you'll have to get a job. What can you do?

TOM. I finished high school, but I don't know what I can do.

JOE. Sometimes when you think about it, what do you think you'd like to do?

TOM. Just sit around like you, Joe, and have somebody run errands for me and drink champagne and take things easy and never be broke and never worry about money.

JOE. That's a noble ambition.

NICK (*to* JOE). How do you do it?

JOE. I really don't know, but I think you've got to have the full co-operation of the Good Lord.

NICK. I can't understand the way you talk.

TOM. Joe, shall I go back and see if I can get her to stop crying?

JOE. Give me a hand and I'll go with you.

TOM (*amazed*). What! You're going to get up already?

JOE. She's crying, isn't she?

TOM. She's crying. Worse than ever now.

JOE. I thought the toys would stop her.

TOM. I've seen you sit in one place from four in the morning till two the next morning.

JOE. At my best, Tom, I don't travel by foot. That's all. Come on. Give me a hand. I'll find some way to stop her from crying.

TOM (*helping* JOE). Joe, I never did tell you. You're a different kind of a guy.

JOE (*swiftly, a little angry*). Don't be silly. I don't understand things. I'm trying to understand them.

> [JOE *is a little drunk. They go out together. The*
> *lights go down slowly, while* WESLEY *plays the piano,*
> *and come up slowly on:*]

ACT III

꒰ Scene: *A cheap bed in Nick's to indicate Room 21 of the New York Hotel, upstairs, around the corner from Nick's. The bed can be at the center of Nick's, or up on the little stage. Everything in Nick's is the same, except that all the people are silent, immobile, and in darkness except* WESLEY, *who is playing the piano softly and sadly.* KITTY DUVAL, *in a dress she has carried around with her from the early days in Ohio, is seated on the bed, tying a ribbon in her hair. She looks at herself in a hand mirror. She is deeply grieved at the change she sees in herself. She takes off the ribbon, angry and hurt. She lifts a book from the bed and tries to read. She begins to sob again. She picks up an old picture of herself and looks at it. Sobs harder than ever, falling on the bed and burying her face. There is a knock, as if at the door.*

KITTY (*sobbing*). Who is it?
TOM'S VOICE. Kitty, it's me. Tom. Me and Joe.
        [JOE, *followed by* TOM, *comes to the bed quietly.* JOE
        is holding a rather large toy carousel. JOE *studies*
        KITTY *a moment. He sets the toy carousel on the*
        floor, at the foot of KITTY'S *bed.*]
TOM (*standing over* KITTY *and bending down close to her*). Don't cry
   any more, Kitty.
KITTY (*not looking, sobbing*). I don't like this life.
        [JOE *starts the carousel, which makes a strange, sor-*
        rowful, tinkling music. The music begins slowly, be-
        comes swift, gradually slows down, and ends. JOE
        himself is interested in the toy, watches and listens to
        it carefully.]

TOM (*eagerly*). Kitty. Joe got up from his chair at Nick's just to get you a toy and come here. This one makes music. We rode all over town in a cab to get it. Listen.

[KITTY *sits up slowly, listening, while* TOM *watches her. Everything happens slowly and somberly.* KITTY *notices the photograph of herself when she was a little girl. Lifts it, and looks at it again.*]

TOM (*looking*). Who's that little girl, Kitty?

KITTY. That's me. When I was seven.

[KITTY *hands the photo to* TOM.]

TOM (*looking, smiling*). Gee, you're pretty, Kitty.

[JOE *reaches up for the photograph, which* TOM *hands to him.* TOM *returns to* KITTY, *whom he finds as pretty now as she was at seven.* JOE *studies the photograph.* KITTY *looks up at* TOM. *There is no doubt that they really love one another.* JOE *looks up at them.*]

KITTY. Tom?

TOM (*eagerly*). Yeah, Kitty.

KITTY. Tom, when you were a little boy what did you want to be?

TOM (*a little bewildered, but eager to please her*). What, Kitty?

KITTY. Do you remember when you were a little boy?

TOM (*thoughtfully*). Yeah, I remember sometimes, Kitty.

KITTY. What did you want to be?

TOM (*looks at* JOE. JOE *holds* TOM's *eyes a moment. Then* TOM *is able to speak*). Sometimes I wanted to be a locomotive engineer. Sometimes I wanted to be a policeman.

KITTY. I wanted to be a great actress. (*She looks up into* TOM's *face.*) Tom, didn't you ever want to be a doctor?

TOM (*looks at* JOE. JOE *holds* TOM's *eyes again, encouraging* TOM *by his serious expression to go on talking*). Yeah, now I remember. Sure, Kitty. I wanted to be a doctor—*once.*

KITTY (*smiling sadly*). I'm so glad. Because I wanted to be an actress and have a young doctor come to the theater and see me and fall in love with me and send me flowers.

[JOE *pantomimes to* TOM, *demanding that he go on talking.*]

TOM. I would do that, Kitty.

KITTY. I wouldn't know how it was, and then one day I'd see him in the street and fall in love with him. I wouldn't know *he* was the one who was in love with me. I'd think about him all the time. I'd dream about him. I'd dream of being near him the rest of my life. I'd dream of having children that looked like him. I wouldn't be an actress all the time. Only until I found him and fell in love with him. After that we'd take a train and go to beautiful cities and see the wonderful people everywhere and give money to the poor and whenever people were sick he'd go to them and make them well again.

[TOM *looks at* JOE, *bewildered, confused, and full of
sorrow.* KITTY *is deep in memory, almost in a trance.*]

JOE (*gently*). Talk to her, Tom. Be the wonderful young doctor she
dreamed about and never found. Go ahead. Correct the errors of
the world.

TOM. Joe. (*Pathetically.*) I don't know what to say.

[*There is rowdy singing in the hall. A loud young*
VOICE *sings: "Sailing, sailing, over the bounding
main."*]

VOICE. Kitty. Oh, Kitty! (KITTY *stirs, shocked, coming out of the
trance.*) Where the hell are you? Oh, Kitty.

[TOM *jumps up, furiously.*]

TOM (*to* JOE). Joe, I'll kill him.

KITTY (*fully herself again, terribly frightened*). Who is it?

[*She looks long and steadily at* TOM *and* JOE. TOM *is
standing, excited and angry.* JOE *is completely at
ease, his expression full of pity.* KITTY *buries her face
in the bed.*]

JOE (*gently*). Tom. Just take him away.

VOICE. Here it is. Number 21. Three naturals. Heaven. My blue heaven.
The west, a nest, and you. Just Molly and me. (*Tragically.*) Ah, to
hell with everything.

[*A young* SAILOR, *a good-looking boy of no more
than twenty or so, who is only drunk and lonely,
comes to the bed, singing sadly.*]

SAILOR. Hi-ya, Kitty. (*Pause.*) Oh. Visitors. Sorry. A thousand apologies. (*To* KITTY.) I'll come back later.

TOM (*taking him by the shoulders, furiously*). If you do, I'll kill you.

[JOE *holds* TOM. TOM *pushes the frightened boy
away.*]

JOE (*somberly*). Tom. You stay here with Kitty. I'm going down to
Union Square to hire an automobile. I'll be back in a few minutes.
We'll ride out to the ocean and watch the sun go down. Then we'll
ride down the Great Highway to Half Moon Bay. We'll have supper
down there, and you and Kitty can dance.

TOM (*stupefied, unable to express his amazement and gratitude*). Joe,
you mean you're going to go on an errand for *me?* You mean you're
not going to send me?

JOE. That's right.

[*He gestures toward* KITTY, *indicating that* TOM *shall
talk to her, protect the innocence in her which is in
so much danger when* TOM *isn't near, which* TOM
loves so deeply. JOE *leaves.* TOM *studies* KITTY, *his*

face becoming childlike and somber. He sets the carousel into motion, listens, watching KITTY, *who lifts herself slowly, looking only at* TOM. TOM *lifts the turning carousel and moves it slowly toward* KITTY, *as though the toy were his heart. The piano music comes up loudly and the lights go down, while* HARRY *is heard dancing swiftly.*]

BLACKOUT

ACT IV

🦆 Scene: *A little later.* WESLEY, *the colored boy, is at the piano.*
HARRY *is on the little stage, dancing.* NICK *is behind the bar. The* ARAB
is in his place. KIT CARSON *is asleep on his folded arms. The* DRUNKARD
*comes in. Goes to the telephone for the nickel that might be in the
return chute.* NICK *comes to take him out. He gestures for* NICK *to hold
on a minute. Then produces a half dollar.* NICK *goes behind the bar to
serve the* DRUNKARD *whisky.*

THE DRUNKARD. To the old, God bless them. (*Another.*) To the new,
God love them. (*Another.*) To—children and small animals, like
little dogs that don't bite. (*Another. Loudly.*) To reforestation.
(*Searches for money. Finds some.*) To—President Taft. (*He goes
out.*)
> [*The telephone rings.*]

KIT CARSON (*jumping up, fighting*). Come on, *all* of you, if you're look-
ing for trouble. I never asked for quarter and I always gave it.
NICK (*reproachfully*). Hey, Kit Carson.
DUDLEY (*on the phone*). Hello. Who? Nick? Yes. He's here. (*To* NICK.)
It's for you. I think it's important.
NICK (*going to the phone*). Important! *What's* important?
DUDLEY. He sounded like big shot.
NICK. Big *what?* (*To* WESLEY *and* HARRY.) Hey, you. Quiet. I want to
hear this important stuff.
> [WESLEY *stops playing the piano.* HARRY *stops
> dancing.* KIT CARSON *comes close to* NICK.]

KIT CARSON. If there's anything I can do, name it. I'll do it for you. I'm
fifty-eight years old; been through three wars; married four times;
the father of countless children whose *names* I don't even know. I've

got no money. I live from hand to mouth. But if there's anything I
can do, name it. I'll do it.

NICK (*patiently*). Listen, Pop. For a moment, please sit down and go
back to sleep—*for me.*

KIT CARSON. I can do that, too.

> [*He sits down, folds his arms, and puts his head into
> them. But not for long. As* NICK *begins to talk, he
> listens carefully, gets to his feet, and then begins to
> express in pantomime the moods of each of* NICK'S
> *remarks.*]

NICK (*on phone*). Yeah? (*Pause.*) Who? Oh, I see. (*Listens.*) Why
don't you leave them alone? (*Listens.*) The church people? Well, to
hell with the church people. I'm a Catholic myself. (*Listens.*) All
right. I'll send them away. I'll tell them to lay low for a couple of
days. Yeah, I know how it is. (NICK'S *daughter* ANNA *comes in
shyly, looking at her father, and stands unnoticed by the piano.*)
What? (*Very angry.*) Listen. I don't like that Blick. He was here this
morning, and I told him not to come back. I'll keep the girls out of
here. You keep Blick out of here. (*Listens.*) I know his brother-in-
law is important, but I don't want him to come down here. He looks
for trouble everywhere, and he always finds it. I don't break any
laws. I've got a dive in the lousiest part of town. Five years nobody's
been robbed, murdered, or gypped. I leave people alone. Your
swanky joints uptown make trouble for you every night. (NICK
gestures to WESLEY—*keeps listening on the phone—puts his hand
over the mouthpiece. To* WESLEY *and* HARRY.) Start playing again.
My ears have got a headache. Go into your dance, son. (WESLEY
begins to play again. HARRY *begins to dance.* NICK, *into the mouthpiece.*) Yeah. I'll keep them out. Just see that Blick doesn't come
around and start something. (*Pause.*) O.K. (*He hangs up.*)

KIT CARSON. Trouble coming?

NICK. That lousy Vice Squad again. It's that gorilla Blick.

KIT CARSON. Anybody at all. You can count on me. What kind of
a gorilla is this gorilla Blick?

NICK. Very dignified. Toenails on his fingers.

ANNA (*to* KIT CARSON, *with great, warm, beautiful pride, pointing at*
NICK). That's my father.

KIT CARSON (*leaping with amazement at the beautiful voice, the
wondrous face, the magnificent event*). Well, bless your heart, child.
Bless your lovely heart. I had a little daughter point me out in a
crowd once.

NICK (*surprised*). Anna. What the hell are you doing here? Get back
home where you belong and help Grandma cook me some supper.

> [ANNA *smiles at her father, understanding him, know-
> ing that his words are words of love. She turns and*

> *goes, looking at him all the way out, as much as to say that she would cook for him the rest of her life.* NICK *stares at the swinging doors.* KIT CARSON *moves toward them, two or three steps.* ANNA *pushes open one of the doors and peeks in, to look at her father again. She waves to him. Turns and runs.* NICK *is very sad. He doesn't know what to do. He gets a glass and a bottle. Pours himself a drink. Swallows some. It isn't enough, so he pours more and swallows the whole drink.*]

NICK (*to himself*). My beautiful, beautiful baby. Anna, she is you again. (*He brings out a handkerchief, touches his eyes, and blows his nose.* KIT CARSON *moves close to* NICK, *watching* NICK's *face.* NICK *looks at him. Loudly, almost making* KIT *jump.*) You're broke, aren't you?

KIT CARSON. Always. Always.

NICK. All right. Go into the kitchen and give Sam a hand. Eat some food and when you come back you can have a couple of beers.

KIT CARSON (*studying* NICK). Anything at all. I know a good man when I see one. (*He goes.*)

> [ELSIE MANDELSPIEGEL *comes into Nick's. She is a beautiful, dark girl, with a sorrowful, wise, dreaming face, almost on the verge of tears, and full of pity. There is an aura of dream about her. She moves softly and gently, as if everything around her were unreal and pathetic.* DUDLEY *doesn't notice her for a moment or two. When he does finally see her, he is so amazed he can barely move or speak. Her presence has the effect of changing him completely. He gets up from his chair, as if in a trance, and walks toward her, smiling sadly.*]

ELSIE (*looking at him*). Hello, Dudley.

DUDLEY (*brokenhearted*). Elsie.

ELSIE. I'm sorry. (*Explaining.*) So many people are sick. Last night a little boy died. I love you, but—— (*She gestures, trying to indicate how hopeless love is. They sit down.*)

DUDLEY (*staring at her, stunned and quieted*). Elsie. You'll never know how glad I am to see you. Just to *see* you. (*Pathetically.*) I was afraid I'd never see you again. It was driving me crazy. I didn't want to live. Honest. (*He shakes his head mournfully, with dumb and beautiful affection. Two streetwalkers come in, and pause near* DUDLEY, *at the bar.*) I know. You told me before, but I can't help it, Elsie. I love you.

ELSIE (*quietly, somberly, gently, with great compassion*). I know you love me, and I love you, but don't you see love is impossible in this world?

DUDLEY. Maybe it isn't, Elsie.

ELSIE. Love is for birds. They have wings to fly away on when it's time for flying. For tigers in the jungle because they don't know their end. We know *our* end. Every night I watch over poor, dying men. I hear them breathing, crying, talking in their sleep. Crying for air and water and love, for mother and field and sunlight. We can never know love or greatness. We *should* know both.

DUDLEY (*deeply moved by her words*). Elsie, I love you.

ELSIE. You want to live. *I* want to live, too, but where? Where can we escape our poor world?

DUDLEY. Elsie, we'll find a place.

ELSIE (*smiling at him*). All right. We'll try again. We'll go together to a room in a cheap hotel, and dream that the world is beautiful, and that living is full of love and greatness. But in the morning, can we forget debts, and duties, and the cost of ridiculous things?

DUDLEY (*with blind faith*). Sure we can, Elsie.

ELSIE. All right, Dudley. Of course. Come on. The time for the new pathetic war has come. Let's hurry, before they dress you, stand you in line, hand you a gun, and have you kill and be killed.

> [ELSIE *looks at him gently, and takes his hand.*
> DUDLEY *embraces her shyly, as if he might hurt her.*
> *They go, as if they were a couple of young animals.*
> *There is a moment of silence. One of the streetwalkers*
> *bursts out laughing.*]

KILLER. Nick, what the hell kind of a joint are you running?

NICK. Well, it's not out of the world. It's on a street in a city, and people come and go. They bring whatever they've got with them and they say what they must say. (*Remembering.*) Oh yeah. Finnegan telephoned.

KILLER. That mouse in elephant's body?

THE OTHER STREETWALKER. What the hell does *he* want?

NICK. Spend your time at the movies for the next couple of days.

KILLER. They're all lousy. (*Mocking.*) All about love.

NICK. Lousy or not lousy, for a couple of days the flatfoots are going to be romancing you, so stay out of here, and lay low.

KILLER. I always was a pushover for a man in uniform, with a badge, a club and a gun.

> [KRUPP *comes into the place. The girls put down*
> *their drinks.*]

NICK. O.K., get going.

> [*The girls begin to leave and meet* KRUPP.]

THE OTHER STREETWALKER. We was just going.

KILLER. We was formerly models at Magnin's.

[*They go.*]

KRUPP (*at the bar*). The strike isn't enough, so they've got to put us on the tails of the girls, too. I don't know. I wish to God I was back in the Sunset holding the hands of kids going home from school, where I belong. I don't like trouble. Give me a beer. (NICK *gives him a beer. He drinks some.*) Right now, McCarthy, my best friend, is with sixty strikers who want to stop the finks who are going to try to unload the *Mary Luckenbach* tonight. Why the hell McCarthy ever became a longshoreman instead of a professor of some kind is something I'll never know.

NICK. Cowboys and Indians, cops and robbers, longshoremen and finks.

KRUPP. They're all guys who are trying to be happy—trying to make a living, support a family, bring up children, enjoy sleep. Go to a movie, take a drive on Sunday. They're all good guys, so out of nowhere comes trouble. All they want is a chance to get out of debt and relax in front of a radio while Amos and Andy go through their act. What the hell do they always want to make trouble for? I been thinking everything over, Nick, and you know what I think?

NICK. No. What?

KRUPP. I think we're all crazy. It came to me while I was on my way to Pier 27. All of a sudden it hit me like a ton of bricks. A thing like that never happened to me before. Here we are in this wonderful world, full of all the wonderful things—here we are—all of us, and look at us. Just look at us. We're crazy. We're nuts. We've got everything, but we always feel lousy and dissatisfied just the same.

NICK. Of course we're crazy. Even so, we've got to go on living together. (*He waves at the people in his joint.*)

KRUPP. There's no hope. I don't suppose it's right for an officer of the law to feel the way I feel, but, by God, right or not right, that's how I feel. Why are we all so lousy? This is a good world. It's wonderful to get up in the morning and go out for a little walk and smell the trees and see the streets and the kids going to school and the clouds in the sky. It's wonderful just to be able to move around and whistle a song if you feel like it, or maybe try to sing one. This is a nice world. So why do they make all the trouble?

NICK. I don't know. Why?

KRUPP. We're crazy, that's why. We're no good any more. All the corruption everywhere. The poor kids selling themselves. A couple of years ago they were in grammar school. Everybody trying to get a lot of money in a hurry. Everybody betting the horses. Nobody going quietly for a little walk to the ocean. Nobody taking things easy and not wanting to make some kind of a killing. Nick, I'm going to quit being a cop. Let somebody else keep law and order. The stuff I hear about at headquarters. I'm thirty-seven years old, and I still can't get used to it. The only trouble is, the wife'll raise hell.

NICK. Ah, the wife.

KRUPP. She's a wonderful woman, Nick. We've got two of the swellest boys in the world. Twelve and seven years old.

[*The* ARAB *gets up and moves closer to listen.*]

NICK. I didn't know that.

KRUPP. Sure. But what'll I do? I've wanted to quit for seven years. I wanted to quit the day they began putting me through the school. I didn't quit. What'll I do if I quit? Where's money going to be coming in from?

NICK. That's one of the reasons we're all crazy. We don't know where it's going to be coming in from, except from wherever it happens to be coming in from at the time, which we don't usually like.

KRUPP. Every once in a while I catch myself being mean, hating people just because they're down and out, broke and hungry, sick or drunk. And then when I'm with the stuffed shirts at headquarters, all of a sudden I'm nice to them, trying to make an impression. On who? People I don't like. And I feel disgusted. (*With finality.*) I'm going to quit. That's all. Quit. Out. I'm going to give them back the uniform and the gadgets that go with it. I don't want any part of it. This is a good world. What do they want to make all the trouble for all the time?

ARAB (*quietly, gently, with great understanding*). No foundation. All the way down the line.

KRUPP. What?

ARAB. No foundation. No foundation.

KRUPP. I'll say there's no foundation.

ARAB. All the way down the line.

KRUPP (*to* NICK). Is that all he ever says?

NICK. That's all he's been saying *this* week.

KRUPP. What is he, anyway?

NICK. He's an Arab, or something like that.

KRUPP. No, I mean what's he do for a living?

NICK (*to* ARAB). What do you do for a living, brother?

ARAB. Work. Work all my life. All my life, work. From small boy to old man, work. In old country, work. In new country, work. In New York. Pittsburgh. Detroit. Chicago. Imperial Valley. San Francisco. Work. No beg. Work. For what? Nothing. Three boys in old country. Twenty years, not see. Lost. Dead. Who knows? What. Whatnot. No foundation. All the way down the line.

KRUPP. What'd he say last week?

NICK. Didn't say anything. Played the harmonica.

ARAB. Old country song, I play. (*He brings a harmonica from his back pocket.*)

KRUPP. Seems like a nice guy.

NICK. Nicest guy in the world.

KRUPP (*bitterly*). But crazy. Just like all the rest of us. Stark raving
mad.

> [WESLEY *and* HARRY *long ago stopped playing and
> dancing. They sat at a table together and talked for a
> while, then began playing casino or rummy. When
> the* ARAB *begins his solo on the harmonica, they stop
> their game to listen.*]

WESLEY. You hear that?

HARRY. That's *something*.

WESLEY. That's crying. That's crying.

HARRY. I want to make people laugh.

WESLEY. That's deep, deep crying. That's crying a long time ago. That's
crying a thousand years ago. Some place five thousand miles away.

HARRY. Do you think you can play to that?

WESLEY. I want to *sing* to that, but I can't *sing*.

HARRY. You try and play to that. I'll try to dance.

> [WESLEY *goes to the piano, and after closer listening,
> he begins to accompany the harmonica solo.* HARRY
> *goes to the little stage and after a few efforts begins
> to dance to the song. This keeps up quietly for some
> time.* KRUPP *and* NICK *have been silent, and deeply
> moved.*]

KRUPP (*softly*). Well, anyhow, Nick.

NICK. Hmmmmmmmm?

KRUPP. What I said. Forget it.

NICK. Sure.

KRUPP. It gets me down once in a while.

NICK. No harm in talking.

KRUPP (*the policeman again, loudly*). Keep the girls out of here.

NICK (*loud and friendly*). Take it easy.

> [*The music and dancing are now at their height.*]

ACT V

Scene: That evening. Foghorns are heard throughout the scene. A man in evening clothes and a top hat, and his woman, also in evening clothes, are entering.

WILLIE is still at the marble game. NICK is behind the bar. JOE is at his table, looking at the book of maps of the countries of Europe. The box containing the revolver and the box containing the cartridges are on the table, beside his glass. He is at peace, his hat tilted back on his head, a calm expression on his face. TOM is leaning against the bar, dreaming of love and KITTY. The ARAB is gone. WESLEY and HARRY are gone. KIT CARSON is watching the boy at the marble game.

LADY. Oh, come on, please.
　　　　[*The gentleman follows miserably. The* SOCIETY MAN
　　　　and WIFE *take a table.* NICK *gives them a menu. Out-*
　　　　side, in the street, the Salvation Army people are
　　　　playing a song. Big drum, tambourines, cornet, and
　　　　singing. They are singing "The Blood of the Lamb."
　　　　The music and words come into the place faintly and
　　　　comically. This is followed by an old sinner testifying.
　　　　It is the DRUNKARD. *His words are not intelligible,*
　　　　but his message is unmistakable. He is saved. He
　　　　　　　wants to sin no more. And so on.]
DRUNKARD (*testifying, unmistakably drunk*). Brothers and sisters. I
　　was a sinner. I chewed tobacco and chased women. Oh, I sinned,
　　brothers and sisters. And then I was saved. Saved by the Salvation
　　Army, God forgive me.
JOE. Let's see now. Here's a city. Pribor. Czechoslovakia. Little, lovely,

lonely Czechoslovakia. I wonder what kind of a place Pribor was? (*Calling.*) Pribor! *Pribor!*

[TOM *leaps.*]

LADY. What's the matter with him?

MAN (*crossing his legs, as if he ought to go to the men's room*). Drunk.

TOM. Who you calling, Joe?

JOE. Pribor.

TOM. Who's Pribor?

JOE. He's a Czech. And a Slav. A Czechoslovakian.

LADY. How interesting.

MAN (*uncrosses his legs*). He's drunk.

JOE. Tom, Pribor's a city in Czechoslovakia.

TOM. Oh. (*Pause.*) You sure were nice to her, Joe.

JOE. Kitty Duval? She's one of the finest people in the world.

TOM. It sure was nice of you to hire an automobile and take us for a drive along the ocean front and down to Half Moon Bay.

JOE. Those three hours were the most delightful, the most somber, and the most beautiful I have ever known.

TOM. Why, Joe?

JOE. Why? I'm a student (*Lifting his voice.*), Tom. (*Quietly.*) I'm a student. I study all things. All. All. And when my study reveals something of beauty in a place or in a person where by all rights only ugliness or death should be revealed, then I know how full of goodness this life is. And that's a good thing to know. That's a truth I shall always seek to verify.

LADY. Are you *sure* he's drunk?

MAN (*crossing his legs*). He's either drunk or just naturally crazy.

TOM. Joe?

JOE. Yeah.

TOM. You won't get sore or anything?

JOE (*impatiently*). What is it, Tom?

TOM. Joe, where do you get all that money? You paid for the automobile. You paid for supper and the two bottles of champagne at the Half Moon Bay Restaurant. You moved Kitty out of the New York Hotel around the corner to the St. Francis Hotel on Powell Street. I saw you pay her rent. I saw you give her money for new clothes. Where do you get all that money, Joe? Three years now and I've never asked.

JOE (*looking at* TOM *sorrowfully, a little irritated, not so much with* TOM *as with the world and himself, his own superiority. He speaks clearly, slowly and solemnly*). Now don't be a fool, Tom. Listen carefully. If anybody's got any money—to hoard or to throw away —you can be sure he stole it from other people. Not from rich people who can spare it, but from poor people who can't. From their lives and from their dreams. I'm no exception. I *earned* the money I throw away. I stole it like everybody else does. I hurt people to get it. Loafing around this way, I *still* earn money. The money itself earns *more*. I *still* hurt people. I don't know who they are, or where they are. If I did, I'd feel worse than I do. I've got a Christian conscience in a world that's got no conscience at all. The world's trying to get some sort of a *social* conscience, but it's having a devil of a time trying to do *that*. I've got money. I'll always have money, as long as this world stays the way it is. I don't work. I don't make anything. (*He sips.*) I drink. I worked when I was a kid. I worked *hard*. I mean hard, Tom. People are supposed to enjoy living. I got tired. (*He lifts the gun and looks at it while he talks.*) I decided to get even on the world. Well, you can't enjoy living unless you work. Unless you do something. I don't do anything. I don't *want* to do anything any more. There isn't anything I can do that won't make me feel embarrassed. Because I can't do simple, good things. I haven't the patience. And I'm too smart. Money is the guiltiest thing in the world. It stinks. Now, don't ever bother me about it again.

TOM. I didn't mean to make you feel bad, Joe.

JOE (*slowly*). Here. Take this gun out in the street and give it to some worthy holdup man.

LADY. What's he saying?

MAN (*uncrosses his legs*). You wanted to visit a honky-tonk. Well, *this* is a honky-tonk. (*To the world.*) Married twenty-eight years and she's still looking for adventure.

TOM. How should I know who's a holdup man?

JOE. Take it away. Give it to somebody.

TOM (*bewildered*). Do I *have* to *give* it to somebody?

JOE. Of course.

TOM. Can't I take it back and get some of our money?

JOE. Don't talk like a businessman. Look around and find somebody who appears to be in need of a gun and give it to him. It's a good gun, isn't it?

TOM. The man said it was, but how can I tell who needs a gun?

JOE. Tom, you've seen good people who needed guns, haven't you?

TOM. I don't remember. Joe, I might give to the wrong kind of guy. He might do something crazy.

JOE. All right. I'll find somebody myself. (TOM *rises.*) Here's some money. Go get me this week's *Life, Liberty, Time,* and six or seven packages of chewing gum.

TOM (*swiftly, in order to remember each item*). *Life, Liberty, Time,* and six or seven packages of chewing gum?

JOE. That's right.

TOM. All that chewing gum? What kind?

JOE. Any kind. Mix 'em up. All kinds.

TOM. Licorice, too?

JOE. Licorice, by all means.

TOM. Juicy Fruit?

JOE. Juicy Fruit.

ГOM. Tutti-Frutti?

JOE. Is there such a gum?

TOM. I think so.

JOE. All right. Tutti-Frutti, too. Get *all* the kinds. Get as many kinds as they're selling.

TOM. *Life, Liberty, Time,* and all the different kinds of gum. (*He begins to go.*)

JOE (*calling after him loudly*). Get some jelly beans too. All the different colors.

TOM. All right, Joe.

JOE. And the longest panatela cigar you can find. Six of them.

TOM. Panatela. I got it.

JOE. Give a news kid a dollar.

TOM. O.K., Joe.

JOE. Give some old man a dollar.

TOM. O.K., Joe.

JOE. Give them Salvation Army people in the street a couple of dollars and ask them to sing that song that goes—— (*He sings loudly.*) Let the lower lights be burning, send a gleam across the wave.

TOM (*swiftly*). Let the lower lights be burning, send a gleam across the wave.

JOE. That's it. (*He goes on with the song, very loudly and religiously.*) Some poor, dying, struggling seaman, you may rescue, you may save. (*Halts.*)

TOM. O.K., Joe, I got it. *Life, Liberty, Time,* all the kinds of gum they're selling, jelly beans, six panatela cigars, a dollar for a news kid, a dollar for an old man, two dollars for the Salvation Army. (*Going.*) Let the lower lights be burning, send a gleam across the wave.

JOE. That's it.

LADY. He's absolutely insane.

MAN (*wearily crossing his legs*). You asked me to take you to a honky-tonk instead of to the Mark Hopkins. You're *here* in a honky-tonk. I can't help it if he's crazy. Do you want to go back to where people *aren't* crazy?

LADY. No, not just yet.

MAN. Well, all right then. Don't be telling me every minute that he's crazy.

LADY. You needn't be huffy about it.

> [*The* MAN *refuses to answer, uncrosses his legs.*
> *When* JOE *began to sing,* KIT CARSON *turned away*

*from the marble game and listened. While the man
and woman are arguing he comes over to* JOE'S
table.]

KIT CARSON. Presbyterian?

JOE. I attended a Presbyterian Sunday school.

KIT CARSON. Fond of singing?

JOE. On occasion. Have a drink?

KIT CARSON. Thanks.

JOE. Get a glass and sit down.

[KIT CARSON *gets a glass from* NICK, *returns to the
table, sits down.* JOE *pours him a drink, they touch
glasses just as the Salvation Army people begin to
fulfill the request. They sip some champagne, and
at the proper moment begin to sing the song together, sipping champagne, raising hell with the tune,
swinging it, and so on. The* SOCIETY LADY *joins them,
and is stopped by her husband.*]

JOE. Always was fond of that song. Used to sing it at the top of my
voice. Never saved a seaman in my life.

KIT CARSON (*flirting with the* SOCIETY LADY, *who loves it*). I saved a
seaman once. Well, he wasn't exactly a seaman. He was a darky
named Wellington. Heavy-set sort of a fellow. Nice personality, but
no friends to speak of. Not until I came along, at any rate. In New
Orleans. In the summer of the year 1899. No. Ninety-eight. I was
a lot younger of course, and had no mustache, but was regarded
by many people as a man of means.

JOE. Know anything about guns?

KIT CARSON (*flirting*). All there is to know. Didn't fight the Ojibways
for nothing. Up there in the Lake Takalooca Country, in Michigan.
(*Remembering.*) Along about in 1881 or two. Fought 'em right
up to the shore of the Lake. Made 'em swim for Canada. One fellow
in particular, an Indian named Harry Daisy.

JOE (*opening the box containing the revolver*). What sort of gun
would you say this is? Any good?

KIT CARSON (*at sight of the gun, leaping*). Yep. That looks like a
pretty nice hunk of shooting iron. That's a six-shooter. Shot a man
with a six-shooter once. Got him through the palm of his right
hand. Lifted his arm to wave to a friend. Thought it was a bird.
Fellow named, I believe, Carroway. Larrimore Carroway.

JOE. Know how to work one of these things? (*He offers* KIT CARSON
the revolver, which is old and enormous.)

KIT CARSON (*laughing at the absurd question*). Know how to work it?
Hand me that little gun, son, and I'll show you all about it. (JOE
hands KIT *the revolver. Importantly.*) Let's see now. This is probably a new kind of six-shooter. After my time. Haven't nicked an

Indian in years. I believe this here place is supposed to move out. (*He fools around and gets the barrel out for loading.*) That's it. There it is.

JOE. Look all right?

KIT CARSON. It's a good gun. You've got a good gun there, son. I'll explain it to you. You see these holes? Well, that's where you put the cartridges.

JOE (*taking some cartridges out of the box*). Here. Show me how it's done.

KIT CARSON (*a little impatiently*). Well, son, you take 'em one by one and put 'em in the holes, like this. There's one. Two. Three. Four. Five. Six. Then you get the barrel back in place. Then cock it. Then all you got to do is aim and fire.

> [*He points the gun at the* LADY *and* GENTLEMAN,
> *who scream and stand up, scaring* KIT CARSON *into*
> *paralysis. The gun is loaded, but uncocked.*]

JOE. It's all set?

KIT CARSON. Ready to kill.

JOE. Let me hold it.

> [KIT *hands* JOE *the gun. The* LADY *and* GENTLEMAN
> *watch, in terror.*]

KIT CARSON. Careful now, son. Don't cock it. Many a man's lost an eye fooling with a loaded gun. Fellow I used to know named Danny Donovan lost a nose. Ruined his whole life. Hold it firm. Squeeze the trigger. Don't snap it. Spoils your aim.

JOE. Thanks. Let's see if I can unload it. (*He begins to unload it.*)

KIT CARSON. Of course you can.

> [JOE *unloads the revolver, looks at it very closely,*
> *puts the cartridges back into the box.*]

JOE (*looking at the gun*). I'm mighty grateful to you. Always wanted to see one of those things close up. Is it really a good one?

KIT CARSON. It's a beaut, son.

JOE (*aims the empty gun at a bottle on the bar*). Bang!

WILLIE (*at the marble game, as the machine groans*). Oh boy! (*Loudly, triumphantly.*) There you are, Nick. Thought I couldn't do it, hey? *Now*, watch. (*The machine begins to make a special kind of noise. Lights go on and off. Some red, some green. A bell rings loudly six times.*) One. Two. Three. Four. Five. Six. (*An American flag jumps up.* WILLIE *comes to attention. Salutes.*) Oh boy, what a beautiful country. (*A loud music-box version of the song "America."* JOE, KIT, *and the* LADY *get to their feet. Singing.*) My country, 'tis of thee, sweet land of liberty, of thee I sing. (*Everything quiets down. The flag goes back into the machine.* WILLIE *is thrilled, amazed, delighted. Everybody has watched the*

*performance of the defeated machine from wherever he happened
to be when the performance began.* WILLIE, *looking around at
everybody, as if they had all been on the side of the machine.*)
O.K. How's that? I knew I could do it. (*To* NICK.) Six nickels.
(NICK *hands him six nickels.* WILLIE *goes over to* JOE *and* KIT.)
Took me a little while, but I finally did it. It's scientific, really.
With a little skill a man can make a modest living beating the marble
games. Not that that's what I want to do. I just don't like the idea
of anything getting the best of me. A machine or anything else.
Myself, I'm the kind of a guy who makes up his mind to do some-
thing, and then goes to work and does it. There's no other way
a man can be a success at anything. (*Indicating the letter F on his
sweater.*) See that letter? That don't stand for some little-bitty high
school somewhere. That stands for *me.* Faroughli. Willie Faroughli.
I'm an Assyrian. We've got a civilization six or seven centuries old,
I think. Somewhere along in there. Ever hear of Osman? Harold
Osman? He's an Assyrian, too. He's got an orchestra down in
Fresno. (*He goes to the* LADY *and* GENTLEMAN.) I've never seen
you before in my life, but I can tell from the clothes you wear and
the company you keep (*Graciously indicating the* LADY.) that you're
a man who looks every problem straight in the eye, and then goes
to work and *solves* it. I'm that way myself. Well. (*He smiles beautifully, takes the* GENTLEMAN's *hand furiously.*) It's been wonderful
talking to a nicer type of people for a change. Well. I'll be seeing
you. So long. (*He turns, takes two steps, returns to the table. Very
politely and seriously.*) Good-by, lady. You've got a good man
there. Take good care of him.

       [WILLIE *goes, saluting* JOE *and the world.*]

KIT CARSON (*to* JOE). By God, for a while there I didn't think that
    young Assyrian was going to do it. That fellow's got something.

       [TOM *comes back with the magazines and other stuff.*]

JOE. Get it all?

TOM. Yeah. I had a little trouble finding the jelly beans.

JOE. Let's take a look at them.

TOM. These are the jelly beans.

       [JOE *puts his hand into the cellophane bag and takes
       out a handful of the jelly beans, looks at them,
       smiles, and tosses a couple into his mouth.*]

JOE. Same as ever. Have some. (*He offers the bag to* KIT.)

KIT CARSON (*flirting*). Thanks! I remember the first time I ever ate
    jelly beans. I was six, or at the most seven. Must have been in
    (*Slowly.*) eighteen—seventy-seven. Seven or eight. Baltimore.

JOE. Have some, Tom.

       [TOM *takes some.*]

TOM. Thanks, Joe.

JOE. Let's have some of that chewing gum. (*He dumps all the packages of gum out of the bag onto the table.*)

KIT CARSON (*flirting*). Me and a boy named Clark. Quinton Clark. Became a Senator.

JOE. Yeah. Tutti-Frutti all right. (*He opens a package and folds all five pieces into his mouth.*) Always wanted to see how many I could chew at one time. Tell you what, Tom. I'll bet I can chew more at one time than you can.

TOM (*delighted*). All right.

> [*They both begin to fold gum into their mouths.*]

KIT CARSON. I'll referee. Now, one at a time. How many you got?

JOE. Six.

KIT CARSON. All right. Let Tom catch up with you.

JOE (*while* TOM's *catching up*). Did you give a dollar to a news kid?

TOM. Yeah, sure.

JOE. What'd he say?

TOM. Thanks.

JOE. What sort of a kid was he?

TOM. Little, dark kid. I guess he's Italian.

JOE. Did he seem pleased?

TOM. Yeah.

JOE. That's good. Did you give a dollar to an old man?

TOM. Yeah.

JOE. Was he pleased?

TOM. Yeah.

JOE. Good. How many you got in your mouth?

TOM. Six.

JOE. All right. I got six, too. (*Folds one more in his mouth.* TOM *folds one too.*)

KIT CARSON. Seven. Seven each. (*They each fold one more into their mouths, very solemnly, chewing them into the main hunk of gum.*) Eight. Nine. Ten.

JOE (*delighted*). Always wanted to do this. (*He picks up one of the magazines.*) Let's see what's going on in the world. (*He turns the pages, and keeps folding gum into his mouth and chewing.*)

KIT CARSON. Eleven. Twelve.

> [KIT *continues to count while* JOE *and* TOM *continue the contest. In spite of what they are doing, each is very serious.*]

TOM. Joe, what'd you want to move Kitty into the St. Francis Hotel for?

JOE. She's a better woman than any of them tramp society dames that hang around that lobby.

TOM. Yeah, but do you think she'll feel at home up there?

JOE. Maybe not at first, but after a couple of days she'll be all right. A nice big room. A bed for sleeping in. Good clothes. Good food. She'll be all right, Tom.

TOM. I hope so. Don't you think she'll get lonely up there with nobody to talk to?

JOE (*looking at* TOM *sharply, almost with admiration, pleased but severe*). There's nobody *anywhere* for *her* to talk to—except *you.*

TOM (*amazed and delighted*). Me, Joe?

JOE (*while* TOM *and* KIT CARSON *listen carefully,* KIT *with great appreciation*). Yes, you. By the grace of God, you're the other half of that girl. Not the angry woman that swaggers into this waterfront dive and shouts because the world has kicked her around. *Anybody* can have *her.* You belong to the little kid in Ohio who once dreamed of living. Not with her carcass, for *money,* so she can have food and clothes, and pay rent. With *all* of her. I put her in that hotel so she can have a chance to gather herself together again. She can't do that in the New York Hotel. You saw what happens there. There's nobody anywhere for her to talk to, except you. They all make her talk like a streetwalker. After a while, she'll *believe* them. Then she won't be able to remember. She'll get lonely. Sure. People can get lonely for *misery,* even. I want her to go on being lonely for *you,* so she can come together again the way she was meant to be from the beginning. Loneliness is good for people. Right now it's the only thing for Kitty. Any more licorice?

TOM (*dazed*). What? Licorice? (*Looking around busily.*) I guess we've chewed all the licorice in. We still got Clove, Peppermint, Doublemint, Beechnut, Teaberry, and Juicy Fruit.

JOE. Licorice used to be my favorite. Don't worry about her, Tom, she'll be all right. You really want to marry her, don't you?

TOM (*nodding*). Honest to God, Joe. (*Pathetically.*) Only I haven't got any money.

JOE. Couldn't you be a prize fighter or something like that?

TOM. Naaaah. I couldn't hit a man if I wasn't sore at him. He'd have to do something that made me hate him.

JOE. You've got to figure out something to do that you won't mind doing very much.

TOM. I wish I could, Joe.

JOE (*thinking deeply; suddenly*). Tom, would you be embarrassed driving a truck?

TOM (*hit by a thunderbolt*). Joe, I never thought of that. I'd like that. Travel. Highways. Little towns. Coffee and hot cakes. Beautiful valleys and mountains and streams and trees and daybreak and sunset.

JOE. There *is* poetry in it, at that.

TOM. Joe, that's just the kind of work I *should* do. Just sit there and travel, and look, and smile, and bust out laughing. Could Kitty go with me, sometimes?

JOE. I don't know. Get me the phone book. Can you drive a truck?

TOM. Joe, you know I can drive a truck, or any kind of thing with a motor and wheels.

[TOM *takes* JOE *the phone book.* JOE *turns the pages.*]

JOE (*looking*). Here! Here it is. Tuxedo 7900. Here's a nickel. Get me that number.

[TOM *goes to telephone, dials the number.*]

TOM. Hello.

JOE. Ask for Mr. Keith.

TOM (*mouth and language full of gum*). I'd like to talk to Mr. Keith. (*Pause.*) Mr. Keith.

JOE. Take that gum out of your mouth for a minute.

[TOM *removes the gum.*]

TOM. Mr. Keith. Yeah. That's right. Hello, Mr. Keith?

JOE. Tell him to hold the line.

TOM. Hold the line, please.

JOE. Give me a hand, Tom. (TOM *helps* JOE *to the telephone. At the phone, wad of gum in his fingers delicately.*) Keith? Joe. Yeah. Fine. Forget it. (*Pause.*) Have you got a place for a good driver? (*Pause.*) I don't think so. (*To* TOM.) You haven't got a driver's license, have you?

TOM (*worried*). No. But I can get one, Joe.

JOE (*at the phone*). No, but he can get one easy enough. To hell with the union. He'll join later. All right, call him a vice-president and say he drives for relaxation. Sure. What do you mean? Tonight? I don't know why not. San Diego? All right, let him start driving without a license. What the hell's the difference? Yeah. Sure. Look him over. Yeah. I'll send him right over. Right. (*He hangs up.*) Thanks. (*To the telephone.*)

TOM. Am I going to get the job?

JOE. He wants to take a look at you.

TOM. Do I look all right, Joe?

JOE (*looking at him carefully*). Hold up your head. Stick out your chest. How do you feel?

[TOM *does these things.*]

TOM. Fine.

JOE. You *look* fine, too. (JOE *takes his wad of gum out of his mouth and wraps the* Liberty *magazine around it.*) You win, Tom. Now, look. (*He bites off the tip of a very long panatela cigar, lights it, and hands one to* TOM, *and another to* KIT.) Have yourselves a pleasant smoke. Here. (*He hands two more to* TOM.) Give those slummers one each. (*He indicates the* SOCIETY LADY *and* GENTLE-MAN.)

[TOM *goes over and without a word gives a cigar
each to the* MAN *and the* LADY. *The* MAN *is offended;
he smells and tosses aside his cigar. The* WOMAN
*looks at her cigar a moment, then puts the cigar in
her mouth.*]

MAN. What do you think you're doing?

LADY. Really, dear. I'd like to.

MAN. Oh, this is too much.

LADY. I'd *really*, really like to, dear.

[*She laughs, puts the cigar in her mouth. Turns to*
KIT. *He spits out tip. She does the same.*]

MAN (*loudly*). The mother of five grown men, and she's still looking
for *romance*. (*Shouts as* KIT *lights her cigar.*) No. I forbid it.

JOE (*shouting*). What's the matter with you? Why don't you leave
her alone? What are you always pushing your women around for?
(*Almost without a pause.*) Now, look, Tom. (*The* LADY *puts the
lighted cigar in her mouth, and begins to smoke, feeling wonderful.*)
Here's ten bucks.

TOM. Ten bucks?

JOE. He may want you to get into a truck and begin driving to San
Diego tonight.

TOM. Joe, I got to tell Kitty.

JOE. I'll tell her.

TOM. Joe, take care of her.

JOE. She'll be all right. Stop worrying about her. She's at the St.
Francis Hotel. Now look. Take a cab to Townsend and Fourth.
You'll see the big sign. Keith Motor Transport Company. He'll be
waiting for you.

TOM. O.K., Joe. (*Trying hard.*) Thanks, Joe.

JOE. Don't be silly. Get going.

[TOM *goes. The* LADY *starts puffing on the cigar. As*
TOM *goes,* WESLEY *and* HARRY *come in together.*]

NICK. Where the hell have you been? We've got to have some entertainment around here. Can't you see them fine people from uptown?
(*He points at the* SOCIETY LADY *and* GENTLEMAN.)

WESLEY. You said to come back at ten for the second show.

NICK. Did I say that?

WESLEY. Yes, sir, Mr. Nick, that's exactly what you said.

HARRY. Was the first show all right?

NICK. That wasn't a show. There was no one here to see it. How
can it be a show when no one sees it? People are afraid to come
down to the water front.

HARRY. Yeah. We were just down to Pier 27. One of the longshoremen
and a cop had a fight and the cop hit him over the head with a
blackjack. We saw it happen, didn't we?

WESLEY. Yes, sir, we was standing there looking when it happened.

NICK (*a little worried*). Anything else happen?

WESLEY. They was all talking.

HARRY. A man in a big car came up and said there was going to be a meeting right away and they hoped to satisfy everybody and stop the strike.

WESLEY. Right away. *Tonight.*

NICK. Well, it's about time. Them poor cops are liable to get nervous and—shoot somebody. (*To* HARRY, *suddenly.*) Come back here. I want you to tend bar for a while. I'm going to take a walk over to the pier.

HARRY. Yes, sir.

NICK (*to the* SOCIETY LADY *and* GENTLEMAN). You society people made up your minds yet?

LADY. Have you champagne?

NICK (*indicating* JOE). What do you think he's pouring out of that bottle, water or something?

LADY. Have you a chill bottle?

NICK. I've got a dozen of them chilled. He's been drinking champagne here all day and all night for a month now.

LADY. May we have a bottle?

NICK. It's six dollars.

LADY. I think we can manage.

MAN. I don't know. I *know* I don't know. [NICK *takes off his coat and helps* HARRY *into it.* HARRY *takes a bottle of champagne and two glasses to the* LADY *and the* GENTLEMAN, *dancing, collects six dollars, and goes back behind the bar, dancing.* NICK *gets his coat and hat.*]

NICK (*to* WESLEY). Rattle the keys a little, son. Rattle the keys.

WESLEY. Yes, sir, Mr. Nick.

[NICK *is on his way out. The* ARAB *enters.*]

NICK. Hi-ya, Mahmed.

ARAB. No foundation.

NICK. All the way down the line. (*He goes.*)

[WESLEY *is at the piano, playing quietly. The* ARAB *swallows a glass of beer, takes out his harmonica, and begins to play.* WESLEY *fits his playing to the* ARAB'S. KITTY DUVAL, *strangely beautiful, in new clothes, comes in. She walks shyly, as if she were embarrassed by the fine clothes, as if she had no right to wear them. The* LADY *and* GENTLEMAN *are very impressed.* HARRY *looks at her with amazement.* JOE *is reading* Time *magazine.* KITTY *goes to his table.* JOE *looks up from the magazine, without the least amazement.*]

JOE. Hello, Kitty.

KITTY. Hello, Joe.

JOE. It's nice seeing you again.

KITTY. I came in a cab.

JOE. You been crying again? (KITTY *can't answer. To* HARRY.) Bring a glass.

> [HARRY *comes over with a glass.* JOE *pours* KITTY *a drink.*]

KITTY. I've got to talk to you.

JOE. Have a drink.

KITTY. I've never been in burlesque. We were just poor.

JOE. Sit down, Kitty.

KITTY (*sits down*). I tried other things.

JOE. Here's to you, Katerina Koranovsky. Here's to you. And Tom.

KITTY (*sorrowfully*). Where *is* Tom?

JOE. He's getting a job tonight driving a truck. He'll be back in a couple of days.

KITTY (*sadly*). I told him I'd marry him.

JOE. He wanted to see you and say good-by.

KITTY. He's too good for me. He's like a little boy. (*Wearily.*) I'm—— Too many things have happened to me.

JOE. Kitty Duval, you're one of the few truly innocent people I have ever known. He'll be back in a couple of days. Go back to the hotel and wait for him.

KITTY. That's what I mean. I can't stand being alone. I'm no good. I tried very hard. I don't know what it is. I miss—— (*She gestures.*)

JOE (*gently*). Do you really want to come back here, Kitty?

KITTY. I don't know. I'm not sure. Everything *smells* different. I don't know how to feel, or what to think. (*Gesturing pathetically.*) I know I don't belong there. It's what I've wanted all my life, but it's too *late*. I try to be happy about it, but all I can do is remember everything and cry.

JOE. I don't know what to tell you, Kitty. I didn't mean to hurt you.

KITTY. You haven't hurt me. You're the only person who's ever been good to me. I've never known anybody like you. I'm not sure about love any more, but I know I love you, and I know I love Tom.

JOE. I love you too, Kitty Duval.

KITTY. He'll want babies. I know he will. I know *I* will, too. Of course I will. I can't—— (*She shakes her head.*)

JOE. Tom's a baby himself. You'll be very happy together. He wants you to ride with him in the truck. Tom's good for you. You're good for Tom.

KITTY (*like a child*). Do you want me to go back and wait for him?

JOE. I can't *tell* you what to do. I think it would be a good idea, though.

KITTY. I wish I could tell you how it makes me feel to be alone. It's almost worse.

JOE. It might take a whole week, Kitty. (*He looks at her sharply, at the arrival of an idea.*) Didn't you speak of reading a book? A book of poems?

KITTY. I didn't know what I was saying.

JOE (*trying to get up*). Of course you knew. I think you'll like poetry. Wait here a minute, Kitty. I'll go see if I can find some books.

KITTY. All right, Joe.

> [*He walks out of the place, trying very hard not to wobble. Foghorn. Music. The* NEWSBOY *comes in. Looks for* JOE. *Is brokenhearted because* JOE *is gone.*]

NEWSBOY (*to the* SOCIETY GENTLEMAN). Paper?

MAN (*angry*). No.

> [*The* NEWSBOY *goes to the* ARAB.]

NEWSBOY. Paper, mister?

ARAB (*irritated*). No foundation.

NEWSBOY. What?

ARAB (*very angry*). No foundation.

> [*The* NEWSBOY *starts out, turns, looks at the* ARAB, *shakes his head.*]

NEWSBOY. No foundation? How do you figure?

> [BLICK *and* TWO COPS *enter.*]

NEWSBOY (*to* BLICK). Paper, mister?

> [BLICK *pushes him aside. The* NEWSBOY *goes.*]

BLICK (*walking authoritatively about the place, to* HARRY). Where's Nick?

HARRY. He went for a walk.

BLICK. Who are you?

HARRY. Harry.

BLICK (*to the* ARAB *and* WESLEY). Hey, you. Shut up. (*The* ARAB *stops playing the harmonica,* WESLEY *the piano.* BLICK *studies* KITTY.) What's your name, sister?

KITTY (*looking at him*). Kitty Duval. What's it to you?

> [KITTY'S *voice is now like it was at the beginning of the play: tough, independent, bitter, and hard.*]

BLICK (*angry*). Don't give me any of your gutter lip. Just answer my questions.

KITTY. You go to hell, you.

BLICK (*coming over, enraged*). Where do you live?

KITTY. The New York Hotel. Room 21.

BLICK. Where do you work?

KITTY. I'm not working just now. I'm looking for work.

BLICK. What kind of work? (KITTY *can't answer.*) What kind of work? (KITTY *can't answer. Furiously.*) WHAT KIND OF WORK?

> [KIT CARSON *comes over.*]

KIT CARSON. You can't talk to a lady that way in *my* presence.

[BLICK *turns and stares at* KIT. *The* COPS *begin to move from the bar.*]

BLICK (*to the* COPS). It's all right, boys. I'll take care of this. (*To* KIT.) What'd you say?

KIT CARSON. You got no right to hurt people. Who are *you?*

[BLICK, *without a word, takes* KIT *to the street. Sounds of a blow and a groan.* BLICK *returns, breathing hard.*]

BLICK (*to the* COPS). O.K., boys. You can go now. Take care of him. Put him on his feet and tell him to behave himself from now on. (*To* KITTY *again.*) Now answer my question. What kind of work?

KITTY (*quietly*). You know what kind of work I do. And I know what kind you do.

MAN (*shocked and really hurt*). Excuse me, officer, but it seems to me that your attitude——

BLICK. Shut up.

MAN (*quietly*). ——is making the poor child say things that are not true.

BLICK. Shut up, I said.

LADY. Well. (*To the* MAN.) Are you going to stand for such insolence?

BLICK (*to the* MAN, *who is standing*). Are you?

MAN (*taking the woman's arm*). I'll get a divorce. I'll start life all over again. (*Pushing the woman.*) Come on. Get the hell out of here!

[*The* MAN *hurries his woman out of the place,* BLICK *watching them go.*]

BLICK (*to* KITTY). Now. Let's begin again, and see that you tell the truth. What's your name?

KITTY. Kitty Duval.

BLICK. Where do you live?

KITTY. Until this evening I lived at the New York Hotel. Room 21. This evening I moved to the St. Francis Hotel.

BLICK. Oh. To the St. Francis Hotel. Nice place. Where do you work?

KITTY. I'm looking for work.

BLICK. What kind of work do you do?

KITTY. I'm an actress.

BLICK. I see. What movies have I seen you in?

KITTY. I've worked in burlesque.

BLICK. You're a liar.

[WESLEY *stands, worried and full of dumb resentment.*]

KITTY (*pathetically, as at the beginning of the play*). It's the truth.

BLICK. What are you doing here?

KITTY. I came to see if I could get a job here.

BLICK. Doing what?

KITTY. Singing—and—dancing.

BLICK. You can't sing or dance. What are you lying for?
KITTY. I can. I sang and danced in burlesque all over the country.
BLICK. You're a liar.
KITTY. I said lines, too.
BLICK. So you danced in burlesque?
KITTY. Yes.
BLICK. All right. Let's see what you did.
KITTY. I can't. There's no music, and I haven't got the right clothes.
BLICK. There's music. (*To* WESLEY.) Put a nickel in that phonograph.
 (WESLEY *can't move.*) Come on. Put a nickel in that phonograph.
 (WESLEY *does so. To* KITTY.) All right. Get up on that stage and do
 a hot little burlesque number. (KITTY *stands. Walks slowly to the
 stage, but is unable to move.* JOE *comes in, holding three books.*)
 Get going, now. Let's see you dance the way you did in burlesque,
 all over the country.

> [KITTY *tries to do a burlesque dance. It is beautiful in
> a tragic way.*]

BLICK. All right, start taking them off!

> [KITTY *removes her hat and starts to remove her
> jacket.* JOE *moves closer to the stage, amazed.*]

JOE (*hurrying to* KITTY). Get down from there. (*He takes* KITTY *into
 his arms. She is crying. To* BLICK.) What the hell do you think you're
 doing!
WESLEY (*like a little boy, very angry*). It's that man, Blick. *He* made
 her take off her clothes. He beat up the old man, too.

> [BLICK *pushes* WESLEY *off as* TOM *enters.* BLICK *be-
> gins beating up* WESLEY.]

TOM. What's the matter, Joe? What's happened?
JOE. Is the truck out there?
TOM. Yeah, but what's happened? Kitty's crying again!
JOE. You driving to San Diego?
TOM. Yeah, Joe. But what's he doing to that poor colored boy?
JOE. Get going. Here's some money. Everything's O.K. (*To* KITTY.)
 Dress in the truck. Take these books.
WESLEY'S VOICE. You can't hurt me. You'll get yours. You wait and
 see.
TOM. Joe, he's hurting that boy. I'll kill him!
JOE (*pushing* TOM). Get out of here! Get married in San Diego. I'll
 see you when you get back. (TOM *and* KITTY *go.* NICK *enters and
 stands at the lower end of bar.* JOE *takes the revolver out of his
 pocket. Looks at it.*) I've always wanted to kill somebody, but I never
 knew who it should be.

> [*He cocks the revolver, stands real straight, holds it in
> front of him firmly, and walks to the door. He stands
> a moment watching* BLICK, *aims very carefully, and*

pulls the trigger. There is no shot. NICK *runs over and grabs the gun, and takes* JOE *aside.*]

NICK. What the hell do you think you're doing?

JOE (*casually, but angry*). That dumb Tom. Buys a six-shooter that won't even shoot once.

[JOE *sits down, dead to the world.* BLICK *comes out, panting for breath.* NICK *looks at him. He speaks slowly.*]

NICK. Blick! I told you to stay out of here! Now get out of here. (*He takes* BLICK *by the collar, tightening his grip as he speaks, and pushing him out.*) If you come back again, I'm going to take you in that room where you've been beating up that colored boy, and I'm going to murder you—slowly—with my hands. Beat it! (*He pushes* BLICK *out. To* HARRY.) Go take care of the colored boy.

[HARRY *runs out.* WILLIE *returns and doesn't sense that anything is changed.* WILLIE *puts another nickel into the machine, but he does so very violently. The consequence of this violence is that the flag comes up again.* WILLIE, *amazed, stands at attention and salutes. The flag goes down. He shakes his head.*]

WILLIE (*thoughtfully*). As far as I'm concerned, this is the *only* country in the world. If you ask me, *nuts* to Europe! (*He is about to push the slide in again when the flag comes up again. Furiously, to* NICK, *while he salutes and stands at attention, pleadingly.*) Hey, Nick. This machine is out of order.

NICK (*somberly*). Give it a whack on the side.

[WILLIE *does so. A hell of a whack. The result is, the flag comes up and down, and* WILLIE *keeps saluting.*]

WILLIE (*saluting*). Hey, Nick. Something's wrong.

[*The machine quiets down abruptly.* WILLIE *very stealthily slides a new nickel in, and starts a new game. From a distance two pistol shots are heard, each carefully timed.* NICK *runs out. The* NEWSBOY *enters, crosses to* JOE'S *table, senses something is wrong.*]

NEWSBOY (*softly*). Paper, mister?

[JOE *can't hear him. The* NEWSBOY *backs away, studies* JOE, *wishes he could cheer* JOE *up. Notices the phonograph, goes to it and puts a coin in it, hoping music will make* JOE *happier. The* NEWSBOY *sits down. Watches* JOE. *The music begins. "The Missouri Waltz." The* DRUNKARD *comes in and walks around. Then sits down.* NICK *comes back.*]

NICK (*delighted*). Joe, Blick's dead! Somebody just shot him, and none of the cops are trying to find out who.

[JOE *doesn't hear.* NICK *steps back, studying* JOE.]

NICK (*shouting*). Joe.

JOE (*looking up*). What?

NICK. Blick's dead.

JOE. Blick? Dead? Good! That goddamn gun wouldn't go off. I *told* Tom to get a good one.

NICK (*picking up the gun and looking at it*). Joe, you wanted to kill that guy! (HARRY *returns.* JOE *puts the gun in his coat pocket.*) I'm going to buy you a bottle of champagne.

[NICK *goes to the bar.* JOE *rises, takes his hat from the rack, puts his coat on. The* NEWSBOY *jumps up, helps* JOE *with the coat.*]

NICK. What's the matter, Joe?

JOE. Nothing. Nothing.

NICK. How about the champagne?

JOE. Thanks. (*Going.*)

NICK. It's not eleven yet. Where you going, Joe?

JOE. I don't know. Nowhere.

NICK. Will I see you tomorrow?

JOE. I don't know. I don't think so.

[KIT CARSON *enters, walks to* JOE. JOE *and* KIT *look at one another knowingly.*]

JOE. Somebody just shot a man. How are you feeling?

KIT. Never felt better in my life. (*Loudly, bragging, but somber.*) I shot a man once. In San Francisco. Shot him two times. In 1939, I think it was. In October. Fellow named Blick or Glick or something like that. Couldn't stand the way he talked to ladies. Went up to my room and got my old pearl-handled revolver and waited for him on Pacific Street. Saw him walking, and let him have it, two times. Had to throw the beautiful revolver into the Bay.

[HARRY, NICK, *the* ARAB, *and the* DRUNKARD *close in around him.* JOE *searches his pockets, brings out the revolver, puts it in* KIT'S *hand, looks at him with great admiration and affection,* JOE *walks slowly to the stairs leading to the street, turns and waves.* KIT, *and then one by one everybody else, waves, and the marble game goes into its beautiful American routine again: flag, lights, and music. The play ends.*]

QUESTIONS

ACT I

1. Is Saroyan being entirely ironic when he describes the contest between Willie and the pinball machine as a "great drama"? What values does

Willie stand for in this contest, and what does the machine represent?

2. Would it be impossible to convey on the stage some of the informa-
    tion Saroyan provides in his stage descriptions? For example, how
    could a director translate into stage terms the information Saroyan
    provides about Kitty Duval's attitude and beauty?

3. In his directions for living printed at the beginning of the play,
    Saroyan says, "Be the inferior of no man, nor of any man be the
    superior." Does Joe live up to these directions? Do the others who
    wander into Nick's bar?

4. What is the significance of Dudley R. Bostwick's getting the wrong
    number, then making the date with Lorene, and Lorene's appearance
    when she arrives at the bar?

5. Through the last part of the act Joe plays with the mechanical toys on
    the table. How does this "act out" what has been going on in the bar?
    This is Joe's image of life in Nick's, but is it entirely a true image?

6. Before Blick's entrance a number of strange and apparently dissimilar
    people have shown up in Nick's. What do all these people have in
    common? Do they share a motive, i.e., are they all trying to do the
    same thing?

7. How does Saroyan dramatize the fact that Blick and what he repre-
    sents bring life to a stop?

ACT II

8. Characters in a play often create for themselves a small world within
    the larger one in which they actually live (Hedda Gabler's drawing
    room, for example). What is the meaning in this play of setting that
    smaller world in a honky-tonk? How does this tavern differ from The
    Boar's Head in *I Henry IV*?

9. How does Saroyan make real the larger world that begins just outside
    the doors of the bar? What kind of a world is it? Would you say that
    the bar is related to the larger world of this play in the same way that
    Hedda Gabler's drawing room is related to the world outside it?

10. What is the meaning of Joe's remaining seated at the table while
    everyone else moves about? In answering this question you will find it
    helpful to consider "dancing" carefully.

11. Can you see any relation between Joe's attitudes, as expressed in
    language, and his actions when he does get up?

12. What is the philosophy of "the what and the what-not"? Is this the
    view of life implicit in the play and does it explain which actions are
    valuable and which are not? Does the "what" need the "what-not" in
    this play in order to exist? To answer this last question consider who
    represents the "what" and who the "what-not" and how they interact.

13. "Living is an art. It's not bookkeeping." Is this as true of the other
    characters as it is of Kit Carson? How does the character of Kit
    Carson bring together and focus the sense of personality and life in
    America that is everywhere in the play?

ACT III

14. Is the musical carousel a good visual image of life as it is portrayed in the play?

15. In what ways does Kitty's room at the New York Hotel contrast with Nick's bar? What kind of set and lighting effects would you use to make clear these differences?

ACT IV

16. Why doesn't Elsie want to marry Dudley? How do her reasons further expand the meaning of the world outside the bar?

17. How are Elsie's objections overcome? Are there other instances of this same power at work in the play?

18. What is the meaning of the entrance of the two streetwalkers while Elsie and Dudley are arguing?

19. Can any sense be made of the Arab's repeated statement, "No foundation," and, if so, does it provide any insights into the meaning of the play?

ACT V

20. What contrast of values is achieved by juxtaposing the Salvation Army outside with Joe inside looking at the atlas? (Czechoslovakia had just been given to Germany when this play was written.)

21. Do you see any significance in the titles of the magazines Joe sends Tom out to buy? any irony? Why the chewing gum? Look back to see if there is any pattern to the objects Tom is sent out for—any progression that parallels the movement of the play?

22. The pinball machine's paying off is a magnificent piece of theater, but is it only that? Has Saroyan made of Willie and the machine a symbol of what happens in the play?

23. Compare Blick's approach to the stories Kitty tells about her life with the way Joe responds to them. Does Blick represent just brutality and cruelty?

24. In tragedy would Joe's gun misfire? Is the good luck that it does not fire "unrealistic"? Even if so, is the view of the way the world operates, symbolized by the misfire, unrealistic?

25. The play ends with Kit Carson killing Blick, the "unreal" destroying the "real." How does this concluding event sum up the plot of the play? Could the action of the play be described as a series of attempts "to kill Blick"?

26. Why does the Arab not say, "No foundation" at the end of the play?

27. What is the meaning of the fact that Kit Carson can kill Blick, but Joe cannot?

THE MISANTHROPE

BY

MOLIÈRE

Molière, whose real name was Jean-Baptiste Poquelin (1622–73), was one of the great actors of his day and the greatest of all French comic playwrights. His father was upholsterer to the French king, Louis XIV, and after a half-hearted attempt to study law, Molière followed for a brief time his father's trade. He seems to have been what would be described now as "stage-struck," and about 1642 joined a company of players. The company failed in Paris and set off for the provinces, where they toured from 1645 to 1658. During this time Molière learned the trade of actor and became the leading player of his company, but he wrote only a few short plays. On their return to Paris, Molière and his company found favor with the King as a result of a farce of Molière's presented at a royal performance. From this time on their fortune was assured, and Molière, apparently encouraged by the King's kindness, produced a series of great comedies such as *The School for Wives* (1662), *The Misanthrope* (1666), *Tartuffe* (1667), *The Miser* (1668), *The Bourgeois Gentleman* (1670), and *The Hypochondriac* (1673). He died shortly after playing the leading role in a performance of this last play.

Molière was a comic dramatist. Each of his plays celebrates the triumph of pleasure, good sense, and the socially useful over stupidity, pride, rigidity, and selfishness. Like all comedies, his plays show the value of *what works* in life. The establishment of transcendental values, the probing of ultimate moral problems, and the search for absolute truths are left to tragedy. But Molière was aware of the claim of ideals, and in *The Misanthrope* he arranges a confrontation of the tragic and comic values. Behind the two chief characters of the play, Alceste and Philinte, Molière places an obviously imperfect, perhaps even a corrupt, world. Beneath their elegant manners and polished language, the fashionable gentlemen and ladies of the Paris of Louis XIV are bores, flirts, hypocrites, clotheshorses, sycophants, and plain fools. They write bad poetry and insist on being praised for it; they ruin reputations under cover of pretended friendship; they seek their own advancement by means of bribes and flattery; they spend "three quarters of an hour spitting into a well, so as to make circles in the water." There may be a few good people in it, but on the whole Philinte's summation catches this world nicely:

> This is a low, conniving age indeed;
> Nothing but trickery prospers nowadays,
> And people ought to mend their shabby ways.
> Yes, man's a beastly creature; . . .

The question posed by the play is, "How are we to act in such a world?" and this gigantic problem is made dramatically manageable by narrowing it to a consideration of two crucial areas of human activity—social relationships and love.

Most of the characters are blissfully unaware of any gap between their manners and their morals, between their masks and the realities of their natures. Since they observe all the social proprieties, they are able to assume that they are proper people, even while indulging in the most vicious activities. Both Philinte and Alceste recognize these imperfections, but the conclusions they draw are quite different. The discovery of human imperfection is no surprise to Philinte. This is the way people are, always have been, and always will be. This is human nature: we might as well be shocked that the "vulture dines upon the dead." Since these are the facts of human nature, it is of no use to rail at mankind, "The world won't change, whatever you say or do." Recognizing this, Philinte adjusts his conduct accordingly. He greets effusively a man whose name he scarcely knows; he praises extravagantly the sonnet of a rhyming peer; he compliments bores on their wit and decayed belles on their beauty. Since bribes and flattery are necessary to win a judgment in court, he recommends bribes and flattery to the man engaged in lawsuits. And he does all this not for personal gain, but in the name of a realistic value: society. If everyone were absolutely frank and truthful society would degenerate into open warfare:

> Wouldn't the social fabric come undone
> If we were wholly frank with everyone?

Philinte is a man, as he says, of "pliant rectitude," but his opposite, the man with green ribbons, Alceste, is stiff and rigid and rude. He rejects Philinte's social argument and argues for absolute standards. The basis of his conduct is quite simple: he sees the truth, that men are knaves and fools, and he acts in conformity with this truth. He will not stoop to curry favor or to flatter man or poet. Where he finds deceit he exposes it; what he feels he says; what he knows he acts upon. The man of truth is one who displays his "inmost heart" in everything he does and says. And the truth admits no paltering: right is right and wrong is wrong. His disgust with mankind is limitless. Having discovered that there is a great deal of folly in the world, he sweeps on to the conclusion that "all are corrupt." He would agree with the satirist Persius who shouts, "Who is there who has not the ears of an ass?" Rigid integrity, frankness, reliance on self—these are his most apparent and his most engaging qualities, but they get him into frequent trouble and disrupt the smooth surface of society.

The conflicting points of view represented by Alceste and Philinte are also present—though with darker overtones—in Shakespeare's *Hamlet,* the play that follows *The Misanthrope* in this volume. These two plays throw a great deal of light on one another and offer between them a good illustration of the difference between comedy and tragedy.

CHARACTERS

ALCESTE, *in love with Célimène*
PHILINTE, *Alceste's friend*
ORONTE, *in love with Célimène*
CÉLIMÈNE, *Alceste's beloved*
ÉLIANTE, *Célimène's cousin*
ARSINOÉ, *a friend of Célimène's*
ACASTE }*marquesses*
CLITANDRE }
BASQUE, *Célimène's servant*
A GUARD *of the Marshalsea*
DUBOIS, *Alceste's valet*

The scene throughout is in Célimène's house at Paris.

ACT I

Scene 1   PHILINTE, ALCESTE.

PHILINTE. Now, what's got into you?

ALCESTE (*seated*).   Kindly leave me alone.

PHILINTE. Come, come, what is it? This lugubrious tone . . .

ALCESTE. Leave me, I said; you spoil my solitude.

PHILINTE. Oh, listen to me, now, and don't be rude.

ALCESTE. I choose to be rude, Sir, and to be hard of hearing.

PHILINTE. These ugly moods of yours are not endearing;
 Friends though we are, I really must insist . . .

ALCESTE (*abruptly rising*). Friends? Friends, you say? Well, cross me
 off your list.
 I've been your friend till now, as you well know;
 But after what I saw a moment ago
 I tell you flatly that our ways must part.
 I wish no place in a dishonest heart.

PHILINTE. Why, what have I done, Alceste? Is this quite just?

ALCESTE. My God, you ought to die of self-disgust.
 I call your conduct inexcusable, Sir,
 And every man of honor will concur.
 I see you almost hug a man to death,
 Exclaim for joy until you're out of breath,
 And supplement these loving demonstrations
 With endless offers, vows, and protestations;
 Then when I ask you "Who was that?" I find
 That you can barely bring his name to mind!
 Once the man's back is turned, you cease to love him,
 And speak with absolute indifference of him!
 By God, I say it's base and scandalous
 To falsify the heart's affections thus;
 If I caught myself behaving in such a way,
 I'd hang myself for shame, without delay.

PHILINTE. It hardly seems a hanging matter to me;

      I hope that you will take it graciously
      If I extend myself a slight reprieve,
      And live a little longer, by your leave.
ALCESTE. How dare you joke about a crime so grave?
PHILINTE. What crime? How else are people to behave?
ALCESTE. I'd have them be sincere, and never part
      With any word that isn't from the heart.
PHILINTE. When someone greets us with a show of pleasure,
      It's but polite to give him equal measure,
      Return his love the best that we know how,
      And trade him offer for offer, vow for vow.
ALCESTE. No, no, this formula you'd have me follow,
      However fashionable, is false and hollow,
      And I despise the frenzied operations
      Of all these barterers of protestations,
      These lavishers of meaningless embraces,
      These utterers of obliging commonplaces,
      Who court and flatter everyone on earth
      And praise the fool no less than the man of worth.
      Should you rejoice that someone fondles you,
      Offers his love and service, swears to be true,
      And fills your ears with praises of your name,
      When to the first damned fop he'll say the same?
      No, no: no self-respecting heart would dream
      Of prizing so promiscuous an esteem;
      However high the praise, there's nothing worse
      Than sharing honors with the universe.
      Esteem is founded on comparison:
      To honor all men is to honor none.
      Since you embrace this indiscriminate vice,
      Your friendship comes at far too cheap a price;
      I spurn the easy tribute of a heart
      Which will not set the worthy man apart:
      I choose, Sir, to be chosen; and in fine,
      The friend of mankind is no friend of mine.
PHILINTE. But in polite society, custom decrees
      That we show certain outward courtesies. . . .
ALCESTE. Ah, no! we should condemn with all our force
      Such false and artificial intercourse.
      Let men behave like men; let them display
      Their inmost hearts in everything they say;
      Let the heart speak, and let our sentiments
      Not mask themselves in silly compliments.
PHILINTE. In certain cases it would be uncouth
      And most absurd to speak the naked truth;

With all respect for your exalted notions,
It's often best to veil one's true emotions.
Wouldn't the social fabric come undone
If we were wholly frank with everyone?
Suppose you met with someone you couldn't bear;
Would you inform him of it then and there?

ALCESTE. Yes.

PHILINTE.   Then you'd tell old Emilie it's pathetic
The way she daubs her features with cosmetic
And plays the gay coquette at sixty-four?

ALCESTE. I would.

PHILINTE.   And you'd call Dorilas a bore,
And tell him every ear at court is lame
From hearing him brag about his noble name?

ALCESTE. Precisely.

PHILINTE.   Ah, you're joking.

ALCESTE.   *Au contraire:*
In this regard there's none I'd choose to spare.
All are corrupt; there's nothing to be seen
In court or town but aggravates my spleen.
I fall into deep gloom and melancholy
When I survey the scene of human folly,
Finding on every hand base flattery,
Injustice, fraud, self-interest, treachery. . . .
Ah, it's too much; mankind has grown so base,
I mean to break with the whole human race.

PHILINTE. This philosophic rage is a bit extreme;
You've no idea how comical you seem;
Indeed, we're like those brothers in the play
Called *School for Husbands*, one of whom was prey . . .

ALCESTE. Enough, now! None of your stupid similes.

PHILINTE. Then let's have no more tirades, if you please.
The world won't change, whatever you say or do;
And since plain speaking means so much to you,
I'll tell you plainly that by being frank
You've earned the reputation of a crank,
And that you're thought ridiculous when you rage
And rant against the manners of the age.

ALCESTE. So much the better; just what I wish to hear.
No news could be more grateful to my ear.
All men are so detestable in my eyes,
I should be sorry if they thought me wise.

PHILINTE. Your hatred's very sweeping, is it not?

ALCESTE. Quite right: I hate the whole degraded lot.

PHILINTE. Must all poor human creatures be embraced,

Without distinction, by your vast distaste?
Even in these bad times, there are surely a few . . .
ALCESTE. No, I include all men in one dim view:
    Some men I hate for being rogues; the others
    I hate because they treat the rogues like brothers,
    And, lacking a virtuous scorn for what is vile,
    Receive the villain with a complaisant smile.
    Notice how tolerant people choose to be
    Toward that bold rascal who's at law with me.
    His social polish can't conceal his nature;
    One sees at once that he's a treacherous creature;
    No one could possibly be taken in
    By those soft speeches and that sugary grin.
    The whole world knows the shady means by which
    The low-brow's grown so powerful and rich,
    And risen to a rank so bright and high
    That virtue can but blush, and merit sigh.
    Whenever his name comes up in conversation,
    None will defend his wretched reputation;
    Call him knave, liar, scoundrel, and all the rest,
    Each head will nod, and no one will protest.
    And yet his smirk is seen in every house,
    He's greeted everywhere with smiles and bows,
    And when there's any honor that can be got
    By pulling strings, he'll get it, like as not.
    My God! It chills my heart to see the ways
    Men come to terms with evil nowadays;
    Sometimes, I swear, I'm moved to flee and find
    Some desert land unfouled by humankind.
PHILINTE. Come, let's forget the follies of the times
    And pardon mankind for its petty crimes;
    Let's have an end of rantings and of railings,
    And show some leniency toward human failings.
    This world requires a pliant rectitude;
    Too stern a virtue makes one stiff and rude;
    Good sense views all extremes with detestation,
    And bids us to be noble in moderation.
    The rigid virtues of the ancient days
    Are not for us; they jar with all our ways
    And ask of us too lofty a perfection.
    Wise men accept their times without objection,
    And there's no greater folly, if you ask me,
    Than trying to reform society.
    Like you, I see each day a hundred and one
    Unhandsome deeds that might be better done,

But still, for all the faults that meet my view,
I'm never known to storm and rave like you.
I take men as they are, or let them be,
And teach my soul to bear their frailty;
And whether in court or town, whatever the scene,
My phlegm's as philosophic as your spleen.

ALCESTE. This phlegm which you so eloquently commend,
Does nothing ever rile it up, my friend?
Suppose some man you trust should treacherously
Conspire to rob you of your property,
And do his best to wreck your reputation?
Wouldn't you feel a certain indignation?

PHILINTE. Why, no. These faults of which you so complain
Are part of human nature, I maintain,
And it's no more a matter for disgust
That men are knavish, selfish and unjust,
Than that the vulture dines upon the dead,
And wolves are furious, and apes ill-bred.

ALCESTE. Shall I see myself betrayed, robbed, torn to bits,
And not . . . Oh, let's be still and rest our wits.
Enough of reasoning, now. I've had my fill.

PHILINTE. Indeed, you would do well, Sir, to be still.
Rage less at your opponent, and give some thought
To how you'll win this lawsuit that he's brought.

ALCESTE. I assure you I'll do nothing of the sort.

PHILINTE. Then who will plead your case before the court?

ALCESTE. Reason and right and justice will plead for me.

PHILINTE. Oh, Lord. What judges do you plan to see?

ALCESTE. Why, none. The justice of my cause is clear.

PHILINTE. Of course, man; but there's politics to fear. . . .

ALCESTE. No, I refuse to lift a hand. That's flat.
I'm either right, or wrong.

PHILINTE.   Don't count on that.

ALCESTE. No, I'll do nothing.

PHILINTE.   Your enemy's influence
Is great, you know . . .

ALCESTE.   That makes no difference.

PHILINTE. It will; you'll see.

ALCESTE.   Must honor bow to guile?
If so, I shall be proud to lose the trial.

PHILINTE. Oh, really . . .

ALCESTE.   I'll discover by this case
Whether or not men are sufficiently base
And impudent and villainous and perverse
To do me wrong before the universe.

PHILINTE. What a man!
ALCESTE.   Oh, I could wish, whatever the cost,
    Just for the beauty of it, that my trial were lost.
PHILINTE. If people heard you talking so, Alceste,
    They'd split their sides. Your name would be a jest.
ALCESTE. So much the worse for jesters.
PHILINTE.   May I enquire
    Whether this rectitude you so admire,
    And these hard virtues you're enamored of
    Are qualities of the lady whom you love?
    It much surprises me that you, who seem
    To view mankind with furious disesteem,
    Have yet found something to enchant your eyes
    Amidst a species which you so despise.
    And what is more amazing, I'm afraid,
    Is the most curious choice your heart has made.
    The honest Éliante is fond of you,
    Arsinoé, the prude, admires you too;
    And yet your spirit's been perversely led
    To choose the flighty Célimène instead,
    Whose brittle malice and coquettish ways
    So typify the manners of our days.
    How is it that the traits you most abhor
    Are bearable in this lady you adore?
    Are you so blind with love that you can't find them?
    Or do you contrive, in her case, not to mind them?
ALCESTE. My love for that young widow's not the kind
    That can't perceive defects; no, I'm not blind.
    I see her faults, despite my ardent love,
    And all I see I fervently reprove.
    And yet I'm weak; for all her falsity,
    That woman knows the art of pleasing me,
    And though I never cease complaining of her,
    I swear I cannot manage not to love her.
    Her charm outweighs her faults; I can but aim
    To cleanse her spirit in my love's pure flame.
PHILINTE. That's no small task; I wish you all success.
    You think then that she loves you?
ALCESTE.   Heavens, yes!
    I wouldn't love her did she not love me.
PHILINTE. Well, if her taste for you is plain to see,
    Why do these rivals cause you such despair?
ALCESTE. True love, Sir, is possessive, and cannot bear
    To share with all the world. I'm here today
    To tell her she must send that mob away.

PHILINTE. If I were you, and had your choice to make,
    Éliante, her cousin, would be the one I'd take;
    That honest heart, which cares for you alone,
    Would harmonize far better with your own.
ALCESTE. True, true: each day my reason tells me so;
    But reason doesn't rule in love, you know.
PHILINTE. I fear some bitter sorrow is in store;
    This love . . .

Scene 2   ORONTE, ALCESTE, PHILINTE.

ORONTE (*to* ALCESTE). The servants told me at the door
    That Éliante and Célimène were out,
    But when I heard, dear Sir, that you were about,
    I came to say, without exaggeration,
    That I hold you in the vastest admiration,
    And that it's always been my dearest desire
    To be the friend of one I so admire.
    I hope to see my love of merit requited,
    And you and I in friendship's bond united.
    I'm sure you won't refuse—if I may be frank—
    A friend of my devotedness—and rank.
        [*During this speech of* ORONTE'S, ALCESTE *is ab-*
        stracted, and seems unaware that he is being spoken
        to. He only breaks off his reverie when ORONTE *says:*]
    It was for you, if you please, that my words were intended.
ALCESTE. For me, Sir?
ORONTE.   Yes, for you. You're not offended?
ALCESTE. By no means. But this much surprises me. . . .
    The honor comes most unexpectedly. . . .
ORONTE. My high regard should not astonish you;
    The whole world feels the same. It is your due.
ALCESTE. Sir . . .
ORONTE.   Why, in all the State there isn't one
    Can match your merits; they shine, Sir, like the sun
ALCESTE. Sir . . .
ORONTE.   You are higher in my estimation
    Than all that's most illustrious in the nation.
ALCESTE. Sir . . .
ORONTE.   If I lie, may heaven strike me dead!
    To show you that I mean what I have said,
    Permit me, Sir, to embrace you most sincerely,

And swear that I will prize our friendship dearly.
Give me your hand. And now, Sir, if you choose,
We'll make our vows.

ALCESTE.   Sir . . .

ORONTE.   What! You refuse?

ALCESTE. Sir, it's a very great honor you extend:
But friendship is a sacred thing, my friend;
It would be profanation to bestow
The name of friend on one you hardly know.
All parts are better played when well-rehearsed;
Let's put off friendship, and get acquainted first.
We may discover it would be unwise
To try to make our natures harmonize.

ORONTE. By heaven! You're sagacious to the core;
This speech has made me admire you even more.
Let time, then, bring us closer day by day;
Meanwhile, I shall be yours in every way.
If, for example, there should be anything
You wish at court, I'll mention it to the King.
I have his ear, of course; it's quite well known
That I am much in favor with the throne.
In short, I am your servant. And now, dear friend,
Since you have such fine judgment, I intend
To please you, if I can, with a small sonnet
I wrote not long ago. Please comment on it,
And tell me whether I ought to publish it.

ALCESTE. You must excuse me, Sir; I'm hardly fit
To judge such matters.

ORONTE.   Why not?

ALCESTE.   I am, I fear,
Inclined to be unfashionably sincere.

ORONTE. Just what I ask; I'd take no satisfaction
In anything but your sincere reaction.
I beg you not to dream of being kind.

ALCESTE. Since you desire it, Sir, I'll speak my mind.

ORONTE. *Sonnet*. It's a sonnet. . . . *Hope* . . . The poem's addressed
To a lady who wakened hopes within my breast.
Hope . . . this is not the pompous sort of thing,
Just modest little verses, with a tender ring.

ALCESTE. Well, we shall see.

ORONTE.   *Hope* . . . I'm anxious to hear
Whether the style seems properly smooth and clear,
And whether the choice of words is good or bad.

ALCESTE. We'll see, we'll see.

ORONTE.   Perhaps I ought to add

That it took me only a quarter-hour to write it.
ALCESTE. The time's irrelevant, Sir: Kindly recite it.
ORONTE (*reading*).

> *Hope comforts us awhile, 'tis true,*
> *Lulling our cares with careless laughter,*
> *And yet such joy is full of rue,*
> *My Phyllis, if nothing follows after.*

PHILINTE. I'm charmed by this already; the style's delightful.
ALCESTE (*sotto voce, to* PHILINTE). How can you say that? Why the
  thing is frightful.

ORONTE.   *Your fair face smiled on me awhile,*
> *But was it kindness so to enchant me?*
> *'Twould have been fairer not to smile,*
> *If hope was all you meant to grant me.*

PHILINTE. What a clever thought! How handsomely you phrase it!
ALCESTE (*sotto voce, to* PHILINTE). You know the thing is trash. How
  dare you praise it?

ORONTE.   *If it's to be my passion's fate*
> *Thus everlastingly to wait,*
> *Then death will come to set me free:*
> *For death is fairer than the fair;*
> *Phyllis, to hope is to despair*
> *When one must hope eternally.*

PHILINTE. The close is exquisite—full of feeling and grace.
ALCESTE (*sotto voce, aside*). Oh, blast the close; you'd better close your
  face
  Before you send your lying soul to hell.
PHILINTE. I can't remember a poem I've liked so well.
ALCESTE (*sotto voce, aside*). Good Lord!
ORONTE (*to* PHILINTE).   I fear you're flattering me a
  bit.
PHILINTE. Oh, no!
ALCESTE (*sotto voce, aside*).
            What else d'you call it, you hypocrite?
ORONTE (*to* ALCESTE). But you, Sir, keep your promise now: don't
  shrink
  From telling me sincerely what you think.
ALCESTE. Sir, these are delicate matters; we all desire
  To be told that we've the true poetic fire.
  But once, to one whose name I shall not mention,
  I said, regarding some verse of his invention,

That gentlemen should rigorously control
That itch to write which often afflicts the soul;
That one should curb the heady inclination
To publicize one's little avocation;
And that in showing off one's works of art
One often plays a very clownish part.

ORONTE. Are you suggesting in a devious way
    That I ought not . . .

ALCESTE.   Oh, that I do not say.
    Further, I told him that no fault is worse
    Than that of writing frigid, lifeless verse,
    And that the merest whisper of such a shame
    Suffices to destroy a man's good name.

ORONTE. D'you mean to say my sonnet's dull and trite?

ALCESTE. I don't say that. But I went on to cite
    Numerous cases of once-respected men
    Who came to grief by taking up the pen.

ORONTE. And am I like them? Do I write so poorly?

ALCESTE. I don't say that. But I told this person, "Surely
    You're under no necessity to compose;
    Why you should wish to publish, heaven knows.
    There's no excuse for printing tedious rot
    Unless one writes for bread, as you do not.
    Resist temptation, then, I beg of you;
    Conceal your pastimes from the public view;
    And don't give up, on any provocation,
    Your present high and courtly reputation,
    To purchase at a greedy printer's shop
    The name of silly author and scribbling fop."
    These were the points I tried to make him see.

ORONTE. I sense that they are also aimed at me;
    But now—about my sonnet—I'd like to be told . . .

ALCESTE. Frankly, that sonnet should be pigeonholed.
    You've chosen the worst models to imitate.
    The style's unnatural. Let me illustrate:

        For example, *Your fair face smiled on me awhile,*
        Followed by, *'Twould have been fairer not to smile!*
        Or this: *such joy is full of rue;*
        Or this: *For death is fairer than the fair;*
        Or, *Phyllis, to hope is to despair*
            When one must hope eternally!

This artificial style, that's all the fashion,
Has neither taste, nor honesty, nor passion;
It's nothing but a sort of wordy play,

And nature never spoke in such a way.
What, in this shallow age, is not debased?
Our fathers, though less refined, had better taste;
I'd barter all that men admire today
For one old love song I shall try to say:

> *If the King had given me for my own*
> *Paris, his citadel,*
> *And I for that must leave alone*
> *Her whom I love so well,*
> *I'd say then to the Crown,*
> *Take back your glittering town;*
> *My darling is more fair, I swear,*
> *My darling is more fair.*

The rhyme's not rich, the style is rough and old,
But don't you see that it's the purest gold
Beside the tinsel nonsense now preferred,
And that there's passion in its every word?

> *If the King had given me for my own*
> *Paris, his citadel,*
> *And I for that must leave alone*
> *Her whom I love so well,*
> *I'd say then to the Crown,*
> *Take back your glittering town;*
> *My darling is more fair, I swear,*
> *My darling is more fair.*

There speaks a loving heart. (*To* PHILINTE) You're laughing, eh?
Laugh on, my precious wit. Whatever you say,
I hold that song's worth all the bibelots
That people hail today with ah's and oh's.

ORONTE. And I maintain my sonnet's very good.

ALCESTE. It's not at all surprising that you should.
You have your reasons; permit me to have mine
For thinking that you cannot write a line.

ORONTE. Others have praised my sonnet to the skies.

ALCESTE. I lack their art of telling pleasant lies.

ORONTE. You seem to think you've got no end of wit.

ALCESTE. To praise your verse, I'd need still more of it.

ORONTE. I'm not in need of your approval, Sir.

ALCESTE. That's good; you couldn't have it if you were.

ORONTE. Come now, I'll lend you the subject of my sonnet;
I'd like to see you try to improve upon it.

ALCESTE. I might, by chance, write something just as shoddy;

But then I wouldn't show it to everybody.
ORONTE. You're most opinionated and conceited.
ALCESTE. Go find your flatterers, and be better treated.
ORONTE. Look here, my little fellow, pray watch your tone.
ALCESTE. My great big fellow, you'd better watch your own.
PHILINTE (*stepping between them*). Oh, please, please, gentlemen! This
    will never do.
ORONTE. The fault is mine, and I leave the field to you.
    I am your servant, Sir, in every way.
ALCESTE. And I, Sir, am your most abject valet.

Scene 3   PHILINTE, ALCESTE.

PHILINTE. Well, as you see, sincerity in excess
    Can get you into a very pretty mess;
    Oronte was hungry for appreciation. . . .
ALCESTE. Don't speak to me.
PHILINTE.   What?
ALCESTE.   No more conversation.
PHILINTE. Really, now . . .
ALCESTE.   Leave me alone.
PHILINTE.   If I . . .
ALCESTE.   Out of my sight!
PHILINTE. But what . . .
ALCESTE.   I won't listen.
PHILINTE.   But . . .
ALCESTE.   Silence!
PHILINTE.   Now, is it polite . . .
ALCESTE. By heaven, I've had enough. Don't follow me.
PHILINTE. Ah, you're just joking. I'll keep you company.

ACT II

Scene 1 ⚬⚬ ALCESTE, CÉLIMÈNE.

ALCESTE. Shall I speak plainly, Madam? I confess
    Your conduct gives me infinite distress,
    And my resentment's grown too hot to smother.
    Soon, I foresee, we'll break with one another.
    If I said otherwise, I should deceive you;
    Sooner or later, I shall be forced to leave you,
    And if I swore that we shall never part,
    I should misread the omens of my heart.
CÉLIMÈNE. You kindly saw me home, it would appear,
    So as to pour invectives in my ear.
ALCESTE. I've no desire to quarrel. But I deplore
    Your inability to shut the door
    On all these suitors who beset you so.
    There's what annoys me, if you care to know.
CÉLIMÈNE. Is it my fault that all these men pursue me?
    Am I to blame if they're attracted to me?
    And when they gently beg an audience,
    Ought I to take a stick and drive them hence?
ALCESTE. Madam, there's no necessity for a stick;
    A less responsive heart would do the trick.
    Of your attractiveness I don't complain;
    But those your charms attract, you then detain
    By a most melting and receptive manner,
    And so enlist their hearts beneath your banner.
    It's the agreeable hopes which you excite
    That keep these lovers round you day and night;
    Were they less liberally smiled upon,
    That sighing troop would very soon be gone.
    But tell me, Madam, why it is that lately
    This man Clitandre interests you so greatly?
    Because of what high merits do you deem

Him worthy of the honor of your esteem?
Is it that your admiring glances linger
On the splendidly long nail of his little finger?
Or do you share the general deep respect
For the blond wig he chooses to affect?
Are you in love with his embroidered hose?
Do you adore his ribbons and his bows?
Or is it that this paragon bewitches
Your tasteful eye with his vast German breeches?
Perhaps his giggle, or his falsetto voice,
Makes him the latest gallant of your choice?

CÉLIMÈNE. You're much mistaken to resent him so.
Why I put up with him you surely know:
My lawsuit's very shortly to be tried,
And I must have his influence on my side.

ALCESTE. Then lose your lawsuit, Madam, or let it drop;
Don't torture me by humoring such a fop.

CÉLIMÈNE. You're jealous of the whole world, Sir.

ALCESTE.   That's true,
Since the whole world is well-received by you.

CÉLIMÈNE. That my good nature is so unconfined
Should serve to pacify your jealous mind;
Were I to smile on one, and scorn the rest,
Then you might have some cause to be distressed.

ALCESTE. Well, if I mustn't be jealous, tell me, then,
Just how I'm better treated than other men.

CÉLIMÈNE. You know you have my love. Will that not do?

ALCESTE. What proof have I that what you say is true?

CÉLIMÈNE. I would expect, Sir, that my having said it
Might give the statement a sufficient credit.

ALCESTE. But how can I be sure that you don't tell
The selfsame thing to other men as well?

CÉLIMÈNE. What a gallant speech! How flattering to me!
What a sweet creature you make me out to be!
Well then, to save you from the pangs of doubt,
All that I've said I hereby cancel out;
Now, none but yourself shall make a monkey of you:
Are you content?

ALCESTE.   Why, why am I doomed to love you?
I swear that I shall bless the blissful hour
When this poor heart's no longer in your power!
I make no secret of it: I've done my best
To exorcise this passion from my breast;
But thus far all in vain; it will not go;
It's for my sins that I must love you so.

CÉLIMÈNE. Your love for me is matchless, Sir; that's clear.
ALCESTE. Indeed, in all the world it has no peer;
     Words can't describe the nature of my passion,
     And no man ever loved in such a fashion.
CÉLIMÈNE. Yes, it's a brand-new fashion, I agree:
     You show your love by castigating me,
     And all your speeches are enraged and rude.
     I've never been so furiously wooed.
ALCESTE. Yet you could calm that fury, if you chose.
     Come, shall we bring our quarrels to a close?
     Let's speak with open hearts, then, and begin . . .

Scene 2   CÉLIMÈNE, ALCESTE, BASQUE.

CÉLIMÈNE. What is it?
BASQUE.   Acaste is here.
CÉLIMÈNE.   Well, send him in.

Scene 3   CÉLIMÈNE, ALCESTE.

ALCESTE. What! Shall we never be alone at all?
     You're always ready to receive a call,
     And you can't bear, for ten ticks of the clock,
     Not to keep open house for all who knock.
CÉLIMÈNE. I couldn't refuse him: he'd be most put out.
ALCESTE. Surely that's not worth worrying about.
CÉLIMÈNE. Acaste would never forgive me if he guessed
     That I consider him a dreadful pest.
ALCESTE. If he's a pest, why bother with him then?
CÉLIMÈNE. Heavens! One can't antagonize such men;
     Why, they're the chartered gossips of the court,
     And have a say in things of every sort.
     One must receive them, and be full of charm;
     They're no great help, but they can do you harm,
     And though your influence be ever so great,
     They're hardly the best people to alienate.
ALCESTE. I see, dear lady, that you could make a case
     For putting up with the whole human race;
     These friendships that you calculate so nicely . . .

Scene 4 ✑ ALCESTE, CÉLIMÈNE, BASQUE.

BASQUE. Madam, Clitandre is here as well.
ALCESTE. Precisely.
CÉLIMÈNE. Where are you going?
ALCESTE. Elsewhere.
CÉLIMÈNE. Stay.
ALCESTE. No, no.
CÉLIMÈNE. Stay, Sir.
ALCESTE. I can't.
CÉLIMÈNE. I wish it.
ALCESTE. No, I must go.
　I beg you, Madam, not to press the matter;
　You know I have no taste for idle chatter.
CÉLIMÈNE. Stay: I command you.
ALCESTE. No, I cannot stay.
CÉLIMÈNE. Very well; you have my leave to go away.

Scene 5 ✑ ÉLIANTE, PHILINTE, ACASTE, CLITANDRE, ALCESTE,
　　　　BASQUE.

ÉLIANTE (to CÉLIMÈNE). The Marquesses have kindly come to call.
　Were they announced?
CÉLIMÈNE. Yes. Basque, bring chairs for all.
　　[BASQUE provides the chairs, and exits.]
　(To ALCESTE.) You haven't gone?
ALCESTE. No; and I shan't depart
　Till you decide who's foremost in your heart.
CÉLIMÈNE. Oh, hush.
ALCESTE. It's time to choose; take them, or me.
CÉLIMÈNE. You're mad.
ALCESTE. I'm not, as you shall shortly see.
CÉLIMÈNE. Oh?
ALCESTE. You'll decide.
CÉLIMÈNE. You're joking now, dear friend.
ALCESTE. No, no; you'll choose; my patience is at an end.
CLITANDRE. Madam, I come from court, where poor Cléonte
　Behaved like a perfect fool, as is his wont.
　Has he no friend to counsel him, I wonder,
　And teach him less unerringly to blunder?
CÉLIMÈNE. It's true, the man's a most accomplished dunce;

His gauche behavior charms the eye at once;
And every time one sees him, on my word,
His manner's grown a trifle more absurd.

ACASTE. Speaking of dunces, I've just now conversed
With old Damon, who's one of the very worst;
I stood a lifetime in the broiling sun
Before his dreary monologue was done.

CÉLIMÈNE. Oh, he's a wondrous talker, and has the power
To tell you nothing hour after hour:
If, by mistake, he ever came to the point,
The shock would put his jawbone out of joint.

ÉLIANTE (*to* PHILINTE). The conversation takes its usual turn,
And all our dear friends' ears will shortly burn.

CLITANDRE. Timante's a character, Madam.

CÉLIMÈNE.   Isn't he, though?
A man of mystery from top to toe,
Who moves about in a romantic mist
On secret missions which do not exist.
His talk is full of eyebrows and grimaces;
How tired one gets of his momentous faces;
He's always whispering something confidential
Which turns out to be quite inconsequential;
Nothing's too slight for him to mystify;
He even whispers when he says "good-by."

ACASTE. Tell us about Géralde.

CÉLIMÈNE.   That tiresome ass.
He mixes only with the titled class,
And fawns on dukes and princes, and is bored
With anyone who's not at least a lord.
The man's obsessed with rank, and his discourses
Are all of hounds and carriages and horses;
He uses Christian names with all the great,
And the word Milord, with him, is out of date.

CLITANDRE. He's very taken with Bélise, I hear.

CÉLIMÈNE. She is the dreariest company, poor dear.
Whenever she comes to call, I grope about
To find some topic which will draw her out,
But, owing to her dry and faint replies,
The conversation wilts, and droops, and dies.
In vain one hopes to animate her face
By mentioning the ultimate commonplace;
But sun or shower, even hail or frost
Are matters she can instantly exhaust.
Meanwhile her visit, painful though it is,
Drags on and on through mute eternities,

And though you ask the time, and yawn, and yawn,
She sits there like a stone and won't be gone.

ACASTE. Now for Adraste.

CÉLIMÈNE.   Oh, that conceited elf
Has a gigantic passion for himself;
He rails against the court, and cannot bear it
That none will recognize his hidden merit;
All honors given to others give offense
To his imaginary excellence.

CLITANDRE. What about young Cléon? His house, they say,
Is full of the best society, night and day.

CÉLIMÈNE. His cook has made him popular, not he:
It's Cléon's table that people come to see.

ÉLIANTE. He gives a splendid dinner, you must admit.

CÉLIMÈNE. But must he serve himself along with it?
For my taste, he's a most insipid dish
Whose presence sours the wine and spoils the fish.

PHILINTE. Damis, his uncle, is admired no end.
What's your opinion, Madam?

CÉLIMÈNE.   Why, he's my friend.

PHILINTE. He seems a decent fellow, and rather clever.

CÉLIMÈNE. He works too hard at cleverness, however.
I hate to see him sweat and struggle so
To fill his conversation with bons mots.
Since he's decided to become a wit
His taste's so pure that nothing pleases it;
He scolds at all the latest books and plays,
Thinking that wit must never stoop to praise,
That finding fault's a sign of intellect,
That all appreciation is abject,
And that by damning everything in sight
One shows oneself in a distinguished light.
He's scornful even of our conversations:
Their trivial nature sorely tries his patience;
He folds his arms, and stands above the battle,
And listens sadly to our childish prattle.

ACASTE. Wonderful, Madam! You've hit him off precisely.

CLITANDRE. No one can sketch a character so nicely.

ALCESTE. How bravely, Sirs, you cut and thrust at all
These absent fools, till one by one they fall:
But let one come in sight, and you'll at once
Embrace the man you lately called a dunce,
Telling him in a tone sincere and fervent
How proud you are to be his humble servant.

CLITANDRE. Why pick on us? *Madame's* been speaking, Sir,

And you should quarrel, if you must, with her.

ALCESTE. No, no, by God, the fault is yours, because
You lead her on with laughter and applause,
And make her think that she's the more delightful
The more her talk is scandalous and spiteful.
Oh, she would stoop to malice far, far less
If no such claque approved her cleverness.
It's flatterers like you whose foolish praise
Nourishes all the vices of these days.

PHILINTE. But why protest when someone ridicules
Those you'd condemn, yourself, as knaves or fools?

CÉLIMÈNE. Why, Sir? Because he loves to make a fuss.
You don't expect him to agree with us,
When there's an opportunity to express
His heaven-sent spirit of contrariness?
What other people think, he can't abide;
Whatever they say, he's on the other side;
He lives in deadly terror of agreeing;
'Twould make him seem an ordinary being.
Indeed, he's so in love with contradiction,
He'll turn against his most profound conviction
And with a furious eloquence deplore it,
If only someone else is speaking for it.

ALCESTE. Go on, dear lady, mock me as you please;
You have your audience in ecstasies.

PHILINTE. But what she says is true: you have a way
Of bridling at whatever people say;
Whether they praise or blame, your angry spirit
Is equally unsatisfied to hear it.

ALCESTE. Men, Sir, are always wrong, and that's the reason
That righteous anger's never out of season;
All that I hear in all their conversation
Is flattering praise or reckless condemnation.

CÉLIMÈNE. But . . .

ALCESTE.   No, no, Madam, I am forced to state
That you have pleasures which I deprecate,
And that these others, here, are much to blame
For nourishing the faults which are your shame.

CLITANDRE. I shan't defend myself, Sir; but I vow
I'd thought this lady faultless until now.

ACASTE. I see her charms and graces, which are many;
But as for faults, I've never noticed any.

ALCESTE. I see them, Sir; and rather than ignore them,
I strenuously criticize her for them.
The more one loves, the more one should object

To every blemish, every least defect.
Were I this lady, I would soon get rid
Of lovers who approved of all I did,
And by their slack indulgence and applause
Endorsed my follies and excused my flaws.

CÉLIMÈNE. If all hearts beat according to your measure,
The dawn of love would be the end of pleasure;
And love would find its perfect consummation
In ecstasies of rage and reprobation.

ÉLIANTE. Love, as a rule, affects men otherwise,
And lovers rarely love to criticize.
They see their lady as a charming blur,
And find all things commendable in her.
If she has any blemish, fault, or shame,
They will redeem it by a pleasing name.
The pale-faced lady's lily-white, perforce;
The swarthy one's a sweet brunette, of course;
The spindly lady has a slender grace;
The fat one has a most majestic pace;
The plain one, with her dress in disarray,
They classify as *beauté négligée;*
The hulking one's a goddess in their eyes,
The dwarf, a concentrate of Paradise;
The haughty lady has a noble mind;
The mean one's witty, and the dull one's kind;
The chatterbox has liveliness and verve,
The mute one has a virtuous reserve.
So lovers manage, in their passion's cause,
To love their ladies even for their flaws.

ALCESTE. But I still say . . .

CÉLIMÈNE.   I think it would be nice
To stroll around the gallery once or twice.
What! You're not going, Sirs?

CLITANDRE AND ACASTE.   No, Madam, no.

ALCESTE. You seem to be in terror lest they go.
Do what you will, Sirs; leave, or linger on,
But I shan't go till after you are gone.

ACASTE. I'm free to linger, unless I should perceive
Madame is tired, and wishes me to leave.

CLITANDRE. And as for me, I needn't go today
Until the hour of the King's *coucher.*

CÉLIMÈNE (*to* ALCESTE). You're joking, surely?

ALCESTE.   Not in the least; we'll see
Whether you'd rather part with them, or me.

Scene 6 ⤝ ALCESTE, CÉLIMÈNE, ÉLIANTE, ACASTE, PHILINTE,
CLITANDRE, BASQUE.

BASQUE (*to* ALCESTE). Sir, there's a fellow here who bids me state
That he must see you, and that it can't wait.
ALCESTE. Tell him that I have no such pressing affairs.
BASQUE. It's a long tailcoat that this fellow wears,
With gold all over.
CÉLIMÈNE (*to* ALCESTE). You'd best go down and see.
Or—have him enter.

Scene 7 ⤝ ALCESTE, CÉLIMÈNE, ÉLIANTE, ACASTE, PHILINTE,
CLITANDRE, GUARD.

ALCESTE (*confronting the* GUARD). Well, what do you want with me?
Come in, Sir.
GUARD.   I've a word, Sir, for your ear.
ALCESTE. Speak it aloud, Sir; I shall strive to hear.
GUARD. The Marshals have instructed me to say
You must report to them without delay.
ALCESTE. Who? Me, Sir?
GUARD.   Yes, Sir; you.
ALCESTE.   But what do they want?
PHILINTE (*to* ALCESTE). To scotch your silly quarrel with Oronte.
CÉLIMÈNE (*to* PHILINTE). What quarrel?
PHILINTE.   Oronte and he have fallen out
Over some verse he spoke his mind about;
The Marshals wish to arbitrate the matter.
ALCESTE. Never shall I equivocate or flatter!
PHILINTE. You'd best obey their summons; come, let's go.
ALCESTE. How can they mend our quarrel, I'd like to know?
Am I to make a cowardly retraction,
And praise those jingles to his satisfaction?
I'll not recant; I've judged that sonnet rightly.
It's bad.
PHILINTE.   But you might say so more politely. . . .
ALCESTE. I'll not back down; his verses make me sick.
PHILINTE. If only you could be more politic!
But come, let's go.
ALCESTE.   I'll go, but I won't unsay
A single word.
PHILINTE.   Well, let's be on our way.

ALCESTE. Till I am ordered by my lord the King
    To praise that poem, I shall say the thing
    Is scandalous, by God, and that the poet
    Ought to be hanged for having the nerve to show it.
          [*To* CLITANDRE *and* ACASTE, *who are laughing.*]
    By heaven, Sirs, I really didn't know
    That I was being humorous.
CÉLIMÈNE.   Go, Sir, go;
    Settle your business.
ALCESTE.   I shall, and when I'm through,
    I shall return to settle things with you.

ACT III

Scene 1 ⤜ᗏ CLITANDRE, ACASTE.

CLITANDRE. Dear Marquess, how contented you appear;
　　All things delight you, nothing mars your cheer.
　　Can you, in perfect honesty, declare
　　That you've a right to be so debonair?
ACASTE. By Jove, when I survey myself, I find
　　No cause whatever for distress of mind.
　　I'm young and rich; I can in modesty
　　Lay claim to an exalted pedigree;
　　And owing to my name and my condition
　　I shall not want for honors and position.
　　Then as to courage, that most precious trait,
　　I seem to have it, as was proved of late
　　Upon the field of honor, where my bearing,
　　They say, was very cool and rather daring.
　　I've wit, of course; and taste in such perfection
　　That I can judge without the least reflection,
　　And at the theater, which is my delight,
　　Can make or break a play on opening night,
　　And lead the crowd in hisses or bravos,
　　And generally be known as one who knows.
　　I'm clever, handsome, gracefully polite;
　　My waist is small, my teeth are strong and white;
　　As for my dress, the world's astonished eyes
　　Assure me that I bear away the prize.
　　I find myself in favor everywhere,
　　Honored by men, and worshiped by the fair;

And since these things are so, it seems to me
I'm justified in my complacency.
CLITANDRE. Well, if so many ladies hold you dear,
Why do you press a hopeless courtship here?
ACASTE. Hopeless, you say? I'm not the sort of fool
That likes his ladies difficult and cool.
Men who are awkward, shy, and peasantish
May pine for heartless beauties, if they wish,
Grovel before them, bear their cruelties,
Woo them with tears and sighs and bended knees,
And hope by dogged faithfulness to gain
What their poor merits never could obtain.
For men like me, however, it makes no sense
To love on trust, and foot the whole expense.
Whatever any lady's merits be,
I think, thank God, that I'm as choice as she;
That if my heart is kind enough to burn
For her, she owes me something in return;
And that in any proper love affair
The partners must invest an equal share.
CLITANDRE. You think, then, that our hostess favors you?
ACASTE. I've reason to believe that that is true.
CLITANDRE. How did you come to such a mad conclusion?
You're blind, dear fellow. This is sheer delusion.
ACASTE. All right, then: I'm deluded and I'm blind.
CLITANDRE. Whatever put the notion in your mind?
ACASTE. Delusion.
CLITANDRE.   What persuades you that you're right?
ACASTE. I'm blind.
CLITANDRE.   But have you any proofs to cite?
ACASTE. I tell you I'm deluded.
CLITANDRE.   Have you, then,
Received some secret pledge from Célimène?
ACASTE. Oh, no: she scorns me.
CLITANDRE.   Tell me the truth, I beg.
ACASTE. She just can't bear me.
CLITANDRE.   Ah, don't pull my leg.
Tell me what hope she's given you, I pray.
ACASTE. I'm hopeless, and it's you who win the day.
She hates me thoroughly, and I'm so vexed
I mean to hang myself on Tuesday next.
CLITANDRE. Dear Marquess, let us have an armistice
And make a treaty. What do you say to this?
If ever one of us can plainly prove

That Célimène encourages his love,
The other must abandon hope, and yield,
And leave him in possession of the field.
ACASTE. Now, there's a bargain that appeals to me;
    With all my heart, dear Marquess, I agree.
    But hush.

Scene 2 *o⅚* CÉLIMÈNE, ACASTE, CLITANDRE.

CÉLIMÈNE. Still here?
CLITANDRE.   'Twas love that stayed our feet.
CÉLIMÈNE. I think I heard a carriage in the street.
    Whose is it? D'you know?

Scene 3 *o⅚* CÉLIMÈNE, ACASTE, CLITANDRE, BASQUE.

BASQUE.   Arsinoé is here,
    Madame.
CÉLIMÈNE.   Arsinoé, you say? Oh, dear.
BASQUE. Éliante is entertaining her below.
CÉLIMÈNE. What brings the creature here, I'd like to know?
ACASTE. They say she's dreadfully prudish, but in fact
    I think her piety . . .
CÉLIMÈNE.   It's all an act.
    At heart she's worldly, and her poor success
    In snaring men explains her prudishness.
    It breaks her heart to see the beaux and gallants
    Engrossed by other women's charms and talents,
    And so she's always in a jealous rage
    Against the faulty standards of the age.
    She lets the world believe that she's a prude
    To justify her loveless solitude,
    And strives to put a brand of moral shame
    On all the graces that she cannot claim.
    But still she'd love a lover; and Alceste
    Appears to be the one she'd love the best.
    His visits here are poison to her pride;
    She seems to think I've lured him from her side;
    And everywhere, at court or in the town,
    The spiteful, envious woman runs me down.
    In short, she's just as stupid as can be,

Vicious and arrogant in the last degree,
And . . .

Scene 4   ARSINOÉ, CÉLIMÈNE, CLITANDRE, ACASTE.

CÉLIMÈNE. Ah! What happy chance has brought you here?
    I've thought about you ever so much, my dear.
ARSINOÉ. I've come to tell you something you should know.
CÉLIMÈNE. How good of you to think of doing so!
          [CLITANDRE and ACASTE go out, laughing.]

Scene 5   ARSINOÉ, CÉLIMÈNE.

ARSINOÉ. It's just as well those gentlemen didn't tarry.
CÉLIMÈNE. Shall we sit down?
ARSINOÉ.   That won't be necessary.
    Madam, the flame of friendship ought to burn
    Brightest in matters of the most concern,
    And as there's nothing which concerns us more
    Than honor, I have hastened to your door
    To bring you, as your friend, some information
    About the status of your reputation.
    I visited, last night, some virtuous folk,
    And, quite by chance, it was of you they spoke;
    There was, I fear, no tendency to praise
    Your light behavior and your dashing ways.
    The quantity of gentlemen you see
    And your by now notorious coquetry
    Were both so vehemently criticized
    By everyone, that I was much surprised.
    Of course, I needn't tell you where I stood;
    I came to your defense as best I could,
    Assured them you were harmless, and declared
    Your soul was absolutely unimpaired.
    But there are some things, you must realize,
    One can't excuse, however hard one tries,
    And I was forced at last into conceding
    That your behavior, Madam, is misleading,
    That it makes a bad impression, giving rise
    To ugly gossip and obscene surmise,
    And that if you were more *overtly* good,

You wouldn't be so much misunderstood.
Not that I think you've been unchaste—no! no!
The saints preserve me from a thought so low!
But mere good conscience never did suffice:
One must avoid the outward show of vice.
Madam, you're too intelligent, I'm sure,
To think my motives anything but pure
In offering you this counsel—which I do
Out of a zealous interest in you.

CÉLIMÈNE. Madam, I haven't taken you amiss;
I'm very much obliged to you for this;
And I'll at once discharge the obligation
By telling you about *your* reputation.
You've been so friendly as to let me know
What certain people say of me, and so
I mean to follow your benign example
By offering you a somewhat similar sample.
The other day, I went to an affair
And found some most distinguished people there
Discussing piety, both false and true.
The conversation soon came round to you.
Alas! Your prudery and bustling zeal
Appeared to have a very slight appeal.
Your affectation of a grave demeanor,
Your endless talk of virtue and of honor,
The aptitude of your suspicious mind
For finding sin where there is none to find,
Your towering self-esteem, that pitying face
With which you contemplate the human race,
Your sermonizings and your sharp aspersions
On people's pure and innocent diversions—
All these were mentioned, Madam, and, in fact,
Were roundly and concertedly attacked.
"What good," they said, "are all these outward shows,
When everything belies her pious pose?
She prays incessantly; but then, they say,
She beats her maids and cheats them of their pay;
She shows her zeal in every holy place,
But still she's vain enough to paint her face;
She holds that naked statues are immoral,
But with a naked *man* she'd have no quarrel."
Of course, I said to everybody there
That they were being viciously unfair;
But still they were disposed to criticize you,
And all agreed that someone should advise you

To leave the morals of the world alone,
And worry rather more about your own.
They felt that one's self-knowledge should be great
Before one thinks of setting others straight;
That one should learn the art of living well
Before one threatens other men with hell,
And that the Church is best equipped, no doubt,
To guide our souls and root our vices out.
Madam, you're too intelligent, I'm sure,
To think my motives anything but pure
In offering you this counsel—which I do
Out of a zealous interest in you.

ARSINOÉ. I dared not hope for gratitude, but I
Did not expect so acid a reply;
I judge, since you've been so extremely tart,
That my good counsel pierced you to the heart.

CÉLIMÈNE. Far from it, Madam. Indeed, it seems to me
We ought to trade advice more frequently.
One's vision of oneself is so defective
That it would be an excellent corrective.
If you are willing, Madam, let's arrange
Shortly to have another frank exchange
In which we'll tell each other, *entre nous,*
What you've heard tell of me, and I of you.

ARSINOÉ. Oh, people never censure you, my dear;
It's me they criticize. Or so I hear.

CÉLIMÈNE. Madam, I think we either blame or praise
According to our taste and length of days.
There is a time of life for coquetry,
And there's a season, too, for prudery.
When all one's charms are gone, it is, I'm sure,
Good strategy to be devout and pure:
It makes one seem a little less forsaken.
Some day, perhaps, I'll take the road you've taken:
Time brings all things. But I have time aplenty,
And see no cause to be a prude at twenty.

ARSINOÉ. You give your age in such a gloating tone
That one would think I was an ancient crone;
We're not so far apart, in sober truth,
That you can mock me with a boast of youth!
Madam, you baffle me. I wish I knew
What moves you to provoke me as you do.

CÉLIMÈNE. For my part, Madam, I should like to know
Why you abuse me everywhere you go.
Is it my fault, dear lady, that your hand

Is not, alas, in very great demand?
If men admire me, if they pay me court
And daily make me offers of the sort
You'd dearly love to have them make to you,
How can I help it? What would you have me do?
If what you want is lovers, please feel free
To take as many as you can from me.

ARSINOÉ. Oh, come. D'you think the world is losing sleep
Over that flock of lovers which you keep,
Or that we find it difficult to guess
What price you pay for their devotedness?
Surely you don't expect us to suppose
Mere merit could attract so many beaux?
It's not your virtue that they're dazzled by;
Nor is it virtuous love for which they sigh.
You're fooling no one, Madam; the world's not blind;
There's many a lady heaven has designed
To call men's noblest, tenderest feelings out,
Who has no lovers dogging her about;
From which it's plain that lovers nowadays
Must be acquired in bold and shameless ways,
And only pay one court for such reward
As modesty and virtue can't afford.
Then don't be quite so puffed up, if you please,
About your tawdry little victories;
Try, if you can, to be a shade less vain,
And treat the world with somewhat less disdain.
If one were envious of your amours,
One soon could have a following like yours;
Lovers are no great trouble to collect
If one prefers them to one's self-respect.

CÉLIMÈNE. Collect them then, my dear; I'd love to see
You demonstrate that charming theory;
Who knows, you might . . .

ARSINOÉ.   Now, Madam, that will do;
It's time to end this trying interview.
My coach is late in coming to your door,
Or I'd have taken leave of you before.

CÉLIMÈNE. Oh, please don't feel that you must rush away;
I'd be delighted, Madam, if you'd stay.
However, lest my conversation bore you,
Let me provide some better company for you;
This gentleman, who comes most apropos,
Will please you more than I could do, I know.

Scene 6 ᰍᨖ ALCESTE, CÉLIMÈNE, ARSINOÉ.

CÉLIMÈNE. Alceste, I have a little note to write
    Which simply must go out before tonight;
    Please entertain *Madame;* I'm sure that she
    Will overlook my incivility.

Scene 7 ᰍᨖ ALCESTE, ARSINOÉ.

ARSINOÉ. Well, Sir, our hostess graciously contrives
    For us to chat until my coach arrives;
    And I shall be forever in her debt
    For granting me this little tête-à-tête.
    We women very rightly give our hearts
    To men of noble character and parts,
    And your especial merits, dear Alceste,
    Have roused the deepest sympathy in my breast.
    Oh, how I wish they had sufficient sense
    At court, to recognize your excellence!
    They wrong you greatly, Sir. How it must hurt you
    Never to be rewarded for your virtue!
ALCESTE. Why, Madam, what cause have I to feel aggrieved?
    What great and brilliant thing have I achieved?
    What service have I rendered to the King
    That I should look to him for anything?
ARSINOÉ. Not everyone who's honored by the State
    Has done great services. A man must wait
    Till time and fortune offer him the chance.
    Your merit, Sir, is obvious at a glance,
    And . . .
ALCESTE.   Ah, forget my merit; I'm not neglected.
    The court, I think, can hardly be expected
    To mine men's souls for merit, and unearth
    Our hidden virtues and our secret worth.
ARSINOÉ. *Some* virtues, though, are far too bright to hide;
    Yours are acknowledged, Sir, on every side.
    Indeed, I've heard you warmly praised of late
    By persons of considerable weight.
ALCESTE. This fawning age has praise for everyone,
    And all distinctions, Madam, are undone.
    All things have equal honor nowadays,

And no one should be gratified by praise.
To be admired, one only need exist,
And every lackey's on the honors list.
ARSINOÉ. I only wish, Sir, that you had your eye
On some position at court, however high;
You'd only have to hint at such a notion
For me to set the proper wheels in motion;
I've certain friendships I'd be glad to use
To get you any office you might choose.
ALCESTE. Madam, I fear that any such ambition
Is wholly foreign to my disposition.
The soul God gave me isn't of the sort
That prospers in the weather of a court.
It's all too obvious that I don't possess
The virtues necessary for success.
My one great talent is for speaking plain;
I've never learned to flatter or to feign;
And anyone so stupidly sincere
Had best not seek a courtier's career.
Outside the court, I know, one must dispense
With honors, privilege, and influence;
But still one gains the right, foregoing these,
Not to be tortured by the wish to please.
One needn't live in dread of snubs and slights,
Nor praise the verse that every idiot writes,
Nor humor silly Marquesses, nor bestow
Politic sighs on Madam So-and-So.
ARSINOÉ. Forget the court, then; let the matter rest.
But I've another cause to be distressed
About your present situation, Sir.
It's to your love affair that I refer.
She whom you love, and who pretends to love you,
Is, I regret to say, unworthy of you.
ALCESTE. Why, Madam! Can you seriously intend
To make so grave a charge against your friend?
ARSINOÉ. Alas, I must. I've stood aside too long
And let that lady do you grievous wrong;
But now my debt to conscience shall be paid:
I tell you that your love has been betrayed.
ALCESTE. I thank you, Madam; you're extremely kind.
Such words are soothing to a lover's mind.
ARSINOÉ. Yes, though she *is* my friend, I say again
You're very much too good for Célimène.
She's wantonly misled you from the start.
ALCESTE. You may be right; who knows another's heart?

But ask yourself if it's the part of charity
To shake my soul with doubts of her sincerity.

ARSINOÉ. Well, if you'd rather be a dupe than doubt her,
That's your affair. I'll say no more about her.

ALCESTE. Madam, you know that doubt and vague suspicion
Are painful to a man in my position;
It's most unkind to worry me this way
Unless you've some real proof of what you say.

ARSINOÉ. Sir, say no more: all doubt shall be removed,
And all that I've been saying shall be proved.
You've only to escort me home, and there
We'll look into the heart of this affair.
I've ocular evidence which will persuade you
Beyond a doubt, that Célimène's betrayed you.
Then, if you're saddened by that revelation,
Perhaps I can provide some consolation.

ACT IV

Scene 1 ✤ ÉLIANTE, PHILINTE.

PHILINTE. Madam, he acted like a stubborn child;
    I thought they never would be reconciled;
    In vain we reasoned, threatened, and appealed;
    He stood his ground and simply would not yield.
    The Marshals, I feel sure, have never heard
    An argument so splendidly absurd.
    "No, gentlemen," said he, "I'll not retract.
    His verse is bad: extremely bad, in fact.
    Surely it does the man no harm to know it.
    Does it disgrace him, not to be a poet?
    A gentleman may be respected still,
    Whether he writes a sonnet well or ill.
    That I dislike his verse should not offend him;
    In all that touches honor, I commend him;
    He's noble, brave, and virtuous—but I fear
    He can't in truth be called a sonneteer.
    I'll gladly praise his wardrobe; I'll endorse
    His dancing, or the way he sits a horse;
    But, gentlemen, I cannot praise his rhyme.
    In fact, it ought to be a capital crime
    For anyone so sadly unendowed
    To write a sonnet, and read the thing aloud."
    At length he fell into a gentler mood
    And, striking a concessive attitude,
    He paid Oronte the following courtesies:
    "Sir, I regret that I'm so hard to please,
    And I'm profoundly sorry that your lyric
    Failed to provoke me to a panegyric."
    After these curious words, the two embraced,
    And then the hearing was adjourned—in haste.

ÉLIANTE. His conduct has been very singular lately;
        Still, I confess that I respect him greatly.
        The honesty in which he takes such pride
        Has—to my mind—its noble, heroic side.
        In this false age, such candor seems outrageous;
        But I could wish that it were more contagious.

PHILINTE. What most intrigues me in our friend Alceste
        Is the grand passion that rages in his breast.
        The sullen humors he's compounded of
        Should not, I think, dispose his heart to love;
        But since they do, it puzzles me still more
        That he should choose your cousin to adore.

ÉLIANTE. It does, indeed, belie the theory
        That love is born of gentle sympathy,
        And that the tender passion must be based
        On sweet accords of temper and of taste.

PHILINTE. Does she return his love, do you suppose?

ÉLIANTE. Ah, that's a difficult question, Sir. Who knows?
        How can we judge the truth of her devotion?
        Her heart's a stranger to its own emotion.
        Sometimes it thinks it loves, when no love's there;
        At other times it loves quite unaware.

PHILINTE. I rather think Alceste is in for more
        Distress and sorrow than he's bargained for;
        Were he of my mind, Madam, his affection
        Would turn in quite a different direction,
        And we would see him more responsive to
        The kind regard which he receives from you.

ÉLIANTE. Sir, I believe in frankness, and I'm inclined,
        In matters of the heart, to speak my mind.
        I don't oppose his love for her; indeed,
        I hope with all my heart that he'll succeed,
        And were it in my power, I'd rejoice
        In giving him the lady of his choice.
        But if, as happens frequently enough
        In love affairs, he meets with a rebuff—
        If Célimène should grant some rival's suit—
        I'd gladly play the role of substitute;
        Nor would his tender speeches please me less
        Because they'd once been made without success.

PHILINTE. Well, Madam, as for me, I don't oppose
        Your hopes in this affair; and heaven knows
        That in my conversations with the man
        I plead your cause as often as I can.
        But if those two should marry, and so remove

> All chance that he will offer you his love,
> Then I'll declare my own, and hope to see
> Your gracious favor pass from him to me.
> In short, should you be cheated of Alceste,
> I'd be most happy to be second best.

ÉLIANTE. Philinte, you're teasing.

PHILINTE.   Ah, Madam, never fear;
> No words of mine were ever so sincere,
> And I shall live in fretful expectation
> Till I can make a fuller declaration.

Scene 2 ✦ ALCESTE, ÉLIANTE, PHILINTE.

ALCESTE. Avenge me, Madam! I must have satisfaction,
> Or this great wrong will drive me to distraction!

ÉLIANTE. Why, what's the matter? What's upset you so?

ALCESTE. Madam, I've had a mortal, mortal blow.
> If Chaos repossessed the universe,
> I swear I'd not be shaken any worse.
> I'm ruined. . . . I can say no more. . . . My soul . . .

ÉLIANTE. Do try, Sir, to regain your self-control.

ALCESTE. Just heaven! Why were so much beauty and grace
> Bestowed on one so vicious and so base?

ÉLIANTE. Once more, Sir, tell us. . . .

ALCESTE.   My world has gone to wrack;
> I'm—I'm betrayed; she's stabbed me in the back:
> Yes, Célimène (who would have thought it of her?)
> Is false to me, and has another lover.

ÉLIANTE. Are you quite certain? Can you prove these things?

PHILINTE. Lovers are prey to wild imaginings
> And jealous fancies. No doubt there's some mistake. . . .

ALCESTE. Mind your own business, Sir, for heaven's sake.
>   [*To* ÉLIANTE.]
> Madam, I have the proof that you demand
> Here in my pocket, penned by her own hand.
> Yes, all the shameful evidence one could want
> Lies in this letter written to Oronte—
> Oronte! whom I felt sure she couldn't love,
> And hardly bothered to be jealous of.

PHILINTE. Still, in a letter, appearances may deceive;
> This may not be so bad as you believe.

ALCESTE. Once more I beg you, Sir, to let me be;
> Tend to your own affairs; leave mine to me.

ÉLIANTE. Compose yourself; this anguish that you feel . . .
ALCESTE. Is something, Madam, you alone can heal.
    My outraged heart, beside itself with grief,
    Appeals to you for comfort and relief.
    Avenge me on your cousin, whose unjust
    And faithless nature has deceived my trust;
    Avenge a crime your pure soul must detest.
ÉLIANTE. But how, Sir?
ALCESTE.   Madam, this heart within my breast
    Is yours; pray take it; redeem my heart from her,
    And so avenge me on my torturer.
    Let her be punished by the fond emotion,
    The ardent love, the bottomless devotion,
    The faithful worship which this heart of mine
    Will offer up to yours as to a shrine.
ÉLIANTE. You have my sympathy, Sir, in all you suffer;
    Nor do I scorn the noble heart you offer;
    But I suspect you'll soon be mollified,
    And this desire for vengeance will subside.
    When some belovèd hand has done us wrong
    We thirst for retribution—but not for long;
    However dark the deed that she's committed,
    A lovely culprit's very soon acquitted.
    Nothing's so stormy as an injured lover,
    And yet no storm so quickly passes over.
ALCESTE. No, Madam, no—this is no lovers' spat;
    I'll not forgive her; it's gone too far for that;
    My mind's made up; I'll kill myself before
    I waste my hopes upon her any more.
    Ah, here she is. My wrath intensifies.
    I shall confront her with her tricks and lies,
    And crush her utterly, and bring you then
    A heart no longer slave to Célimène.

Scene 3   CÉLIMÈNE, ALCESTE.

ALCESTE (*aside*). Sweet heaven, help me to control my passion.
CÉLIMÈNE (*aside*). Oh, Lord.
            [*To* ALCESTE.]
            Why stand there staring in that fashion?
    And what d'you mean by those dramatic sighs,
    And that malignant glitter in your eyes?

ALCESTE. I mean that sins which cause the blood to freeze
  Look innocent beside your treacheries;
  That nothing Hell's or Heaven's wrath could do
  Ever produced so bad a thing as you.
CÉLIMÈNE. Your compliments were always sweet and pretty.
ALCESTE. Madam, it's not the moment to be witty.
  No, blush and hang your head; you've ample reason,
  Since I've the fullest evidence of your treason.
  Ah, this is what my sad heart prophesied;
  Now all my anxious fears are verified;
  My dark suspicion and my gloomy doubt
  Divined the truth, and now the truth is out.
  For all your trickery, I was not deceived;
  It was my bitter stars that I believed.
  But don't imagine that you'll go scot-free;
  You shan't misuse me with impunity.
  I know that love's irrational and blind;
  I know the heart's not subject to the mind,
  And can't be reasoned into beating faster;
  I know each soul is free to choose its master;
  Therefore had you but spoken from the heart,
  Rejecting my attentions from the start,
  I'd have no grievance, or at any rate
  I could complain of nothing but my fate.
  Ah, but so falsely to encourage me—
  That was a treason and a treachery
  For which you cannot suffer too severely,
  And you shall pay for that behavior dearly.
  Yes, now I have no pity, not a shred;
  My temper's out of hand; I've lost my head;
  Shocked by the knowledge of your double-dealings,
  My reason can't restrain my savage feelings;
  A righteous wrath deprives me of my senses,
  And I won't answer for the consequences.
CÉLIMÈNE. What does this outburst mean? Will you please explain?
  Have you, by any chance, gone quite insane?
ALCESTE. Yes, yes, I went insane the day I fell
  A victim to your black and fatal spell,
  Thinking to meet with some sincerity
  Among the treacherous charms that beckoned me.
CÉLIMÈNE. Pooh. Of what treachery can you complain?
ALCESTE. How sly you are, how cleverly you feign!
  But you'll not victimize me any more.
  Look: here's a document you've seen before.
  This evidence, which I acquired today,

Leaves you, I think, without a thing to say.
CÉLIMÈNE. Is this what sent you into such a fit?
ALCESTE. You should be blushing at the sight of it.
CÉLIMÈNE. Ought I to blush? I truly don't see why.
ALCESTE. Ah, now you're being bold as well as sly;
    Since there's no signature, perhaps you'll claim . . .
CÉLIMÈNE. I wrote it, whether or not it bears my name.
ALCESTE. And you can view with equanimity
    This proof of your disloyalty to me!
CÉLIMÈNE. Oh, don't be so outrageous and extreme.
ALCESTE. You take this matter lightly, it would seem.
    Was it no wrong to me, no shame to you,
    That you should send Oronte this billet-doux?
CÉLIMÈNE. Oronte! Who said it was for him?
ALCESTE.   Why, those
    Who brought me this example of your prose.
    But what's the difference? If you wrote the letter
    To someone else, it pleases me no better.
    My grievance and your guilt remain the same.
CÉLIMÈNE. But need you rage, and need I blush for shame,
    If this was written to a *woman* friend?
ALCESTE. Ah! Most ingenious. I'm impressed no end;
    And after that incredible evasion
    Your guilt is clear. I need no more persuasion.
    How dare you try so clumsy a deception?
    D'you think I'm wholly wanting in perception?
    Come, come, let's see how brazenly you'll try
    To bolster up so palpable a lie:
    Kindly construe this ardent closing section
    As nothing more than sisterly affection!
    Here, let me read it. Tell me, if you dare to,
    That this is for a woman . . .
CÉLIMÈNE.   I don't care to.
    What right have you to badger and berate me,
    And so highhandedly interrogate me?
ALCESTE. Now, don't be angry; all I ask of you
    Is that you justify a phrase or two . . .
CÉLIMÈNE. No, I shall not. I utterly refuse,
    And you may take those phrases as you choose.
ALCESTE. Just show me how this letter could be meant
    For a woman's eyes, and I shall be content.
CÉLIMÈNE. No, no, it's for Oronte; you're perfectly right.
    I welcome his attentions with delight,
    I prize his character and his intellect,
    And everything is just as you suspect.

Come, do your worst now; give your rage free rein;
But kindly cease to bicker and complain.

ALCESTE (*aside*). Good God! Could anything be more inhuman?
Was ever a heart so mangled by a woman?
When I complain of how she has betrayed me,
She bridles, and commences to upbraid me!
She tries my tortured patience to the limit;
She won't deny her guilt; she glories in it!
And yet my heart's too faint and cowardly
To break these chains of passion, and be free,
To scorn her as it should, and rise above
This unrewarded, mad, and bitter love.

[*To* CÉLIMÈNE.]

Ah, traitress, in how confident a fashion
You take advantage of my helpless passion,
And use my weakness for your faithless charms
To make me once again throw down my arms!
But do at least deny this black transgression;
Take back that mocking and perverse confession;
Defend this letter and your innocence,
And I, poor fool, will aid in your defense.
Pretend, pretend, that you are just and true,
And I shall make myself believe in you.

CÉLIMÈNE. Oh, stop it. Don't be such a jealous dunce,
Or I shall leave off loving you at once.
Just why should I *pretend*? What could impel me
To stoop so low as that? And kindly tell me
Why, if I loved another, I shouldn't merely
Inform you of it, simply and sincerely!
I've told you where you stand, and that admission
Should altogether clear me of suspicion;
After so generous a guarantee,
What right have you to harbor doubts of me?
Since women are (from natural reticence)
Reluctant to declare their sentiments,
And since the honor of our sex requires
That we conceal our amorous desires,
Ought any man for whom such laws are broken
To question what the oracle has spoken?
Should he not rather feel an obligation
To trust that most obliging declaration?
Enough, now. Your suspicions quite disgust me;
Why should I love a man who doesn't trust me?
I cannot understand why I continue,
Fool that I am, to take an interest in you.

I ought to choose a man less prone to doubt,
And give you something to be vexed about.
ALCESTE. Ah, what a poor enchanted fool I am;
    These gentle words, no doubt, were all a sham;
    But destiny requires me to entrust
    My happiness to you, and so I must.
    I'll love you to the bitter end, and see
    How false and treacherous you dare to be.
CÉLIMÈNE. No, you don't really love me as you ought.
ALCESTE. I love you more than can be said or thought;
    Indeed, I wish you were in such distress
    That I might show my deep devotedness.
    Yes, I could wish that you were wretchedly poor,
    Unloved, uncherished, utterly obscure;
    That fate had set you down upon the earth
    Without possessions, rank, or gentle birth;
    Then, by the offer of my heart, I might
    Repair the great injustice of your plight;
    I'd raise you from the dust, and proudly prove
    The purity and vastness of my love.
CÉLIMÈNE. This is a strange benevolence indeed!
    God grant that I may never be in need. . . .
    Ah, here's Monsieur Dubois, in quaint disguise.

Scene 4 ᴥᵹ CÉLIMÈNE, ALCESTE, DUBOIS.

ALCESTE. Well, why this costume? Why those frightened eyes?
    What ails you?
DUBOIS.   Well, Sir, things are most mysterious.
ALCESTE. What do you mean?
DUBOIS.   I fear they're very serious.
ALCESTE. What?
DUBOIS.   Shall I speak more loudly?
ALCESTE.   Yes; speak out.
DUBOIS. Isn't there someone here, Sir?
ALCESTE.   Speak, you lout!
    Stop wasting time.
DUBOIS.   Sir, we must slip away.
ALCESTE. How's that?
DUBOIS.   We must decamp without delay.
ALCESTE. Explain yourself.
DUBOIS.   I tell you we must fly.

ALCESTE. What for?

DUBOIS.   We mustn't pause to say good-by.

ALCESTE. Now what d'you mean by all of this, you clown?

DUBOIS. I mean, Sir, that we've got to leave this town.

ALCESTE. I'll tear you limb from limb and joint from joint
    If you don't come more quickly to the point.

DUBOIS. Well, Sir, today a man in a black suit,
    Who wore a black and ugly scowl to boot,
    Left us a document scrawled in such a hand
    As even Satan couldn't understand.
    It bears upon your lawsuit, I don't doubt;
    But all hell's devils couldn't make it out.

ALCESTE. Well, well, go on. What then? I fail to see
    How this event obliges us to flee.

DUBOIS. Well, Sir: an hour later, hardly more,
    A gentleman who's often called before
    Came looking for you in an anxious way.
    Not finding you, he asked me to convey
    (Knowing I could be trusted with the same)
    The following message. . . . Now, what *was* his name?

ALCESTE. Forget his name, you idiot. What did he say?

DUBOIS. Well, it was one of your friends, Sir, anyway.
    He warned you to begone, and he suggested
    That if you stay, you may well be arrested.

ALCESTE. What? Nothing more specific? Think, man, think!

DUBOIS. No, Sir. He had me bring him pen and ink,
    And dashed you off a letter which, I'm sure,
    Will render things distinctly less obscure.

ALCESTE. Well—let me have it!

CÉLIMÈNE.   What *is* this all about?

ALCESTE. God knows; but I have hopes of finding out.
    How long am I to wait, you blitherer?

DUBOIS (*after a protracted search for the letter*). I must have left it on
    your table, Sir.

ALCESTE. I ought to . . .

CÉLIMÈNE.   No, no, keep your self-control;
    Go find out what's behind his rigmarole.

ALCESTE. It seems that fate, no matter what I do,
    Has sworn that I may not converse with you;
    But, Madam, pray permit your faithful lover
    To try once more before the day is over.

ACT V

Scene 1 ☙ ALCESTE, PHILINTE.

ALCESTE. No, it's too much. My mind's made up, I tell you.
PHILINTE. Why should this blow, however hard, compel you . . .
ALCESTE. No, no, don't waste your breath in argument;
  Nothing you say will alter my intent;
  This age is vile, and I've made up my mind
  To have no further commerce with mankind.
  Did not truth, honor, decency, and the laws
  Oppose my enemy and approve my cause?
  My claims were justified in all men's sight;
  I put my trust in equity and right;
  Yet, to my horror and the world's disgrace,
  Justice is mocked, and I have lost my case!
  A scoundrel whose dishonesty is notorious
  Emerges from another lie victorious!
  Honor and right condone his brazen fraud,
  While rectitude and decency applaud!
  Before his smirking face, the truth stands charmed,
  And virtue conquered, and the law disarmed!
  His crime is sanctioned by a court decree!
  And not content with what he's done to me,
  The dog now seeks to ruin me by stating
  That I composed a book now circulating,
  A book so wholly criminal and vicious
  That even to speak its title is seditious!
  Meanwhile Oronte, my rival, lends his credit
  To the same libelous tale, and helps to spread it!
  Oronte! a man of honor and of rank,
  With whom I've been entirely fair and frank;
  Who sought me out and forced me, willy-nilly,
  To judge some verse I found extremely silly;
  And who, because I properly refused

    To flatter him, or see the truth abused,
    Abets my enemy in a rotten slander!
    There's the reward of honesty and candor!
    The man will hate me to the end of time
    For failing to commend his wretched rhyme!
    And not this man alone, but all humanity
    Do what they do from interest and vanity;
    They prate of honor, truth, and righteousness,
    But lie, betray, and swindle nonetheless.
    Come then: man's villainy is too much to bear;
    Let's leave this jungle and this jackal's lair.
    Yes! treacherous and savage race of men,
    You shall not look upon my face again.

PHILINTE. Oh, don't rush into exile prematurely;
    Things aren't as dreadful as you make them, surely.
    It's rather obvious, since you're still at large,
    That people don't believe your enemy's charge.
    Indeed, his tale's so patently untrue
    That it may do more harm to him than you.

ALCESTE. Nothing could do that scoundrel any harm:
    His frank corruption is his greatest charm,
    And, far from hurting him, a further shame
    Would only serve to magnify his name.

PHILINTE. In any case, his bald prevarication
    Has done no injury to your reputation,
    And you may feel secure in that regard.
    As for your lawsuit, it should not be hard
    To have the case reopened, and contest
    This judgment . . .

ALCESTE.   No, no, let the verdict rest.
    Whatever cruel penalty it may bring,
    I wouldn't have it changed for anything.
    It shows the times' injustice with such clarity
    That I shall pass it down to our posterity
    As a great proof and signal demonstration
    Of the black wickedness of this generation.
    It may cost twenty thousand francs; but I
    Shall pay their twenty thousand, and gain thereby
    The right to storm and rage at human evil,
    And send the race of mankind to the devil.

PHILINTE. Listen to me. . . .

ALCESTE.   Why? What can you possibly say?
    Don't argue, Sir; your labor's thrown away.
    Do you propose to offer lame excuses
    For men's behavior and the times' abuses?

PHILINTE. No, all you say I'll readily concede:
This is a low, conniving age indeed;
Nothing but trickery prospers nowadays,
And people ought to mend their shabby ways.
Yes, man's a beastly creature; but must we then
Abandon the society of men?
Here in the world, each human frailty
Provides occasion for philosophy,
And that is virtue's noblest exercise;
If honesty shone forth from all men's eyes,
If every heart were frank and kind and just,
What could our virtues do but gather dust
(Since their employment is to help us bear
The villainies of men without despair)?
A heart well-armed with virtue can endure. . . .

ALCESTE. Sir, you're a matchless reasoner, to be sure;
Your words are fine and full of cogency;
But don't waste time and eloquence on me.
My reason bids me go, for my own good.
My tongue won't lie and flatter as it should;
God knows what frankness it might next commit,
And what I'd suffer on account of it.
Pray let me wait for Célimène's return
In peace and quiet. I shall shortly learn,
By her response to what I have in view,
Whether her love for me is feigned or true.

PHILINTE. Till then, let's visit Éliante upstairs.

ALCESTE. No, I am too weighed down with somber cares.
Go to her, do; and leave me with my gloom
Here in the darkened corner of this room.

PHILINTE. Why, that's no sort of company, my friend;
I'll see if Éliante will not descend.

Scene 2   CÉLIMÈNE, ORONTE, ALCESTE.

ORONTE. Yes, Madam, if you wish me to remain
Your true and ardent lover, you must deign
To give me some more positive assurance.
All this suspense is quite beyond endurance.
If your heart shares the sweet desires of mine,
Show me as much by some convincing sign;
And here's the sign I urgently suggest:

That you no longer tolerate Alceste,
But sacrifice him to my love, and sever
All your relations with the man forever.

CÉLIMÈNE. Why do you suddenly dislike him so?
You praised him to the skies not long ago.

ORONTE. Madam, that's not the point. I'm here to find
Which way your tender feelings are inclined.
Choose, if you please, between Alceste and me,
And I shall stay or go accordingly.

ALCESTE (*emerging from the corner*). Yes, Madam, choose; this gen-
tleman's demand
Is wholly just, and I support his stand.
I too am true and ardent; I too am here
To ask you that you make your feelings clear.
No more delays, now; no equivocation;
The time has come to make your declaration.

ORONTE. Sir, I've no wish in any way to be
An obstacle to your felicity.

ALCESTE. Sir, I've no wish to share her heart with you;
That may sound jealous, but at least it's true.

ORONTE. If, weighing us, she leans in your direction . . .

ALCESTE. If she regards you with the least affection . . .

ORONTE. I swear I'll yield her to you there and then.

ALCESTE. I swear I'll never see her face again.

ORONTE. Now, Madam, tell us what we've come to hear.

ALCESTE. Madam, speak openly and have no fear.

ORONTE. Just say which one is to remain your lover.

ALCESTE. Just name one name, and it will all be over.

ORONTE. What! Is it possible that you're undecided?

ALCESTE. What! Can your feelings possibly be divided?

CÉLIMÈNE. Enough: this inquisition's gone too far:
How utterly unreasonable you are!
Not that I couldn't make the choice with ease;
My heart has no conflicting sympathies;
I know full well which one of you I favor,
And you'd not see me hesitate or waver.
But how can you expect me to reveal
So cruelly and bluntly what I feel?
I think it altogether too unpleasant
To choose between two men when both are present;
One's heart has means more subtle and more kind
Of letting its affections be divined,
Nor need one be uncharitably plain
To let a lover know he loves in vain.

ORONTE. No, no, speak plainly; I for one can stand it.

I beg you to be frank.

ALCESTE.   And I demand it.
The simple truth is what I wish to know,
And there's no need for softening the blow.
You've made an art of pleasing everyone,
But now your days of coquetry are done:
You have no choice now, Madam, but to choose,
For I'll know what to think if you refuse;
I'll take your silence for a clear admission
That I'm entitled to my worst suspicion.

ORONTE. I thank you for this ultimatum, Sir,
And I may say I heartily concur.

CÉLIMÈNE. Really, this foolishness is very wearing:
Must you be so unjust and overbearing?
Haven't I told you why I must demur?
Ah, here's Éliante; I'll put the case to her.

Scene 3: ÉLIANTE, PHILINTE, CÉLIMÈNE, ORONTE, ALCESTE.

CÉLIMÈNE. Cousin, I'm being persecuted here
By these two persons, who, it would appear,
Will not be satisfied till I confess
Which one I love the more, and which the less,
And tell the latter to his face that he
Is henceforth banished from my company.
Tell me, has ever such a thing been done?

ÉLIANTE. You'd best not turn to me; I'm not the one
To back you in a matter of this kind:
I'm all for those who frankly speak their mind.

ORONTE. Madam, you'll search in vain for a defender.

ALCESTE. You're beaten, Madam, and may as well surrender.

ORONTE. Speak, speak, you must; and end this awful strain.

ALCESTE. Or don't, and your position will be plain.

ORONTE. A single word will close this painful scene.

ALCESTE. But if you're silent, I'll know what you mean.

Scene 4 ✦ ARSINOÉ, CÉLIMÈNE, ÉLIANTE, ALCESTE, PHI-
LINTE, ACASTE, CLITANDRE, ORONTE.

ACASTE (*to* CÉLIMÈNE). Madam, with all due deference, we two
Have come to pick a little bone with you.

CLITANDRE (*to* ORONTE *and* ALCESTE). I'm glad you're present, Sirs; as
     you'll soon learn,
     Our business here is also your concern.
ARSINOÉ (*to* CÉLIMÈNE). Madam, I visit you so soon again
     Only because of these two gentlemen,
     Who came to me indignant and aggrieved
     About a crime too base to be believed.
     Knowing your virtue, having such confidence in it,
     I couldn't think you guilty for a minute,
     In spite of all their telling evidence;
     And, rising above our little difference,
     I've hastened here in friendship's name to see
     You clear yourself of this great calumny.
ALCESTE. Yes, Madam, let us see with what composure
     You'll manage to respond to this disclosure.
     You lately sent Clitandre this tender note.
CLITANDRE. And this one, for Acaste, you also wrote.
ACASTE (*to* ORONTE *and* ALCESTE). You'll recognize this writing, Sirs,
     I think;
     The lady is so free with pen and ink
     That you must know it all too well, I fear.
     But listen: this is something you should hear.

> *How absurd you are to condemn my lightheartedness in so-
> ciety, and to accuse me of being happiest in the company of
> others. Nothing could be more unjust; and if you do not come
> to me instantly and beg pardon for saying such a thing, I shall
> never forgive you as long as I live. Our big bumbling friend the
> Viscount . . .*

What a shame that he's not here.

> *Our big bumbling friend the Viscount, whose name stands first
> in your complaint, is hardly a man to my taste; and ever since
> the day I watched him spend three-quarters of an hour spitting
> into a well, so as to make circles in the water, I have been unable
> to think highly of him. As for the little Marquess . . .*

In all modesty gentlemen, that is I.

> *As for the little Marquess, who sat squeezing my hand for such
> a long while yesterday, I find him in all respects the most trifling
> creature alive; and the only things of value about him are his
> cape and his sword. As for the man with the green ribbons . . .*

               [*To* ALCESTE.]
It's your turn now, Sir.

As for the man with the green ribbons, he amuses me now and then with his bluntness and his bearish ill-humor; but there are many times indeed when I think him the greatest bore in the world. And as for the sonneteer . . .

[*To* ORONTE.]

Here's your helping.

And as for the sonneteer, who has taken it into his head to be witty, and insists on being an author in the teeth of opinion, I simply cannot be bothered to listen to him, and his prose wearies me quite as much as his poetry. Be assured that I am not always so well-entertained as you suppose; that I long for your company, more than I dare to say, at all these entertainments to which people drag me; and that the presence of those one loves is the true and perfect seasoning to all one's pleasures.

CLITANDRE. And now for me.

Clitandre, whom you mention, and who so pesters me with his saccharine speeches, is the last man on earth for whom I could feel any affection. He is quite mad to suppose that I love him, and so are you, to doubt that you are loved. Do come to your senses; exchange your suppositions for his; and visit me as often as possible, to help me bear the annoyance of his unwelcome attentions.

It's a sweet character that these letters show,
And what to call it, Madam, you well know.
Enough. We're off to make the world acquainted
With this sublime self-portrait that you've painted.
ACASTE. Madam, I'll make you no farewell oration;
No, you're not worthy of my indignation.
Far choicer hearts than yours, as you'll discover,
Would like this little Marquess for a lover.

Scene 5 ❧ CÉLIMÈNE, ÉLIANTE, ARSINOÉ, ALCESTE, ORONTE, PHILINTE.

ORONTE. So! After all those loving letters you wrote,
You turn on me like this, and cut my throat!
And your dissembling, faithless heart, I find,
Has pledged itself by turns to all mankind!
How blind I've been! But now I clearly see;

I thank you, Madam, for enlightening me.
My heart is mine once more, and I'm content;
The loss of it shall be your punishment.
                    [*To* ALCESTE.]
Sir, she is yours; I'll seek no more to stand
Between your wishes and this lady's hand.

Scene 6 ᦍ CÉLIMÈNE, ÉLIANTE, ARSINOÉ, ALCESTE, PHILINTE.

ARSINOÉ (*to* CÉLIMÈNE). Madam, I'm forced to speak. I'm far too stirred
  To keep my counsel, after what I've heard.
  I'm shocked and staggered by your want of morals.
  It's not my way to mix in others' quarrels;
  But really, when this fine and noble spirit,
  This man of honor and surpassing merit,
  Laid down the offering of his heart before you,
  How *could* you . . .
ALCESTE.   Madam, permit me, I implore you,
  To represent myself in this debate.
  Don't bother, please, to be my advocate.
  My heart, in any case, could not afford
  To give your services their due reward;
  And if I chose, for consolation's sake,
  Some other lady, 'twould not be you I'd take.
ARSINOÉ. What makes you think you could, Sir? And how dare you
  Imply that I've been trying to ensnare you?
  If you can for a moment entertain
  Such flattering fancies, you're extremely vain.
  I'm not so interested as you suppose
  In Célimène's discarded gigolos.
  Get rid of that absurd illusion, do.
  Women like me are not for such as you.
  Stay with this creature, to whom you're so attached;
  I've never seen two people better matched.

Scene 7 ᦍ CÉLIMÈNE, ÉLIANTE, ALCESTE, PHILINTE.

ALCESTE (*to* CÉLIMÈNE). Well, I've been still throughout this exposé,
  Till everyone but me has said his say.

Come, have I shown sufficient self-restraint?
And may I now . . .
CÉLIMÈNE.   Yes, make your just complaint.
Reproach me freely, call me what you will;
You've every right to say I've used you ill.
I've wronged you, I confess it; and in my shame
I'll make no effort to escape the blame.
The anger of those others I could despise;
My guilt toward you I sadly recognize.
Your wrath is wholly justified, I fear;
I know how culpable I must appear,
I know all things bespeak my treachery,
And that, in short, you've grounds for hating me.
Do so; I give you leave.
ALCESTE.   Ah, traitress—how,
How should I cease to love you, even now?
Though mind and will were passionately bent
On hating you, my heart would not consent.

[*To* ÉLIANTE *and* PHILINTE.]

Be witness to my madness, both of you;
See what infatuation drives one to;
But wait; my folly's only just begun,
And I shall prove to you before I'm done
How strange the human heart is, and how far
From rational we sorry creatures are.

[*To* CÉLIMÈNE.]

Woman, I'm willing to forget your shame,
And clothe your treacheries in a sweeter name;
I'll call them youthful errors, instead of crimes,
And lay the blame on these corrupting times.
My one condition is that you agree
To share my chosen fate, and fly with me
To that wild, trackless, solitary place
In which I shall forget the human race.
Only by such a course can you atone
For those atrocious letters; by that alone
Can you remove my present horror of you,
And make it possible for me to love you.
CÉLIMÈNE. What! *I* renounce the world at my young age,
And die of boredom in some hermitage?
ALCESTE. Ah, if you really loved me as you ought,
You wouldn't give the world a moment's thought;
Must you have me, and all the world beside?
CÉLIMÈNE. Alas, at twenty one is terrified
Of solitude. I fear I lack the force

And depth of soul to take so stern a course.
But if my hand in marriage will content you,
Why, there's a plan which I might well consent to,
And . . .
ALCESTE.   No, I detest you now. I could excuse
Everything else, but since you thus refuse
To love me wholly, as a wife should do,
And see the world in me, as I in you,
Go! I reject your hand, and disenthrall
My heart from your enchantments, once for all.

Scene 8 ⚬⚬ ÉLIANTE, ALCESTE, PHILINTE.

ALCESTE (*to* ÉLIANTE). Madam, your virtuous beauty has no peer;
Of all this world, you only are sincere;
I've long esteemed you highly, as you know;
Permit me ever to esteem you so,
And if I do not now request your hand,
Forgive me, Madam, and try to understand.
I feel unworthy of it; I sense that fate
Does not intend me for the married state,
That I should do you wrong by offering you
My shattered heart's unhappy residue,
And that in short . . .
ÉLIANTE.   Your argument's well taken:
Nor need you fear that I shall feel forsaken.
Were I to offer him this hand of mine,
Your friend Philinte, I think, would not decline.
PHILINTE. Ah, Madam, that's my heart's most cherished goal,
For which I'd gladly give my life and soul.
ALCESTE (*to* ÉLIANTE *and* PHILINTE). May you be true to all you now
    profess,
And so deserve unending happiness.
Meanwhile, betrayed and wronged in everything,
I'll flee this bitter world where vice is king,
And seek some spot unpeopled and apart
Where I'll be free to have an honest heart.
PHILINTE. Come, Madam, let's do everything we can
To change the mind of this unhappy man.

QUESTIONS

ACT I

1. What basic attitudes toward society are voiced by Alceste and Philinte?
2. What arguments are presented by each to support his understanding of proper social conduct? Which argument of Philinte's is the most convincing?
3. Consider Alceste's line, "The friend of mankind is no friend of mine." Does it suggest that Alceste's reasons for criticizing Philinte's behavior are more complicated than he himself is aware of? Can you find other lines that suggest an ambivalence of motive?
4. Is Philinte also suspect in this way? Do any lines suggest that he is something more than charitable and agreeable?
5. In what way is Scene 2 an *acting out* of certain theories of conduct discussed in Scene 1?
6. Oronte's poem is a conventional seventeenth-century love poem, which expresses all the standard sentiments and employs the typical devices of that poetry. As it stands, however, is it a remarkably bad poem? Why is its "conventionality" alone enough to damn it in Alceste's eyes?
7. Examine Alceste's specific criticism of Oronte's sonnet and try to define the type of critic he is. Does his literary criticism parallel his social criticism?
8. What kind of poetry does Alceste prefer? Is the poem he recites noticeably better than Oronte's? in what ways? Can it be argued that it is just as false an image of human nature?

ACT II

9. How does Alceste's attitude toward love resemble his attitude toward society and literature?
10. Having answered the above question, can you describe the principle on which Molière is constructing his plot?
11.   I fall into deep gloom and melancholy
        When I survey the scene of human folly,
        Finding on every hand base flattery,
        Injustice, fraud, self-interest, treachery. . . .

    This is Alceste's description (I.1) of the social scene in which he lives. How does Molière manage to present this scene to us without actually introducing a great number of characters and a wide variety of actions on stage? Is Alceste's estimation of his society accurate?
12. In what ways does Éliante's description of the ways in which the lover sees his beloved ("the swarthy one's a sweet brunette," etc.) ally her with Philinte?

ACT III

13. Does Arsinoé resemble Alceste in any way? Does she differ? What do the resemblances and differences tell us about Alceste?

14. Wilbur's verse form (the heroic couplet) in this translation does not exactly catch the tone of the original, but it is close enough so that we can talk with reasonable assurance about the effect of the verse. Is it appropriate in this play that everyone should make use of the *same* verse form, and in most places the same meter? What does the constant use of the heroic couplet suggest about the nature of the characters who speak in this form? To answer this last question adequately it will be necessary to define the outstanding features of the heroic couplet.

15. Does Alceste's reaction to Arsinoé prove anything that Célimène has previously said about him? Logically, shouldn't he agree with Arsinoé's view of a world blind to merit?

ACT IV

16. No question troubles Alceste more than whether or not Célimène loves him. Is it possible to answer this question from the play? Is it perhaps characteristic of Alceste that he asks it and expects an absolute answer?

17. Consider carefully Éliante's opinion about whether or not Célimène loves Alceste (IV.1) in the speech beginning, "How can we judge the truth of her devotion?" Does Éliante have a truer understanding of human nature than Alceste?

18. Contrast Éliante and Philinte's opinions about the nature of love with those of Célimène and Alceste.

19. Do you find instances in which Alceste's language betrays him? Is his style often too high for the subject he is dealing with?

20. "The true center of *The Misanthrope* is Célimène. She embodies all the contradictions, the confusions, the weaknesses, and the glories of human nature. She is a dreadful scandalmonger who needs only be given a name to dissect the character; she is a flirt who cannot resist captivating any man who comes near her, only to make a joke of him in turn for the next man she encounters; she is an outrageous liar; and she is a vicious infighter in the drawing room, never hesitating to use the low verbal blow to cripple her opponent. All of this is no doubt bad, but Célimène is also alive and attractive: she is beautiful; she has spirit and style; she is witty; and she is courageous. Whatever she does, she does with breathtaking elegance. In her person she sums up the world that comedy always presents—amoral, energetic, intensely vital, and filled with promise for those who understand her rightly." Do you agree with this statement about Célimène? If so, how does her character help us understand all the other characters in the play?

21. What bearing does the comic exchange between Alceste and his servant at the end of Act IV have on the previous discussion between Alceste and Célimène?

22. In the discussion between Célimène and Alceste about love are there any indications that Alceste's love is not so pure as he believes, that he "unconsciously" seeks in his relationship with Célimène satisfaction of some other needs than are usual in a lover? If you find evidence of such darker motivations, can you tie them to the ambivalent motives that appear in his attitude toward society in Act I?

ACT V

23. Does Alceste actually enjoy losing his law case?

24. At the end of Act V, Scene 1, Alceste removes himself to a dark corner of the room to sit alone. In what ways does this "visual imagery" define his nature and relations with the world?

25. Is Célimène being truthful when she tells Oronte and Alceste, "I know full well which one of you I favor"?

26. In what ways is the condition Alceste attaches to his offer to marry Célimène typical of him? How are we to understand her refusal?

27. At the end of the play Alceste leaves to "seek some spot unpeopled and apart," some "wild, trackless, solitary place/In which I shall forget the human race." This desert is Molière's one symbol used to represent the "world" that exists outside the polished society of court and town. Describe the contrast between the social and natural worlds and discuss the meaning of this juxtaposition.

28. Does Molière present any way of life or any person as perfect?

29. Critics from Molière's day to the present have been passionately divided on the question of the hero of the play. Some have seen Alceste as a man of courage and sensitivity caught in a morally corrupt world that he cannot change. Others have seen Alceste as something of a fool and have taken the urbane and reasonable Philinte as the true hero. Which view is correct in your opinion? In answering this question the most important consideration is that you decide *how* it can be *meaningfully* answered. What grounds are provided by Molière for making a decision?

30. Dramatic characters often are expressions of single, isolated tendencies or attitudes that in living people exist in combination, and often in opposition, with other tendencies. What two common human tendencies do Alceste and Philinte represent?

THE TRAGEDY OF
HAMLET
PRINCE OF DENMARK

BY

WILLIAM SHAKESPEARE

Hamlet does not require the kind of introduction given the other plays in this volume. It is the most famous and the most prized of all English plays. Nearly everyone can quote several passages from it. Many of its phrases have become a permanent part of the English language because they catch so perfectly some of the crucial facts of existence: "To be or not to be," "hoist by his own petard," "we know what we are but not what we may be," "readiness is all." Yet in another way it remains the least known of plays, for it seems both bottomless in its presentation of human nature, and infinitely complex in its depiction of life.

What is most necessary, but most difficult to achieve, for an understanding of *Hamlet* is some sense of it as a whole, some ability to hold in our minds that sweep of events which leads from a bleak, cold battlement on the edge of an impenetrable darkness to the "stage" on which the body of Hamlet is placed, which also opens onto the impenetrable darkness. Between these two darknesses the full life of man is played out with all of its hopes, its losses, its searchings, its pride and hatred of self, its love and agony. Before us in the lighted space of Elsinore we see for an instant the full range of humanity: the sensual, crafty, politically effective Claudius; the unreflective, optimistic Gertrude; the foolish-wise counsellor Polonius; the innocent, trusting, obedient daughter Ophelia; the fiery young man of fashion Laertes; his grotesque parody, the courtier Osric; the affable, self-seeking, but vaguely uneasy opportunists Rosencrantz and Guilden-stern; the cracker-barrel philosopher, the insensitive gravedigger; the heroic voice of the past, old Hamlet; the silent, trustworthy Horatio, unmoved by his grim world; and, finally, that mixture of all qualities, Hamlet himself.

Such a play as this serves well as a capstone for the plays that have gone before it because all of the dramatic techniques discussed earlier and illustrated in the other plays are brought to their fulfillment here. Here every resource of the theater is used to create character and bring into being the world in which the characters move. Here the plot is not only the shape the dramatist gives to events, but it is also the very subject of the play. And here the magnificent use of the theater coupled with an unparalleled command of language lays down level after level of meaning until the central action of the play gathers into itself all of human life. But beyond providing superb examples of the use of the elements of drama, *Hamlet* examines the validity of these devices and of the play form itself as a way of mirroring reality. Hamlet's attempts to stage a play, *The Death of Priam,* and *The Murder of Gonzago,* his advice to players, and his frequent arrange-ment of scenes are all efforts not only "to catch the conscience of the King," but also to "catch" the world aright, to "show" it as it really is. Similarly, the use of words connected with the theater such as *play, act, perform,* and *pretend* raise the question of just what each of these words does mean, in life and in the theater. Ultimately, each of the plays within the play falls short of the truth and in doing so reveals the limitations of certain dramatic devices. Yet the play *Hamlet* taken as a whole transcends these limitations, and no more instructive in-troduction to the nature of drama could be found than an examination of the differences between *The Death of Priam* and *Hamlet,* or Ham-let's instructions to the actors on how to play their parts and the way that the *dramatis personae* do *in fact* play their parts.

DRAMATIS PERSONAE

CLAUDIUS, *King of Denmark*
HAMLET, *son to the late, and nephew to the present King*
POLONIUS, *Lord Chamberlain*
HORATIO, *friend to Hamlet*
LAERTES, *son to Polonius*
VOLTIMAND ⎫
CORNELIUS ⎪
ROSENCRANTZ ⎬ *courtiers*
GUILDENSTERN ⎪
OSRIC ⎪
A GENTLEMAN ⎭
A PRIEST
MARCELLUS ⎫ *officers*
BERNARDO ⎭
FRANCISCO, *a soldier*
REYNALDO, *servant to Polonius*
PLAYERS
TWO CLOWNS, *gravediggers*
FORTINBRAS, *Prince of Norway*
A CAPTAIN
ENGLISH AMBASSADORS
GERTRUDE, *Queen of Denmark, and mother to Hamlet*
OPHELIA, *daughter to Polonius*
LORDS, LADIES, OFFICERS, SOLDIERS, SAILORS, MESSENGERS, *and other* ATTENDANTS
GHOST *of Hamlet's father*

SCENE —— *Denmark.*

From Shakespeare: The Complete Works edited by G. B. Harrison, copyright 1948, 1952 by Harcourt, Brace & World, Inc. and reprinted with their permission. Line numbers do not represent the actual lineation of this edition but are keyed to the Globe Shakespeare to provide for easy cross reference to other editions of the play.

ACT I

Scene 1 🦢 *Elsinore. A platform° before the castle.*

[FRANCISCO *at his post. Enter to him* BERNARDO.]

BERNARDO. Who's there?

FRANCISCO. Nay, answer me. Stand, and unfold yourself.°

BERNARDO. Long live the King!°

FRANCISCO. Bernardo?

BERNARDO. He.   5

FRANCISCO. You come most carefully upon your hour.

BERNARDO. 'Tis now struck twelve. Get thee to bed, Francisco.

FRANCISCO. For this relief much thanks. 'Tis bitter cold,
  And I am sick at heart.

BERNARDO. Have you had quiet guard?

FRANCISCO.   Not a mouse stirring.   10

BERNARDO. Well, good night.
  If you do meet Horatio and Marcellus,
  The rivals° of my watch, bid them make haste.

FRANCISCO. I think I hear them. Stand, ho! Who is there?

  [*Enter* HORATIO *and* MARCELLUS.]

HORATIO. Friends to this ground.

MARCELLUS.   And liegemen° to the Dane.   15

FRANCISCO. Give you good night.

MARCELLUS.   Oh, farewell, honest soldier.
  Who hath relieved you?

FRANCISCO.   Bernardo hath my place.
  Give you good night.   [*Exit.*]

MARCELLUS.   Holloa! Bernardo!

BERNARDO.   Say,
  What, is Horatio there?

Act I, Sc. 1: s.d., **platform:** the level place on the ramparts where the cannon were mounted.   **2. unfold yourself:** reveal who you are.   **3. Long . . . King:** probably the password for the night.   **13. rivals:** partners.   **15. liegemen:** loyal subjects.

HORATIO.   A piece of him.
BERNARDO. Welcome, Horatio. Welcome, good Marcellus.   20
MARCELLUS. What, has this thing appeared again tonight?
BERNARDO. I have seen nothing.
MARCELLUS. Horatio says 'tis but our fantasy,°
    And will not let belief take hold of him
    Touching this dreaded sight twice seen of us,   25
    Therefore I have entreated him along
    With us to watch the minutes of this night,
    That if again this apparition come,
    He may approve our eyes° and speak to it.
HORATIO. Tush, tush, 'twill not appear.
BERNARDO.   Sit down awhile,   30
    And let us once again assail your ears,
    That are so fortified against our story,
    What we have two nights seen.
HORATIO.   Well, sit we down,
    And let us hear Bernardo speak of this.
BERNARDO. Last night of all,   35
    When yond same star that's westward from the pole°
    Had made his course to illume° that part of heaven
    Where now it burns, Marcellus and myself,
    The bell then beating one——
                [*Enter* GHOST.]
MARCELLUS. Peace, break thee off. Look where it comes again!   40
BERNARDO. In the same figure, like the King that's dead.
MARCELLUS. Thou art a scholar.° Speak to it, Horatio.
BERNARDO. Looks it not like the King? Mark it, Horatio.
HORATIO. Most like. It harrows° me with fear and wonder.
BERNARDO. It would be spoke to.
MARCELLUS.   Question it, Horatio.   45
HORATIO. What art thou that usurp'st this time of night,
    Together with° that fair and warlike form
    In which the majesty of buried Denmark°
    Did sometimes march? By Heaven I charge thee, speak!
MARCELLUS. It is offended.
BERNARDO.   See, it stalks away!   50
HORATIO. Stay! Speak, speak! I charge thee, speak!
                [*Exit* GHOST.]

---

23. **fantasy:** imagination.   29. **approve our eyes:** verify what we have seen.
36. **pole:** Polestar.   37. **illume:** light.   42. **scholar:** As Latin was the proper
language in which to address and exorcise evil spirits, a scholar was necessary.
44. **harrows:** distresses; lit., plows up.   47. **Together with:** i.e., appearing in.
48. **majesty . . . Denmark:** the dead King.

MARCELLUS. 'Tis gone, and will not answer.

BERNARDO. How now, Horatio! You tremble and look pale.
Is not this something more than fantasy?
What think you on 't? 55

HORATIO. Before my God, I might not this believe
Without the sensible and true avouch
Of mine own eyes.°

MARCELLUS. Is it not like the King?

HORATIO. As thou art to thyself.
Such was the very armor he had on 60
When he the ambitious Norway combated.
So frowned he once when, in an angry parle,°
He smote the sledded Polacks° on the ice.
'Tis strange.

MARCELLUS. Thus twice before, and jump at this dead hour,° 65
With martial stalk hath he gone by our watch.

HORATIO. In what particular thought to work I know not,
But in the gross and scope° of my opinion
This bodes some strange eruption° to our state.

MARCELLUS. Good now, sit down and tell me, he that knows, 70
Why this same strict and most observant watch
So nightly toils° the subject° of the land;
And why such daily cast of brazen cannon
And foreign mart° for implements of war;
Why° such impress° of shipwrights, whose sore task 75
Does not divide the Sunday from the week;
What might be toward,° that this sweaty haste
Doth make the night joint laborer with the day.
Who is't that can inform me?

HORATIO. That can I,
At least the whisper goes so. Our last King, 80
Whose image even but now appeared to us,
Was, as you know, by Fortinbras of Norway,
Thereto pricked° on by a most emulate° pride,

57–58. Without . . . eyes: unless my own eye had vouched for it. sensible:
perceived by my senses. 62. parle: parley. 63. sledded Polacks: There has
been much controversy about this phrase. Q1 and Q2 read "sleaded Pollax,"
F1 reads "sledded Pollax." Either the late King smote his heavy (leaded)
poleax on the ice, or else he attacked the Poles in their sledges. There is no
further reference to this incident. 65. jump . . . hour: just at deep midnight. 68. gross . . . scope: general conclusion. 69. eruption: violent disturbance. 72. toils: wearies. subject: subjects. 74. foreign mart: purchase
abroad. 75–78. Why . . . day: i.e., workers in shipyards and munition factories are working night shifts and Sundays. impress: conscription. toward:
in preparation. 83. pricked: spurred. emulate: jealous.

Dared to the combat, in which our valiant Hamlet—
For so this side of our known world esteemed him—   85
Did slay this Fortinbras. Who° by a sealed compact,°
Well ratified by law and heraldry,°
Did forfeit, with his life, all those his lands
Which he stood seized of° to the conqueror.
Against the which, a moiety competent°   90
Was gagèd° by our King, which had returned
To the inheritance of Fortinbras
Had he been vanquisher, as by the same covenant
And carriage of the article designed°
His fell to Hamlet. Now, sir, your Fortinbras,   95
Of unimprovèd° mettle° hot and full,
Hath in the skirts° of Norway here and there
Sharked° up a list of lawless resolutes,°
For food and diet,° to some enterprise
That hath a stomach° in 't. Which is no other—   100
As it doth well appear unto our state—
But to recover of us, by strong hand
And terms compulsatory,° those foresaid lands
So by his father lost. And this, I take it,
Is the main motive of our preparations,   105
The source of this our watch and the chief head°
Of this posthaste and romage° in the land.
BERNARDO. I think it be no other but e'en so.
Well may it sort° that this portentous figure
Comes armèd through our watch, so like the King   110
That was and is the question of these wars.
HORATIO. A mote° it is to trouble the mind's eye.
In the most high and palmy° state of Rome,
A little ere the mightiest Julius fell,
The graves stood tenantless, and the sheeted° dead   115

86–95. Who . . . Hamlet: i.e., before the combat it was agreed that the vic-
tor should win the lands of the vanquished. 86. sealed compact: formal
agreement. 87. heraldry: The heralds were responsible for arranging formal
combats. 89. seized of: possessed of, a legal term. 90. moiety competent:
adequate portion. 91. gaged: pledged. 94. carriage . . . designed: fulfillment of the clause in the agreement. 96. unimproved mettle: untutored, wild
material, nature. 97. skirts: outlying parts. 98. Sharked: collected indis-
criminately, as a shark bolts its prey. lawless resolutes: gangsters. 99. diet:
maintenance. 100. stomach: resolution. 103. terms compulsatory: force.
106. chief head: main purpose. 107. posthaste . . . romage: urgency and
bustle. 109. Well . . . sort: it would be a natural reason. 112. mote: speck
of dust. 113. palmy: flourishing. 115. sheeted: in their shrouds.

Did squeak and gibber° in the Roman streets.
As stars° with trains of fire and dews of blood,
Disasters° in the sun, and the moist star°
Upon whose influence Neptune's empire stands
Was sick almost to doomsday with eclipse.   120
And even the like precurse° of fierce events,
As harbingers° preceding still the fates
And prologue to the omen° coming on,
Have Heaven and earth together demonstrated
Unto our climatures° and countrymen.   125
[*Re-enter* GHOST.] But soft, behold! Lo where it comes again!
I'll cross it,° though it blast me. Stay, illusion!
If thou hast any sound, or use of voice,
Speak to me.
If° there be any good thing to be done   130
That may to thee do ease and grace to me,°
Speak to me.
If thou art privy to° thy country's fate,
Which, happily,° foreknowing may avoid,
Oh, speak!   135
Or if thou hast uphoarded in thy life
Extorted° treasure in the womb of earth,
For which, they say, you spirits oft walk in death,
Speak of it. Stay, and speak! [*The cock crows.*°] Stop it,
    Marcellus.
MARCELLUS. Shall I strike at it with my partisan?°   140
HORATIO. Do, if it will not stand.
BERNARDO.   'Tis here!
HORATIO.   'Tis here!
MARCELLUS. 'Tis gone!   [*Exit* GHOST.]
    We do it wrong, being so majestical,

116. gibber: utter strange sounds.   117. As stars: The sense of the passage is
here broken; possibly a line has been omitted after l. 116.   118. Disasters:
unlucky signs. moist star: the moon, which influences the tides.   121. pre-
curse: forewarning.   122. harbingers: forerunners. The harbinger was an officer of the Court who was sent ahead to make the arrangements when the
Court went on progress.   123. omen: disaster.   125. climatures: regions.
127. cross it: stand in its way.   130–39. If . . . speak: In popular belief
there were four reasons why the spirit of a dead man should *walk:* (a) to reveal a secret, (b) to utter a warning, (c) to reveal concealed treasure, (d)
to reveal the manner of its death. Horatio thus adjures the ghost by three potent reasons, but before he can utter the fourth the cock crows.   131. grace
to me: bring me into a state of spiritual grace.   133. Extorted: evilly acquired.
139. s.d., cock crows: i.e., a sign that dawn is at hand. See ll. 147–64.   140.
partisan: a spear with a long blade.

　　　To offer it the show of violence,
　　　For it is as the air invulnerable,　　　　　　　　　145
　　　And our vain blows malicious mockery.
BERNARDO. It was about to speak when the cock crew.
HORATIO. And then it started like a guilty thing
　　　Upon a fearful° summons. I have heard
　　　The cock, that is the trumpet to the morn,　　　150
　　　Doth with his lofty and shrill-sounding throat
　　　Awake the god of day, and at his warning,
　　　Whether in sea or fire, in earth or air,
　　　The extravagant and erring° spirit hies
　　　To his confíne.° And of the truth herein　　　155
　　　This present object made probation.°
MARCELLUS. It faded on the crowing of the cock.
　　　Some say that ever 'gainst° that season comes
　　　Wherein Our Saviour's birth is celebrated,
　　　The bird of dawning singeth all night long.　　　160
　　　And then, they say, no spirit dare stir abroad,
　　　The nights are wholesome, then no planets° strike,
　　　No fairy takes° nor witch hath power to charm,
　　　So hallowed and so gracious is the time.
HORATIO. So have I heard and do in part believe it.　　　165
　　　But look, the morn, in russet mantle clad,
　　　Walks o'er the dew of yon high eastward hill.
　　　Break we our watch up, and by my advice
　　　Let us impart what we have seen tonight
　　　Unto young Hamlet, for upon my life,　　　170
　　　This spirit, dumb to us, will speak to him.
　　　Do you consent we shall acquaint him with it,
　　　As needful in our loves, fitting our duty?
MARCELLUS. Let's do 't, I pray. And I this morning know
　　　Where we shall find him most conveniently.　　　[*Exeunt.*]　　　175

---

149. fearful: causing fear. **154. extravagant . . . erring:** both words mean "wandering." **155. confine:** place of confinement. **156. probation:** proof. **158. 'gainst:** in anticipation of. **162. planets:** Planets were supposed to bring disaster. **163. takes:** bewitches.

Scene 2 ✌ *A room of state in the castle.*

[*Flourish.*° *Enter the* KING, QUEEN, HAMLET, POLONIUS,
LAERTES, VOLTIMAND, CORNELIUS, LORDS, *and* ATTENDANTS.]
KING. Though yet of Hamlet our dear brother's death
 The memory be green,° and that it us befitted
 To bear our hearts in grief and our whole kingdom
 To be contracted in one brow of woe,°
 Yet so far hath discretion° fought with nature°   5
 That we with wisest sorrow think on him,
 Together with remembrance of ourselves.
 Therefore our sometime sister,° now our Queen,
 The imperial jointress° to this warlike state,
 Have we, as 'twere with a defeated joy—   10
 With an auspicious and a dropping eye,°
 With mirth in funeral and with dirge in marriage,
 In equal scale weighing delight and dole°—
 Taken to wife. Nor have we herein barred
 Your better wisdoms,° which have freely gone   15
 With this affair along. For all, our thanks.
 Now follows that you know. Young Fortinbras,
 Holding a weak supposal° of our worth,
 Or thinking by our late dear brother's death
 Our state to be disjoint and out of frame,   20

Sc. 2: s.d., **Flourish:** fanfare of trumpets. 2. **green:** fresh. 4. **contracted
. . . woe:** i.e., every subject's forehead should be puckered with grief. 5.
discretion: common sense. **nature:** natural sorrow. 8. **sister:** i.e., my
brother's sister. 9. **jointress:** partner by marriage. 11. **auspicious . . .
eye:** an eye at the same time full of joy and of tears. 13. **dole:** grief. 14–15.
barred . . . wisdoms: i.e., in taking this step we have not shut out your advice. As is obvious throughout the play, the Danes chose their King by election and not by right of birth. See V.2.65, 366. 18. **weak supposal:** poor
opinion.

Colleagued with the dream of his advantage,°
He hath not failed to pester us with message
Importing the surrender of those lands
Lost by his father, with all bonds of law,°
To our most valiant brother. So much for him.   25
Now for ourself, and for this time of meeting.
Thus much the business is: We have here writ
To Norway, uncle of young Fortinbras—
Who, impotent and bedrid, scarcely hears
Of this his nephew's purpose—to suppress   30
His further gait° herein, in that the levies,
The lists° and full proportions,° are all made
Out of his subject.° And we here dispatch
You, good Cornelius, and you, Voltimand,
For bearers of this greeting to old Norway,   35
Giving to you no further personal power
To business with the King more than the scope°
Of these delated articles° allow.
Farewell, and let your haste commend° your duty.
CORNELIUS & VOLTIMAND. In that and all things will we show our
          duty.   40
KING. We doubt it nothing. Heartily farewell.
                    [*Exeunt* VOLTIMAND *and* CORNELIUS.]
And now, Laertes, what's the news with you?
You told us of some suit°—what is 't, Laertes?
You cannot speak of reason to the Dane
And lose your voice. What wouldst thou beg, Laertes,   45
That shall not be my offer, not thy asking?
The head is not more native° to the heart,
The hand more instrumental° to the mouth,
Than is the throne of Denmark to thy father.
What wouldst thou have, Laertes?
LAERTES.   My dread° lord,   50
Your leave and favor to return to France,
From whence though willingly I came to Denmark

---

21. **Colleagued . . . advantage:** uniting himself with this dream that here
was a good opportunity.   24. **with . . . law:** legally binding, as already explained in I.1.80–95.   31. **gait:** progress.   32. **lists:** rosters. **proportions:** military establishments.   33. **subject:** subjects.   37. **scope:** limit.   38. **delated articles:** detailed instructions. Claudius is following usual diplomatic procedure.
Ambassadors sent on a special mission carried with them a letter of introduction and greeting to the King of the foreign Court and detailed instructions
to guide them in the negotiations.   39. **commend:** display; lit., recommend.
43. **suit:** petition.   47. **native:** closely related.   48. **instrumental:** serviceable.
50. **dread:** dreaded, much respected.

To show my duty in your coronation,
Yet now, I must confess, that duty done,
My thoughts and wishes bend again toward France   55
And bow them to your gracious leave and pardon.
KING. Have you your father's leave? What says Polonius?
POLONIUS. He hath, my lord, wrung from me my slow leave
By laborsome petition, and at last
Upon his will° I sealed my hard consent.°   60
I do beseech you give him leave to go.
KING. Take thy fair hour, Laertes, time be thine,
And thy best graces spend° it at thy will!
But now, my cousin° Hamlet, and my son——
HAMLET. [Aside] A little more than kin and less than kind.°   65
KING. How is it that the clouds still hang on you?
HAMLET. Not so, my lord. I am too much i' the sun.
QUEEN. Good Hamlet, cast thy nighted color° off,
And let thine eye look like a friend on Denmark.
Do not forever with thy vailèd lids°   70
Seek for thy noble father in the dust.
Thou know'st 'tis common—all that lives must die,
Passing through nature to eternity.
HAMLET. Aye, madam, it is common.
QUEEN.   If it be,
Why seems it so particular with thee?   75
HAMLET. Seems, madam! Nay, it is. I know not "seems."
'Tis not alone my inky cloak, good Mother,
Nor customary suits of solemn black,
Nor windy suspiration of forced breath—
No, nor the fruitful river° in the eye,   80
Nor the dejected havior of the visage,°
Together with all forms, moods, shapes of grief—
That can denote me truly. These indeed seem,
For they are actions that a man might play.°
But I have that within which passeth show,   85
These but the trappings° and the suits of woe.
KING. 'Tis sweet and commendable in your nature, Hamlet,
To give these mourning duties to your father.

60. will: desire. sealed . . . consent: agreed to, but with great reluctance.
63. best . . . spend: i.e., use your time well.   64. cousin: kinsman. The word
was used for any near relation.   65. A . . . kind: too near a relation (uncle-
father) and too little natural affection. kind: affectionate.   68. nighted color:
black. Hamlet alone is in deep mourning; the rest of the Court wear gay
clothes.   70. vailed lids: lowered eyelids.   80. fruitful river: stream of tears.
81: dejected . . . visage: downcast countenance.   84. play: act, as in a play.
86. trappings: ornaments.

But you must know your father lost a father,
That father lost, lost his, and the survivor bound   90
In filial obligation for some term
To do obsequious sorrow.° But to perséver
In obstinate condolement° is a course
Of impious stubbornness, 'tis unmanly grief.
It shows a will most incorrect to Heaven,   95
A heart unfortified,° a mind impatient,
An understanding simple and unschooled.
For what we know must be and is as common
As any the most vulgar° thing to sense,
Why should we in our peevish opposition   100
Take it to heart? Fie! 'Tis a fault to Heaven,
A fault against the dead, a fault to nature,
To reason most absurd, whose common theme
Is death of fathers, and who still hath cried,
From the first corse° till he that died today,   105
"This must be so." We pray you throw to earth
This unprevailing° woe, and think of us
As of a father. For let the world take note,
You are the most immediate° to our throne,
And with no less nobility of love   110
Than that which dearest father bears his son
Do I impart toward you. For your intent
In going back to school° in Wittenberg,
It is most retrograde° to our desire.
And we beseech you bend you° to remain   115
Here in the cheer and comfort of our eye,
Our chiefest courtier, cousin, and our son.
QUEEN. Let not thy mother lose her prayers, Hamlet.
   I pray thee, stay with us, go not to Wittenberg.
HAMLET. I shall in all my best obey you, madam.   120
KING. Why, 'tis a loving and a fair reply.
   Be as ourself in Denmark. Madam, come,
   This gentle and unforced accord of Hamlet
   Sits smiling to my heart. In grace whereof,
   No jocund health that Denmark drinks today   125

---

92. obsequious sorrow: the sorrow usual at funerals.   **93. obstinate condolement:** lamentation disregarding the will of God.   **96. unfortified:** not strengthened with the consolation of religion.   **99. vulgar:** common.   **105. corse:** corpse. There is unconscious irony in this remark, for the first corpse was that of Abel, also slain by his brother.   **107. unprevailing:** futile.   **109. most immediate:** next heir.   **113. school:** university.   **114. retrograde:** contrary.   **115. bend you:** incline.

But the great cannon° to the clouds shall tell,
And the King's rouse° the Heaven shall bruit° again,
Respeaking earthly thunder. Come away.
                             [Flourish. Exeunt all but HAMLET.]
HAMLET. Oh, that this too too solid flesh would melt,
    Thaw, and resolve itself into a dew!   130
    Or that the Everlasting had not fixed
    His canon° 'gainst self-slaughter! Oh, God! God!
    How weary, stale, flat, and unprofitable
    Seem to me all the uses° of this world!
    Fie on 't, ah, fie! 'Tis an unweeded garden,   135
    That grows to seed, things rank° and gross in nature
    Possess it merely.° That it should come to this!
    But two months dead! Nay, not so much, not two.
    So excellent a King, that was, to this,
    Hyperion° to a satyr.° So loving to my mother   140
    That he might not beteem° the winds of heaven
    Visit her face too roughly. Heaven and earth!
    Must I remember? Why, she would hang on him
    As if increase of appetite had grown
    By what it fed on. And yet within a month——   145
    Let me not think on 't.—Frailty, thy name is woman!—
    A little month, or ere those shoes were old
    With which she followed my poor father's body,
    Like Niobe° all tears.—Why she, even she—
    Oh, God! A beast that wants discourse of reason°   150
    Would have mourned longer—married with my uncle,
    My father's brother, but no more like my father
    Than I to Hercules. Within a month,
    Ere yet the salt of most unrighteous tears
    Had left the flushing in her gallèd° eyes,   155
    She married. Oh, most wicked speed, to post°
    With such dexterity° to incestuous sheets!
    It is not, nor it cannot, come to good.
    But break, my heart, for I must hold my tongue!

126. great cannon: This Danish custom of discharging cannon when the King proposed a toast was much noted by Englishmen.   **127. rouse:** deep drink. **bruit:** sound loudly, echo.   **132. canon:** rule, law.   **134. uses:** ways.   **136. rank:** coarse.   **137. merely:** entirely.   **140. Hyperion:** the sun god. **satyr:** a creature half man, half goat—ugly and lecherous.   **141. beteem:** allow.   **149. Niobe:** She boasted of her children, to the annoyance of the goddess Artemis, who slew them all. Thereafter Niobe became so sorrowful that she changed into a rock everlastingly dripping water.   **150. wants . . . reason:** is without ability to reason.   **155. galled:** sore.   **156. post:** hasten.   **157. dexterity:** nimbleness.

[Enter HORATIO, MARCELLUS, *and* BERNARDO.]

HORATIO. Hail to your lordship!

HAMLET.   I am glad to see you well.   160
    Horatio—or I do forget myself.

HORATIO. The same, my lord, and your poor servant ever.

HAMLET. Sir, my good friend—I'll change that name° with you.
    And what make you from Wittenberg, Horatio?
    Marcellus?   165

MARCELLUS. My good lord?

HAMLET. I am very glad to see you. [*To* BERNARDO] Good even,
    sir.
    But what, in faith, make you from Wittenberg?

HORATIO. A truant disposition, good my lord.

HAMLET. I would not hear your enemy say so,   170
    Nor shall you do my ear that violence
    To make it truster of your own report
    Against yourself. I know you are no truant.
    But what is your affair in Elsinore?
    We'll teach you to drink deep° ere you depart.   175

HORATIO. My lord, I came to see your father's funeral.

HAMLET. I pray thee do not mock me, fellow student.
    I think it was to see my mother's wedding.

HORATIO. Indeed, my lord, it followed hard upon.

HAMLET. Thrift, thrift, Horatio! The funeral baked meats   180
    Did coldly furnish forth the marriage tables.°
    Would I had met my dearest° foe in Heaven
    Or ever I had seen that day, Horatio!
    My father!—Methinks I see my father.

HORATIO. Oh, where, my lord?

HAMLET.   In my mind's eye, Horatio.   185

HORATIO. I saw him once. He was a goodly King.

HAMLET. He was a man, take him for all in all.
    I shall not look upon his like again.

HORATIO. My lord, I think I saw him yesternight.

HAMLET. Saw? Who?   190

HORATIO. My lord, the King your father.

HAMLET.   The King my father!

HORATIO. Season your admiration° for a while
    With an attent° ear till I may deliver,

---

164. that name: i.e., friend.   **175. drink deep:** For more on the drunken habits
of the Danes, see I.4.8–38.   **180–81. Thrift . . . tables:** they hurried on the
wedding for economy's sake, so that the remains of food served at the funeral
might be used cold for the wedding. **baked meats:** feast.   **182. dearest:** best-
hated.   **192. Season . . . admiration:** moderate your wonder.   **193. attent:**
attentive.

Upon the witness of these gentlemen,
This marvel to you.
HAMLET.   For God's love, let me hear.   195
HORATIO. Two nights together had these gentlemen,
    Marcellus and Bernardo, on their watch
    In the dead vast and middle of the night,°
    Been thus encountered. A figure like your father,
    Armèd at point exactly, cap-a-pie,°
    Appears before them and with solemn march
    Goes slow and stately by them. Thrice he walked
    By their oppressed and fear-surprisèd eyes
    Within his truncheon's° length, whilst they, distilled°
    Almost to jelly with the act of fear,   205
    Stand dumb, and speak not to him. This to me
    In dreadful secrecy impart they did,
    And I with them the third night kept the watch.
    Where, as they had delivered, both in time,
    Form of the thing, each word made true and good,   210
    The apparition comes. I knew your father.
    These hands are not more like.
HAMLET.   But where was this?
MARCELLUS. My lord, upon the platform where we watched.
HAMLET. Did you not speak to it?
HORATIO.   My lord, I did,
    But answer made it none. Yet once methought   215
    It lifted up it° head and did address
    Itself to motion, like as it would speak.
    But even then the morning cock crew loud,
    And at the sound it shrunk in haste away
    And vanished from our sight.
HAMLET.   'Tis very strange.   220
HORATIO. As I do live, my honored lord, 'tis true,
    And we did think it writ down in our duty
    To let you know of it.
HAMLET. Indeed, indeed, sirs, but this troubles me.
    Hold you the watch tonight?
MARCELLUS & BERNARDO.   We do, my lord.   225
HAMLET. Armed, say you?
MARCELLUS & BERNARDO. Armed, my lord.
HAMLET.   From top to toe?
MARCELLUS & BERNARDO. My lord, from head to foot.

---

198. **dead . . . night:** deep, silent midnight. 200. **at . . . cap-a-pie:** complete in every detail, head to foot. 204. **truncheon:** a general's staff. **distilled:** melted. 216. **it:** its.

HAMLET. Then saw you not his face?
HORATIO. Oh yes, my lord, he wore his beaver° up.
HAMLET. What, looked he frowningly?   230
HORATIO. A countenance more in sorrow than in anger.
HAMLET. Pale, or red?
HORATIO. Nay, very pale.
HAMLET.   And fixed his eyes upon you?
HORATIO. Most constantly.
HAMLET.   I would I had been there.   235
HORATIO. It would have much amazed you.
HAMLET. Very like, very like. Stayed it long?
HORATIO. While one with moderate haste might tell° a hundred.
MARCELLUS & BERNARDO. Longer, longer.
HORATIO. Not when I saw 't.
HAMLET.   His beard was grizzled?° No?   240
HORATIO. It was as I have seen it in his life,
    A sable silvered.°
HAMLET.   I will watch tonight.
    Perchance 'twill walk again.
HORATIO.   I warrant it will.
HAMLET. If it assume my noble father's person,
    I'll speak to it though Hell itself should gape   245
    And bid me hold my peace. I pray you all,
    If you have hitherto concealed this sight,
    Let it be tenable° in your silence still,
    And whatsoever else shall hap tonight,
    Give it an understanding, but no tongue.   250
    I will requite° your loves. So fare you well.
    Upon the platform, 'twixt eleven and twelve,
    I'll visit you.
ALL.   Our duty to your Honor.
HAMLET. Your loves, as mine to you. Farewell.
                    [*Exeunt all but* HAMLET.]
    My father's spirit in arms! All is not well.   255
    I doubt° some foul play. Would the night were come!
    Till then sit still, my soul. Foul deeds will rise,
    Though all the earth o'erwhelm them, to men's eyes.
                                        [*Exit.*]

---

229. beaver: front part of the helmet, which could be raised.   238. tell:
count.   240. grizzled: gray.   242. sable silvered: black mingled with white.
248. tenable: held fast.   251. requite: repay.   256. doubt: suspect.

Scene 3 ⚹ *A room in* POLONIUS'S *house.*

[*Enter* LAERTES *and* OPHELIA.]

LAERTES. My necessaries° are embarked. Farewell.
    And, Sister, as the winds give benefit
    And convoy is assistant,° do not sleep,
    But let me hear from you.

OPHELIA.   Do you doubt that?

LAERTES. For Hamlet, and the trifling of his favor,°   5
    Hold it a fashion and a toy in blood,°
    A violet in the youth of primy° nature,
    Forward, not permanent, sweet, not lasting,
    The perfume and suppliance of a minute°—
    No more.

OPHELIA. No more but so?

LAERTES.   Think it no more.   10
    For Nature crescent does not grow alone
    In thews and bulk,° but as this temple° waxes
    The inward service of the mind and soul
    Grows wide withal. Perhaps he loves you now,
    And now no soil nor cautel° doth besmirch   15
    The virtue of his will.° But you must fear,
    His greatness weighed,° his will is not his own,
    For he himself is subject to his birth.
    He may not, as unvalued persons do,
    Carve° for himself, for on his choice depends   20
    The safety and health of this whole state,

Scn. 3: 1. necessaries: baggage. 3. convoy . . . assistant: means of conveyance is available. 5. favor: i.e., toward you. 6. toy in blood: trifling impulse. 7. primy: springtime; i.e., youthful. 8. perfume . . . minute: perfume which lasts only for a minute. 11–12. For . . . bulk: for natural growth is not only in bodily bulk. 12. temple: i.e., the body. 15. cautel: deceit. 16. will: desire. 17. His . . . weighed: when you consider his high position. 20. Carve: choose.

And therefore must his choice be circumscribed°
Unto the voice and yielding of that body
Whereof he is the head. Then if he says he loves you,
It fits your wisdom so far to believe it   25
As he in his particular act and place
May give his saying deed, which is no further
Than the main voice of Denmark goes withal.
Then weigh what loss your honor may sustain
If with too credent° ear you list his songs,   30
Or lose your heart, or your chaste treasure° open
To his unmastered importunity.
Fear it, Ophelia, fear it, my dear sister,
And keep you in the rear° of your affection,
Out of the shot and danger of desire.   35
The chariest maid is prodigal enough
If she unmask her beauty to the moon.
Virtue itself 'scapes not calumnious strokes.
The canker galls the infants° of the spring
Too oft before their buttons° be disclosed,   40
And in the morn and liquid dew of youth
Contagious blastments° are most imminent.
Be wary, then, best safety lies in fear.
Youth to itself rebels, though none else near.°
OPHELIA. I shall the effect of this good lesson keep   45
    As watchman to my heart. But, good my brother,
    Do not, as some ungracious pastors do,
    Show me the steep and thorny way to Heaven
    Whilst, like a puffed° and reckless libertine,
    Himself the primrose path of dalliance° treads   50
    And recks not his own rede.°
LAERTES.   Oh, fear me not.
    I stay too long. But here my father comes.
    [*Enter* POLONIUS.] A double blessing is a double grace,
    Occasion smiles° upon a second leave.
POLONIUS. Yet here, Laertes! Aboard, aboard, for shame!   55
    The wind sits in the shoulder of your sail
    And you are stayed° for. There, my blessing with thee!

22. circumscribed: restricted.   **30. credent:** credulous.   **31. chaste treasure:** the treasure of your chasity.   **34. in . . . rear:** i.e., farthest from danger.   **39. canker . . . infants:** maggot harms the unopened buds.   **40. buttons:** buds.   **42. Contagious blastments:** infectious blasts.   **44. though . . . near:** without anyone else to encourage it.   **49. puffed:** panting.   **50. primrose . . . dalliance:** i.e., the pleasant way of love-making.   **51. recks . . . rede:** takes no heed of his own advice.   **54. Occasion smiles:** i.e., here is a happy chance.   **57. stayed:** waited.

And these few precepts in thy memory
Look thou charácter.° Give thy thoughts no tongue,
Nor any unproportioned° thought his act.   60
Be thou familiar, but by no means vulgar.
Those friends thou hast, and their adoption tried,°
Grapple them to thy soul with hoops of steel,
But do not dull thy palm with entertainment°
Of each newhatched unfledged° comrade. Beware   65
Of entrance to a quarrel, but being in,
Bear 't that the opposèd may beware of thee.
Give every man thy ear, but few thy voice.°
Take each man's censure,° but reserve thy judgment.
Costly thy habit° as thy purse can buy,   70
But not expressed in fancy°—rich, not gaudy.
For the apparel oft proclaims the man,
And they in France of the best rank and station
Are of a most select and generous chief in that.°
Neither a borrower nor a lender be,   75
For loan oft loses both itself and friend
And borrowing dulls the edge of husbandry.°
This above all: To thine own self be true,
And it must follow, as the night the day,
Thou canst not then be false to any man.   80
Farewell. My blessing season° this in thee!
LAERTES. Most humbly do I take my leave, my lord.
POLONIUS. The time invites you. Go, your servants tend.°
LAERTES. Farewell, Ophelia, and remember well
What I have said to you.
OPHELIA.   'Tis in my memory locked,   85
And you yourself shall keep the key of it.
LAERTES. Farewell.   [*Exit.*]
POLONIUS. What is 't, Ophelia, he hath said to you?
OPHELIA. So please you, something touching the Lord Hamlet.
POLONIUS. Marry,° well bethought.°   90

---

59. **character:** inscribe.   60. **unproportioned:** unsuitable.   62. **adoption tried:**
friendship tested by experience.   64. **dull . . . entertainment:** let your hand
grow callous with welcome.   65. **unfledged:** lit., newly out of the egg, immature.   68. **Give . . . voice:** listen to everyone but commit yourself to few.
69. **censure:** opinion.   70. **habit:** dress.   71. **expressed in fancy:** fantastic.
74. **Are . . . that:** A disputed line; this is the F1 reading. Q2 reads "Or of
the most select and generous, chief in that"; i.e., the best noble and gentle
families are very particular in their dress. **generous:** of gentle birth.   77.
husbandry: economy.   81. **season:** bring to fruit.   83. **tend:** attend.   90.
Marry: Mary, by the Virgin Mary. **well bethought:** well remembered.

'Tis told me he hath very oft of late
Given private time to you, and you yourself
Have of your audience been most free and bounteous.
If it be so—as so 'tis put on me,
And that in way of caution—I must tell you   95
You do not understand yourself so clearly
As it behooves° my daughter and your honor.
What is between you? Give me up the truth.

OPHELIA. He hath, my lord, of late made many tenders°
Of his affection to me.   100

POLONIUS. Affection! Pooh! You speak like a green girl,
Unsifted° in such perilous circumstance.
Do you believe his tenders, as you call them?

OPHELIA. I do not know, my lord, what I should think.

POLONIUS. Marry, I'll teach you. Think yourself a baby   105
That you have ta'en these tenders° for true pay,
Which are not sterling.° Tender yourself more dearly,
Or—not to crack the wind of° the poor phrase,
Running it thus—you'll tender me a fool.

OPHELIA. My lord, he hath importuned me with love   110
In honorable fashion.

POLONIUS. Aye, fashion° you may call it. Go to, go to.

OPHELIA. And hath given countenance to his speech,° my lord,
With almost all the holy vows of Heaven.

POLONIUS. Aye, springes° to catch woodcocks.° I do know,   115
When the blood burns, how prodigal° the soul
Lends the tongue vows. These blazes,° daughter,
Giving more light than heat, extinct in both,
Even in their promise as it is a-making,
You must not take for fire. From this time   120
Be something scanter of your maiden presence,
Set your entreatments at a higher rate
Than a command to parley.° For Lord Hamlet,
Believe so much in him, that he is young,
And with a larger tether° may he walk   125
Than may be given you. In few,° Ophelia,

97. behooves: is the duty of. 99. tenders: offers. 102. Unsifted: untried.
106–609. tenders . . . tender: Polonius puns on "tenders," counters (used
for money in games); "tender," value; "tender," show. 107. sterling: true
currency. 108. crack . . . of: i.e., ride to death. 112. fashion: mere
show. 113. given . . . speech: confirmed his words. 115. springes: snares.
woodcocks: foolish birds. 116. prodigal: extravagantly. 117. blazes: flashes,
quickly extinguished (*extinct.*) 122–23. Set . . . parley: when you are asked
to see him do not regard it as a command to negotiate. parley: meeting to
discuss terms. 125. tether: rope by which a grazing animal is fastened to
its peg. 126. In few: in short.

Do not believe his vows, for they are brokers,°
Not of that dye which their investments° show,
But mere implorators° of unholy suits,
Breathing like sanctified and pious bawds°   130
The better to beguile. This is for all.
I would not, in plain terms, from this time forth
Have you so slander any moment leisure°
As to give words or talk with the Lord Hamlet.
Look to 't, I charge you. Come your ways.   135
OPHELIA. I shall obey, my lord.   [*Exeunt.*]

Scene 4 ⌁ *The platform.*

[*Enter* HAMLET, HORATIO, *and* MARCELLUS.]
HAMLET. The air bites shrewdly.° It is very cold.
HORATIO. It is a nipping and an eager° air.
HAMLET. What hour now?
HORATIO.   I think it lacks of twelve.
MARCELLUS. No, it is struck.
HORATIO. Indeed? I heard it not. It then draws near the season   5
     Wherein the spirit held his wont to walk.
     [*A flourish of trumpets, and ordnance shot off within.*°]
     What doth this mean, my lord?
HAMLET. The King doth wake° tonight and takes his rouse,°
     Keeps wassail,° and the swaggering upspring reels.°
     And as he drains his draughts of Rhenish° down,   10
     The kettledrum and trumpet thus bray out
     The triumph of his pledge.
HORATIO.   Is it a custom?

127. **brokers:** traveling salesmen.   128. **investments:** garments.   129. **im-plorators:** men who solicit.   130. **bawds:** keepers of brothels. F1 and Q2 read "bond," an easy misprint for "baud"—the Elizabethan spelling of "bawd." 133. **slander . . . leisure:** misuse any moment of leisure.
     Sc. 4: 1. **shrewdly:** bitterly.   2. **eager:** sharp.   6. **s.d., within:** off stage. 8. **wake:** "makes a night of it." **rouse:** See I.2.127, n.   9. **wassail.** revelry. **swaggering . . . reels:** reel in a riotous dance.   10. **Rhenish:** Rhine wine.

HAMLET. Aye, marry, is 't.
    But to my mind, though I am native here
    And to the manner born, it is a custom   15
    More honored in the breach than the observance.
    This heavy-headed revel° east and west
    Makes us traduced and taxed of° other nations.
    They clepe° us drunkards, and with swinish phrase
    Soil our addition,° and indeed it takes   20
    From our achievements, though performed at height,°
    The pith and marrow of our attribute.°
    So oft it chances in particular men,
    That for some vicious mole° of nature in them,
    As in their birth—wherein they are not guilty,   25
    Since nature cannot choose his origin—
    By the o'ergrowth of some complexion,°
    Oft breaking down the pales° and forts of reason,
    Or by some habit that too much o'erleavens°
    The form of plausive° manners, that these men—   30
    Carrying, I say, the stamp of one defect,
    Being Nature's livery,° or Fortune's star°—
    Their virtues else—be they as pure as grace,
    As infinite as man may undergo—
    Shall in the general censure take corruption   35
    From that particular fault. The dram of eale
    Doth all the noble substance of a doubt
    To his own scandal.°

                 [*Enter* GHOST.]
HORATIO.   Look, my lord, it comes!

---

17. heavy-headed revel: drinking which produces a thick head.   **18. traduced . . . of:** disgraced and censured by.   **19. clepe:** call.   **20. soil . . . addition:** smirch our honor. **addition:** lit., title of honor added to a man's name.   **21. though . . . height:** though of the highest merit.   **22: pith . . . attribute:** essential part of our honor due to our achievements because of our reputation for drunkenness.   **24. mole:** blemish.   **27. o'ergrowth . . . complexion:** some quality allowed to overbalance the rest.   **28. pales:** defenses. **29. o'erleavens:** mixes with.   **30. plausive:** agreeable.   **32. Nature's livery:** i. e., inborn. **Fortune's star:** the result of ill luck.   **36–38. The . . . scandal:** This is the most famous of all disputed passages in Shakespeare's plays. The general meaning is clear: "a small portion of evil brings scandal on the whole substance, however noble." "Eale" is an Elizabethan spelling and pronunciation of "evil," as later in Q2 (II.2.628); "deale" is the spelling and pronunciation of "Devil." The difficulty lies in "of a doubt," which is obviously a misprint of some such word as "corrupt"; but to be satisfactory it must fit the meter and be a plausible misprint. So far, although many guesses have been made, none is wholly convincing. The best is perhaps "often dout"— often put out.

HAMLET. Angels and ministers of grace defend us!
    Be thou a spirit of health or goblin damned.°   40
    Bring with thee airs from Heaven or blasts from Hell,
    Be thy intents wicked or charitable,
    Thou comest in such a questionable° shape
    That I will speak to thee. I'll call thee Hamlet,
    King, Father, royal Dane. Oh, answer me!   45
    Let me not burst in ignorance, but tell
    Why thy canónized° bones, hearsèd° in death,
    Have burst their cerements,° why the sepulcher
    Wherein we saw thee quietly inurned°
    Hath oped his ponderous and marble jaws   50
    To cast thee up again. What may this mean,
    That thou, dead corse, again, in complete steel,°
    Revisit'st thus the glimpses of the moon,
    Making night hideous, and we fools° of nature
    So horridly to shake our disposition°   55
    With thoughts beyond the reaches of our souls?
    Say, why is this? Wherefore? What should we do?
            [GHOST *beckons* HAMLET.]
HORATIO. It beckons you to go away with it,
    As if it some impartment° did desire
    To you alone.
MARCELLUS.   Look with what courteous action   60
    It waves you to a more removèd ground.
    But do not go with it.
HORATIO.   No, by no means.
HAMLET. It will not speak. Then I will follow it.
HORATIO. Do not, my lord.
HAMLET.   Why, what should be the fear?
    I do not set my life at a pin's fee,°   65
    And for my soul, what can it do to that,
    Being a thing immortal as itself?
    It waves me forth again. I'll follow it.
HORATIO. What if it tempt you toward the flood, my lord,
    Or to the dreadful summit of the cliff   70

40. spirit . . . damned: a holy spirit or damned fiend. Hamlet, until convinced at the end of the play scene (III.2.298), is perpetually in doubt
whether the ghost which he sees is a good spirit sent to warn him, a devil
sent to tempt him into some damnable action, or a hallucinaion created by
his own diseased imagination. See II.2.627-32. **43. questionable:** inviting
question. **47. canonized:** buried with full rites according to the canon of the
Church. **hearsed:** buried. **48. cerements:** waxen shroud, used to wrap the
bodies of the illustrious dead. **49. inurned:** buried. **52. complete steel:** full
armor. **54. fools:** dupes. **55. disposition:** nature. **59. impartment:** communication. **65. fee:** value.

That beetles o'er° his base into the sea,
And there assume some other horrible form
Which might deprive your sovereignty of reason°
And draw you into madness? Think of it.
The very place puts toys of desperation,°   75
Without more motive, into every brain
That looks so many fathoms to the sea
And hears it roar beneath.
HAMLET.   It waves me still.
    Go on. I'll follow thee.
MARCELLUS. You shall not go, my lord.
HAMLET.   Hold off your hands.   80
HORATIO. Be ruled. You shall not go.
HAMLET.   My fate cries out,
    And makes each petty artery in this body
    As hardy as the Nemean lion's nerve.°
    Still am I called. Unhand me, gentlemen.
    By Heaven, I'll make a ghost of him that lets° me!   85
    I say, away! Go on. I'll follow thee.
                          [*Exeunt* GHOST *and* HAMLET.]
HORATIO. He waxes desperate with imagination.
MARCELLUS. Let's follow. 'Tis not fit thus to obey him.
HORATIO. Have after. To what issue will this come?
MARCELLUS. Something is rotten in the state of Denmark.   90
HORATIO. Heaven will direct it.
MARCELLUS.   Nay, let's follow him. [*Exeunt*.]

Scene 5 ◆ *Another part of the platform.*

                      [*Enter* GHOST *and* HAMLET.]
HAMLET. Whither wilt thou lead me? Speak. I'll go no further.
GHOST. Mark me.
HAMLET.   I will.
GHOST.   My hour is almost come

71. beetles o'er: juts out over.   73. sovereignty of reason: control of your reason over your actions.   75. toys of desperation: desperate fancies.   83.
Nemean . . . nerve: sinew of a fierce beast slain by Hercules.   85. lets:
hinders.

When I to sulphurous and tormenting flames
Must render up myself.
HAMLET.   Alas, poor ghost!
GHOST. Pity me not, but lend thy serious hearing   5
To what I shall unfold.
HAMLET.   Speak. I am bound to hear.
GHOST. So art thou to revenge, when thou shalt hear.
HAMLET. What?
GHOST. I am thy father's spirit,
Doomed for a certain term to walk the night   10
And for the day confined to fast in fires
Till the foul crimes done in my days of nature
Are burnt and purged away. But that I am forbid
To tell the secrets of my prison house,
I could a tale unfold whose lightest word   15
Would harrow up thy soul, freeze thy young blood,
Make thy two eyes, like stars,° start from their spheres,°
Thy knotted and combinèd° locks to part
And each particular° hair to stand an° end
Like quills upon the fretful porpentine.°   20
But this eternal blazon° must not be
To ears of flesh and blood. List, list, oh, list!
If thou didst ever thy dear father love——
HAMLET. Oh, God!
GHOST. Revenge his foul and most unnatural murder.   25
HAMLET. Murder!
GHOST. Murder most foul, as in the best° it is,
But this most foul, strange, and unnatural.
HAMLET. Haste me to know 't, that I, with wings as swift
As meditation or the thoughts of love,   30
May sweep to my revenge.
GHOST.   I find thee apt,
And duller shouldst thou be than the fat° weed
That roots itself in ease° on Lethe wharf°
Wouldst thou not stir in this. Now, Hamlet, hear.
'Tis given out that, sleeping in my orchard,   35
A serpent stung me—so the whole ear of Denmark
Is by a forgèd process° of my death

Sc. 5: **17. stars:** planets. **spheres:** the courses of planets in the heavens. **18. knotted . . . combined:** the hair that lies together in a mass. **19. particular:** individual. **an:** on. **20. porpentine:** porcupine. **21. eternal blazon:** description of eternity. **27. in . . . best:** i.e., murder is foul even when there is a good excuse. **32. fat:** thick, slimy, motionless. **33. in ease:** undisturbed. **Lethe wharf:** the bank of Lethe, the river of forgetfulness in the underworld. **37. forged process:** false account.

Rankly abused. But know, thou noble youth,
The serpent that did sting thy father's life
Now wears his crown.
HAMLET.   Oh, my prophetic soul!   40
My uncle!
GHOST. Aye, that incestuous, that adulterate beast,
With witchcraft of his wit, with traitorous gifts—
O wicked wit and gifts, that have the power
So to seduce!—won to his shameful lust   45
The will of my most seeming-virtuous Queen.
O Hamlet, what a falling-off was there!
From me, whose love was of that dignity
That it went hand in hand even with the vow
I made to her in marriage, and to decline   50
Upon a wretch whose natural gifts were poor
To those of mine!
But virtue, as it never will be moved
Though lewdness court it in a shape of Heaven,°
So Lust, though to a radiant angel linked,   55
Will sate itself° in a celestial bed
And prey on garbage.
But soft! Methinks I scent the morning air.
Brief let me be. Sleeping within my orchard,
My custom always of the afternoon,   60
Upon my secure hour° thy uncle stole
With juice of cursèd hebenon° in a vial,
And in the porches° of my ears did pour
The leperous distillment,° whose effect
Holds such an enmity with blood of man   65
That swift as quicksilver it courses through
The natural gates and alleys of the body,
And with a sudden vigor it doth posset°
And curd, like eager° droppings into milk,
The thin and wholesome blood. So did it mine,   70
And a most instant tetter barked° about,
Most lazarlike,° with vile and loathsome crust,
All my smooth body.
Thus was I, sleeping, by a brother's hand
Of life, of crown, of Queen, at once dispatched—   75

---

54. lewdness . . . Heaven: though wooed by Lust disguised as an angel.
56. sate itself: gorge.   61. secure hour: time of relaxation.   62. hebenon:
probably henbane, a poisonous plant.   63. porches: entrances.   64. leperous
distillment: distillation causing leprosy.   68. posset: curdle.   69. eager: acid.
71. tetter barked: eruption formed a bark.   72. lazarlike: like leprosy.

Cut off even in the blossoms of my sin,°
Unhouseled, disappointed, unaneled,°
No reckoning made, but sent to my account
With all my imperfections on my head.   80
Oh, horrible! Oh, horrible, most horrible!
If thou hast nature° in thee, bear it not.
Let not the royal bed of Denmark be
A couch for luxury° and damned incest.
But, howsoever thou pursuest this act,   85
Taint not thy mind, nor let thy soul contrive
Against thy mother aught. Leave her to Heaven
And to those thorns that in her bosom lodge
To prick and sting her. Fare thee well at once!
The glowworm shows the matin° to be near,
And 'gins to pale his uneffectual° fire.   90
Adieu, adieu, adieu! Remember me.   [*Exit.*]
HAMLET. O all you host of Heaven! O earth! What else?
And shall I couple Hell? Oh, fie! Hold, hold, my heart,
And you, my sinews, grow not instant old
But bear me stiffly up. Remember thee!   95
Aye, thou poor ghost, while memory holds a seat
In this distracted globe.° Remember thee!
Yea, from the table° of my memory
I'll wipe away all trivial fond° recórds,
All saws° of books, all forms,° all pressures° past,   100
That youth and observation copied there,
And thy commandment all alone shall live
Within the book and volume of my brain,
Unmixed with baser matter. Yes, by Heaven!
O most pernicious woman!   105
O villain, villain, smiling, damnèd villain!
My tables—meet it is I set it down
[*Writing*] That one may smile, and smile, and be a villain.
At least I'm sure it may be so in Denmark.
So, Uncle, there you are. Now to my word.°   110
It is "Adieu, adieu! Remember me."
I have sworn 't.

76. Cut . . . sin: cut off in a state of sin and so in danger of damnation. See III.3.80–86.   77. Unhouseled . . . unaneled: without receiving the sacrament of penance, not properly prepared, unanointed—without extreme unction.   81. nature: natural feelings.   83. luxury: lust.   89. matin: morning.
90. uneffectual: made ineffectual by daylight.   97. globe: i.e., head.   98. table: notebook. Intellectual young men carried notebooks in which they recorded good sayings and notable observations. See III.2.42, n.   99. fond: trifling.   100. saws: wise sayings. forms: images in the mind. pressures: impressions.   110. word: cue.

HORATIO & MARCELLUS. [*Within*] My lord, my lord!
[Enter HORATIO and MARCELLUS.]

MARCELLUS.   Lord Hamlet!
HORATIO.   Heaven secure him!
HAMLET. So be it!
MARCELLUS. Illo, ho, ho,° my lord!   115
HAMLET. Hillo, ho, ho, boy! Come, bird, come.
MARCELLUS. How is 't, my noble lord?
HORATIO.   What news, my lord?
HAMLET. Oh, wonderful!
HORATIO. Good my lord, tell it.
HAMLET.   No, you will reveal it.
HORATIO. Not I, my lord, by Heaven.
MARCELLUS.   Nor I, my lord.   120
HAMLET. How say you, then, would heart of man once think it?
    But you'll be secret?
HORATIO & MARCELLUS.   Aye, by Heaven, my lord.
HAMLET. There's ne'er a villain dwelling in all Denmark
    But he's an arrant° knave.
HORATIO. There needs no ghost, my lord, come from the grave   125
    To tell us this.
HAMLET.   Why, right, you are i' the right.
    And so, without more circumstance° at all,
    I hold it fit that we shake hands and part—
    You as your business and desire shall point you,
    For every man hath business and desire,   130
    Such as it is. And for my own poor part,
    Look you, I'll go pray.
HORATIO. These are but wild and whirling° words, my lord.
HAMLET. I'm sorry they offend you, heartily,
    Yes, faith, heartily.
HORATIO.   There's no offense, my lord.   135
HAMLET. Yes, by Saint Patrick, but there is, Horatio,
    And much offense too. Touching this vision here,
    It is an honest° ghost, that let me tell you.
    For your desire to know what is between us,
    O'ermaster 't as you may. And now, good friends,   140
    As you are friends, scholars, and soldiers,
    Give me one poor request.
HORATIO. What is 't, my lord? We will.
HAMLET. Never make known what you have seen tonight.
HORATIO & MARCELLUS. My lord, we will not.

115. Illo . . . ho: the falconer's cry to recall the hawk.   **124. arrant:** out-and-out.   **127. circumstance:** ceremony.   **133. whirling:** violent.   **138. honest:** true. See I.4.40, n.

HAMLET.   Nay, but swear 't.
HORATIO.
                                                      In faith,   145
    My lord, not I.
MARCELLUS.   Nor I, my lord, in faith.
HAMLET. Upon my sword.
MARCELLUS.   We have sworn, my lord, already.
HAMLET. Indeed, upon my sword,° indeed.
GHOST. [*Beneath*] Swear.
HAMLET. Ah, ha, boy! Say'st thou so? Art thou there, true-
    penny?°   150
    Come on. You hear this fellow in the cellarage.
    Consent to swear.
HORATIO.   Propose the oath, my lord.
HAMLET. Never to speak of this that you have seen,
    Swear by my sword.
GHOST. [*Beneath*] Swear.   155
HAMLET. *Hic et ubique?*° Then we'll shift our ground.
    Come hither, gentlemen,
    And lay your hands again upon my sword.
    Never to speak of this that you have heard,
    Swear by my sword.   160
GHOST. [*Beneath*] Swear.
HAMLET. Well said, old mole! Canst work i' the earth so fast?
    A worthy pioner!° Once more remove,° good friends.
HORATIO. Oh, day and night, but this is wondrous strange!
HAMLET. And therefore as a stranger give it welcome.   165
    There are more things in Heaven and earth, Horatio,
    Than are dreamt of in your philosophy.
    But come,
    Here, as before, never, so help you mercy,
    How strange or odd soe'er I bear myself,   170
    As I perchance hereafter shall think meet
    To put an antic disposition° on,
    That you, at such times seeing me, never shall,
    With arms encumbered° thus, or this headshake,
    Or by pronouncing of some doubtful phrase,   175
    As "Well, well, we know," or "We could an if we would,"
    Or "If we list to speak," or "There be, an if they might,"
    Or such ambiguous giving out, to note
    That you know aught of me. This not to do,

---

148. upon . . . sword: on the cross made by the hilt of the sword; but for
soldiers the sword itself was a sacred object.   **150. truepenny:** old boy.   **156.**
Hic et ubique: here and everywhere.   **163. pioner:** miner. **remove:** move.
172. antic disposition: mad behavior.   **174. encumbered:** folded.

So grace and mercy at your most need help you,   180
    Swear.
GHOST. [*Beneath*] Swear.
HAMLET. Rest, rest, perturbèd spirit! [*They swear.*] So, gentle-
    men,
    With all my love I do commend me to you.
    And what so poor a man as Hamlet is   185
    May do to express his love and friending° to you,
    God willing, shall not lack. Let us go in together.
    And still your fingers on your lips, I pray.
    The time is out of joint. Oh, cursèd spite
    That ever I was born to set it right!   190
    Nay, come, let's go together.   [*Exeunt.*]

186. friending: friendship.

ACT II

Scene 1 ✧ *A room in* POLONIUS'S *house.*

[*Enter* POLONIUS *and* REYNALDO.]

POLONIUS. Give him this money and these notes, Reynaldo.

REYNALDO. I will, my lord.

POLONIUS. You shall do marvelous wisely, good Reynaldo,
    Before you visit him, to make inquire
    Of his behavior.

REYNALDO.   My lord, I did intend it.   5

POLONIUS. Marry, well said, very well said. Look you, sir,
    Inquire me first what Danskers° are in Paris,
    And how, and who, what means,° and where they keep,°
    What company, at what expense, and finding
    By this encompassment and drift of question°   10
    That they do know my son, come you more nearer
    Than your particular demands will touch it.°
    Take you, as 'twere, some distant knowledge of him,
    As thus, "I know his father and his friends,
    And in part him." Do you mark this, Reynaldo?   15

REYNALDO. Aye, very well, my lord.

POLONIUS. "And in part him, but," you may say, "not well.
    But if 't be he I mean, he's very wild,
    Addicted so and so"—and there put on him
    What forgeries° you please. Marry, none so rank°   20
    As may dishonor him, take heed of that,
    But, sir, such wanton, wild, and usual slips
    As are companions noted and most known
    To youth and liberty.

Act II, Sc. 1: 7. **Danskers:** Danes.   8. **what means:** what their income is.
keep: live.   10. **encompassment . . . question:** roundabout method of questioning.   12. **your . . . it:** i.e., you won't get at the truth by straight questions.   20. **forgeries:** inventions. **rank:** gross.

REYNALDO.   As gaming, my lord.

POLONIUS. Aye, or drinking, fencing,° swearing, quarreling,   25
  Drabbing.° You may go so far.

REYNALDO. My lord, that would dishonor him.

POLONIUS. Faith, no, as you may season° it in the charge.
  You must not put another scandal on him,
  That he is open to incontinency.°   30
  That's not my meaning. But breathe his faults so quaintly°
  That they may seem the taints of liberty,
  The flash and outbreak of a fiery mind,
  A savageness in unreclaimèd° blood,
  Of general assault.°

REYNALDO.   But, my good lord——   35

POLONIUS. Wherefore should you do this?

REYNALDO.   Aye, my lord,
  I would know that.

POLONIUS.   Marry, sir, here's my drift,°
  And I believe it is a fetch of warrant.°
  You laying these slight sullies° on my son,
  As 'twere a thing a little soiled i' the working,   40
  Mark you,
  Your party in converse, him you would sound,
  Having ever seen° in the prenominate° crimes
  The youth you breathe of guilty, be assured
  He closes with you in this consequence°—   45
  "Good sir," or so, or "friend," or "gentleman,"
  According to the phrase or the addition°
  Of man and country.

REYNALDO.   Very good, my lord.

POLONIUS. And then, sir, does he this—he does—   50
  What was I about to say? By the mass, I was about
  to say something. Where did I leave?

REYNALDO. At "closes in the consequence," at "friend or so," and
  "gentleman."

POLONIUS. At "closes in the consequence," aye, marry,
  He closes with you thus: "I know the gentleman.   55

25. **fencing:** A young man who haunted fencing schools would be regarded
as quarrelsome and likely to belong to the sporting set. 26. **Drabbing:** whoring. 28. **season:** qualify. 30. **open . . . incontinency:** So long as Laertes
does his drabbing inconspicuously Polonius would not be disturbed. 31.
quaintly: skillfully. 34. **unreclaimed:** naturally wild. 35. **Of . . . assault:**
common to all men. 37. **drift:** intention. 38. **fetch . . . warrant:** trick war-
ranted to work. 39. **sullies:** blemishes. 43. **Having . . . seen:** if ever he
has seen. **prenominate:** aforementioned. 45. **closes . . . consequence:** follows up with this reply. 47. **addition:** title. See I.4.20.

I saw him yesterday, or t'other day,
Or then, or then, with such, or such, and, as you say,
There was a' gaming, there o'ertook in 's rouse,
There falling out at tennis."° Or perchance,
"I saw him enter such a house of sale,"   60
Videlicet,° a brothel, or so forth.
See you now,
Your bait of falsehood takes this carp of truth.
And thus do we of wisdom and of reach,°
With windlasses° and with assays of bias,°   65
By indirections find directions out.°
So, by my former lecture and advice,
Shall you my son. You have me, have you not?
REYNALDO. My lord, I have.
POLONIUS.   God be wi' ye, fare ye well.
REYNALDO. Good my lord!   70
POLONIUS. Observe his inclination in° yourself.
REYNALDO. I shall, my lord.
POLONIUS. And let him ply his music.
REYNALDO.   Well, my lord.
POLONIUS. Farewell!   [*Exit* REYNALDO.]
[*Enter* OPHELIA.] How now, Ophelia! What's the matter?
OPHELIA. Oh, my lord, my lord, I have been so affrighted!   75
POLONIUS. With what, i' the name of God?
OPHELIA. My lord, as I was sewing in my closet,°
     Lord Hamlet, with his doublet° all unbraced,
     No hat upon his head, his stockings fouled,
     Ungartered and down-gyved° to his ankle,   80
     Pale as his shirt, his knees knocking each other,
     And with a look so piteous in purport
     As if he had been loosèd out of Hell
     To speak of horrors, he comes before me.
POLONIUS. Mad for thy love?
OPHELIA.   My lord, I do not know,   85
     But truly I do fear it.
POLONIUS.   What said he?

59. tennis: Visitors to France were much impressed by the enthusiasm of all classes of Frenchmen for tennis, which in England was mainly a courtier's game. **61. Videlicet:** namely, "viz." **64. wisdom . . . reach:** of far-reaching wisdom. **65. windlasses:** roundabout methods. **assays of bias:** making our bowl take a curved course. **66. indirections . . . out:** by indirect means come at the direct truth. **71. in:** for. **77. closet:** private room. **78. doublet:** the short close-fitting coat which was braced to the hose by laces. When a man was relaxing or careless of appearance, he *unbraced,* as a modern man takes off his coat. **80. down-gyved:** hanging around his ankles like fetters.

OPHELIA. He took me by the wrist and held me hard.
    Then goes he to the length of all his arm,
    And with his other hand thus o'er his brow,
    He falls to such perusal of my face   90
    As he would draw it. Long stayed he so.
    At last, a little shaking of mine arm,
    And thrice his head thus waving up and down,
    He raised a sigh so piteous and profound
    As it did seem to shatter all his bulk   95
    And end his being. That done, he lets me go.
    And with his head over his shoulder turned,
    He seemed to find his way without his eyes;
    For out o' doors he went without their helps,
    And to the last bended their light on me.   100
POLONIUS. Come, go with me. I will go seek the King.
    This is the very ecstasy° of love,
    Whose violent property fordoes° itself
    And leads the will to desperate undertakings
    As oft as any passion under heaven   105
    That does afflict our natures. I am sorry.
    What, have you given him any hard words of late?
OPHELIA. No, my good lord, but, as you did command,
    I did repel his letters and denied
    His access to me.
POLONIUS.   That hath made him mad.   110
    I am sorry that with better heed and judgment
    I had not quoted° him. I feared he did but trifle
    And meant to wreck thee, but beshrew° my jealousy!
    By Heaven, it is as proper° to our age
    To cast beyond ourselves° in our opinions   115
    As it is common for the younger sort
    To lack discretion. Come, go we to the King.
    This must be known, which, being kept close, might move
    More grief to hide than hate to utter love.°
    Come.   [*Exeunt.*]   120

---

102. **ecstasy:** frenzy.   103. **property fordoes:** natural quality destroys.   **112. quoted:** observed carefully.   **113. beshrew:** a plague on.   **114. proper:** natural.   **115. cast . . . ourselves:** be too clever.   **118–19. which . . . love:** by being kept secret it may cause more sorrow than it will cause anger by being revealed; i.e., the King and Queen may be angry at the thought of the Prince's marrying beneath his proper rank.

Scene 2 🙞🙜 *A room in the castle.*

[*Flourish. Enter* KING, QUEEN, ROSENCRANTZ,
GUILDENSTERN, *and* ATTENDANTS.]

KING. Welcome, dear Rosencrantz and Guildenstern!
Moreover° that we much did long to see you,
The need we have to use you did provoke
Our hasty sending. Something have you heard
Of Hamlet's transformation—so call it,   5
Sith° nor the exterior nor the inward man
Resembles that it was. What it should be,
More than his father's death, that thus hath put him
So much from the understanding of himself
I cannot dream of. I entreat you both   10
That, being of so young days brought up with him
And sith so neighbored to his youth and havior°
That you vouchsafe your rest° here in our Court
Some little time, so by your companies
To draw him on to pleasures, and to gather   15
So much as from occasion you may glean,
Whether aught to us unknown afflicts him thus
That opened lies within our remedy.°
QUEEN. Good gentlemen, he hath much talked of you,
And sure I am two men there art not living   20
To whom he more adheres.° If it will please you
To show us so much gentry° and good will
As to expend your time with us a while
For the supply and profit of our hope,°

Sc. 2: 2. **Moreover:** in addition to the fact that. 6. **Sith:** since. 12.
neighbored . . . havior: so near to his youthful manner of living. 13. **vouchsafe . . . rest:** consent to stay. 18. **opened . . . remedy:** if revealed, might
be put right by us. 21. **To . . . adheres:** whom he regards more highly.
22. **gentry:** courtesy. 24. **supply . . . hope:** to bring a profitable conclusion
to our hope.

Your visitation shall receive such thanks   25
As fits a king's remembrance.

ROSENCRANTZ.   Both your Majesties
Might, by the sovereign power you have of us,
Put your dread pleasures more into command
Than to entreaty.

GUILDENSTERN.   But we both obey,
And here give up ourselves, in the full bent°   30
To lay our service freely at your feet,
To be commanded.

KING. Thanks, Rosencrantz and gentle Guildenstern.

QUEEN. Thanks, Guildenstern and gentle Rosencrantz.
And I beseech you instantly to visit   35
My too-much-changèd son. Go, some of you,
And bring these gentlemen where Hamlet is.

GUILDENSTERN. Heavens make our presence and our practices
Pleasant and helpful to him!

QUEEN.   Aye, amen!

[Exeunt ROSENCRANTZ, GUILDENSTERN,
and some ATTENDANTS.]

[Enter POLONIUS.]

POLONIUS. The ambassadors from Norway, my good lord,   40
Are joyfully returned.

KING. Thou still° hast been the father of good news.

POLONIUS. Have I, my lord? I assure my good liege
I hold my duty as I hold my soul,
Both to my God and to my gracious King.   45
And I do think, or else this brain of mine
Hunts not the trail of policy so sure
As it hath used to do,° that I have found
The very cause of Hamlet's lunacy.

KING. Oh, speak of that. That do I long to hear.   50

POLONIUS. Give first admittance to the ambassadors.
My news shall be the fruit° to that great feast.

KING. Thyself do grace° to them and bring them in.

[Exit POLONIUS.]

He tells me, my dear Gertrude, he hath found
The head and source of all your son's distemper.°   55

QUEEN. I doubt it is no other but the main,°

---

30. **in . . . bent:** stretched to our uttermost. **42. still:** always. **47–48. Hunts . . . do:** is not so good at following the scent of political events as it used to be. **52. fruit:** the dessert, which comes at the end of the feast. **53. do grace:** honor; i.e., by escorting them into the royal presence. **55. distemper:** mental disturbance. **56. main:** principal cause.

His father's death and our o'erhasty marriage.
KING. Well, we shall sift him.
          [*Re-enter* POLONIUS, *with* VOLTIMAND *and* CORNELIUS.]
                         Welcome, my good friends!
Say, Voltimand, what from our brother Norway?
VOLTIMAND. Most fair return of greetings and desires.   60
     Upon our first,° he sent out to suppress
     His nephew's levies, which to him appeared
     To be a preparation 'gainst the Polack,
     But better looked into, he truly found
     It was against your Highness, whereat, grieved   65
     That so his sickness, age, and impotence
     Was falsely borne in hand,° sends out arrests
     On Fortinbras; which he, in brief, obeys,
     Receives rebuke from Norway, and in fine°
     Makes vow before his uncle never more   70
     To give the assay of arms° against your Majesty.
     Whereon old Norway, overcome with joy,
     Gives him three thousand crowns in annual fee
     And his commission to employ those soldiers,
     So levied as before, against the Polack.   75
     With an entreaty, herein further shown, [*Giving a paper*]
     That it might please you to give quiet pass°
     Through your dominions for this enterprise,
     On such regards of safety and allowance°
     As therein are set down.
KING.   It likes° us well,   80
     And at our more considered time we'll read,
     Answer, and think upon this business.
     Meantime we thank you for your well-took labor.
     Go to your rest. At night we'll feast together.
     Most welcome home!
                         [*Exeunt* VOLTIMAND *and* CORNELIUS.]
POLONIUS.   This business is well ended.   85
     My liege, and madam, to expostulate°
     What majesty should be, what duty is,
     Why day is day, night night, and time is time,
     Were nothing but to waste night, day, and time.
     Therefore, since brevity is the soul of wit   90
     And tediousness the limbs and outward flourishes,°

61. first: i.e., audience.   67. borne in hand: imposed upon.   69. in fine: in
the end.   71. give . . . arms: make an attack.   77. quiet pass: unmolested
passage.   79. regards . . . allowance: safeguard and conditions.   80. likes:
pleases.   86. expostulate: indulge in an academic discussion.   91. flourishes:
ornaments.

    I will be brief. Your noble son is mad.
    Mad call I it, for to define true madness,
    What is 't but to be nothing else but mad?
    But let that go.
QUEEN.   More matter, with less art.°   95
POLONIUS. Madam, I swear I use no art at all.
    That he is mad, 'tis true. 'Tis true 'tis pity,
    And pity 'tis 'tis true—a foolish figure,°
    But farewell it, for I will use no art.
    Mad let us grant him, then. And now remains   100
    That we find out the cause of this effect,
    Or rather say the cause of this defect,
    For this effect defective comes by cause.
    Thus it remains and the remainder thus.
    Perpend.°   105
    I have a daughter—have while she is mine—
    Who in her duty and obedience, mark,
    Hath given me this. Now gather and surmise.°
    [*Reads*.]
    "To the celestial, and my soul's idol, the most beautified°
       Ophelia—"   110
    That's an ill phrase, a vile phrase, "beautified" is a vile
    phrase. But you shall hear. Thus: [*Reads*.]
    "In her excellent white bosom, these," and so forth.
QUEEN. Came this from Hamlet to her?
POLONIUS. Good madam, stay awhile, I will be faithful.   115
    [*Reads*.] "Doubt thou the stars are fire,
          Doubt that the sun doth move,
          Doubt truth to be a liar,
          But never doubt I love.
    "Oh dear Ophelia, I am ill at these numbers,° I have not   120
    art to reckon my groans, but that I love thee best, believe it.
    Adieu.
       "Thine evermore, most dear lady, whilst this
                  machine° is to him, HAMLET."
    This is obedience hath my daughter shown me,   125
    And more above, hath his solicitings,
    As they fell out by time, by means and place,
    All given to mine ear.
KING.   But how hath she
    Received his love?

---

95. art: ornament. **98. figure:** i.e., a figure of speech. **105. Perpend:** note carefully. **108. surmise:** guess the meaning. **110. beautified:** beautiful. **120. numbers:** verses. **124. machine:** i.e., body, an affected phrase.

POLONIUS.   What do you think of me?
KING. As of a man faithful and honorable.   130
POLONIUS. I would fain prove so. But what might you think,
     When I had seen this hot love on the wing—
     As I perceived it, I must tell you that,
     Before my daughter told me—what might you
     Or my dear Majesty your Queen here think   135
     If I had played the desk or table book,°
     Or given my heart awinking, mute and dumb,
     Or looked upon this love with idle sight—
     What might you think? No, I went round° to work,
     And my young mistress thus I did bespeak:°   140
     "Lord Hamlet is a Prince, out of thy star.°
     This must not be." And then I prescripts° gave her
     That she should lock herself from his resort,
     Admit no messengers, receive no tokens.
     Which done, she took the fruits of my advice.   145
     And he, repulsèd, a short tale to make,
     Fell into a sadness, then into a fast,
     Thence to a watch, thence into a weakness,
     Thence to a lightness,° and by this declension°
     Into the madness wherein now he raves   150
     And all we mourn for.
KING. Do you think this?
QUEEN.   It may be, very like.
POLONIUS. Hath there been such a time, I'd fain know that,
     That I have positively said " 'Tis so"
     When it proved otherwise?
KING.   Not that I know.   155
POLONIUS. [*Pointing to his head and shoulder*.] Take this from
     this, if this be otherwise.
     If circumstances lead me, I will find
     Where truth is hid, though it were hid indeed
     Within the center.°
KING.   How may we try it further?

136. desk . . . book: i.e., acted as silent go-between (desks and books being natural post offices for a love letter), or been a recipient of secrets but
took no action (as desks and notebooks are the natural but inanimate places
for keeping secrets). 139. round: straight. 140. bespeak: address. 141.
out . . . star: above your destiny. 142. prescripts: instructions. 147–49.
Fell . . . lightness: Hamlet's case history, according to Polonius, develops
by stages—melancholy, loss of appetite, sleeplessness, physical weakness,
mental instability, and finally madness. 149. declension: decline. 159. center: the very center of the earth, regarded before Copernicus as the center of
the Universe.

POLONIUS. You know sometimes he walks four hours together   160
    Here in the lobby.
QUEEN.   So he does indeed.
POLONIUS. At such a time I'll loose° my daughter to him.
    Be you and I behind an arras° then.
    Mark the encounter. If he love her not,
    And be not from his reason fall'n thereon,   165
    Let me be no assistant for a state,
    But keep a farm and carters.°
KING.   We will try it.
QUEEN. But look where sadly the poor wretch comes reading.
POLONIUS. Away, I do beseech you, both away.
    I'll board° him presently.   [*Exeunt* KING, QUEEN,   170
                                and ATTENDANTS.]
    [*Enter* HAMLET, *reading*.] Oh, give me leave. How does my
    good Lord Hamlet?
HAMLET. Well, God-a-mercy.
POLONIUS. Do you know me, my lord?
HAMLET. Excellent well. You are a fishmonger.°
POLONIUS. Not I, my lord.   175
HAMLET. Then I would you were so honest a man.
POLONIUS. Honest, my lord!
HAMLET. Aye, sir, to be honest, as this world goes, is to be one
    man picked out of ten thousand.
POLONIUS. That's very true, my lord.   180
HAMLET. For if the sun breed maggots° in a dead dog, being a
    god° kissing carrion°——Have you a daughter?
POLONIUS. I have, my lord.   184
HAMLET. Let her not walk i' the sun. Conception is a blessing,
    but not as your daughter may conceive—friend, look to 't.
POLONIUS. [*Aside*] How say you by that? Still harping on my
    daughter. Yet he knew me not at first, he said I was a fish-
    monger. He is far gone, far gone. And truly in my youth I
    suffered much extremity for love, very near this. I'll speak to
    him again.—What do you read, my lord?   193
HAMLET. Words, words, words.
POLONIUS. What is the matter, my lord?
HAMLET. Between who?   196
POLONIUS. I mean the matter that you read, my lord.

---

162. loose: turn loose.   **163. arras:** tapestry hanging.   **167. keep . . . carters:**
i.e., turn country squire—like Justice Shallow. See *II Hen IV*.   **170. board:**
accost.   **174. fishmonger:** Hamlet is now in his "antic disposition," enjoying
himself by fooling Polonius.   **181. sun . . . maggots:** a general belief. Cf.
Ant & Cleo, II.7.29–31.   **182. god:** Q2 and F1 read "good." **carrion:** flesh.

HAMLET. Slanders, sir. For the satirical rogue says here that old
    men have gray beards, that their faces are wrinkled, their
    eyes purging thick amber and plum-tree gum, and that they
    have a plentiful lack of wit, together with most weak hams.°
    All which, sir, though I most powerfully and potently be-
    lieve, yet I hold it not honesty to have it thus set down;
    for yourself, sir, should be old as I am if like a crab you
    could go backward.   206

POLONIUS. [*Aside*] Though this be madness, yet there is method°
    in 't.—Will you walk out of the air, my lord?

HAMLET. Into my grave.

POLONIUS. Indeed, that's out of the air. [*Aside*] How pregnant°   212
    sometimes his replies are! A happiness° that often mad-
    ness hits on, which reason and sanity could not so pros-
    perously be delivered of. I will leave him, and suddenly con-
    trive the means of meeting between him and my daughter.
    —My honorable lord, I will most humbly take my leave
    of you.   218

HAMLET. You cannot, sir, take from me anything that I will more
    willingly part withal—except my life, except my life, except
    my life.   215

POLONIUS. Fare you well, my lord.

HAMLET. These tedious old fools!

        [*Enter* ROSENCRANTZ *and* GUILDENSTERN.]

POLONIUS. You go to seek the Lord Hamlet. There he is.

ROSENCRANTZ. [*To* POLONIUS] God save you, sir!   225

                        [*Exit* POLONIUS.]

GUILDENSTERN. My honored lord!

ROSENCRANTZ. My most dear lord!

HAMLET. My excellent good friends!° How dost thou, Guilden-   228
    stern? Ah, Rosencrantz! Good lads, how do you both?

ROSENCRANTZ. As the indifferent° children of the earth.

GUILDENSTERN. Happy in that we are not overhappy.
    On Fortune's cap we are not the very button.°

HAMLET. Nor the soles of her shoe?

ROSENCRANTZ. Neither, my lord.   235

HAMLET. Then you live about her waist, or in the middle of her
    favors?

GUILDENSTERN. Faith, her privates° we.

202. **hams:** knee joints.   208. **method:** order, sense.   212. **pregnant:** apt,
meaningful.   212. **happiness:** good turn of phrase.   228. **My . . . friends:**
As soon as Polonius has gone, Hamlet drops his assumed madness and greets
Rosencrantz and Guildenstern naturally.   231. **indifferent:** neither too great
nor too little.   233. **button:** i.e., at the top.   238. **privates:** with a pun on
"private parts" and "private," not concerned with politics.

HAMLET. In the secret parts of Fortune? Oh, most true, she is a
    strumpet. What's the news?   240

ROSENCRANTZ. None, my lord, but that the world's grown honest.

HAMLET. Then is Doomsday near. But your news is not true. Let
    me question more in particular. What have you, my good
    friends, deserved at the hands of Fortune, that she sends you
    to prison hither?   247

GUILDENSTERN. Prison, my lord!

HAMLET. Denmark's a prison.

ROSENCRANTZ. Then is the world one.

HAMLET. A goodly one, in which there are many confines,°
    wards,° and dungeons, Denmark being one o' the worst.

ROSENCRANTZ. We think not so, my lord.   254

HAMLET. Why, then 'tis none to you, for there is nothing either
    good or bad but thinking makes it so. To me it is a prison.

ROSENCRANTZ. Why, then your ambition° makes it one. 'Tis too
    narrow for your mind.   259

HAMLET. Oh, God, I could be bounded in a nutshell and count
    myself a king of infinite space were it not that I have bad
    dreams.

GUILDENSTERN. Which dreams indeed are ambition, for the very
    substance of the ambitious° is merely the shadow of a dream.

HAMLET. A dream itself is but a shadow.   265

ROSENCRANTZ. Truly, and I hold ambition of so airy and light a
    quality that it is but a shadow's shadow.

HAMLET. Then are our beggars bodies, and our monarchs and
    outstretched heroes the beggars' shadows.° Shall we to the
    Court? For, by my fay,° I cannot reason.°   271

ROSENCRANTZ & GUILDENSTERN. We'll wait upon you.°

HAMLET. No such matter. I will not sort° you with the rest of my
    servants, for, to speak to you like an honest man, I am most
    dreadfully attended.° But in the beaten way of friendship,
    what make you at Elsinore?   278

ROSENCRANTZ. To visit you, my lord, no other occasion.

HAMLET. Beggar that I am, I am even poor in thanks, but I thank
    you. And sure, dear friends, my thanks are too dear a half-

---

252. confines: places of confinement. **wards:** cells. **258. your ambition:**
Rosencrantz is feeling after one possible cause of Hamlet's melancholy—
thwarted ambition. **264. substance . . . ambitious:** that on which an ambitious man feeds his fancies. **269–71. Then . . . shadows:** i.e., by your
reasoning beggars are the only men of substance, for kings and heroes are
by nature ambitious and therefore "the shadows of a dream." **outstretched:**
of exaggerated reputation. **271. fay:** faith. **272. reason:** argue. **273. wait
. . . you:** be your servants. **274. sort:** class. **276. dreadfully attended:** my
attendants are a poor crowd.

penny.° Were you not sent for? Is it your own inclining?
Is it a free visitation?° Come, deal justly with me. Come,
come. Nay, speak.   285

GUILDENSTERN. What should we say, my lord?

HAMLET. Why, anything, but to the purpose.° You were sent for,
and there is a kind of confession in your looks which your
modesties have not craft enough to color.° I know the good
King and Queen have sent for you.

ROSENCRANTZ. To what end, my lord?   292

HAMLET. That you must teach me. But let me conjure° you, by
the rights of our fellowship,° by the consonancy° of our
youth, by the obligation of our ever preserved love, and by
what more dear a better proposer could charge you withal,
be even° and direct with me, whether you were sent for,
or no.   299

ROSENCRANTZ. [Aside to GUILDENSTERN] What say you?

HAMLET. [Aside] Nay, then, I have an eye of you.—If you love
me, hold not off.

GUILDENSTERN. My lord, we were sent for.   303

HAMLET. I will tell you why. So shall my anticipation prevent
your discovery, and your secrecy to the King and Queen
molt no feather.° I have of late—but wherefore I know not
—lost all my mirth, forgone all custom of exercises, and
indeed it goes so heavily with my disposition that this goodly
frame the earth seems to me a sterile promontory. This   310
most excellent canopy,° the air, look you, this brave o'erhanging firmament,° this majestical roof fretted° with
golden fire—why, it appears no other thing to me than a
foul and pestilent congregation of vapors. What a piece of
work is a man! How noble in reason! How infinite in fac-   315
ulty!° In form and moving° how express° and admirable!
In action how like an angel! In apprehension how like a god!
The beauty of the world! The paragon of animals! And yet,
to me, what is this quintessence° of dust? Man delights not
me—no, nor woman neither, though by your smiling you   320

---

282. too . . . halfpenny: not worth a halfpenny. 283. free visitation: voluntary visit. 287. anything . . . purpose: anything so long as it is not true.
290. color: conceal. 294. conjure: make solemn appeal to. fellowship: comradeship. 295. consonancy: concord. 298. even: straight. 304–06. So
. . . feather: i.e., so by my telling you first you will not be obliged to betray
the secrets of the King. prevent: forestall. molt no feather: be undisturbed.
311. canopy: covering. 312. firmament: sky. 313. fretted: ornamented.
316. faculty: power of the mind. 317. moving: movement. express: exact.
319. quintessence: perfection; the fifth essence, which would be left if the
four elements were taken away.

seem to say so.

ROSENCRANTZ. My lord, there was no such stuff in my thoughts.

HAMLET. Why did you laugh, then, when I said "Man delights not me"?

ROSENCRANTZ. To think, my lord, if you delight not in man, what lenten entertainment° the players shall receive from you. We coted° them on the way, and hither are they coming to offer you service.   331

HAMLET. He that plays the King shall be welcome, His Majesty shall have tribute of me. The adventurous knight shall use his foil and target,° the lover shall not sigh gratis, the humorous man° shall end his part in peace, the clown shall make those laugh whose lungs are tickle o' the sere,° and the lady shall say her mind freely or the blank verse shall halt° for 't. What players are they?   340

ROSENCRANTZ. Even those you were wont to take such delight in, the tragedians of the city.

HAMLET. How chances it they travel? Their residence, both in reputation and profit, was better both ways.°   345

ROSENCRANTZ. I° think their inhibition° comes by the means of the late innovation.°

HAMLET. Do they hold the same estimation they did when I was in the city? Are they so followed?

ROSENCRANTZ. No, indeed are they not.   350

HAMLET. How comes it? Do they grow rusty?

ROSENCRANTZ. Nay, their endeavor keeps in the wonted pace.° But there is, sir, an eyrie° of children, little eyases,° that cry out on the top of question° and are most tyrannically° clapped for 't. These are now the fashion, and so berattle° 356 the common stages°—so they call them—that many wearing rapiers are afraid of goose quills° and dare scarce come

329. **lenten entertainment:** mager welcome.   330. **coted:** overtook.   334. **foil . . . target:** rapier and small shield.   335. **humorous man:** the man who specializes in character parts; e.g., Jaques in *AYLI*.   338. **are . . . sere:** explode at a touch. The *sere* is part of the trigger mechanism of a gun which if "ticklish" will go off at a touch.   340. **halt:** limp.   343–45. **Their . . . way:** i.e., if they stayed in the city, it would bring them more profit and fame.   346–79. **I . . . too:** This is one of the several topical references in *Hamlet*. In 1600 and 1601 there was fierce competition between the professional players and the two companies of boy actors, formed from the choir boys of the royal chapels and St. Paul's.   346. **inhibition:** formal prohibition.   347. **innovation:** riot.   352–53. **endeavor . . . pace:** they try as hard as ever.   353. **eyrie:** nest.   354. **eyases:** young hawks.   354. **cry . . . question:** either "cry in a shrill voice" or perhaps "cry out the latest detail of the dispute."   355. **tyrannically:** outrageously.   356. **berattle:** abuse.   357. **common stages:** the professional players. The boys acted in "private" playhouses.   359. **goose quills:** pens; i.e., of such as Ben Jonson.

thither.   360

HAMLET. What, are they children? Who maintains 'em? How
    are they escoted?° Will they pursue the quality° no longer
    than they can sing? Will they not say afterward, if they
    should grow themselves to common players—as it is most
    like if their means are no better—their writers do them
    wrong to make them exclaim against their own succession?°   368

ROSENCRANTZ. Faith, there has been much to-do on both sides,
    and the nation holds it no sin to tarre° them to con-
    troversy. There was for a while no money bid for argu-
    ment° unless the poet and the player went to cuffs° in the
    question.

HAMLET. Is 't possible?   373

GUILDENSTERN. Oh, there has been much throwing-about of
    brains.

HAMLET. Do the boys carry it away?

ROSENCRANTZ. Aye, that they do, my lord, Hercules and his
    load° too.   379

HAMLET. It is not very strange, for my uncle is King of Den-
    mark, and those that would make mows° at him while my
    father lived give twenty, forty, fifty, a hundred ducats apiece
    for his picture in little. 'Sblood,° there is something in this
    more than natural, if philosophy could find it out.   385

    [*Flourish of trumpets within.*]

GUILDENSTERN. There are the players.

HAMLET. Gentlemen, you are welcome to Elsinore. Your hands.
    Come then. The appurtenance of welcome is fashion and
    ceremony.° Let me comply° with you in this garb,° lest my
    extent° to the players—which, I tell you, must show fairly   390
    outward—should more appear like entertainment° than
    yours. You are welcome. But my uncle-father and aunt-
    mother are deceived.

GUILDENSTERN. In what, my dear lord?   395

HAMLET. I am but mad north-northwest.° When the wind is

---

362. escoted: paid.   **363. quality:** acting profession.   **368. exclaim . . . succession:** abuse the profession to which they will afterward belong.   **370. tarre:**
urge on to fight; generally used of encouraging a dog.   **372. argument:** plot
of a play. See III.2.242.   **372–73. went to cuffs:** boxed each other's ears.
378–79. Hercules . . . load: Hercules carrying the globe on his shoulders
was the sign of the Globe Playhouse.   **381. mows:** grimaces.   **384. 'Sblood:**
by God's blood.   **388–89. appurtenance . . . ceremony:** that which pertains
to welcome is formal ceremony.   **389. comply:** use the formality of welcome;
i.e., shake hands with you.   **390. garb:** fashion.   **extent:** outward behavior.
392. entertainment: welcome.   **396. north-northwest:** i.e., 327° (out of 360°)
of the compass.

southerly,° I know a hawk from a handsaw.°
[*Re-enter* POLONIUS.]
POLONIUS. Well be with you, gentlemen!
HAMLET. Hark you, Guildenstern, and you too—at each ear a
hearer. That great baby you see there is not yet out of his
swaddling clouts.°   401
ROSENCRANTZ. Happily he's the second time come to them, for
they say an old man is twice a child.
HAMLET. I will prophesy he comes to tell me of the players, mark
it. You say right, sir. O' Monday morning, 'twas so in-
deed.   407
POLONIUS. My lord, I have news to tell you.
HAMLET. My lord, I have news to tell you. When Roscius° was
an actor in Rome——
POLONIUS. The actors are come hither, my lord.
HAMLET. Buzz, buzz!°
POLONIUS. Upon my honor——   413
HAMLET. Then came each actor on his ass——
POLONIUS. The° best actors in the world, either for tragedy,
comedy, history, pastoral, pastoral-comical, historical-pasto-
ral, tragical-historical, tragical-comical-historical-pastoral,
scene individable° or poem unlimited.° Seneca cannot be
too heavy, nor Plautus° too light. For the law of writ° and   420
the liberty,° these are the only men.
HAMLET. O Jephthah,° judge of Israel, what a treasure hadst
thou!
POLONIUS. What a treasure had he, my lord?
HAMLET. Why,   425
"One° fair daughter, and no more,
The which he lovèd passing well."

397. **wind is southerly:** The south wind was considered unhealthy.   396–97.
hawk . . . handsaw: Either "handsaw" is a corruption of "heronshaw," heron,
or a hawk is a tool like a pickax. The phrase means "I'm not so mad as you
think."   401. **clouts:** clothes.   410. **Roscius:** the most famous of Roman actors.   412. **Buzz, buzz:** slang for "stale news."   415–21. **The . . . men:**
Polonius reads out the accomplishments of the actors from the license which
they have presented him.   418. **scene individable:** i.e., a play preserving the
unities.   418–19. **poem unlimited:** i.e., a play which disregards the rules.
419–20. **Seneca . . . Plautus:** the Roman writers of tragedy and comedy
with whose plays every educated man was familiar.   420. **law of writ:** the
critical rules; i.e., classical plays. **liberty:** plays freely written; i.e., "modern"
drama.   422. **Jephthah:** The story of Jephthah is told in Judges, Chapter 11.
He vowed that if successful against the Ammonites he would sacrifice the
first creature to meet him on his return, which was his daughter.   426–37.
One . . . was: Quotations from a ballad of Jephthah.

POLONIUS. [*Aside*] Still° on my daughter.

HAMLET. Am I not i' the right, old Jephthah?

POLONIUS. If you call me Jephthah, my lord, I have a daughter
that I love passing well.   431

HAMLET. Nay, that follows not.

POLONIUS. What follows, then, my lord?

HAMLET. Why,

                "As by lot, God wot,"°   435
and then you know,
                "It came to pass, as most like it was—"
the first row° of the pious chanson° will show you more, for
look where my abridgement° comes. [*Enter four or five*   439
PLAYERS.] You are welcome, masters, welcome all. I am glad
to see thee well. Welcome, good friends. Oh, my old friend!°
Why, thy face is valanced° since I saw thee last. Comest thou
to beard° me in Denmark? What, my young lady° and mistress! By 'r Lady, your ladyship is nearer to Heaven than
when I saw you last, by the altitude of a chopine.° Pray God   446
your voice, like a piece of uncurrent gold, be not cracked
within the ring.° Masters, you are all welcome. We'll e'en to
't like French falconers,° fly at anything we see. We'll have
a speech straight. Come, give us a taste of your quality°—
come, a passionate speech.   453

FIRST PLAYER. What speech, my good lord?

HAMLET. I heard thee speak me a speech once, but it was never
acted, or if it was, not above once; for the play, I remember, pleased not the million, 'twas caviar° to the general.°
But it was—as I received it, and others, whose judgments
in such matters cried in the top of mine°—an excellent play,
well digested° in the scenes, set down with as much mod-   460
esty° as cunning. I remember one said there were no sallets°

---

428. Still: always.   435. wot: knows.   438. row: line.   pious chanson: godly
poem.   439. abridgement: entertainment.   441. old friend: i.e., the leading
player.   442. valanced: bearded. A valance is a fringe hung round the sides
and bottom of a bed.   443. beard: dare, with a pun on "valanced." young
lady: i.e., the boy who takes the woman's parts.   446. chopine: lady's shoe
with thick cork sole.   447. cracked . . . ring: Before coins were milled on
the rim they were liable to crack. When the crack reached the ring surrounding the device, the coin was no longer valid.   450. French falconers: They
were famous for their skill in hawking.   452. quality: skill as an actor.   457.
caviar: sturgeon's roe, a Russian delicacy not then appreciated (or known)
by any but gourmets.   general: common herd.   459. cried . . . mine: surpassed mine.   460. digested: composed.   461. modesty: moderation.   462.
sallets: tasty bits.

in the lines to make the matter savory, nor no matter in the
phrase that might indict the author of affection,° but called
it an honest method, as wholesome as sweet, and by very   465
much more handsome than fine.° One speech in it I chiefly
loved. 'Twas Aeneas' tale to Dido,° and thereabout of it especially where he speaks of Priam's° slaughter. If it live in
your memory, begin at this line—let me see, let me see—   471
    "The rugged Pyrrhus,° like th' Hyrcanian beast,°—"
It is not so. It begins with "Pyrrhus."
    "The° rugged Pyrrhus, he whose sable° arms,
    Black as his purpose, did the night resemble   475
    When he lay couchèd in the ominous° horse,°
    Hath now this dread and black complexion smeared
    With heraldry° more dismal. Head to foot
    Now is he total gules, horridly tricked
    With blood of fathers, mothers, daughters, sons,   480
    Baked and impasted° with the parching streets
    That lend a tyrannous and a damnèd light
    To their lord's murder. Roasted in wrath and fire,
    And thus o'ersized with coagulate gore,°
    With eyes like carbuncles, the hellish Pyrrhus   485
    Old grandsire Priam seeks."
So, proceed you.
POLONIUS. 'Fore God, my lord, well spoken, with good accent and
    good discretion.
FIRST PLAYER.   "Anon he finds him   490
    Striking too short at Greeks. His antique sword,
    Rebellious to his arm, lies where it falls,

463–64. phrase . . . affection: nothing in the language which could charge
the author with affectation. 466. fine: subtle. 467. Aeneas' . . . Dido: the
story of the sack of Troy as told by Aeneas to Dido, Queen of Carthage. The
original is in Virgil's *Aeneid*. A similar speech occurs in Marlowe's play *Dido,
Queen of Carthage*. 469. Priam: the old King of Troy. 472. Pyrrhus: the
son of Achilles, one of the Greeks concealed in the Wooden Horse. 472.
Hyrcanian beast: the tiger. 474–541. The . . . gods: The speech may be
from some lost play of *Dido and Aeneas*, but more likely it is Shakespeare's
own invention. It is written in the heavy elaborate style still popular in the
dramas of the Admiral's Men. The first player delivers it with excessive gesture
and emotion. 474. sable: black. 476. ominous: fateful. horse: the Wooden
Horse by which a small Greek force was enabled to make a secret entry into
Troy. 478. heraldry: painting. The image of heraldic painting is kept up in
gules (the heraldic term for red) and *tricked* (painted). 481. impasted:
turned into a crust by the heat of the burning city. 484. o'ersized . . . gore:
covered over with congealed blood.

Repugnant to command.° Unequal matched,
Pyrrhus at Priam drives, in rage strikes wide,
But with the whiff and wind of his fell sword 495
The unnerved father falls. Then senseless Ilium,°
Seeming to feel this blow, with flaming top
Stoops to his base,° and with a hideous crash
Takes prisoner Pyrrhus' ear. For, lo! his sword,
Which was declining° on the milky° head 500
Of reverend Priam, seemed i' the air to stick.
So as a painted tyrant° Pyrrhus stood,
And like a neutral to his will and matter,°
Did nothing.
But as we often see, against° some storm 505
A silence in the heavens, the rack° stand still,
The bold winds speechless and the orb° below
As hush as death, anon the dreadful thunder
Doth rend the region°—so after Pyrrhus' pause
Arousèd vengeance sets him new awork. 510
And never did the Cyclops'° hammers fall
On Mars's armor, forged for proof eterne,°
With less remorse° than Pyrrhus' bleeding sword
Now falls on Priam.
Out, out, thou strumpet, Fortune! All you gods, 515
In general synod° take away her power,
Break all the spokes and fellies° from her wheel,
And bowl the round nave° down the hill of Heaven
As low as to the fiends!"
POLONIUS. This is too long. 520
HAMLET. It shall to the barber's, with your beard. Prithee, say on.
     He's for a jig° or a tale of bawdry, or he sleeps. Say on.
     Come to Hecuba.
FIRST PLAYER. "But who, oh, who had seen the mobled°
     Queen—" 525
HAMLET. "The mobled Queen"?

---

493. Repugnant to command: refusing to be used.   **496. Ilium:** the citadel
of Troy.   **498. stoops . . . base:** collapses.   **500. declining:** bending toward.
milky: milk-white.   **502. painted tyrant:** as in the painting of a tyrant.   **503.**
neutral . . . matter: one midway (*neutral*) between his desire (*will*) and
action (*matter*).   **505. against:** just before.   **506. rack:** the clouds in the
upper air.   **507. orb:** world.   **509. region:** the country round.   **511. Cyclops':**
of Titans, giants who aided Vulcan, the blacksmith god, to make armor for
Mars, the war god.   **512. proof eterne:** everlasting protection.   **513. re-**
morse: pity.   **516. synod:** council.   **517. fellies:** the pieces forming the circumference of a wooden wheel.   **518. nave:** center of the wheel.   **522. jig:**
bawdy dance.   **525. mobled:** muffled.

POLONIUS. That's good, "mobled Queen" is good.

FIRST PLAYER. "Run barefoot up and down, threatening the flames
    With bisson rheum,° a clout° upon that head
    Where late the diadem stood, and for a robe,   530
    About her lank and all o'erteemèd° loins
    A blanket, in the alarm of fear caught up.
    Who this had seen, with tongue in venom steeped
    'Gainst Fortune's state would treason have pronounced.°
    But if the gods themselves did see her then,   535
    When she saw Pyrrhus make malicious sport
    In mincing with his sword her husband's limbs,
    The instant burst of clamor that she made,
    Unless things mortal move them not at all,
    Would have made milch° the burning eyes of Heaven   540
    And passion in the gods."

POLONIUS. Look whether he has not turned his color and has tears
    in 's eyes. Prithee, no more.

HAMLET. 'Tis well; I'll have thee speak out the rest of this soon.
    Good my lord, will you see the players well bestowed?° Do
    you hear, let them be well used, for they are the abstract
    and brief chronicles of the time.° After your death you 550
    were better have a bad epitaph than their ill report while
    you live.

POLONIUS. My lord, I will use them according to their desert.°

HAMLET. God's bodykins,° man, much better. Use every man
    after his desert and who shall 'scape whipping? Use them
    after your own honor and dignity. The less they deserve,
    the more merit is in your bounty. Take them in.

POLONIUS. Come, sirs.   559

HAMLET. Follow him, friends. We'll hear a play tomorrow. [*Exit*
    POLONIUS *with all the* PLAYERS *but the* FIRST.] Dost thou
    hear me, old friend? Can you play *The Murder of Gonzago*?

FIRST PLAYER. Aye, my lord.   564

HAMLET. We'll ha 't tomorrow night. You could, for a need, study
    a speech of some dozen or sixteen lines which I would set
    down and insert in 't, could you not?

---

529. bisson rheum: blinding moisture. **clout:** rag. **531. o'erteemed:** exhausted by bearing children; she had borne fifty-two. **533–34. Who . . . pronounced:** anyone who had seen this sight would with bitter words have uttered treason against the tyranny of Fortune. **540. milch:** milky, i.e., dripping moisture. **548. bestowed:** housed. **549–50. abstract . . . time:** they summarize and record the events of our time. Elizabethan players were often in trouble for too saucily commenting on their betters in plays dealing with history or contemporary events and persons. **552. desert:** rank. **553. God's bodykins:** by God's little body.

FIRST PLAYER. Aye, my lord.   569
HAMLET. Very well. Follow that lord, and look you mock him
    not. [*Exit* FIRST PLAYER.] My good friends, I'll leave you till
    night. You are welcome to Elsinore.
ROSENCRANTZ. Good my lord!   574
HAMLET. Aye, so, God be wi' ye! [*Exeunt* RESENCRANTZ *and*
    GUILDENSTERN.] Now I am alone.
    Oh, what a rogue and peasant slave am I!
    Is it not monstrous that this player here,
    But in a fiction, in a dream of passion,°
    Could force his soul so to his own conceit°
    That from her working° all his visage wanned,°   580
    Tears in his eyes, distraction° in 's aspect,°
    A broken voice, and his whole function° suiting
    With forms to his conceit? And all for nothing!
    For Hecuba!
    What's Hecuba to him or he to Hecuba,   585
    That he should weep for her? What would he do
    Had he the motive and the cue for passion
    That I have? He would drown the stage with tears
    And cleave the general ear° with horrid speech,
    Make mad the guilty and appal the free,°   590
    Confound the ignorant, and amaze indeed
    The very faculties of eyes and ears.
    Yet I,
    A dull and muddy-mettled° rascal, peak,°
    Like John-a-dreams,° unpregnant of my cause,°   595
    And can say nothing—no, not for a King
    Upon whose property° and most dear life
    A damned defeat° was made. Am I a coward?
    Who° calls me villain? Breaks my pate across?
    Plucks off my beard and blows it in my face?   600
    Tweaks me by the nose? Gives me the lie i' the throat
    As deep as to the lungs? Who does me this?
    Ha!

---

578. dream of passion: imaginary emotion.   **579. conceit:** imagination.   **580. her working:** i.e., the effect of imagination. **wanned:** went pale.   **581. distraction:** frenzy. **aspect:** countenance.   **582. function:** behavior.   **589. general ear:** ears of the audience.   **590. free:** innocent.   **594. muddy-mettled:** made of mud, not iron. **peak:** mope.   **595. John-a-dreams:** "Sleepy Sam." **unpregnant . . . cause:** barren of plans for vengeance.   **597. property:** personality, life.   **598. defeat:** ruin.   **599–602. Who . . . this:** Hamlet runs through all the insults which provoked a resolute man to mortal combat. **pate:** head. **lie . . . throat:** the bitterest of insults.

'Swounds,° I should take it. For it cannot be
But I am pigeon-livered° and lack gall°　　　　　605
To make oppression bitter, or ere this
I should have fatted all the region kites
With this slave's offal.° Bloody, bawdy villain!
Remorseless, treacherous, lecherous, kindless° villain!
Oh, vengeance!　　　　　610
Why, what an ass am I! This is most brave,
That I, the son of a dear father murdered,
Prompted to my revenge by Heaven and Hell,
Must, like a whore, unpack my heart with words
And fall a-cursing like a very drab,°　　　　　615
A scullion!°
Fie upon 't! Foh! About, my brain! Hum, I have heard
That guilty creatures sitting at a play
Have by the very cunning of the scene
Been struck so to the soul that presently°　　　　　620
They have proclaimed their malefactions;°
For murder, though it have no tongue, will speak
With most miraculous organ. I'll have these players
Play something like the murder of my father
Before mine uncle. I'll observe his looks,　　　　　625
I'll tent° him to the quick. If he but blench,°
I know my course. The° spirit that I have seen
May be the Devil, and the Devil hath power
To assume a pleasing shape. Yea, and perhaps
Out of my weakness and my melancholy,　　　　　630
As he is very potent with such spirits,
Abuses me to damn me.° I'll have grounds°
More relative than this.° The play's the thing
Wherein I'll catch the conscience of the King.

　　　　　　　　　　　　　　　　[*Exit.*]

604. 'Swounds: by God's wounds. **605. pigeon-livered:** "as gentle as a dove." **gall:** spirit. **606–08. I . . . offal:** before this I would have fed this slave's (i.e., the King's) guts to the kites. **fatted:** made fat. **609. kindless:** unnatural. **615. drab:** "moll." **616. scullion:** the lowest of the kitchen servants. **620. presently:** immediately. **621. proclaimed . . . malefactions:** shouted out their crimes. **626. tent:** probe. **blench:** flinch. **627–32. The . . . me:** an illusion sent by the Devil, or caused by acute melancholy. **632. Abuses . . . me:** i.e., deceives me so that I may commit the sin of murder which will bring me to damnation. **grounds:** reasons for action. **633. relative . . . this:** i.e., more convincing than the appearance of a ghost.

ACT III

Scene 1 ⌘ *A room in the castle.*

[*Enter* KING, QUEEN, POLONIUS, OPHELIA, ROSENCRANTZ,
and GUILDENSTERN.]

KING. And can you, by no drift of circumstance,°
    Get from him why he puts on this confusion,
    Grating° so harshly all his days of quiet
    With turbulent and dangerous lunacy?
ROSENCRANTZ. He does confess he feels himself distracted,   5
    But from what cause he will by no means speak.
GUILDENSTERN. Nor do we find him forward to be sounded,°
    But, with a crafty madness, keeps aloof
    When we would bring him on to some confession
    Of his true state.
QUEEN.   Did he receive you well?   10
ROSENCRANTZ. Most like a gentleman.
GUILDENSTERN. But with much forcing of his disposition.°
ROSENCRANTZ. Niggard of question,° but of our demands
    Most free in his reply.
QUEEN.   Did you assay him
    To any pastime?°   15
ROSENCRANTZ. Madam, it so fell out that certain players
    We o'erraught° on the way. Of these we told him,
    And there did seem in him a kind of joy
    To hear of it. They are about the Court,
    And, as I think, they have already order   20
    This night to play before him.

Act III, Sc. 1: 1. **drift of circumstance:** circumstantial evidence, hint. **3. grating:** disturbing. **7. forward . . . sounded:** eager to be questioned. **12. much . . . disposition:** making a great effort to be civil to us. **13. Niggard of question:** not asking many questions. **14–15. Did . . . pastime:** Did you try to interest him in any amusement. **17. o'erraught:** overtook.

POLONIUS.   'Tis most true.
And he beseeched me to entreat your Majesties
To hear and see the matter.
KING. With all my heart, and it doth much content me
To hear him so inclined.   25
Good gentlemen, give him a further edge,°
And drive his purpose on to these delights.
ROSENCRANTZ. We shall, my lord.
             [*Exeunt* ROSENCRANTZ *and* GUILDENSTERN.]
KING.   Sweet Gertrude, leave us too,
For we have closely° sent for Hamlet hither,
That he, as 'twere by accident, may here   30
Affront° Ophelia.
Her father and myself, lawful espials,°
Will so bestow ourselves that, seeing unseen,
We may of their encounter frankly judge
And gather by him, as he is behaved,°   35
If 't be the affliction of his love or no
That thus he suffers for.
QUEEN.   I shall obey you.
And for your part, Ophelia, I do wish
That your good beauties be the happy cause
Of Hamlet's wildness. So shall I hope your virtues   40
Will bring him to his wonted way° again,
To both your honors.
OPHELIA. Madam, I wish it may.   [*Exit* QUEEN.]
POLONIUS. Ophelia, walk you here. Gracious,° so please you,
We will bestow ourselves. [*To* OPHELIA] Read on this book,°
That show of such an exercise may color   45
Your loneliness. We are oft to blame in this—
'Tis too much proved—that with devotion's visage°
And pious action we do sugar o'er
The Devil himself.
KING. [*Aside*] Oh, 'tis too true!
How smart a lash that speech doth give my conscience!   50
The harlot's cheek, beautied with plastering art,
Is not more ugly to the thing that helps it°

---

26. edge: encouragement. 29. closely: secretly. 31. Affront: encounter.
32. lawful espials: who are justified in spying on him. 35. by . . . behaved:
from him, from his behavior. 41. wonted way: normal state. 43. Gracious:
your Majesty—addressed to the King. 44. book: i.e., of devotions. 47. devotion's visage: an outward appearance of religion. 52. ugly . . . it: i.e.,
lust, which is the cause of its artificial beauty.

Than is my deed to my most painted° word.
Oh, heavy burden!
POLONIUS. I hear him coming. Let's withdraw, my lord.   55
                    [*Exeunt* KING *and* POLONIUS.]
                    [*Enter* HAMLET.°]
HAMLET. To be, or not to be—that is the question.
          Whether 'tis nobler in the mind to suffer
          The slings and arrows of outrageous° fortune,
          Or to take arms against a sea° of troubles
          And by opposing end them. To die, to sleep—   60
          No more, and by a sleep to say we end
          The heartache and the thousand natural shocks
          That flesh is heir to. 'Tis a consummation°
          Devoutly to be wished. To die, to sleep,
          To sleep—perchance to dream. Aye, there's the rub,°   65
          For in that sleep of death what dreams may come
          When we have shuffled off this mortal coil°
          Must give us pause. There's the respect°
          That makes calamity of so long life.°
          For who would bear the whips and scorns of time,   70
          The oppressor's wrong, the proud man's contumely°
          The pangs of déspised love, the law's delay,
          The insolence of office° and the spurns
          That patient merit of the unworthy takes,°
          When he himself might his quietus° make   75
          With a bare bodkin?° Who would fardels° bear,
          To grunt and sweat under a weary life,
          But that the dread of something after death,
          The undiscovered country from whose bourn°
          No traveler returns, puzzles the will,°   80
          And makes us rather bear those ills we have
          Than fly to others that we know not of?

---

53. painted: i.e., false.   **55. s.d., Enter Hamlet:** In Q1 the King draws attention to Hamlet's approach with the words "See where he comes poring upon a book." Hamlet is again reading, and is too much absorbed to notice Ophelia. **58. outrageous:** cruel.   **59. sea:** i.e., an endless turmoil.   **63. consummation:** completion.   **65. rub:** impediment.   **67. shuffled . . . coil:** cast off this fuss of life.   **68. respect:** reason.   **69. makes . . . life:** makes it a calamity to have to live so long.   **71. contumely:** insulting behavior.   **73. insolence of office:** insolent behavior of government officials.   **73–74. spurns . . . takes:** insults which men of merit have patiently to endure from the unworthy. **75. quietus:** discharge.   **76. bodkin:** dagger. **fardels:** burdens, the coolie's pack.   **79. bourn:** boundary.   **80. will:** resolution, ability to act.

Thus° conscience does make cowards of us all,
And thus the native hue° of resolution
Is sicklied o'er with the pale cast° of thought, 85
And enterprises of great pitch° and moment
With this regard their currents turn awry
And lose the name of action.°—Soft you now!
The fair Ophelia! Nymph, in thy orisons°
Be all my sins remembered.

OPHELIA. Good my lord, 90
How does your Honor for this many a day?

HAMLET. I humbly thank you—well, well, well.

OPHELIA. My lord, I have remembrances of yours
That I have longed long to redeliver.
I pray you now receive them.

HAMLET. No, not I. 95
I never gave you aught.

OPHELIA. My honored lord, you know right well you did,
And with them words of so sweet breath composed
As made the things more rich. Their perfume lost,
Take these again, for to the noble mind 100
Rich gifts wax poor when givers prove unkind.
There, my lord.

HAMLET. Ha, ha! Are you honest?°

OPHELIA. My lord?

HAMLET. Are you fair? 105

OPHELIA. What means your lordship?

HAMLET. That if you be honest and fair, your honesty should
admit no discourse to your beauty.°

OPHELIA. Could beauty, my lord, have better commerce than with
honesty? 110

HAMLET. Aye, truly, for the power of beauty will sooner trans-
form honesty from what it is to a bawd° than the force of
honesty can translate beauty into his likeness. This was
sometime a paradox,° but now the time gives it proof. I did
love you once. 116

OPHELIA. Indeed, my lord, you made me believe so.

HAMLET. You should not have believed me, for virtue cannot so

---

83–88. Thus . . . action: the religious fear that death may not be the end
makes men shrink from heroic actions.   84. native hue: natural color.   85.
cast: color.   86. pitch: height; used of the soaring flight of a hawk.   87–88.
With . . . action: by brooding on this thought great enterprises are diverted
from their course and fade away.   89. orisons: prayers.   103. honest: chaste.
107–08. That . . . beauty: if you are chaste and beautiful your chasity should
have nothing to do with your beauty—because (so Hamlet thinks in his bitterness) beautiful women are seldom chaste.   112. bawd: brothel-keeper.
115. paradox: statement contrary to accepted opinion.

inoculate our old stock but we shall relish° of it. I loved
you not.   120

OPHELIA. I was the more deceived.

HAMLET. Get thee to a nunnery. Why wouldst thou be a breeder
of sinners? I am myself indifferent honest,° but yet I could   124
accuse me of such things that it were better my mother had
not borne me. I am very proud, revengeful, ambitious, with
more offenses at my beck° than I have thoughts to put them
in, imagination to give them shape, or time to act them in.
What should such fellows as I do crawling between heaven
and earth? We are arrant knaves all. Believe none of us. Go
thy ways to a nunnery.° Where's your father?   132

OPHELIA. At home, my lord.

HAMLET. Let the doors be shut upon him, that he may play the
fool nowhere but in 's own house. Farewell.   137

OPHELIA. Oh, help him, you sweet Heavens!

HAMLET. If thou dost marry, I'll give thee this plague for thy
dowry: Be thou as chaste as ice, as pure as snow—thou
shalt not escape calumny.° Get thee to a nunnery, go. Fare-   141
well. Or if thou wilt needs marry, marry a fool, for wise
men know well enough what monsters° you make of them.
To a nunnery, go, and quickly too. Farewell.

OPHELIA. O heavenly powers, restore him!   147

HAMLET. I have heard of your paintings° too, well enough. God
hath given you one face and you make yourselves another.
You jig,° you amble,° and you lisp,° and nickname God's
creatures, and make your wantonness your ignorance.° Go
to, I'll no more on 't—it hath made me mad. I say we will
have no more marriages. Those that are married already, all
but one, shall live; the rest shall keep as they are. To a nun-   156
nery, go.   [*Exit.*]

OPHELIA. Oh, what a noble mind is here o'erthrown!
The courtier's, soldier's, scholar's, eye, tongue, sword—
The expectancy and rose° of the fair state,   160
The glass° of fashion and the mold of form,°

---

120. relish: have some trace.   **123–24. indifferent honest:** moderately honorable.   **127. at . . . beck:** waiting to come when I beckon.   **132. nunnery:**
i.e., a place where she will be removed from temptation.   **141. calumny:**
slander.   **145. monsters:** horned beasts, cuckolds—husbands, deceived by
their wives, who were supposed to wear invisible horns.   **148. paintings:**
using make-up.   **150. jig:** dance lecherously. **amble:** walk artificially.   **151.
lisp:** talk affectedly.   **152–53. nickname . . . ignorance:** give things indecent
names and pretend to be too simple to understand their meanings.   **160. expectancy . . . rose:** bright hope. The rose is used as a symbol for beauty and
perfection. Cf. *I Hen IV*, I.3.175.   **161. glass:** mirror. **mold of form:** perfect
pattern of manly beauty.

The observed of all observers—quite, quite down!
And I, of ladies most deject and wretched,
That sucked the honey of his music vows,
Now see that noble and most sovereign reason,   165
Like sweet bells jangled, out of tune and harsh,
That unmatched° form and feature of blown° youth
Blasted with ecstasy.° Oh, woe is me,
To have seen what I have seen, see what I see!
                    [*Re-enter* KING *and* POLONIUS.]
KING. Love! His affections° do not that way tend,   170
Nor what he spake, though it lacked form a little,
Was not like madness. There's something in his soul
O'er which his melancholy sits on brood,°
And I do doubt the hatch and the disclose°
Will be some danger. Which for to prevent,   175
I have in quick determination
Thus set it down: He shall with speed to England,
For the demand of our neglected tribute.
Haply° the seas and countries different
With variable objects° shall expel   180
This something-settled° matter in his heart
Whereon his brains still beating puts him thus
From fashion of himself.° What think you on 't?
POLONIUS. It shall do well. But yet do I believe
The origin and commencement of his grief   185
Sprung from neglected love. How now, Ophelia!
You need not tell us what Lord Hamlet said,
We heard it all. My lord, do as you please,
But, if you hold it fit, after the play
Let his Queen mother all alone entreat him   190
To show his grief. Let her be round° with him,
And I'll be placed, so please you, in the ear
Of all their conference. If she find him not,
To England send him, or confine him where
Your wisdom best shall think.
KING.   It shall be so.   195
Madness in great ones must not unwatched go.   [*Exeunt.*]

---

167. unmatched: unmatchable. **blown:** perfect, like an open flower at its best. **168. Blasted . . . ecstasy:** ruined by madness. **170. affections:** state of mind. **173. sits . . . brood:** sits hatching. **174. doubt . . . disclose:** suspect the brood which will result. **179. Haply:** perhaps. **180. variable objects:** novel sights. **181. something-settled:** somewhat settled; i.e., not yet incurable. **182–83. puts . . . himself:** i.e., separates him from his normal self. **191. round:** direct.

Scene 2 &&& *A hall in the castle.*

[*Enter* HAMLET *and* PLAYERS.]

HAMLET. Speak the speech,° I pray you, as I pronounced it to
you, trippingly° on the tongue. But if you mouth° it, as
many of your players do, I had as lief° the town crier spoke
my lines. Nor do not saw the air too much with your hand,
thus, but use all gently. For in the very torrent, tempest,   5
and, as I may say, whirlwind of passion, you must acquire
and beget a temperance that may give it smoothness. Oh, it
offends me to the soul to hear a robustious° periwig-pated°
fellow tear a passion to tatters, to very rags, to split the ears   10
of the groundlings,° who for the most part are capable of
nothing but inexplicable dumb shows° and noise. I would
have such a fellow whipped for o'erdoing Termagant°—   15
it out-Herods Herod. Pray you, avoid it.

FIRST PLAYER. I warrant your Honor.

HAMLET. Be not too tame neither, but let your own discretion be
your tutor. Suit the action to the word, the word to the action, with this special observance, that you o'erstep not the   20
modesty of nature. For anything so overdone is from° the
purpose of playing, whose end, both at the first and now,
was and is to hold as 'twere the mirror up to Nature—to
show Virtue her own feature, scorn her own image, and   25

Sc. 2: 1. the speech: which he has written. See ll. 266–67. The whole passage which follows is Shakespeare's own comment on the actor's art and states
the creed and practice of his company as contrasted with the more violent
methods of Edward Alleyn and his fellows of the Admiral's company.   2.
trippingly: smoothly, easily.   3. mouth: "ham" it.   4. lief: soon.   9. robus-
tious: ranting.   10. periwig-pated: wearing a wig.   11. groundlings: the
poorer spectators, who stood in the yard of the playhouse.   14. dumb shows:
an old-fashioned dramatic device, still being used by the Admiral's Men:
before a tragedy, and sometimes before each act, the characters mimed the
action which was to follow. See later, l. 145.   15. Termagant: God of the
Saracens, who, like Herod, was presented in early stage plays as a roaring
tyrant.   22. from: contrary to.

the very age and body of the time his form and pressure.° Now this overdone or come tardy off, though it make the unskillful laugh, cannot but make the judicious grieve, the censure of the which one° must in your allowance o'erweigh 30 a whole theater of others. Oh, there be players° that I have seen play, and heard others praise—and that highly, not to speak it profanely—that neither having the accent of Christians nor the gait of Christian, pagan, nor man, have so strutted and bellowed that I have thought some of Nature's 35 journeymen° had made men, and not made them well, they imitated humanity so abominably.

FIRST PLAYER. I hope we have reformed that indifferently° with 41 us, sir.

HAMLET. Oh, reform it altogether. And let those that play your clowns° speak no more than is set down for them. For there be of them that will themselves laugh, to set on some quantity of barren spectators to laugh too, though in the mean- 45 time some necessary question of the play be then to be considered. That's villainous, and shows a most pitiful° ambition in the fool that uses it. Go, make you ready. [*Exeunt* 50 PLAYERS. *Enter* POLONIUS, ROSENCRANTZ, *and* GUILDENSTERN.] How now, my lord! Will the King hear this piece of work?

POLONIUS. And the Queen too, and that presently.

HAMLET. Bid the players make haste. [*Exit* POLONIUS.] Will you two help to hasten them? 55

ROSENCRANTZ & GUILDENSTERN. We will, my lord.

        [*Exeunt* ROSENCRANTZ *and* GUILDENSTERN.]

HAMLET. What ho! Horatio!

        [*Enter* HORATIO.]

HORATIO. Here, sweet lord, at your service.

HAMLET. Horatio, thou art e'en as just a man

26–27. very . . . pressure: an exact reproduction of the age. **form:** shape. **pressure:** imprint (of a seal). **30. the . . . one:** i.e., the judicious spectator. **31. there . . . players:** An obvious attack on Alleyn. **36. journeymen:** hired workmen, not masters of the trade. **41. indifferently:** moderately. **42–43. those . . . clowns:** a hit at Will Kempe, the former clown of Shakespeare's company, now with a rival company. Q1 adds the passage "And then you have some again that keep one suit of jests, as a man is known by one suit of apparel, and gentlemen quote his jests down in their tables before they come to the play, as thus: 'Cannot you stay till I eat my porridge?' and 'You owe me a quarter's wages,' and 'My coat wants a cullison,' and 'Your beer is sour,' and blabbering with his lips, and thus keeping in his cinquepace of jests, when God knows the warm clown cannot make a jest unless by chance, as the blind man catcheth a hare. Masters tell him of it." **49. pitiful:** contemptible.

As e'er my conversation coped° withal.   60
HORATIO. Oh, my dear lord——
HAMLET.   Nay, do not think I flatter,
    For what advancement° may I hope from thee,
    That no revénue hast but thy good spirits
    To feed and clothe thee? Why should the poor be flattered?
    No, let the candied° tongue lick absurd pomp   65
    And crook the pregnant hinges of the knee
    Where thrift may follow fawning.° Dost thou hear?
    Since my dear soul was mistress of her choice
    And could of men distinguish, her election
    Hath sealed° thee for herself. For thou hast been   70
    As one in suffering all that suffers nothing,
    A man that fortune's buffets and rewards
    Hast ta'en with equal thanks. And blest are those
    Whose blood and judgment are so well commingled
    That they are not a pipe° for fortune's finger   75
    To sound what stop she please. Give me that man
    That is not passion's slave, and I will wear him
    In my heart's core—aye, in my heart of heart,
    As I do thee. Something too much of this.
    There is a play tonight before the King.   80
    One scene of it comes near the circumstance
    Which I have told thee of my father's death.
    I prithee when thou seest that act afoot,
    Even with the very comment° of thy soul
    Observe my uncle. If his occulted° guilt   85
    Do not itself unkennel° in one speech
    It is a damnèd ghost° that we have seen
    And my imaginations are as foul
    As Vulcan's° stithy.° Give him heedful note,°
    For I mine eyes will rivet to his face,   90
    And after we will both our judgments join
    In censure of his seeming.°
HORATIO.   Well, my lord.
    If he steal aught the whilst this play is playing,
    And 'scape detecting, I will pay the theft.
HAMLET. They are coming to the play. I must be idle.°   95

60. coped: met.   62. advancement: promotion.   65. candied: sugared over
with hypocrisy.   66–67. crook . . . fawning: bend the ready knees whenever gain will follow flattery.   70. sealed: set a mark on.   75. pipe: an instrument that varies its notes.   84. comment: close observation.   85. occulted:
concealed.   86. unkennel: come to light; lit., force a fox from his hole.   87.
damned ghost: See II.2.627.   89. Vulcan: the blacksmith god. stithy: smithy.
heedful note: careful observation.   92. censure . . . seeming: judgment on
his looks.   95. be idle: seem crazy.

Get you a place.

> [*Danish march. A flourish. Enter* KING, QUEEN,
> POLONIUS, OPHELIA, ROSENCRANTZ, GUILDENSTERN,
> *and other* LORDS *attendant, with the* GUARD
> *carrying torches.*]

KING. How fares our cousin Hamlet?

HAMLET. Excellent, i' faith, of the chameleon's dish. I eat the
air, promise-crammed. You cannot feed capons so.°   100

KING. I have nothing with this answer,° Hamlet. These words are
not mine.

HAMLET. No, nor mine now. [*To* POLONIUS] My lord, you played
once i' the university, you say?

POLONIUS. That did I, my lord, and was accounted a good actor.   106

HAMLET. What did you enact?

POLONIUS. I did enact Julius Caesar. I was killed i' the Capitol.
Brutus killed me.

HAMLET. It was a brute part of him to kill so capital a calf there.
Be the players ready?   111

ROSENCRANTZ. Aye, my lord, they stay upon your patience.°

QUEEN. Come hither, my dear Hamlet, sit by me.

HAMLET. No, good Mother, here's metal more attractive.   117

POLONIUS. [*To the* KING] Oh ho! Do you mark that?

HAMLET. Lady, shall I lie in your lap?

> [*Lying down at* OPHELIA's *feet*]

OPHELIA. No, my lord.   120

HAMLET. I mean, my head upon your lap?

OPHELIA. Aye, my lord.

HAMLET. Do you think I meant country matters?°

OPHELIA. I think nothing, my lord.

HAMLET. That's a fair thought to lie between maids' legs.   126

OPHELIA. What is, my lord?

HAMLET. Nothing.

OPHELIA. You are merry, my lord.

HAMLET. Who, I?

OPHELIA. Aye, my lord.

HAMLET. Oh God, your only jig-maker.° What should a man do   132

98–100. Excellent . . . so: Hamlet takes "fare" literally as "what food are you
eating." The chameleon was supposed to feed on air. **promise-crammed:**
stuffed, like a fattened chicken (*capon*)—but with empty promises.   **101. I
. . . answer:** I cannot make any sense of your answer.   **103. nor . . . now:**
i.e., once words have left the lips they cease to belong to the speaker.   **112.
stay . . . patience:** wait for you to be ready.   **123. country matters:** something indecent.   **132. jig-maker:** composer of jigs.

but be merry? For look you how cheerfully my mother
looks, and my father died within 's two hours.

OPHELIA. Nay, 'tis twice two months, my lord.

HAMLET. So long? Nay, then, let the Devil wear black, for I'll
have a suit of sables.° Oh heavens! Die two months ago,   138
and not forgotten yet? Then there's hope a great man's
memory may outlive his life half a year. But, by 'r Lady,
he must build churches then, or else shall he suffer not
thinking on, with the hobbyhorse,° whose epitaph is "For,
oh, for oh, the hobbyhorse is forgot."   145

[*Hautboys*° *play. The dumb show enters.*° *Enter a* KING *and
a* QUEEN *very lovingly, the* QUEEN *embracing him and he
her. She kneels, and makes show of protestation unto him.
He takes her up, and declines his head upon her neck, lays
him down upon a bank of flowers. She, seeing him asleep,
leaves him. Anon comes in a fellow, takes off his crown,
kisses it, and pours poison in the* KING's *ears, and exit. The*
QUEEN *returns, finds the* KING *dead, and makes passionate
action. The Poisoner, with some two or three Mutes, comes
in again, seeming to lament with her. The dead body is carried away. The Poisoner woos the* QUEEN *with gifts. She
seems loath and unwilling awhile, but in the end accepts his
love.*   Exeunt.]

OPHELIA. What means this, my lord?

HAMLET. Marry, this is miching mallecho.° It means mischief.

OPHELIA. Belike this show imports the argument° of the play.   149

[*Enter* PROLOGUE.]

HAMLET. We shall know by this fellow. The players cannot keep
counsel, they'll tell all.

OPHELIA. Will he tell us what this show meant?

HAMLET. Aye, or any show that you'll show him. Be not you
ashamed to show, he'll not shame to tell you what it
means.

---

138. **suit of sables:** a quibble on "sable," black, and "sable," gown trimmed
with sable fur, worn by wealthy old gentlemen.   144. **hobbyhorse:** imitation
horse worn by performers in a morris dance, an amusement much disapproved
of by the godly.   145. **s.d., Hautboys:** oboes. **The dumb show enters:** Critics
have been disturbed because this dumb show cannot be exactly paralleled in
any other Elizabethan play, and because the King is apparently not disturbed
by it. Shakespeare's intention, however, in presenting a play within a play is
to produce something stagy and artificial compared with the play proper.
Moreover, as Hamlet has already complained, dumb shows were often inexplicable.   147. **miching mallecho:** slinking mischief.   149. **argument:** plot.
She too is puzzled by the dumb show.

OPHELIA. You are naught,° you are naught. I'll mark the play.   157
PROLOGUE.   For us, and for our tragedy,
                 Here stooping to your clemency,
                 We beg your hearing patiently.
HAMLET. Is this a prologue, or the posy of a ring?°   162
OPHELIA. 'Tis brief, my lord.
HAMLET. As woman's love.
              [*Enter two* PLAYERS, KING *and* QUEEN.]
PLAYER KING. Full° thirty times hath Phoebus' cart° gone round   165
    Neptune's° salt wash and Tellus'° orbèd ground,
    And thirty dozen moons with borrowed sheen°
    About the world have times twelve thirties been,
    Since love our hearts and Hymen° did our hands
    Unite commutual° in most sacred bands.   170
PLAYER QUEEN. So many journeys may the sun and moon
    Make us again count o'er ere love be done!
    But, woe is me, you are so sick of late,
    So far from cheer and from your former state,
    That I distrust° you. Yet, though I distrust,   175
    Discomfort you, my lord, it nothing must.
    For women's fear and love holds quantity°
    In neither aught or in extremity.°
    Now what my love is, proof hath made you know,
    And as my love is sized, my fear is so.   180
    Where love is great, the littlest doubts are fear,
    Where little fears grow great, great love grows there.
PLAYER KING. Faith, I must leave thee,° love, and shortly too,
    My operant powers° their functions leave to do.
    And thou shalt live in this fair world behind,   185
    Honored, beloved, and haply one as kind
    For husband shalt thou——
PLAYER QUEEN.   Oh, confound the rest!
    Such love must needs be treason in my breast.
    In second husband let me be accurst!
    None wed the second but who killed the first.   190
HAMLET. [*Aside*] Wormwood,° wormwood.

157. naught: i.e., disgusting.   **162. posy . . . ring:** It was a pretty custom to inscribe rings with little mottoes or messages, which were necessarily brief. **165–238. Full . . . twain:** The play is deliberately written in crude rhyming verse, full of ridiculous and bombastic phrases.   **165. Phoebus' cart:** the chariot of the sun.   **166. Neptune:** the sea god. **Tellus:** the earth goddess.   **167. borrowed sheen:** light borrowed from the sun.   **169. Hymen:** god of marriage.   **170. commutual:** mutually.   **175. distrust:** am anxious about.   **177. quantity:** proportion.   **178. In . . . extremity:** either nothing or too much. **183. leave thee:** i.e., die.   **184. operant powers:** bodily strength.   **191. Wormwood:** bitterness.

PLAYER QUEEN. The instances° that second marriage move
Are base respects of thrift,° but none of love.
A second time I kill my husband dead
When second husband kisses me in bed.   195
PLAYER KING. I do believe you think what now you speak,
But what we do determine oft we break.
Purpose is but the slave to memory,
Of violent birth but poor validity,
Which now, like fruit unripe, sticks on the tree   200
But fall unshaken when they mellow be.
Most necessary 'tis that we forget
To pay ourselves what to ourselves is debt.
What to ourselves in passion we propose,
The passion ending, doth the purpose lose.   205
The violence of either grief or joy
Their own enactures° with themselves destroy.
Where joy most revels, grief doth most lament,
Grief joys, joy grieves, on slender accident.
This world is not for aye,° nor 'tis not strange   210
That even our loves should with our fortunes change,
For 'tis a question left us yet to prove
Whether love lead fortune or else fortune love.
The great man down, you mark his favorite flies:
The poor advanced makes friends of enemies.   215
And hitherto doth love on fortune tend,
For who not needs shall never lack a friend,
And who in want a hollow friend doth try
Directly seasons° him his enemy.
But, orderly to end where I begun,   220
Our wills and fates do so contráry run
That our devices still are overthrown,
Out thoughts are ours, their ends none of our own.
So think thou wilt no second husband wed,
But die thy thoughts when thy first lord is dead.   225
PLAYER QUEEN. Nor earth to me give food nor Heaven light!
Sport and repose lock from me day and night!
To desperation turn my trust and hope!
An anchor's° cheer in prison be my scope!
Each opposite that blanks° the face of joy   230
Meet what I would have well and it destroy!
Both here and hence pursue me lasting strife
If, once a widow, ever I be wife!

192. **instances:** arguments.   193. **respects of thrift:** considerations of gain.
207. **enactures:** performances.   210. **aye:** ever.   219. **seasons:** ripens into.
229. **anchor:** anchorite, hermit.   230. **blanks:** makes pale.

HAMLET. If she should break it now!

PLAYER KING. 'Tis deeply sworn. Sweet, leave me here a while.   235
My spirits grow dull, and fain I would beguile
The tedious day with sleep.   [*Sleeps.*]

PLAYER QUEEN.   Sleep rock thy brain,
And never come mischance between us twain!   [*Exit.*]

HAMLET. Madam, how like you this play?

QUEEN. The lady doth protest too much, methinks.   240

HAMLET. Oh, but she'll keep her word.

KING. Have you heard the argument?° Is there no offense in 't?

HAMLET. No, no, they do but jest, poison in jest—no offense i'
the world.   245

KING. What do you call the play?

HAMLET. *The Mousetrap.*° Marry, how? Tropically.° This play is
the image of a murder done in Vienna. Gonzago is the
Duke's name, his wife, Baptista. You shall see anon. 'Tis a
knavish piece of work, but what o' that? Your Majesty, and   250
we that have free° souls, it touches us not. Let the galled
jade wince, our withers are unwrung.°
[*Enter* LUCIANUS.] This is one Lucianus, nephew to the King.

OPHELIA. You are as good as a chorus,° my lord.   255

HAMLET. I could interpret between you and your love, if I could
see the puppets dallying.°

OPHELIA. You are keen, my lord, you are keen.

HAMLET. It would cost you a groaning to take off my edge.   260

OPHELIA. Still better, and worse.

HAMLET. So you must take your husbands.° Begin, murderer.
Pox, leave thy damnable faces and begin. Come, the croak-
ing raven doth bellow for revenge.

LUCIANUS. Thoughts black, hands apt, drugs fit, and time agreeing,   266
Confederate season, else no creature° seeing,

---

242. argument: plot. When performances were given at Court it was sometimes customary to provide a written or printed synopsis of the story for the
distinguished spectators.   **247. Mousetrap:** The phrase was used of a device
to entice a person to his own destruction (OED).   **248. Tropically:** figura-
tively, with a pun on "trap."   **252. free:** innocent.   **252–53. galled . . . unwrung:** let a nag with a sore back flinch when the saddle is put on; our shoulders (being ungalled) feel no pain.   **255. chorus:** the chorus sometimes introduced the characters and commented on what was to follow. See, for instance, the Chorus in *Hen V.*   **257. puppets dallying:** Elizabethan puppets
were crude marionettes, popular at fairs. While the figures were put through
their motions, the puppet master explained what was happening.   **262. So
. . . husbands:** i.e., as the marriage service expresses it, "for better, for
worse."   **267. confederate . . . creature:** the opportunity conspiring with
me, no other creature.

Thou mixture rank of midnight weeds collected,
With Hecate's ban° thrice blasted, thrice infected,
Thy natural magic and dire property°   270
On wholesome life usurp immediately.
          [*Pours the poison into the sleeper's ear.*]
HAMLET. He poisons him i' the garden for his estate.° His name's
     Gonzago. The story is extant, and written in very choice
     Italian. You shall see anon how the murderer gets the love
     of Gonzago's wife.
OPHELIA. The King rises.   276
HAMLET. What, frighted with false fire!°
QUEEN. How fares my lord?
POLONIUS. Give o'er the play.
KING. Give me some light. Away!   280
POLONIUS. Lights, lights, lights!
          [*Exeunt all but* HAMLET *and* HORATIO.]
HAMLET.   "Why, let the stricken deer go weep,
               The hart ungallèd play,
          For some must watch while some must sleep.
               Thus runs the world away."   285
     Would not this, sir, and a forest of feathers°—if the rest
     of my fortunes turn Turk° with me—with two Provincial
     roses° on my razed° shoes, get me a fellowship° in a cry°
     of players, sir?
HORATIO. Half a share.   290
HAMLET. A whole one, I.
               "For thou dost know, O Damon° dear,
                  This realm dismantled° was
               Of Jove himself, and now reigns here
                  A very, very—pajock."°   295
HORATIO. You might have rhymed.
HAMLET. O good Horatio, I'll take the ghost's word for a thou-
     sand pound. Didst perceive?
HORATIO. Very well, my lord.
HAMLET. Upon the talk of the poisoning?   300
HORATIO. I did very well note him.
HAMLET. Ah, ha! Come, some music! Come, the recorders!°

269. Hecate's ban: the curse of Hecate, goddess of witchcraft.   **270. property:**
nature.   **273. estate:** kingdom.   **277. false fire:** a mere show.   **286. forest of
feathers:** set of plumes, much worn by players. **287. turn Turk:** turn heathen,
and treat me cruelly.   **288. Provincial roses:** rosettes, worn on the shoes.
razed: slashed, ornamented with cuts.   **289. fellowship:** partnership. **cry:** pack.
292. Damon: Damon and Pythias were types of perfect friends.   **293. dis-
mantled:** robbed.   **295. pajock:** peacock, a strutting, lecherous bird. These
verses, and the lines above, may have come from some ballad, otherwise lost.
303. recorders: wooden pipes.

"For if the King like not the comedy,
　　Why then, belike, he likes it not, perdy."°   305
Come, some music!
　　　[*Re-enter* ROSENCRANTZ *and* GUILDENSTERN.]
GUILDENSTERN. Good my lord, vouchsafe me a word with you.
HAMLET. Sir, a whole history.
GUILDENSTERN. The King, sir——   310
HAMLET. Aye, sir, what of him?
GUILDENSTERN. Is in his retirement marvelous distempered.°
HAMLET. With drink, sir?
GUILDENSTERN. No, my lord, rather with choler.°   315
HAMLET. Your wisdom should show itself more richer to signify
　　this to the doctor, for for me to put him to his purgation°
　　would perhaps plunge him into far more choler.   319
GUILDENSTERN. Good my lord, put your discourse into some
　　frame,° and start not so wildly from my affair.
HAMLET. I am tame, sir. Pronounce.
GUILDENSTERN. The Queen your mother, in most great affliction
　　of spirit, hath sent me to you.
HAMLET. You are welcome.   325
GUILDENSTERN. Nay, good my lord, this courtesy is not of the
　　right breed. If it shall please you to make me a wholesome
　　answer, I will do your mother's commandment. If not, your
　　pardon and my return shall be the end of my business.   330
HAMLET. Sir. I cannot.
GUILDENSTERN. What, my lord?
HAMLET. Make you a wholesome answer, my wit's diseased. But,
　　sir, such answer as I can make you shall command, or
　　rather, as you say, my mother. Therefore no more, but to
　　the matter. My mother, you say——   337
ROSENCRANTZ. Then thus she says. Your behavior hath struck
　　her into amazement and admiration.°
HAMLET. Oh, wonderful son that can so astonish a mother! But
　　is there no sequel at the heels of this mother's admiration?
　　Impart.   342
ROSENCRANTZ. She desires to speak with you in her closet ere
　　you go to bed.
HAMLET. We shall obey, were she ten times our mother. Have
　　you any further trade with us?
ROSENCRANTZ. My lord, you once did love me.   348

---

305. **perdy:** by God.　312. **distempered:** disturbed; but Hamlet takes the
word in its other sense of "drunk."　315. **choler:** anger, which Hamlet again
pretends to understand as meaning "biliousness."　317–18. **put . . . purga-
tion:** "give him a dose of salts."　321. **frame:** shape; i.e., "please talk sense."
339. **admiration:** wonder.

HAMLET. So I do still, by these pickers and stealers.°

ROSENCRANTZ. Good my lord, what is your cause of distemper?
You do surely bar the door upon your own liberty if you
deny your griefs° to your friend.

HAMLET. Sir, I lack advancement.°   354

ROSENCRANTZ. How can that be when you have the voice of the
King himself for your succession in Denmark?

HAMLET. Aye, sir, but "While the grass grows"°—the proverb   359
is something musty. [*Re-enter* PLAYERS *with recorders.*] Oh,
the recorders! Let me see one. To withdraw° with you——
why do you go about to recover the wind° of me, as if you
would drive me into a toil?°

GUILDENSTERN. O my lord, if my duty be too bold, my love is
too unmannerly.°   365

HAMLET. I do not well understand that. Will you play upon this
pipe?

GUILDENSTERN. My lord, I cannot.

HAMLET. I pray you.

GUILDENSTERN. Believe me, I cannot.   370

HAMLET. I do beseech you.

GUILDENSTERN. I know no touch of it, my lord.

HAMLET. It is as easy as lying. Govern these ventages° with your   374
fingers and thumb, give it breath with your mouth, and it
will discourse most eloquent music. Look you, these are the
stops.

GUILDENSTERN. But these cannot I command to any utterance of
harmony, I have not the skill.

HAMLET. Why, look you now, how unworthy a thing you make
of me! You would play upon me, you would seem to know   380
my stops, you would pluck out the heart of my mystery,
you would sound me from my lowest note to the top of my
compass—and there is much music, excellent voice, in this
little organ—yet cannot you make it speak. 'Sblood, do you
think I am easier to be played on than a pipe? Call me what

---

349. pickers . . . stealers: i.e., hands—an echo from the Christian's duty in
the catechism to keep his hands "from picking and stealing." **353. deny . . .
griefs:** refuse to tell your troubles. **354. advancement:** promotion. Hamlet
harks back to his previous interview with Rosencrantz and Guildenstern. See
II.2.258. **358. While . . . grows:** the proverb ends "the steed starves."
361. withdraw: go aside. Hamlet leads Guildenstern to one side of the stage.
362. recover . . . wind: a hunting metaphor; approach me with the wind
against you. **363. toil:** net. **364-65. if . . . unmannerly:** if I exceed my
duty by asking these questions, then my affection for you shows lack of manners; i.e., forgive me if I have been impertinent. **374. ventages:** holes, stops.

instrument you will, though you can fret° me, you cannot
play upon me. [*Re-enter* POLONIUS.] God bless you, sir!   390
POLONIUS. My lord, the Queen would speak with you, and
presently.
HAMLET. Do you see yonder cloud that's almost in shape of a
camel?
POLONIUS. By the mass, and 'tis like a camel indeed.   395
HAMLET. Methinks it is like a weasel.
POLONIUS. It is backed like a weasel.
HAMLET. Or like a whale?
POLONIUS. Very like a whale.
HAMLET. Then I will come to my mother by and by. Then fool   400
me to the top of my bent.° I will come by and by.
POLONIUS. I will say so.   [*Exit* POLONIUS.]
HAMLET. "By and by" is easily said. Leave me, friends.
                       [*Exeunt all but* HAMLET.]
'Tis now the very witching time° of night,   406
When churchyards yawn and Hell itself breathes out
Contagion° to this world. Now could I drink hot blood,
And do such bitter business as the day   409
Would quake to look on. Soft! Now to my mother.
O heart, lose not thy nature, let not ever
The soul of Nero° enter this firm bosom.
Let me be cruel, not unnatural.
I will speak daggers to her, but use none.
My tongue and soul in this be hypocrites,   415
How in my words soever she be shent,°
To give them seals° never, my soul, consent!   [*Exit.*]

389. fret: annoy, with a pun on the frets or bars on stringed instruments by
which the fingering is regulated.   **401. top . . . bent:** See II.2.30, n.   **406.**
witching time: when witches perform their foul rites.   **408. Contagion:** infection.   **412. Nero:** Nero killed his own mother. Hamlet is afraid that in the
interview to come he will lose all self-control.   **416. shent:** rebuked.   **417.**
give . . . seals: ratify words by actions.

Scene 3 ⚶ *A room in the castle.*

[*Enter* KING, ROSENCRANTZ, *and* GUILDENSTERN.]

KING. I like him not, nor stands it safe with us
    To let his madness range.° Therefore prepare you.
    I your commission will forthwith dispatch,
    And he to England shall along with you.
    The terms of our estate° may not endure   5
    Hazard so near us as doth hourly grow
    Out of his lunacies.
GUILDENSTERN.   We will ourselves provide.°
    Most holy and religious fear° it is
    To keep those many many bodies safe
    That live and feed upon your Majesty.   10
ROSENCRANTZ. The single and peculiar° life is bound
    With all the strength and armor of the mind
    To keep itself from noyance,° but much more
    That spirit upon whose weal° depends and rests
    The lives of many. The cease of majesty°   15
    Dies not alone, but like a gulf° doth draw
    What's near it with it. It is a massy° wheel
    Fixed on the summit of the highest mount,
    To whose huge spokes ten thousand lesser things
    Are mortised° and adjoined; which, when it falls,   20
    Each small annexment, petty consequence,°
    Attends° the boisterous ruin. Never alone
    Did the King sigh but with a general groan.
KING. Arm you, I pray you, to this speedy voyage,
    For we will fetters put upon this fear,   25

Sc. 3: 2. range: roam freely.   **5. terms . . . estate:** i.e., one in my position.
7. ourselves provide: make our preparations.   **8. fear:** anxiety.   **11. peculiar:**
individual.   **13. noyance:** injury.   **14. weal:** welfare.   **15. cease of majesty:**
death of a king.   **16. gulf:** whirlpool.   **17. massy:** massive.   **20. mortised:**
firmly fastened.   **21. annexment . . . consequence:** attachment, smallest
thing connected with it.   **22. Attends:** waits on, is involved in.

Which now goes too free-footed.

ROSENCRANTZ & GUILDENSTERN.   We will haste us.

[*Exeunt* ROSENCRANTZ *and* GUILDENSTERN.]

[*Enter* POLONIUS.]

POLONIUS. My lord, he's going to his mother's closet.
Behind the arras I'll convey myself
To hear the process.° I'll warrant she'll tax° him home.
And, as you said,° and wisely was it said,   30
'Tis meet that some more audience than a mother,
Since nature makes them partial, should o'erhear
The speech, of vantage.° Fare you well, my liege.
I'll call upon you ere you go to bed
And tell you what I know.

KING.   Thanks, dear my lord.   [*Exit* POLONIUS.]   35
Oh, my offense is rank,° it smells to Heaven.
It hath the primal eldest curse° upon 't,
A brother's murder. Pray can I not,
Though inclination be as sharp as will.°
My stronger guilt defeats my strong intent,   40
And like a man to double business bound,
I stand in pause where I shall first begin,
And both neglect. What if this cursèd hand
Were thicker than itself with brother's blood,
Is there not rain enough in the sweet heavens   45
To wash it white as snow? Whereto serves mercy
But to confront the visage of offense?°
And what's in prayer but this twofold force,
To be forestallèd° ere we come to fall
Or pardoned being down? Then I'll look up,   50
My fault is past. But oh, what form of prayer
Can serve my turn? "Forgive me my foul murder"?
That cannot be, since I am still possessed
Of those effects° for which I did the murder—
My crown, mine own ambition, and my Queen.   55
May one be pardoned and retain the offense?°
In the corrupted currents° of this world
Offense's gilded hand may shove by justice,
And oft 'tis seen the wicked prize° itself

---

29. process: proceeding. **tax:** censure. **30. as . . . said:** Actually Polonius
himself had said it (III.1.189–93). **33. of vantage:** from a place of vantage;
i.e., concealment. **36. rank:** foul. **37. primal . . . curse:** the curse laid
upon Cain, the first murderer, who also slew his brother. **39. will:** desire.
47. confront . . . offense: look crime in the face. **49. forestalled:** prevented.
54. effects: advantages. **56. offense:** i.e., that for which he has offended.
57. currents: courses, ways. **59. wicked prize:** the proceeds of the crime.

Buys out the law. But 'tis not so above.   60
There is no shuffling, there the action lies
In his true nature,° and we ourselves compelled
Even to the teeth and forehead° of our faults
To give in evidence. What then? What rests?
Try what repentance can. What can it not?   65
Yet what can it when one cannot repent?
Oh, wretched state! Oh, bosom black as death!
Oh, limèd° soul, that struggling to be free
Art more engaged!° Help, angels! Make assay!°
Bow, stubborn knees, and heart with strings of steel,   70
Be soft as sinews of the newborn babe!
All may be well.   [*Retires and kneels.*]

               [*Enter* HAMLET.]

HAMLET. Now might I do it pat, now he is praying,
And now I'll do 't. And so he goes to Heaven,
And so am I revenged. That would be scanned: 75
A villain kills my father, and for that
I, his sole son, do this same villain send
To Heaven.
Oh, this is hire and salary,° not revenge.
He took my father grossly,° full of bread,   80
With all his crimes broad blown, as flush° as May,
And how his audit° stands who knows save Heaven?
But in our circumstance and course of thought,°
'Tis heavy with him. And am I then revenged,
To take him in the purging of his soul,   85
When he is fit and seasoned,° for his passage?
No.
Up, sword, and know thou a more horrid hent.°
When he is drunk asleep, or in his rage,
Or in the incestuous pleasure of his bed—   90
At gaming, swearing, or about some act
That has no relish of salvation in 't—
Then trip him, that his heels may kick at Heaven
And that his soul may be as damned and black
As Hell, whereto it goes. My mother stays.   95
This physic but prolongs thy sickly days.   [*Exit.*]

61–62. there . . . nature: in Heaven the case is tried on its own merits.   **63. teeth . . . forehead:** i.e., face to face.   **68. limed:** caught as in birdlime.   **69. engaged:** stuck fast. **assay:** attempt.   **79. hire . . . salary:** i.e., a kind action deserving pay.   **80. grossly:** i.e., when he was in a state of sin. See I.5.74–80.   **81. broad . . . flush:** in full blossom, as luxuriant.   **82. audit:** account.   **93. circumstance . . . thought:** as it appears to my mind.   **86. seasoned:** ripe.   **88. hent:** opportunity.

KING. [*Rising*] My words fly up, my thoughts remain below.
　　Words without thoughts never to Heaven go.　　[*Exit.*]

Scene 4 ✑ *The* QUEEN'S *closet.*

[*Enter* QUEEN *and* POLONIUS.]
POLONIUS. He will come straight. Look you lay home to° him.
　　Tell him his pranks have been too broad° to bear with,
　　And that your grace hath screened and stood between
　　Much heat and him. I'll sconce me° even here.
　　Pray you, be round with him.　　　　　　　　　　　　5
HAMLET. [*Within*] Mother, Mother, Mother!
QUEEN.　　　　　　　　　　　　　I'll warrant you,
　　Fear me not. Withdraw, I hear him coming.
　　　　　[POLONIUS *hides behind the arras.*]
　　　　　　　[*Enter* HAMLET.]
HAMLET. Now, Mother, what's the matter?
QUEEN. Hamlet, thou hast thy father much offended.
HAMLET. Mother, you have my father much offended.　　10
QUEEN. Come, come, you answer with an idle° tongue.
HAMLET. Go, go, you question with a wicked tongue.
QUEEN. Why, how now, Hamlet!
HAMLET.　　　　　　　　　　What's the matter now?
QUEEN. Have you forgot me?
HAMLET.　　　　　　　　No, by the rood,° not so.
　　You are the Queen, your husband's brother's wife,　　15
　　And—would it were not so!—you are my mother.
QUEEN. Nay, then, I'll set those to you that can speak.
HAMLET. Come, come, and sit you down. You shall not budge,
　　You go not till I set you up a glass°
　　Where you may see the inmost part of you.　　　　　20
QUEEN. What wilt thou do? Thou wilt not murder me?

Sc. 4: 1. lay . . . to: be strict with.　2. broad: unrestrained. Polonius is
thinking of the obvious insolence of the remarks about second marriage in the
play scene.　4. sconce me: hide myself.　11. idle: foolish.　14. rood: crucifix.
19. glass: looking-glass.

          Help, help, ho!
POLONIUS. [*Behind*] What ho! Help, help, help!
HAMLET. [*Drawing*] How now! A rat? Dead, for a ducat dead!
          [*Makes a pass through the arras.*]
POLONIUS. [*Behind*] Oh, I am slain!   [*Falls and dies.*]
QUEEN.   Oh me, what hast thou done?   25
HAMLET. Nay, I know not. Is it the King?
QUEEN. Oh, what a rash and bloody deed is this!
HAMLET. A bloody deed! Almost as bad, good Mother,
          As kill a king and marry with his brother.
QUEEN. As kill a king!
HAMLET.   Aye, lady, 'twas my word.   30
          [*Lifts up the arras and discovers* POLONIUS.]
Thou wretched, rash, intruding fool, farewell!
I took thee for thy better. Take thy fortune.
Thou find'st to be too busy is some danger.
Leave wringing of your hands. Peace! Sit you down,
And let me wring your heart. For so I shall   35
If it be made of penetrable stuff,
If damnèd custom have not brassed° it so
That it be proof and bulwark against sense.
QUEEN. What have I done that thou darest wag thy tongue
          In noise so rude against me?
HAMLET.   Such an act   40
That blurs the grace and blush of modesty,
Calls virtue hypocrite, takes off the rose
From the fair forehead of an innocent love,
And sets a blister° there—makes marriage vows
As false as dicers' oaths. Oh, such a deed   45
As from the body of contraction° plucks
The very soul, and sweet religion makes
A rhapsody of words.° Heaven's face doth glow,
Yea, this solidity and compound mass,°
With tristful visage, as against the doom,°   50
Is thought-sick at the act.
QUEEN.   Aye me, what act
That roars so loud and thunders in the index?°
HAMLET. Look here upon this picture,° and on this,

37. **brassed:** made brazen; i.e., impenetrable.   44. **sets a blister:** brands as a harlot; see IV.5.118, n.   46. **contraction:** the marriage contract.   48. **rhapsody of words:** string of meaningless words.   49. **solidity . . . mass:** i.e., solid earth.   50. **tristful . . . doom:** sorrowful face, as in anticipation of Doomsday.   52. **in . . . index:** i.e., if the beginning (*index*, i.e., table of contents) is so noisy, what will follow?   53. **picture:** Modern producers usually interpret the pictures as miniatures, Hamlet wearing one of his father, Gertrude one of Claudius. In the eighteenth century, wall portraits were used.

The counterfeit presentment° of two brothers.
See what a grace was seated on this brow—   55
Hyperion's curls, the front° of Jove himself,
An eye like Mars, to threaten and command,
A station° like the herald Mercury°
New-lighted° on a heaven-kissing hill,
A combination° and a form indeed   60
Where every god did seem to set his seal°
To give the world assurance of a man.
This was your husband. Look you now what follows.
Here is your husband, like a mildewed ear,
Blasting his wholesome brother. Have you eyes?   65
Could you on this fair mountain leave to feed
And batten° on this moor? Ha! Have you eyes?
You cannot call it love, for at your age
The heyday° in the blood is tame, it's humble,
And waits upon the judgment. And what judgment   70
Would step from this to this? Sense° sure you have,
Else could you not have motion.° But sure that sense
Is apoplexed;° for madness would not err,
Nor sense to ecstasy° was ne'er so thralled°
But it reserved some quantity of choice   75
To serve in such a difference.° What devil was 't
That thus hath cozened° you at hoodman-blind?°
Eyes without feeling, feeling without sight,
Ears without hands or eyes, smelling sans° all,
Or but a sickly part of one true sense   80
Could not so mope.°
Oh, shame! Where is thy blush? Rebellious° Hell,
If thou canst mutine° in a matron's bones,
To flaming youth let virtue be as wax
And melt in her own fire. Proclaim no shame   85

---

54. counterfeit presentment: portrait. **56. front:** forehead. **58. station:** figure; lit., standing. **Mercury:** messenger of the gods, and one of the most beautiful. **59. New-lighted:** newly alighted. **60. combination:** i.e., of physical qualities. **61. set . . . seal:** guarantee as a perfect man. **67. batten:** glut yourself. **69. heyday:** excitement. **71. Sense:** feeling. **72. motion:** desire. **73. apoplexed:** paralyzed. **74. ecstasy:** excitement, passion. See II.1.102. **thralled:** enslaved. **76. serve . . . difference:** to enable you to see the difference between your former and your present husband. **77. cozened:** cheated. **hoodman-blind:** blind-man's-buff. **79. sans:** without. **81. mope:** be dull. **82–88. Rebellious . . . will:** i.e., if the passion (*Hell*) of a woman of your age is uncontrollable (*rebellious*), youth can have no restraints; there is no shame in a young man's lust when the elderly are just as eager and their reason (which should control desire) encourages them. **83. mutine:** mutiny.

When the compulsive ardor° gives the charge,
Since frost itself as actively doth burn,
And reason panders° will.

QUEEN.   O Hamlet, speak no more.
Thou turn'st mine eyes into my very soul,
And there I see such black and grainèd° spots   90
As will not leave their tinct.°

HAMLET.   Nay, but to live
In the rank sweat of an enseamèd° bed,
Stewed in corruption, honeying and making love
Over the nasty sty——

QUEEN.   Oh, speak to me no more,
These words like daggers enter in my ears.   95
No more, sweet Hamlet!

HAMLET.   A murderer and a villain,
A slave that is not twentieth part the tithe°
Of your precedent° lord, a vice of kings,°
A cutpurse° of the empire and the rule,
That from a shelf the precious diadem stole   100
And put it in his pocket!

QUEEN.   No more!

HAMLET. A king of shreds and patches——
[*Enter* GHOST] Save me, and hover o'er me with your wings,
You heavenly guards! What would your gracious figure?

QUEEN. Alas, he's mad!   105

HAMLET. Do you not come your tardy son to chide
That, lapsed in time and passion, lets go by
The important acting of your dread command?°
Oh, say!

GHOST. Do not forget. This visitation   110
Is but to whet thy almost blunted purpose.
But look, amazement on thy mother sits.
Oh, step between her and her fighting soul.
Conceit° in weakest bodies strongest works.
Speak to her, Hamlet.

HAMLET.   How is it with you, lady?   115

QUEEN. Alas, how is 't with you
That you do bend your eye on vacancy°
And with the incorporal° air do hold discourse?

86. compulsive ardor: compelling lust.   **88. panders:** acts as go-between.
90. grained: dyed in the grain.   **91. tinct:** color.   **92. enseamed:** greasy.   **97.
tithe:** tenth part.   **98. precedent:** former. **vice of kings:** caricature of a king.
99. cutpurse: thief.   **107–08. That . . . command:** who has allowed time to
pass and passion to cool, and neglects the urgent duty of obeying your dread
command.   **114. Conceit:** imagination.   **117. vacancy:** empty space.   **118.
incorporal:** bodiless.

Forth at your eyes your spirits wildly peep,
And as the sleeping soldiers in the alarm,   120
Your bedded° hairs, like life in excrements,°
Start up and stand an° end. O gentle son,
Upon the heat and flame of thy distemper°
Sprinkle cool patience. Whereon do you look?
HAMLET. On him, on him! Look you how pale he glares!   125
His form and cause conjoined,° preaching to stones,
Would make them capable.° Do not look upon me,
Lest with this piteous action you convert
My stern effects.° Then what I have to do
Will want true color—tears perchance for blood.   130
QUEEN. To whom do you speak this?
HAMLET.   Do you see nothing there?
QUEEN. Nothing at all, yet all that is I see.
HAMLET. Nor did you nothing hear?
QUEEN.   No, nothing but ourselves.
HAMLET. Why, look you there! Look how it steals away!
My father, in his habit as he lived!   135
Look where he goes, even now, out at the portal!

                                        [*Exit* GHOST.]

QUEEN. This is the very coinage of your brain.
This bodiless creation ecstasy°
Is very cunning in.
HAMLET.   Ecstasy!
My pulse, as yours, doth temperately keep time,   140
And makes as healthful music. It is not madness
That I have uttered. Bring me to the test
And I the matter will reword, which madness
Would gambol° from. Mother, for love of grace,
Lay not that flattering unction° to your soul,   145
That not your trespass but my madness speaks.
It will but skin and film the ulcerous place,
Whiles rank corruption, mining° all within,
Infects unseen. Confess yourself to Heaven,
Repent what's past, avoid what is to come,   150
And do not spread the compost° on the weeds
To make them ranker. Forgive me this my virtue,

---

121. bedded: evenly laid. **excrements:** anything that grows out of the body, such as hair or fingernails; here hair. **122. an:** on. **123. distemper:** mental disturbance. **126. form . . . conjoined:** his appearance and the reason for his appearance joined. **127. capable:** i.e., of feeling. **128–29. convert . . . effects:** change the stern action which should follow. **138. ecstasy:** madness. **144. gambol:** start away. **145. unction:** healing ointment. **148. mining:** undermining. **151. compost:** manure.

For in the fatness° of these pursy° times
Virtue itself of vice must pardon beg—
Yea, curb° and woo for leave to do him good.   155
QUEEN. O Hamlet, thou hast cleft my heart in twain.
HAMLET. Oh, throw away the worser part of it,
 And live the purer with the other half.
 Good night. But go not to my uncle's bed.
 Assume a virtue if you have it not.   160
 That° monster, custom, who all sense doth eat,
 Of habits devil,° is angel yet in this,
 That to the use° of actions fair and good
 He likewise gives a frock or livery
 That aptly° is put on. Refrain tonight,   165
 And that shall lend a kind of easiness
 To the next abstinence, the next more easy.
 For use almost can change the stamp° of nature,
 And either the Devil,° or throw him out
 With wondrous potency. Once more, good night.   170
 And when you are desirous to be blest,
 I'll blessing beg of you. For this same lord,
          [*Pointing to* POLONIUS]
 I do repent; but Heaven hath pleased it so,
 To punish me with this, and this with me,
 That I must be their scourge and minister.   175
 I will bestow° him, and will answer well
 The death I gave him. So again good night.
 I must be cruel only to be kind.
 Thus bad begins, and worse remains behind.
 One word more, good lady.
QUEEN.   What shall I do?   180
HAMLET. Not this, by no means, that I bid you do.
 Let the bloat° king tempt you again to bed,
 Pinch wanton° on your cheek, call you his mouse,
 And let him, for a pair of reechy° kisses
 Or paddling in your neck with his damned fingers,   185
 Make you to ravel° all this matter out,
 That I essentially am not in madness,

153. **fatness:** grossness. **pursy:** bloated. **155. curb:** bow low. **161–65. That . . . on:** i.e., custom (bad habits) like an evil monster destroys all sense of good and evil, but yet can become an angel (good habits) when it makes us perform good actions as mechanically as we put on our clothes. **162. devil:** This is the Q2 reading; the passage is omitted in F1. Probably the word should be "evil." **163. use:** practice. **165. aptly:** readily. **168. stamp:** impression. **169. either the Devil:** some verb such as "shame" or "curb" has been omitted. **176. bestow:** get rid of. **182. bloat:** bloated. **183. wanton:** lewdly. **184. reechy:** foul. **186. ravel:** unravel, reveal.

But mad in craft. 'Twere good you let him know.
For who that's but a Queen, fair, sober, wise,
Would from a paddock,° from a bat, a gib,°   190
Such dear concernings° hide? Who would do so?
No, in despite° of sense and secrecy,
Unpeg the basket on the house's top,
Let the birds fly, and like the famous ape,°
To try conclusions,° in the basket creep   195
And break your own neck down.
QUEEN. Be thou assured if words be made of breath
    And breath of life, I have no life to breathe
    What thou hast said to me.
HAMLET. I must to England. You know that?
QUEEN.   Alack,   200
    I had forgot. 'Tis so concluded on.
HAMLET. There's letters sealed, and my two schoolfellows,
    Whom I will trust as I will adders fanged,
    They bear the mandate.° They must sweep my way,
    And marshal me to knavery. Let it work,   205
    For 'tis the sport to have the enginer°
    Hoist with his own petar.° And 't shall go hard
    But I will delve one yard below their mines
    And blow them at the moon: Oh, 'tis most sweet
    When in one line two crafts° directly meet.   210
    This man shall set me packing.
    I'll lug the guts into the neighbor room.
    Mother, good night. Indeed this counselor
    Is now most still, most secret, and most grave
    Who was in life a foolish prating knave.   215
    Come, sir, to draw toward an end with you.
    Good night, Mother.   [*Exeunt severally,*°
                                    HAMLET *dragging in* POLONIUS.]

190. paddock: toad.   gib: tomcat.   191. dear concernings: important matters.
192. despite: spite.   194. famous ape: The story is not known, but evidently
told of an ape that let the birds out of their cage and, seeing them fly, crept
into the cage himself and jumped out, breaking his own neck.   195. try conclusions: repeat the experiment.   204. mandate: command.   206. enginer:
engineer.   207. petar: petard, land mine.   210. crafts: devices.   217. s.d.,
Exeunt severally: i.e., by separate exits. In F1 there is no break here. The King
enters as soon as Hamlet has dragged the body away. Q2 marks the break.
The act division was first inserted in a quarto of 1676.

ACT IV

Scene 1 ᴥᵹ *A room in the castle.*

[*Enter* KING, QUEEN, ROSENCRANTZ, *and* GUILDENSTERN.]
KING. There's matter° in these sighs, these profound heaves,
You must translate. 'Tis fit we understand them.
Where is your son?
QUEEN. Bestow this place° on us a little while.
              [*Exeunt* ROSENCRANTZ *and* GUILDENSTERN.]
Ah, mine own lord, what have I seen tonight!   5
KING. What, Gertrude? How does Hamlet?
QUEEN. Mad as the sea and wind when both contend
Which is the mightier. In his lawless fit,
Behind the arras hearing something stir,
Whips out his rapier, cries "A rat, a rat!"   10
And in this brainish apprehension° kills
The unseen good old man.
KING.   Oh, heavy deed!
It had been so with us had we been there.
His liberty is full of threats to all,
To you yourself, to us, to everyone.   15
Alas, how shall this bloody deed be answered?
It will be laid to us, whose providence°
Should have kept short,° restrained and out of haunt,°
This mad young man. But so much was our love
We would not understand what was most fit,   20
But, like the owner of a foul disease,
To keep it from divulging° let it feed
Even on the pith° of life. Where is he gone?

Act IV, Sc. 1: 1. **matter:** something serious. **4. Bestow . . . place:** give
place, leave us. **11. brainish apprehension:** mad imagination. **17. providence:** foresight. **18. short:** confined. **out of haunt:** away from others. **22.
divulging:** becoming known. **23. pith:** marrow.

QUEEN. To draw apart the body he hath killed,
    O'er whom his very madness, like some ore   25
    Among a mineral of metals base,
    Shows itself pure. He weeps for what is done.
KING. O Gertrude, come away!
    The sun no sooner shall the mountains touch
    But we will ship him hence. And this vile deed   30
    We must, with all our majesty and skill,
    Both countenance° and excuse. Ho, Guildenstern!
        [*Re-enter* ROSENCRANTZ *and* GUILDENSTERN.]
    Friends both, go join you with some further aid.
    Hamlet in madness hath Polonius slain,
    And from his mother's closet hath he dragged him.   35
    Go seek him out, speak fair, and bring the body
    Into the chapel. I pray you, haste in this.
        [*Exeunt* ROSENCRANTZ *and* GUILDENSTERN.]
    Come, Gertrude, we'll call up our wisest friends,
    And let them know both what we mean to do
    And what's untimely done,°   40
    Whose whisper o'er the world's diameter
    As level as the cannon to his blank°
    Transports his poisoned shot, may miss our name
    And hit the woundless air. Oh, come away!
    My soul is full of discord and dismay.   [*Exeunt.*]   45

Scene 2 ᴥᶟ *Another room in the castle.*

        [*Enter* HAMLET.]
HAMLET. Safely stowed.
ROSENCRANTZ & GUILDENSTERN. [*Within*] Hamlet! Lord Hamlet!
HAMLET. But soft, what noise? Who calls on Hamlet?
    Oh, here they come.
        [*Enter* ROSENCRANTZ *and* GUILDENSTERN.]
ROSENCRANTZ. What have you done, my lord, with the dead body?   5

32. countenance: take responsibility for.   **40. done:** A half-line has been
omitted. Some editors fill the gap with "So, haply slander."   **42. blank:** target.

HAMLET. Compounded it with dust, whereto 'tis kin.
ROSENCRANTZ. Tell us where 'tis, that we may take it thence
   And bear it to the chapel.
HAMLET. Do not believe it.
ROSENCRANTZ. Believe what?   10
HAMLET. That I can keep your counsel and not mine own. Besides, to be demanded of a sponge! What replication° should
   be made by the son of a king?
ROSENCRANTZ. Take you me for a sponge, my lord?   15
HAMLET. Aye, sir, that soaks up the King's countenance,° his
   rewards, his authorities. But such officers do the King best
   service in the end. He keeps them, like an ape, in the corner
   of his jaw, first mouthed, to be last swallowed. When he
   needs what you have gleaned, it is but squeezing you and,
   sponge, you shall be dry again.   23
ROSENCRANTZ. I understand you not, my lord.
HAMLET. I am glad of it. A knavish speech sleeps in a foolish
   ear.°
ROSENCRANTZ. My lord, you must tell us where the body is, and
   go with us to the King.   28
HAMLET. The body is with the King, but the King is not with the
   body.° The King is a thing——
GUILDENSTERN. A thing, my lord?
HAMLET. Of nothing. Bring me to him. Hide fox, and all after.°   33
                                                   [*Exeunt.*]

Scene 3 ✒ *Another room in the castle.*

[*Enter* KING, *attended.*]
KING. I have sent to seek him, and to find the body.
   How dangerous is it that this man goes loose!

Sc. 2: 14. replication: answer. 17. countenance: favor. 25–26. A . . .
ear: a fool never understands the point of a sinister speech. 29–30. The . . .
body: Hamlet deliberately bewilders his companions. 32–33. Hide . . .
after: a form of the game of hide-and-seek. With these words Hamlet runs
away from them.

Yet must not we put the strong law on him.
He's loved of the distracted° multitude,
Who like not in their judgment but their eyes;°   5
And where 'tis so, the offender's scourge° is weighed,
But never the offense. To bear° all smooth and even,
This sudden sending him away must seem
Deliberate pause.° Diseases desperate grown
By desperate appliance are relieved,   10
Or not at all.
[*Enter* ROSENCRANTZ.] How now! What hath befall'n?
ROSENCRANTZ. Where the dead is bestowed, my lord,
    We cannot get from him.
KING.   But where is he?
ROSENCRANTZ. Without, my lord, guarded, to know your pleasure.
KING. Bring him before us.   15
ROSENCRANTZ. Ho, Guildenstern! Bring in my lord.
                [*Enter* HAMLET *and* GUILDENSTERN.]
KING. Now, Hamlet, where's Polonius?
HAMLET. At supper.
KING. At supper! Where?
HAMLET. Not where he eats, but where he is eaten. A certain con-   20
    vocation of politic worms° are e'en at him. Your worm is
    your only emperor for diet. We fat all creatures else to fat
    us, and we fat ourselves for maggots. Your fat king and
    your lean beggar is but variable service,° two dishes, but to
    one table. That's the end.   26
KING. Alas, alas!
HAMLET. A man may fish with the worm that hath eat of a king,
    and eat of the fish that hath fed of that worm.
KING. What dost thou mean by this?
HAMLET. Nothing but to show you how a king may go a pro-
    gress° through the guts of a beggar.
KING. Where is Polonius?   34
HAMLET. In Heaven—send thither to see. If your messenger find
    him not there, seek him i' the other place yourself. But in-
    deed if you find him not within this month, you shall nose
    him as you go up the stairs into the lobby.   39
KING. [*To some* ATTENDANTS] Go seek him there.
HAMLET. He will stay till you come.   [*Exeunt* ATTENDANTS.]

Sc. 3: 4. distracted: bewildered. 5. like . . . eyes: whose likings are
swayed not by judgment but by looks. 6. scourge: punishment. 7. bear:
make. 9. Deliberate pause: the result of careful planning. 21. convocation
. . . worms: an assembly of political-minded worms. 25. variable service:
choice of alternatives. 33. go a progress: make a state journey.

KING. Hamlet, this deed, for thine especial safety,
    Which we do tender,° as we dearly grieve
    For that which thou hast done, must send thee hence
    With fiery quickness. Therefore prepare thyself.   45
    The bark is ready and the wind at help,°
    The associates tend,° and every thing is bent°
    For England.
HAMLET.   For England?
KING.   Aye, Hamlet.
HAMLET.   Good.
KING. So is it if thou knew'st our purposes.
HAMLET. I see a cherub that sees them. But, come, for England!
    Farewell, dear Mother.   51
KING. Thy loving father, Hamlet.
HAMLET. My mother. Father and mother is man and wife, man
    and wife is one flesh, and so, my mother. Come, for Eng-
    land!   [*Exit.*]
KING. Follow him at foot,° tempt° him with speed aboard.   56
    Delay it not, I'll have him hence tonight.
    Away! For everything is sealed and done
    That else leans on the affair. Pray you make haste.
               [*Exeunt* ROSENCRANTZ *and* GUILDENSTERN.]
    And, England, if my love thou hold'st at aught—   60
    As my great power thereof may give thee sense,
    Since yet thy cicatrice° looks raw and red
    After the Danish sword, and thy free awe°
    Pays homage to us—thou mayst not coldly set
    Our sovereign process,° which imports at full,   65
    By letters congruing° to that effect,
    The present° death of Hamlet. Do it, England,
    For like the hectic° in my blood he rages,
    And thou must cure me. Till I know 'tis done,
    Howe'er my haps,° my joys were ne'er begun.   [*Exit.*]   70

---

43. tender: regard highly.   **46. at help:** favorable.   **47. associates tend:** your companions are waiting. **bent:** ready.   **56. at foot:** at his heels. **tempt:** entice. **62. cicatrice:** scar. There is nothing in the play to explain this incident.   **63. free awe:** voluntary submission.   **64–65. coldly . . . process:** hesitate to carry out our royal command.   **66. congruing:** agreeing.   **67. present:** immediate.   **68. hectic:** fever.   **70. Howe'er my haps:** whatever may happen to me.

Scene 4 ⚬ఢ *A plain in Denmark.*

[*Enter* FORTINBRAS, *a* CAPTAIN *and* SOLDIERS, *marching.*]
FORTINBRAS. Go, Captain, from me greet the Danish King.
    Tell him that by his license Fortinbras
    Craves the conveyance of a promised march°
    Over his kingdom. You know the rendezvous.
    If that His Majesty would aught with us,   5
    We shall express our duty in his eye,°
    And let him know so.
CAPTAIN.   I will do 't, my lord.
FORTINBRAS. Go softly on.
                    [*Exeunt* FORTINBRAS *and* SOLDIERS.]
     [*Enter* HAMLET, ROSENCRANTZ, GUILDENSTERN, *and others.*]
HAMLET. Good sir, whose powers° are these?
CAPTAIN. They are of Norway, sir.   10
HAMLET. How purposed, sir, I pray you?
CAPTAIN. Against some part of Poland.
HAMLET. Who commands them, sir?
CAPTAIN. The nephew to old Norway, Fortinbras.
HAMLET. Goes it against the main° of Poland, sir,   15
    Or for some frontier?
CAPTAIN. Truly to speak, and with no addition,°
    We go to gain a little patch of ground
    That hath in it no profit but the name.
    To pay five ducats, five, I would not farm it,   20
    Nor will it yield to Norway or the Pole
    A ranker° rate should it be sold in fee.°
HAMLET. Why, then the Polack never will defend it.
CAPTAIN. Yes, it is already garrisoned.
HAMLET. Two thousand souls and twenty thousand ducats   25
    Will not debate the question of this straw.

    Sc. 4: 3. Craves . . . march: asks for permission to transport his army, as
had already been promised. See II.2.76–82.   **6. in . . . eye:** before his eyes;
i.e., in person.   **9. powers:** forces.   **15. main:** mainland.   **17. addition:** exaggeration.   **22. ranker:** richer. **in fee:** with possession as freehold.

This is the imposthume of° much wealth and peace,
That inward breaks, and shows no cause without
Why the man dies. I humbly thank you, sir.
CAPTAIN. God be wi' you, sir.   [*Exit.*]
ROSENCRANTZ.   Will 't please you go, my lord?   30
HAMLET. I'll be with you straight. Go a little before.
                              [*Exeunt all but* HAMLET.]
How° all occasions do inform against° me
And spur my dull revenge! What is a man
If his chief good and market° of his time
Be but to sleep and feed? A beast, no more.   35
Sure, He that made us with such large discourse,
Looking before and after,° gave us not
That capability and godlike reason
To fust° in us unused. Now whether it be
Bestial oblivion, or some craven scruple   40
Of thinking too precisely on the event—
A thought which, quartered, hath but one part wisdom
And ever three parts coward—I do not know
Why yet I live to say "This thing's to do,"
Sith I have cause, and will, and strength, and means   45
To do 't. Examples gross° as earth exhort me.
Witness this army, of such mass and charge,°
Led by a delicate and tender Prince
Whose spirit with divine ambition puffed
Makes mouths at the invisible event,°   50
Exposing what is mortal and unsure
To all that fortune, death, and danger dare,
Even for an eggshell.° Rightly to be great
Is not to stir without great argument,
But greatly to find quarrel in a straw   55
When honor's at the stake.° How stand I then,
That have a father killed, a mother stained,
Excitements of my reason and my blood,
And let all sleep while to my shame I see
The imminent death of twenty thousand men   60
That for a fantasy and trick° of fame

27. **imposthume of:** inward swelling caused by.   **32–66. How . . . worth:**
The soliloquy and all the dialogue after the exit of Fortinbras are omitted in
F1.   **32. inform against:** accuse.   **34. market:** profit.   **36–37. such . . .
after:** intelligence that enables us to consider the future and the past.   **39.
fust:** grow musty.   **46. gross:** large.   **47. charge:** expense.   **50. Makes . . .
event:** mocks at the unseen risk.   **53. eggshell:** i.e., worthless trifle.   **53–56.
Rightly . . . stake:** true greatness is a matter of fighting not for a mighty
cause but for the merest trifle when honor is concerned.   **61. fantasy . . .
trick:** illusion and whim.

Go to their graves like beds, fight for a plot
Whereon the numbers cannot try the cause,°
Which is not tomb enough and continent°
To hide the slain? Oh, from this time forth,   65
My thoughts be bloody or be nothing worth!

                                        [*Exit.*]

Scene 5 ᦥ *Elsinore. A room in the castle.*

                    [*Enter* QUEEN, HORATIO, *and a* GENTLEMAN.]
QUEEN. I will not speak with her.
GENTLEMAN. She is importunate, indeed distract.°
    Her mood will needs be pitied.
QUEEN.   What would she have?
GENTLEMAN. She speaks much of her father, says she hears
    There's tricks° i' the world, and hems° and beats her heart,   5
    Spurns enviously° at straws, speaks things in doubt
    That carry but half-sense. Her speech is nothing,
    Yet the unshaped use° of it doth move
    The hearers to collection.° They aim° at it,
    And botch° the words up fit to their own thoughts,   10
    Which, as her winks and nods and gestures yield them,
    Indeed would make one think there might be thought,
    Though nothing sure, yet much unhappily.
HORATIO. 'Twere good she were spoken with, for she may strew
    Dangerous conjectures in ill-breeding minds.   15
QUEEN. Let her come in.   [*Exit* GENTLEMAN.]
    [*Aside*] To my sick soul, as sin's true nature is,
    Each toy° seems prologue to some great amiss.°
    So full of artless jealousy° is guilt,

63. **Whereon . . . cause:** a piece of ground so small that it would not hold
the combatants.   64. **continent:** large enough to contain.
    Sc. 5: 2. distract: out of her mind.   5. **tricks:** trickery. **hems:** makes signifi-
cant noises.   6. **Spurns enviously:** kicks spitefully.   8. **unshaped use:** disorder.   9. **collection:** i.e., attempts to find a sinister meaning. **aim:** guess.   10.
botch: patch.   18. **toy:** trifle. **amiss:** calamity.   19. **artless jealousy:** clumsy
suspicion.

It spills itself in fearing to be spilt.°   20
   [*Re-enter* GENTLEMAN, *with* OPHELIA.°]
OPHELIA. Where is the beauteous Majesty of Denmark?
QUEEN. How now, Ophelia!
OPHELIA. [*Sings.*]
    "How should I your truelove know
     From another one?
     By his cockle hat° and staff   25
     And his sandal shoon."°
QUEEN. Alas, sweet lady, what imports this song?
OPHELIA. Say you? nay, pray you, mark. [*Sings.*]
    "He is dead and gone, lady,
     He is dead and gone,   30
     At his head a grass-green turf,
     At his heels a stone."
  Oh, oh!
QUEEN. Nay, but, Ophelia——
OPHELIA.   Pray you, mark. [*Sings.*]
  "White his shroud as the mountain snow——"   35
     [*Enter* KING.]
QUEEN. Alas, look here, my lord.
OPHELIA. [*Sings.*]
    "Larded° with sweet flowers,
     Which bewept to the grave did go
     With truelove showers."°
KING. How do you, pretty lady?   40
OPHELIA. Well, God 'ild° you! They say the owl was a baker's
  daughter.° Lord, we know what we are but know not what
  we may be. God be at your table!
KING. Conceit upon her father.   45
OPHELIA. Pray you let's have no words of this, but when they
  ask you what it means, say you this [*Sings*]:
    "Tomorrow is Saint Valentine's day,°
     All in the morning betime,

20. It . . . split: guilt reveals itself by its efforts at concealment. 20. s.d.,
Re-enter . . . Ophelia: Q1 notes "Enter Ophelia playing on a lute, and her
hair down, singing." 25. cockle hat: a hat adorned with a cockleshell worn
by pilgrims. 26. sandal shoon: sandals, the proper footwear of pilgrims. 37.
Larded: garnished. 39. truelove showers: the tears of his faithful love. 41.
'ild (yield): reward. 41–42. owl . . . daughter: An allusion to a legend
that Christ once went into a baker's shop and asked for bread. The baker's
wife gave him a piece but was rebuked by her daughter for giving him too
much. Thereupon the daughter was turned into an owl. 48. Saint . . . day:
February 14, the day when birds are supposed to mate. According to the old
belief the first single man then seen by a maid is destined to be her husband.

And I a maid at your window,   50
    To be your Valentine.

"Then up he rose, and donned his clothes,
    And dupped° the chamber door,
    Let in the maid, that out a maid
        Never departed more."   55

KING. Pretty Ophelia!

OPHELIA. Indeed, la, without an oath, I'll make an end on 't.
    [*Sings.*]
            "By Gis° and by Saint Charity,
                Alack, and fie for shame!   60
            Young men will do 't, if they come to 't,
                By cock, they are to blame.
            Quoth she, before you tumbled me,
                You promised me to wed."

He answers:
            "So would I ha' done, by yonder sun,   65
                An thou hadst not come to my bed."

KING. How long hath she been thus?

OPHELIA. I hope all will be well. We must be patient. But I can-
    not choose but weep to think they should lay him i' the cold
    ground. My brother shall know of it. And so I thank you   70
    for your good counsel. Come, my coach! Good night, ladies,
    good night, sweet ladies, good night, good night.   [*Exit.*]

KING. Follow her close,° give her good watch, I pray you.   75
                                        [*Exit* HORATIO.]
    Oh, this is the poison of deep grief. It springs
    All from her father's death. O Gertrude, Gertrude,
    When sorrows come, they come not single spies,°
    But in battalions! First, her father slain.
    Next, your son gone, and he most violent author°   80
    Of his own just remove. The people muddied,
    Thick and unwholesome in their thoughts and whispers,
    For good Polonius' death. And we have done but greenly°
    In huggermugger° to inter him. Poor Ophelia
    Divided from herself and her fair judgment,°   85
    Without the which we are pictures,° or mere beasts.

---

53. dupped: opened.   **59–62. Gis . . . cock:** for "Jesus" and "God," both
words being used instead of the sacred names, like the modern "Jeez" and
"Gee."   **74. close:** closely.   **78. spies:** scouts.   **80. author:** cause.   **83. done
. . . greenly:** shown immature judgment.   **84. huggermugger:** secret haste,
"any which way."   **85. Divided . . . judgment:** no longer able to use her
judgment.   **86. pictures:** lifeless imitations.

Last, and as much containing as all these,
Her brother is in secret come from France,
Feeds on his wonder, keeps himself in clouds,
And wants not buzzers° to infect his ear   90
With pestilent speeches of his father's death,
Wherein necessity, of matter beggared,
Will nothing stick our person to arraign°
In ear and ear. O my dear Gertrude, this,
Like to a murdering piece,° in many places   95
Gives me superfluous death.   [*A noise within*]
QUEEN.   Alack, what noise is this?
KING. Where are my Switzers?° Let them guard the door.
     [*Enter another* GENTLEMAN.] What is the matter?
GENTLEMAN.   Save yourself, my lord.
The ocean, overpeering of his list,°
Eats not the flats° with more impetuous haste   100
Than young Laertes, in a riotous head,°
O'erbears your officers. The rabble call him lord,
And as the world were now but to begin,
Antiquity forgot, custom not known,
The ratifiers and props of every word,°   105
They cry "Choose we—Laertes shall be King!"
Caps, hands, and tongues applaud it to the clouds—
"Laertes shall be King, Laertes King!"
QUEEN. How cheerfully on the false trail they cry!
     Oh, this is counter,° you false Danish dogs! [*Noise within*]   110
KING. The doors are broke.
          [*Enter* LAERTES, *armed*, DANES *following*.]
LAERTES. Where in this King? Sirs, stand you all without.
DANES. No, let's come in.
LAERTES.   I pray you, give me leave.
DANES. We will, we will.   [*They retire without the door.*]
LAERTES. I thank you. Keep the door. O thou vile King,   115
     Give me my father!
QUEEN.   Calmly, good Laertes.
LAERTES. That drop of blood that's calm proclaims me bastard,

---

90. buzzers: scandalmongers. **92–93. Wherein . . . arraign:** in which, knowing nothing of the true facts, he must necessarily accuse us. **95. murdering piece:** cannon loaded with grapeshot. **97. Switzers:** Swiss bodyguard. **99. overpeering . . . list:** looking over its boundary; i.e., flooding the mainland. **100. Eats . . . flats:** floods not the flat country. **101. in . . . head:** with a force of rioters. **104–05. Antiquity . . . word:** forgetting ancient rule and ignoring old custom, by which all promises must be maintained. **110. counter:** in the wrong direction of the scent.

Cries cuckold° to my father, brands the harlot°
Even here, between the chaste unsmirchèd brows
Of my true mother.

KING.   What is the cause, Laertes,   120
That thy rebellion looks so giantlike?
Let him go, Gertrude. Do not fear° our person.
There's such divinity doth hedge a king°
That treason can but peep° to what it would,
Acts little of his will. Tell me, Laertes,   125
Why thou art thus incensed. Let him go, Gertrude.
Speak, man.

LAERTES. Where is my father?

KING.   Dead.

QUEEN.   But not by him.

KING. Let him demand his fill.

LAERTES. How came he dead? I'll not be juggled with.   130
To Hell, allegiance! Vows, to the blackest devil!
Conscience and grace, to the profoundest pit!
I dare damnation. To this point I stand,
That both the worlds I give to negligence.°
Let come what comes, only I'll be revenged   135
Most throughly° for my father.

KING.   Who shall stay you?

LAERTES. My will, not all the world.
And for my means, I'll husband° them so well
They shall go far with little.

KING.   Good Laertes,
If you desire to know the certainty   140
Of your dear father's death, is 't writ in your revenge
That swoopstake,° you will draw both friend and foe,
Winner and loser?

LAERTES. None but his enemies.

KING.   Will you know them, then?

LAERTES. To his good friends thus wide I'll ope my arms,   145
And like the kind life-rendering pelican,°
Repast° them with my blood.

KING.   Why, now you speak

---

118. **cuckold:** a husband deceived by his wife. **brands . . . harlot:** Convicted harlots were branded with a hot iron. Cf. III.4.44.   122. **fear:** fear for.   123. **divinity . . . king:** divine protection surrounds a king as with a hedge.   124. **peep:** look over, not break through.   134. **That . . . negligence:** I do not care what happens to me in this world or the next.   136. **throughly:** thoroughly.   138. **husband:** use economically.   142. **swoopstake:** "sweeping the board."   146. **life-rendering pelican:** The mother pelican was supposed to feed her young with blood from her own breast.   147. **Repast:** feed.

Like a good child and a true gentleman.
That I am guiltless of your father's death,
And am most sensibly° in grief for it,   150
It shall as level° to your judgment pierce
As day does to your eye.
DANES. [*Within*]   Let her come in.
LAERTES. How now! What noise is that?
    [*Re-enter* OPHELIA.] O heat, dry up my brains! Tears seven
     times salt
    Burn out the sense and virtue of mine eye!   155
    By Heaven, thy madness shall be paid with weight
    Till our scale turn the beam.° O rose of May!°
    Dear maid, kind sister, sweet Ophelia!
    Oh heavens! Is 't possible a young maid's wits
    Should be as mortal as an old man's life?   160
    Nature is fine in love, and where 'tis fine
    It sends some precious instance of itself
    After the thing it loves.°
OPHELIA. [*Sings.*] "They bore him barefaced on the bier,
        Hey non nonny, nonny, hey nonny,   165
        And in his grave rained many a tear——"
    Fare you well, my dove!
LAERTES. Hadst thou thy wits and didst persuade revenge,
    It could not move thus.
OPHELIA. [*Sings.*]   "You must sing down a-down   170
        An you call him a-down-a."
    Ah, how the wheel° becomes it! It is the false steward, that
    stole his master's daughter.
LAERTES. This nothing's more than matter.°   174
OPHELIA. There's° rosemary, that's for remembrance—pray you,
    love, remember. And there is pansies, that's for thoughts.

---

150. sensibly: feelingly.   151. level: clearly.   157. turn . . . beam: weigh
down the beam of the scale. rose of May: perfection of young beauty. See
III:1.160.   161–63. Nature . . . loves: i.e., her love for her father was so
exquisite that she has sent her sanity after him. Laertes, especially in moments
of emotion, is prone to use highly exaggerated speech.   172. wheel: explained
variously as the spinning wheel, Fortune's wheel, or the refrain. The likeliest
explanation is that she breaks into a little dance at the words "You must sing,"
and that the *wheel* is the turn as she circles round.   174. This . . . matter:
this nonsense means more than sense.   175–85. There's . . . died: In the
language of flowers, each has its peculiar meaning, and Ophelia distributes
them appropriately: for her brother rosemary (remembrance) and pansies
(thoughts); for the King fennel (flattery) and columbine (thanklessness);
for the Queen rue, called also herb o' grace (sorrow), and daisy (light of
love). Neither is worthy of violets (faithfulness).

LAERTES. A document° in madness, thoughts and remembrance
    fitted.   179
OPHELIA. There's fennel for you, and columbines. There's rue for
    you, and here's some for me—we may call it herb of grace
    o' Sundays. Oh, you must wear your rue with a difference.
    There's a daisy. I would give you some violets, but they
    withered all when my father died. They say a' made a good
    end. [*Sings.*]   186
          "For bonny sweet Robin is all my joy."
LAERTES. Thought and affliction, passion, Hell itself,
    She turns to favor° and to prettiness.
OPHELIA. [*Sings.*] "And will a' not come again?   190
        And will a' not come again?
          No, no, he is dead,
          Go to thy deathbed,
          He never will come again.

          "His beard was as white as snow,   195
          All flaxen was his poll.°
          He is gone, he is gone,
          And we cast away moan.
          God ha' mercy on his soul! "
And of all Christian souls, I pray God. God be wi' you.
                                      [*Exit.*]
LAERTES. Do you see this, O God?   201
KING. Laertes, I must commune with your grief,
    Or you deny me right. Go but apart,
    Make choice of whom your wisest friends you will,
    And they shall hear and judge 'twixt you and me.   205
    If by direct or by collateral° hand
    They find us touched,° we will our kingdom give,
    Our crown, our life, and all that we call ours,
    To you in satisfaction. But if not,
    Be you content to lend your patience to us   210
    And we shall jointly labor with your soul
    To give it due content.
LAERTES.   Let this be so.
    His means of death, his obscure funeral,°
    No trophy, sword, nor hatchment° o'er his bones,

---

178. document: instruction.   **189. favor:** charm.   **196. flaxen . . . poll:** white
as flax was his head.   **206. collateral:** i.e., as an accessory.   **207. touched:**
implicated.   **213. obscure funeral:** Men of rank were buried with much ostentation. To bury Polonius "huggermugger" was thus an insult to his memory and to his family.   **214. hatchment:** device of the coat of arms carried
in a funeral and hung up over the tomb.

No noble rite nor formal ostentation,°   215
Cry to be heard, as 'twere from Heaven to earth,
That I must call 't in question.
KING.   So you shall,
And where the offense is let the great ax fall.
I pray you, go with me.   [*Exeunt.*]

Scene 6 ⤳ *Another room in the castle.*

[*Enter* HORATIO *and a* SERVANT.]
HORATIO. What are they that would speak with me?
SERVANT. Seafaring men, sir. They say they have letters for you.
HORATIO. Let them come in.   [*Exit* SERVANT.]
    I do not know from what part of the world
    I should be greeted, if not from Lord Hamlet.   5
                    [*Enter* SAILORS.]
FIRST SAILOR. God bless you, sir.
HORATIO. Let Him bless thee too.
FIRST SAILOR. He shall, sir, an 't please Him. There's a letter for
    you, sir. It comes from the ambassador that was bound for
    England—if your name be Horatio, as I am let to know   10
    it is.
HORATIO. [*Reads.*] "Horatio, when thou shalt have overlooked°
    this, give these fellows some means° to the King. They have
    letters for him. Ere we were two days old at sea, a pirate of
    very warlike appointment° gave us chase. Finding ourselves   16
    too slow of sail, we put on a compelled valor, and in the
    grapple I boarded them. On the instant they got clear of
    our ship, so I alone became their prisoner. They have dealt
    with me like thieves of mercy; but they knew what they did   20
    —I am to do a good turn for them. Let the King have the
    letters I have sent, and repair thou to me with as much speed
    as thou wouldest fly death. I have words to speak in thine

---

215. formal ostentation: ceremony properly ordered.
    Sc. 6: 13. overlooked: read. means: access.   16. appointment: equipment.

ear will make thee dumb, yet are they much too light for   25
the bore of the matter.° These good fellows will bring thee
where I am. Rosencrantz and Guildenstern hold their course
for England. Of them I have much to tell thee. Farewell.   30
"He that thou knowest thine,
"HAMLET"

Come, I will make you way for these your letters,
And do 't the speedier that you may direct me
To him from whom you brought them.   [*Exeunt.*]

Scene 7 ✑ *Another room in the castle.*

[*Enter* KING *and* LAERTES.]

KING. Now must your conscience my acquittance seal,°
 And you must put me in your heart for friend,
 Sith you have heard, and with a knowing ear,
 That he which hath your noble father slain
 Pursued my life.
LAERTES.   It well appears. But tell me   5
 Why you proceeded not against these feats,°
 So crimeful and so capital° in nature,
 As by your safety, wisdom, all things else,
 You mainly were stirred up.
KING.   Oh, for two special reasons,
 Which may to you perhaps seem much unsinewed,°   10
 But yet to me they're strong. The Queen his mother
 Lives almost by his looks, and for myself—
 My virtue or my plague, be it either which—
 She's so conjunctive° to my life and soul
 That as the star° moves not but° in his sphere,   15
 I could not but by her. The other motive

26. too . . . matter: i.e., words fall short, like a small shot fired from a cannon with too wide a bore.
 Sc. 7: 1. my . . . seal: acquit me. 6. feats: acts. 7. capital: deserving death. 10. unsinewed: weak, flabby. 14. conjunctive: joined inseparably.
15. moves . . . but: moves only in. star: planet.

Why to a public count° I might not go
Is the great love the general gender° bear him,
Who, dipping all his faults in their affection,°
Would, like the spring that turneth wood to stone,°   20
Convert his gyves to graces.° So that my arrows,
Too slightly timbered° for so loud a wind,
Would have reverted to my bow again
And not where I had aimed them.

LAERTES. And so have I a noble father lost,   25
A sister driven into desperate terms,°
Whose worth, if praises may go back again,°
Stood challenger on mount of all the age
For her perfections.° But my revenge will come.

KING. Break not your sleeps for that. You must not think   30
That we are made of stuff so flat and dull
That we can let our beard be shook with danger
And think it pastime. You shortly shall hear more.°
I loved your father, and we love ourself,
And that, I hope, will teach you to imagine——   35
[*Enter a* MESSENGER, *with letters.*] How now! What news?

MESSENGER.   Letters, my lord, from Hamlet.
This to your Majesty, this to the Queen.

KING. From Hamlet! Who brought them?

MESSENGER. Sailors, my lord, they say—I saw them not.
They were given me by Claudio, he received them   40
Of him that brought them.

KING. Laertes, you shall hear them.
Leave us.   [*Exit* MESSENGER.]
[*Reads*] "High and Mighty, you shall know I am set naked°
on your kingdom. Tomorrow shall I beg leave to see your   45
kingly eyes, when I shall, first asking your pardon thereunto,
recount the occasion of my sudden and more strange return.
                            "HAMLET"
What should this mean? Are all the rest come back?
Or is it some abuse,° and no such thing?   50

---

17. **count:** trial.   18. **general gender:** common people.   19. **dipping . . . affection:** gilding his faults with their love.   20. **like . . . stone:** In several places in England there are springs of water so strongly impregnated with lime that they will quickly cover with stone anything placed under them.   21. **Convert . . . graces:** regard his fetters as honorable ornaments.   22. **timbered:** shafted. A light arrow is caught by the wind and blown back.   26. **terms:** condition.   27. **if . . . again:** if one may praise her for what she used to be.   28–29. **Stood . . . perfections:** i.e., her worth challenged the whole world to find one as perfect.   33. **hear more:** i.e., when news comes from England that Hamlet is dead.   45. **naked:** destitute.   50. **abuse:** attempt to deceive.

LAERTES. Know you the hand?

KING. 'Tis Hamlet's character.° "Naked! "
  And in a postscript here, he says "alone."
  Can you advise me?

LAERTES. I'm lost in it, my lord. But let him come.   55
  It warms the very sickness in my heart
  That I shall live and tell him to his teeth
  "Thus didest thou."

KING.   If it be so, Laertes—
  As how should it be so, how otherwise?—
  Will you be ruled by me?

LAERTES.   Aye, my lord,   60
  So you will not o'errule° me to a peace.

KING. To thine own peace. If he be now returned,
  As checking at° his voyage, and that he means
  No more to undertake it, I will work him
  To an exploit now ripe in my device,   65
  Under the which he shall not choose but fall.
  And for his death no wind of blame shall breathe,
  But even his mother shall uncharge the practice°
  And call it accident.

LAERTES.   My lord, I will be ruled,
  The rather if you could devise it so   70
  That I might be the organ.°

KING.   It falls right.
  You have been talked of since your travel much,
  And that in Hamlet's hearing, for a quality
  Wherein they say you shine. Your sum of parts°
  Did not together pluck such envy from him   75
  As did that one, and that in my regard
  Of the unworthiest siege.°

LAERTES.   What part is that, my lord?

KING. A very ribbon in the cap of youth,
  Yet needful too; for youth no less becomes
  The light and careless livery that it wears   80
  Than settled age his sables and his weeds,°
  Importing health and graveness. Two months since,
  Here was a gentleman of Normandy.
  I've seen myself, and served against, the French,

52. character: handwriting. 61. o'errule: command. 63. checking at: swerving aside from, like a hawk that leaves the pursuit of his prey. 68. uncharge . . . practice: not suspect that his death was the result of the plot. 71. organ: instrument. 74. sum of parts: accomplishments as a whole. 77. siege: seat, place. 81. sables . . . weeds: dignified robes. See III.2.138.

And they can well° on horseback; but this gallant   85
Had witchcraft in 't, he grew unto his seat,
And to such wondrous doing brought his horse
As had he been incorpsed and deminatured°
With the brave beast. So far he topped my thought°
That I, in forgery of shapes and tricks,°   90
Come short of what he did.

LAERTES.   A Norman was 't?

KING. A Norman.

LAERTES. Upon my life, Lamond.

KING.   The very same.

LAERTES. I know him well. He is the brooch° indeed
And gem of all the nation.   95

KING. He made confession° of you,
And gave you such a masterly report
For art and exercise in your defense,
And for your rapier most especial,
That he cried out 'twould be a sight indeed   100
If one could match you. The scrimers° of their nation.
He swore, had neither motion, guard, nor eye
If you opposed them. Sir, this report of his
Did Hamlet so envenom° with his envy
That he could nothing do but wish and beg   105
Your sudden coming o'er, to play with him.
Now, out of this——

LAERTES.   What out of this, my lord?

KING. Laertes, was your father dear to you?
Or are you like the painting° of a sorrow,
A face without a heart?

LAERTES.   Why ask you this?   110

KING. Not that I think you did not love your father,
But that I know love is begun by time,
And that I see, in passages of proof,°
Time qualifies° the spark and fire of it.
There lives within the very flame of love   115
A kind of wick or snuff° that will abate it.
And nothing is at a like goodness still,°

85. can well: can do well. 88. incorpsed . . . deminatured: of one body.
89. topped my thought: surpassed what I could imagine. 90. forgery . . .
tricks: imagination of all kinds of fancy tricks. shapes: fancies. 94. brooch:
ornament. 96. confession: report. 101. scrimers: fencers. 104. envenom:
poison. 109. painting: i.e., imitation. 113. passages of proof: experiences
which prove. 114. qualifies: diminishes. 116. snuff: Before the invention
of self-consuming wicks for candles, the wick smoldered and formed a ball
of soot which dimmed the light and gave out a foul smoke. 117. still: always.

For goodness, growing to a pleurisy,°
Dies in his own too much. That we would do
We should do when we would; for this "would" changes   120
And hath abatements and delays as many
As there are tongues, are hands, are accidents,
And then this "should" is like a spendthrift° sigh
That hurts by easing. But to the quick o' the ulcer.°
Hamlet comes back. What would you undertake   125
To show yourself your father's son in deed
More than in words?
LAERTES.   To cut his throat i' the church.°
KING. No place indeed should murder sanctuarize,°
Revenge should have no bounds. But, good Laertes,
Will you do this, keep close within your chamber.   130
Hamlet returned shall know you are come home.
We'll put on those° shall praise your excellence
And set a double varnish on the fame
The Frenchman gave you, bring you in fine° together
And wager on your heads. He, being remiss,°   135
Most generous° and free from all contriving,°
Will not peruse the foils, so that with ease,
Or with a little shuffling, you may choose
A sword unbated,° and in a pass of practice°
Requite him for your father.
LAERTES.   I will do 't,   140
And for that purpose I'll anoint my sword.
I bought an unction° of a mountebank°
So mortal that but dip a knife in it,
Where it draws blood no cataplasm° so rare,
Collected from all simples° that have virtue   145
Under the moon,° can save the thing from death
That is but scratched withal. I'll touch my point
With this contagion, that if I gall° him slightly,
It may be death.

---

118. **pleurisy**: fullness.   123. **spendthrift**: wasteful, because sighing was supposed to be bad for the blood.   124. **quick . . . ulcer**: i.e., to come to the real issue. **quick**: flesh, sensitive part.   127. **cut . . . church**: i.e., to commit murder in a holy place, which would bring Laertes in danger of everlasting damnation; no crime could be worse.   128. **sanctuarize**: give sanctuary to.   132. **put . . . those**: set on some.   134. **fine**: short.   135. **remiss**: careless.   136. **generous**: noble. **contriving**: plotting.   139. **unbated**: not blunted, with a sharp point. **pass of practice**: treacherous thrust.   142. **unction**: poison. **mountebank**: quack doctor.   144. **cataplasm**: poultice.   145. **simples**: herbs. **146. Under . . . moon**: herbs collected by moonlight were regarded as particularly potent.   148. **gall**: break the skin.

KING.   Let's further think of this,
    Weigh what convenience both of time and means   150
    May fit us to our shape.° If this should fail,
    And that our drift look through our bad performance,°
    'Twere better not assayed. Therefore this project
    Should have a back or second, that might hold
    If this did blast in proof.° Soft! Let me see—   155
    We'll make a solemn wager on your cunnings.
    I ha 't.
    When in your motion you are hot and dry—
    As make your bouts° more violent to that end—
    And that he calls for drink, I'll have prepared him   160
    A chalice° for the nonce,° whereon but sipping,
    If he by chance escape your venomed stuck,°
    Our purpose may hold there. But stay, what noise?
    [*Enter* QUEEN.] How now, sweet Queen!
QUEEN. One woe doth tread upon another's heel,
    So fast they follow. Your sister's drowned, Laertes.   165
LAERTES. Drowned! Oh, where?
QUEEN. There is a willow grows aslant a brook
    That shows his hoar° leaves in the glassy stream.
    There with fantastic garlands did she come
    Of crowflowers, nettles, daisies, and long purples   170
    That liberal° shepherds give a grosser name,
    But our cold maids do dead-men's-fingers call them.
    There on the pendent° boughs her coronet weeds°
    Clambering to hang, an envious sliver° broke,
    When down her weedy trophies and herself   175
    Fell in the weeping brook. Her clothes spread wide,
    And mermaidlike a while they bore her up—
    Which time she chanted snatches of old tunes,
    As one incapable° of her own distress,
    Or like a creature native and indued°   180
    Unto that element. But long it could not be
    Till that her garments, heavy with their drink,

150–51. Weigh . . . shape: consider the best time and method of carrying
out our plan.   **152. drift . . . performance:** intention be revealed through
bungling.   **155. blast in proof:** break in trial, like a cannon which bursts
when being tested.   **159. bouts:** attacks, in the fencing match.   **161. chalice:**
cup. **nonce:** occasion.   **162. stuck:** thrust.   **168. hoar:** gray. The underside
of the leaves of the willow are silver-gray.   **171. liberal:** coarse-mouthed.
173. pendent: hanging over the water. **coronet weeds:** wild flowers woven
into a crown.   **174. envious sliver:** malicious branch.   **179. incapable:** not
realizing.   **180. indued:** endowed; i.e., a creature whose natural home is
the water (*element*).

Pulled the poor wretch from her melodious lay°
To muddy death.
LAERTES.   Alas, then, she is drowned!
QUEEN. Drowned, drowned.   185
LAERTES. Too much of water hast thou, poor Ophelia,
And therefore I forbid my tears. But yet
It is our trick°—Nature her custom holds,
Let shame say what it will. When these° are gone,
The woman will be out.° Adieu, my lord.   190
I have a speech of fire that fain° would blaze
But that this folly douts° it.   [Exit.]
KING.   Let's follow, Gertrude.
How much I had to do to calm his rage!
Now fear I this will give it start again,
Therefore let's follow.   [Exeunt.]   195

183. **lay:** song.   187–88. **But . . . trick:** it is our habit; i.e., to break into
tears at great sorrow.   189. **these:** i.e., my tears.   190. **woman . . . out:**
I shall be a man again.   191. **fain:** willingly.   192. **douts:** puts out.

ACT V

Scene 1 ⚫ *A churchyard.*

[*Enter two* CLOWNS,° *with spades, etc.*]

FIRST CLOWN. Is she to be buried in Christian burial° that willfully seeks her own salvation?

SECOND CLOWN. I tell thee she is, and therefore make her grave
straight.° The crowner° hath sat on her, and finds it Chris-
tian burial.   5

FIRST CLOWN. How can that be, unless she drowned herself in her
own defense?

SECOND CLOWN. Why, 'tis found so.

FIRST CLOWN. It must be "se offendendo,"° it cannot be else.
For here lies the point. If I drown myself wittingly,° it   10
argues an act, and an act hath three branches—it is to act,
to do, and to perform. Argal,° she drowned herself wittingly.

SECOND CLOWN. Nay, but hear you, goodman delver.°   15

FIRST CLOWN. Give me leave. Here lies the water, good. Here
stands the man, good. If the man go to this water and
drown himself, it is will he, nill he° he goes, mark you that;
but if the water come to him and drown him, he drowns not
himself. Argal, he that is not guilty of his own death
shortens not his own life.   22

SECOND CLOWN. But is this law?

Act V, Sc. 1: s.d., Clowns: countrymen. See Gen. Intro. p. xiii.   **1. Christian burial:** Suicides were not allowed burial in consecrated ground, but were
buried at crossroads. The gravediggers and the priest are professionally
scandalized that Ophelia should be allowed Christian burial solely because
she is a lady of the Court.   **4. straight:** straightway. **crowner:** coroner.   **9. se
offendendo:** for *defendendo*, in self-defense.   **11. wittingly:** with full knowledge.   **12. Argal:** for the Latin *ergo*, therefore.   **15. delver:** digger.   **18. will
he, nill he:** willy-nilly, whether he wishes or not.

FIRST CLOWN. Aye, marry, is 't, crowner's quest° law.

SECOND CLOWN. Will you ha' the truth on 't? If this had not been
a gentlewoman, she should have been buried out o' Chris-
tian burial.   28

FIRST CLOWN. Why, there thou say'st. And the more pity that
great folks should have countenance° in this world to drown
or hang themselves more than their even° Christian. Come,
my spade. There is no ancient gentlemen but gardeners,
ditchers, and gravemakers. They hold up° Adam's profes-   35
sion.

SECOND CLOWN. Was he a gentleman?

FIRST CLOWN. A' was the first that ever bore arms.°

SECOND CLOWN. Why, he had none.   39

FIRST CLOWN. What, art a heathen? How dost thou understand
the Scripture? The Scripture says Adam digged. Could
he dig without arms? I'll put another question to thee. If
thou answerest me not to the purpose, confess thyself——

SECOND CLOWN. Go to.   45

FIRST CLOWN. What is he that builds stronger than either the
mason, the shipwright, or the carpenter?

SECOND CLOWN. The gallows-maker, for that frame outlives a
thousand tenants.   50

FIRST CLOWN. I like thy wit well, in good faith. The gallows does
well, but how does it well? It does well to those that do ill.
Now thou dost ill to say the gallows is built stronger than
the church; argal, the gallows may do well to thee. To 't
again, come.   56

SECOND CLOWN. Who builds stronger than a mason, a shipwright,
or a carpenter?

FIRST CLOWN. Aye, tell me that, and unyoke.°

SECOND CLOWN. Marry, now I can tell.   60

FIRST CLOWN. To 't.

SECOND CLOWN. Mass,° I cannot tell.

        [*Enter* HAMLET *and* HORATIO, *afar off.*]

FIRST CLOWN. Cudgel thy brains no more about it, for your dull
ass will not mend his pace with beating, and when you are
asked this question next, say "A gravemaker." The houses
that he makes last till Doomsday. Go, get thee to Yaughan,°   67
fetch me a stoup° of liquor.   [*Exit* SECOND CLOWN.]

        [FIRST CLOWN *digs, and sings.*]

---

24. quest: inquest.   **30. countenance:** favor.   **33. even:** fellow.   **35. hold
up:** support.   **38. bore arms:** had a coat of arms—the outward sign of a
gentleman.   **59. unyoke:** finish the job, unyoking the plow oxen being the
end of the day's work.   **62. Mass:** by the mass.   **67. Yaughan:** apparently an
innkeeper near the Globe Theatre.   **68. stoup:** large pot.

"In youth,° when I did love, did love,
  Methought it was very sweet,
To contract; oh, the time, for-a my behoove,°   71
  Oh, methought, there-a was nothing-a meet."
HAMLET. Has this fellow no feeling of his business, that he sings
  at grave-making?
HORATIO. Custom hath made it in him a property of easiness.°
HAMLET. 'Tis e'en so. The hand of little employment hath the
  daintier sense.°   78
FIRST CLOWN. [Sings.] "But age, with his stealing steps,
    Hath clawed me in his clutch,
    And hath shipped me intil the land°
    As if I had never been such."
            [Throws up a skull.]
HAMLET. That skull had a tongue in it, and could sing once. How
  the knave jowls° it to the ground, as if it were Cain's jaw-   84
  bone, that did the first murder! It might be the pate of a
  politician which this ass now o'erreaches°—one that would
  circumvent° God, might it not?
HORATIO. It might, my lord.   89
HAMLET. Or of a courtier, which could say "Good morrow, sweet
  lord! How dost thou, good lord?" This might be my lord
  Such-a-one that praised my lord Such-a-one's horse when he
  meant to beg it, might it not?
HORATIO. Aye, my lord.   95
HAMLET. Why, e'en so. And now my Lady Worm's chapless,°
  and knocked about the mazzard° with a sexton's spade.
  Here's fine revolution, an we had the trick to see 't. Did
  these bones cost no more the breeding but to play at log-
  gats° with 'em? Mine ache to think on 't.   100
FIRST CLOWN. [Sings.] "A pickax and a spade, a spade,
    For and a shrouding sheet—
    Oh, a pit of clay for to be made
    For such a guest is meet."   105
            [Throws up another skull.]
HAMLET. There's another. Why may not that be the skull of a

69–105. In youth . . . meet: The song which the gravedigger sings without
much care for accuracy or sense was first printed in *Tottel's Miscellany*,
1558. 71. behoove: benefit. 75–76. property of easiness: careless habit.
77–78. hand . . . sense: those who have little to do are the most sensitive.
81. shipped . . . land: shoved me into the ground. 84. jowls: dashes. 87.
o'erreaches: gets the better of. circumvent: get around. 97. chapless: without jaws. mazzard: head, a slang word; lit., drinking-bowl. 100. loggats: a
a game in which billets of wood or bones were stuck in the ground and
knocked over by throwing at them.

lawyer?° Where be his quiddities now, his quillets, his cases,
his tenures, and his tricks? Why does he suffer this rude
knave now to knock him about the sconce° with a dirty   110
shovel, and will not tell him of his action of battery? Hum!
This fellow might be in 's time a great buyer of land, with
his statutes, his recognizances, his fines, his double vouchers,
his recoveries. Is this the fine° of his fines and the recovery   115
of his recoveries, to have his fine pate full of fine dirt? Will
his vouchers vouch him no more of his purchases, and
double ones too, than the length and breadth of a pair of
indentures? The very conveyances of his lands will hardly lie
in this box,° and must the inheritor himself have no more,   120
ha?
HORATIO. Not a jot more, my lord.
HAMLET. Is not parchment made of sheepskins?
HORATIO. Aye, my lord, and of calfskins too.
HAMLET. They are sheep and calves which seek out assurance
in that. I will speak to this fellow. Whose grave's this, sirrah?
FIRST CLOWN. Mine, sir. [Sings.]
    "Oh, a pit of clay for to be made
        For such a guest is meet."   129
HAMLET. I think it be thine indeed, for thou liest in 't.
FIRST CLOWN. You lie out on 't, sir, and therefore 'tis not yours.
For my part, I do not lie in 't, and yet it is mine.   135
HAMLET. Thou dost lie in 't, to be in 't and say it is thine. 'Tis
for the dead, not for the quick, therefore thou liest.
FIRST CLOWN. 'Tis a quick lie, sir, 'twill away again, from me to
you.   140
HAMLET. What man dost thou dig it for?
FIRST CLOWN. For no man, sir.
HAMLET. What woman, then?
FIRST CLOWN. For none, neither.
HAMLET. Who is to be buried in 't?   145
FIRST CLOWN. One that was a woman, sir, but, rest her soul, she's
dead.
HAMLET. How absolute° the knave is! We must speak by the
card,° or equivocation° will undo us. By the Lord, Horatio,   149
this three years I have taken note of it—the age is grown

107–18. lawyer . . . indentures: Hamlet strings out a number of the legal
phrases loved by lawyers: *quiddities:* subtle arguments; *quillets:* quibbles;
tenures: titles to property; *tricks:* knavery; *statutes:* bonds; *recognizances:*
obligations; *fines:* conveyances; *vouchers:* guarantors; *recoveries:* transfers;
indentures: agreements.   110. sconce: head; lit., blockhouse.   114. fine: ending.   120. box: coffin.   148. absolute: exact.   149. by . . . card: exactly.
The card is the mariner's compass. equivocation: speaking with a double
sense. The word was much discussed when *Hamlet* was written.

so picked° that the toe of the peasant comes so near the
heel of the courtier, he galls his kibe.° How long hast thou
been a gravemaker?   154

FIRST CLOWN. Of all the days i' the year, I came to 't that day
that our last King Hamlet o'ercame Fortinbras.

HAMLET. How long is that since?

FIRST CLOWN. Cannot you tell that? Every fool can tell that. It
was that very day that young Hamlet was born, he that is
mad, and sent into England.   164

HAMLET. Aye, marry, why was he sent into England?

FIRST CLOWN. Why, because a' was mad. A' shall recover his wits
there, or, if a' do not, 'tis no great matter there.

HAMLET. Why?

FIRST CLOWN. 'Twill not be seen in him there—there the men are
as mad as he.   170

HAMLET. How came he mad?

FIRST CLOWN. Very strangely, they say.

HAMLET. How "strangely"?

FIRST CLOWN. Faith, e'en with losing his wits.

HAMLET. Upon what ground?

FIRST CLOWN. Why, here in Denmark. I have been sexton here,
man and boy, thirty years.°   177

HAMLET. How long will a man lie i' the earth ere he rot?

FIRST CLOWN. I' faith, if a' be not rotten before a' die—as we
have many pocky° corses nowadays that will scarce hold
the laying in—a' will last you some eight year or nine year.
A tanner will last you nine year.

HAMLET. Why he more than another?   185

FIRST CLOWN. Why, sir, his hide is so tanned with his trade that
a' will keep out water a great while, and your water is a sore
decayer of your whoreson° dead body. Here's a skull now.   189
This skull has lain in the earth three and twenty years.

HAMLET. Whose was it?

FIRST CLOWN. A whoreson mad fellow's it was. Whose do you
think it was?

HAMLET. Nay, I know not.   195

---

151. picked: refined. **151–53. toe . . . kibe:** i.e., the peasant follows the
courtier so closely that he rubs the courtier's heel into a blister. From about
1598 onward, writers, especially dramatists, often satirized the practice of
yeoman farmers grown rich from war profits in sending their awkward sons
to London to learn gentlemanly manners. Ben Jonson portrays two specimens
in Stephen in *Every Man in His Humour* and Sogliardo in *Every Man out of
His Humour.* **177. thirty years:** The Clown's chronology has puzzled critics,
for the general impression is that Hamlet was much younger. **181. pocky:**
suffering from the pox (venereal disease). **189. whoreson:** bastard, "son
of a bitch."

FIRST CLOWN. A pestilence on him for a mad rogue! A' poured a
flagon of Rhenish on my head once. This same skull, sir,
was Yorick's skull, the King's jester.

HAMLET. This?

FIRST CLOWN. E'en that.

HAMLET. Let me see. [*Takes the skull.*] Alas, poor Yorick! I knew
him, Horatio—a fellow of infinite jest, of most excellent
fancy. He hath borne me on his back a thousand times, and 205
now how abhorred in my imagination it is! My gorge rises°
at it. Here hung those lips that I have kissed I know not how
oft. Where be your gibes now? Your gambols? Your songs?
Your flashes of merriment that were wont to set the table on
a roar? Not one now, to mock your own grinning? Quite 210
chopfallen?° Now get you to my lady's chamber and tell her,
let her paint an inch thick, to his favor° she must come—
make her laugh at that. Prithee, Horatio, tell me one thing.

HORATIO. What's that, my lord? 217

HAMLET. Dost thou think Alexander looked o' this fashion i' the
earth?

HORATIO. E'en so.

HAMLET. And smelt so? Pah!   [*Puts down the skull.*]

HORATIO. E'en so, my lord.

HAMLET. To what base uses we may return, Horatio! Why may
not imagination trace the noble dust of Alexander till he find
it stopping a bunghole?° 226

HORATIO. 'Twere to consider too curiously° to consider so.

HAMLET. No, faith, not a jot, but to follow him thither with
modesty° enough and likelihood to lead it. As thus: Alexander died, Alexander was buried, Alexander returneth into
dust; the dust is earth; of earth we make loam;° and why of
that loam, whereto he was converted, might they not stop a
beer barrel? 235

    "Imperious Caesar, dead and turned to clay,
    Might stop a hole to keep the wind away.
    Oh, that that earth which kept the world in awe
    Should patch a wall to expel the winter's flaw!" °

But soft! But soft! Aside—here comes the King.

    [*Enter* PRIESTS,° *etc., in procession; the corpse of*

---

206. My . . . rises: I feel sick. **gorge:** throat. **212. chopfallen:** downcast,
with a pun on "chapless," (see l. 97). **213. favor:** appearance, especially
in the face. **226. bunghole:** the hole in a beer barrel. **227. curiously:**
precisely. **230. with modesty:** without exaggeration. **233. loam:** mixture of
clay and sand, used in plastering walls. **239. flaw:** blast. **240. s.d., Enter
Priests.** The stage directions in early texts are less elaborate. Q2 notes, curtly,
Enter K.Q. Laertes and the corse. F1 has *Enter King, Queen, Laertes, and*

Ophelia, LAERTES *and* MOURNERS *following;*
   KING, QUEEN, *their trains, etc.*]
The Queen, the courtiers—who is this they follow?
And with such maimèd° rites? This doth betoken°   242
The corse they follow did with desperate hand
Fordo° its own life. 'Twas of some estate.°
Couch° we awhile, and mark.   [*Retiring with* HORATIO.]
LAERTES. What ceremony else?
HAMLET. That is Laertes, a very noble youth. Mark.
LAERTES. What ceremony else?
FIRST PRIEST. Her obsequies have been as far enlarged
   As we have warranty.° Her death was doubtful,   250
   And but that great command o'ersways the order,°
   She should in ground unsanctified have lodged
   Till the last trumpet; for° charitable prayers,
   Shards,° flints, and pebbles should be thrown on her.
   Yet here she is allowed her virgin crants,°   255
   Her maiden strewments° and the bringing home
   Of bell and burial.
LAERTES. Must there no more be done?
FIRST PRIEST.   No more be done.
   We should profane the service of the dead
   To sing a requiem and such rest to her   260
   As to peace-parted souls.°
LAERTES.   Lay her i' the earth.
   And from her fair and unpolluted flesh
   May violets spring! I tell thee, churlish priest,
   A ministering angel shall my sister be
   When thou liest howling.
HAMLET.   What, the fair Ophelia!   265
QUEEN. [*Scattering flowers*] Sweets to the sweet. Farewell!
   I hoped thou shouldst have been my Hamlet's wife,
   I thought thy bride bed to have decked, sweet maid,

a coffin, with Lords attendant. Q1 prints *Enter King and Queen, Laertes
and other lords, with a Priest after the coffin.* This probably was how the
scene was originally staged. The modern directions ignore the whole significance of the "maimed rites"—Ophelia's funeral is insultingly simple.
242. maimed: curtailed. **betoken:** indicate. **244. Fordo:** destroy. **estate:** high
rank. **245. Couch:** lie down. **249–50. Her . . . warranty:** the funeral rites
have been as complete as may be allowed. **251. but . . . order:** if the King's
command had not overruled the proper procedure. **253. for:** instead of.
254. Shards: pieces of broken crockery. **255. crants:** wreaths of flowers—a
sign that she had died unwed. **256. maiden strewments:** the flowers strewn
on the corpse of a maiden. **261. peace-parted souls:** souls which departed
in peace, fortified with the rites of the Church.

And not have strewed thy grave.

LAERTES.   Oh, treble woe
Fall ten times treble on that cursèd head   270
Whose wicked deed thy most ingenious sense°
Deprived thee of! Hold off the earth a while
Till I have caught her once more in mine arms.
        [Leaps into the grave.]
Now pile your dust upon the quick° and dead
Till of this flat a mountain you have made   275
To o'ertop old Pelion° or the skyish° head
Of blue Olympus.

HAMLET. *[Advancing]* What is he whose grief
Bears such an emphasis? Whose phrase of sorrow
Conjures the wandering stars and makes them stand°
Like wonder-wounded hearers? This is I,   280
Hamlet the Dane.   *[Leaps into the grave.]*

LAERTES. The Devil take thy soul!   *[Grappling with him]*

HAMLET.   Thou pray'st not well.
I prithee, take thy fingers from my throat,
For though I am not splenitive° and rash,
Yet have I in me something dangerous,   285
Which let thy wisdom fear. Hold off thy hand.

KING. Pluck them asunder.

QUEEN.   Hamlet, Hamlet!

ALL.   Gentlemen——

HORATIO. Good my lord, be quiet.
      [The ATTENDANTS *part them, and they come out
          of the grave.]*

HAMLET. Why, I will fight with him upon this theme
Until my eyelids will no longer wag.   290

QUEEN. O my son, what theme?

HAMLET. I loved Ophelia. Forty thousand brothers
Could not, with all their quantity of love,
Make up my sum. What wilt thou do for her?

KING. Oh, he is mad, Laertes.   295

QUEEN. For love of God, forbear him.°

HAMLET. 'Swounds,° show me what thou'lt do.

---

271. most . . . sense: lively intelligence. **274. quick:** living. **276. Pelion:**
When the giants fought against the gods in order to reach Heaven, they tried
to pile Mount Pelion and Mount Ossa on Mount Olympus, the highest mountain in Greece. **skyish:** reaching the sky. **279. stand:** stand still. **284. spleni-**
tive: hot-tempered. **296. forbear him:** leave him alone. **297–307. 'Swounds**
. . . thou: Hamlet in his excitement cries out that if Laertes wishes to make
extravagant boasts of what he will do to show his sorrow, he will be even
more extravagant.

Woo 't weep? Woo 't fight? Woo 't fast? Woo 't tear thyself?
Woo 't drink up eisel?° Eat a crocodile?
I'll do 't. Dost thou come here to whine?   300
To outface° me with leaping in her grave?
Be buried quick with her, and so will I.
And if thou prate of mountains, let them throw
Millions of acres on us, till our ground,
Singeing his pate against the burning zone,   305
Make Ossa° like a wart! Nay, an thou 'lt mouth,
I'll rant as well as thou.
QUEEN.   This is mere madness.
And thus awhile the fit will work on him.
Anon, as patient as the female dove
When that her golden couplets° are disclosed,°   310
His silence will sit drooping.
HAMLET.   Hear you, sir.
What is the reason that you use me thus?
I loved you ever. But it is no matter,
Let Hercules himself do what he may,
The cat will mew and dog will have his day.°   [Exit.]   315
KING. I pray thee, good Horatio, wait upon him.   [Exit HORATIO.]
    [To LAERTES] Strengthen your patience in our last night's
        speech.
We'll put the matter to the present push.°
Good Gertrude, set some watch over your son.
This grave shall have a living monument.°   320
An hour of quiet shortly shall we see,
Till then, in patience our proceeding be.   [Exeunt.]

---

299. **eisel:** vinegar.   301. **outface:** browbeat.   306. **Ossa:** See l. 276, n.   310.
couplets: eggs, of which the dove lays two only. **disclosed:** hatched.   314–15.
Let . . . day: i.e., let this ranting hero have his turn; mine will come sometime.   318. **push:** test; lit., thrust of a pike.   320. **living monument:** with
the double meaning of "lifelike memorial" and "the death of Hamlet."

Scene 2 ꮠ *A hall in the castle.*

[*Enter* HAMLET *and* HORATIO.]

HAMLET. So much for this, sir. Now shall you see the other.
You do remember all the circumstance?

HORATIO. Remember it, my lord!

HAMLET. Sir, in my heart there was a kind of fighting
That would not let me sleep. Methought I lay   5
Worse than the mutines in the bilboes.° Rashly,
And praised be rashness for it, let us know,
Our indiscretion sometime serves us well
When our deep plots do pall.° And that should learn° us
There's a divinity that shapes our ends,   10
Roughhew them how we will.°

HORATIO.   That is most certain.

HAMLET. Up from my cabin,
My sea gown° scarfed° about me, in the dark
Groped I to find out them,° had my desire,
Fingered their packet, and in fine withdrew   15
To mine own room again, making so bold,
My fears forgetting manners, to unseal
Their grand commission where I found, Horatio—
Oh royal knavery!—an exact command,
Larded° with many several sorts of reasons,   20
Importing Denmark's health and England's too,
With, ho! such bugs° and goblins in my life°
That, on the supervise,° no leisure bated,°
No, not to stay the grinding of the ax,

Sc. 2: **6. mutines . . . bilboes:** mutineers in the shackles used on board ship. **9. pall:** fail. **learn:** teach. **10–11. There's . . . will:** though we may make the rough beginning, God finishes our designs. **13. sea gown:** a thick coat with a high collar worn by seamen. **scarfed:** wrapped. **14. them:** i.e., Rosencrantz and Guildenstern. **20. Larded:** garnished. **22. bugs:** bugbears. **in my life:** so long as I was alive. **23. supervise:** reading. **bated:** allowed.

My head should be struck off.
HORATIO.   Is 't possible?   25
HAMLET. Here's the commission. Read it at more leisure
　　But wilt thou hear me how I did proceed?
HORATIO. I beseech you.
HAMLET. Being thus benetted round with villainies—
　　Ere I could make a prologue to my brains,   30
　　They had begun the play—I sat me down,
　　Devised a new commission, wrote it fair.
　　I once did hold it, as our statists° do,
　　A baseness to write fair, and labored much
　　How to forget that learning, but, sir, now   35
　　It did me yeoman's service.° Wilt thou know
　　The effect of what I wrote?
HORATIO.   Aye, good my lord.
HAMLET. An earnest conjuration from the King,
　　As England was his faithful tributary,
　　As love between them like the palm might flourish,   40
　　As peace should still her wheaten garland wear
　　And stand a comma 'tween their amities,°
　　And many suchlike "Ases"° of great charge,°
　　That, on the view and knowing of these contents,
　　Without debatement° further, more or less,   45
　　He should the bearers put to sudden death,
　　Not shriving time allowed.°
HORATIO.   How was this sealed?
HAMLET. Why, even in that was Heaven ordinant.°
　　I had my father's signet in my purse,
　　Which was the model° of that Danish seal—   50
　　Folded the writ° up in the form of the other,
　　Subscribed° it, gave 't the impression,° placed it safely,

---

33. statists: statesmen. As scholars who have had to read Elizabethan documents know, the more exalted the writer, the worse his handwriting. As a girl Queen Elizabeth wrote a beautiful script; as Queen her letters are as illegible as any. All but the most confidential documents were copied out in a fair hand by a secretary. **36. yeoman's service:** faithful service. The most reliable English soldiers were yeomen—farmers and their men. **42. stand . . . amities:** be a connecting link of their friendship. **43. "Ases":** Official documents were written in flowery language full of metaphorical clauses beginning with "As." Hamlet puns on "asses." **great charge:** "great weight" and "heavy burden." **45. debatement:** argument. **47. Not . . . allowed:** without giving them time even to confess their sins. **48. ordinant:** directing, in control. **50. model:** copy. **51. writ:** writing. **52. Subscribed:** signed. **impression:** of the seal.

The changeling° never known. Now the next day
Was our sea fight, and what to this was sequent°
Thou know'st already.   55
HORATIO. So Guildenstern and Rosencrantz go to 't.
HAMLET. Why, man, they did make love to this employment.
They are not near my conscience, their defeat°
Does by their own insinuation° grow.
'Tis dangerous when the baser nature comes   60
Between the pass and fell incensèd points
Of mighty opposites.°
HORATIO.   Why, what a King is this!
HAMLET. Does it not, think'st thee, stand me now upon—
He that hath killed my King and whored my mother.
Popped in between the election and my hopes,°   65
Thrown out his angle° for my proper° life,
And with such cozenage°—is 't not perfect conscience,
To quit° him with this arm? And is 't not to be damned,
To let this canker° of our nature come
In further evil?   70
HORATIO. It must be shortly known to him from England
What is the issue of the business there.
HAMLET. It will be short. The interim° is mine,
And a man's life's no more than to say "One."
But I am very sorry, good Horatio,   75
That to Laertes I forgot myself,
For by the image of my cause I see
The portraiture of his. I'll court his favors.
But, sure, the bravery° of his grief did put me
Into a towering passion.
HORATIO.   Peace! Who comes here?   80
                    [Enter OSRIC.°]
OSRIC. Your lordship is right welcome back to Denmark.
HAMLET. I humbly thank you, sir. Dost know this water fly?°

---

53. changeling: lit., an ugly child exchanged by the fairies for a fair one. **54. sequent:** following. **58. defeat:** destruction. **59. by . . . insinuation:** because they insinuated themselves into this business. **60–62. 'Tis . . . opposites:** it is dangerous for inferior men to interfere in a duel between mighty enemies. **pass:** thrust. **fell:** fierce. **65. Popped . . . hopes:** As is from time to time shown in the play, the Danes chose their King by election. **66. angle:** fishing rod and line. **proper:** own. **67. cozenage:** cheating. **68. quit:** pay back. **69. canker:** maggot. See I.3.39. **73. interim:** interval—between now and the news from England. **79. bravery:** excessive show. **80. s.d., Osric:** Osric is a specimen of the fashionable, effeminate courtier. He dresses prettily and talks the jargon of his class, which at this time affected elaborate and allusive metaphors and at all costs avoided saying plain things plainly. **83. water fly:** a useless little creature that flits about.

HORATIO. No, my good lord.

HAMLET. Thy state is the more gracious,° for 'tis a vice to know   85
him. He hath much land, and fertile. Let a beast be lord of
beasts and his crib shall stand at the King's mess.° 'Tis a
chough,° but, as I say, spacious° in the possession of dirt.   90

OSRIC. Sweet lord, if your lordship were at leisure, I should impart a thing to you from His Majesty.

HAMLET. I will receive it, sir, with all diligence of spirit. Put
your bonnet to his right use,° 'tis for the head.   95

OSRIC. I thank your lordship, it is very hot.

HAMLET. No, believe me, 'tis very cold. The wind is northerly.

OSRIC. It is indifferent° cold, my lord, indeed.   100

HAMLET. But yet methinks it is very sultry and hot, for my complexion——

OSRIC. Exceedingly, my lord. It is very sultry, as 'twere—I cannot
tell how. But, my lord, His Majesty bade me signify to you
that he has laid a great wager on your head. Sir, this is the
matter——

HAMLET. I beseech you, remember——   108

     [HAMLET *moves him to put on his hat.*]

OSRIC. Nay, good my lord, for mine ease, in good faith. Sir, here
is newly come to Court Laertes—believe me, an absolute°
gentleman, full of most excellent differences,° of very soft
society° and great showing.° Indeed, to speak feelingly° of   114
him, he is the card or calendar of gentry,° for you shall find
in him the continent of what part a gentleman would see.°

HAMLET. Sir,° his definement suffers no perdition in you, though
I know to divide him inventorially would dizzy the arithmetic of memory, and yet but yaw neither, in respect of his

---

85. Thy . . . gracious: you are in the better state.   **88–89. Let . . . mess:**
i.e., any man, however low, who has wealth enough will find a good place
at Court. **crib:** manger. **mess:** table.   **89. chough:** jackdaw.   **90. spacious:**
wealthy.   **95. Put . . . use:** i.e., put your hat on your head. Osric is so nice-
mannered that he cannot bring himself to wear his hat in the presence of
the Prince.   **100. indifferent:** moderately.   **111. absolute:** perfect.   **112. differences:** qualities peculiar to himself. **soft society:** gentle breeding.   **112–13.
great showing:** distinguished appearance.   **113. feelingly:** with proper appreciation.   **114. card . . . gentry:** the very fashion plate of what a gentleman should be.   **115–16. continent . . . see:** all the parts that should be
in a perfect gentleman.   **117–25. Sir . . . more:** Hamlet retorts in similar
but even more extravagant language. This is too much for Osric (and for
most modern readers). Hamlet's words may be paraphrased: "Sir, the description of this perfect gentleman loses nothing in your account of him;
though I realize that if one were to try to enumerate his excellences, it would
exhaust our arithmetic, and yet"—here he changes the image to one of sailing—"we should still lag behind him as he outsails us. But in the true
vocabulary of praise, I take him to be a soul of the greatest worth, and his

quick sail. But in the verity of extolment, I take him to be a   120
soul of great article, and his infusion of such dearth and
rareness as, to make true diction of him, his semblable is his
mirror, and who else would trace him, his umbrage—nothing more.   125

OSRIC. Your lordship speaks most infallibly of him.

HAMLET. The concernancy,° sir? Why do we wrap the gentleman
in our more rawer breath?°

OSRIC. Sir?°   129

HORATIO. Is 't not possible to understand in another tongue?
You will do 't, sir, really.

HAMLET. What imports the nomination° of this gentleman?   133

OSRIC. Of Laertes?

HORATIO. His purse is empty already, all's golden words are spent.

HAMLET. Of him, sir.

OSRIC. I know you are not ignorant——

HAMLET. I would you did, sir. Yet, in faith, if you did, it would
not much approve° me. Well, sir?   141

OSRIC. You are not ignorant of what excellence Laertes is——

HAMLET. I dare not confess that, lest I should compare with him
in excellence, but to know a man well were to know himself.

OSRIC. I mean, sir, for his weapon,° but in the imputation° laid
on him by them, in his meed° he's unfellowed.°   150

HAMLET. What's his weapon?

OSRIC. Rapier and dagger.

HAMLET. That's two of his weapons, but, well.

OSRIC. The King, sir, hath wagered with him six Barbary horses,
against the which he has imponed,° as I take it, six French   156
rapiers and poniards, with their assigns,° as girdle, hanger,°
and so—three of the carriages, in faith, are very dear to
fancy,° very responsive to° the hilts, most delicate carriages, and of very liberal conceit.°   160

perfume"—i.e., his personal essence—"so scarce and rare that to speak truly
of him, the only thing like him is his own reflection in his mirror, and everyone else who tries to follow him merely his shadow." **yaw:** fall off from the
course laid. **verity . . . extolment:** in true praise. **infusion:** essence. **semblable:**
resemblance. **trace:** follow. **umbrage:** shadow. **127. concernancy:** i.e., what
is all this talk about? **127–28. Why . . . breath:** why do we discuss the
gentleman with our inadequate voices? **129. Sir:** Osric is completely baf-
fled. **133. nomination:** naming. **141. approve:** commend. **148. his
weapon:** i.e., skill with his weapon. **149. imputation:** reputation. **meed:**
merit. **150. unfellowed:** without an equal. **156. imponed:** laid down as a
stake. **157. assigns:** that which goes with them. **hanger:** straps by which the
scabbard was hung from the belt. **158–59. dear to fancy:** of beautiful
design. **159. responsive to:** matching. **160. liberal conceit:** elaborately
artistic.

HAMLET. What call you the carriages?

HORATIO. I knew you must be edified by the margent° ere you had done.

OSRIC. The carriages, sir, are the hangers. 164

HAMLET. The phrase would be more germane° to the matter if we could carry a cannon by our sides. I would it might be hangers till then. But, on—six Barbary horses against six French swords, their assigns, and three liberal-conceited carriages. That's the French bet against the Danish. Why is this "imponed," as you call it? 171

OSRIC. The King, sir, hath laid, sir, that in a dozen passes between yourself and him, he shall not exceed you three hits. He hath laid on twelve for nine,° and it would come to immediate trial if your lordship would vouchsafe the answer.

HAMLET. How if I answer no? 177

OSRIC. I mean, my lord, the opposition of your person in trial.

HAMLET. Sir, I will walk here in the hall. If it please His Majesty, it is the breathing-time of day with me.° Let the foils be 182 brought, the gentleman willing, and the King hold his purpose, I will win for him an I can. If not, I will gain nothing but my shame and the odd hits.

OSRIC. Shall I redeliver you e'en so?

HAMLET. To this effect, sir, after what flourish° your nature will. 187

OSRIC. I commend my duty to your lordship.

HAMLET. Yours, yours. [*Exit* OSRIC.] He does well to commend it himself, there are no tongues else for 's turn.

HORATIO. This lapwing° runs away with the shell on his head.

HAMLET. He did comply with his dug° before he sucked it. Thus 195 has he—and many more of the same breed that I know the drossy° age dotes on—only got the tune of the time and outward habit of encounter,° a kind of yesty collection° which carries them through and through the most fond° and winnowed° opinions—and do but blow them to their trial, 200

---

162. edified . . . margent: informed by the notes. In Shakespeare's time the notes were often printed in the margin. **165. germane:** related. **174–75. twelve . . . nine:** i.e., Laertes will hit Hamlet twelve times before Hamlet hits him nine times. **181–82. breathing-time . . . me:** time when I take exercise. **187. flourish:** fanfare, elaborate phrasing. **193. lapwing:** a pretty, lively little bird. It is so lively that it can run about the moment it is hatched. **195. did . . . dug:** was ceremonious with the nipple; i.e., behaved in this fantastic way from his infancy. See II.2.389. **197. drossy:** scummy, frivolous. **198–99. tune . . . encounter:** i.e., they sing the same tune as everyone else and have the same society manners. **199. yesty collection:** frothy catchwords. **200. fond:** foolish. **201. winnowed:** light as chaff. Winnowing in the process of fanning the chaff from the grain.

the bubbles are out.°

[*Enter a* LORD.]

LORD. My lord, His Majesty commended him to you by young
    Osric, who brings back to him that you attend him in the
    hall. He sends to know if your pleasure hold to play with
    Laertes, or that you will take longer time.   207

HAMLET. I am constant to my purposes, they follow the King's
    pleasure. If his fitness speaks, mine is ready, now or when-
    soever, provided I be so able as now.

LORD. The King and Queen and all are coming down.

HAMLET. In happy time.°   214

LORD. The Queen desires you to use some gentle entertainment°
    to Laertes before you fall to play.

HAMLET. She well instructs me.   [*Exit* LORD.]

HORATIO. You will lose this wager, my lord.   219

HAMLET. I do not think so. Since he went into France I have been
    in continual practice, I shall win at the odds. But thou
    wouldst not think how ill all's here about my heart—but it
    is no matter.

HORATIO. Nay, good my lord——

HAMLET. It is but foolery, but it is such a kind of gaingiving° as   226
    would perhaps trouble a woman.

HORATIO. If your mind dislike anything, obey it. I will forestall
    their repair hither and say you are not fit.

HAMLET. Not a whit, we defy augury.° There's special providence   230
    in the fall of a sparrow.° If it be now, 'tis not to come; if
    it be not to come, it will be now; if it be not now, yet it will
    come. The readiness is all. Since no man has aught of what
    he leaves, what is 't to leave betimes? Let be.   235

    [*Enter* KING, QUEEN, LAERTES, *and* LORDS, OSRIC *and
    other* ATTENDANTS *with foils; a table and flagons of
    wine on it.*]

KING. Come, Hamlet, come, and take this hand from me.

    [*The* KING *puts* LAERTES' *hand into* HAMLET'S.]

HAMLET. Give me your pardon, sir. I've done you wrong,
    But pardon 't, as you are a gentleman.
    This presence° knows,
    And you must needs have heard, how I am punished   240

201–02. do . . . out: force them to make sense of their words and they are
deflated, as Hamlet has just deflated Osric.   **214. In . . . time:** at a good
moment.   **215–16. gentle entertainment:** kindly treatment; i.e., be reconciled
after the brawl in the churchyard.   **226. gaingiving:** misgiving.   **230. augury:**
omens.   **231. special . . . sparrow:** The idea comes from Matthew 10:29.
"Are not two sparrows sold for a farthing? and one of them shall not fall to
the ground without your Father."   **239. presence:** the whole Court.

With sore distraction. What I have done
That might your nature, honor, and exception°
Roughly awake, I here proclaim was madness.
Was 't Hamlet wronged Laertes? Never Hamlet.
If Hamlet from himself be ta'en away,°   245
And when he's not himself does wrong Laertes,
Then Hamlet does it not, Hamlet denies it.
Who does it, then? His madness. If 't be so,
Hamlet is of the faction that is wronged,
His madness is poor Hamlet's enemy.   250
Sir, in this audience
Let my disclaiming from a purposed evil°
Free me so far in your most generous thoughts
That I have shot mine arrow o'er the house,
And hurt my brother.

LAERTES.   I am satisfied in nature,   255
Whose motive, in this case, should stir me most
To my revenge. But in my terms of honor
I stand aloof, and will no reconcilement
Till by some elder masters of known honor
I have a voice and precedent of peace   260
To keep my name ungored.° But till that time
I do receive your offered love like love
And will not wrong it.

HAMLET.   I embrace it freely,
And will this brother's wager frankly play.
Give us the foils. Come on.

LAERTES.   Come, one for me.   265

HAMLET. I'll be your foil,° Laertes. In mine ignorance
Your skill shall, like a star i' the darkest night,
Stick° fiery off indeed.

LAERTES.   You mock me, sir.

HAMLET. No, by this hand.

KING. Give them the foils, young Osric. Cousin Hamlet,   270
You know the wager?

HAMLET.   Very well, my lord.
Your Grace has laid the odds o' the weaker side.

---

242. exception: resentment. 245. If . . . away: i.e., Hamlet mad is not
Hamlet. 252. Let . . . evil: let my declaration that I did not intend any
harm. 255-61. I . . . ungored: I bear you no grudge so far as concerns
my personal feelings, which would most readily move me to vengeance; but
as this matter touches my honor, I cannot accept your apology until I have
been assured by those expert in matters of honor that I may so do without
loss of reputation. 266. foil: Hamlet puns on the other meaning of foil—tin
foil set behind a gem to give it luster. 268. Stick . . . off: shine out.

KING. I do not fear it, I have seen you both.
 But since he is bettered,° we have therefore odds.
LAERTES. This is too heavy, let me see another.   275
HAMLET. This likes° me well. These foils have all a length?°
     [*They prepare to play.*]
OSRIC. Aye, my good lord.
KING. Set me the stoups° of wine upon that table.
 If Hamlet give the first or second hit,
 Or quit° in answer of the third exchange,   280
 Let all the battlements their ordnance fire.
 The King shall drink to Hamlet's better breath,
 And in the cup a union° shall he throw
 Richer than that which four successive kings
 In Denmark's crown have worn. Give me the cups, 285
 And let the kettle° to the trumpet speak,
 The trumpet to the cannoneer without,
 The cannon to the Heavens, the Heaven to earth,
 "Now the King drinks to Hamlet." Come, begin,
 And you, the judges, bear a wary eye.   290
HAMLET. Come on, sir.
LAERTES.   Come, my lord.   [*They play.*]
HAMLET.   One.
LAERTES.   No.
HAMLET.   Judgment.
OSRIC. A hit, a very palpable° hit.
LAERTES.   Well, again.
KING. Stay, give me drink. Hamlet, this pearl is thine°—
 Here's to thy health.
   [*Trumpets sound, and cannon shot off within.*]
      Give him the cup.
HAMLET. I'll play this bout first. Set it by a while. 295
 Come. [*They play.*] Another hit, what say you?
LAERTES. A touch, a touch, I do confess.
KING. Our son shall win.
QUEEN.   He's fat° and scant of breath.
 Here, Hamlet, take my napkin, rub thy brows.
 The Queen carouses to thy fortune, Hamlet.   300
HAMLET. Good madam!
KING.   Gertrude, do not drink.
QUEEN. I will, my lord, I pray you pardon me. [*She drinks.*]

---

274. bettered: considered your superior. **276. likes:** pleases. **have . . . length:** are all of equal length. **278. stoups:** drinking-vessels. **280. quit:** strike back. **283. union:** a large pearl. **286. kettle:** kettledrum. **292. palpable:** clear. **293. this . . . thine:** With these words the King drops the poisoned pearl into the cup intended for Hamlet. **298. fat:** out of condition.

KING. [*Aside*] It is the poisoned cup, it is too late.
HAMLET. I dare not drink yet, madam—by and by.
QUEEN. Come, let me wipe thy face.   305
LAERTES. My lord, I'll hit him now.
KING.   I do not think 't.
LAERTES. [*Aside*] And yet 'tis almost against my conscience.
HAMLET. Come, for the third, Laertes. You but dally.°
   I pray you pass with your best violence,
   I am afeard you make a wanton of me.°   310
LAERTES. Say you so? Come on.   [*They play.*]
OSRIC. Nothing, neither way.
LAERTES. Have at you now!
   [LAERTES *wounds* HAMLET; *then, in scuffling, they change*
      rapiers, and HAMLET *wounds* LAERTES.]
KING.   Part them, they are incensed.
HAMLET. Nay, come, again.   [*The* QUEEN *falls.*]
OSRIC.   Look to the Queen there, ho!
HORATIO. They bleed on both sides. How is it, my lord?   325
OSRIC. How is 't, Laertes?
LAERTES. Why, as a woodcock to mine own springe,° Osric,
   I am justly killed with mine own treachery.
HAMLET. How does the queen?
KING.   She swounds to see them bleed.
QUEEN. No, no, the drink, the drink!—O my dear Hamlet—   320
   The drink, the drink! I am poisoned.   [*Dies.*]
HAMLET. Oh, villainy! Ho! Let the door be locked.
   Treachery! Seek it out.   [LAERTES *falls.*]
LAERTES. It is here, Hamlet. Hamlet, thou art slain.
   No medicine in the world can do thee good,   315
   In thee there is not half an hour of life.
   The treacherous instrument is in thy hand,
   Unbated and envenomed. The foul practice
   Hath turned itself on me. Lo, here I lie
   Never to rise again. Thy mother's poisoned.   330
   I can no more. The King, the King's to blame.
HAMLET. The point envenomed too!
   Then, venom, to thy work.   [*Stabs the* KING.]
ALL. Treason! Treason!
KING. Oh, yet defend me, friends, I am but hurt.   335
HAMLET. Here, thou incestuous, murderous, damnèd Dane,
   Drink off this potion. Is thy union° here?
   Follow my mother.   [KING *dies.*]

308. dally: play. 310. make . . . me: treat me like a child by letting me win. 317. springe: snare. 337. union: pearl, as in l. 283.

LAERTES.   He is justly served.
It is a poison tempered° by himself.
Exchange forgiveness with me, noble Hamlet.   340
Mine and my father's death come not upon thee,°
Nor thine on me!   [*Dies.*]
HAMLET. Heaven make thee free of it!° I follow thee.
I am dead, Horatio. Wretched Queen, adieu!
You that look pale and tremble at this chance,   345
That are but mutes or audience to this act,
Had I but time—as this fell° sergeant,° Death,
Is strict in his arrest—oh, I could tell you——
But let it be. Horatio, I am dead,
Thou livest. Report me and my cause aright   350
To the unsatisfied.°
HORATIO.   Never believe it.
I am more an antique Roman° than a Dane.
Here's yet some liquor left.
HAMLET.   As thou 'rt a man,
Give me the cup. Let go—by Heaven, I'll have 't.
O good Horatio, what a wounded name,   355
Things standing thus unknown, shall live behind me!
If thou didst ever hold me in thy heart,
Absent thee from felicity a while,
And in this harsh world draw thy breath in pain
To tell my story.   [*March afar off, and shot within*]
What warlike noise is this?   360
OSRIC. Young Fortinbras, with conquest come from Poland,
To the ambassadors of England gives
This warlike volley.
HAMLET.   Oh, I die, Horatio,
The potent poison quite o'ercrows° my spirit.
I cannot live to hear the news from England,   365
But I do prophesy the election° lights
On Fortinbras. He has my dying voice.°
So tell him, with the occurrents, more and less,
Which have solicited.° The rest is silence.   [*Dies.*]
HORATIO. Now cracks a noble heart. Good night, sweet Prince,   370
And flights of angels sing thee to thy rest!   [*March within.*]

339. tempered: mixed.   341. come . . . thee: are not on your head.   343.
Heaven . . . it: God forgive you.   347. fell: dread. sergeant: the officer of
the Court who made arrests.   351. unsatisfied: who do not know the truth.
352. antique Roman: like Cato and Brutus, who killed themselves rather
than survive in a world which was unpleasing to them.   364. o'ercrows:
overpowers.   366. election: as King of Denmark. See l. 65 above.   367.
voice: support.   368–69. occurrents . . . solicited: events great and small
which have caused me to act.

Why does the drum come hither?
[*Enter* FORTINBRAS, *and the* ENGLISH AMBASSADORS, *with*
drum, colors, and ATTENDANTS.]
FORTINBRAS. Where is this sight?
HORATIO.   What is it you would see?
If aught of woe or wonder, cease your search.
FORTINBRAS. This quarry cries on havoc.° O proud Death,   375
What feast is toward° in thine eternal cell
That thou so many princes at a shot
So bloodily hast struck?
FIRST AMBASSADOR.   The sight is dismal,
And our affairs from England come too late.
The ears are senseless that should give us hearing,   380
To tell him his commandment is fulfilled,
That Rosencrantz and Guildenstern are dead.
Where should we have our thanks?
HORATIO.   Not from his mouth
Had it the ability of life to thank you.
He never gave commandment for their death.   385
But since, so jump° upon this bloody question,°
You from the Polack wars, and you from England,
Are here arrived, give order that these bodies
High on a stage be placèd to the view,
And let me speak to the yet unknowing world   390
How these things came about. So shall you hear
Of carnal, bloody, and unnatural acts,
Of accidental judgments, casual slaughters,
Of deaths put on by cunning and forced cause,
And, in this upshot, purposes mistook   395
Fall'n on the inventors' heads.° All this can I
Truly deliver.
FORTINBRAS.   Let us haste to hear it,
And call the noblest to the audience.
For me, with sorrow I embrace my fortune.
I have some rights of memory° in this kingdom,   400

---

375. quarry . . . havoc: heap of slain denotes a pitiless slaughter. See *Caesar*,
III.1.273.   376. toward: being prepared.   386. jump: exactly. See I.1.65.
question: matter.   392–96. carnal . . . heads: These lines sum up the whole
tragedy: Claudius' adultery with Gertrude, his murder of his brother, the
death of Ophelia due to an accident, that of Polonius by casual chance,
Hamlet's device which caused the deaths of Rosencrantz and Guildenstern,
the plan which went awry and caused the deaths of Claudius and Laertes.
400. rights of memory: rights which will be remembered; i.e., with the dis-
appearance of all the family of the original King Hamlet the situation re-
verts to what it was before the death of Fortinbras' father. See I.1.80–95.

Which now to claim my vantage° doth invite me.
HORATIO. Of that I shall have also cause to speak,
    And from his mouth whose voice will draw on more.°
    But let this same be presently performed,
    Even while men's minds are wild, lest more mischance   405
    On plots and errors happen.
FORTINBRAS.   Let four captains
    Bear Hamlet, like a soldier, to the stage.
    For he was likely, had he been put on,°
    To have proved most royally. And for his passage
    The soldiers' music and the rites of war   410
    Speak loudly for him.
    Take up the bodies. Such a sight as this
    Becomes the field, but here shows much amiss.
    Go, bid the soldiers shoot.
        [*A dead march. Exeunt, bearing off the bodies;*
          after which a peal of ordnance is shot off.]

401. vantage: i.e., my advantage, there being none to dispute my claim.
403. voice . . . more: i.e., Hamlet's dying voice will strengthen your claim.
408. had . . . on: had he become King.

QUESTIONS

ACT I

1. Scene 1 provides very little information and does not introduce the major figures of the play. It does set the atmosphere and introduce us to the "world" in which the action is to occur. Examine the details that compose the scene—e.g., a soldier on watch, a ghost, a discussion of political troubles—and try to describe what kind of world is built up here.
2. In the second scene the action shifts from the dark battlements to the brilliant center of the Danish court, the King's council chamber. Contrast the two scenes and discuss the different attitudes toward the world and its problems shown in each.
3. It has often been remarked that Claudius is an exceptionally capable king and politician. How does this impression of Claudius emerge in his first long speech? Take into account not only the way he deals with problems but the *style* of his speech—his diction, images, and rhythms.
4. Claudius offers Hamlet some perfectly sound advice about how to

take the death of a father, but it rings false. What is there about his way of delivering these truisms that suggests they are meaningless?

5. Contrast the rhythms of Hamlet's first soliloquy, "Oh, that this too too solid flesh," with those of Claudius' first speech. How does Hamlet's speech suggest a compulsive concern? What is the compulsion?

6. At the end of the first soliloquy, what does Hamlet decide he must do about this "unweeded garden" of the world?

7. Compose a picture of old Hamlet from the information provided in Horatio and Hamlet's discussion of him and from what he tells us about himself, both directly and in his style of speaking, in his appearance on the battlements. Compare him with Claudius, the new king; with Hamlet, his son.

8. Scene 3 offers a good picture of the Polonius family, who are to play a prominent part in coming events. Look carefully at all the advice Laertes and Polonius offer on various subjects and describe their approach to the world and their understanding of human nature. Would you call them sensitive or practical? What does this scene gain in meaning by being placed between two scenes involving a ghost come back from another world to speak of the corruption in this one?

9. In lines 24–35 of Scene 4 Hamlet defines the tragic flaw, that weakness or failing supposedly found in all tragic heroes which is said to bring about their downfall. Is this applicable to Hamlet? Has any weakness of character led him into this desperate situation of being asked to kill a king and of standing in danger of his life from the clever, suspicious man who has killed his father, married his mother, and stolen his throne?

10. Compare Hamlet's attitude in Scene 5 (lines 92–112), just after the Ghost has sworn him to revenge, with his attitude in the final lines of the scene: "Oh, cursèd spite/That ever I was born to set it right!" Where else do we see this fluctuation or mixture of motives in Hamlet? What two major conflicting forces are at work deep in his mind? Are they symbolized by his two professions: the prince of Denmark and the student at Wittenberg?

ACT II

11. Polonius' description of his method for discovering truth,

> With windlasses and with assays of bias,
> By indirections find directions out,

defines very nicely the way the court, in which he is chief counsellor, operates. Find other examples of this movement by "indirection." Why is it necessary in this world?

12. How does Hamlet "find directions out" as described by Ophelia (lines 87–119)? How does this differ from the practice of the court?

13. Why do Ophelia's rejection of Hamlet and the spying of his old friends, Rosencrantz and Guildenstern, seem to Hamlet dreadful breaches of trust? How do all three justify their actions?

14. Critics have been painfully anxious to settle the question of Hamlet's madness. Looking at the way he manages Polonius and Rosencrantz and Guildenstern in these scenes, can you see any evidence for arguing that Hamlet is truly mad? Can you see, perhaps, why in a world so practical and "sane" as Elsinore he might be considered mad?

15. How do Rosencrantz and Guildenstern betray their true motives?

16. In what ways does Hamlet's famous speech, "What a piece of work is a man" (2.304-22), explain his melancholy? Compare the beliefs he once held about man and the world with the realities of Elsinore.

23. One critic has suggested that the dominant tone of *Hamlet* is set by the frequent questions asked, ranging from such apparently trivial ones as, "Who's there"—the opening line of the play—to such gigantic questions as, "What should such fellows as I do crawling between earth and heaven?" Select several of Hamlet's most crucial questions, discuss them, and show how the issues they raise are central to the play.

ACT III

24. Hamlet uses the play within the play to trap Claudius, and it works marvelously well. Does this play also say certain things about human nature, human will, and man's fate that are applicable to the larger play, *Hamlet*?

25. How does Claudius' prayer (Scene 3) complicate his character?

26. Consider carefully the reason why Claudius cannot truly pray for forgiveness. Does this identify the force in life that Claudius represents? If so, does this illuminate other actions and statements of the King? Does it make understandable the things Hamlet says about him?

27. Can it be said that Hamlet sets up for his mother another little play within the play, which is intended to have the same results as *The Murder of Gonzago*?

28. What do you make of Gertrude's inability to see the Ghost and her remark, "yet all that is I see"? What does this tell us about her? Does the ability to see the Ghost begin to take on special meaning?

29. In what ways does the stabbing of Polonius through the arras manifest in action what Hamlet has been attempting to do throughout the play?

30. Can Hamlet's jokes about the body of Polonius be understood as mere signs of madness? What state of mind has he arrived at by now?

31. Why are Fortinbras and his army so attractive to Hamlet? Does his description of them also contain criticism, of which Hamlet seems unaware?

ACT IV

32. Ophelia is the most pitiful figure in the play, and her madness and death are the direct results of the conflict between those "mighty opposites," Claudius and Hamlet. What point do you think Shakespeare is making here about the position of innocence and dutifulness in this world?

33. Describe the ways in which Laertes' situation, when he returns in Act IV, parallels Hamlet's in Act I.

34. Do the parallel situations and Laertes' response to his situation in any way counter the frequent argument that Hamlet should not have delayed a moment in seeking his revenge?

ACT V

35. Compare Hamlet's attitude when he leaves for England at the end of Act III with his attitude when he appears again at the beginning of Act V. What sort of change has he undergone?

26. How is this change reflected in his very complicated attitude toward the fact of death as it is presented in the graveyard?

37. Why does Hamlet consider Laertes' conduct at the grave of Ophelia outrageous and exaggerated? Is the gravedigger's approach to death just as exaggerated in another way?

37. How did Hamlet escape the plot the King had laid to murder him? Does this teach him to regard his function in life in a different way?

38. Why does Osric seem so grotesque and outrageously comic in these particular circumstances?

39. Could the Hamlet of Act I have faced the duel with Laertes and said simply, "the readiness is all"? Could it be said that "character" has ceased to be more important than "plot" once this statement is made?

40. What do you make of the irony that so long as Hamlet actively pursues his revenge and lays careful plans, he never succeeds, but once he comes to accept situations as they are offered and to meet them as best he can, he achieves his revenge?

41. Does the King's final scheme for killing Hamlet sum up his methods of operation? Consider carefully the way in which he is linked with poison throughout the play.

42. Is Hamlet's death in vain? Is it an unqualified triumph?

43. Are Fortinbras and old Hamlet in any ways alike?

44. What values do the antagonists, Claudius and Hamlet, represent? Would a comparison with Creon and Antigone be at all enlightening?

PART
III

GLOSSARY

Glossary

I   THEATERS

The only requirements of a theater are that it provide a place for the
actors to work and that it permit the audience to see and hear the play.
Yet every great culture has built its own particular theater. Radical
changes in belief about the function of the drama seem to be accompanied by radical changes in the physical construction and arrangement of theaters. It would appear from this that the shape of a theater
and the arrangement of its parts in some way reflects, or gives physical
form to, the view of life offered in the plays written for that theater.
The theater, we might say, is part of the symbolic statement made
about man and his world in any play performed in it; and it follows
that in reading plays we must have some idea of the theater for which
they were planned.

Evidence about the theaters of the past is often sketchy, and the
descriptions that follow are not to be taken as precise re-creations of
any particular theater. Instead, what is offered is a description of a
type of theater, a listing of the major features that would have been
found in some form in most of the theaters of a given age.

THE GREEK THEATER: Greek drama apparently origi-
nated in religious festivals which celebrated and attempted to ensure
the fertility of the land and the well-being of its people. These rituals
were originally connected with the worship of the god Dionysus, a
nature god who, like the fields, died and was reborn each year. The
details of these festivals are extremely obscure, but most authorities
speculate that they involved singing and dancing by a chorus, but did
not employ individual actors until a very late date. Thespis—from
whom our word *Thespian* comes—is said to have been the first to

introduce the individual actor in performances of plays in the sixth century B.C. About 534 B.C. the Athenian ruler Pisistratus instituted a competition among playwrights at the annual festival of Dionysus held during March-April. (There was another Dionysiac festival, the *Lenaea,* held earlier in the year, at which only comedies were presented originally.) At this festival three days were given to showing tragedies. The cost of these performances was shared by the state and by a prominent citizen, chosen by lot, called the *choregus.* First, second, and third prizes were awarded the dramatists whose works were considered the best. Aeschylus, Sophocles, and Euripides—the three tragic authors whose works have, in part, survived—were apparently the most frequent winners during the fifth century, the great age of Athenian drama.

From these few facts emerges a concept of theater that seems strange to the modern reader accustomed to thinking of plays as private ventures put on to make money by providing entertainment and, sometimes, instruction. Athenian theatrical productions were civic occasions attended by nearly the entire free population of the city. The prizes and the method of financing the productions further suggest an attempt to encourage artistic excellence, as if the greatness and health of the state depended to some degree on the writing of great drama. Beyond this, the fact that the plays were presented during a religious celebration hints that, in origin at least, plays were considered semireligious rites dealing with the relations of men and the gods.

The physical theater in which these plays were performed consisted basically of three parts: the auditorium, the orchestra, and the stage. The auditorium was semicircular and built up of tiers of seats, first of wood and later of stone, cut into a hillside. At the bottom of the semicircle and within its arms was the orchestra, a round space in which the chorus danced and sang. Behind the orchestra—and somewhat later in development—was a rectangular building known as the *skene.* In front of the skene was a row of pillars, the proscenium. Scholars differ on whether the actors performed in front of the proscenium (between the orchestra and the row of pillars), or whether a raised stage was supported by the pillars of the proscenium and the front of the upper portion of the skene.

This was a very simple theater, yet it provided everything needed for performance. It also dictated the fundamentals of Greek drama: a chorus between the audience and one or more actors moving before a scene suggesting the town square and palace of a Greek city-state.

Closest to the audience was the chorus, at one time a group of fifty men, but ordinarily in the fifth century not more than twelve. The chorus usually chanted and moved in unison, but in most plays there was a chorus leader who had individual lines and addressed the actors directly. When the chorus was not speaking it remained in the orches-

tra watching the actors. The function of the chorus varies from playwright to playwright—Euripides nearly eliminated it from any serious
part in his plays—and even from play to play, but ordinarily this
group represented the people or, more specifically, the elders of the
city. Theirs was the voice of bewilderment in times of trouble, of
caution in times of prosperity, of traditional wisdom, and of helpless
sorrow for the suffering that was taking place on the stage beyond
them.

At the farthest reach of the theater stood those isolated individuals,
the two or three actors who played all the single parts. Their heroic
size was magnified by the *cothurnus,* the elevated shoe or "tragic
boot," worn in tragedy; their expressions of pain and determination
were fixed and exaggerated by startling masks; and their proportions
and magnificence were extended by padded, brilliantly colored costumes. Behind them was first the palace, the symbol of the earthly
authority and rule they exercised, and then the open sky where dwelt
those mysterious powers controlling human fate with which the hero,
as the representative of his people, had to struggle.

THE MEDIEVAL THEATER: Medieval drama originated
in the church; all over Europe in the eleventh and twelfth centuries
brief liturgical plays presenting the events of the Resurrection and
the birth of Christ were performed at Easter and Christmas for the
instruction of the laity. During the next few hundred years religious
drama spread beyond the church to the town squares, to wagon-stages
hauled through the streets of the cities, and to other suitable playing
places; at the same time, the subject matter of these plays expanded
to include dramatizations of the principal events of the Bible—*mystery plays;* the events of saints' lives—*miracle plays;* and ultimately
allegorical presentations of moral problems and religious doctrine—
morality plays. Everyman belongs to this last category, which marks
the most advanced stage of medieval drama before it gave way to
the secular, professional drama of the Renaissance.

While medieval "theaters" were set up anywhere a suitable playing
space could be found—the aisles and chapels of a cathedral, the open
square of a town, the elevated platform of a pageant wagon and the
adjacent street, or even a flat field—these theaters do have certain
common features. The first and most striking is the use of *mansions*
or small houses placed around the edge of the "stage." These were
basically small canvas booths of some sort; they could be either very
plain or elaborately constructed to resemble the places they represented,
e.g., the Temple in Jerusalem, Heaven, or the Mouth of Hell. These
were the *places,* the locales, representing some specific region or condition of being, and every character in a play had his particular mansion. In *Everyman,* though we have no exact information on how the

play was staged, there were presumably several of these mansions, perhaps lined up side by side at the back of the playing area, and each was designated as the house of a particular character. From this house he came onto the stage for his dealings with Everyman, and into it he retired when his business was finished. The grave into which Everyman goes at the end of the play was probably another mansion, rather than a simulated grave.

The open area between or in front of the mansions—aisle, street, or square—was neutral ground, unlocalized in space or time. Across it the devils moved from Hell to collect their victims, here Herod raged and ranted, and here the Wise Men from the East traveled from their mansion to the manger at Bethlehem. The chief point to be made about this open playing area is that it was all places at all times and could, therefore, be turned into any given place at any time when a particular character walked onto it. At one moment God might create the world on it, and in the next moment it would become the field in which Cain slew Abel.

This theater is characteristically medieval in its mingling of the specific and the timeless, the specific mansions and the open, unlocalized stage. The same kind of mingling is to be found in the stage effects. This theater was not pale and abstract but lively and spectacular. The Holy Ghost was represented by a container of flaming spirits lowered on stage; tree leaves and flowers were designed to open at the word of God; the grotesque monster's mouth representing the entrance to Hell opened and closed and belched smoke; realistic and bloody tortures were simulated on stage; heads appeared to be struck off and to spurt blood; and the costumes of the actors were elaborate and highly colored. Yet these intensely realistic effects, which suggest an apprehension of the objective world so powerful and immediate that it gives even the mysteries of the Christian religion flamboyant, substantial forms, existed together in a most unrealistic arrangement of space and time. The Garden of Eden and the Throne of God on Judgment Day would appear on the same stage simultaneously, and the Creation and the Crucifixion, presented as realistically as possible, could take place on the same ground in a short space of time. This blending of the ideal and the actual worlds is duplicated also in the characterization and language of the plays. The man who drives the nails through Christ's hands speaks with the voice of a Yorkshire carpenter and grumbles about the poor work done by those who made the cross. An abstract personification of some quality such as Mercy will speak in the familiar and earthy tones of a good-hearted neighbor woman. In the medieval theater, as in the medieval world, the abstract ideal and the solid, immediate world were equally real, and they fitted neatly together in drama, and philosophy, since both were expressions on different levels of being of the same ultimate, unchanging reality.

THE ELIZABETHAN THEATER: The first Elizabethan
public theater, designed and erected solely for the purpose of producing
plays, was built as a private, money-making enterprise in 1576, north of
the city of London. Although we know the names of many Elizabethan
theaters, our information about their exact dimensions, their seating
capacity, and their stage features is very limited. Most of what we
do know comes from a copy of a drawing of the Swan Theater made
by a Dutch traveler, from two builders' contracts for the erection of
theaters, and from the plays themselves, which often suggest the type
of stage necessary for their production. Out of these diverse materials
emerge a few general facts that the modern reader—who is likely to
think that any theater built before our own century must have been
crude and small—needs to know. All references to Elizabethan theaters, however, suggest that they were very ornate and richly decorated
buildings. Second, they were in many cases quite large buildings, providing standing and seating room for between two and three thousand
people. Third, the audience was made up of a cross section of the
citizens of London, not just the apprentices and lower classes. The
Elizabethan theater, like the Greek, was a truly public theater where
the central values of the nation and the concerns of all classes of
citizens were staged.

The outer frame of the theater was circular or many-sided. On
one side was a gate through which the playgoer could pass by paying
a penny. Once inside, he could stand in what was known as the "pit,"
an unroofed open area occupying the center of the building. Around
him, forming the interior of the walls, rose three or four galleries of
seats. These were, of course, more comfortable places from which to
see the play, and they were roofed. Entrance to the gallery required
an additional payment of a penny or two. At the front of the pit, and
projecting out into it, was the platform stage, supported on trestles
or posts covered with cloth or palings. This stage was quite large; the
one contract we have that supplies dimensions stipulates that the stage
be 43 feet wide and 27½ feet deep. One or more traps opened from
the stage into the space below, which was called the "cellarage" or
"hell." Above the stage, supported by pillars resting on the stage or
cantilevered out from the roof, was a cover known as the "shadow"
or the "heavens." The first function of this shadow was to protect the
players and their expensive costumes from the English rain, but it was
also painted underneath with elaborate representations of the stars,
the planets, and the signs of the zodiac.

At the rear of the stage rose the front wall of the "tiring house,"
or what would now be called "backstage." The front wall of the
tiring house had one or more doors to allow the actors to enter and
exit. Available evidence suggests that in the center of this wall there
was some provision for a small "inner stage." Whether this was a

built-in recess or some temporary tent-like arrangement, we do not
know for certain. The one drawing we have of the interior of an
Elizabethan theater shows nothing on this wall but two large doors.
Some plays, however, make it clear that a small curtained area at
stage rear was often required for production. Above this area, and
connected with the platform stage by some manner of stairs or ladder,
was the "upper stage," a narrow gallery running the width of the stage,
which was used for balcony and battlement scenes. Above this was
the "musicians' gallery," a small balcony for the orchestra, which
provided the frequent music required in Elizabethan plays. Somewhere
above or to the rear of the musicians' gallery was the sound-effects
and machinery room. Here cannonballs were rolled down wooden
troughs to create the sound of thunder, fireworks were set off to suggest
lightning, and the pulleys and ropes that were used for such spectacular effects as lowering gods to the stage and sending spirits flying
through the air were housed.

Add to all these features of the Elizabethan stage the gorgeous and
expensive costumes the actors wore, and it becomes clear that this
theater, far from being crude and improvised, was in fact extremely
advanced and sophisticated. But it was not a realistic theater. It used
little scenery, and it made no attempt to recreate an exact illusion of
life. The stage was unlocalized—i.e. it was not restricted to any particular place or time—so any part of the eternal human drama might
be presented without concern for the limitations imposed by common-
sense notions about time, space, and probability. On this stage a
thirteen-year-old girl, Juliet, could rise to the heights of love and idealism; an entire life could pass during the two-hours' playing time; and
blank verse could magically shift the scene in a moment's time from
the coast of England to a battlefield in France.

To understand what the Elizabethan theater was truly like, we need
to turn away from maps, building contracts, and sketches, and try to
discover the symbolic values of the details of that theater—how it
looked not to the literal eye, but to the eye of the imagination that
sees in the parts suggestions of the whole and in imperfect material
matter the rough shape of ideal forms. Fortunately, we can see the
Elizabethan theater in just this way. The voice is Hamlet's:

. . . this goodly frame the earth seems to me a sterile promontory. This
most excellent canopy, the air, look you, this brave o'erhanging firmament,
this majestical roof fretted with golden fire—why, it appears no other thing
to me than a foul and pestilent congregation of vapors. What a piece of
work is a man! How noble in reason! How infinite in faculty! In form and
moving how express and admirable! In action how like an angel! In apprehension how like a god! The beauty of the world! The paragon of
animals!

As Hamlet speaks these words, his finger travels from one part of the theater to the other, and he calls out their symbolic values. "This goodly frame" is "the earth"—frame was the technical term used for the outer walls of the auditorium. He moves next to the shadow, or heavens, overhead, "this most excellent canopy, the air," and details the beauty of the constellations painted on it. Then he descends to the stage itself, pointing to the richly costumed, graceful actors, "What a piece of work is a man! . . . In form and moving how express and admirable! In action how like an angel!" Below him, and unmentioned, is hell, from which he has already, perhaps, had a visitor, and into which, as to the heavens above, a quick passage was always available in the Elizabethan theater. The name of the theater in which Hamlet first spoke these lines was the *Globe,* and in each of its details, like other Elizabethan theaters, it was a little globe mirroring the great globe on which it was modeled.

THE THEATER OF MODERN REALISM: This type of theater is not a descendant of the Elizabethan theater with its un-localized stage, but the product of a separate line of development that began in Italy in the late Renaissance. Its form was stabilized during the nineteenth century, and it is ideally suited for the presentation of realistic drama, such as Ibsen's *Hedda Gabler,* where the illusion is carefully maintained that the play shows life exactly as it appears to the eyes of common sense.

Since this theater is still the standard type, only a brief description of its physical features will be necessary. The auditorium is covered—in contrast to the Greek and Elizabethan theaters—and seats are provided for the entire audience. The stage does not extend out into the audience but is entirely recessed into the back wall. Its front is framed by what is known as the "proscenium arch." Perspective scenery is used back of the arch to give the set a realistic appearance, usually of the inside of a room furnished appropriately. The effect achieved in this way is one of a "real" room with the fourth wall cut away. Since the audience sits in darkness with only the stage lighted, the illusion is furthered that the events on stage are "a slice of life," which the spectators are privileged to witness without themselves being seen. In other words, the theater of modern realism tries to deny the fact that it is a *theater,* a place of pretense and show. Instead it attempts to be a "candid camera," which catches real people doing real things in real settings. Realistic acting styles in which the actor *becomes* the character he plays, sets in which walls are realistically solid and water actually flows from faucets, technical effects that reproduce on stage the phenomena of life, costumes that are historically accurate down to the last button, and lifelike makeup—all have grown up in the last hundred years to intensify the impression that what we see on stage is not an image of reality, but reality itself.

During the same time that the theater of realism was perfected, some men of the theater who wished to return once more to a frankly illusionistic stage have conducted a continuing series of experiments with different types of nonrealistic techniques. The revolt against realism has not succeeded—the realistic theater is still standard—but it continues, and it is not unusual today to find stages that project out into the audience; theaters in the round, where the actors are surrounded by auditors; bare stages with no scenery at all; and scenery that is symbolic rather than realistic. Our own age, it would seem, is in the process of constructing a new type of theater in response to its changed sense of the world, but it is not clear yet just what form this attempt will take.

II TYPES OF DRAMA

ALLEGORY: A work in which abstract qualities and values are presented as characters and a definite system of thought is dramatized. In *Everyman* Death and Fellowship, for example, become characters; and the play works out in dramatic terms the Christian doctrine of salvation. It is sometimes difficult to tell at just what point an allegorical figure becomes a true "character," since every personage in all plays represents to some degree a general quality of human nature. King Lear's daughters are distinct characters, but they are also representations of some general attitudes.

BURLESQUE: A satiric treatment of some well-known play, or a style of play in which themes and conventions are treated in such a way as to make them ridiculous. High burlesque results when something is shown in a form to which it aspires but which is obviously grander than it deserves—the ward politician in the robes of a king. Low burlesque works in the opposite way—a great general dressed as a butcher.

COMEDY: A form concerned not so much with the individual as with the welfare of society and the human race. It envisions a beneficent world and a nature that, while tricky, is ultimately bounteous and rewarding. Man's function in comedy is to adjust himself to the world and to enjoy it. The marks of comedy are (1) a tendency to

present rather simple, straightforward characters given to a few traditional vices or virtues; (2) the classification of characters into a few
types—lawyer, doctor, merchant, chief—who do the same things over
and over; (3) concentration on man as a social creature by showing
him usually as part of a group—seldom alone as in tragedy; (4) the
use of a familiar type of story, usually involving love, which suggests
that what has happened before is still happening and will happen
again; (5) a plot that is rather loosely put together and that is apt
to involve unexpected and unprepared-for events; (6) a pursuit not
of truth but of some very worldly goal such as wealth, pleasure, or
sex; (7) an eventual triumph of youth over age, flexibility and wit
over rigidity and dogmatism, life over death; (8) a happy conclusion,
which usually is expressed in a wedding, a feast, or a dance—all symbols of social agreement.

D R A M A : A serious play that cannot properly be called tragedy.
The French term for this type of play is *drame*.

E N T E R T A I N M E N T : A general category for works whose
only function is to provide amusement.

E X P R E S S I O N I S M : The opposite of naturalism. While naturalism concentrates on the external details of reality and environment,
to reflect the naturalistic belief that these are the shaping forces in
life, expressionism presents directly the internal life of man and shows
the world as he experiences it. The term was first used to describe
plays written in the late nineteenth century, but can be applied to any
play—*Everyman,* for example—in which mental experience is openly
staged. In expressionism the primary fact of life becomes the world
not as it objectively is but as it subjectively is perceived.

F A R C E : Ludicrous exaggeration of comic actions. Usually defined
as "highly improbable actions and situations," farce is better understood as a dramatic technique that permits the author to show,
without concern for realism, human foolishness and ineffectiveness. It
is quite closely related to parody and burlesque.

H I S T O R Y   P L A Y (sometimes also referred to as a *chronicle
play*): A play in which the playwright dramatizes one or more historical events (as in *I Henry IV,* for example), but in history plays of the
first order a comic or tragic pattern is usually imposed on the historical
events.

M E L O D R A M A : An extension into the realm of the improbable
—but not necessarily the untrue. What farce is to comedy, melodrama

is to tragedy. The distinguishing marks of melodrama are an excess of pathetic situations and a thinness of characterization. In melodrama the plot is stressed at the expense of character, which means that the persons of the play have little effect on their destiny. They suffer without acting.

MIME: What the Elizabethans called a "dumb show." A good example occurs in *Hamlet* where the play within the play is introduced with a dumb show. Essentially, miming is acting without words; every actor mimes, and every playwright makes use of this "language of the body."

MIRACLE PLAY: A type of medieval play dramatizing a saint's life or some miraculous event of Christian history.

MORALITY PLAY: Any allegorical drama that was written in England in the fifteenth and sixteenth centuries to dramatize Christian moral problems. See ALLEGORY.

MYSTERY PLAY: A medieval dramatization of the events of the Bible. They were presented in a series beginning with Creation and ending with the Last Judgment. The craft guilds undertook the expense and labor of constructing the wagons on which the plays were performed and of acting them out; hence the name "mystery plays," *mystery* being a synonym for *craft* or *skill*.

NATURALISM: The opposite of expressionism. The term was first employed in the late nineteenth century to describe such plays as Strindberg's *The Father* or Zola's *Thérèse Raquin*, which reproduced the realistic appearance of the world and dramatized the theories of naturalistic philosophy. But any play that shows men as the victims of their environment, the creations of their social and natural world, may be properly called naturalistic.

PROBLEM PLAY: Thesis play, propaganda play, play with a message, or social drama are variant terms. The common denominator here is an attempt on the part of the author to set up some specific contemporary problem and provide, explicitly or implicitly, a solution to it by recommending a course of action. In contrast to a play like, say, *The Misanthrope*, which dramatizes a continuing human problem without advising us on what to do to find a solution, a problem play is constructed to persuade us to think and act in a particular manner.

REALISM: A difficult term, which should always be handled with a great deal of care. After all, what is reality? Since every work of art is an imitation of the real, not itself the real, realism can only be a relative term when applied to plays, pictures, and poems. But realism can be a useful descriptive term if we remember that it refers only to approximations of the world. Generally, it applies to works that present us with an image of what we ordinarily see and hear. No poetic play, for example, can strictly be called realistic since people do not ordinarily speak in verse.

S Y M B O L I S M : Generally speaking, the antithesis of realism, because in it objects, actions and characters are not created to give the illusion of immediate reality, but to reflect or define some truth that lies below the surface of things as we usually see them. Poetic drama is thus one kind of symbolism. Expressionism is another. More recently the term symbolism has been restricted in dramatic criticism to the endowing of various objects in a play with particular, but unspecified, significance. The toys and the pinball machine in *The Time of Your Life* are examples of symbolism in this narrowed sense.

T R A G E D Y : Commonly taken to mean any unhappy or painful situation, particularly if it involves death. But while pain, suffering, and death are prominent parts of literary tragedy, the tragic experience as it is presented in great art is much more complicated. Essentially, literary tragedy deals with the great individual at war with himself, with his society and with the world around him. He seeks for something as a person that the rest of life denies, but that he knows he must achieve in order to fulfill himself; and he persists in his search while more ordinary men give in. Therefore he must commit himself to some course of action, he must *do* something; and once he commits himself, he releases certain powers, brings himself into conflict with forces whose existence he had hitherto not suspected, and he necessarily abides the consequences. And so he stumbles forward into his suffering, holding to an ideal which has by now become so qualified and complex that the hero himself is no longer certain of it. In the end he usually achieves something of value by his struggles. He may in the most optimistic of tragedies bring about the reformation of a kingdom or free an entire people from terror and plague. In darker tragedies he may do no more than discover the truth about himself or by some final, desperate act validate his own worth and freedom. But no matter what he discovers, the price the tragic man pays for the discovery is almost impossibly high—usually it is his life. Tragedy celebrates our lives as individuals, those hopes and ideals that comprise our personal selves; it shows the difficulty of realizing this individuality, and accepts the double nature of enlightenment—at once the price and the reward of man's struggle with his limitations. On the other hand, comedy, to which tragedy should be contrasted, shows man as a member of society, of the human race, of life itself, and submerges his individuality in the pattern of a continuing world.

TRAGICOMEDY: The mixing of comedy and tragedy. Formal Renaissance critics insisted that tragedy and comedy should not properly be mixed, that kings and clowns did not belong on the same stage. But the English playwrights quite happily joined the two forms in a single play—as in *I Henry IV*. The immediate reason for doing so was probably to provide the audience with the pleasures of both comedy and tragedy; but more serious authors then and now mix the two forms because they wish to show life as being both comic and tragic at once.

III   CRITICAL TERMS

ANTICLIMAX: When conflicting forces fail to come into open confrontation or to arrive at a conclusive decision. The anticlimax is popularly believed to be a sign of poor plotting, but *The Cherry Orchard* presents a series of anticlimaxes. The skillful dramatist can always use this device to mirror a world in which people never press on to logical or emotional conclusions.

ASIDE: Lines spoken by an actor that are by convention heard only by the audience, not by the other actors on stage. The aside is basically a device for presenting thought.

ATMOSPHERE: A vague term used to describe the "quality" built up in a play by language, scenery, costumes, etc. For example, we might say that the series of unanswered questions coupled with the cold, dark battlements in the first scene of *Hamlet* build up an atmosphere of mystery and fear. It would be more precise and useful to say that the characters live in a mysterious world in which they grope for information.

BATHOS: A descent from the sublime to the ridiculous. A plot is bathetic when it tumbles from the serious to the ridiculous: when, for example, in *The Misanthrope,* two ladies begin by offering one another the highest moral advice in the most elevated tones and end up squabbling.

CATASTROPHE: A word that usually means disaster of any kind, but which technically refers to that point in the play where one of the conflicting forces or persons triumphs over the other. This ordinarily occurs near or at the end of the play. *Dénouement* is a synonym, but more neutral in its implications, for catastrophe, which means literally, "to turn downwards."

CATHARSIS: A term used by Aristotle in his *Poetics* to describe the purging of the feelings of pity and fear, which, according to him, should be experienced by the audience at the conclusion of a tragedy. Aristotle also argued that the production of this effect was the proper end of tragedy.

CHORUS: The group of dancers and singers, usually representing the elders of the community, used in Greek tragedy and comedy. Their number varied from twelve to fifty at different times.

CLIMAX: The high point of the action in the play toward which events have been building throughout, the point at which the character sees that what he thinks he has been doing is not what he has *in fact* been doing. At this point the relations of the chief character to the other characters undergo a sharp change.

COMIC RELIEF: A device by which the dramatist, who has presented very serious and tragic matters for some time, affords his audience a rest by inserting a comic scene; this is how affective critics— those who try to describe a play by the feelings it creates in the audience—account for comic relief. The Falstaff scenes in *I Henry IV* would by this critical approach be styled comic relief. But in well-constructed plays the comic scenes usually handle in a different way the same themes and problems dealt with in the preceding "serious" scenes. Comic perspective would be an apter term for this dramatic technique.

CONTRAST: One of the artist's principal techniques for establishing meaning. Basically, contrast is the juxtaposition of unlikes so that each will question the other and throw it into relief. Black and white, hate and love, Falstaff and Hotspur, Alceste and Philinte— these are all effective contrasts.

CONVENTIONS: Shorthand ways of saying things, present in every art, which, because we are accustomed to them, we take for granted and often fail to notice. The Japanese theatergoer has no trouble accepting the convention of his theater that hopping up and down on one leg represents running a considerable distance. In the same way we accept the conventions of our theater: we can accept the passage of several days in the space of three-hours' playing time; we pretend that the characters speaking their thoughts aloud in asides and soliloquies are thinking rather than speaking; and we allow the one scene to be changed to another while we wait.

DÉNOUEMENT: Literally, the untying or unraveling of the plot. The point at which the meaning of past events becomes clear. See CATASTROPHE.

DEUS EX MACHINA: The "God from the Machine," the term used in dramatic criticism for the unanticipated intervention of some outside force or person to tie up the plot. The term originates in the occasional practice in the Greek theater of solving the problems of the plot and bringing the play to a conclusion by lowering a god onto the stage by some mechanical device. The god then dispensed justice and brought the play to an end. The term now is used to refer to the use of any person or piece of information hitherto unmentioned in the play to bring it to an end. A rich uncle returning unexpectedly in the last act, the discovery of an unknown will, a fortunate coincidence, or some quirk of fate—these are all instances of the *deus ex machina*. Plays using this device are said to be badly plotted, since the conclusion is supposed to grow, properly, out of character and what has gone before. But comedy frequently ends with the introduction of some variety of deus ex machina because it presents a world in which there are always fortuitous happenings.

DRAMATIS PERSONAE: The persons of the drama. A useful term for distinguishing the characters of the play from real people.

EPISODIC PLOT: A type of plot in which events are not part of a cause and effect pattern, but are related in some other manner, or not related at all. *Mother Courage* is a good example of a play with an episodic plot: twelve different scenes in which the same thing happens again and again in different ways, but one event does not cause the next. Yet it has a unity. It is a serial representation of the same view of life. The revue (a series of unrelated skits) is a good example of an inferior episodic plot.

EXPOSITION: Technically, the opening part of the play, devoted to introducing the characters and providing the necessary background information about them. Exposition can, however, take place at any point in the play or throughout it. But the term as it is ordinarily used is a mechanical one which suggests that a playwright stops his action for a time while he contrives some way of providing necessary information. A skillful playwright, however, will keep his play in movement at all times, and the statement of background material by the characters will be used as continuing demonstrations of their motives. When Hedda Gabler tells us about her earlier relationship with Eilert Lövborg, she is providing background information that helps us understand what is taking place, but she is also acting out her desire for freedom by proxy from the restraints imposed by polite society.

F A B L E : The traditional English name for the story of the play or the plot. Aristotle's term for the fable was *mythos*, the myth.

F A L L I N G   A C T I O N : That section of the play which comes between the catastrophe and the end.

F O R E S H A D O W I N G (*prolepsis*): Traditionally, obvious hints of what will come. A clear example of foreshadowing is Prince Hal's statement in the mock-court scene of *I Henry IV* that he will banish Falstaff when he becomes king. When he is crowned, he does so. But in most plays of the first order, some kind of foreshadowing is omnipresent. Every act of Hedda Gabler's, for example, tells us what she will eventually do. If a character is consistent, then his end is contained, foreshadowed, in his beginning. Heavy use of foreshadowing emphasizes the role of fate in a play.

I M A G E R Y : The general term for comparisons: metaphor, simile, personification, analogue, symbol, etc. Since all art is an attempt to find a suitable image for an unknown or unidentified quality, the subject of imagery is as wide as art itself. But ordinarily dramatic critics use the term to mean only those comparisons that are made in the language of the play. See page 19.

I R O N Y : A device by which what seems to be and what is are in some way opposed. Dramatists use irony frequently to portray situations in which men pretend to be something they are not, or in which they think they are doing something when in fact they are doing something else. At any time irony appears, character becomes complicated because irony creates two levels of being, "seems" and "is."

O B L I G A T O R Y   S C E N E : A relic of nineteenth-century French dramatic criticism. This term originally referred to a mechanical, contrived scene that the audience was led to expect. If, for example, a man seduced a woman and then left her at the beginning of a play, the audience, in this theater, would expect that there would inevitably be a child and that ultimately the child and the father would meet. The meeting would be the obligatory scene. This describes the mechanical plotting of many so-called well made plays. More usefully, the obligatory scene is the event compelled by the logic of the play, the full and clear expression of motives and conflicts that have been present in the play in one form or another from the outset. Thus Hedda Gabler's suicide and the confrontation of Hal and Hotspur are obligatory scenes. It should be noticed that comedy often refuses to supply the obligatory scene, since in comedy, as its spirit Puck says,

> Those things best please me
> That befall preposterously.

P A T H O S : A word that originally meant, in Greek, "enduring" or "suffering." It is correctly applied to circumstances in which characters are forced to accept, helplessly, a fate that no action of theirs has initiated. Excessive pathos exploited for its own sake is usually termed *sentimentality.*

P E R S O N I F I C A T I O N : A character in a play who merely represents some idea or aspect of life, Good Works and Fellowship in *Everyman,* for example. Personifications lack individuality and seem to have no life of their own. It is often extremely difficult, however, to decide whether a figure is a personification or a "character." All dramatic characters are to some degree personifications.

P O I N T   O F   A T T A C K : That point in time at which the playwright picks up events and begins his play. Earlier details necessary to an understanding of the events dramatized are introduced in the dialogue.

P R O B A B I L I T Y : Aristotle's recommendation that events in tragedy should follow one another in a probable and necessary manner. That is, if a character begins as courageous he should not be shown later as cowardly. Probability is perhaps better understood as consistency: what is shown in the beginning should still be there at the end. The characters and events of tragedy are usually, though not always, consistent; but comedy is less likely to deal in the probable.

R E C O G N I T I O N : That point at which a character suddenly sees himself and understands his position truly. Hedda Gabler's recognition occurs when Brack tells her of the manner of Lövborg's death and shows that he intends to use this knowledge for his own benefit. Recognition will usually, though not necessarily, involve a reversal and will occur at the dénouement. But the term *recognition* focuses attention not only on the change of fortune described by reversal and dénouement, but also on the apprehension of that change and its moral implications by the chief character. Recognition is, very simply, the point of full self-awareness.

REVERSAL: An Aristotelian critical term (*peripety*), which refers to the point in a play where affairs turn in an unexpected direction. The reversal occurs in *Oedipus* when it becomes clear that the murderer Oedipus is tracking down is himself, and in *Antigone* when it becomes clear that Creon's actions have destroyed his family and his city rather than saving them. In this book reversal has been treated as one form of dramatic irony.

RISING ACTION: The traditional way of describing the events that come between the joining of the conflict and its climax. In this book, rising action would be described as the increasingly overt expression of the central motives.

SETTING: The equivalent of the "world" of the play. The environment of the characters of the drama created with the physical set, lighting, sound effects, and language.

SOLILOQUY: Monologue. A speech delivered by a character alone on stage, which is, by convention, accepted as voiced thought.

SUSPENSE: A useful critical term only if we assume that the playwright designs his play to hold the attention of the audience by raising questions and anticipations and then delaying their answers and fulfillments. If we assume, however, as most modern critics do, that a good play is not so much concerned with its effect on the audience as it is with staging some truth about life, then the interval between the opening of a line of action and its completion must be understood as some part of the playwright's strategy for giving form to his sense of life. It is a part of what is in this book called the *rhythm of action*.

TEMPO: The timing or over-all plot rhythm of the play. Do events move swiftly or slowly? Is the action maintained at a high level? Does it rise and fall?

THEME: A word used to describe the "meaning" or "central idea" of a play. There is a danger involved in its use, however, for it suggests that the entire play can be reduced to one abstract statement: its theme. In fact, every detail in a well-constructed play contributes to its theme. Statements about the theme of a play should only be thought of as working tools, ways of getting closer to the heart of a play.

TRAGIC FLAW: The weakness or moral failing—pride, envy, temper—that blemishes the tragic hero's otherwise perfect character and causes his difficulties. Since he is "flawed," it follows that his downfall is to some degree just, and that the operation of the universe is therefore moral. This concept of the tragic flaw was believed to have originated with Aristotle, but he actually spoke not of a flaw but of "some human failing or weakness." In other words, the characteristic that involves the tragic hero in his painful destiny need not be a moral failing but simply some limitation common to all men, such as inability to foresee the future or imperfect knowledge of his own nature. Furthermore, there are a great many tragic heroes, Hamlet for example, who are thrust into tragedy for no reason except that they were born. Even in heroes who do seem to be morally culpable in some way, the "flaw" is often the very source of their greatness. Only a god could speak without sounding impossibly smug of the moral flaws of Antigone or Mother Courage.

THE UNITIES: Time, place, and action. Renaissance critics, believing that they were following Aristotle, laid down the rule that plays must observe these unities. That is, a play must limit the time portrayed to twenty-four hours, the place to an area which could reasonably be covered in that time, and the action to the events of one story only.

A   3
B   4
C   5
D   6
E   7
F   8
G   9
H   0
I   1
J   2